More information about this series at http://www.springer.com/series/7899

Communications in Computer and Information Science 956

Commenced Publication in 2007
Founding and Former Series Editors:
Phoebe Chen, Alfredo Cuzzocrea, Xiaoyong Du, Orhun Kara, Ting Liu,
Dominik Ślęzak, and Xiaokang Yang

Editorial Board

Ashish Kumar Luhach · Dharm Singh
Pao-Ann Hsiung · Kamarul Bin Ghazali Hawari
Pawan Lingras · Pradeep Kumar Singh (Eds.)

Advanced Informatics for Computing Research

Second International Conference, ICAICR 2018
Shimla, India, July 14–15, 2018
Revised Selected Papers, Part II

Springer

Editors
Ashish Kumar Luhach
Department of Computer Science
and Engineering
Maharshi Dayanand University
Rohtak, Haryana, India

Dharm Singh
Namibia University of Science
and Technology
Windhoek, Namibia

Pao-Ann Hsiung
National Chung Cheng University
Minxiong Township, Chiayi County
Taiwan

Kamarul Bin Ghazali Hawari
Electrical and Electronics Engineering
Universiti Malaysia Pahang
Pekan, Pahang, Malaysia

Pawan Lingras
Saint Mary's University
Halifax, NS, Canada

Pradeep Kumar Singh
Department of Computer Science
and Engineering
Jaypee University of Information
Technology
Kandaghat, India

ISSN 1865-0929   ISSN 1865-0937 (electronic)
Communications in Computer and Information Science
ISBN 978-981-13-3142-8   ISBN 978-981-13-3143-5 (eBook)
https://doi.org/10.1007/978-981-13-3143-5

Library of Congress Control Number: 2018960620

This Springer imprint is published by the registered company Springer Nature Singapore Pte Ltd.
The registered company address is: 152 Beach Road, #21-01/04 Gateway East, Singapore 189721, Singapore

Preface

The Second International Conference on Advanced Informatics for Computing Research (ICAICR 2018) targeted state-of-the-art as well as emerging topics pertaining to advanced informatics for computing research and its implementation for engineering applications. The objective of this international conference is to provide opportunities for the researchers, academics, industry professionals, and students to interact and exchange ideas, experience, and expertise in the current trends and strategies in information and communication technologies. Moreover, participants were informed about current and emerging technological developments in the field of advanced informatics and its applications, which were thoroughly explored and discussed.

ICAICR 2018 was held during July 14–15 in Shimla, India, in association with Namibia University of Science and Technology and technically sponsored by the CSI Chandigarh Chapter and Southern Federal University, Russia.

We are very thankful to our valuable authors for their contribution and our Technical Program Committee for their immense support and motivation for making the first edition of ICAICR 2018 a success. We are also grateful to our keynote speakers for sharing their precious work and enlightening the delegates of the conference. We express our sincere gratitude to our publication partner, Springer, for believing in us.

July 2018

Ashish Kumar Luhach
Dharm Singh
Pao-Ann Hsiung
Kamarul Bin Ghazali Hawari
Pawan Lingras
Pradeep Kumar Singh

Organization

Conference General Chair

Pao-ann Hsiung   National Chung Cheng University, Taiwan

Conference Chairs

Kamarul Bin Ghazali Hawari	Universiti Malaysia Pahang, Malaysia
Dharm Singh	Namibia University of Science and Technology, Namibia

Conference Co-chairs

Pljonkin Anton	Southern Federal University, Russia
Ashish kr. Luhach (Professional Member of CSI)	Maharishi Dayanand University, Rohtak, India
Pardeep Kumar Singh (Professional Member of CSI)	Jaypee University of Information Technology, Solan, India

Technical Program Committee

Chairs

Pawan Lingras	Saint Mary's University, Canada
Pelin Angin	Purdue University, USA

Co-chairs

Vivek Kumar Sehgal	Jaypee University of Information Technology, India
Ritesh Chugh	CQ University, Australia
Ioan-Cosmin Mihai	A.I. Cuza Police Academy, Romania
Abhijit Sen	Kwantlen Polytechnic University, Canada

Members

K. T. Arasu	Wright State University Dayton, Ohio, USA
Mohammad Ayoub Khan	Taibah University, Kingdom of Saudi Arabia
Rumyantsev Konstantin	Southern Federal University, Russia
Wen-Juan Hou	National Taiwan Normal University, Taiwan
Syed Akhat Hossain	Daffodil University, Dhaka, Bangladesh
Zoran Bojkovic	University of Belgrade, Serbia
Sophia Rahaman	Manipal University, Dubai

Thippeswamy Mn	University of KwaZulu-Natal, South Africa
Lavneet Singh	University of Canberra, Australia
Pao-ann Hsiung	National Chung Cheng University, Taiwan
Wei Wang	Xi'an Jiaotong-Liverpool University, China
Mohd. Helmey Abd Wahab	Universiti Tun Hussein Onn, Malaysia
Andrew Ware	University of South Wales, UK
Shireen Panchoo	University of Technology, Mauritius
Sumathy Ayyausamy	Manipal University, Dubai
Kamarul Bin Ghazali Hawari	Universiti Malaysia Pahang, Malaysia
Dharm Singh	Namibia University of Science and Technology, Namibia
Adel Elmaghraby	University of Louisville, USA
Almir Pereira Guimaraes	Federal University of Alagoas, Brazil
Fabrice Labeau	McGill University, Canada
Abbas Karimi	IAU, Arak, Iran
Kaiyu Wan	Xi'an Jiaotong-Liverpool University, China
Pao-Ann Hsiung	National Chung Cheng University, Taiwan
Paul Macharia	Data Manager, Kenya
Yong Zhao	University of Electronic Science and Technology of China, China
Upasana G. Singh	University of KwaZulu-Natal, South Africa
Basheer Al-Duwairi	Jordan University of Science and Technology, Jordan
M. Najam-ul-Islam	Bahria University, Pakistan
Ritesh Chugh	CQ University Sydney, Australia
Yao-Hua Ho	National Taiwan Normal University, Taiwan
Pawan Lingras	Saint Mary's University, Canada
Poonam Dhaka	University of Namibia, Namibia
Amirrudin Kamsin	University of Malaya, Malaysia
Ashish kr. Luhach	Maharishi Dayanand University, Rohtak, India
Pelin Angin	Purdue University, USA
Indra Seher	CQ University Sydney, Australia
Adel Elmaghraby	University of Louisville, USA
Sung-Bae Cho	Yonsei University, Seoul, Korea
Dong Fang	Southeast University, China
Huy Quan Vu	Victoria University, Australia
Basheer Al-Duwairi	JUST, Jordan
Sugam Sharma	Iowa State University, USA
Yong Wang	University of Electronic Science and Technology of China, China
T. G. K. Vasista	King Saud University, Saudi Arabia
Nalin Asanka Gamagedara Arachchilage	University of New South Wales, Australia
Durgesh Samadhiya	National Applied Research Laboratories, Taiwan
Akhtar Kalam	Victoria University, Australia
Ajith Abraham (Director)	MIR Labs, USA
Runyao Duan	Tsinghua University, China

Miroslav Skoric	IEEE Section, Austria
Al-Sakib Khan Pathan	IIU, Malaysia
Arunita Jaekal	Windsor University, Canada
Pei Feng	Southeast University, China
Ioan-Cosmin Mihai	A.I. Cuza Police Academy, Romania
Abhijit Sen	Kwantlen Polytechnic University, Canada
R. B. Mishra	Indian Institute of Technology, IIT (BHU), India
Bhaskar Bisawas	Indian Institute of Technology, IIT (BHU), India

Contents – Part II

Hardware

Information Systems

Networks

Security and Privacy

Contents – Part I

Hardware

Small–Signal Gain Investigation of Folded Cascode Op-Amps

Anil Sharma[✉] and Tripti Sharma

ECE Department, Chandigarh University, Gharuan, India
anilsharma1780.as@gmail.com, tripsha@gmail.com

Abstract. A low voltage and high gain folded cascode Operational-Amplifier with Cross-coupling in the output stage is analyzed. Small signal gain investigation is performed to find the frequency dependent parameter i.e. gain (A_v). Furthermore, Conventional cascode Operational-Amplifier is contrasted with the improved folded cascode Operational-Amplifier. This analysis demonstrates that the gain of the Operational-Amplifier with Cross-Coupling in output stage is significantly higher than the gain obtained from conventional cascode Op-Amp. Cascode structure presents various advantages, for example, increased gain, low power and it is utilized to increase the ICMR. Further Cross-Coupling is utilized to enhance the gain.

Keywords: CMOS · Tans-conductance · Low power · Gain
DC (direct-coupled) unity gain frequency · Cascode stage
ICMR (input common mode range)

1 Introduction

In the recent years, rapid development in CMOS technology has made analog IC's to dominate the existing marketplace in providing low cost, superior frameworks with minimum feature size in the market [1] and [2].

The prime restriction to low power frameworks is the requirement of threshold voltage (V_t) which is vital for the MOSFET to operate. For CMOS operational-Amplifiers to work at low voltages the constraint of V_t needs to be scaled down [3] and [4]. With scaling techniques, length of the transistor downsizes, supply voltage downsizes, however the threshold voltage scaling rate isn't identical [5]. To reduce the effects of threshold voltage, depletion NMOS transistors were used with body driven PMOS differential pair [6]. Power dissipation diminution in analog circuits does not primarily reduce when supply voltage is low therefore design must be kept as simple as possible [7]. The inclination towards trimming down of the supply potential is a characteristic approach towards bringing down the power utilization in digital circuits while, supply diminution presents numeral challenges in the analog IC designing [8]. To reduce supply voltage, native transistors [9] were utilized instead of NMOS and PMOS transistors but it degrades the overall performance of the circuit.

To eliminate the effect of V_t, body driven MOSFETs can be utilized [3] and [4]. Diverse Operational-Amplifiers utilizing body driven techniques have been accounted and presented the concern about reduced trans-conductance. The diminished input

© Springer Nature Singapore Pte Ltd. 2019
A. K. Luhach et al. (Eds.): ICAICR 2018, CCIS 956, pp. 3–14, 2019.
https://doi.org/10.1007/978-981-13-3143-5_1

Trans-conductance has its effect on various Op-Amp parameters such as reduced gain and gain bandwidth product. Although, this approach reduces the problem of latch up prevailing in gate driven approach. To improve the trans-conductance, partial positive feedback can be utilized [10].

Application Specific Integrated Circuits (ASIC's) are progressively becoming mixed signal types to realize system on chip (SOC) and extensively utilized building block is Op-Amp [11], [12] and [13]. The realization of an Operational amplifier with ideal prerequisites in an IC influences the complete performance of the framework [14]. Designing an Op-Amp as per the prerequisite application has turned out to be worth mentioning. The growing demand of compact hardware gadgets influences the designer's imagination in developing low power and low voltage IC's [15].

Operational amplifier (Op-Amp) is a multistage device with high gain, infinite impedance at input side and zero impedance at the output side [16]. The Op-Amp design poses a great challenge because with each new technology node supply voltage and channel lengths are trim down [17].

Operational amplifier is a DC high gain amplifier. Op-Amp is considered as the fundamental circuit in analog circuits [18]. Direct-coupled amplifiers are the one that can amplify the signals having frequency as low as zero [19] and [20]. The Op-Amps ideally can amplify signals of any frequency with equal gain, therefore they have infinite bandwidth.

The Op-Amp is undeniably an essential device within analog frameworks [21] and [22]. Op-Amp, a three-terminal device shown in Fig. 1 comprises of input differential stage, differential to single ended stage and buffer stage at output. The amplified differential input appears at the output terminal.

2   Conventional Cascode Op-Amp

Cascode Op-Amp revealed in Fig. 1 comprises of N-channel transistors in the differential pair. Transistors M_{n1} and M_{n2} forms N-channel pairs to which the input is applied and folded cascode is achieved by connecting M_{n6} and M_{n7} transistors with them. V_{OUT} is the single-ended output of the Cascode Op-Amp. M_{n3} Forms the current source transistor providing biasing to the input pair. M_{n4}, M_{n5}, forms the current mirrors and acts as load. Whereas M_{n8}, M_{n9} M_{n10} and M_{n11} forms the cascode current mirror [1].

Figure 2 reveals the ac analysis model for the Op-Amp shown in Fig. 1 and is further utilized to achieve the ac analysis parameters of this pair shown below:

Assuming the two transistors in differential pair to be identical i.e. $M_{n1} = M_{n2}$.
Therefore, $g_{mn1} = g_{mn2} = g_{mn}$

Where g_{mn1} is transconductance of M_{n1} transistor.
g_{mn2} is transconductance of M_{n2} transistor.

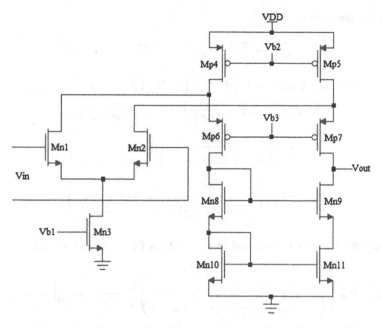

Fig. 1. Conventional cascode Op-Amp [1]

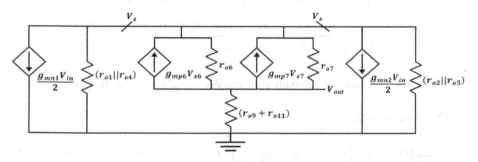

Fig. 2. Small signal equivalent of conventional cascode stage

Total current flowing is given as

$$\frac{g_{mn1}V_{in}}{2} + \frac{V_s}{(r_{o1}||r_{o4})} + \frac{V_{out}}{(r_{o9}+r_{o11})} + \frac{g_{mn2}V_{in}}{2} + \frac{V_s}{(r_{o2}||r_{o5})} = 0$$

$$\left(\frac{g_{mn1}V_{in}}{2} + \frac{g_{mn2}V_{in}}{2}\right) + \left(\frac{V_s}{(r_{o1}||r_{o4})} + \frac{V_s}{(r_{o2}||r_{o5})}\right) = -\frac{V_{out}}{(r_{o9}+r_{o11})} \qquad (2.1)$$

$$g_{mn}V_{in} + \frac{V_s}{(r_{o1}||r_{o4})||(r_{o2}||r_{o5})} = -\frac{V_{out}}{(r_{o9}+r_{o11})}$$

Also we can write;

$$-g_{mp6}V_{s6} + \frac{(V_s - V_{out})}{r_{o6}} - g_{mp7}V_{s7} + \frac{(V_s - V_{out})}{r_{o7}} = \frac{V_{out}}{(r_{o9} + r_{o11})}$$

$$V_{s6} = V_{s7} = V_s$$

$$-(g_{mp6} + g_{mp7})V_s + V_s\left(\frac{1}{r_{o6}} + \frac{1}{r_{o7}}\right) - V_{out}\left(\frac{1}{r_{o6}} + \frac{1}{r_{o7}}\right) = \frac{V_{out}}{(r_{o9} + r_{o11})}$$

$$\left(-g_{mp6} - g_{mp7} + \frac{1}{(r_{o6}||r_{o7})}\right)V_s = \frac{V_{out}}{(r_{o9} + r_{o11})||(r_{o6}||r_{o7})}$$

$$V_s = V_{out}\left(\frac{1}{\left(-g_{mp6} - g_{mp7} + \frac{1}{(r_{o6}||r_{o7})}\right)(r_{o9} + r_{o11})||(r_{o6}||r_{o7})}\right) \tag{2.2}$$

$$V_s = -V_{out}\left(\frac{1}{\left(g_{mp6} + g_{mp7} - \frac{1}{(r_{o6}||r_{o7})}\right)(r_{o9} + r_{o11})||(r_{o6}||r_{o7})}\right)$$

Putting the value of V_s obtained in Eq. (2.2) in Eq. (2.1) and we get;

$$g_{mn}V_{in} - V_{out}\left(\frac{1}{\left(g_{mp6} + g_{mp7} - \frac{1}{(r_{o6}||r_{o7})}\right)(r_{o9} + r_{o11})||(r_{o6}||r_{o7})}\right)\left[\frac{1}{(r_{o1}||r_{o4})||(r_{o2}||r_{o5})}\right] = -\frac{V_{out}}{(r_{o9} + r_{o11})}$$

$$\frac{V_{out}}{V_{in}} = \frac{-g_{mn}}{\left\{\frac{1}{(r_{o9} + r_{o11})} - \frac{1}{\left(g_{mp6} + g_{mp7} - \frac{1}{(r_{o6}||r_{o7})}\right)[(r_{o9} + r_{o11})||(r_{o6}||r_{o7})](r_{o1}||r_{o4})||(r_{o2}||r_{o5})}\right\}}$$

$$|A_v| = \frac{g_{mn}(r_{o9} + r_{o11})\left(g_{mp6} + g_{mp7} - \frac{1}{(r_{o6}||r_{o7})}\right)[(r_{o9} + r_{o11})||(r_{o6}||r_{o7})](r_{o1}||r_{o4})||(r_{o2}||r_{o5})}{\left(g_{mp6} + g_{mp7} - \frac{1}{(r_{o6}||r_{o7})}\right)[(r_{o9} + r_{o11})||(r_{o6}||r_{o7})](r_{o1}||r_{o4})||(r_{o2}||r_{o5}) - (r_{o9} + r_{o11})}$$

Neglecting the series combination of resistors $(r_{o9} + r_{o11})$ as the value will be small,

Therefore we get;

$$|A_v| = \frac{g_{mn}(r_{o9} + r_{o11})\left(g_{mp6} + g_{mp7} - \frac{1}{(r_{o6}||r_{o7})}\right)[(r_{o9} + r_{o11})||(r_{o6}||r_{o7})](r_{o1}||r_{o4})||(r_{o2}||r_{o5})}{\left(g_{mp6} + g_{mp7} - \frac{1}{(r_{o6}||r_{o7})}\right)[(r_{o9} + r_{o11})||(r_{o6}||r_{o7})](r_{o1}||r_{o4})||(r_{o2}||r_{o5})}$$

Above equation further reduces to:

$$|A_v| = g_{mn}(r_{o9} + r_{o11}) \tag{2.3}$$

Where $|A_v|$ is the gain of the cascode Operational-Amplifier.

g_{mn} Represents the effective transconductance of input differential pair.

$(r_{o9} + r_{o11})$ Represents series connection of drain resistances of M_{n9} and M_{n11}.

From Eq. (2.3), it is apparent that gain has linear relationship with the effective trans-conductance of the NMOS transistors in the input pair multiplied by a factor represented by series combination of drain resistances of transistors in cascode current mirror pair.

3 Folded Cascode Op-Amp

The cascode Op-Amps presents some shortcomings such as reduced output voltage swings and reduced speed. These shortcomings were reduced by using folding technique and folded cascode Op-Amps are used. In N-channel or P-channel cascode pair, the input differential pair is substituted by converse pair converting voltage at input into current. An important property of such Op-Amps is that they maintain the ICMR close to the supply rails.

Figure 3 reveals the topology of the chosen two stage folded cascode Operational Amplifier which comprises of bias control circuitry, differential amplifier and second gain stage [21]. The bias circuitry is utilized to set up accurate operating point for every transistor to be in saturation.

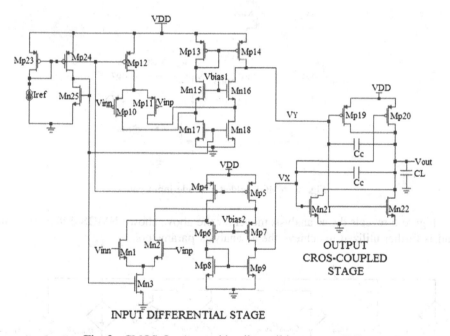

Fig. 3. CMOS Op-Amp with rail-to-rail input stage [21]

The differential amplifier used is folded cascode differential amplifier. Cascode structure presents various advantages such as increased gain, and it is used to enhance the input CM range. Two differential amplifiers are used in the input stage namely PMOS folded cascode differential amplifier which is used to cover negative supply rail and second one is NMOS folded cascode differential amplifier which is used to cover positive supply rail. The differential outputs are input to the second gain stage which consists of cross coupled stage. This stage adds on to the gain obtained from input stage, thus increasing the overall gain.

The two stage Rail-to-Rail folded cascode Op-Amp is revealed in the Fig. 3 comprises of two gain stages. Initial stage is differential stage and the subsequent gain stage is Cross-Coupled stage which adds on into the gain obtained from first stage. Input differential pair comprises of NMOS pair and PMOS pair to reach either of the supply rails and theses are analyzed further as below:

(a) **NMOS Pair**

NMOS pair revealed in Fig. 4 [21] comprises of N-channel transistors in the differential pair. Transistors M_{n1} and M_{n2} forms N-channel pairs to which the input is applied and folded cascode is achieved by connecting M_{n6} and M_{n7} transistors with them. V_X is the output of the NMOS differential pair. M_{n3} Forms the tail current transistor. M_{n4}, M_{n5}, M_{n8} and M_{n9} forms the current mirrors.

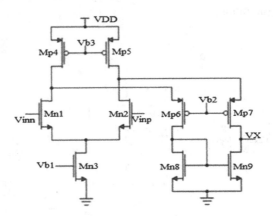

Fig. 4. NMOS folded cascode input pair

Figure 5 reveals the ac analysis model for the above shown NMOS differential pair and is further utilized to achieve the ac analysis parameters.

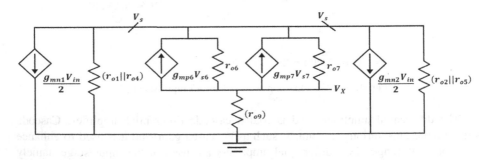

Fig. 5. Small signal equivalent for NMOS differential pair

Assuming the two transistors in differential pair to be identical i.e. $M_{n1} = M_{n2}$. Therefore, $g_{mn1} = g_{mn2} = g_{mn}$

Where g_{mn1} is transconductance of M_{n1} transistor.
g_{mn2} is transconductance of M_{n2} transistor.

Also

$$V_{inn} = V_{inp} = \frac{V_{in}}{2}$$

Total current flowing is given as

$$\frac{g_{mn1}V_{in}}{2} + \frac{V_s}{(r_{o1}||r_{o4})} + \frac{V_X}{(r_{o9})} + \frac{g_{mn2}V_{in}}{2} + \frac{V_s}{(r_{o2}||r_{o5})} = 0$$

$$\left(\frac{g_{mn1}V_{in}}{2} + \frac{g_{mn2}V_{in}}{2}\right) + \left(\frac{V_s}{(r_{o1}||r_{o4})} + \frac{V_s}{(r_{o2}||r_{o5})}\right) = -\frac{V_X}{(r_{o9})} \qquad (3.1)$$

$$g_{mn}V_{in} + \frac{V_s}{[(r_{o1}||r_{o4})||(r_{o2}||r_{o5})]} = -\frac{V_X}{(r_{o9})}$$

Also we can write;

$$g_{mp6}V_{s6} + \frac{(V_s-V_X)}{r_{o6}} + g_{mp7}V_{s7} + \frac{(V_s-V_X)}{r_{o7}} = \frac{V_X}{(r_{o9})}$$

$$V_{s6} = V_{s7} = V_s$$

$$-\left(g_{mp6} + g_{mp7}\right)V_s + \left(\frac{V_s}{r_{o6}} + \frac{V_s}{r_{o7}}\right) - \left(\frac{V_X}{r_{o6}} + \frac{V_X}{r_{o7}}\right) = \frac{V_X}{(r_{o9})}$$

$$\left(-g_{mp6} - g_{mp7} + \left(\frac{1}{r_{o6}||r_{o7}}\right)\right)V_s = V_X\left[\frac{1}{r_{o6}||r_{o7}||r_{o9}}\right]$$

$$V_s = -V_X\left(\frac{1}{\left(g_{mp6} + g_{mp7} - \left(\frac{1}{r_{o6}||r_{o7}}\right)\right)(r_{o6}||r_{o7}||r_{o9})}\right)$$

Put Eq. (3.2) in Eq. (3.1) and we get;

$$g_{mn}V_{in} - V_X\left(\frac{1}{\left(g_{mp6} + g_{mp7} - \left(\frac{1}{r_{o6}||r_{o7}}\right)\right)(r_{o6}||r_{o7}||r_{o9})}\right)\left[\frac{1}{((r_{o1}||r_{o4})||(r_{o2}||r_{o5}))}\right] = -\frac{V_X}{(r_{o9})}$$

$$(3.2)$$

$$V_X = -\frac{g_{mn}V_{in}r_{o9}\left(g_{mp6} + g_{mp7} - \left(\frac{1}{r_{o6}||r_{o7}}\right)\right)(r_{o6}||r_{o7}||r_{o9})((r_{o1}||r_{o4})||(r_{o2}||r_{o5}))}{\left(\left(g_{mp6} + g_{mp7} - \left(\frac{1}{r_{o6}||r_{o7}}\right)\right)(r_{o6}||r_{o7}||r_{o9})((r_{o1}||r_{o4})||(r_{o2}||r_{o5})) - (r_{o9})\right)}$$

Neglecting (r_{o9}) resistor as the value will be small,

$$V_X = -\frac{g_{mn}V_{in}r_{o9}\left(g_{mp6} + g_{mp7} - \left(\frac{1}{r_{o6}||r_{o7}}\right)\right)(r_{o6}||r_{o7}||r_{o9})((r_{o1}||r_{o4})||(r_{o2}||r_{o5}))}{\left(\left(g_{mp6} + g_{mp7} - \left(\frac{1}{r_{o6}||r_{o7}}\right)\right)(r_{o6}||r_{o7}||r_{o9})((r_{o1}||r_{o4})||(r_{o2}||r_{o5}))\right)}$$

Above equation further reduces

$$V_X = -g_{mn}V_{in}(r_{o9}) \tag{3.3}$$

Where V_X represents the output from NMOS differential pair.

g_{mn} Represents the effective transconductance of input differential pair.

(r_{o9}) Represents drain resistances of M_{n9}.

(b) **PMOS Pair**

PMOS pair revealed in Fig. 6 [21] comprises of P-channel transistors in the differential pair. Transistors M_{n10} and M_{n11} forms P-channel pairs to which the input is applied and folded cascode is achieved by connecting M_{n15} and M_{n16} transistors. V_Y is the output of the PMOS differential pair. M_{n12} forms the tail current transistor. M_{n13}, M_{n14}, M_{n17} and M_{n18} forms the current mirrors.

Figure 7 reveals the ac analysis model for the above shown NMOS differential pair and is further utilized to carry out the ac analysis of this pair shown below:

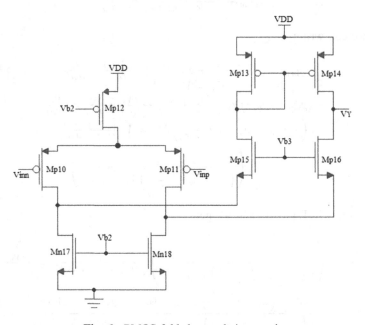

Fig. 6. PMOS folded cascode input pair

Assuming the two PMOS transistors in differential pair to be identical i.e.$M_{p10} = M_{p11}$.

Therefore, $g_{mp10} = g_{mp11} = g_{mn}$

Where g_{mp10} is transconductance of M_{p10} transistor.

g_{mp11} is transconductance of M_{p11} transistor.

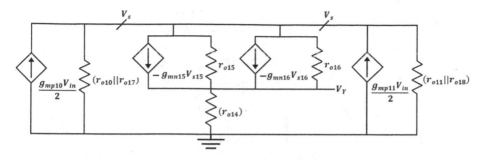

Fig. 7. Small signal equivalent for PMOS differential pair

Also

$$V_{inn} = V_{inp} = \frac{V_{in}}{2}$$

V_{inn} and V_{inp} are the two input voltages to the differential amplifier.

Similarly for PMOS pair, the output equation can be obtained in the same manner as obtained for NMOS pair above and

$$V_Y = -g_{mp}V_{in}(r_{o14}) \tag{3.4}$$

Where V_Y represents the output from PMOS differential pair.

g_{mp} represents the effective transconductance of input differential pair. (r_{o14}) represents drain resistances of M_{p14} and V_{in} is the input voltage.

(c) Output Stage

The output stage comprises of Cross-Coupling stage which in turn enhances the overall gain. This stage increases the transconductance of the MOSFETs and enhances the gain of the Operational amplifier with modest current consumption [21].

In Fig. 8 [21], V_X and V_Y are the outputs from the differential pair which are input to cross coupled output stage. g_{mp19} and g_{mp20} are P-channel transistors & g_{mn21} and g_{mn22} are N-channel transistors in the output stage. Gates of g_{mp19} and g_{mn22} are connected to each other and V_X is applied to their gates. Gates of g_{mp20} and g_{mn21} are connected to each other and V_Y is applied to their gates. This forms cross coupling in the output stage which enhances the gain of the Operational-Amplifier. C_c is the coupling capacitor used for stability reasons.

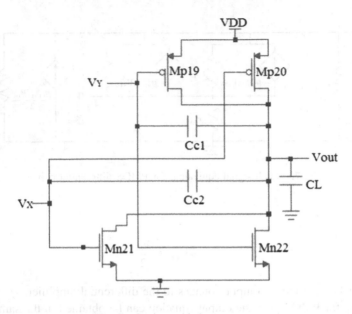

Fig. 8. Cross-coupled output stage

Figure 9 reveals the ac analysis model for the above shown NMOS differential pair and is further utilized to carry out the ac analysis of this pair shown below:

Total current in the paths is given as

$$g_{mn23}V_X + g_{mn22}V_Y + g_{mp20}V_X + g_{mp19}V_Y + \frac{V_{OUT}}{(r_{o19}||r_{o20}||r_{o23}||r_{o22})} = 0$$

$$(g_{mn23} + g_{mp20})V_X + (g_{mn22} + g_{mp19})V_Y = -\frac{V_{OUT}}{(r_{o19}||r_{o20}||r_{o23}||r_{o22})}$$

$$(g_{mn23} + g_{mp20})(-g_{mn}V_{in}(r_{o9})) + (g_{mn22} + g_{mp19})(-g_{mp}V_{in}(r_{o14})) = -\frac{V_{OUT}}{(r_{o19}||r_{o20}||r_{o23}||r_{o22})}$$

$$\{(g_{mn23} + g_{mp20})(g_{mn}(r_{o9})) + (g_{mn22} + g_{mp19})(g_{mp}(r_{o14}))\}(r_{o19}||r_{o20}||r_{o23}||r_{o22}) = \frac{V_{OUT}}{V_{in}}$$

$$A_v = \{(g_{mn23} + g_{mp20})(g_{mn}(r_{o9})) + (g_{mn22} + g_{mp19})(g_{mp}(r_{o14}))\}(r_{o19}||r_{o20}||r_{o23}||r_{o22})$$

$$(3.5)$$

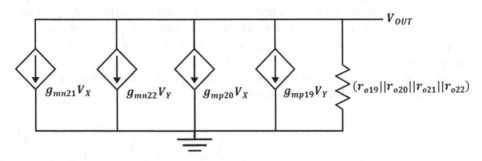

Fig. 9. Small signal equivalent of cross-coupled stage

Where A_v represents the gain of the Rail-to-Rail Op-Amp with Cross-Coupled stage.

$r_{o19} \| r_{o20} \| r_{o23} \| r_{o22}$ Represents parallel combination of transistors in output stage. g_{mp19} & g_{mp20} are the transconductance of PMOS transistors in output stage. g_{mn23} & g_{mn22} are the transconductance of NMOS transistors in output stage.

Table 1. Comparison between different Op-Amps

Parameter	Conventional cascode OP-AMP [1]	Folded cascode OP-AMP [21]
Gain	$\lvert A_v \rvert = g_{mn}(r_{o9} + r_{o11})$	$A_v = \{ (g_{mn23} + g_{mp20})(g_{mn}(r_{o9})) + (g_{mn22} + g_{mp19})(g_{mp}(r_{o14})) \}(r_{o19} \| r_{o20} \| r_{o23} \| r_{o22})$

4 Conclusion

In folded cascode Operational-Amplifier, NMOS and PMOS differential pairs are utilized to reach either of the suppy Rails ie V_{DD} or V_{SS}. These pair compose the initial stage and provide high gain and high CMRR. Subsequent stage is formed by Cross-Coupled stage which improves the trans-conductance of the Op-Amp and in turn improves several parameters to a certain extent. On comparing Eqs. (2.3) and (3.5) it can be infered that the gain obtained in folded cascode Operational-Amplifier with Cross-Coupled output stage is much higher than the conventional cascode Op-Amp due to the fact that the transconductances g_{mp19}, g_{mp20} and g_{mn22}, g_{mn23} of output stage transistors elevates the gain.

Table 1 shows the contrast between conventional cascode and folded cascode with cross coupled stage.

References

1. Razavi, B.: Design of Analog CMOS Integrated Circuits, 27th edn. McGraw-Hill Education, New York (2013)
2. Baker, J.R.: CMOS Circuit Design, Layout, and Simulation, 2nd edn (2013)
3. Raikos, G., Vlassis, S., Psychalinos, C.: 0.5 V bulk-driven analog building blocks. AEU - Int. J. Electron. Commun. 66(11), 920–927 (2012)
4. Blalock, B., Allen, P., Rincon-Mora, G.: Designing 1-V op amps using standard digital CMOS technology. IEEE Trans. Circ. Syst. II: Analog Digit. Sig. Process. 45(7), 769–780 (1998)
5. Duque-Carrillo, J., Ausin, J., Torelli, G., Valverde, J., Deminguez, M.: 1-V rail-to-rail operational amplifiers in standard CMOS technology. IEEE J. Solid-State Circ. 35(1), 33–44 (2000)
6. Stockstad, T., Yoshizawa, H.: A 0.9-V 0.5-µA rail-to-rail CMOS operational amplifier. IEEE J. Solid-State Circ. 37(3), 286–292 (2002)

7. Yu, C.-M., Lin, Z.-M., Chen, J.-D.: A low voltage high unity-gain bandwidth CMOS OP-AMP. In: Proceedings oh the 2004 IEEE Asia-Pacific Conference on Circuits and Systems (2004)
8. Schlögl, F., Zimmermann, H.: Low-voltage operational amplifier in 0.12 μm digital CMOS technology. IEEE Proc.-Circ. Devices Syst 151(5), 395 (2004)
9. Chatterjee, S., Tsividis, Y., Kinget, P.: 0.5-V analog circuit techniques and their application in OTA and filter design. IEEE J. Solid. State. Circ. 40(12), 2373–2387 (2005)
10. Zhao, X., Zhang, Q., Wang, Y., Deng, M.: Transconductance and slew rate improvement technique for current recycling folded cascode amplifier. AEU – Int. J. Electron. Commun. 70(3), 326–330 (2016)
11. Huang, H.-Y., Wang, B.-R., Liu, J.-C.: High-gain and high-bandwidth rail-to-rail operational amplifier with slew rate boost circuit. In: IEEE International Symposium on Circuits and Systems (2006)
12. Carrillo, J., Torelli, G., Prez-Aloe, R., Duque-Carrillo, J.: 1-V rail-to-rail CMOS Op-Amp with improved bulk-driven input stage. IEEE J. Solid-State Circ. 42(3), 508–517 (2007)
13. Lee, E., Lam, A., Li, T.: A 0.65 V rail-to-rail constant gm Op-Amp for biomedical applications. In: 2008 IEEE International Symposium on Circuits and Systems (2008)
14. Pan, S., Chuang, C., Yang, C. Lai, Y.: A novel OTA with dual bulk-driven input stage. In: 2009 IEEE International Symposium on Circuits and Systems (2009)
15. Kargaran, E., Khosrowjerdi, H., Ghaffarzadegan, K.: A 1.5 v high swing ultra-low-power two stage CMOS OP-AMP in 0.18 μm technology. In: 2010 2nd International Conference on Mechanical and Electronics Engineering (2010)
16. Lee, E.: A sub-0.5 V, 1.5 μW rail-to-rail constant gm Op-Amp and its filter application. In: IEEE International Symposium on Circuits and Systems (2012)
17. Guang, Y., Bin, Y.: Design and analysis of a high-gain rail-to-rail operational amplifier. Procedia Eng. 29, 3039–3043 (2012)
18. Kulej, T.: 0.5-V bulk-driven CMOS operational amplifier. IET Circ. Devices Syst. 7(6), 352–360 (2013)
19. Tanaka, A., Qin, Z., Yoshizawa, H.: A 0.5-V 85-nW rail-to-rail operational amplifier with a cross-coupled output stage. In: 2013 IEEE 20th International Conference on Electronics, Circuits, and Systems (ICECS) (2013)
20. Ferreira, L., Sonkusale, S.: A 60-dB Gain OTA Operating at 0.25-V Power Supply in 130-nm Digital CMOS Process. IEEE Trans. Circ. Syst. I: Regul. Pap. 61(6), 1609–1617 (2014)
21. Qin, Z., Tanaka, A., Takaya, N., Yoshizawa, H.: 0.5-V 70-nW rail-to-rail operational amplifier using a cross-coupled output stage. IEEE Trans. Circ. Syst. II: Express Briefs 63(11), 1009–1011 (2016)
22. Sheeparamatti, A., Bhat, M.V., Srivatsa, M.P., Nithin, M.: Design of 3.3 V rail to rail operational amplifier for high resolution ADC driver amplifier. In: International Conference on Innovative Mechanisms for Industry Applications (ICIMIA 2017), Bangalore, India, pp. 317–321 2017

Analysis of the Impact of Diverse Pulse Shaping Filters on BER of GFDM System Incorporated with MRC Diversity Combining Scheme

Pawan Kumar[(⊠)] and Lavish Kansal

Lovely Professional University, Phagwara, India
pawankumar945@gmail.com, lavish.15911@lpu.co.in

Abstract. With the passage of previous several decades it is analyzed that the upcoming generation of mobile communication should provide high data rates as well as capacity of data transmission. As far as Generalized Frequency Division Multiplexing (GFDM) is concerned, the pulse shaping filters plays a significant role in it. The Bit Error Rate (BER) performance of GFDM is worse as compared to OFDM due to the lack of initial orthogonality in the subcarriers. This can be made better with the usage of different pulse shaping filter. This paper presents the implementation of the Raised Cosine (RC), Square Root Raised Cosine (SRRC) and Gaussian filter along with the MRC combining scheme of MIMO for GFDM. The simulation results show that the different SNR values can be obtained for the respective BER in GFDM.

Keywords: OFDM · GFDM · BER · RC · SRRC · MRC

1 Introduction

In the today's scenario, the Fifth Generation (5G) of cellular communication systems are expected to handle the various parameters for betterment of services. It should have less latency and must be reliable and efficient. The OFDM has found specifically its application into a lot of wireless standards like WiMAX, DVB-T and LTE. The 5G systems introduce new requirements for the current communication system which are not efficiently handled by the OFDM. And due to the need of orthogonality in the OFDM, we cannot vary the system performance beyond a certain level in OFDM. The OOB emission and PAPR of OFDM are quite high [1]. This demands channel filtering in order to cope up with the emission masks that are set by the authorized and regulatory bodies. The cyclic prefixes used in the OFDM require a larger bandwidth.

The most common waveform contender for 5G is GFDM. The main concept that distinguishes it from OFDM is that the subcarriers used in GFDM are not initially orthogonal [2]. With the introduction of GFDM, it was analyzed that it uses only one cyclic prefix for the overall message signal. This reduces the wastage of bandwidth up to a greater extent [3]. Further the implementation of MIMO makes the GFDM system to achieve the higher data rates. MRC is one of the combining schemes that help GFDM to achieve the different BER with respect to the various pulse shaping filters as

© Springer Nature Singapore Pte Ltd. 2019
A. K. Luhach et al. (Eds.): ICAICR 2018, CCIS 956, pp. 15–29, 2019.
https://doi.org/10.1007/978-981-13-3143-5_2

compared to the OFDM. The various pulse shaping filters that are used for GFDM are raised cosine, square root raised cosine and Gaussian filters. In MRC, all the signals are combined in a weighted and co-phased manner. In other words, the weight of significant magnitude is multiplied to the signal strengths in this combining scheme. This is done for achieving the higher SNR at the receiver during all the times. From the various simulations it is proved that the MRC performance is better as compared to the equal gain combining and selection combining. Moreover, the PAPR of the GFDM can be reduced furthermore with the usage of various PAPR reduction schemes like clipping, companding and precoding (Fig. 1).

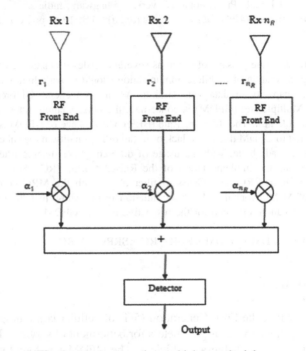

Fig. 1. Maximum ratio combining methodology

2 Related Work

Cho et al. [1] tells that in order to communicate via the single carrier transmission, we require nyquist bandwidth in order to get the symbol transferred per unit time. These systems have the frequency selectivity issue and it can be eradicated with the usage of multiple carriers for the data transmission. Zhou et al. [2] described zero padded Orthogonal Frequency Division Multiplexing (ZPOFDM) as a substitute to conventional OFDM technology. It is brought to notice that when communication is done under water, the guard interval can be very long. And that may consume more transmission power in case of CP-OFDM. In contrast to that ZP-OFDM not only saves the transmission power in that case but also reduces the duty cycle of the practical transducer. Being a combination of a large number of modulated signals, OFDM signal may show the high PAPR. Hanzo et al. [3] tells that the high amplitude variations from small instantaneous power values to large power values under the traversal of time domain signal may leads to the high value of out of band radiation. This OOB emission can be avoided by not letting the power amplifiers to reach up to their saturation state. Therefore, these operate along with the so called back-off.

The reasons behind the selection of GFDM for the implementation of 5G includes it attractive properties. The main attraction of GFDM is that while addressing the limitations of the OFDM, it also preserves most of the advantageous properties of it. The bandwidth efficiency of it can be clearly analyzed by the fact that it uses only one CP at its transmitter. Practically, when 4-DPSK is implemented in alliance with PTS-OFDM along with the subcarriers, it is found that redundancy is $R_{ap} = 2(V - 1)$ which was independently of W as per the opinions of Muller et al. [4]. Where V is depicting the number of sub blocks used in PTS and W is depicting the admitted angles for b_μ^v which must not be quite high. Also, Re et al. [5] tells that the direct sequence code division multiple access systems provide better performance as compared to the OFDM. In the proposed system a non-negligible portion of the noise power is focused in narrow band interference. As a result of that under the small values of SNR, we can obtain better performance. Farhang et al. [6] proposed the transceiver model for GFDM in which separate FFT is utilized at the transmitter side and separate IFFT at the receiver side. For improving the flexibility of the GFDM two approaches of subcarriers are introduced by Gasper et al. [7]. The first approach shows that GFDM signal is best fitted in the LTE grid. This reduces the latency of the GFDM by the factor of 15. The second approach shows that the latency of signaling in 5G may be smaller by the current LTE systems. This can be 10 times smaller than current LTE systems. Sharifian et al. [8] discussed that circular pulse shaping is used in GFDM in order to make the system compatible with the new applications of 5G networks like Machine to Machine communications (M2M) and Internet of Things (IoT).

In order to get a multiplexing technique that should be potent enough against the frequency selective channels, the combination of GFDM and WHT can be used as per Michailow et al. [9]. This is proved by comparing the BER of the GFDM with the WHT-GFDM under the frequency selective channels. Matthe et al. [10] proposed Alamouti-STC for GFDM along with the Maximum Ratio Combining receiver (MRC) structure. If the dirichlet pulse is used in GFDM, it can make the system orthogonal and we can reach up to the BER level of OFDM system under the presence of AWGN as per the Matthe et al. [11] point of view. While considering the asynchronous systems, ROC curves are drawn for the GFDM as well as for the OFDM. And the results proved that the ROCsensing performance is better in the GFDM, when the GFDM transmission of the messages is sensed by the GFDM receiver that is brought to our notice by Datta et al. [12]. The ZF receiver needs to cancel more ICI and ISI as per the traditional way of approaching the high values of complex valued samples and roll off factors. This leads to the noise amplification but with the wider opening as well as the dense sampling of continuous time Zak transform in the transmitter filter, the values that are contained in Discrete Zak Transform (DZT) leads to zero and this will constitute the high values of the DZT for the dual window as per opinions the of Matthe et al. [13].

Bandari et al. [14] tells that Offset Quadrature Amplitude Modulation (OQAM) is the concept that can improve the Symbol Error Rate (SER) and mitigate the interference effect. The proposed GFDM/OQAM model shows that it can outperform the conventional GFDM model by improving the SER performance of the system. Zhong et al. [15] described about the usage of combination of GFDM and the time reversal space time coding in order to cancel the degradation of the error performance that existed due to the presence of frequency selective channels. Carrick et al. [16] proposed a new Frequency Shift Filter (FRESH) in order to deal with the time varied spectral redundancy. This type of filter helps in creating such multicarrier waveforms that are reliable and resistant to the frequency selective fading. OFDM and GFDM are the waveforms in which we can analyze the impact of Timing Offset (TO), Carrier Frequency Offset (CFO) and phase noise. Lim et al. [17] provided the signal to interference ratio (SIR) analysis for the four classified cases of the TO. The SIR of GFDM is degraded slowly as compared to the OFDM because of its robustness against the timing offsets.

Kumar et al. [18] described GFDM as a multi branch multicarrier filter bank approach in which pulse shaping is provided in time domain to every subcarrier. Na et al. [19] also considered GFDM as a competent candidate for 5G waveforms. Along with these Michallow et al. [20] tells that Space Time Coding (STC) can be used along with the Generalized Frequency Division Multiplexing (GFDM) in order to achieve diversity in the system. Jaborri et al. [21] took the concept of spatial multiplexing into consideration for the performance evaluation of MIMO-GFDM. The PAPR reduction techniques also plays a significant role in GFDM. Sendrei et al. [22] told that clipping technique produces non-linear degradation of the signal. It will affect the BER of the signal. The usage of iterative reception structure for nonlinear noise mitigation eradicates this problem and improves the system performance. Ortega et al. [23] says that the companding technique can also be used along with clipping method for the immunity of the small signals from the noise in GFDM. This makes the GFDM signals performance even better. Overall, we can say that the GFDM is a technique which have the competency to replace the OFDM by providing better results for the 5G applications.

3   Generalized Frequency Division Multiplexing

Generalized Frequency Division Multiplexing (GFDM) is the recently proposed technique that has many attractive properties. It preserves the advantages of the OFDM while removing the limitations of it. For the past several years, OFDM was the choice of technology for wireless as well as wired system [4]. The GFDM transmit signal can be represented by the below given expression:

$$X(n) = \sum_{(m=0)}^{(M-1)} \sum_{(k=0)}^{(N-1)} d[m]g[(n - mN)mod\ M * N]\ ej2\pi kn/N \qquad (1)$$

Where, d[m] = QAM modulated data stream
n = 0, ..., M * N − 1
M = symbols that are added during CP insertions
M * N = length of samples.

While selecting the subcarrier frequencies it is taken care that all the all the sub carriers should be orthogonal among themselves [5]. That mean there will be no cross talk between the sub channels and the guard band between the carriers is not required. For the orthogonality it is required that the spacing of the subcarrier is:

$$\Delta f = kT \tag{2}$$

Where k = positive integer
T = useful symbol duration.

The overall spectrum of the OFDM is generally white that provides it benign interference properties which are electromagnetic in nature with respect to the co-channel users. A timing window can be used for smoothing the transition between the GFDM blocks. The definition of time window is given as:

$$W(n) = \begin{cases} Wrise[n] & 0 \leq n < Nw \\ 1 & Nw \leq n \leq Ncp + N \\ Wfall[n] & Ncp + N < n < Ncp + N + Nw \end{cases} \tag{3}$$

Where $W_{rise}[n]$ = ramp up segment of time window
$W_{fall}[n]$ = ramp down segment of time window.

4   GFDM System Model

The block diagram of GFDM transmitter can be assumed as a synthesis filter bank with the circular filtering present in it. In the first step of the GFDM transmitter section, the stream d = $[d_0^T, \ldots\ldots\ldots\ldots, d_{N-1}^T]^T$ of QAM modulated symbols is divided into a low rate sub-stream whose rate is N times smaller than that of d [6]. Here M is the number of data symbols that are taken over every band of subcarrier which is given by:

$$dkT = [dk[0], \ldots\ldots\ldots\ldots\ldots, dk[M-1]] \tag{4}$$

In order to place it differently, dkT is sent over m^{th} time slot and k^{th} subcarrier. Generally we can use the QAM [7], QPSK and OQAM in the block diagram of GFDM. In oversampling the sampling of the signal is done with a sampling frequency higher than the Nyquist rate. Upsampling is the process of the conversion of the rate of messages from the considered rate to the other arbitrary rate. Mathematically both of these do the same operations. The nyquist rate is given as the twice of the maximum frequency of the signal given as (Fig. 2):

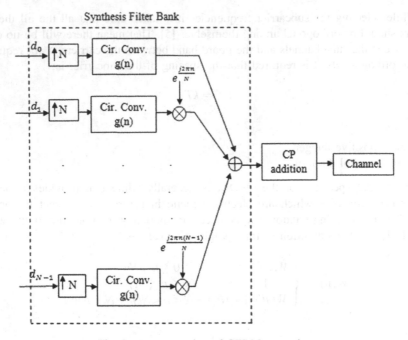

Fig. 2. Representation of GFDM transmitter

$$Nyquist\ rate = 2\ *\ maximum\ freq.\ of\ the\ signal \tag{5}$$

Circular convolution is performed between the two periodic sequences having period N which is varying from 0 to N − 1 [9]. Let us consider h[n] is the impulse response of the given LTI system and x[n] be the input vector. Then we can compute its response or output y[n] as:

$$y[n] = \sum_{-\infty}^{\infty} x[k]h[n-k] = \sum_{-\infty}^{\infty} h[k]x[n-k] \tag{6}$$

Where h[n] = the impulse response of the given LTI system
x [n] = the input vector
y [n] = the input vector.

This expression represents the linear convolution. In circular convolution, IFFT of the multiplication of the FFT of the considered two padded matrix is performed. In Cyclic prefix insertion, 1/4 of the message bits are added to the front portion of the message bitsin order to avoid the interference between the adjacent channels. In spite of adding cyclic prefix to every subcarrier we add only one cyclic prefix to the combination of subcarriers in GFDM [10] (Fig. 3).

Cyclic Prefix	Payload

Fig. 3. Cyclic prefix addition to the payload

A Matched filter Receiver (MF) is the receiver that is used at the receiver end to maximize the signal to the noise ratio per individual subcarrier [11]. Zero Forcing Receiver (ZF) can be represented in the form of matrix that will further increase the noise power to cancel out the self-interference. Linear Minimum Mean Square Error (MMSE) helps in the balancing of the self-interference. It outperforms the ZF and MF at the price of the increased complexity (Fig. 4).

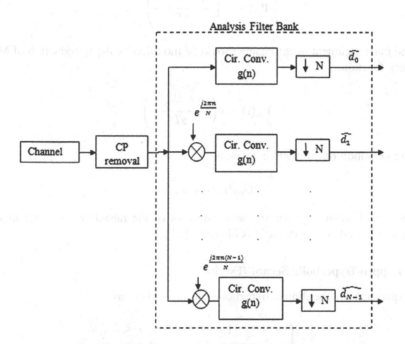

Fig. 4. Representation of GFDM receiver

5 Pulse Shaping Filters Used in GFDM

In the practice of maximizing the SNR, we actually introduce self-interference at receiver under the usage of non-orthogonal pulses in GFDM. The various pulse shaping filters used for GFDM are explained as follows:

5.1   Root Raised Cosine

Root Raised Cosine (RRC) is that category of pulse shaping filter that is well defined by the Raised Cosine (RC) function in the time domain along with the roll off factor equal to α [14–21]. The expression for the RRC filters is as follows:

$$
\mathrm{grc}(t) = \begin{cases} 1, & |t| \leq \frac{(1-\alpha)T}{2} \\ \frac{1}{2}[1 + \cos(\pi P_{rc}(t))], & \frac{(1-\alpha)T}{2} < |t| \leq \frac{(1+\alpha)T}{2} \\ 0, & otherwise \end{cases} \tag{7}
$$

Where $P_{rc}(t)$ = inner argument of the cosine

$$
P_{rc}(t) = \left(\frac{|t| - \frac{(1-\alpha)T}{2}}{\alpha T} \right) \tag{8}
$$

The inner argument of the cosine should be modified by the introduction of Meyer auxiliary function as

$$
P_{rc}(t) = v \left(\frac{|t| - \frac{(1-\alpha)T}{2}}{\alpha T} \right) \tag{9}
$$

The definition of the RRC is given as

$$
G_{rrc}(t) = \sqrt{g_{rc}(t)} \tag{10}
$$

In other word when we perform the square root of the raised cosine (RC) then the square root raised cosine (SRRC) is obtained [22].

5.2   Flipped-Hyperbolic Secant (Fsech)

The expression for the flipped hyperbolic secant is given as

$$
g(t) = \begin{cases} 1, & |t| \leq \frac{(1-\alpha)T}{2} \\ [1 - \mathrm{sech}(\rho * p_1(t))], & \frac{(1-\alpha)T}{2} < |t| \leq \frac{T}{2} \\ \mathrm{sech}(\rho * p_2(t))), & \frac{T}{2} < |t| \leq \frac{(1+\alpha)T}{2} \\ 0, & \frac{(1+\alpha)T}{2} < |t| \end{cases} \tag{11}
$$

Where sech = hyperbolic secant function

$$
\rho = \ln \left(\sqrt{3} + 2 \right) \Big/ \alpha * \frac{T}{2}
$$

$p_1(t)$, $p2(t)$ = inner arguments of the hyperbolic function

$$p_1(t) = \frac{(1+\alpha)T}{2} - |t| \tag{12}$$

and

$$p_2(t) = ((|t| - (\frac{(1-\alpha)T}{2})) \tag{13}$$

Let us consider the Meyer auxiliary function $\upsilon(x)$ [22]. After that the modified equation with the inner arguments of the hyperbolic secant function $p_1(t)$ and $p_2(t)$ will be given as:

$$p_1(t) = v((\frac{(1+\alpha)T}{2} - |t|)) \tag{14}$$

and

$$p_2(t) = v((|t| - (\frac{(1-\alpha)T}{2}))) \tag{15}$$

5.3   Flipped-Inverse Hyperbolic Secant (Farcsech)

When the independent frequency variable is interchanged with the time variable then we got the time domain expression if Farcsech is obtained [22]. This expression is given as:

$$g(t) = \begin{cases} 1, & |t| \le \frac{(1-\alpha)T}{2} \\ [arcsech((1/\rho) * p_1 * (t))], & \frac{(1-\alpha)T}{2} < |t| \le \frac{T}{2} \\ \left[1 - arcsech\left(\left(\frac{1}{\rho}\right) * p_2(t)\right)\right], & \frac{T}{2} < |t| \le \frac{(1+\alpha)T}{2} \\ 0, & \frac{(1+\alpha)T}{2} < |t| \end{cases} \tag{16}$$

Where arcsech = inverse hyperbolic secant function

$$\rho = \ln\left(\sqrt{3}+2\right)\Big/\alpha * \frac{T}{2}$$

p_1 and p_2 = inner arguments of the inverse hypeolic function

$$p_1(t) = ((|t| - \frac{(1-\alpha)T}{2})) \tag{17}$$

and

$$p_2(t) = ((\frac{(1+\alpha)T}{2} - |t|))$$ (18)

Let us consider the Meyer auxiliary function v(x). The modified equation with the inner arguments of the inverse hyperbolic secant function $P_1(t)$ and $P_2(t)$ will be given as:

$$p_1(t) = v((\frac{(1+\alpha)T}{2} - |t|))$$ (19)

and

$$p_2(t) = v((|t| - \frac{(1-\alpha)T}{2}))$$ (20)

5.4   Xia Pulse

The Xia pulse shaping filter can be implemented by using two orders of it. The 1st and 4th order of the Xia are mathematically given as
The first order Xia is as follows

$$G_{xia}[f] = \frac{1}{2}\left[1 - e^{-j\pi lin\alpha\left(\frac{f}{M}\right)sign(f)}\right]$$ (21)

and
   The 4th order of Xia is as follows

$$G_{xia4}[f] = \frac{1}{2}\left[1 - e^{-j\pi p^4 lin\alpha\left(\frac{f}{M}\right)sign(f)}\right]$$ (22)

5.5   Gaussian Pulse

When the truncation of the sampled version of the continuous time impulse response of Gaussian filter is done then we obtain the FIR Gaussian filter and is shown as the below given expression:

$$h(t) = \left(\frac{\sqrt{\pi}}{a}e^{\frac{-(\pi t)^2}{a^2}}\right)$$ (23)

The parameter 'a' is related to 3 db bandwidth symbol time product (B * T_s) of Gaussian filter

$$a = \frac{1}{BT_s}\sqrt{\frac{\log 2}{2}}$$ (24)

5.6   Dirichlet Pulse

Dirichlet pulse shaping filter is the special case of the Xia pulse when the roll off approaches to zero [19, 20]. It is generally a perfect rectangular function that may be represented in the frequency domain with the width of M frequency bins. These bins are basically located near the DC bin in order to get the time domain response as dirichlet response [21, 22]. This is the pulse shaping filter which actually helps in making the subcarriers orthogonal and is mathematically represented as:

$$[g_f]_l = \sqrt{K} \sum_{k=0}^{M-1} \delta_{lk}, \quad l = 0, 1, \ldots \ldots, D - 1 \tag{25}$$

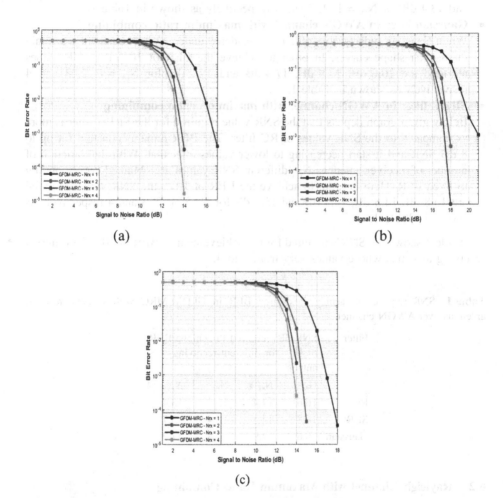

(a)

(b)

(c)

Fig. 5. BER vs. SNR comparison for GFDM system augmented with MRC diversity combining technique over AWGN channel for varying receiving antennas (a) RC filter (b) Gaussian filter (c) SRRC filter

6 Result Discussion

6.1 AWGN Channel with Maximum Ratio Combining

AWGN channel is the channel which is defined by the linear addition of the white noise along with the Gaussian distribution of the amplitude. The explanation of AWGN channel simulation along with MRC-GFDM is given below:

- **RC filter in AWGN channel with maximum ratio combining**
  The relation between the BER and SNR for MRC technique is investigated in the Fig. 5. As the value of N_{rx} is increased the SNR starts decreasing. In order to achieve the BER of 10^{-3} the SNR values required are 16.6 dB, 14.4 dB, 13.8 dB and 13.4 dB for $N_{rx} = 1, 2, 3$ and 4 respectively as shown in Table 1.
- **Gaussian filter in AWGN channel with maximum ratio combining**
  When Gaussian pulse shaping filter is considered under AWGN channel, we obtain the similar shape curves. In order to achieve the BER of 10^{-3} the SNR values required are 20.6 dB, 17.9 dB, 17.4 dB and 17.2 dB for $N_{rx} = 1, 2, 3$ and 4 respectively as shown in Table 1.
- **SRRC filter in AWGN channel with maximum ratio combining**
  Below given graph depicts that the SNR value required for the SRRC filter is more as compared to the SNR values of RC filter. The BER remains constant for up to 8 dB SNR and it start decreasing to lower values after that. With the variation of number of receiver antennas N_{rx}, different SNR values are obtained corresponding to fixed BER. Here in order to achieve the BER of 10^{-3}, the SNR values required are 16.8 dB, 14.5 dB, 14.4 dB and 13.7 dB for $N_{rx} = 1, 2, 3$ and 4 respectively as shown in Table 1.

Table 1 shows the SNR's required for the achievement of BER of 10^{-3} for different receiving antennas whose values vary from 1 to 4.

Table 1. SNR required to achieve a desired BER in GFDM-MRC with variable receiver antennas over AWGN channel

Filter	SNR(dB) required to achieve BER of 10^{-3} for different receiving antennas			
	$N_{rx} = 1$	$N_{rx} = 2$	$N_{rx} = 3$	$N_{rx} = 4$
RC	16.6	14.4	13.8	13.4
SRRC	16.8	14.5	14.4	13.7
Gaussian	20.6	17.9	17.4	17.2

6.2 Rayleigh Channel with Maximum Ratio Combining

Rayleigh channel is the channel in which the signal magnitude varies randomly according to the Rayleigh distribution. The explanation of Rayleigh channel simulation along with MRC-GFDM is given below:

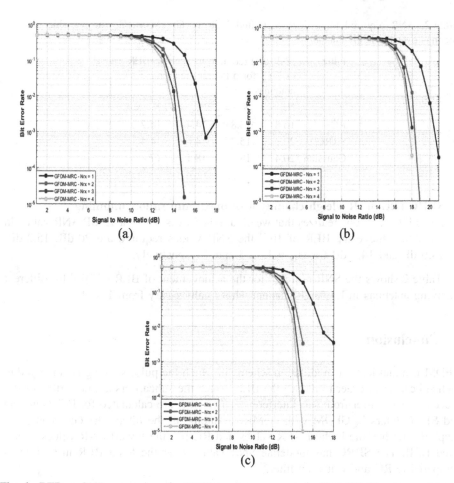

Fig. 6. BER vs. SNR comparison for GFDM system augmented with MRC diversity combining technique over Rayleigh channel for varying receiving antennas (a) RC filter (b) Gaussian filter (c) SRRC filter

- **RC filter in Rayleigh channel with maximum ratio combining**
  In order to achieve the BER of 10^{-3}, the SNR values required are 16.8 dB, 14.8 dB, 14.4 dB and 14.2 dB for $N_{rx} = 1$, 2, 3 and 4 respectively. These SNR values are high as compared to the SNR values that are obtained in the previous simulations for AWGN channel using RC filter as shown in Table 2.
- **Gaussian filter in Rayleigh channel with maximum ratio combining**
  From the simulations we conclude that using Gaussian pulse shaping filter under the Rayleigh channel we obtain the least BER approximately near about 19 dB SNR as shown in Fig. 6(b). In order to achieve the BER of 10^{-3} the SNR values required are 20.4 dB, 18.3 dB, 18.1 dB and 17.8 dB for $N_{rx} = 1$, 2, and 4 respectively as shown in Table 2.

Table 2. SNR required to achieve a desired BER in GFDM-MRC with variable receiver antennas over Rayleigh channel

Filter	SNR(dB) required to achieve BER of 10^{-3} for different receiving antennas			
	$N_{rx} = 1$	$N_{rx} = 2$	$N_{rx} = 3$	$N_{rx} = 4$
RC	16.8	14.8	14.4	14.2
SRRC	20	15.2	14.6	14.4
Gaussian	20.4	18.3	18.1	17.8

- **SRRC filter in Rayleigh channel with maximum ratio combining**
  From Fig. 6(c), one realizes that we obtain the lowest BER at 15 dB SNR value. In order to achieve the BER of 10^{-3} the SNR values required are 20 dB, 15.2 dB, 14.6 dB and 14.4 dB for $N_{rx} = 1$, 2, 3 and 4 respectively.

Table 2 shows the SNR required for the achievement of BER of 10^{-3} for different receiving antennas in Rayleigh channel whose values vary from 1 to 4.

7 Conclusion

GFDM is a multicarrier modulation scheme in which the pulse shaping is employed to each subcarrier in order to reduce the BER. Since the subcarriers are not orthogonally spaced, it may suffer from self-interference. The BER are calculated for RC, Gaussian and SRRC filters in GFDM with theMRC. Among all the filters, the Gaussian pulse shaping filter has the highest SNR values and RC has the lowest SNR values over a fixed BER. The SRRC has moderate SNR values over the fixed BER in GFDM as compared to RC and Gaussian filter.

References

1. Cho, Y.S., Kim, J., Yang, W.Y., Kang, C.G.: MIMO-OFDM Wireless Communications with MATLAB. Wiley, Hoboken (2010)
2. Zhou, S., Wang, Z.: OFDM for Underwater Acoustic Communications. Wiley, Hoboken (2014)
3. Hanzo, L., Keller, T.: OFDM and MC-CDMA: A Primer. Wiley, Hoboken (2006)
4. Muller, S.H., Huber, J.B.: A novel peak power reduction scheme for OFDM. In: 8th International Symposium on Personal, Indoor and Mobile Radio Communications, Finland, pp. 1090–1094. IEEE Press, (1997)
5. Re, E.D., Fantacci, R., Morosi, S., Seravalle, R.: Comparison of CDMA and OFDM techniques for downstream power-line communications on low voltage grid. IEEE Trans. Power Delivery **18**, 1104–1109 (2003)
6. Farhang, A., Marchetti, N., Doyle, L.E.: Low complexity transceiver design for GFDM. IEEE Trans. Sig. Process. **64**, 1507–1518 (2016)

7. Gasper, I., Mendes, L., Matthe, M., Michailow, N., Festag, A., Fettweis, G.: LTE-compatible 5G PHY based on generalized frequency division multiplexing. In:11th International Symposium on Wireless Communications Systems, Spain, pp. 209–213. IEEE Press (2014)
8. Sharifian, Z., Omidi, M., Farhang, A., Sourck, H.S.: Polynomial-based compressing and iterative expanding for PAPR reduction in GFDM. In: 23rd Iranian Conference on Electrical Engineering, Iran, pp. 518–523. IEEE Press (2015)
9. Michailow, N., Mendes, L., Matthe, M., Gaspar, I., Festag, A., Fettweis, G.: Robust WHT-GFDM for the next generation of wireless networks. IEEE Commun. Lett. **19**, 106–109 (2014)
10. Matthe, M., Mendes, L.L., Fettweis, G.: Space-time coding for generalized frequency division multiplexing. In: 20th European Wireless conference, Spain, pp. 1–5. IEEE Press (2010)
11. Matthe, M., Michailow, N., Gaspar, I., Fettweis, G.: Influence of pulse shaping on bit error rate performance and out of band radiation of generalized frequency division multiplexing. In: IEEE International Conference on Communications Workshops, Australia, pp. 43–48. IEEE Press (2014)
12. Datta, R., Michailow, N., Krone, S., Lentmaier M., Fettweis, G.: Generalized frequency division multiplexing in cognitive radio. In: 20th European Signal Processing Conference, Romania, pp. 2679–2683. IEEE Press (2016)
13. Matthe, M., Mendes, L.L., Fettweis, G.: Generalized frequency division multiplexing in a Gabor transform setting. IEEE Commun. Lett. **18**, 1379–1382 (2014)
14. Bandari, S.K., Vakamulla, V.M., Drosopoulos, A.: GFDM/OQAM performance analysis under nakagami fading channels. Phys. Commun. **26**, 162–169 (2018)
15. Zhong, Z., Guo, J.: Bit error rate analysis of a MIMO-generalized frequency division multiplexing scheme for 5th generation cellular systems. In: IEEE International Conference on Electronic Information and Communication Technology, China, pp. 62–68. IEEEPress (2016)
16. Carrick, M., Reed, J.H.: Improved GFDM equalization in severe frequency selective fading. In: IEEE 38th Sarnoff Symposium, USA, pp. 1–6. IEEE Press (2017)
17. Lim, B., Ko, C.: SIR analysis of OFDM and GFDM waveforms with timing offset, CFO and phase noise. IEEE Trans. Wirel. Commun. **16**, 6979–6990 (2017)
18. Kumar, A., Magarini, M., Bregni, S.: Improving GFDM symbol error rate performance using "Better than Nyquist" pulse shaping filters. IEEE Latin Am. Trans. **15**, 1244–1249 (2017)
19. Na, Z., et al.: Turbo receiver channel estimation for GFDM-based cognitive radio networks. IEEE Access **6**, 9926–9935 (2018)
20. Michailow, N., et al.: generalized frequency division multiplexing for 5th generation cellular networks. IEEE Trans. Commun. **62**, 3045–3061 (2014)
21. Juboori, G.A., Doufexi, A., Nix, A.R.: System level 5G evaluation of MIMO-GFDM in an LTE-A platform. In: 24th International Conference on Telecommunications, Cyprus, pp. 1–5. IEEE Press (2017)
22. Sendrei, L., Marchevsky, S., Michailow, N., Fettweis, G.: Iterative receiver for clipped GFDM signals. In: 24th International Conference Radioelektronika, Slovakia, pp. 1–4. IEEE Press (2014)
23. Ortega, A., Fabbri, L., Tralli,V.: Performance evaluation of GFDM over nonlinear channel. In: International Conference on Information and Communication Technology Convergence (ICTC), South Korea, pp. 12–17. IEEE Press (2016)

Comparative Analysis of KALMAN and Least Square for DWT Based MIMO-OFDM System

Neha Awasthi[✉] and Sukesha Sharma

UIET, Panjab University, Chandigarh, India
neha.27lawasthi@gmail.com, er_sukesha@yahoo.com

Abstract. In this paper the BER performance of LS and KALMAN is calculated, Channel estimation is done by implementation of DWT based MIMO OFDM system and is performed by simple substitution of FFT with DWT in new system framework. Channel estimation is used to recover the transmitted data. Simulations are done in MATLAB and performances are investigated with different modulations like QPSK (Quadrature Phase Shift Keying), QAM (Quadrature Amplitude Modulation), and BPSK (Binary Phase Shift Keying) for LS and KALMAN filter.

Keywords: Channel estimation · Least square · KALMAN · DWT
Bit error rate

1 Introduction

In a wireless communication system, for the design of receiver channel estimation (which reduces noise and interference) plays an important role to recover the transmitted data, trace channel and to improve receiver demodulation ability. Discrete wavelet (DW) helps in attaining high data rate transmission. Channel estimation is done by inserting pilot symbols. Two methods for inserting it are comb-type pilot and block type pilot [1]. Comb type pilot includes a higher degree of transmission rate hence provides better signal to noise ratio [2]. Wavelet-based OFDM satisfies the condition of orthogonality and whose related wavelet transform is orthogonal is called an orthogonal wavelet [3, 4]. In this investigation, the signal is decomposed into frequency components and different modulation schemes used are QAM, BPSK, QPSK. QAM uses four phases and finite range of a minimum of two amplitudes and two phases. In BPSK, two phases are used. BPSK separate bits by shifting the carriers by 180° [3]. The rate at which error occur is called BER. BER is expressed in terms of percentage and a unitless quantity. It is influenced by distortion, interference, transmission channel, noise, wireless multipath fading. QAM, BPSK, QPSK these are different modulation techniques which reduce the bit error rate. The result presented in this paper is simulated using MATLAB software.

A. K. Luhach et al. (Eds.): ICAICR 2018, CCIS 956, pp. 30–38, 2019.
https://doi.org/10.1007/978-981-13-3143-5_3

2 Implementation of the DWT Based MIMO-OFDM System

For the transmission and reception of binary data, the system uses modulator/demodulator concept to evaluate the BER. The binary data mapped into multi-amplitude and multiphase signals. After the insertion of pilots, inverse discrete wavelet transform (IDWT) transforms the data sequence into the time domain signal and then convert parallel to serial. At the receiver, noise added into a transmitted signal and then convert the signal from serial to parallel form [5]. For de-multiplexing of the received signal, the data is sent to the DWT block. After DWT data is recovered, transforming the signal into the frequency domain and then pilot signals are extracted. And then convert the signal from parallel to serial form [6]. After that signal will be demodulated and then binary data is received on the receiver. The input data bits are grouped and mapped into multi-amplitude and the mapped data symbols'$\psi(n)$' are transformed and combined to form a signal '$P(n)$' is written as:

$$P(n) = IDWT\{\psi(n)\} \tag{1}$$

$$\psi(n) = e^{j2\pi n/Tu(t-Ts)} \tag{2}$$

where, 'u' is transmission time, 't' is time and 'T_s' is Total time, '$\psi(n)$' is Subcarrier pulse (mother wavelet) vector form, signal '$P(n)$' can be written as:

$$P(n) = [P(0), P(1), \ldots \ldots \ldots P(N-1)] \tag{3}$$

where, 'N' is the number of subcarriers, then symbol '$P(n)$' is transmitted through frequency selective multipath fading channel and is written as:

$$Z(n) = P(n) * b(n) + W(n) \tag{4}$$

where, 'n' is Impulse response, '*' is convolution operator, '$W(n)$' is AWGN. Signal '$b(n)$' is transmitted through multipath fading channel with AWGN and channel impulse response is expressed as:

$$b(n) = \sum_{v=0}^{v-1} b_p b(t - T_v) + W(n) \tag{5}$$

where, 'b_P' is complex channel impulse response, 'v' is a number of the propagation path, '$W(n)$' is additive white Gaussian noise, 'T_v' is propagation time, 'b' is transmitted signal. In vector form, channel impulse response is written as:

$$b(n) = [b(0), b(1), \ldots \ldots, b(N-1)] \tag{6}$$

Again, by utilizing DWT at the receiver side reverse method is done. The Signals are handled by the demodulator for information recovery. After serial to parallel conversion DWT (discrete wavelet transform) is done and is written as:

$$Y(k) = DWT[P(n)] = (Y(n), \psi(n))$$

$$= 2^{-n/2} \sum_{n-\infty}^{\infty} P(n)\psi(2^{-n}n - k) \tag{7}$$

where 'Ψ' is the mother wavelet function, '2^{-n}' and '$n-k$' are shifting and scaling parameters. The signal '$Y(k)$' can be composed in the frequency domain is written as:

$$Y(k) = P(k)b(k) + W(k) \tag{8}$$

where, '$P(k)$', '$W(k)$' and '$b(k)$' are discrete wavelet transform of '$P(n)$', '$W(n)$' and '$b(n)$' respectively. The signal is assessed by partitioning the received signal with the transmitted signal and the received signal with estimated channel response is written as:

$$P(k) = Z(k)/b(k) \quad \text{where, } k = 0, 1, \ldots (N-1) \tag{9}$$

where '$P(k)$' is the estimate of transmitted signal OFDM signal. De-mapping of the signal yield the output information.

3 Least Square Estimator and KALMAN Filter

The least square estimator is characterized as the proportion between the input data sequence and the output. The least square has low complexity. By using a mathematical function to determine a line of best fit by diminishing the sum of squares of errors the least square technique is utilized [7, 8]. Transmitted data is represented as:

$$Ix = [I(0)\ I(1)\ I(2).\ldots\ldots\ldots\ldots\ldots I(n-1)] \tag{10}$$

Where, '$n-1$' represents 'n^{th}' bit from total transmitted bits. The received signal is represented as:

$$Jx = [J(0)\ J(1)\ J(2).\ldots\ldots\ldots\ldots\ldots J(n-1)] \tag{11}$$

$$b(k) = Ix/Jx \tag{12}$$

Due to low complexity least square can be implemented easily. But least square suffers from high mean square error. To overcome this problem KALMAN technique can be used [9]. To provides an efficient computation KALMAN filter contain a set of mathematical equations. To evaluate the state estimate and to minimize the mean square error KALMAN filter is used. To filter the impurities in the linear system KALMAN filter is an effective method [10]. KALMAN filter maintains the estimations of past, present, and future states. The KALMAN filter is an iterative mathematical process that uses consecutive data inputs and a set of equations to quickly estimate the position, true values, the velocity of the object being measured when the measured values contain unpredicted or random error, uncertainty or variation. KALMAN filter algorithm is used and is expressed as:

$$Zr(m) = b(0)\,P(m) + b(0)\,P(m-1) + \ldots\ldots b(m-N+1) + W(n) \qquad (13)$$

In vector form, OFDM symbol is expressed as:

$$Zr = [Z(0), Z(1), \ldots\ldots\ldots\ldots, Z(N-1)]^T \qquad (14)$$

In vector form, AWGN can be expressed as:

$$W(m) = [W(0),\ W(1),\ \ldots\ldots W(N-1)]^T \qquad (15)$$

The state space model 'U(r)' is expressed as:

$$U(r) = [b_{r-1}b_y]^T_{LX1} \qquad (16)$$

Where, LX1 is the channel tap vector.

$$b_r(L) = a1 b_{r-1}(L) + a2 b_{r-2}(L) + E_r(L) \qquad (17)$$

where, 'E_r' is the modeling noise vector and a1 and a2 are the coefficients. By using Eqs. (6) and (17):

$$br = [br(0),\ br(1),\ \ldots br(L-1)]^T \qquad (18)$$

$$b_{r-1} = [b_{r-1}(0),\ b_{r-1}(1), \ldots, b_{r-1}(L-1)]_{LX1} \qquad (19)$$

From Eq. (17), provides the process equation is written as: (Fig. 1)

$$Ur = DUr - 1 + Er \qquad (20)$$

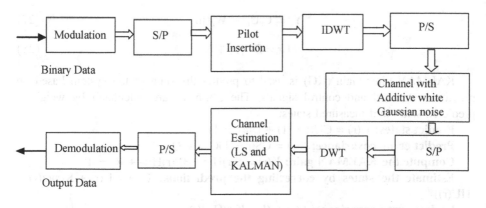

Fig. 1. DWT based MIMO-OFDM system.

By using Eqs. (13) and (17)

$$E_r = [E_r(0), E_r(1), \ldots E_r(L-1)] \tag{21}$$

$$Y_r = C_r U_r + W_r(m) \tag{22}$$

where, 'C_r' is the measurement matrix and is formed by augmenting with null matrix and is expressed as:

$$C_r = [0_{NXL} \quad C_r]_{NX2L} \tag{23}$$

here, C_r is a NX2L matrix of transmitted symbol.

$$C_r = \begin{bmatrix} P_r(0) & P_{r-1}(N-1) & P_{r-1}(N-L+1) \\ P_r(1) & P_r(0) & P_{r-1}(N-L+1) \\ Pr(N-1) & Pr(N-2) & Pr(N-L) \end{bmatrix} \tag{24}$$

By using Eq. (13)

$$Z_r(m) = b_r(0)P(m) + b_r(1)P(m-1) + \ldots\ldots\ldots + b_r(L-1)P(m-L+1) + W_r(m) \tag{25}$$

$$\begin{bmatrix} P_r(0) \\ P_r(1) \\ P_r(N-1) \end{bmatrix} = \begin{bmatrix} P_r(0) & P_{r-1}(N-1) & P_{r-1}(N-L+1) \\ P_r(1) & P_r(0) & P_{r-1}(N-L+1) \\ P_r(N-1) & P_r(N-2) & P_n(N-L) \end{bmatrix} \begin{bmatrix} b_r(0) \\ b_r(1) \\ b_r(L-1) \end{bmatrix} + W_r(m) \tag{26}$$

KALMAN algorithm works in two groups one is Prediction Equation and the other one is Update equation. For state space model Eqs. (20) and (23) form the process equation and measurement equation and is written as:

$$Y_r = C_r U_r + W_r(m) \tag{27}$$

$$U_r = DU_{r-1} + E_r \tag{28}$$

KALMAN filter Gain (KG) is used to predict the state of the system based on previous estimated and control signals. The estimates are calculated by weighing predicted states and measured states:

Predict states: $U(r) = CU(r-1) + Du(r-1)$

Predict error covariance: $S(r) = CS(r-1)C > + Q$

Compute the KALMAN gain: $K(r) = S(r)H > (HP(r)H > + R) - 1$

Estimate the states by correcting the predictions: $U(r) = U(r) + K(r)(z(r) - HU(r))$

Update error covariance: $S(r) = (I - K(r)H)S(r)$

3.1   DWT Based MIMO OFDM

DWT has been presented as a versatile and efficient technique for decomposition of the signal [10]. DWT is utilized as a part of OFDM system to the improvement of BER and throughput performance [11]. In DWT based MIMO-OFDM system there is no need to add cyclic prefix and it offers the investigation of the signal in both frequency and in the time domain [12]. The execution of the DWT based MIMO-OFDM is gotten by just replacement of FFT/IFFT block with DWT/IDWT.

4   Simulation and Result

The BER performance of LS and KALMAN using different modulations is shown in the figures (Figs. 2, 3 and 4) and (Tables 1, 2 and 3).

Table 1. Different channel parameters for simulation.

Simulation parameters	Value (DWT based MIMO-OFDM)
Modulation	QAM, PSK, QPSK
Subcarriers	64, 128, 256
No. of symbols	100
Constellation	64
Type of channel	AWGN/Rayleigh flat fading
SNR range	[0:2:40]

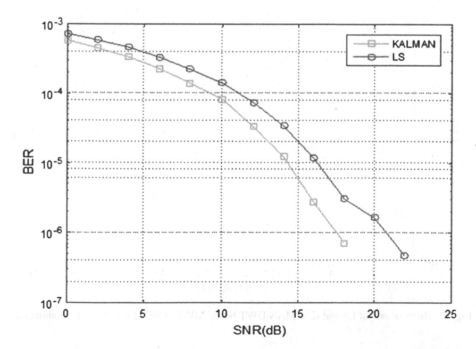

Fig. 2. Bit error rate of LS and KALMAN DWT based MIMO-OFDM using QAM modulation.

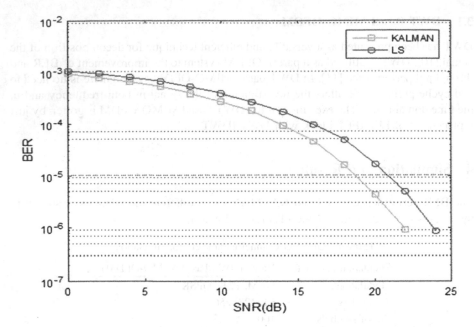

Fig. 3. Bit error rate of LS and KALMAN DWT based MIMO-OFDM using QPSK modulation.

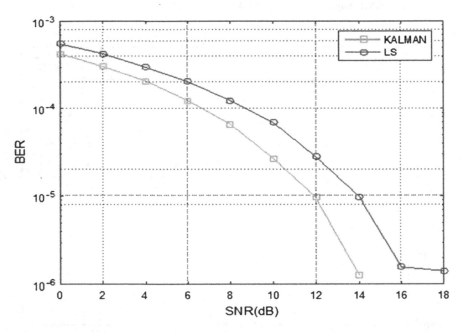

Fig. 4. Bit error rate of LS and KALMAN DWT based MIMO-OFDM using BPSK modulation.

Table 2. QAM, BPSK and QPSK in KALMAN graph for bit error rate of proposed work, implemented in MATLAB.

SNR (in dB)	Bit error rate		
	KALMAN		
	QAM	BPSK	QPSK
0	.0009290	.0004272	.0005794
2	.0007747	.0003075	.0004480
4	.0006490	.0002077	.0003353
6	.0005150	.0001225	.0002261
8	.0003844	.0006539	.0001407
10	.0002675	.00002648	.00008148
12	.0001792	.000009609	.00003304
14	.00009375	.000001250	.00001234
16	.00004617	0	.000002734
18	.00001609	0	.0000007031
20	.000004296	0	0
22	.0000009375	0	0

Table 3. QAM, BPSK and QPSK in least square graph for bit error rate of proposed work, implemented in MATLAB.

SNR (in dB)	Bit error rate		
	Least square		
	QAM	BPSK	QPSK
0	.00100	.0005628	.0007219
2	.0009254	.0004282	.0005883
4	.0007860	.0003019	.0004616
6	.0006521	.0002046	.0003314
8	.0005129	.0001225	.0002256
10	.0003824	.00006937	.0001422
12	.0002645	.00002804	.00007343
14	.0001700	.000009687	.00003398
16	.00009593	.000001562	.00001164
18	.00004960	.000001406	.000003046
20	.000001687	0	.000001640
22	.000005000	0	.0000004687
23	.0000008593	0	0

5 Conclusion

After performing the proposed work to estimate the BER with channel estimation, QAM, BPSK, QPSK. The KALMAN algorithm reduces more error as compared to LS algorithm thus for transmission of digital data KALMAN algorithm is an efficient solution. SNR is directly proportional to data rate and BER is inversely proportional to the SNR The transmitted signal goes through numerous reflection, refraction, multipath fading, and propagation. So at the receiver side theses effects of channel needs to minimized to recover the actual signal. By using DWT in MIMO-OFDM system the BER and the throughput performance is improved. In this, it has been observed that the accuracy of KALMAN is better and BER is minimum than that of LS Estimator by using QAM, BPSK, QPSK modulations.

References

1. Weeks, M.: Digital Signal Processing using MATLAB and the Wavelets. Georgia State University, Atlanta (2007)
2. Beek, V., De Kate, S., Sandell, M., Wilson, S.K.: On channel estimation in OFDM systems, 0–5 (1995). https://doi.org/10.1109/VETEC.1995.504981
3. Zaier, A., Boualleque, R.: Channel estimation study for block type pilot insertion in OFDM system under slowly time-varying conditions, vol. 3, no. 6, November 2011
4. Vamsidhar, A., Rajesh Kumar, P., Raja Rajeswari, K.: A new approach to investigation of discrete wavelet-based multiuser MIMO-OFDM for BPSK modulation scheme. In: Satapathy, S.C., Bhateja, V., Chowdary, P.S.R., Chakravarthy, V.V.S.S.S., Anguera, J. (eds.) Proceedings of 2nd International Conference on Micro-Electronics, Electromagnetics and Telecommunications. LNEE, vol. 434, pp. 323–332. Springer, Singapore (2018). https://doi.org/10.1007/978-981-10-4280-5_34
5. Asadi, A., Tazehkand, B.M.: A new method to channel estimation in OFDM. Int. J. Digit. Inf. Wirel. Commun. (IJDIWC) 3(1), 1–9 (2013). ISSN 2225-658X
6. Madan Kumar, L., Homayeun, N.: A review of wavelets for digital wireless communication. Wirel. Pers. Commun. 37(3–4), 387–420 (2006)
7. Bouchlel, A., Sakle, A., Mansouri, N.: Performance comparison of DWT based MIMOOFDM and FFT based MIMO-OFDM (2005)
8. Moqbel, M.A.M., Wangdong, W., Ali, A.Z.: MIMO channel estimation using the LS and MMSE algorithm. Hunan University, Changsha, Hunan, China
9. IOSR J. Electron. Commun. Eng. (IOSR-JECE), 12(1), 13–22 (2017). Hajjah University, Hajjah, Yemen. e-ISSN 2278-2834, p-ISSN 2278-8735, ver. II
10. Gupta, A.K., Pathela, M., Kumar, A.: Kalman filtering based channel estimation for MIMOOFDM. Dehradun Int. J. Comput. Appl. 53(15) (2012). 0975–8887
11. Lakshmanan, M.K., Nikookar, H.: A review of wavelets for digital wireless communication. Wirel. Pers. Commun. 37, 387–420 (2006)
12. Nallanathan, A., Sen, Q.S.: Adaptive channel estimation and interference cancellation in space-time coded OFDM systems. In: IEEE 59th Vehicular Technology Conference, vol. 3, pp. 1760–1764 (2004)
13. Kumbasar, V., et al.: Optimization of wavelet-based OFDM for multipath powerline channel by genetic algorithm. Wirel. Commun. Mob. Comput. 9(9), 1243–1250 (2009)
14. Anuradha, Kumar, N.: BER analysis of conventional and wavelet-based OFDM in LTE using different modulation techniques. In: Proceedings of Engineering and Computational Sciences (RAECS), UIET Panjab University Chandigarh, India, pp. 1–4. IEEE, March 2014
15. Hussain, A.: Studies on DWT-OFDM and FFT-OFDM systems. In: ICCCP (2009)

Equivalent Circuit Modelling
for Unimorph and Bimorph Piezoelectric
Energy Harvester

Prateek Asthana$^{(\boxtimes)}$, Apoorva Dwivedi, and Gargi Khanna

Department of Electronics and Communication Engineering,
National Institute of Technology, Hamirpur, India
prateekasthana1989@gmail.com, apoorva.dwivedi07@gmail.com,
gargikhanna20@gmail.com

Abstract. Piezoelectricity is a growing area of energy harvesting research. Piezoelectric energy harvester (PEH) generally use cantilever structures in unimorph and bimorph configuration. These harvester sense the mechanical vibration and convert them into usable electric energy. In this work, an analytical model displaying the characteristics of PEH with resonant frequency, tip deflections and output power have been determined. Analytical model is in close agreement with the FEM simulation model having an error of about 5%. In order to bridge the gap between FEM simulation and energy harvesting circuitry an equivalent electrical model for the energy harvester is developed. Resonant frequency determined from the equivalent model is 87.12 Hz, whereas from FEM model and analytical model are 90.56 Hz and 93.32 Hz respectively.

Keywords: Equivalent circuitry · Piezoelectric energy harvester
Vibration · Analytical modeling · Resonant frequency
Renewable energy

1 Introduction

Wireless sensing devices and portable electronics require periodically maintained external power supply throughout their lifetime. Self powered wireless sensing devices are being developed for low power applications. There are many methods to harvest energy like solar, wind, vibration etc. A promising source of energy is vibration which can be used to harvest power for wireless sensors [1]. There are three ways to harvest vibration energy from the environment to power wireless sensing nodes i.e. electrostatics, capacitive and piezoelectric. Among these methods piezoelectric is the most reliable and robust technique to harvest vibrations. Piezoelectric energy harvesting involves simple structure, low cost, no electromagnetic interference, easiness to fabricate and a high energy density compared to the other two vibration techniques [2]. Vibration energy harvesting has been

Supported by MEITY.

© Springer Nature Singapore Pte Ltd. 2019
A. K. Luhach et al. (Eds.): ICAICR 2018, CCIS 956, pp. 39–49, 2019.
https://doi.org/10.1007/978-981-13-3143-5_4

Table 1. Device parameters for piezoelectric energy harvester

Parameter name	Parameter symbol	Parameter value [mm]
Length of device	L	40
Length of piezo	L_p	40
Width of device	w_d	4
Thickness of piezo	t_p	0.06
Thickness of substrate	t_s	0.04
Length of proof mass	L_m	9
Thickness of proof mass	t_m	4

area of research for the past few years, with a lot of emphasis being given to piezoelectric materials. Modeling of piezoelectric materials has been a focus of research over the past few years [3]. Despite the research a model relating material properties and power output for the harvester in an easy manner is not available. The present research work is aimed on the development of a new model for evaluating the output power of the piezoelectric energy harvester using analogies to electronic circuit theory. The model, initially, relies on equivalent circuit representation of electromechanical transducers. The equivalent circuit representation can model electromechanical transducers (i.e. electrical and mechanical domains), using simple circuit elements, giving an analogy in the differential equations describing both domains, and couple both domains by an ideal electromechanical transformer [4].

SPICE (Simulated Program with Integrated Circuit Emphasis) and FEA (Finite element analysis) have been utilized to model electrical and mechanical properties of a Piezoelectric energy harvester (PEH). Open circuit and short circuit voltage can be estimated with finite analysis. For system with weak electromechanical coupling these results can be directly applied [5]. But when there is strong coupling, mechanical vibrations are effected by backward coupling, which causes inconsistencies in voltage and current values. In order to bridge this gap between SPICE and FEA an Equivalent circuit model (ECM) is developed, which could estimate the performance of PEH accurately.

2 Analytical Model

Characteristics of a PEH can be realized with the help of an analytical model. Several coupled and uncoupled lumped and distributed models have been developed in the past few years. Distributed model based on Rayleigh-Ritz and Euler Bernoulli theorem give an appropriate analysis of the harvester under ambient vibration conditions. Ertuk and Inman [5] reviewed many models and addressed the issues in distributed modeling of PEH. A brief description of the distributed parameter model of simple cantilevered unimorph harvester has been provided with calculation of tip deflection as well as generated power output have been

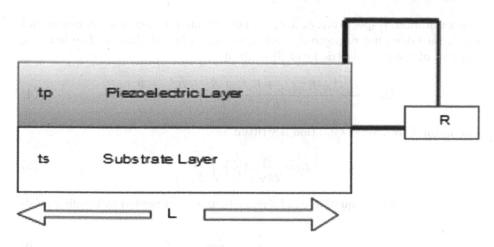

Fig. 1. A Piezoelectric unimorph energy harvester [2]

derived. The energy harvester in a bimorph configuration can be derived similarly. Table 1 describes the device parameters for PEH.

Unimorph Cantilever PEH

A rectangular shaped unimorph cantilever based PEH is shown in Fig. 1. Beam is longitudinally uniform in density. Following assumptions are made in the analytical modeling on the constitutive piezoelectricity relations: (a) Beam assumption for Euler-Bernoulli; (b) negligible air damping for external excitation; (c) proportional damping (i.e., viscous air damping and strain rate damping are assumed to be proportional to bending stiffness and mass per length); and (d) uniform electric field through the piezoelectric thickness [6]. The piezoelectric constitutive equations are given as:

$$\sigma = dE + sX \tag{1}$$

$$D = \epsilon E + dX \tag{2}$$

where s is elasticity modulus and σ is stress that is dependent on electric field E and strain X while d is the piezoelectric constant. Electric field and strain determine the dielectric displacement D. ϵ is absolute permittivity of the piezoelectric material. Assumptions (a) and (b) determine the governing equation of mechanical motion is,

$$\frac{\partial^2 M(x,t)}{\partial x^2} + c_a \frac{\partial w_{rel}(x,t)}{\partial t} + m \frac{\partial^2 w_{rel}(x,t)}{\partial t^2} +$$

$$c_s I \frac{\partial^5 w_{rel}(x,t)}{\partial t \partial x^4} = -m \frac{\partial^2 w_b(x,t)}{\partial t^2} \tag{3}$$

where I is moment of inertia of beam; $M(x,t)$ is the internal bending moment of the beam; $w_{rel}(xt)$ and $w_b(xt)$ are deflection relative to the base motion and base excitation, respectively; c_a & c_s are coefficients for viscous air damping and strain rate damping respectively and m is mass per unit length. The bending moment of the piezoelectric layer [7] is given by:

$$D_p = \frac{E_p^2 t_p^4 + E_{np}^2 t_{np}^4 + E_p t_{np}(2t_p^2 + 2t_{np}^2 + 3t_p t_{np})}{12(E_p t_p + E_{np} t_{np})} \qquad (4)$$

The natural transverse vibration is written as:

$$f_i = \frac{v_i^2}{2\pi\sqrt{2}}\left(\frac{h}{l_b^2}\right)\sqrt{\frac{e_T}{\rho}} \qquad (5)$$

The Bernoulli-Euler equation can be derived in a term related to bending modulus as,

$$f_i = \frac{v_i^2}{2\pi l_b^2}\sqrt{\frac{D}{m_w}} \qquad (6)$$

with v_i for the first three modes are: $v_1 = 1.8751$, $v_2 = 4.6941$ and $v_3 = 7.857$ The first natural frequency of the unimorph structure is calculated as:

$$f_N = \frac{0.1615}{l_b^2}\sqrt{\frac{D_p}{m}} \qquad (7)$$

The natural frequency of cantilever with proof mass, f_M is:

$$f_M = f_N\sqrt{\frac{m_{eff}}{m_{eff} + M_t}} \qquad (8)$$

M_t is the additional proof mass while the effective mass at the tip of the cantilever structure is m_{eff}. Effective mass is given by:

$$m_{eff} = 0.236\rho_b w_b h_b l_b \qquad (9)$$

Tip deflection of the unimorph cantilever is given by:

$$W_D = \frac{Ymw^2}{k\sqrt{[1 - (\frac{\omega}{\omega_n})^2]^2 + (\zeta\frac{\omega}{\omega_n})^2}} \qquad (10)$$

where, $Y = \frac{a}{\omega^2}$ and ζ is damping coefficient. The primary focus of the work is on the bimorph energy harvester as it provides better power density then the unimorph energy harvester.

Bimorph Cantilever PEH

A bimorph is constructed with a substrate in center sandwiched between two piezoelectric layers as shown in Fig. 2. Thickness of piezoelectric layer is t_p while that for substrate layer is t_s. The piezoelectric layers are electrically shorted in series with layers being poled towards the substructure. In order to tune cantilever a proof mass M_t is placed at tip of cantilever (x = L). The parameters

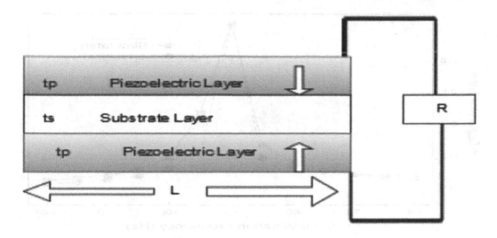

Fig. 2. A Piezoelectric bimorph energy harvester

with the subscripts s and p refer to substrate and piezoelectric, respectively. Total base movement can be described by:

$$w_b(x,t) = xh(t) + g(t) \qquad (11)$$

Beam motion of a bimorph cantilever for series connected piezoelectric layer is given by:

$$YI\frac{\partial^4 w_r el(x,t)}{\partial x^4} + c_a\frac{\partial w_{rel}(x,t)}{\partial t} + kv(t)(\frac{d\delta(x)}{dx} - \frac{d\delta(x-L)}{dx}) +$$
$$m\frac{\partial^2 w_{rel}(x,t)}{\partial t^2} + c_{sI}\frac{\partial^5 w_{rel}(x,t)}{\partial t\partial x^4} = -[m + M_t\delta(x-L)\frac{\partial^2 w_b(x,t)}{\partial t^2}] \qquad (12)$$

c_{sI} and c_a are coefficient for strain rate and viscous air dampening. Piezoelectric coupling term k, m is mass per unit length [8]. $v(t)$ is the voltage over the piezoelectric layers in accordance with Dirac delta function δ. The bending stiffness term YI of the cantilever is given by:

$$YI = \frac{2b}{3}[Y_s\frac{t_s^3}{8} + c_{11}^E((t_p + \frac{t_s}{2})^3 - \frac{t_s^3}{8})] \qquad (13)$$

where c_{11}^E is elastic constant at constant E-field while Y_s is Young's modulus for the substructure. t_s and t_p are thickness of substructure and piezoelectric layers respectively, and width of the cantilever is b.

Air damping constitutes to about 10% of total damping when the harvester is working in air, hence proportional damping exists in the system making the c_{sI} = c_a = 0. When harvester is working in higher viscosity fluids, these constants have to be considered [8]. The piezoelectric coupling coefficient k is given by:

$$k = \frac{d_{31}c_{11}(h_p + h_s)b}{2} \qquad (14)$$

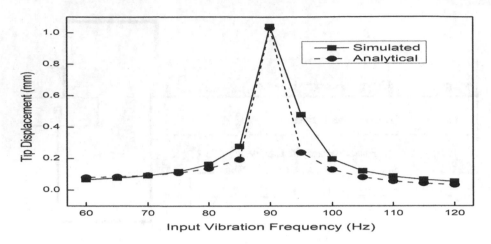

Fig. 3. A Piezoelectric bimorph energy harvester

Mass per unit length m for bimorph is:

$$m = b(\rho_s h_s + 2\rho_p h_p) \tag{15}$$

The resonant frequency for the bimorph cantilever can be calculated using Eqs. (7) and (15). Assuming proportional damping in beam, the response of system can be evaluated by an absolute convergent series of eigen value functions [7]:

$$\omega_{rel}^s = \Sigma_{r=1}^{\infty} \phi_r(x)\eta_r(t) \tag{16}$$

The mass-normalized eigenfunction $\phi_r(x)$ beam deflection in its rth mode, and modal mechanical function $\eta_r(t)$ describes amplitude of deflection over time. Tip deflection of unimorph cantilever with varying input vibration frequency is depicted in Fig. 3 based on:

$$W_D = \frac{Ymw^2}{k\sqrt{[1 - (\frac{\omega}{\omega_n})^2]^2 + (2\zeta\frac{\omega}{\omega_n})^2}} \tag{17}$$

2.1 Output Power

System's output power depends on amount of charge developed on the piezoelectric layer and due to the applied mechanical stress,

$$Q_3 = 2 \int_0^L D_3 w_s dx \tag{18}$$

By solving (1), (2), (10), (17) and (18) we obtain

$$Q_3 = 2w_s \int_0^L (d_{31}\sigma_1 + \epsilon_1^\sigma \frac{I_r R}{t_p}) \tag{19}$$

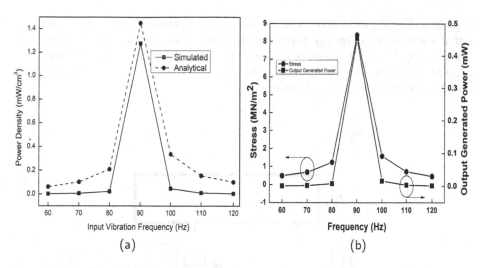

Fig. 4. (a) The frequency vs the power density, (b) the stress and generated output power for the input vibration frequency

Current is defined as the charge per unit area; hence, differentiating and solving (19) gives:

$$I_r(f) = \frac{d_{31}E_p t_n w_s (\frac{f}{f_n})^2 m a l_p}{4EI\sqrt{X + (1 - (\frac{f}{f_n})^2)^2}}$$

(20)

The average power dissipated in the load resistor R can be determined:

$$P_{avg}(f) = \frac{(I_r(f))^2 R}{2}$$

(21)

By using (20) in (21) we obtain

$$P_{avg}(f) = \frac{d_{31}^2 E_p^2 t_n^2 w_s(a)^2 m^2 (\frac{f^3}{f_n})^2 l_p R}{32(EI)^2((1 - (\frac{f}{f_n})^2)^2 + X)}$$

(22)

where

$$l_p = (4L^2 + 6Ll_m + 3l_m^2)^2$$

and

$$X = (2\zeta \frac{f}{f_n})^2 (1 + \frac{2\epsilon_p^\sigma w_s L f R}{t_p})$$

Power density from the analytical model Eq. (22) is compared with the FEM model in Fig. 4a and stress developed on the piezoelectric layer is converted into outout power as shown in Fig. 4b.

3   Equivalent Circuit Modeling

A PEH is generally connected to a resistive load, the power drop across the resistive load can be determined by analytical model and system-level FEA.

In practical application non-linear electric components such as rectifier and regulator are included in energy harvesting circuits. These circuits also have storage elements [9]. Energy harvesters having complex geometries cannot be modeled using analytical model and FEA. For these complex structures equivalent circuit modeling is the most appropriate method.

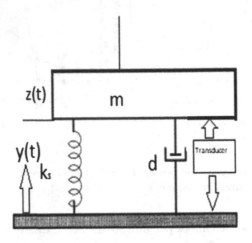

Fig. 5. Mass spring damper equivalent

3.1   Mechanical Equivalent

A mass spring damper system can be used to model PEH as shown in Fig. 5. Mass of the PEH system is m, k_s is the spring constant and d is damping coefficient. Harmonic movement of frame is y(t) while z(t) is relative motion of seismic mass [10]. Transfer function for the system is given by:

$$ma = m\ddot{z} + d\dot{z} + k_s z + F_e \tag{23}$$

$$a(t) = \ddot{y}(t) = \hat{a}\sin(\omega t)$$

External force applied on the harvester is ma. Damping force is F_e.

$$ma = m\ddot{z} + (d_e + d)\dot{z} + k_s z \tag{24}$$

Taking laplace transform,

$$ms^2 y = ms^2 z + (d + d_e)sz + k_s z \tag{25}$$

The dimensionless electrical & mechanical damping coefficient is given by:

$$\zeta_e = \frac{d_e}{2m\omega_n} \quad and \quad \zeta_d = \frac{d}{2m\omega_n} \tag{26}$$

Transfer function,

$$\frac{Z(s)}{y(s)} = \frac{s^2}{s^2 + 2\omega_n(\zeta_d + \zeta_e)s + \omega_n^2} \tag{27}$$

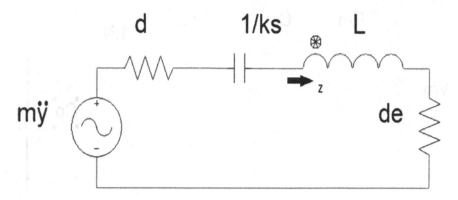

Fig. 6. Electrical equivalent of energy harvester

3.2 Electrical Equivalent

Electrical analogy is used to determine the equivalent circuit of the energy harvester. Mechanical force is represented as voltage, while electric current acts as mechanical velocity [11,12]. From (1) and (2) the electrical equivalent circuit is given in Fig. 6. Electrical circuit parameter can be determined in terms of energy harvester design parameters.

$$k_s = \frac{3YI}{L^2} \tag{28}$$

$$L = m_{eq} = \frac{33}{140}mL + M_t \tag{29}$$

where m is the mass per unit length of beam and M_t is mass of proof mass kept at tip of beam. Resistive component values can be determined from Eq. (26). The circuit above only represents the mechanical part of the harvester. Mechanical domain coupling to the electrical domain using electromechanical is established with the help of a transformer having winding ratio $1 : N$ as shown in Fig. 7. Electromechanical coupling coefficient is defined as k_{31}^2,

$$k_{31}^2 = \frac{d_{31}^2}{A_{33}^T s_{11}^E} \tag{30}$$

Transformer coupling N is defined in terms of design parameters,

$$N = \frac{d_{31}w}{s_{11}^E} \tag{31}$$

A simplified model is also derived with RLC circuit components can also be used as an electrical equivalent circuit for PEH as shown in Fig. 8.

$$V_{mc} = \frac{ma}{N} \tag{32}$$

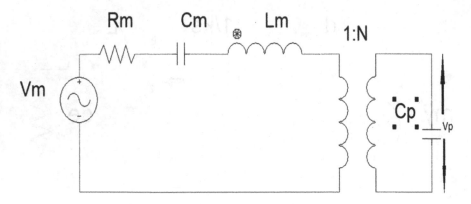

Fig. 7. Coupled electromechanical system

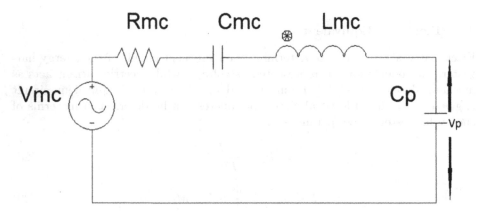

Fig. 8. Simplified electromechanical equivalent circuit

$$R_{mc} = \frac{d}{N^2} \tag{33}$$

$$L_{mc} = \frac{m_{eq}}{N^2} \tag{34}$$

$$C_{mc} = \frac{N^2}{k_s} \tag{35}$$

Using the electrical equivalent circuit model resonant frequency of the harvester can be determined as

$$\omega_n = \frac{1}{2\pi\sqrt{L_{mc}C_{mc}}} \tag{36}$$

for the bimorph energy harvester the resonant frequency using the electrical equivalent circuit is determined as 90.12 Hz.

4   Conclusion

An effective analytical model determining the resonant frequency, tip displacement and output generated power for the PEH has been described. The model matches the simulation result with a maximum error of 5%. An electrical equivalent circuit for the energy harvester is also emulated. The circuit consists of Resistor, Capacitor, Inductor with coupling being represented by a transformer. The resonant frequency from equivalent circuit is 87.12 Hz, while those from FEM and analytical model is 90.56 Hz and 93.32 Hz.

References

1. Beeby, S.P., Tudor, M.J., White, N.: Energy harvesting vibration sources for microsystems applications. Meas. Sci. Technol. **17**(12), R175 (2006)
2. Kim, S.G., Priya, S., Kanno, I.: Piezoelectric MEMS for energy harvesting. MRS Bull. **37**(11), 1039–1050 (2012)
3. Sodano, H.A., Inman, D.J., Park, G.: Comparison of piezoelectric energy harvesting devices for recharging batteries. J. Intell. Mater. Syst. Struct. **16**(10), 799–807 (2005)
4. Aghakhani, A., Basdogan, I.: Equivalent impedance electroelastic modeling of multiple piezo-patch energy harvesters on a thin plate with ac-dc conversion. IEEE/ASME Trans. Mechatron. **22**(4), 1575–1584 (2017)
5. Erturk, A., Inman, D.J.: A distributed parameter electromechanical model for cantilevered piezoelectric energy harvesters. J. Vib. Acoust. **130**(4), 041002 (2008)
6. Liu, H., Tay, C.J., Quan, C., Kobayashi, T., Lee, C.: Piezoelectric MEMS energy harvester for low-frequency vibrations with wideband operation range and steadily increased output power. J. Microelectromech. Syst. **20**(5), 1131–1142 (2011)
7. Yi, J.W., Shih, W.Y., Shih, W.H.: Effect of length, width, and mode on the mass detection sensitivity of piezoelectric unimorph cantilevers. J. Appl. Phys. **91**(3), 1680–1686 (2002)
8. Li, Z., Zhou, G., Zhu, Z., Li, W.: A study on the power generation capacity of piezoelectric energy harvesters with different fixation modes and adjustment methods. Energies **9**(2), 98 (2016)
9. Tilmans, H.A.: Equivalent circuit representation of electromechanical transducers: I. Lumped-parameter systems. J. Micromech. Microeng. **6**(1), 157 (1996)
10. Caliò, R.: Piezoelectric energy harvesting solutions. Sensors **14**(3), 4755–4790 (2014)
11. Hehn, T., Manoli, Y.: Piezoelectricity and energy harvester modelling. CMOS Circuits for Piezoelectric Energy Harvesters. SSAM, vol. 38, pp. 21–40. Springer, Dordrecht (2015). https://doi.org/10.1007/978-94-017-9288-2_2
12. De Giuseppe, G., Centuori, A., Malvasi, A.: An improved PZT cantilever spice model for practical energy harvesting circuits simulations and measurements. Measurement **98**, 374–383 (2017)

Exact BER for MDPSK and MPSK over Generalized Rician Fading Channel

Veenu Kansal, Rajanbir Singh, and Simranjit Singh$^{(\boxtimes)}$

Department of ECE, Punjabi University, Patiala, India
veenukansal@outlook.com, rajanbir_singh@outlook.com,
simranjit@live.com

Abstract. Generalized Rician fading (GR) channel model is the parent model of existing fading models which are special cases of this fading channel. The exact performance evaluation for different types of modulation schemes over generalized fading channel is of great interest and importance. In this paper, exact error probability results for M-ary differential phase shift keying (MDPSK) and M-ary phase shift keying (MPSK) over the GR fading channel are derived. This fading channel provides improved average symbol error probability (ASEP) when compared with other fading channels. The obtained analytical results provide the performance evaluation of the given fading channel. The accuracy of analytical results is justified magnificently by MATLAB simulations.

Keywords: MPSK · MDPSK · Rician fading · Nakagami-m fading
Generalized Rician fading

1 Introduction

Mobile communication systems work at high frequencies as the available bandwidth at lower portion of spectrum is very less to adequately provide mobile services. On the other hand at high frequencies complex problems come into picture and mobility of users further worsens the condition [1, 2]. The performance of wireless systems degrades due to fading. Most common fading distributions that describe the statistics of the mobile radio signal are Rayleigh, Rician and Nakagami-m, TWDP fading [3–12].

GR fading channel is not very extensively studied in literature. In [3], an analysis on symbol error probability (SEP) with maximal ratio combining (MRC) diversity reception over GR fading channels was considered for different M-ary modulation schemes. The second order statistics i.e. level crossing rate (LCR) and average duration of fades (ADF) were also considered.

The bit error rate (BER) performance of Gray-coded quadrature amplitude modulation (QAM) with MRC diversity reception was evaluated in [5]. A new method was developed to calculate the conditional probability of correlated, independent and non-identically distributed (i.n.d) Rician fading. In [6], the authors examined the M-ary QAM MIMO-OFDM systems by calculate the outage probability and the BER by using the moment generating function (MGF) approach. Authors in [7] deduced that exact average error rate expressions employing non-coherent equal-gain diversity.

© Springer Nature Singapore Pte Ltd. 2019
A. K. Luhach et al. (Eds.): ICAICR 2018, CCIS 956, pp. 50–62, 2019.
https://doi.org/10.1007/978-981-13-3143-5_5

Orthogonal space-time block coded (OSTBC) OFDM systems over GR fading channel were analyzed in [8]. The MGF of SNR was calculated and used to calculate the BER, pairwise error probability (PEP) and outage probability. In [9], the SER for equal gain combining (EGC) over GR fading channel was evaluated with considering the effect of correlation between diversity branches. The authors provided a detail analysis of lower and upper bounds on the joint probability distribution function (PDF) of fading amplitudes. With the use of these joint PDF bounds, asymptotically tight SEP bounds for EGC with pre-detection combining were developed. Asymptotic error performance for EGC and SC expressions was generalized in [10]. The authors presented the expression of asymptotic error rate in terms of infinite series. By terminating the series at a particular point the authors were successful in achieving more accuracy than asymptotic rate. In [12], analysis for selection combiner output (SCO) for single-user cumulative distribution functions (CDFs) of multivariate correlated and identically distributed GR fading for different no. of degree of freedom is done.

From the literature survey, we can conclude that most of the work done in past was on diversity and not much of the work is done exclusively on modulations schemes over the GR fading channel. The organisation of this paper is as follows. The PDF of fading model is discussed in Sect. 2. The closed-form ASEP expressions are calculated in Sect. 3. In Sect. 4, the results are plotted for the derived expressions. The veracity of derived results is verified by the simulation results which are performed by using MATLAB software. In Sect. 5, the concluding remarks about the paper are made.

2 System Model

A. Generalized Rician Fading PDF

The envelope of the received signal follows the GR fading distribution. A GR random variable can be constructed from n Gaussian random variables as $X = \sqrt{\sum_{i=1}^{n} X_i^2}$ where X_i $\{i = 1, 2 \dots n\}$ are independent Gaussians have mean m_i and common variance $\sigma^2 = 1/2$ i.e., $X_i \sim N(0, 1/2)$. This fading model is a general model and includes existing fading models such as Rayleigh, Rician and Nakagami-m as special cases. The PDF of GR random variable is given by [13, 2.464]:

$$p_x(x) = \frac{x^{n/2}}{\sigma^2 s^{n-2/2}} e^{-\frac{x^2+s^2}{2\sigma^2}} I_{\frac{n}{2}-1}\left(\frac{sx}{\sigma^2}\right). \tag{1}$$

where $s = \sqrt{\sum_{i=1}^{n} m_i^2}$ and n is the degrees of freedom of the PDF. $I_\alpha(x)$ is modified Bessel function of first kind and order α given in [14].

B. PDF of Received SNR

The PDF in Eq. (1) can be transformed into SNR form by using the square transformation given in [15]. The PDF in SNR form is given by:

$$p_\gamma(\gamma) = \frac{\Omega^{\frac{n+2}{4}}\gamma^{\frac{n-2}{4}}\exp\left(-\frac{nK}{2}\right)\exp\left(-\frac{\Omega\gamma}{2\sigma^2\bar{\gamma}}\right)I_{\frac{n}{2}-1}\left(\sqrt{\frac{nK\Omega\gamma}{\sigma^2\bar{\gamma}}}\right)}{2(\bar{\gamma})^{\frac{n+2}{4}}(nK)^{\frac{n-2}{4}}(\sigma^2)^{\frac{n+2}{4}}}. \tag{2}$$

where Ω is second moment of GR Fading which is obtained by substituting $n = 2$ in equation [13, 2.3–66].

$$\Omega = E[X^2] = 2\sigma^2 e^{-\frac{s^2}{2\sigma^2}}\frac{n}{2}{}_1F_1\left(1+\frac{n}{2},\frac{n}{2};\frac{s^2}{2\sigma^2}\right). \tag{3}$$

where E[.] is expectation operator and ${}_1F_1(\cdot;\cdot;\cdot)$ is Confluent hypergeometric function. K is Generalized Rician K-factor which represents the ratio of the power of the specular component to the power of diffused components. It is given as $K = \frac{s^2}{n\sigma^2}$.

By express the modified Bessel function into series form, and then the PDF of received SNR becomes:

$$p_\gamma(\gamma) = e^{-\frac{nK}{2}}\sum_{l=0}^{\infty}\frac{\Omega^{l+\frac{n}{2}}(nK)^l}{2^{2l+\frac{n}{2}}\bar{\gamma}^{l+\frac{n}{2}}(\sigma^2)^{l+\frac{n}{2}}l!\Gamma\left(l+\frac{n}{2}\right)}\gamma^{l+\frac{n}{2}-1}e^{-\frac{\Omega\gamma}{2\sigma^2\bar{\gamma}}}. \tag{4}$$

The GR distribution behaves as Rician fading when we put $n = 2$ in (2), and as Rayleigh when $n = 2$, $s_i = 0$ and as Nakagami-m when $n = 2$ m, $s_i = 0$, with m constrained to integer or half integer values.

3 Performance Analysis

The ASEP for various modulations can be evaluated by averaging conditional symbol error probability over the PDF of a fading channel [16] as:

$$P_e = \int_0^\infty P_e(\gamma)p_\gamma(\gamma)d\gamma, \tag{5}$$

where $P_e(\gamma)$ denotes the conditional SEP of an AWGN channel and $p_\gamma(\gamma)$ denotes the PDF of fading channel. The conditional SEP of M-ary modulation schemes can be represented in the generalized form as:

$$P_e(\gamma) = A\int_0^{\pi-\frac{\pi}{M}}\exp(-B(\theta)\gamma)d\theta, \tag{6}$$

The values of A and B depend on different modulation schemes [17] are given in Table 1.

Table 1. Values of A and B for MPSK and MDPSK modulation schemes

Modulation scheme	A	B
MPSK	$1/\pi$	$\dfrac{\sin^2(\pi/M) \times \log_2(M)}{\sin^2(\theta)}$
MDPSK	$1/\pi$	$\dfrac{\sin^2(\pi/M) \times \log_2(M)}{1 + (\cos(\pi/M) \times \cos(\theta))}$

The ASEP for MPSK and MDPSK is calculated by substituting the Eqs. (4) and (6) into (5), to obtain the following equation:

$$
P_e = A \times \exp\left(-\frac{nK}{2}\right) \times \sum_{l=0}^{\infty} \frac{\Omega^{l+\frac{n}{2}}\,(nK)^l}{2^{2l+\frac{n}{2}}\,\bar{\gamma}^{l+\frac{n}{2}}\,(\sigma^2)^{l+\frac{n}{2}}\,l!\;\Gamma\left(l+\frac{n}{2}\right)} \times
$$
$$
\int_0^{\pi-\frac{\pi}{M}} \int_0^{\infty} \gamma^{l+\frac{n}{2}-1} \times \exp\left(-\gamma\left(\frac{\Omega}{2\sigma^2\bar{\gamma}}+B\right)\right)\, d\gamma d\theta
$$

$$(7)$$

The above equation can be evaluated using the formula given in [14, 3.381.4] as

$$
\int_0^{\infty} x^{c-1}\exp(-\mu x)dx = \frac{\Gamma(c)}{\mu^c} \quad ,\text{Re}\,\mu > 0 \text{ and Rec} > 0. \tag{8}
$$

By using the formula given in (8), the inner loop of (7) can be solved as to obtain the ASEP of M-ary modulation scheme over GR fading channel as:

$$
P_e = A \times \sum_{l=0}^{\infty} \frac{(nK)^l \exp\left(-\frac{nK}{2}\right)}{2^l l!} \int_0^{\pi-\frac{\pi}{M}} \left(1+\frac{B}{v}\right)^{-\left(l+\frac{n}{2}\right)} d\theta. \tag{9}
$$

where $v = \frac{\Omega}{2\sigma^2\bar{\gamma}}$.

The equation in (9) can be solved using the popular software MATHEMATICA.

4 Analytical Results and Discussion

The ASEP performance of M-ary modulations is studied by varying fading parameter n and keeping K constant. In Fig. 1, the ASEP expression of 16 PSK and 4-DPSK is drawn with respect to the average SNR for different values of n and for a constant value of $K = 3$ dB. As anticipated, the ASEP decreases as the value of n increases. The simulation results are shown to validate the analytically derived expression for general M-ary modulation schemes over GR fading channel.

The derived results of ASEP for 16 PSK and 4 DPSK are plotted against average SNR for various combinations of fading parameter K and for a constant value of $n = 2$

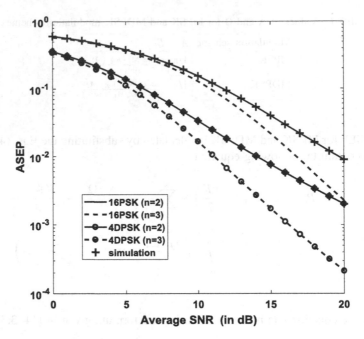

Fig. 1. Exact ASEP and simulation of 4-DPSK and 16-PSK over GR fading with $K = 3$ and different values of n.

in Fig. 2. It can be depicted that when the value of K increases, the ASEP decreases. So the performance of SEP improves with increase in value of specular power 'K' as expected, because increase in the specular power increases the strength of signal, hence reducing the symbol error rate.

In Figs. 3 and 4, the results are plotted for 8PSK and 4PSK modulation against average SNR. The curves are drawn for different values of K and n parameters. From Fig. 3, it can be demonstrated that the performance of system is improved as the degree of freedom increases. Also, it can be depicted that as the modulation order of PSK modulation schemes increases, the system performance degrade. The simulations results are also shown in Fig. 3 which include the Rician fading as special case of GR fading channel when degree of freedom, 'n' = 2. Similarly, in Fig. 4, it can be observed that with increase in specular power by keeping 'n' constant, the system performance improves and error rate decreases.

Further, in Figs. 5 and 6, the ASEP of 8PSK and 16 PSK are plotted against specular power respectively for different values of n parameters by keeping average SNR, $\bar{\gamma} = 10\,dB$. The curve drawn for degree of freedom, $n = 3$ gives better results than $n = 2$. From both Figs. 5 and 6, it can be demonstrated that the ASEP improves by increasing the specular power of the system.

Similarly, the ASEP results for 4-PSK and 2-PSK (is also known as binary phase shift keying (BPSK)) against specular power are drawn in Figs. 7 and 8 respectively for different values of n parameters by keeping average SNR, $\bar{\gamma} = 10\ dB$. It can be observed that the system performance degrades as the degree of freedom and specular

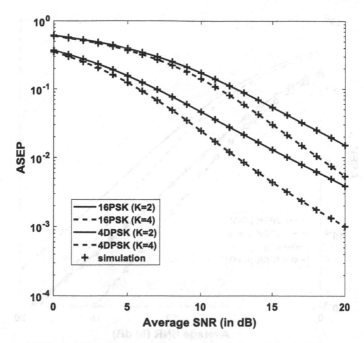

Fig. 2. Exact ASEP of 4-DPSK and 16-PSK over GR fading channel with $n = 2$ and various values of K.

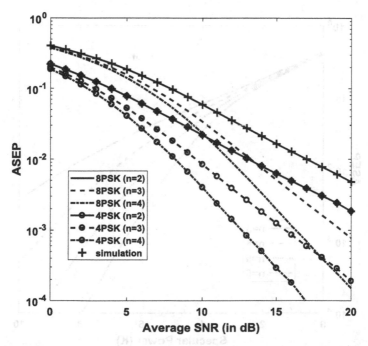

Fig. 3. Exact ASEP and simulation of 4-PSK and 8-PSK over GR fading with $K = 2$ and different values of n.

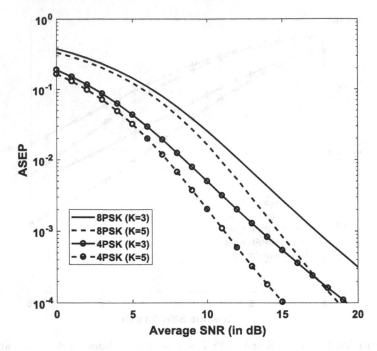

Fig. 4. Exact ASEP of 4-PSK and 8-PSK over GR fading channel with $n = 3$ and various values of K.

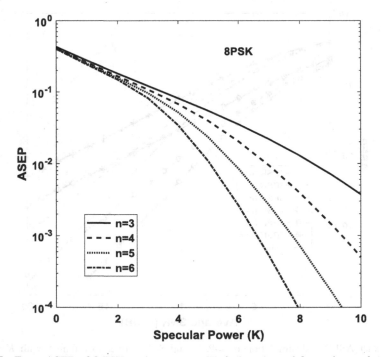

Fig. 5. Exact ASEP of 8-PSK against K over GR fading channel for various values of n

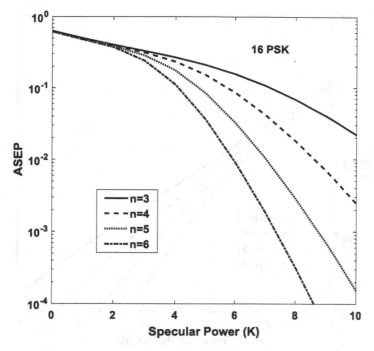

Fig. 6. Exact ASEP of 16-PSK against K over GR fading channel for various values of *n*

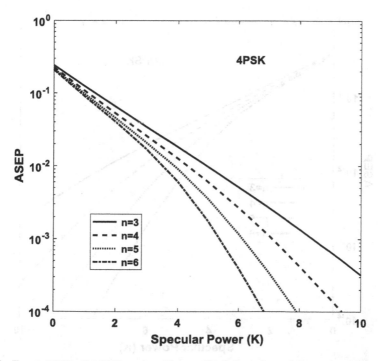

Fig. 7. Exact ASEP of 4-PSK against K over GR fading channel for various values of *n*

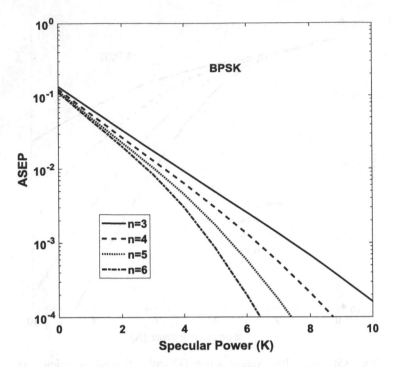

Fig. 8. Exact ASEP of BPSK against K over GR fading channel for various values of *n*

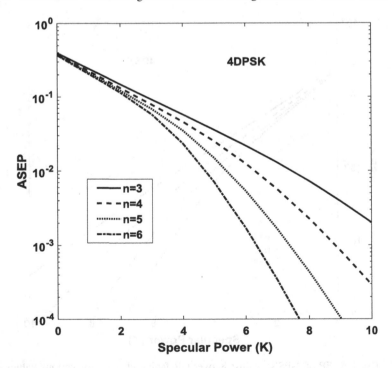

Fig. 9. Exact ASEP of 4-DPSK against K over GR fading channel for various values of *n*

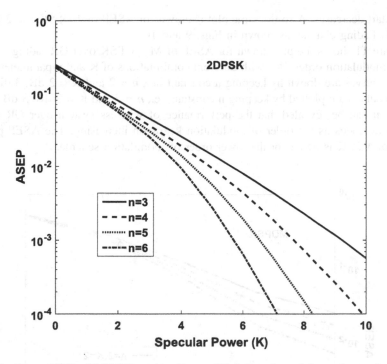

Fig. 10. Exact ASEP of 2-DPSK against K over GR fading channel for various values of n

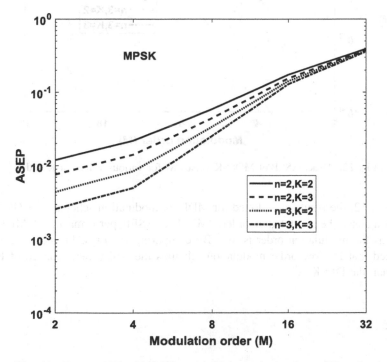

Fig. 11. Exact ASEP of MPSK versus M for various values of K and n

power start decreases. Also the same plot is drawn for ASEP of 4-DPSK and 2-DPSK over GR Fading channel as shown in Figs. 9 and 10.

Figure 11 shows the plot drawn for ASEP of M-ary PSK over GR fading channel against modulation order, 'M' with different combinations of K and n parameters. The first two curves are drawn by keeping n constant i.e., $n = 2$ and K = 2 dB, 3 dB. The last two curves are plotted by keeping n constant i.e., $n = 3$ and K = 2 dB, 3 dB. From Fig. 11, it can be revealed that the performance of wireless system over GR fading channel degrades as the order of modulation keeps on increasing. The ASEP performance of MPSK is better for the lower order of modulation scheme.

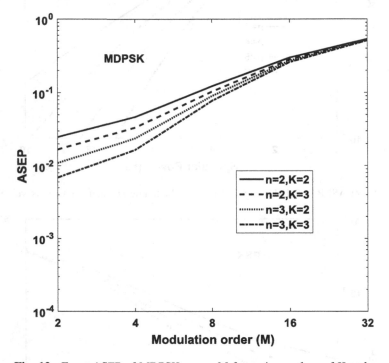

Fig. 12. Exact ASEP of MDPSK versus M for various values of K and n

In Fig. 12, the results are plotted for MDPSK modulation scheme over GR fading channel against the modulation order, 'M'. The ASEP performance of MDPSK is worthy as the modulation order is low. By comparing the Figs. 11 and 12, it can be concluded that for low order modulation schemes the ASEP performance of PSK is better than the DPSK.

5 Conclusion

The analysis for performance of MPSK and MDPSK over GR fading channel is provided in this paper. The expressions of ASEP are derived for both the modulation schemes. The GR fading channel behaves as Rician fading channel for $n = 2$, it gets reduced to Rayleigh for $n = 2$ and $s_i = 0$ and to Nakagami-m for $n = 2$ m, $s_i = 0$. The existing fading models such as Rayleigh, Rician and Nakagami-m fading models are special cases of the GR fading model. Only single integral evaluation was needed to arrive at the analytical results. The derived ASEP results are validate by using MATLAB simulation.

References

1. Herscovici, N., Christodoulou, C.: Fading distributions and co-channel interference in wireless systems. IEEE Antennas and Prop. Mag. **42**(1), 150–159 (2000)
2. Rappaport, T.S.: Wireless Communications: Principles and Practice, 2nd edn. Pearson Education Inc., London (2002)
3. Cheng J., Berger T.: Performance analysis for maximal-ratio combining in correlated generalized Rician fading. In: Proceedings of IEEE Asilomar Conference on Signal, System and Computers, pp. 1672–1675 (2003)
4. Youssef, N., Wangt, C.X., Patzoldt, M., Jaafar, I., Tabbane, S.: On the statistical properties of generalized Rice multipath fading channels. In: Proceedings of IEEE Vehicular Technology Conference, pp. 162–165 (2004)
5. Najafizadeh, L., Tellambura, C.: BER analysis of arbitrary QAM for MRC diversity with imperfect channel estimation in generalized Rician fading channels. IEEE Trans. Commun. **55**(4), 1239–1248 (2006)
6. Loskot, P., Norman, C.: Performance analysis of coded MIMO-OFDM systems over generalized Rician fading channels. In: Proceedings of IEEE Canadian Conference on Electrical and Computer Engineering, pp. 1634–1639 (2006)
7. Radaydeh, R.M., Matalgah, M.M.: Compact formulas for the average error performance of non-coherent M-ary orthogonal signals over generalized Rician, Nakagami-m, and Nakagami-q fading channels with diversity reception. IEEE Trans. Commun. **56**(1), 32–38 (2008)
8. Loskot, P., Beaulieu, N.C.: Approximate performance analysis of coded OSTBC-OFDM systems over arbitrary correlated generalized Rician fading channels. IEEE Trans. Commun. **57**(8), 2235–2238 (2009)
9. Schlenker, J., Cheng, J., Schober, R.: Asymptotically tight error rate bounds for EGC in correlated generalized Rician fading. In: Proceedings of IEEE International Conference on Communications, pp. 3079–3084 (2013)
10. Schlenker, J., Cheng, J., Schober, R.: Improving and bounding asymptotic approximations for diversity combiners in correlated generalized Rician fading. IEEE Trans. Wirel. Commun. **13**(2), 736–748 (2014)
11. Singh, S., Kansal, V.: Performance of M-ary PSK over TWDP fading channels. Int. J. Electron. Lett. **4**(4), 433–437 (2015)
12. Le, K.N.: Selection combiner output distributions of multivariate equally-correlated generalised-Rician fading for any degrees of freedom. IEEE Trans. Veh. Technol. **67**(3), 2761–2765 (2018)

13. Proakis, J.G., Salehi, M.: Digital Communications, 5th edn. The McGraw-Hill, The McGraw-Hill (2008)
14. Gradshteyn, I.S., Ryzhik, I.M.: Table of Integrals, Series, and Products, 6th edn. Academic Press, Cambridge (2000)
15. Simon, M.K., Alouini, M.S.: Digital Communications over Fading Channels, 2nd edn. Wiley-IEEE Press, Hoboken (2004)
16. Goldsmith, A.: Wireless Communications, 2nd edn. Cambridge University Press, Cambridge (2005)
17. Pawula, R.F.: A new formula for MDPSK symbol error probability. IEEE Commun. Lett. 2, 271–272 (1998)

Electrical Signal Analysis of Different Types of Oxygen Efficient Plants

Anurag Kumar[✉], Neetu Sood, and Indu Saini

Department of ECE, Dr. B. R. Ambedkar National Institute of Technology,
Jalandhar 144011, Punjab, India
anuragece23@gmail.com, {soodn,sainii}@nitj.ac.in

Abstract. Plants have an electrical signal, which is a weak signal. These signals vary during the growth of plants, the stress of plant. Environment changes are observed by their electrophysiological signals. Four plants of different species have been connected to channel of BIOPAC MP36 set-up individually at different instant of time, then the signal variations in plants have been observed at different time day(sunlight intensity 60000 lx to 80000 lx) and night (less than 500 lx). However, the statistical parameters of electrical signal like amplitude, mean, variance, RMS value, standard deviation, mean square value etc. have been analyzed. The resulting oxygen efficient plant (Epipremnum aureum, Ocimum tenuiflorum) shows maximum statistical parameters of the electrical signal as compared to other plants like Aloe-Vera and Cord line Fruticosa.

Keywords: Amplitude · Frequency · Mean · Mean square value
RMS value · Standard deviation · Variance

1 Introduction

Stimulation in plants was first observed by scientist Burdon − Sanderson in 1873, after a day its studies in various plants has increased. Many scientists belonging to different times and cultures have clinched a belief that plants have much more intricate abilities than they are perceptible to sense and respond to change in environment stimulus [1]. Electrical signal transmission phenomena occur due to electrophysiological signal, they communicate through air, and roots are the transmission media, they are conscious enough to be aware of surrounding things of environment like - hazard, threats [2]. On earth, everything has energy, and it depends on whatever that utilizes it. The Only matter is all energy pulsating with different frequency, amplitude and statistical parameters like- mean, variance, standard deviation, Mean Square value, RMS values etc. all these values are characterized by continuously monitoring the electrical signal of plants [3, 4]. Electrical signals play important role in many plant photosynthesis relation. Electrocardiogram (ECG) and Electroencephalogram (EEG) are also classified as an electrophysiological recording of human beings. Electrical signals in plants are- Action potential (AP), Variation potential (VP) and local electrical potential

© Springer Nature Singapore Pte Ltd. 2019
A. K. Luhach et al. (Eds.): ICAICR 2018, CCIS 956, pp. 63–73, 2019.
https://doi.org/10.1007/978-981-13-3143-5_6

(LEP) signals. Among these three signal observed in plants, LEP has sub-threshold response induced by change in environmental factors (soil, water, fertility, light, temp, and humidity). LEP is locally generated and not transferred to the other part of the plant, it has tremendous impact on physiology status of the plant [5–8]. Action potential and variation potential are transmitted from stimulated site to the other part of the plant. AP is induced by non-damaging stimuli (cold, mechanical and electrical stimulus). It is like widespread phenomena, which can expeditiously transmit information over long-distance communication in the plant cell. AP follows the all-or-none low (it is independent of the strength of stimulus), in this weaker than a certain threshold cannot trigger AP, but increases above the value of threshold. Because of this, the amplitude does not change as it maintains a constant velocity [9]. The reason of VP in the plant by damaging stimuli (e.g. burning and cutting), it does not follow all-or-none low as the magnitude and shape of VP vary with the intensity of the stimulus. VP depends mainly on the xylem for transmission, which can enters the dead organs inside the plants [10]. Plant electrical signal is a kind of non-linear and non-stationary random signal [11]. It is a kind of weak and low-frequency signal, its amplitude varies due to atmospheric change and its signal is highly noisy.

In this paper, four different types of the plant taken from the different family are clearly explained below.

  i. Epipremnum aureum (Money plant) – Epipremnum aureum is the type of flowering plant which belongs to Araceae family.
 ii. Ocimum tenuiflorum (Tulsi plant) – Ocimum tenuiflorum is commonly known as holy basil in an aromatic perennial plant which belongs to Lamiaceae family.
iii. Aloe Vera plant – Aloe Vera is a succulent plant which belongs to the genus Aloe.
 iv. Cordyline fruticosa (Normal plant) – Cordyline fruticosa is an evergreen plant which belongs to Asparagus family.

The above of these four different types of plant consider as experiment purpose the Epipremnum aureum (Money plant) and Ocimum tenuiflorum (Tulsi plant) are known as oxygen efficient plants, Aloe Vera plant and Cordyline fruticosa are known as a non-oxygen efficient plant.

2 Material Used and Methodology

Recorded the data for four different types of plant, Epipremnum aureum (Money plant), Ocimum tenuiflorum (Tulsi plant), Cordyline Fruticosa (Normal plant), Aloe-Vera by using computer-aided BIOPAC MP36 (Fig. 1e). The signal acquisition set up has been formed in time domain. The temperature of sunlight, PH level of soil, Intensity of sunlight, Humidity of soil, these four parameters have been measured by Pro 4 in 1 soil survey instrument which has been kept maintained throughout the experiment at day and night time. The four parameters for the soil survey is mentioned in Fig. 1e (yellow colour). First of all, place a NaCl electrode near shoot and root of plant-like

Epipremnum aureum (Money plant), Ocimum tenuiflorum (Tulsi plant), Cordyline Fruticosa (Normal plant) and Aloe-Vera. SS2LB connector with 9 pin DIN at one end has been connected to BIOPAC MP36 and 3 pinch leads at other end connected to electrodes placed near shoot, root and ground. Here, with BIOPAC MP36, the positive wire is connected to root, negative wire is connected to shoot and ground wire in the soil of four different types of plants, then signals have been taken from plants at daytime and the same connection has been used for nighttime i.e. in the absence of light, shown in Fig. 1(a)–(d). When a weak stimulus is applied and it does not reach the threshold value, nothing happens. But, when a strong stimulus is applied, it reaches the threshold value and because of driving force it increases membrane potential, it is called action potential. Na+ ions rush into the cell and Na+ channels open and that cause sodium to reach into the cell, as more Na+ ion enter into the cell along with axon, it reaches at equilibrium voltage and gets enough potential, it is called as depolarization. When K+ ion goes outside the cell along with axon then membrane potential decreases, it is called as re-polarization [11]. The depolarization and re polarization mechanism, which is shown in Sect. 2.2 Fig. 2.

In this paper, proper maintain of Pro 4 in 1 soil survey instrument at day and night, in the present of light or absence of light. For oxygen efficient plant at daytime the intensity range between 60000 to 80000 lx (NOR +), temperature of soil 28 °C, PH level of soil 5.5 and humidity of soil 20 to 30% (WET) of Epipremnum aureum (Money plant) and the light intensity range between 60000 to 80000 lx(NOR+), temperature of soil 26 °C, PH level of sail 6.5 and humidity of soil <5% (DRY+) of Ocimum tenuiflorum (Tulsi plant). The non-oxygen efficient plant at daytime the intensity of light range between 60000 to 80000 lx (NOR+), temperature of soil 27 °C, PH level of soil 6.5 and humidity of soil <5% (DRY+) of Aloe Vera plant and the light intensity range between 60000 to 80000 lx, temperature of soil 28 °C, PH level of soil 6.5 and humidity of soil 10 to 20% (NOR) of cordyline fruticosa. In the night, light intensity range between <500 lx (LOW−), temperature of soil 28 °C, PH level of soil 6.5 and humidity of soil 20 to 30% of Epipremnum aureum (Money plant) and intensity of light <5% (DRY+), temperature of soil 26 °C, PH level of soil 6.5 and humidity of soil <5% (DRY+) of Ocimum tenuiflorum (Tulsi plant) and intensity of light range between <500 lx (LOW−), temperature of soil 27 °C, PH level of soil 6.5 and humidity of soil <5% (DRY+) of Aloe Vera plant and intensity of light range between <500 lx (LOW−), temperature of soil 28 °C, PH level of soil 6.5 and humidity of soil 10 to 20% (NOR) of Cordyline fruticosa.

These are above parameters of Pro 4 in 1 soil survey instrument kept it in mind when taken data from plant and no change in environment.

2.1 Experimental Set up

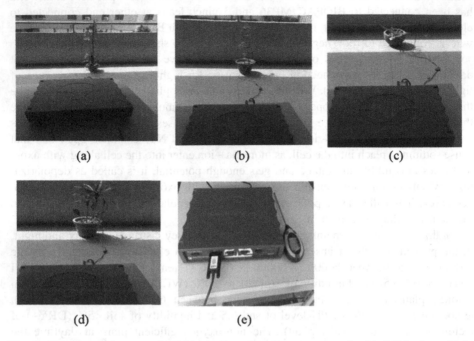

Fig. 1. Experimental set-up (a) Money plant (Epipremnumaureum), (b) Tulsi plant (Ocimumtenuiflorum), (c) Aloe Vera plant, (d) Normal plant (Cordyline Fruicosa), (e) BIOPAC MP36 and Pro 4 in 1soil soil survey instrument.

2.2 Depolarization and Re-polarization Mechanism

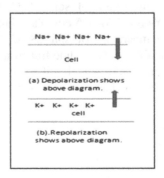

Fig. 2. Depolarization and Re-polarization mechanism (ion exchange) during plant's normal activity.

3   Results and Discussion

The experiment was first performed for four different types of plant like Epipremnum aureum (Maney plant), Ocimum tenuiflorum (Tulsi plant), Cordyline Fruicosa (Normal plant), and Aloe-Vera) at daytime (1:30PM, April 6, 2018) using BIOPAC MP36 hardware and software by continuously monitoring the physiological electrical signal of plant several times. First, an electrical signal has been taken at daytime from money plant (Epipremnum aureum) and observed that its statistical parameter like - amplitude has maximum value of 13.23 mv & minimum value of 7.23 mv, mean is equals to 10.15 mv, Mean Square value is 11.94 mv, rms value is 10.58 mv, standard deviation is 1.15 mv. Then electrical signal of rest three plants has been taken at the same date and time and calculated statistical parameters of electrical signal have been mentioned in Table no. 1.

Second, the electrical signal of plants have been recorded in the absence of sunlight, in dark room at night time (9:30PM, April 6, 2018) and the statistical parameter of electrical signal have been observed. Firstly, money plant (Epipremnum aureum) has been taken and its value like - amplitude has maximum value 16 mv, minimum value 25 mv, mean is 4.17 mv, Mean square Value is 184.17 mv, rms is 13.57 mv, standard deviation is 12.91 mv, variance is 166.76 mv. Then electrical signal of rest three plants have been taken at same date and time, and calculated statistical parameter of electrical signal have been mentioned in Table no. 1 by using Matlab R2015a. software The box plot shows variation of mean of normal plant (Epipremnum aureum) and Tulsi plant (Ocimum tenuiflorum) at different time interval in Figs. 4(b), and (c) shows mean variation of all four plants at daytime (sun intensity 60000 lx to 80000 lx) and at night (less than 500 lx) [12]. The bar-diagram shows that day and night time amplitude variation, the oxygen efficient plant shows maximum amplitude as compare to normal plant and Aloe Vera.

3.1   Waveform of Electrical Signal Four Different Plants at Day and Night in the Time Domain

See Fig. 3.

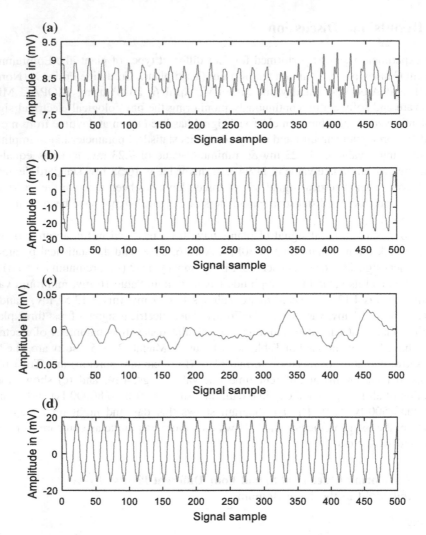

Fig. 3. (a) Money plant electrical signal waveform at daytime (sunlight intensity 60000 to 80000 lx) in the time domain. (b) Money plant electrical signal waveform at nighttime (sunlight intensity less than 500 lx) in the time domain. (c) Tulsi plant electrical signal waveform at daytime (sunlight intensity 60000 to 80000 lx) in the time domain. (d) Tulsi plant electrical signal waveform at night time (sunlight intensity less than 500 lx) in the time domain. (e) Aloe Vera plant electrical signal waveform at daytime (sunlight intensity 60000 to 80000 lx) in the time domain. (f) Aloe Vera plant electrical signal waveform at night time (sunlight intensity 60000 to 80000 lx) in the time domain. (g) Normal plant electrical signal waveform at daytime (sunlight intensity 60000 to 80000 lx) in the time domain. (h) Normal plant electrical signal waveform at nighttime (sunlight intensity 60000 to 80000 lx) in time domain.

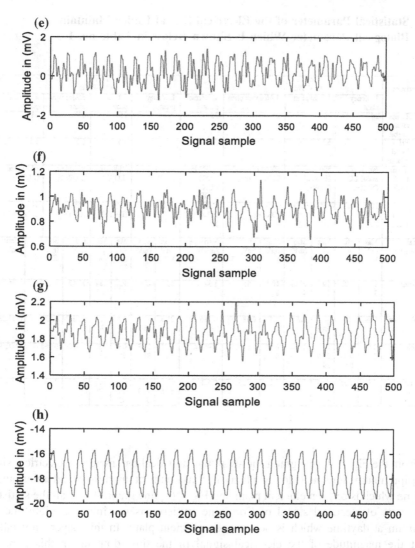

Fig. 3. (*continued*)

3.2 Statistical Parameter of the Electrical Signal Under Maintain Biological Parameter Which Is Shown Below in Table no. 1

Biological characteristics	Day (1:30 PM)				Night (9:30PM)			
	1. Money plant	2.Tulsi plant	3.Aloe vera plant	4. Normal plant	1. Money plant	2.Tulsi plant	3.Aloe vera plant	4. Normal plant
1. Temperature of soil	28	26	27	28	28	26	27	28
2. PH Level of soil	5.5	6.5	6.5	6.5	5.5	6.5	6.5	6.5
3. Intensity of sunlight	60000 to 80000 LUX (NOR+)	60000 to 80000 LUX (NOR+)	60000 to 80000 LUX (NOR+)	60000 to 80000 LUX (NOR+)	<500 Lux (LOW-)	<500 Lux (LOW-)	<500 Lux (LOW-)	<500 Lux (LOW-)
4. Humidity of soil	20 to 30% (WET)	<5% (DRY+)	<5% (DRY+)	10 to 20%(NOR)	20 to 30% (WET)	<5% (DRY+)	<5% (DRY+)	10 to 20%(NOR)

Electrical characteristics	Max (mV)	Min (mV)	Mean (mV)	Msq (mV)	Rms (mV)	Std (mV)	Variance (mV)	Max (mV)	Min (mV)	Mean (mV)	Msq (mV)	Rms (mV)	Std (mV)	Variance (mV)
1. Money plant	13.23	7.23	10.51	111.94	10.58	1.15	1.34	16	-25	12.5	184.17	13.57	12.91	166.76
2. Tulsi plant	9.99	-10	-.0084	0.27	0.431	0.18	0.186	21.31	-23.11	0.84	151.94	12.32	12.29	151.23
3. Aloe Vera	0.575	-0.4382	-0.00029	4*e-4	0.020	0.0198	3.9*e-4	1.7	0.0381	0.915	0.863	0.929	0.160	0.0259
4. Normal plant	5.31	1.55	3.04	9.79	3.12	0.726	0.528	-6.36	-17.76	-10.42	115.70	10.75	2.64	6.98

From the Fig. 4(d) line graph shows all the statistical parameters of electrical signal of Epipremnum aureum (Money plant) is maximum at nighttime and minimum at daytime which is oxygen efficient plant and Fig. 4(e) line graph shows all the statistical parameters of electrical signal of Cordyline fruticosa is maximum at nighttime and minimum at daytime which is non-oxygen efficient plant. In this paper only talking about the magnitude of the electrical signal in the time domain. In this paper all statistical parameters are calculated at 50 Hz of the electrical signal, at daytime the electrical shows the variation at every instant of time and it is not periodically repeated same but when talking about nighttime electrical signal it is repeated continuously at every instant of time, because of that there is no any light intensity present.

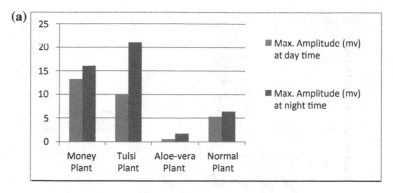

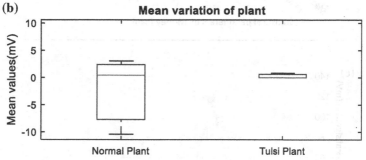

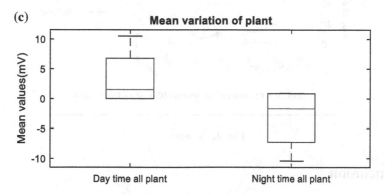

Fig. 4. (a) Bar-diagram shows the amplitude variation at day and night of all four plants. (b) Mean variation of normal plant and Tulsi plant, (c) Mean variation on of all four plants at day and night. (d) Line graph shows the statistical parameters variation due to day and night of Epipremnum aureum. (e) Line graph shows the statistical parameters variation due to day and night of Cordyline fruticosa.

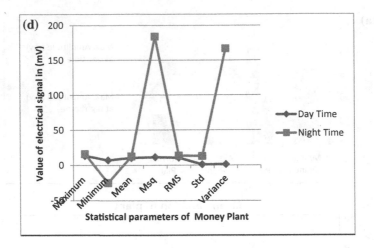

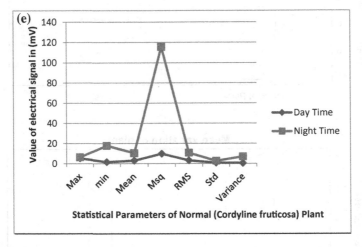

Fig. 4. (*continued*)

4   Conclusion

From the above discussion, it can be concluded that the Money plant and Tulsi (Ocimum tenuiflorum) have oxygen-rich properties and have maximum values of statistical parameter of the electrical signal in time domain analysis as compared to normal plants like Cordyline fruticosa and Aloe-Vera plant, at day time and night time Money plant and Tulsi (Ocimum tenuiflorum) are shows maximum amplitude and other statistical parameter of electrical signal, which we can say that oxygen efficient plants shows maximum value of all statistical parameter from the above discussion. In plants, the cell ion transmission process is done by roots of the plants. Here, from the electrical signal variation of the plant at daytime and nighttime, it can be noticed that plant electrical signals are non- stationary and random signals. For future purpose plants have energy that releases electrons which may be remunerative.

References

1. Davies, E.: Electrical signals in plants: facts and hypotheses. In: Volkov, A.G. (ed.) Plant Electrophysiology, pp. 407–422. Springer, Berlin (2006). https://doi.org/10.1007/978-3-540-37843-3_17
2. Yan, X., et al.: Research progress on electrical signals in higher plants. Prog. Nat. Sci. **19**, 531–541 (2009)
3. Yaddanapudi, K.S., Sood, N., Saini, I: A testimony of inter-plant communication through electrophysiological signal analysis. Commun. Plant Sci. (ISSN 2237-4027)
4. Jingxia, L., Weimin, D.: Study and evalution of plant electrical signal processing method. In: 2011 14th International congress on Image and Signal Processing. IEEE
5. Hu, J.H.: Measurement and research on vegetal bioelectricity under water stress. Dissertation, Jilin University, China (2003)
6. Ren, H.Y., Wang, X.C., Lou, C.H.: The universal existence of electrical signals and its physiological effects in higher plants. Acta Phytophysiol. Sin. **19**(1), 97–101 (1993)
7. Dietrich, P., Sanders, D., Hedrich, R.: The role of ion channels in light dependent stomatal opening. J. Exp. Bot. **52**(363), 1959–1967 (2001)
8. Wu, W.H.: Plant physiology, 1st edn, pp. 72–76. Science Press, Beijing (2003)
9. Dziubinska, H., Trebacz, K., Zawadzki, T.: Transmission route for action potentials and variation potentials in Helianthus annuus L. J. Plant Physiol. **158**, 1167–1172 (2001)
10. Fromm, J., Lautner, S.: Electrical signals and their physiological significance in plants. Plant, Cell Environ. **30**, 249–257 (2007)
11. Zhao, Z.K.: A study on ultra-weak electronic signal in plants. J. China Jiliang Univ. **13**, 253–257 (2002)
12. Takano, T., Xu, C., Funahashi, C., Namba, T., Kaibuchi, K.: Neuronal polarization. Development **142**, 2088–2093 (2015). https://doi.org/10.1242/dev.114454
13. Tian, L., Meng, Q., Li, Y., Li, M., Wang, X., Han, Y.: Time and frequency domain analysis to plant electrical signal of swallow and anthurium under controlled LED environment. In: 2016 12th World Congress on Intelligent Control and Automation (WCICA), 12–15 June 2016, Guilin, China (2016)

A Dual-Band MIMO Antenna Using RF Switch for LTE Mobile Handset Applications

Aahat Gupta$^{(\boxtimes)}$ and Paras Chawla

Chandigarh University, Gharuan, Punjab, India
aahat.gupta@gmail.com

Abstract. A full-duplex conventional radio design communication systems, in which transmitter (Tx) and is active receiver (Rx) are active at same time and the connection between the transmitter and receiver is established by duplex filters. Notwithstanding, an expanding number of long-term evolution (LTE) bands need multiband operation. Consequently front-end design, expand LTE bands. RF antenna with inserted MEM switch at the center of slot. Performance changed by state of MEM switch based on ON/OFF. Transmission line model (TLM) is used to calculate the antenna parameters, antenna model simulated at 3.4 GHz.

Keywords: LTE · MEM switch · RF antenna

1 Introduction

An antenna has very important and indispensable part in WCS. It's coupling device among transmitter and receiver. It's a device radiating or receiving radio waves. Nowadays there is an increasing demand for the antenna with the multiband operation. Hence it has attracted many research scholars to do research for advanced types of antenna. Microstrip patch antenna has the number of advantages and extraordinary features than the conventional antennas. With regards to their geometrical shapes and practical applications, microstrip patch antennas are very efficient and useful. There are dissimilar types of antennas like loop antenna, a reflector antenna, aperture antenna, lens antenna, microstrip patch [1]. Among them, microstrip patch antenna is one of most versatile and conformal antenna. It is easy to design and fabricate.

The concept and fundamental idea of microstrip antenna were created in 1953 [1]. A flat aerial that can be used in Ultra High frequency (UHF) range was invented and patented in 1955 [2]. Through continued research, a thorough and detailed study of microstrip antenna was made only in the year 1970s. By the year 1970, the microstrip antenna had become very popular. That led to the rapid growth of microstrip patch antenna technology.

The first practical microstrip antennas were developed in 1970 [3]. In the meantime, the microstrip patch antenna with various geometrical shapes was invented in 1972 [4]. With the increase in development in wireless communication industry remain to determination the desires for meagre, reconcilable and inexpensive reconfigurable architecture. Wireless systems like cellular systems have become essential as number of

© Springer Nature Singapore Pte Ltd. 2019
A. K. Luhach et al. (Eds.): ICAICR 2018, CCIS 956, pp. 74–85, 2019.
https://doi.org/10.1007/978-981-13-3143-5_7

mobile user increases. Mobile phone acts as a substrate to compliment today's exotic and busy lifestyle and overall usage is going to increase even more in near future [5].

First of all, overall requirements beside general connectivity are quite high like Global Positioning System, Wireless Local Area Network (802.11), and Bluetooth (802.15). From this, it's quite evident that accommodating numerous standards and numerous frequency bands is a big challenge [6–8]. So, the need of the hour is to review all the concepts, designs to use them to build a new better RF front end mobile terminal which would be able to accommodate and operate in different frequency bands. One of such terms also known as the advanced mobile terminal is present in Japan, functions in dissimilar frequency bands and is qualified to WCDMA systems. Working frequencies are 2 GHz, 800 MHz and 1.7 GHz.

Nowadays microstrip patch antennas are commonly used for commercial purposes. They can fix an external of aircraft, satellites, spacecraft, automobiles, missiles, even mobile phones [9]. A microstrip antenna comprises of dielectric substrate which has transmitted patch side of a dielectric substrate and opposite side have a ground plane.

A patch usually made of by copper or gold, which are good conducting materials. The radiating patch can take any shape like elliptical, circular, square, and rectangular and triangular. Among them the rectangular patch and circular patches are very standard because of their easy investigation, and manufacture. These antennas have eye-catching radiation characteristics, as they possess low cross polarization radiation.

Some of important advantages of microstrip patch antenna are as follows. They can be made conformal planar and non-planar surfaces because of its low weight, little volume and thin profile shape. These antennas can fabricate using modern printed-circuit technology. Their fabrication cost is low and mass production of these antennas can be easily done [8].

In specialized devices the planar radio wires are additionally extremely appealing for applications in remote neighborhood (WLAN) frameworks inside the 2.4 GHz & 5.2 GHz, the groups [10–14]. Given the design of an internal antenna for multi-band for cell phone applications. Two antenna segments are framed on both base and best of a similar substrate and unite by metallic stick to get the multi band characteristics [15].

Different reconfigurable RF front-end engineering for upcoming devoid of band cell phone terminals were proposed. The solitary way to design the utilization of the single-band device with the circulated reconfigurable coordinating systems which can possibly accomplish the ideal RF front-end. The first phase are confirming proposed reconfig-urable quad-band design introduced. The design utilizing micro electro mechanical system low temperature and switches technology gets more extreme power included productivity more noteworthy than 44% in the 0.9, 1.5, 2.0, to 2.6-GHz bands [15].

It has exhibited the RF-MEMS tunable channel reasonable innovation in wireless systems in 1.5–2.5 GHz range, and it can bring about a narrowband channel reaction (72 MHz) and low supplement loss (2 dB). Channels can likewise deal with no less than 300 MW of the RF power with down distortion when portrayed utilizing two-tone uti-lizing a WCDMA signal ACPR, and so on. A littler channel can be executed later on with the utilization high dielectric consistent fired substrate. These require higher capacitance loading, which can likewise be accomplished utilizing RF-MEMS devices [16].

The design utilized to execute unique sorts of the tunable filters on several MHz to a couple of GHz extend. A progressed broadband circuit demonstrate exhibited to bundled, hermetically-fixed MEMS the switches Radiant MEMS. The design utilized to actualize three unique sets of tunable filters from many MHz to a couple of GHz range and results in a correct expectation of each channel reaction. Reproduction and estimation come about are in total assertion for a lumped component and a micro strip scale strip planar tunable filter, then the best in class switch design is utilized as a part of recreations. The main RF MEMS switch tunable filter simulation results design and presented [17, 18].

2 Designing of Antenna Structure

The design of single component is appeared given underneath and different measurements the patch antenna. The patch antenna was planned based on TLM. The width of patch is ascertained to begin with, given by,

$$W = \frac{c}{2f}\sqrt{\frac{2}{\epsilon_r + 1}} \tag{1}$$

where, ϵ_r substrate of dielectric constant, W patch width.

As a result of bordering impact, the antenna appearances bigger than the physical measurements. ΔL produces this results in account and can processed to

$$\Delta L = 0.142h\frac{\left(\epsilon_{eff} + 0.3\right)\left(\frac{W}{h} + 0.264\right)}{\left(\epsilon_{eff} - 0.3\right)\left(\frac{W}{h} + 0.8\right)} \tag{2}$$

where, h substrate height and ϵ_{eff} actual dielectric constant assumed:

$$\epsilon_{eff} = \frac{\epsilon_r + 1}{2} + \frac{\epsilon_r - 1}{2}\left\{1 + 12\frac{h}{W}\right\}^{-\frac{1}{2}} \tag{3}$$

When height (h) has reached out by every side of patch, the compelling length is given,

$$L_{eff} = \frac{c}{2f\sqrt{\epsilon_{eff}}} \tag{4}$$

L is Length of Patch resonant given by,

$$L = L_{eff}(\text{length of dielectric constant}) - 2\Delta \tag{5}$$

The dielectric substrate Duroid and height have values respectively $\epsilon_r = 2.2$, h = 1.57 in mm utilized. A microstrip line joined with focal point of the transmitting edges and feed line is a 50 Ω transmission line.

The setup additionally called impedance managing. The impedance Z1 given,

$$Z_l = \sqrt{Z_0 * R_L} \tag{6}$$

where, microstrip feed impedance is Z0 and impedance of patch R_L. The width of transformer is intended by,

$$\frac{width(w)}{height(h)} = \frac{8 * exp(A)}{exp(2A) - 2} \tag{7}$$

where A is given,

$$A = \frac{Z_l}{60} \left\{ \frac{\epsilon_r + 1}{2} \right\}^{\frac{1}{2}} + \frac{\epsilon_r - 1}{\epsilon_r + 1} \left\{ 0.23 + \frac{0.11}{\epsilon_r} \right\} \tag{8}$$

Patch with measurement with length and width

$$a = length/10 \tag{9}$$

$$b = a/10 \tag{10}$$

When the antenna is designed a MEM switch is introduced at the Centre.

2.1   A. Design of Linear Array

As previously mentioned, fundamental component was examined, an array antenna with MEMS switch turn OFF and ON are composed exclusively.

There are four components organized such that all transmission lines are appropriately coordinated.

A frequency is 3.4 GHz for quarter wave transformers utilized, established estimation length is λ/4 or 22 mm. The impedance of stub is computed by formula given as:

$$Z_0^2 = Z_S * Z_L$$

Width of 50 ω line = 4.8 mm. In the measurements of the considerable number of transformers, the exhibit is outlined and is displayed.

3   Simulation and Analysis

This research focused on design, simulate RF Front-End antenna with MEMS Switch for various application of Mobile Devices that will operate in a frequency range 2.36 GHz until 2.4 GHz. All design and prototype of the antenna in this research were constructed using HFSS software.

A result of measurement in this research was focused on three main things which are reflection loss, gain, and SAR value. The simulation parameter and antenna dimensions of designed patch antenna mention below in Table 1:

Table 1. Dimension of antenna designed.

S. No.	Parameter	Value
1.	Dielectric (ϵ) constant	2.2 Duroid
2.	Resonant frequency	3.4 GHz
3.	W_P	34.85 mm
4.	L_P	29.73 mm
5.	W_{QWT}	11.44 mm
6.	L_{QWT}	20.8325 mm
7.	W_{TL} of 50	4.84 mm
8.	L_{TL} of 50 Ω	20 mm
9.	L_S	$L_P/10$
10.	W_S	$L_S/10$

3.1   Antenna Simulation Layout

Figure 1 demonstrates the geometry of the proposed antenna which is used for the LTE smartphones, whose exact configuration and optimized values are mentioned in Table 1. In Fig. 2, represented the single element mobile antenna with MEMS switch. The ground plan of the proposed antenna system is 130×70 antenna size encompassed by the metal material having the height = 5 mm, thickness = 0.3 mm. In this antenna having two non-ground sections of 10×70 mm as well as 5×70 mm respectively, these dimension used for top and bottom edge of present antenna.

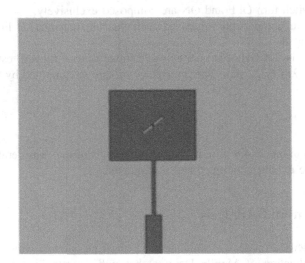

Fig. 1.   Geometry of RF mobile antenna for LTE application.

In the middle of two different non-ground parts, there will be a ground plane system with having length = 115 mm and width = 70 mm. As seen, the Fig. 1 have coaxial feed line is worked to stimulate connected to feed line (point A) with the ground (point B).

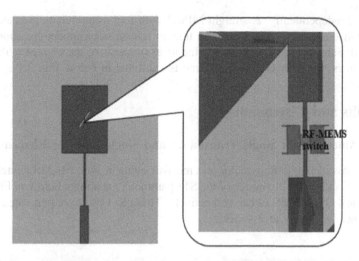

Fig. 2. Layout of RF mobile antenna with MEMS switch.

Here feed line point has 25 mm distance from the edge of antenna presented on system circuit board. In which unbroken metallic rim material directly fed by coaxial feed line which associated with ground and patch. This unbroken metal material is distributed into two stripes like ground and patch.

Here Loop 1 length is around 260 mm that enables to produce circle mode (0.67 GHz) as the crucial method. The high arranged resonant method of the Loop 1, for example, the modes are likewise energized. After that changed the Loop length is around 156 mm (1.13 GHz) that gave two resonant modes. Here two crucial methods of ON Switch and OFF Switch create a wide data transfer capacity to cover the activity.

As previously mentioned, where the fundamental component was talked about a MIMO system receiver with MEMS switch turns OFF and MIMO with MEMS switch

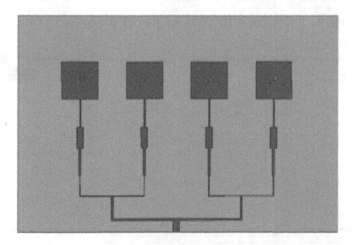

Fig. 3. MIMO array antenna elements

ON planned independently. A straight MIMO with four components indicated. There are four components masterminded such that all transmission model are appropriately coordinated. Subsequent to ascertaining the measurements of the considerable number of transformers, the MIMO is outlined and is exhibited in below Fig. 3.

4 Results and Discussion

4.1 RF Antenna with Single Transmitter and Single Receiver Element

The return loss of single transmitter and receiver element with MEMS switch in both the case OFF and ON. The figures of the S11 parameter are shown below in Figs. 4 and 5 for OFF and ON MEMS switch respectively. These S11 plots are generated based on the resonance frequency at 3.4 GHz.

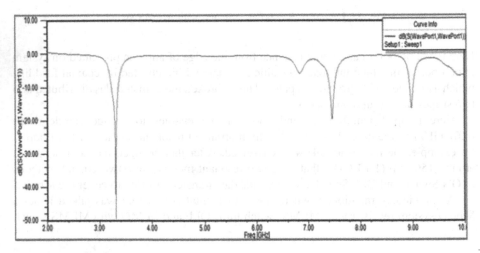

Fig. 4. Return loss of MEMS switch for OFF position at 3.4 GHz.

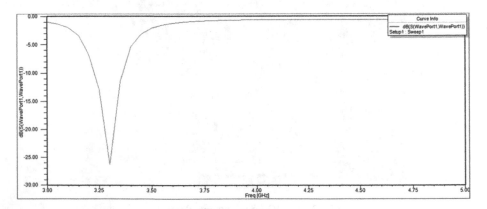

Fig. 5. Return loss parameter of MEMS switch for ON position at 3.4 GHz.

4.2   RF Antenna with MIMO System

MIMO with MEMS Switch with ON Case

Figure 3 demonstrates the MIMO antenna with MEMS switches. The recreated aftereffects of MIMO with MEMS Switch ON case is demonstrated as follows. Figure 6 introduces S11 return loss plot which demonstrates that resonance frequency at 3.43 GHz, in this case, MEMS switches positions are ON.

Figure 7 demonstrating VSWR plot affirms resonance frequency at 3.43 GHz with most minimal estimation of 1.8. Antenna gain of exhibit MIMO antenna 12.4 dBi, 3 dB beam width of MIMO antenna is 22° in the E-plane bringing about higher gain and efficiency. Here we measured all the possible results of the MIMO antenna with MEMS switches.

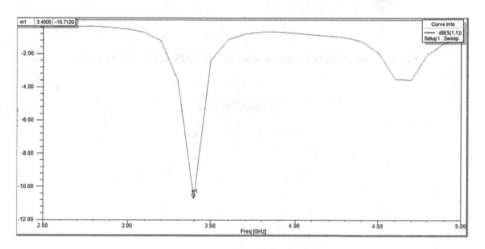

Fig. 6. S11-parameter plot demonstrates MIMO antenna with RF MEMS switch ON.

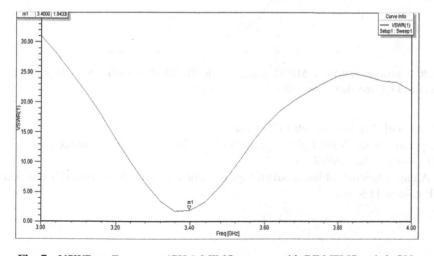

Fig. 7. VSWR vs Frequency (GHz) MIMO antenna with RF MEMS switch ON.

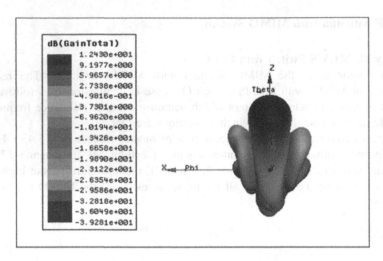

Fig. 8. Gain of MIMO antenna with RF MEEMS switch ON in (dBi).

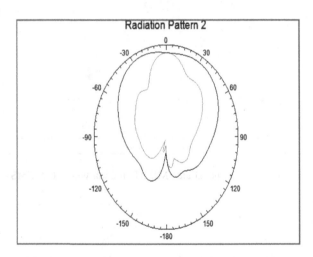

Fig. 9. Radiation pattern of MIMO antenna with RF MEMS switch ON in H-plane (Black Trace) and E-plane (Red Trace). (Color figure online)

MIMO with MEMS Switch OFF Case

S11-parameter and VSWR plot appeared in Figs. 10 and 11, the resonance frequency is 3.43 GHz and the VSWR 1.8.

A gain efficiency of linear MIMO system when it's switching from ON position to OFF case is 11.9 dBi.

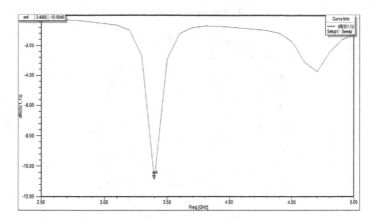

Fig. 10. S-S11 parameter in (dB) vs Frequency (GHz) of MIMO antenna with RF MEMS switch OFF.

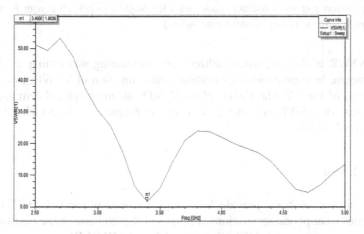

Fig. 11. VSWR vs Frequency (GHz) of MIMO antenna with RF MEMS switch OFF.

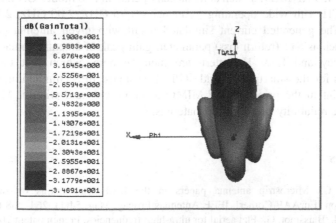

Fig. 12. Gain of MIMO antenna with RF MEMS switch OFF (dBi).

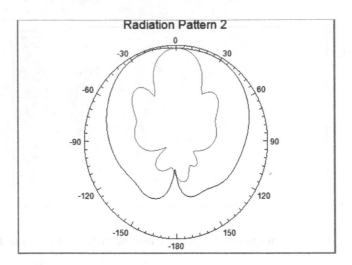

Fig. 13. Radiation pattern of MIMO system with RF MEMS switch OFF with E-plane (Red Trace), H-plane (Black Trace). (Color figure online)

This VSWR is the proportion utilized for coordinating and tuning of the transmitting antenna. In experimental applications, the estimation of VSWR, as a rule, lies in the vicinity of 1 and 2. The VSWR of the MIMO antenna graphical demonstrate that the estimation of VSWR is under 2 at mentions frequencies 1.75 GHz, 2.00 GHz, 2.1 GHz and 2.30 GHz.

5 Conclusion

A mobile antenna capable to provide the multiple numbers of bands for LTE operation under various smartphone applications is proposed. By combining the performance of Single element antenna with MEM Switch and 1 × 4 MIMO RF antenna to each, the proposed MIMO RF MEM switch antenna can operate in two modes ON SWITCH and OFF SWITCH with wide operating frequencies 1.75 GHz, 2.00 GHz, 2.1 GHz and 2.30 GHz. The generated current simulated result with given antenna performance parameter such as S11 (return loss) parameter, gain peak of antenna, radiation pattern, total efficiency and E & H pattern are mention here, which met the complete requirements for the smartphone, and 4G/LTE systems. In accumulation, the highest highlight point in the projected RF MIMO antenna with and without MEM switch possesses the reliability of the metal materials.

References

1. Peixeiro, C.: Microstrip antenna papers in the IEEE transactions on antennas and propagation [EurAAP Corner]. IEEE Antennas Propag. Mag. **54**(1), 264–268 (2012)
2. Gutton, H., Baissinot, G.: Flat aerial for ultra-high frequencies. French patent 703113 (1955)

3. Byron, E.V.: A new flush mounted antenna element for phased array application. Phased Array Antennas, 187–192 (1972)
4. Okazaki, H., Kawai, K., Fukuda, A., Furuta, T., Narahashi, S.: Reconfigurable amplifier towards enhanced selectivity of future multi-band mobile terminals. In: 2010 IEEE International Microwave Workshop Series on RF Front-ends for Software Defined and Cognitive Radio Solutions (IMWS), pp. 1–4. IEEE (2010)
5. Bahramzy, P., et al.: A tunable RF front-end with narrowband antennas for mobile devices. IEEE Trans. Microw. Theory Tech. 63(10), 3300–3310 (2015)
6. Zhang, S., He, S., Zhao, K., Ying, Z.: Multi-band wireless terminals with multiple antennas along an end portion, and related multi-band antenna systems. United States patent US 9,673,520. June 6 2017. Inventors; Sony Corp, Sony Mobile Communications Inc. Assignee
7. Boeck, G., et al.: RF front-end technology for reconfigurable mobile systems. In: Microwave and Optoelectronics Conference, IMOC 2003. Proceedings of the 2003 SBMO/IEEE MTT-S International 20 September 2003, vol. 2, pp. 863–868. IEEE (2003)
8. Shafi, M., et al.: 5G: a tutorial overview of standards, trials, challenges, deployment, and practice. IEEE J. Sel. Areas Commun. 35(6), 1201–1221 (2017)
9. Zheng, M., Wang, H., Hao, Y.: Internal hexa-band folded monopole/dipole/loop antenna with four resonances for mobile device. IEEE Trans. Antennas Propag. 60(6), 2880–2885 (2012)
10. Ban, Y.L., Qiang, Y.F., Chen, Z., Kang, K., Guo, J.H.: A dual-loop antenna design for hepta-band WWAN/LTE metal-rimmed smartphone applications. IEEE Trans. Antennas Propag. 63(1), 48–58 (2015)
11. Yuan, B., Cao, Y., Wang, G., Cui, B.: Slot antenna for metal-rimmed mobile handsets. IEEE Antennas Wirel. Propag. Lett. 11, 1334–1337 (2012)
12. Ishimiya, K., Chiu, C.Y., Takada, J.I.: Multiband loop handset antenna with less ground clearance. IEEE Antennas Wirel. Propag. Lett. 12, 1444–1447 (2013)
13. Wong, K.L., Chen, M.T.: Small-size LTE/WWAN printed loop antenna with an inductively coupled branch strip for bandwidth enhancement in the tablet computer. IEEE Trans. Antennas Propag. 61(12), 6144–6151 (2013)
14. Chaabane, G., Guines, C., Chatras, M., Madrangeas, V., Blondy, P.: Reconfigurable PIFA antenna using RF MEMS switches. In: Proceedings of 9th European Conference Antennas Propagation, Lisbon, Portugal, pp. 1–4 (2015)
15. El-Tanani, M.A., Rebeiz, G.M.: High-performance 1.5–2.5-GHz RF-MEMS tunable filters for wireless applications. IEEE Trans. Microw. Theory Tech. 58(6), 1629–1637 (2010)
16. Ali, T., Muzammil Khaleeq, M., Biradar, R.: A multiband reconfigurable slot antenna for wireless applications. AEU-Int. J. Electron. Commun. 84, 273–280 (2018)
17. Sambhe, V., Awale, R., Wagh, A.: Compact multi-band novel-shaped planar monopole antenna for DCS, bluetooth, and ultra-wide-band applications. J. Eng. 2016(5), 119–123 (2016)
18. Varamini, G., Keshtkar, A., Naser-Moghadasi, M.: Compact and miniaturized microstrip antenna based on fractal and metamaterial loads with reconfigurable qualification. AEU-Int. J. Electron. Commun. 83, 213–221 (2018)

Design and Implementation of a Wideband U Slot Microstrip Patch Antenna Using DGS for C Band

Asmita Rajawat$^{(\boxtimes)}$ and Nikita Saxena$^{(\boxtimes)}$

Electronics and Communication Department,
Amity University, Noida, Uttar Pradesh, India.
arajawat@amity.edu, nikita01saxena01@gmail.com

Abstract. A Wideband Microstrip Patch Antenna has been designed in this paper for C band applications. The designed antenna overcomes the short comings of the narrow band antennas in the communication domain. The narrow impedance bandwidth has been a barrier for microstrip patch antenna's application in wireless communication such as Wifi, LAN, WLAN, Bluetooth, WiMax. They are known for inherently low impedance bandwidth and relatively low efficiency. These design issues have been resolved in the proposed Wideband Microstrip Patch Antenna. The designed antenna has a 'U' shaped slot on the surface of the patch which gives a bandwidth of 450 MHz. This bandwidth has been enhanced by the Defected Ground Structure technique. A 'G' shaped defect has been made on the ground of the Microstrip Patch Antenna. This enhanced the bandwidth by 250 MHz. Thus, the final bandwidth obtained was 700 MHz. Both the designs were implemented and simulated at 5 GHz frequency and RT Duroid with the dielectric constant of 2.2 has been used as the substrate. The designed antenna was found to be suitable for the 5 GHz wireless networking band which comprises of the Wifi and WiMax technologies. It can cater to the various C Band applications. The designs were simulated on the CST Microwave software.

Keywords: Microstrip patch antenna · Gain · Reflection coefficient
Wide band · Defected Ground Structure

1 Introduction

A communication system is said to be a wide band system when its bandwidth significantly exceeds the coherence band width of the system. One such system has been designed in this work as well. Wideband Antennas have a wide number of applications. Military requires a wideband antenna for system agility or multifunctionality of the system. Communication systems having high gain require wideband. One of the latest applications of wideband antenna is the 4G LTE technology. The antennas used here are generally Multiple Input Multiple Output antennas. The designed antenna is a Microstrip Patch Antenna which gives the desired results at 5 GHz frequency. The results have been found to be compatible for the 5 GHz Wireless LAN applications. This LAN has got several advantages as compared to the 2.45 GHz LAN networks.

© Springer Nature Singapore Pte Ltd. 2019
A. K. Luhach et al. (Eds.): ICAICR 2018, CCIS 956, pp. 86–95, 2019.
https://doi.org/10.1007/978-981-13-3143-5_8

The problem of interference and airtime challenges has been resolved, more over it offers a much higher data rate as compared to the 2.45 GHz Wifi LAN. The 5 GHz ISM Band was initially for about 150 MHz which was further extended to 725 MHz of spectrum. Therefore, two designs of Microstrip Patch Antenna applicable for wideband applications have been proposed in this paper. The S11 parameter is below −10 dB along with wide band characteristics, which makes them suitable for many wireless networking applications such as Wifi, WiMax.

1.1 Related Work

In [1] designing of a Dual Band patch antenna with circular slots operating at Wifi frequency was done. Gain of 3.93 dB was obtained at the lower band and a gain of 3.73 dB was obtained for the upper band. The Microstrip Patch Antenna was designed at 2.4 GHz and 3.5 GHz frequency. The main purpose was to cater to the Zigbee and WiMax applications. The concept of IOT has been implemented on the designed antenna [2]. The designed antenna is implemented by cutting 'L' shaped slots on the main patch of the antenna. This showed better return loss and gain along with the dual band characteristics [3]. In [4] the insight of a novel rectangular finite grounded Microstrip Patch antenna with DGS. The designed antenna has the bandwidth of 31% due to the contribution of the DGS. Similarly, size reduction of the Microstrip Patch Antenna is due to the cutting of the slots on the patch of the antenna. The dual band frequency of the Microstrip Patch Antenna was achieved by using the capacitive value which was also used in the structure of artificial magnetic conductor [5]. The two Microstrip Patch Antenna designs have been implemented for the S Band (2 GHz– 3 GHz) and C Band (4 GHz–8 GHz). The designs have been implemented using inverted 'E' slot and 'U' slot to obtain the desired gain and reflection coefficient [6]. The proposed antenna was found to be suitable for compact wireless devices and their various applications. It has a very compact size because of high dielectric constant of the substrate that is 10.2 and loss tangent of 0.0002. The desired resonance was obtained by the removal of the diagonal edges of the patch [7]. The design proposed in [8] has been simulated at 2.45 GHz and 3.5 GHz using the DGS technique. The bandwidth percentage of 13.56% at 2.45 GHz and 10.36% at 3.5 GHz was obtained. [9] proposes a dual band Microstrip Patch Antenna having a wide band of 180 MHz for mobile applications. The obtained results are compatible for devices involving WiMax, Wifi, Bluetooth and WLAN. The proposed design is a dual band antenna working at 3.5 GHz and 5.2 GHz for WiMAx and Wifi applications respectively. The designed antenna has two parallel slots on the ground plane and a 'C' shaped slot on the patch. The results obtained showed low profile, high gain and wide bandwidth for the entire range of frequency [10].

1.2 Contribution

This research work will contribute towards designing and implementation of a Wideband Microstrip Patch Antenna using the inset feed technique. The 'U' slot on the patch and the 'G' shaped defect on the ground have led to the desired results which are applicable for various wireless applications.

1.3 Organization of Paper

The paper has been divided into total four parts. Section 1 containing the Introduction. Section 2 comprises of the proposed Antenna design with the specifications. Section 3 providing the results and discussions obtained from the design and finally Sect. 4 concluding the paper.

2 Proposed Antenna Design

Microstrip antenna is one of the most common and the most widely used antennas in the communication domain. The main reason behind its popularity is the ease of fabrication and low cost. The microstrip antenna is also very compact and gives efficient results at the desired frequencies. The length of the Microstrip Patch Antenna depends upon the dielectric constant of the substrate. If the dielectric constant of the substrate increases the length of the Microstrip patch Antenna decreases. The resonant length of the antenna is slightly less than the actual length of the antenna. The reason behind this difference is the extended electric fringe fields which increase the electrical length of the antenna.

The dimensions of the substrate, ground, patch and the microstrip feed line were calculated using the standard Microstrip Patch Antenna equations. Patch Antenna was designed using RT Duroid as the substrate with dimensions equal to [−W, W] and [−L, L], Copper (annealed) as the ground with dimensions as [−(W + 6 h), (W + 6 h)] and [−(L + 6 h), (L + 6 h)]. The patch was cut on the substrate along with the microstrip line using copper (annealed). The dimensions of the patch and the microstrip feed line were [−W/2, W/2], [−L/2, L/2] and [−Wf/2, Wf/2], [(L/2 − Fi), (Lf + L/2 − Fi)] respectively. W and L are the width and length of the patch, Wf and Lf are the width and length of the feed line and Fi is the inset depth. The frequency and the dielectric constant were taken as 5 GHz and 2.2 respectively. The thickness of the substrate was taken as 3.175 mm. First, a simple Microstrip Patch Antenna was simulated by using the dimensions given in Table 1.

Table 1. Optimized parameters

Ser. no	Parameters	Value (mm)
1	Length of the patch	42
2	Width of the patch	48
3	Width of the feed	7.8
4	Length of the feed	30.6
5	Depth of the feed	10.1
6	Height of the substrate	3.175

The results of this antenna were then enhanced by the implantation of the 'U' shaped slot on the surface of the patch of the antenna. Various slot parameters such as the slot position, width and length were optimized to obtain the wideband characteristics. The position of the slots was chosen according to the areas having maximum surface current density on the surface of the patch. The distance of 5.6 mm from the center of the patch to the vertical slots was optimized for the enhanced bandwidth of the antenna. The width of the slot has to be small with respect to the length of the slot. Since it is a 'U' shaped slot, three slots had to be cut on the surface of the patch as shown in Fig. 1.

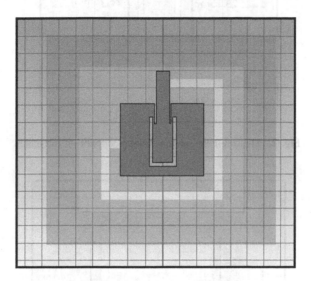

Fig. 1. 'U' shaped slots and the patch of the antenna and the 'G' shaped defect on the ground

Two slots were cut parallel to each other in the vertical plane and the third one was cut horizontally with respect to the patch. Optimization for the width of the slot was carried out between 0.5–3 mm. The broadest bandwidth was obtained at 2 mm width of the slot along with the desired gain. The length of the slot was not found to be such a significant parameter for increasing the bandwidth of the antenna. The optimized 'U' slot is shown in Fig. 2. The obtained bandwidth after this implementation was 450 MHz.

The DGS technique was implemented to further enhance the bandwidth. This technique is known for improving various antenna parameters such as bandwidth, low gain, and cross polarization. When a defect is made on the ground of the antenna, the current distribution on the ground gets altered and hence other parameters also change. Thus, the 'G' shaped slot as shown in Fig. 3 was cut on the ground of the antenna. The width, length and the position of the defect were optimized to obtain the required improvement in bandwidth. The dimensions of the defect are shown in Fig. 3. The integration of the two techniques led to the design of the wideband antenna.

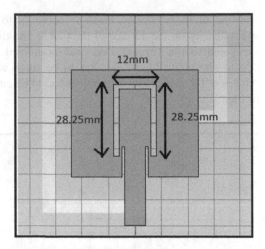

Fig. 2. Measurements of the 'U'-shaped slot on the patch

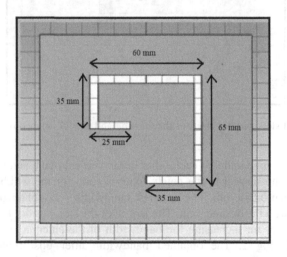

Fig. 3. Measurements of the G shaped DGS

3 Result

The desired results were obtained from the implemented design of the Microstrip Patch Antenna with 'U' slots on the surface of the patch and 'G' shaped DGS. According to the bandwidth obtained the wide band antenna can be used for various wide band applications.

3.1   Reflection Coefficient

The graph given in Figs. 4 and 5 has been plotted between the frequency of simulation and the S11 parameter. Since the S11 parameter is below -10 dB for the frequencies lying in C band, the obtained design can be used for C band applications.

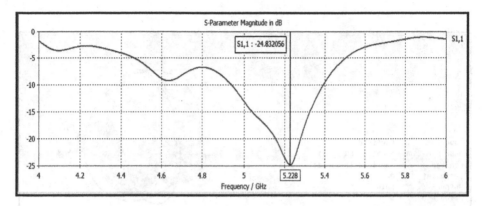

Fig. 4. S_{11} of the antennas operating without DGS

The S11 parameter of the antenna having only 'U' shaped slot on the patch of the antenna was found to be below −10 dB from 4.94 GHz to 5.39 GHz and the bandwidth was found to be 450 MHz as shown in Fig. 4. The plot shows the minimum value of −24.832 dB at 5.228 GHz.

The S11 parameter of the antenna with the 'U' shaped slot on the patch along with the 'G' shaped DGS was found to be below −10 dB from 4.82 GHz to 5.52 GHz and the bandwidth was found to be 700 MHz as shown in Fig. 5. The plot shows the minimum value of −27.9 dB at 5.32 GHz.

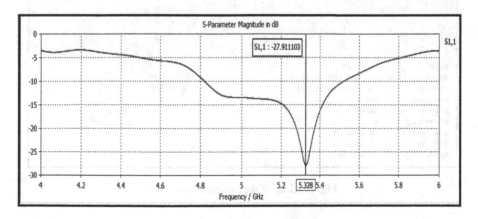

Fig. 5. S_{11} of the antenna operating with DGS

3.2 Gain

Gain defines the transmission power of the antenna. This gain has been enhanced by cutting the U-Shaped Slot on the Patch.

Figure 6 shows the gain of the antenna at 5 GHz frequency. The gain obtained for the antenna having only the 'U' shaped slots was found to be 8.621 dB.

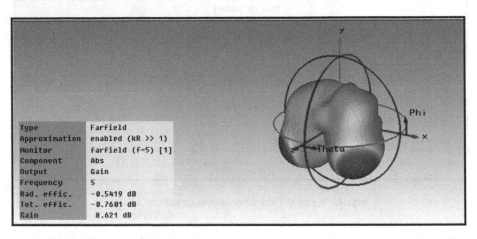

Fig. 6. Gain of the antenna without DGS

Figure 7 shows the gain of the antenna at 5 GHz frequency. The gain obtained for the antenna based on the DGS technique was found to be 7.356 dB.

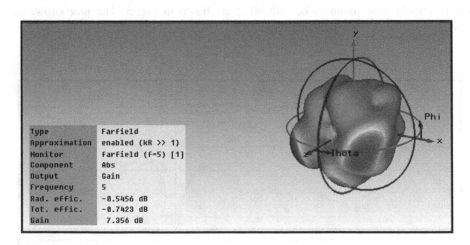

Fig. 7. Gain of the antenna with DGS

3.3 Surface Current

The Surface Current is defined as the flow of current on the patch. Surface Current Density is generally higher at the places where the slots are cut on the surface of the patch. Figures 8 and 9 shows the graph obtained for surface current density for the non DGS antenna and DGS antenna respectively.

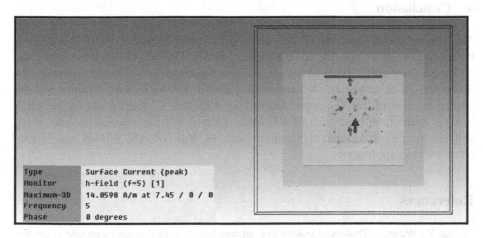

Type	Surface Current (peak)
Monitor	h-field (f=5) [1]
Maximum-3D	14.0598 A/m at 7.45 / 0 / 0
Frequency	5
Phase	0 degrees

Fig. 8. Surface current of the antenna without DGS

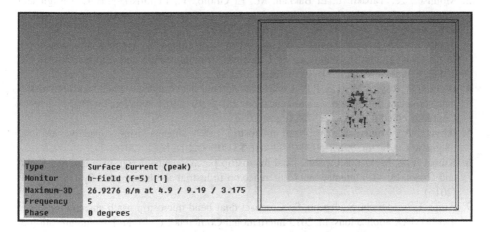

Type	Surface Current (peak)
Monitor	h-field (f=5) [1]
Maximum-3D	26.9276 A/m at 4.9 / 9.19 / 3.175
Frequency	5
Phase	0 degrees

Fig. 9. Surface current of the antenna with DGS

With the implementation of DGS technique the surface current density on the surface of the antenna increased.

Table 2 shows the gain and the bandwidth obtained at 5 GHz frequency for the antenna having the DGS slot and the one without the DGS slot.

Table 2. Gain and bandwidth of the simulated antennas

Ser. no.	Technique used	Gain dB	Bandwidth MHz
1.	Slots on the patch	8.621	450
2.	Slots on the patch and DGS	7.356	700

4 Conclusion

The designing and simulation of the wideband Inset-Fed Microstrip Patch Antenna has been successfully completed. The bandwidth of 450 MHz was obtained by cutting the 'U' shaped slot on the patch of the antenna and this bandwidth was then enhanced by using the DGS technique. A bandwidth gain of 250 MHz was obtained by the implementation of the 'G' shaped DGS along with the 'U' shaped slot on the patch leading to the final bandwidth of 700 MHz. Due to this the antenna becomes more suitable for various C Band applications, such as Wifi, WLAN, WiMax and various other wireless applications.

References

1. Li, Y., Wang, J.: Dual-band leaky-wave antenna based on dual-mode composite microstrip line for microwave and millimeter-wave applications. IEEE Trans. Antennas Propag. **66**, 1660–1668 (2018). https://doi.org/10.1109/TAP.2018.2800705
2. Mounsef, A., Tabakh, I., El Bakkali, M., El Gholb, Y., El Idrissi, N.E.A.: Design and simulation of a dual band microstrip patch antenna for an emergency medical service system, 978-1-5386-2123-3/17/$31.00 © 2017 IEEE (2017)
3. Maity, B.: Design of dual band L-slot microstrip patch antenna for wireless communication. In: 2017 International Conference on Computer Communication and Informatics (ICCCI-2017), Coimbatore, India, 05–07 January 2017
4. Bhunia, S., Roy, A., Sarkar, P.P.: Compact wideband dual frequency (dual band) microstrip patch antenna for wireless communication. In: 2016 URSI Asia-Pacific Radio Science Conference/Seoul, Korea, 21–25 August 2016
5. Ikhyari, A., Munir, A.: Dual-band microstrip patch antenna using capacitive artificial magnetic conductor, 978-1-5090-2649-4/16/$31.00 ©2016 IEEE (2016)
6. Kumar, P.S., Mohan, B.C.: Dual-band microstrip patch antenna design with inverted-E slot and U-slot. In: 11th International Conference on Industrial and Information Systems (ICIIS) (2016)
7. Amal, K.A., Amma, S., Joseph, S.: Compact dual band microstrip patch antenna for Wi-Fi and WiMAX applications. In: 2015 International Conference on Control, Communication & Computing India (ICCC), Trivandrum, 19–21 November 2015
8. Ali, I., Chang, R.Y.: Design of dual-band microstrip patch antenna with defected ground plane for modern wireless applications. In: Research Center for Information Technology Innovation, Academia Sinica, Taiwan. IEEE (2015)

9. Rahman, M.A., Hossain, M., Iqbal, I.S.: Design and performance analysis of a dual-band microstrip patch antenna for mobile WiMAX, WLAN, Wi-Fi and bluetooth applications. In: 3rd International Conference on Informatics, Electronics & Vision (2014)

10. Yassin, A.A., Saeed, R.A., Mokhtar, R.A.: Dual band microstrip patch antenna design using c slot for Wifi and WiMAx Applications. In: 5th International Conference on Computer & Communication Engineering, 978-1-4799-7635-5/14 $31.00 © 2014 IEEE (2014). https://doi.org/10.1109/ICCCE.2014.72

Fractional Order PID Controller Design for DFIG Based Wind Energy Conversion System

Renuka Thakur[✉] and Ritula Thakur

National Institute of Technical Teachers Training and Research, Sector 26,
Chandigarh 160019, India
renukathakur01@gmail.com, ritula.thakur@gmail.com

Abstract. This paper presents the behavior analysis of Fractional order PID controller for DFIG based wind turbine system and its comparison with PID controller. The parameters of FOPID controller are optimally tuned using FPID optimization tool of MATLAB. The optimal power from the wind can be obtained by using different controllers and various control strategies, which are well studied. For this paper vector oriented control scheme is used as the control strategy, in which rotor current dq-axis component controls the active and reactive power independently. The mathematical modeling and simulation of DFIG with its rotor side converter is presented in the MATLAB/SIMULINK environment. The simulation results are performed for 1.5 MW DFIG system to demonstrate the effectiveness of proposed FOPID controller.

Keywords: Fractional order PID controller (FOPID)
Doubly fed induction generator (DFIG) · Grid side converter (GSC)
Rotor side converter (RSC)

1 Introduction

A new report of GWEC (Global wind energy council) stated that the total installed capacity for wind power in the global market is expected to reach over 840 GW by 2022 [1]. Non-conventional sources are gaining importance over the conventional sources. Wind, solar, hydro, geothermal are the examples of non-conventional resources. Wind has become one of the most accessible and promising source of energy. Wind energy is a byproduct of sun and it blows due to change in atmospheric pressure. Wind has emanated as the most suitable source of electrical energy and it is replacing the conventional resources.

There are two modes of operation of wind power turbines, fixed speed operation and variable speed operation [2]. In the past, the use of FSWT (Fixed speed wind turbine) system was more prominent. But no reactive power support and even wind power conversion system provides low efficiency with FSWT system. Also, it imposes mechanical stress on the turbine and maximum power cannot be extracted at varying speed [3]. The limitations of FSWT system are overcome by VSWT (Variable speed wind turbine) system. The maximum power can be extracted at varying speed and provides reduced size of power converter having capacity of 25–30% of rated capacity of DFIG [4].

© Springer Nature Singapore Pte Ltd. 2019
A. K. Luhach et al. (Eds.): ICAICR 2018, CCIS 956, pp. 96–105, 2019.
https://doi.org/10.1007/978-981-13-3143-5_9

This paper presents the vector oriented control (VOC) strategy, where synchronous dq frame is used to define the control system. The synchronous dq frame can be constant to either stator flux [5] or stator voltage [6]. The active and reactive powers can be controlled by rotor current q-axis and d-axis component respectively. For performing VOC strategy, accurate information of stator and rotor parameter of machine is required. The machine torque can be directly controlled using DTC (direct torque control) method. The torque and stator flux information is required to select the appropriate voltage vectors for direct control of torque [7]. Another control scheme is DPC (direct power control). Abad et al. uses DPC, in which inner current loops are not present and power response obtained using DPC is fast and robust [8].

To enhance the system performance various control techniques have been used such as sliding mode controller to exhibit the fast transient response [9]. The use of different control techniques is to regulate the RSC and GSC. RSC regulates the active and reactive power of stator whereas power factor is maintained at unity and dc link voltage is maintained constant through GSC [10]. Hamane et al. performed the comparison of classical PI with Fuzzy-PI controller. The fuzzy PI controller has low dependence on model parameter and gives fast dynamic response [11]. Zolfagiri et al. uses FOPI controller to improve the system robustness and performance [12].

Section 2 discussed the detailed mathematical modeling of DFIG. This section also includes the control strategy for the entire system. Section 3 consists of an overview of FOPID controller and its tuning. Section 4 consists of all simulation results and conclusion of the proposed work is presented in Sect. 5 (Fig. 1).

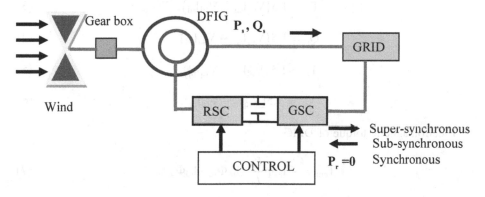

Fig. 1. DFIG based wind energy conversion system.

2 Mathematical Modeling

2.1 Wind Turbine

Power obtained by wind turbine

$$P_t = 0.5\rho\pi R^2 V_w^3 C_p(\lambda, \beta). \tag{1}$$

Above equation signifies that the turbine power is function of (C_p) power coefficient. Where C_p depends upon β and λ [13].

$$\lambda = \frac{Rw_t}{V_w}.\qquad(2)$$

Where,

λ = tip speed ratio
β = pitch angle
R = rotor radius
W_t = turbine speed
V_w = wind speed

For a particular wind speed, there is an optimal λ for a particular β, which provides the maximum power at that particular wind speed. So, to obtain the optimal power from a particular wind speed, it is required to rotate the rotor at optimal speed [14].

2.2 DFIG

The DFIG can be expressed by following equations rotating at w_s speed in synchronous dq reference frame [15].

The stator power and rotor power of DFIG in dq reference frame is expressed as

$$P_s = 1.5\left(V_{sq}I_{sq} + V_{sd}I_{sd}\right).\qquad(3)$$

$$Q_s = 1.5\left(V_{sq}I_{sq} - V_{sd}I_{sd}\right).\qquad(4)$$

$$P_r = 1.5\left(V_{rd}I_{rd} + V_{rq}I_{rq}\right).\qquad(5)$$

$$Q_r = 1.5\left(V_{rq}I_{rd} - V_{rd}I_{rq}\right).\qquad(6)$$

Electromagnetic torque of DFIG

$$T_{em} = -1.5p\frac{L_m}{L_r}\left[I_{rq}\Phi_{sd} - I_{rd}\Phi_{sq}\right].\qquad(7)$$

Where P = Real power, Q = Reactive power, T_{em} = Electromagnetic torque, Φ = Flux, L = Inductance, V = Voltage, I = Current, R = Resistance.

2.3 Control Strategy

For the simplifications in control, the dq reference frame is adopted. The dq frame is synchronously rotating which is used to establish the control of RSC by placing the stator flux vector on the d-axis. Therefore, stator flux becomes as shown below. Besides, stator resistance can be neglected since it is a realistic assumption for the generators used in the wind turbine.

$$\Phi_{sd} = \Phi_s \text{ and } \Phi_{sq} = 0. \tag{8}$$

Modified stator current, voltage and rotor flux are as follows

$$I_{sd} = \frac{\Phi_{sd} - L_m I_{rd}}{L_s} \text{ and } I_{sq} = \frac{L_m I_{rq}}{L_s}. \tag{9}$$

$$V_{sd} = 0 \text{ and } V_{sq} = w_s \Phi_s. \tag{10}$$

$$\Phi_{rd} = L_r \sigma I_{rd} + \frac{L_m}{L_r} \Phi_{sd} \text{ and } \Phi_{rq} = L_r \sigma I_{rq}. \tag{11}$$

Modified rotor voltages are

$$V_{rd} = R_r I_{rd} - s w_s L_r \sigma I_{rq}. \tag{12}$$

$$V_{rq} = R_r I_{rq} + s w_s L_r \sigma I_{rd} + s \frac{L_m}{Ls} V_{sq}. \tag{13}$$

Where $\sigma = 1 - \frac{L_m^2}{L_s L_r}$ which is a dispersion coefficient of DFIG. Equations (12) and (13) represent the relation between dq-axis rotor currents and voltages, where obtained dq-axis rotor voltages applied to control the generator.

Modified stator powers are

$$Ps = 1.5 V_{sq} I_{sq} = -1.5 \frac{L_m}{L_s} V_{sq} I_{rq}. \tag{14}$$

$$Qs = 1.5 V_{sq} I_{sd} = 1.5 V_{sq} \left[\frac{V_{sq}}{L_s w_s} - \frac{L_m}{L_s} I_{rd} \right]. \tag{15}$$

Above Eqs. (14) and (15) represents that the decoupled control of active and reactive power of stator can be achieved by using dq axis component of rotor current.

A block diagram containing the rotor voltage as input and stator power as output is established in Fig. 2 from Eqs. (12), (13), (14), (15). The first order transfer function links the stator powers and rotor voltages. This transfer function depends on the generator parameters like resistance, inductance and slip.

Figure 3 shows the control strategy for RSC of DFIG using fraction order PID controller. The main aim of this part is to achieve the cascaded control of dq-axis rotor currents and voltages. These controlled rotor voltages applied to the generator, which provides the regulated stator powers.

The reference stator powers are measured with actual stators power which provides the reference dq axis rotor current. The reference rotor current in dq-axis is compared with measured dq axis rotor current which gives the - decoupled dq-axis rotor voltage. Using, inverse parks transformation rotor voltage dq-axis components converted to abc components, this provides the controlled PWM switching to the RSC.

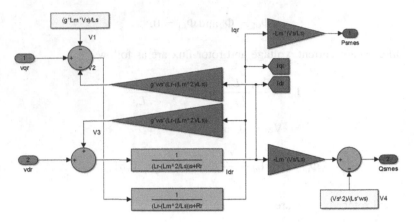

Fig. 2. Mathematical representation of DFIG.

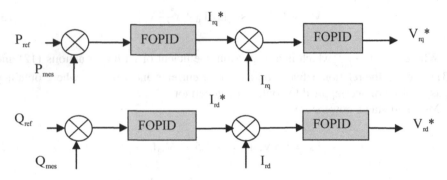

Fig. 3. Control strategy using FOPID controller.

The error between the reference signal and actual signal is required to get minimum value. In this approach, error value is passed through the controller, which should have the appropriate gain to obtain the desired output. So, proper tuning of controller is required to achieve the appropriate gain for the controller.

3   Tuning of FOPID Controller

The attraction of engineering and physics towards the fractional calculus has been increased. Fractional calculus is an old branch of mathematics. In last centuries, it was only studied in mathematics but from last few years the application of fractional calculus emerged into the various field of science and engineering.

The differential equation for $PI^\lambda D^\mu$ controller, for $0 < \lambda < 2$ and $0 < \mu < 2$, in time and frequency domain is given by

$$c(t) = K_p e(t) + K_i D_t^{-\lambda} e(t) + K_d D_t^{\mu} e(t). \tag{16}$$

$$C(s) = K_p + K_i s^{-\lambda} + K_d s^{\mu}. \tag{17}$$

The tuning of FOPID parameters is performed using FPID optimization tool of MATLAB. An optimal control system is obtained by adjusting the parameters so that the performance index reaches to either maximum or minimum value. The objective function is considered as the integral time absolute error (ITAE). ITAE is achieved by adding time weighting to IAE. This is defined as,

$$ITAE = \int_0^t t(|\Delta P| + |\Delta Q| + |\Delta I|). \tag{18}$$

This generally leads to the systems with reasonable transient characteristics. It also has a property that initial large error gets weighted lightly and late occurring error gets penalized heavily. This performance index is minimized using Nelder-Mead method.

Firstly, PID controller parameters are tuned using Ziegler-Nichol's method with the help of integer order PID tuning tool of MATLAB. These parameters are the initial

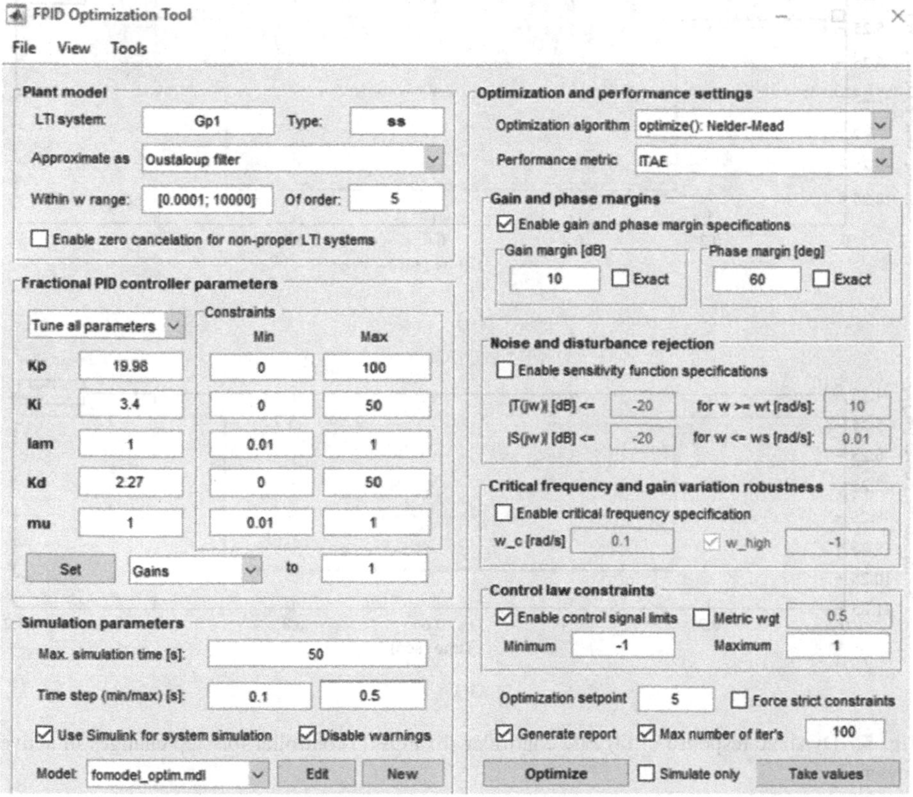

Fig. 4. FPID optimization tool.

assumption for fractional order PID controller. The design of FOPID controller is carried out using fpid_optim tool. where LTI system contains the workspace name of the plant. Type of system can be state space (ss) and transfer function (tf). The desired simulation model is added to this tool by clicking on new.

For this paper, Nelder-Mead optimization algorithm is used with ITAE performance metric. After setting all the parameters of optimization click on optimize to obtain new optimized values for controller parameters as shown in Fig. 4.

4   Simulation Results

The mathematical model of 1.5 MW DFIG and simulation for control scheme has been built in Matlab/Simulink. The control approach is validated by comparing the response of PID and FOPID controller for input reference of stator active and reactive power. The simulation tests have been performed for 1.2 s to analyze the system performance with two different controllers. Dynamic response obtained for the proposed controllers has been presented in Figs. 5 and 6.

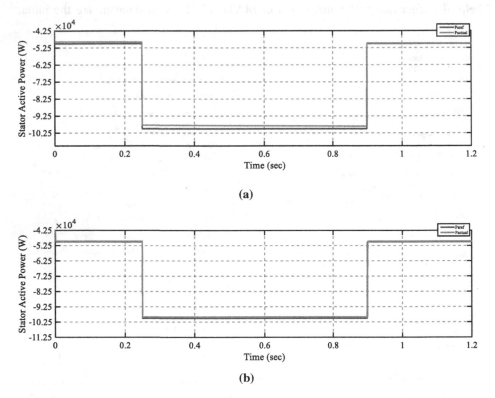

Fig. 5. Dynamic response of (a) PID controller (b) FOPID controller for step changes in active power.

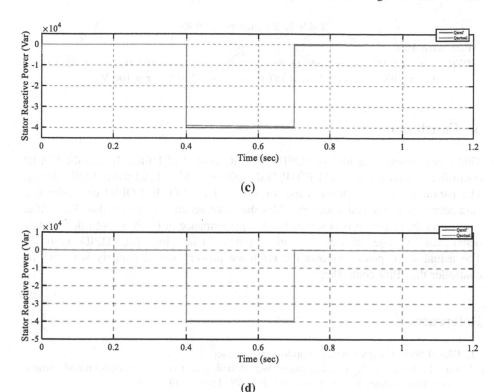

Fig. 6. Dynamic response of (c) PID controller (d) FOPID controller for step changes in reactive power.

4.1 Reference Tracking

The machine is first tested in ideal condition by applying different step input for active and reactive power. The response of both the controller is presented below. The response obtained using FOPID controller is exactly tracking the input reference but the more deviations in the response are observed with PID controller.

4.2 Transient Response

It is clearly observed in the Table 1. that the transient response obtained using FOPID controller is better than PID controller. FOPID controller provides the fast response therefore its settling time and rise time are less as compared to PID controller (Table 2).

Table 1. Time domain specifications for FOPID and PID controller-based system.

Parameters	FOPID controller	PID controller
Rise time (µs)	6.12	9.45
Settling time (µs)	11.9	17.3
Overshoot (%)	0	0
Steady state error	0	0.08

Table 2. Parameters of DFIG

Parameters value	
DFIG	Pm = 1.5 MW, Rs = 0.455 Ω, Rr = 0.19 Ω, p = 2, Ls = 0.07 H, Lr = 0.0213 H, Lm = 0.034 H, s = 0.03, w_s = 157 rad/sec, Vs = 230 V, Vr = 190 V

5 Conclusion

This paper presents the idea of FOPID for RSC control of DFIG. To use the FOPID controller it is required to add FOMCOM toolbox in MATLAB/SIMULINK library. The parameters of system are same for PID and FOPID. In FOPID controller five parameters are optimized which provides the more accurate response than PID. After comparing the results, it is observed that the performance of FOPID controller is much better than PID. The stable and smooth output is obtained by using FOPID controller. The actual stator power follows the reference power more accurately with FOPID controller than PID controller.

References

1. Global Wind Energy Council. http://www.gwec.net
2. Ko, H., Yoon, G., Kyung, N., Hong, W.: Modeling and control of DFIG-based variable speed wind-turbine. Electr. Power Syst. Res. **78**, 1841–1849 (2008)
3. Bharti, O.P.: Controller design of DFIG based wind turbine by using evolutionary soft computational techniques. Eng. Technol. Appl. Sci. Res. **7**(3), 1732–1736 (2017)
4. Elazzaoui, M.: Electrical & electronic systems modeling and control of a wind system based doubly fed induction generator: optimization of the power produced. J. Electr. Electron. Syst. **4**(1), 1–8 (2015)
5. Wang, Z., Sun, Y., Li, G., Ooi, B.T.: Magnitude and frequency control of grid connected doubly fed induction generator based on synchronised model for wind power generation. IET Renew. Power Gener. **4**(3), 232–241 (2010)
6. Akagi, H., Sato, H.: Control and performance of a doubly-fed induction machine intended for a flywheel energy storage system. IEEE Trans. Power Electron. **17**(1), 109–116 (2002)
7. Xu, L., Cartwright, P.: Direct active and reactive power control of DFIG for wind energy generation. IEEE Trans. Energy Convers. **21**(3), 750–758 (2006)
8. Abad, G., Rodriguez, M.A., Iwanski, G., Poza, J.: Direct power control of doubly-fed-induction generator-based wind turbines under unbalanced grid voltage. IEEE Trans. Power Electron. **25**(2), 442–452 (2010)
9. Barkia, A., Bouchiba, N., Sallem, S., Chrifi-alaoui, L., Kammoun, M.B.A.: A comparative study of PI and sliding mode controllers for autonomous wind energy conversion system based on DFIG. In: International Conference on Science and Techniques of Automatic Control Computer Engineering, pp. 612–617, December 2016
10. Tanvir, A., Merabet, A., Beguenane, R.: Real-time control of active and reactive power for doubly fed induction generator (DFIG)-based wind energy conversion system. Energies **8**, 10389–10408 (2015)
11. Hamane, B., Benghanem, M.: Control for variable speed wind turbine driving a doubly fed induction generator using Fuzzy-PI control. Energy Procedia **18**, 476–485 (2012)

12. Zolfaghari, M., Arani, K.A.A., et. al.: A fractional order proportional-integral controller design to improve load sharing between DGs in microgrid. In: Smart Grids Conference (SGC), Kerman, Iran, pp. 1–5 (2016)
13. Unchim, T., Oonsivilai, A.: A study of wind speed characteristic in PI controller based DFIG wind turbine. International Science Index, Electrical and Computer Engineering, vol. 5 (2011)
14. Ganti, V.C., Singh, B., Aggarwal, S.K., Kandpal, T.C.: DFIG-based wind power conversion with grid power leveling for reduced gusts. IEEE Trans. Sustain. Energy 3(1), 12–20 (2012)
15. Ko, H.-S., Yoon, G.-G., Kyung, N.-H., Hong, W.-P.: Modeling and control of DFIG-based variable-speed wind-turbine. Electr. Power Syst. Res. 78(11), 1841–1849 (2008)

Modeling and Validation of Shunt Active Power Filter by Using OPAL-RT

Sanjeev Kumar[✉] and Ritula Thakur

Electrical Engineering Department, National Institute of Technical Teachers
Training and Research, Sector 26, Chandigarh 160019, India
sanjeev.icl6@nitttrchd.ac.in, ritula.thakur@gmail.com

Abstract. Distortion in source current, voltage and power factor is due to non-linear electrical devices used at load side. Which produces harmonic pollution and may damage or responsible for false operation of equipment connected to it. Shunt Active power filters (SAPF) are the emerging devices, which can effectively mitigate harmonics and improves current waveforms and also supplies reactive power to the load. This paper focuses on the design and validation of SAPF based on Instantaneous Reactive Power algorithm to mitigate the current harmonics and Reactive Power Compensation (RPC) which are generated by nonlinear loads. MATLAB/Simulink tool is used for simulate the system and for obtaining the results. For validation of the results real time simulator OP4510 made by OPAL-RT is used which gives actual response of the system. The obtained results are within the limits recommended by IEEE-519 standard (THD < 5%) and also the reactive power demand is almost zero.

Keywords: SAPF · Total harmonic distortion (THD) · OPAL-RT
PQ theory

1 Introduction

In present days, the rapid increment in power electronics devices to boost the controllability and enhance the performance and efficiency of the system mostly in the switching loads (such as, switched mode power supplies (SMPS), and variable frequency devices (VFDs), etc.) are the main cause of harmonic production and source current distortion on power system network. Because of switching the load draws non-sinusoidal harmonic currents. Therefore, harmonics are generated that causes poor power quality and noisy sinusoidal waveform of supply and increase the reactive power demand is the significant main problem for the distributors and consumers of electric power as well [1]. Basically, Harmonics are the sinusoidal part of voltage and current that is the integral multiple of the fundamental frequency [2]. A while ago, passive filters were used to eradicate such issues and enhance the power quality due to their ease of operation and cheaper cost. But there are some major disadvantages like detuning, large size, particular harmonic rejection, resonance, large number of components required etc. To endure those disadvantages a new technique was developed named as Active Power filters. Basis on the connection the active power filters are divided as Series Active Power Filter, Shunt Active Power Filter & Hybrid Filter. The

© Springer Nature Singapore Pte Ltd. 2019
A. K. Luhach et al. (Eds.): ICAICR 2018, CCIS 956, pp. 106–116, 2019.
https://doi.org/10.1007/978-981-13-3143-5_10

power circuit which is commonly used for harmonic nullification and RPC is the SAPF filter because series active filter doesn't have capability for compensation of harmonic currents injected by the load [3].

Figure 1 represents the diagram of compensation technique in Shunt Active Power Filter. The non-linear load draws power from a three-phase source with the SAPF connected to it through coupling inductor. i_s is the supply current, i_L is the load current and i_f is the filter current (compensating current) generated by controlling the SAPF. This compensating current removes the harmonics presents in current mainly presents in the AC mains and forces the supply current to be sinusoidal in nature and in-phase with voltage by providing the filter current equal in magnitude and opposite in phase to the load harmonic current.

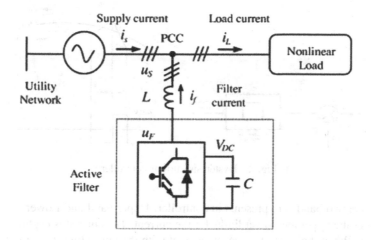

Fig. 1. Basic diagram of Shunt Active Power Filter

The current study is based on designing the SAPF to eradicate various harmonics contents present in current from the system induced by the three-phase diode rectifier with RL load. This paper shows the real time relative study of the system based on Total Harmonic Distortion (%THD) and compensation of Reactive power with or without SAPF [4].

2 Topology

2.1 Instantaneous Real and Reactive Power Theory (IRPT or P-Q Method)

IRPT theory is a powerful technique for defining real and imaginary power instantaneously. IRPT is not used only for mitigation of harmonics but also used for compensation of reactive power and also concerns with the power flow control in the system or transmission line [5]. It can be applied on both the 3-phase three-wire or 3-phase four wire system. In this theory first 3-phase current and voltage waveforms of abc coordinates transformed to αβ0 coordinates and instantaneous powers are defined on these coordinates. The pq theory consist of real matrix that converts 3-phase components into αβ0 stationary reference frames also known as Clark's transformation [6].

2.2 Design of Hysteresis Controller

For generation of accurate gate pulses in a particular sequence for the IGBT based inverter hysteresis band current controller is used. It generates gating signal by comparing the actual current with reference current. Figure 2 shows the Hysteresis controller with switching waveforms.

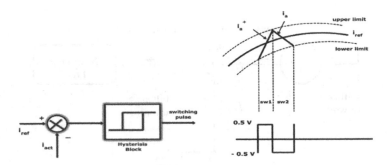

Fig. 2. Hysteresis current controller

There are two bands are presents in controller, Upper band and Lower band. These band defines the upper and lower limits for the current. The current is captured between these limits. When the current comes in contact with the upper limit the lower switches of inverter gets on and the uppers are off. Parallelly the lower switches are turned off when the current comes in contact with lower limit and the reference current always followed by the compensating current. This band is robust and provide excellent dynamic action than any other comparator [7].

3 Mathematical Modelling

3.1 P-Q Method

The relation between a-b-c coordinates and the orthogonal (αβ0) coordinates of 3-phase power system are represented by Clarke's transformation. The matrix for conversion of source voltage into α-β orthogonal coordinates (v_α, v_β) are given below [8]

$$\begin{pmatrix} v_\alpha \\ v_\beta \end{pmatrix} = \sqrt{2/3} \begin{pmatrix} 1 & \frac{1}{2} & -\frac{1}{2} \\ 0 & \frac{\sqrt{3}}{2} & -\frac{\sqrt{3}}{2} \end{pmatrix} \begin{pmatrix} v_{sa} \\ v_{sb} \\ v_{sc} \end{pmatrix}. \tag{1}$$

Similarly, the 3-phase load currents are converted into α-β orthogonal coordinates $(i_{L\alpha}, i_{L\beta})$ as

$$\begin{pmatrix} i_{L\alpha} \\ i_{L\beta} \end{pmatrix} = \sqrt{2/3} \begin{pmatrix} 1 & \frac{1}{2} & -\frac{1}{2} \\ 0 & \frac{\sqrt{3}}{2} & -\frac{\sqrt{3}}{2} \end{pmatrix} \begin{pmatrix} i_{La} \\ i_{Lb} \\ i_{Lc} \end{pmatrix}. \tag{2}$$

From above expressions, the instantaneous power p_L and the instantaneous reactive power q_L flowing through the system are calculated as

$$\begin{pmatrix} p_L \\ q_L \end{pmatrix} = \begin{pmatrix} v_\alpha & v_\beta \\ v_\beta & -v_\alpha \end{pmatrix} \begin{pmatrix} i_{L\alpha} \\ i_{L\beta} \end{pmatrix}. \tag{3}$$

The above real (p_L) and imaginary (q_L) power consists Ac and Dc parts. Let p_L consists of the $\overline{p_L}$ and $\widetilde{p_L}$ and q_L consists $\overline{q_L}$ and $\widetilde{q_L}$ as DC component and the harmonic component respectively, which are expressed as

$$p_L = \overline{p_L} + \widetilde{p_L}. \tag{4}$$

$$q_L = \overline{q_L} + \widetilde{q_L}. \tag{5}$$

After the calculation of p_L and q_L, reference current has been calculated and by taking inverse Clark's transformation the values of compensating currents are obtained as shown below

$$\begin{pmatrix} i_{sa}^* \\ i_{sb}^* \\ i_{sc}^* \end{pmatrix} = \sqrt{2/3} \begin{pmatrix} 1 & 0 \\ -\frac{1}{2} & \frac{\sqrt{3}}{2} \\ -\frac{1}{2} & -\frac{\sqrt{3}}{2} \end{pmatrix} \begin{pmatrix} v_\alpha & v_\beta \\ -v_\beta & v_\alpha \end{pmatrix}^{-1} \begin{pmatrix} p^* \\ q^* \end{pmatrix}. \tag{6}$$

Where, $p^* = \widetilde{p_L} + p_{loss}$ and $q^* = q = 0$ and p_{loss} is the instantaneous active power necessary to adjust the voltage of DC capacitor to its reference value and the compensating current for the mitigation of harmonics is generated. To maintain the value of DC link capacitor to its reference value PI controller is used [9].

3.2 PI Controller

For compensating switching and conduction losses and for maintaining DC bus voltage it is necessary to continuous flow of power through DC capacitor. The difference of actual DC link voltage and reference DC link voltage is passed from a PI controller. The power required by the capacitor to maintain dc-link voltage at a fixed value is proportional to the difference of reference and actual voltages [10].

3.3 DC Bus Voltage

DC bus voltage (V_{DC}) of the SAPF depends upon the line voltage of the system. For a 3-phase voltage source converter, the DC voltage is expressed as

$$V_{DC} = 2\sqrt{2}V_{LL}\big/\left(\sqrt{3}m\right).\tag{7}$$

3.4 DC Link Capacitor and Interfacing Inductor

Based on the principle of instantaneous power the value of DC link capacitor C_{DC} is given by [11]

$$0.5C_{DC}[V_{DC}^2 - V_{DC1}^2] = 3V_{ph}(\text{aI})\text{t}.\tag{8}$$

The value of interfacing inductor is depends on the ripple current I_{crpp}, which is a part of Voltage source converter current seeing approx. 15% current ripple at switching frequency f_s, the value of inductor is given as

$$L_f = \sqrt{3}mV_{DC}\big/(12\text{a}\,f_s I_{crpp}).\tag{9}$$

4 Real-Time Simulation

4.1 Simulation of the System Without Filter

MATLAB simulink model of the system with 3-phase non-linear rectifier and RL load without Active filter is shown in Fig. 3 as-

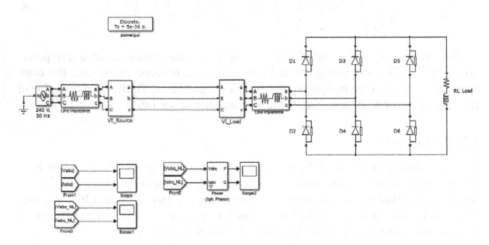

Fig. 3. Simulation circuit for non-linear load without SAPF

The source current is highly distorted due to nonlinear load which gives non sinusoidal waveform of source current and reactive power demand is shown in Figs. 4

and 5 respectively and the FFT analysis gives total harmonic distortion is 26.09% shown in Fig. 6.

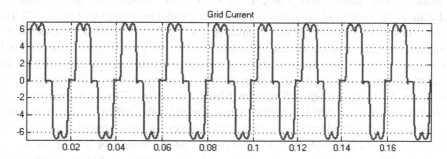

Fig. 4. Source current without SAPF

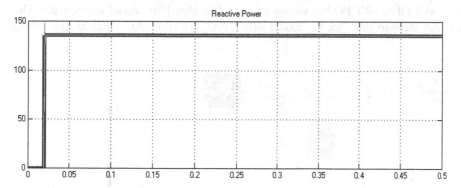

Fig. 5. Reactive power demand without SAPF

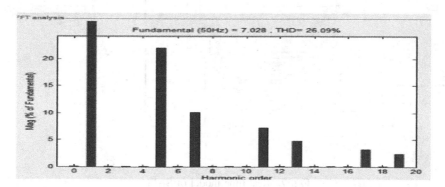

Fig. 6. THD without SAPF

4.2   Real-Time Simulation of the System with Filter Using OP4510

OP4510 is OPAL-RT's the real time simulation tool is completely suitable platform for validation of the models build in MATLAB/SIMULINK. Where user can create master and console subsystem of the model for fast and parallel execution on target. [12] The master subsystem consists all the simulating part or MATLAB/SIMULINK model along with OpCtrl, AnalogOut and AnalogIn blocks of Opal-RT present in Simulink library and console subsystem consists of all the controlling parameters which are required to changes during the operation and all the output results are obtained in this subsystem by using real-time Opcomm block and scope. The real-time model is uploaded on target which is OP4510 simulator through TCP/IP protocol network connection and loopback cable is used to make the connection between the hardware and host computer and with DSO (digital storage oscilloscope) for getting the digital and analog I/O results and waveforms. For real time simulation, MATLAB/Simulink model of proposed system is used [13, 14].

Figures 7 and 8 shows real time simulation of SAPF connected to the non-linear load with OPAL-RT I/O blocks and the complete algorithm model respectively. There are four steps to interface the model with OPAL-RT simulator which are as follows

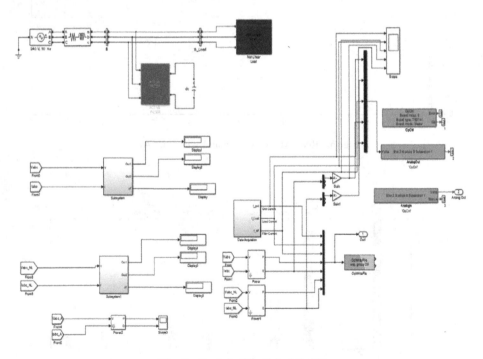

Fig. 7. Real time model of SAPF

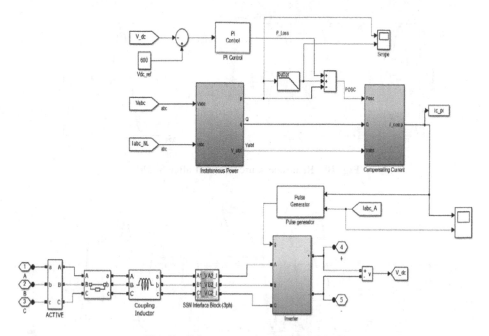

Fig. 8. Sub system of active filter block

1. Edit: - It opens Simulink model directly by RT-software.
2. Build\Compile: Model is transformed into real time and codes are generated.
3. Execute: - Run the simulation on real time target using multiples core.
4. Interact: - Use the graphical interface to change control and acquire data [15].

5 Real Time Results and Discussion

After introducing the SAPF i.e. the pulses is applied to the inverter the real-time source voltage is shown in Fig. 9, real-time source current is shown in Figs. 10, 11 and 12 shows real-time compensation Filter current, Fig. 13 shows Reactive power demand of the system after SAPF and THD present in the system after SAPF has been illustrated in Fig. 14 (Table 1).

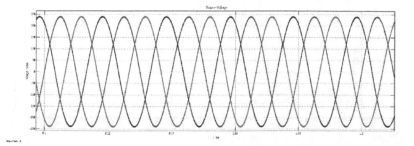

Fig. 9. Real-time source voltage

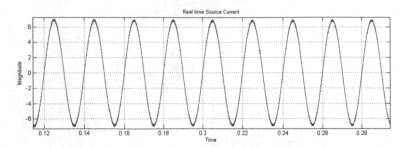

Fig. 10. Real-time source current after SAPF

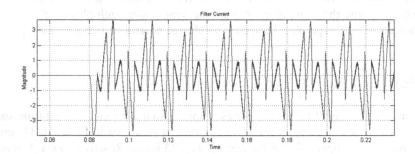

Fig. 11. Real-time source current before and after SAPF

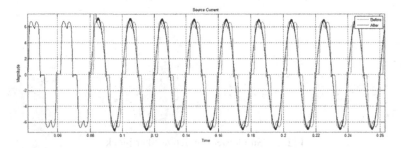

Fig. 12. Real-time filter current of SAPF

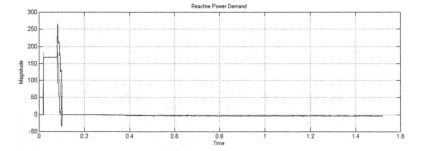

Fig. 13. Real-time reactive power demand after SAPF

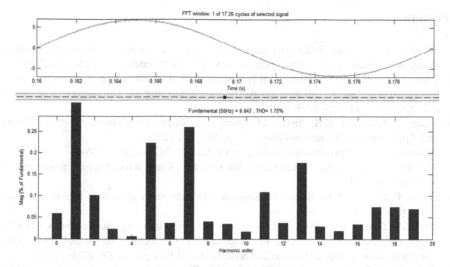

Fig. 14. THD after SAPF

Table 1. Parameters for source voltage, line impedance, load and filter details.

Simulation parameters	Values	Simulation parameters	Values
Source voltage (Vs)	240 V	Optimal values (Kp and Ki)	0.2 and 1.5
Source impedance (Rs; Ls)	0.1 Ω; 0.15 mH	Hysteresis band	±0.2 A
Dc Link voltage (Vdc)	700 V	Load impedance (R; L)	60 Ω; 20 mH
Dc link capacitance (Cdc)	20 μF	Coupling inductor	40 mH

6 Conclusion

This paper develops Instantaneous active and reactive power theory (IRPT) based SAPF under the unbalanced/non-linear load condition for reactive power demand and harmonics nullification and validates the results by preparing real-time simulation of the system with the help of eMEGAsim solver of OPAL-RT in real-time simulator OP4510. The IRPT based SAPF gives better results as the total harmonic distortion (THD) becomes 1.75% which is under the recommendation given by IEEE and reactive power demand almost zero and the power factor becomes unity and the real-time results are also similar to the simulation results.

References

1. Shankar, V.A., Kumar, N.S.: Implementation of shunt active filter for harmonic compensation in a 3 phase 3 wire distribution network. Energy Procedia **117**, 172–179 (2017)
2. Lada, M.Y., Bugis, I., Talib, M.H.N.: Simulation a shunt active power filter using MATLAB/Simulink. In: 4th International Power Engineering and Optimization Conference (PEOCO), pp. 371–375. IEEE (2010)
3. Akagi, H., Watanabe, E.H., Aredes, M.: Shunt active filters. In: Instantaneous Power Theory and Applications to Power Conditioning, pp. 109–220 (2007)
4. Akagi, H.: Active harmonic filters. Proc. IEEE **93**(12), 2128–2141 (2005)
5. Afonso, J.L., Aredes, M., Watanabe, E., Martins, J.S.: Shunt active filter for power quality improvement (2001)
6. Gamit, B.R., Vyas, S.R.: Harmonic elimination in three phase system by means of a shunt active filter (2018)
7. Samal, S., Hota, P.K., Barik, P.K.: Harmonics mitigation by using shunt active power filter under different load condition. In: International Conference on Signal Processing, Communication, Power and Embedded System (SCOPES), pp. 94–98. IEEE (2016)
8. Badgujar, D.S., Varade, K.P., Veeresh, C.: Shunt active filter for power quality improvement. Int. J. Eng. Res. Gen. Sci. **3**(4), 137–148 (2015). ISSN 20912730
9. Singh, B., Chandra, A., Al-Haddad, K.: Power Quality: Problems and Mitigation Techniques. Wiley, New York (2014)
10. Soomro, D.M., Omran, M.A., Alswed, S.K.: Design of a shunt active power filter to mitigate the harmonics caused by nonlinear loads (2006)
11. Singh, B.N., Rastgoufard, P., Singh, B., Chandra, A., Al-Haddad, K.: Design, simulation and implementation of three-pole/four-pole topologies for active filters. IEEE Proc.-Electr. Power Appl. **151**(4), 467–476 (2004)
12. Dubey, A., Chakrabarti, S., Terzija, V.: Testing and validation of a dynamic estimator of states in OPAL-RT real time simulator. In: Power and Energy Society General Meeting, pp. 1–5. IEEE (2017)
13. Patel, A., Mathur, H.D., Bhanot, S.: An improved control method for unified power quality conditioner with unbalanced load. Int. J. Electr. Power Energy Syst. **100**, 129–138 (2018)
14. Bechar, M., Hazzab, A., Habbab, M., Lakhdari, L., Slimi, M.: Real-time control of AC machine drives using RT-LAB package. In: Hajji, B., Tina, G.M., Ghoumid, K., Rabhi, A., Mellit, A. (eds.) ICEERE 2018. LNEE, vol. 519, pp. 533–544. Springer, Singapore (2019). https://doi.org/10.1007/978-981-13-1405-6_62
15. Kumaravel, S., Narayan, R.S., O'Donnell, T., O'Loughlin, C.: Genetic algorithm-based PI tuning of VSC-HVDC system and implementation using OPAL-RT. In: Region 10 Conference, TENCON 2017 IEEE, pp. 2193–2197. IEEE, November 2017

Real Time Simulation of IEEE 9 Bus System for Fault Analysis Using Transient Response

Ankit Kumar Singh$^{(\boxtimes)}$ and Ritula Thakur

Electrical Engineering Department (I&C), National Institute of Technical
Teachers Training and Research, Sector 26, Chandigarh 160019, India
ankit.icl6@nitttrchd.ac.in, ritula.thakur@gmail.com

Abstract. Power system stability is an important aspect of secure and economic power system operation. During designing and planning of the project,
power system studies plays important role. This paper covers the real time
simulation/ modelling of the IEEE 9 bus system using RT lab tools. In this, the
fault is created on different locations in the multi machine system in running
condition and transient stability is analyzed for different load and generating
conditions in real time. Rotor load angle is a reliable indicator to identify the
uncertainty in the system. So change in rotor angle of machines in the system is
used as indicator of the transient stability of the system and to calculate the
measures taken to maintain frequency and system stability. In this way fault
have applied at different location in IEEE 9 bus system and the real time
response have fetched with the help of OP 4510 simulator.

Keywords: Power system stability · Real time simulation · IEEE 9 bus system
RT lab tool · Transient stability · Rotor load angle

1 Introduction

In the present era, there is a need to keep up synchronism on the grounds that the
system is expanding regularly and these outcomes help in bigger machine's installation. Because of this, transient fluctuations are raising persistently in power system [1].
Due to the variation in load, faults, loss excitation and switching operation, distur-
bances in transient are caused. Subsequently, it is very necessary to recover synchronism after aggravations in the system. Thus, intensive investigation of transient stability
is needed to lessen issues, for example, synchronism loss, blackouts etc. [2].

The word stability alludes to build synchronism and the stability limit means
maximum flow of power which is possible or a part at which working of the system is
stable. The Stability in Power system is the nature of power System which allows
system to be in equilibrium under normal working conditions and to recover equilibrium condition after the application of fault [3, 4].

The Stability in Power system can be classified into transient, dynamic and steady
state stability. For small slow disturbance, to retain synchronism between machines, the

© Springer Nature Singapore Pte Ltd. 2019
A. K. Luhach et al. (Eds.): ICAICR 2018, CCIS 956, pp. 117–126, 2019.
https://doi.org/10.1007/978-981-13-3143-5_11

capability of a power system is called Steady state stability. After the initial swing, system achieves the new equilibrium position. In this way the ability of system to achieve synchronism in time, is called Dynamic Stability.

The Power System ability to regain condition of stability and to maintain synchronism after a large disturbance, which arise from general situations like circuit element ON and OFF switching, fault clearing etc, is called Power System Transient Stability. Here, the main significance is given to system transient stability. This implementation of stability is for one swing, a short time period. Transient stability analysis is implemented to determine whether during the first swing the system looses stability or not [5].

Here, the stability analysis is done by using different type of faults. Faults mainly happen when there is a connection establish between phases, insulation deterioration, lightning, falling of trees across lines, wind damage, etc.

In the system swing behavior is resolved with the help of swing equation. This equation describe relative motion between the rotor angle (δ) and the stator field with respect to time [6].

1.1 Real Time Simulator

This paper represent phasor tool development for real time simulation application of eMEGAsim simulator for transient stability. The application of Phasor tool may be for assessments of dynamic security, and test of functionality of hardware e.g. controllers in micro-grids and also for preparing academic laboratories or for operation in industries [7, 8].

The design of phasor tool performs more efficiently for the simulation of power systems at large scale. While, results of simulation verified that effectiveness of Phasor tool is for around 10000 buses for real-time simulation, at OPAL-RT Technologies ongoing research is planned of 20000 buses system for real-time simulation [9]. Moreover, the tool library is enlarging by including suitable models for other power grids components such as HVDC lines and static VAR compensators [10].

2 Problem Formulation

2.1 Transient Stability

In this paper, transient stability analysis has been done for IEEE-9 bus system by introduction of faults at different locations.

Figure 1 represent a synchronous generator model which is attached to an infinite bus by using transmission system [17].

Where E_T = Terminal voltage of Generator, X_g = Internal reactance of Generator, E_g = Internal Voltage of Generator, E_{HV} = High side voltage of step transformer, E_O = System voltage, X_E = External impedance, X_T = Transformer impedance, X_L = Line impedance and P_e = Transferred power.

$$P_e = \frac{E_g E_T}{X_g} \sin \delta \qquad (1)$$

The transferred power is directly proportional to rotor angle δ [11, 12]. A System disturbance can result a variation in flow of power in electrical power system, which result in variation in rotor power angle δ [13]. This is graphically presented in Fig. 2 [17].

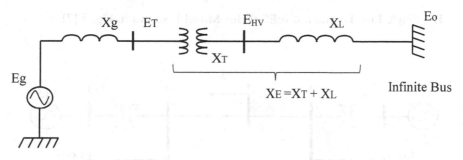

Fig. 1. Synchronous machine connected to infinite bus

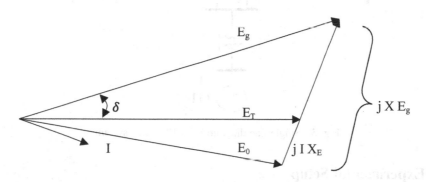

Fig. 2. Vector diagram of synchronous machine

2.2 Methodology

In the case of immediate and large variations, the transient stability analysis perform. As example, fault appearance, or load addition or removal suddenly. In the presence of disturbance, system performance is analyzed with the help of transient stability analysis [14, 15].

Steps involved for transient stability analysis-

1: First of all an IEEE- 9 bus circuit is designed and performed in Matlab/Simulation and analysis of load flow is achieved.
2: Initial parameters of system e.g. frequency, voltages and power angles of bus, generator rotor angles are studied.
3: At specific location in transmission line of system, a balanced 3-phase fault is applied.
4: Model is interfaced with RT Lab simulator and real time response taken and the effect of fault analyzed on the basis of change in rotor angle of machine.

The Single Line Diagram of IEEE 9 Bus Model is shown in Fig. 3 [7].

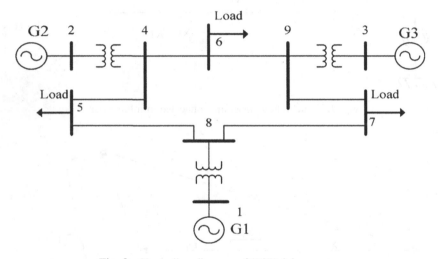

Fig. 3. Single line diagram of IEEE 9 bus system

3 Experimental Setup

3.1 Real Time Simulator (OP 4510)

A computer model of a physical system which can perform with same rate as actual "wall clock" time, is called Real- Time Simulation. In other words, the computer model executes with same rate as actual physical system. It is the necessity of performer to acquire fast and accurate solutions during the process and the OPAL-RT provides an efficient platform. This technology is used by most of the development and research industries to acquire results in real time [16].

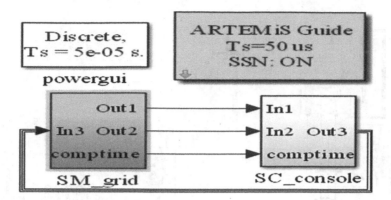

Fig. 4. Top view of MATLAB/SIMULINK model of IEEE 9 bus system with RT lab tools

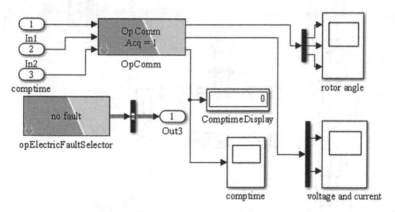

Fig. 5. Console block of MATLAB/SIMULINK model of IEEE 9 bus system with RT lab tools

3.2   Softwares Used

MATLAB/SIMULINK software of Mathworks Ltd. was used for developing the model of IEEE-9 bus system and RT Lab software of OPAL-RT. It was used for real time simulation studies.

MATLAB/SIMULINK based model of Top view, Console block and Master block of IEEE- 9 bus system with RT Lab tools is shown in Figs. 4, 5 and 6 respectively.

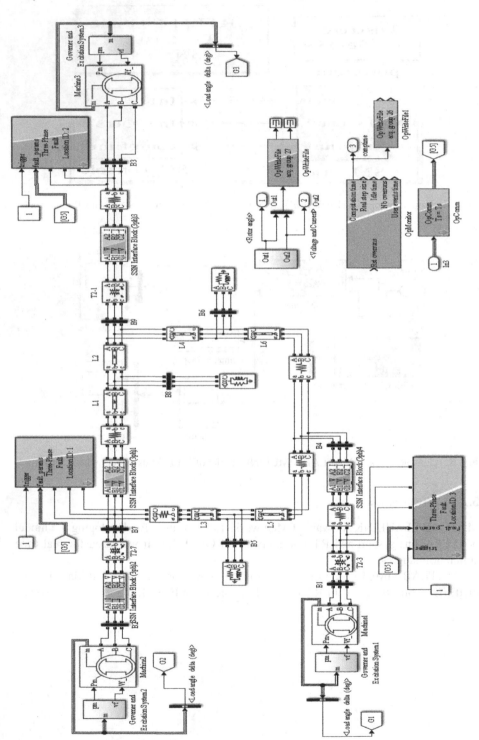

Fig. 6. Master block of MATLAB/SIMULINK model of MM system with RT lab tools

4   Results and Discussions

The transient response of model using real time simulator OP 4510 is shown by Figs. 7, 8 and 9. In the three generators in circuit, generator1, generator2 and generator3 having rating 247.5, 192 and 128 MVA respectively. Each generator is connected to a 100 MVA rating transformer.

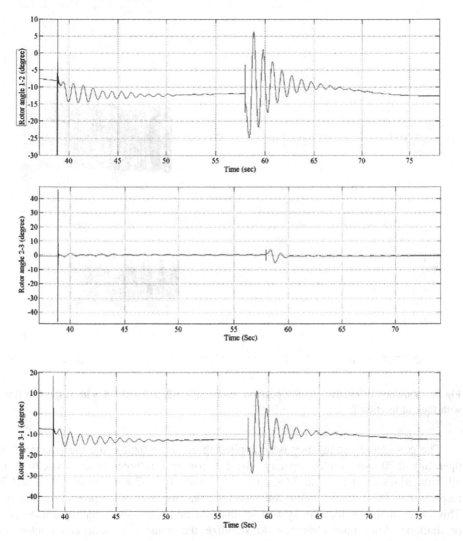

Fig. 7. Variation of relative angular position rotor angle 1-2, 2-3 and 3-1 with respect to time with fault at location 1

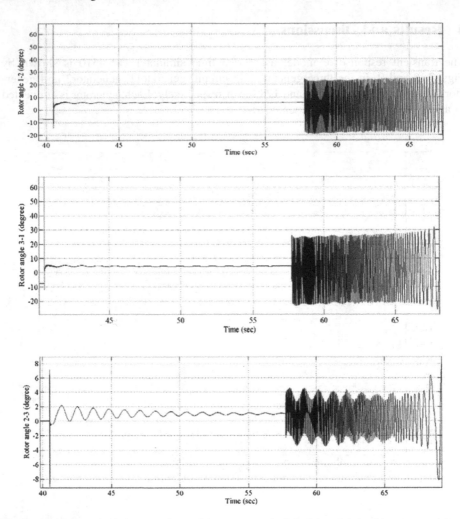

Fig. 8. Variation of relative angular position rotor angle 1-2, 2-3 and 3-1 with respect to time with fault at location 2

The considered contingency is an applied three-phase fault while the generator is operating at 70% of its rated capacity. The duration time in three-phase short-circuit in all simulations is taken 38 to 58 s, 41 to 55 s and 41 to 57 s in location 1, 2 and 3 respectively. This period contains the maximum reaction time of the protection system. This curve indicates that the system is unstable and rotor angle having undamped oscillations. After fault clearance, to stabilize the transients, additional control is required. In Figs. 4, 5 and 6, it is shown that how RT Lab tools are applied in simulation and by interfacing with RT lab simulator the transient response is fetched.

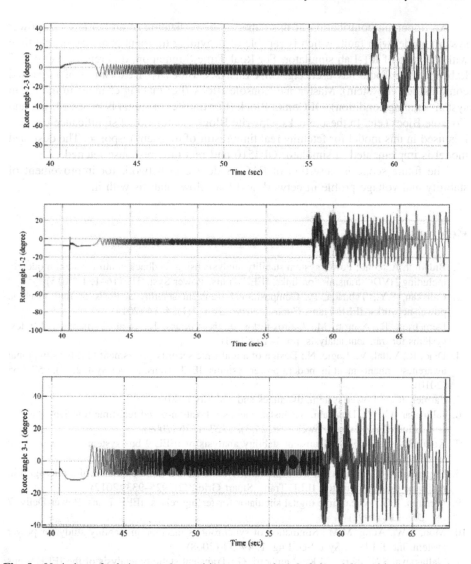

Fig. 9. Variation of relative angular position rotor angle 1-2, 2-3 and 3-1 with respect to time with fault at location 3

5   Conclusion

This paper has demonstrated the real time simulation of transient response of fault applied at different location in IEEE 9 bus system.

The first step in this design approach is to develop IEEE 9 bus model of power system. This model is designed using MATLAB/SIMULATION. It consist of 3 generator source, 3 transformer and 9 buses. After designing, the fault problem was translated into this model at three different locations and then its transient response analysis has performed.

An important contribution of this paper is the realization of an IEEE 9 bus power system model with fault, which is capable of providing transient response in real time with the help of RT-Lab simulator. For Real Time Simulation, different blocks of RT Lab Software Tools has used e.g. SSN Interface Block (For execution of large and complex power system), Master and Console Block (For making changes in model, in system running condition), OPComm Block (For transfer of signal between Master and Console Block) etc. In these blocks, Opwrite Block has important significance because it is used in this model for fetching real time result of transient response. The designed model is implemented in simulator OP4510 and real time response fetched.

The future scope is, insertion of FACTS device in network for improvement of stability and voltage profile in network and load flow analysis with it.

References

1. Bidadfar, A., et al.: Power system stability analysis using feedback control system modeling including HVDC transmission links. IEEE Trans. Power Syst. **31**, 116–124 (2015)
2. Caliskan, S.Y., Tabuada, P.: Compositional transient stability analysis of multimachine power networks. IEEE Trans. Control. Netw. Syst. **1**(1), 4–14 (2014)
3. Demetriou, P., Asprou, M., Quiros-tortos, J., Kyriakides, E., et al.: Dynamic IEEE test systems for transient analysis, pp. 1–10 (2015)
4. Diao, R., Vittal, V., Logic, N.: Design of a real-time security assessment tool for situational awareness enhancement in modern power systems. IEEE Trans. Power Syst. **25**(2), 957–965 (2010)
5. Farmer, R.G.: Power system, dynamics and stability (2001)
6. Jalili-marandi, V., Dinavahi, V.: Instantaneous relaxation-based real-time transient stability simulation. IEEE Trans. Power Syst. **24**(3), 1327–1336 (2009)
7. Kaur, R., Kumar, E.D.: Transient stability analysis of IEEE 9 bus system in power world simulator. Int. J. Eng. Res. Appl. **6**(1), 35–39 (2016)
8. Logenthiran, T., Srinivasan, D.: Multiagent system for real-time operation of a microgrid in real-time digital simulator. IEEE Trans. Smart Grid **3**(2), 925–933 (2012)
9. Mclaren, P.G.: A real time digital simulator for testing relays. IEEE Trans. Power Deliv. **7**(1), 207–213 (1992)
10. Mon, T.W., Aung, M.M.: Simulation of synchronous machine in stability study for power system. Int. J. Electr. Syst. Sci. Eng. **1**, 49–54 (2008)
11. Nallagalva, S.K., Kirar, M.K., Agnihotri, G.: Transient stability analysis of the IEEE 9-bus system electric power system. Int. J. Sci. Eng. Technol. **166**(1), 161–166 (2012)
12. Oluic, M., Ghandhari, M., Berggren, B.: Methodology for rotor angle transient stability assessment in parameter space. IEEE Trans. Power Syst. **8950**(1), 1–10 (2016). https://doi.org/10.1109/TPWRS.2016.2571562
13. Kundur, P.: Definition and classification of power system stability IEEE Trans. Power Syst. **19**(2), 1387–1401 (2004)
14. Roberts, L., Kafanas, G., Champneys, A., di Bernardo, M., Bell, K.: A parametric investigation on the effects of inertia on the stability of power systems (2015)
15. Faruque, M.O., et al.: Real-time simulation technologies for power systems design, testing, and analysis. IEEE Power Energy Technol. Syst. J. **2**(2), 63–73 (2015)
16. Uhlen, K.: Transient stability analysis in multi-terminal VSC- HVDC grids (2016)
17. Basler, M.J., Schaefer, R.C.: Understanding power system stability. In: 2005 58th Annual Conference for Protective Relay Engineers, pp. 46–67. IEEE Transactions (2005)

Low Transconductance OTA Based Active Comb Filter for Biomedical Applications

Anil Kumar Sahu$^{(\boxtimes)}$ and Arvind Kumar Sahu

SSGI/SSTC, Bhilai, India
anilsahu82@gmail.com, arvind100691@gmail.com

Abstract. This paper presents a comb filter to suppress power line interference in biomedical signals. The filter is based on OTA-C topology and the rejection frequency of the filter is tunable by changing the transconductance of the OTA. This filter is designed in Tanner EDA tool in 45 nm technology and is powered by 1.1 V supply. This Designed filter achieves a stop band attenuation of 24 dB for 50 Hz, 150 Hz and 250 Hz frequencies. A comb filter using OTA-C topology is designed. The filter is designed using 45 nm CMOS technology in Tanner EDA tool and simulated using TSPICE simulator. The performance of the filter is as expected. This filter has more number of active components than but has less number of passive components. One more advantage of OTA-C based filter design is that by simply controlling the bias current of OTAs, electronic tuning of filter parameters such as center frequency and quality factor can be achieved. Future scope of this design can be to implement it using low power OTA cell in 14 nm FinFET technology. This way power consumption and chip area will be reduced.

Keywords: Biomedical signal · Comb filter · OTA-C · Power line interference

1 Introduction

Measuring bio-potential signals have become common in neuroscience research, prosthetics and rehabilitation treatment. The most important bio-potential signals are Electroencephalogram (EEG), Electromyogram (EMG), and Electrocardiogram (ECG). These bio-potential signals are in the order of μV and mV and gets contaminated easily against various contaminating signals such as power line harmonics. It is of great challenge to reduce the power consumption while preserving the high performance in portable biomedical monitoring systems. The voltage levels of various biomedical signals are given in Table 1 [2].

The powerline interference (50 Hz/60 Hz and its harmonics) is greater than these biomedical signals [1]. In order to accurately measure these signals there is a need to eliminate this interfering signal. The bandwidth of these bio-potential signal are well below the 1 kHz mark for ECG, EEG, and ERG signals, and extending only up to 3 kHz for EMG signals. To measure bio-potential signals, electrodes are either implanted or measured from the surface of the skin. Therefore, it is observed from the literature that power line harmonics (50 Hz, 150 Hz and 250 Hz) can easily be picked

© Springer Nature Singapore Pte Ltd. 2019
A. K. Luhach et al. (Eds.): ICAICR 2018, CCIS 956, pp. 127–137, 2019.
https://doi.org/10.1007/978-981-13-3143-5_12

Table 1. Voltage level of biopotential signals

Physiological signal	Measurement range
Electroencephalography (EEG)	25–300 μV
Electroretinogram (ERG)	10–1000 μV
Electrogastrogram (EGG)	8–800 μV
Electrocardiography (ECG)	0.6–6 mV
Electromyography (EMG)	0.1–1 mV

up by the electrodes and it has become cumbersome to remove these interferences because the signal voltage level and the noise voltage level are almost same.

The filter implementation of this frequency range requires large time constants which can be easily implemented by using large passive components (resistances and capacitances). But this increases the size of wearable or implantable device, making it obtrusive.

Both analog and digital filters can be used to suppress these powerline interferences. Various methods of noise suppression using analog notch filter at frequency 50 Hz/60 Hz have been described [2–7]. In this paper an active comb filter is proposed. The Filter is based on OTA-C topology, which can be implemented on an IC. This filter attenuates signal at 50 Hz and its odd harmonics at 150 Hz and 250 Hz.

The stopband frequency and quality factor of filter can be easily tuned electronically by adjusting the bias voltage of OTAs.

2 Methodology

2.1 RLC Notch Filter

An RLC second order passive notch filter consists of three elements, a resistor, a capacitor and an inductor as shown in Fig. 1.

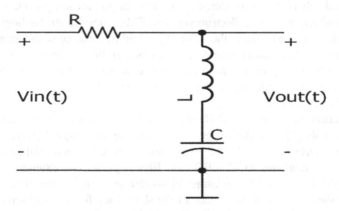

Fig. 1. Simple RLC notch filter.

The transfer function of the filter H(s) is given as

$$H(s) = \frac{s^2LC + 1}{s^2LC + sCR + 1} \qquad (1)$$

The parameters of the filter are obtained as

$$\omega_0 = \frac{1}{\sqrt{LC}} \qquad (2)$$

$$Q_0 = \frac{1}{R}\sqrt{\frac{L}{C}} \qquad (3)$$

$$\Delta f = \frac{R}{L} \qquad (4)$$

By using n-number of such notch filter with different center frequency a comb filter can be designed to remove n-number of harmonics. Comb filter using notch filter is shown in Fig. 2.

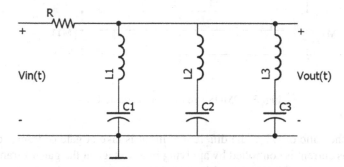

Fig. 2. Comb filter using RLC notch filter.

This comb filter using large passive components are too bulky to be fabricated in an IC. Large valued inductors and resistors can be implemented by using active element such as operational transconductance amplifier (OTA). This way inductors and large valued capacitors and resistors are eliminated.

2.2 OTA

OTA is almost similar to operational amplifiers (OPAMPS), they both have differential input with infinite input impedances. The difference is in the output they produce, OPAMPS produces voltage output with low output impedance and OTAs produces current output with infinite output impedance. One of the advantage of OTA over OPAMP is the transconductance gain (G_m) can be changed electronically by adjusting bias current. The structure of OTA [8] used in this paper is a symmetrical cascade OTA as shown in Fig. 3. Symbolic representation of OTA is show in Fig. 4.

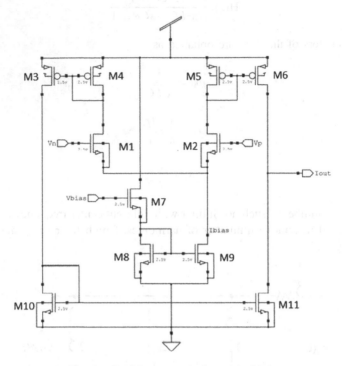

Fig. 3. CMOS symmetrical cascade OTA.

In the schematic of OTA, the differential input is take at gate of transistor M1 and M2. The bias current is controlled by applying bias voltage at the gate of transistor M7. And the p channel MOS transistor M3, M4, M5, M6 acts as active loads.

The relation between transconductance (G_m) and bias current [8] is given as

$$G_m = B\sqrt{2\mu C_{OX}\left(\frac{W}{L}\right)I_B}$$ (5)

where B is constant, μ is mobility of electron, COX is oxide layer capacitance, IB is bias current which can be controlled by controlling Vbias at the gate of transistor M7 in Fig. 3.

Various characteristics of OTA such as variation of transconductance (Gm) with frequency and variation of Gm with Vbias is given in Figs. 5 and 6 respectively.

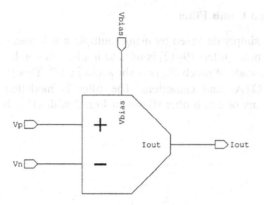

Fig. 4. Symbol of OTA.

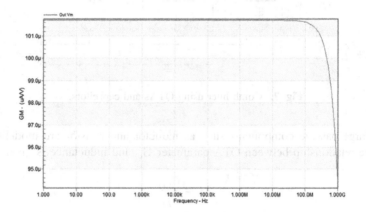

Fig. 5. Variation of G_m with frequency.

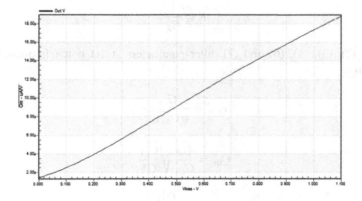

Fig. 6. Variation of G with Vbias.

2.3   OTA-C Based Comb Filter

Comb filter can be simply designed by using multiple notch filters in cascade. Here a cascade of OTA-C notch filters [9–12] is used to implement comb filter. The circuit of comb filter using cascade of notch filters is shown in Fig. 7. This filter consists of only two components, OTAs and capacitors. The filter is modelled by replacing the inductors and resistors of comb filter shown in Fig. 2 with OTA based inductors and resistors.

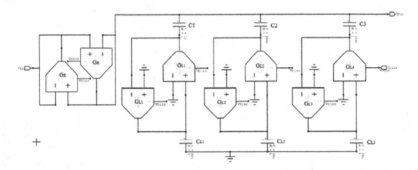

Fig. 7. Comb filter using OTAs and capacitors.

The large passive components such as inductor and resistor are modelled using OTAs, the relationship between OTA parameter G_m and inductance is given as

$$L_1 = \frac{C_{L1}}{G_{L1}^2} \tag{6}$$

and the relationship between resistor and G_m is given as

$$R = \frac{1}{G_R} \tag{7}$$

from Eqs. (2), (3), (4), (6) and (7), filter parameters at 1st notch frequency can be obtained as

$$\omega_{01} = \frac{G_{L1}}{\sqrt{C_{L1}C1}} \tag{8}$$

$$Q_{01} = \frac{G_R}{G_{L1}}\sqrt{\frac{C_{L1}}{C1}} \tag{9}$$

$$\Delta f1 = \frac{G_{L1}^2}{G_R C_{L1}} \tag{10}$$

From the above equation it can be observed that filter parameter can be tuned independently by simply adjusting the Gm of individual OTAs. The Gm of all OTAs used in the comb filter is set to 1.41 μA/V by applying Vbias of 0 V. This gives value of R as 709 kΩ. The value of capacitor CL1 and C1 for notch frequency of 50 Hz are 50 nF and 440 nF respectively. Similarly, capacitor for notch frequency 150 Hz and 250 Hz are selected as CL2 = 55 nF, C2 = 55 nF, CL3 = 31 nF and C3 = 31 nF.

3 Results and Discussion

The performance of the comb filter was evaluated using T-SPICE. The comb filter was simulated using 45 nm technology. The magnitude and phase response of proposed comb filter is shown Fig. 8.

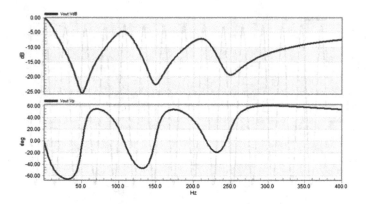

Fig. 8. Magnitude and phase response of comb filter.

The THD of filter at 5 Hz with signal amplitude of 0.5 V is 1.7%. The stopband attenuation obtained by the filter at frequencies 50 Hz, 150 Hz and 250 Hz are 25 dB, 22 dB and 20 dB respectively. The transient response of the filter for sinusoidal signal input of amplitude 1 V and frequency 50 Hz, 150 Hz and 250 Hz are shown in Figs. 9, 10 and 11 respectively.

The average power consumption of this filter is 2.2 mW. Total integrated input noise and output noise of the filter up to frequency of 100 Hz are 2.608 μV and 403.54 nV respectively.

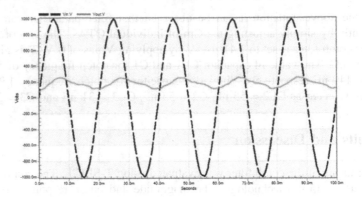

Fig. 9. Filter response for 50 Hz sinusoidal signal.

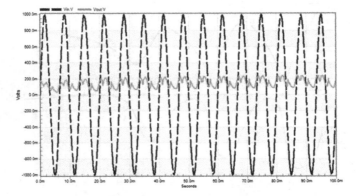

Fig. 10. Filter response for 150 Hz sinusoidal signal.

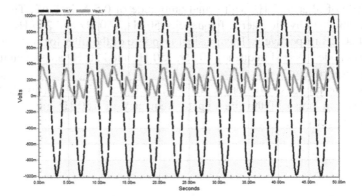

Fig. 11. Filter response for 250 Hz sinusoidal signal.

4 Conclusion and Future Scope

A comb filter using OTA-C topology is designed. The filter is designed using 250 nm CMOS technology in Tanner EDA tool and simulated using TSPICE simulator. The performance of the filter is as expected. This filter has more number of active components than but has less number of passive components. One more advantage of OTA-C based filter design is that by simply controlling the bias current of OTAs, electronic tuning of filter parameters such as center frequency and quality factor can be achieved.

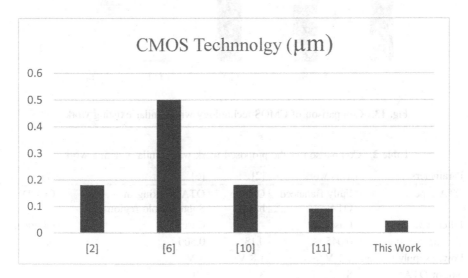

Fig. 12. Comparison of power consumption with similar existing work

Future scope of this design can be to implement it using low power OTA cell in 14 nm FinFET technology. This way power consumption and chip area will be reduced. Figures 12 and 13 shows a comparison of power consumption and CMOS technology with similar existing work respectively. Table 2 reports comparison of the proposed work with similar existing work.

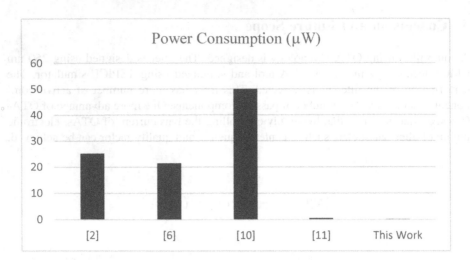

Fig. 13. Comparison of CMOS technology with similar existing work

Table 2. Comparison of the proposed work with similar existing work

Parameters	This work	[2]	[6]	[7]
OTA type	Fully Balanced OTA	Opamp based	OTA working in Subthreshold region	CCCD
Filter type	Cascaded	-	Cascaded	elliptical
Technology (um)	0.045	0.18	0.500	0.6
Power supply voltage	1.1 V	1.8 V	5 V	-
No. of OTAs	8	3 OPAMPs	10	7
Stop band attenuation (dB)	26	55.4	60	32
THD (%)	1.4%	-	<2%	-
Power consumption (mW)	0.225	25.2	21.5	-
Noise at output	400 nV/$\sqrt{Hz}$	-	482 nV/$\sqrt{Hz}$	-

Acknowledgment. I would like to acknowledge my gratitude to a number of people who have helped me in different ways for the successful completion of my thesis. I take this opportunity to express a deep sense of gratitude towards my guide, Mr. Anil Kumar Sahu, Asst. Prof. (ET&T), Shri Shankaracharya Technical Campus, Bhilai for providing excellent guidance, encouragement and inspiration throughout the project work. Without his invaluable guidance, this work would never have been a successful one.

References

1. Huhta, J.C., Webster, J.G.: 60-Hz interference in electrocardiography. IEEE Trans. Biomed. Eng. **20**(2), 91–101 (1973)
2. Li, H., Zhang, J., Wang, L.: A fully integrated continuous-time 50-Hz notch filter with center frequency tunability. In: 33rd Annual International Conference of the IEEE EMBS Boston, Massachusetts, USA, 30 August–3 September 2011 (2011)
3. Piskorowski, J.: Power line interference removal from ECG signal using notch filter with non-zero initial conditions. In: Proceedings of the IEEE International Symposium on Medical Measurements and Application (MeMeA 2012), pp. 1–3. University of Technology, Budapest, May 2012
4. Tsai, C.-T., Chan, H.-L., Tseng, C.-C., Wu, C.-P.: Harmonic interference elimination by an active comb filter [ECG application]. In: Proceedings of 16th Annual International Conference of IEEE Engineering in Medicine and Biology Society, Baltimore, MD, USA, vol. 2, pp. 964–965, November 1994
5. Tsai, C.-D., Chiou, D.-C., Lin, Y.-D., Chan, H.-L., Wu, C.-P.: An active comb filter design for harmonic interference removal. J. Chin. Inst. Eng. **21**(5), 605–610 (1998)
6. Ranjan, R.K., Yalla, S.P., Sorya, S., Paul, S.K.: Active comb filter using operational transconductance amplifier. Act. Passiv. Electron. Compon. **2014**, Article no. 587932, 6 p. (2014). https://doi.org/10.1155/2014/587932
7. Ling, C., Ye, P., Liu, R., Wang, J.: A low-pass power notch filter based on an OTA—C structure for electroencephalogram. In: Proceedings of the International Symposium on Intelligent Signal Processing and Communications Systems (ISPACS 2007), Xiamen, China, pp. 451–453, December 2007. Patent 3 624 12, 16 July 1990
8. Duzenlia, G., Kcili, Y., Kuntmanc, H., Atamanb, A.: On the design of low-frequency filters using CMOS OTAs operating in the subthreshold region. Microelectron. J. **30**(1), 45–54 (1999)
9. Geiger, R.L., Sánchez-Sinencio, E.: Active filter design using operational transconductance amplifiers: a tutorial. IEEE Circuits Devices Mag. **1**(2), 20–32 (1985)
10. Abbasalizadeh, S., Sheikhaei, S., Forouzandeh, B.: A 0.9 V supply OTA in 0.18 μm CMOS technology and its application in realizing a tunable low-pass Gm-C filter for wireless sensor networks. Circuits Syst. Sci. Res. **4**(1), 34–43 (2013)
11. Ma, C.-T., Mak, P.-I., Vai, M.-I., Mak, P.-U.: A 90 nm CMOS bio-potential front end with improved powerline interference rejection. In: International Symposium on Circuits and Systems IEEE, Taipei, 24–27 May 2009, pp. 665–668 (2009)
12. Saberhosseini, S.S., Zabihian, A., Sodagar, A.M.: Low-noise OTA for neural amplifying applications. In: 2012 8th International Caribbean Conference on Devices, Circuits and Systems (ICCDCS) (2012)

Performance Improvement of MIMO-FBMC Systems Using Different Diversity Combining Schemes Through AWGN and Rayleigh Channels

Satwinder Kaur[1], Lavish Kansal[1], Gurjot Singh Gaba[1(✉)],
Mohamed El Bakkali[2], and Faisel Em Tubbal[3,4,5]

[1] School of Electronics and Electrical Engineering, Lovely Professional
University, Phagwara, Punjab, India
satwinderkaur244@yahoo.in, lavish.15911@lpu.co.in,
er.gurjotgaba@gmail.com
[2] Signals, Systems and Components Laboratory, Faculty of Sciences and
Technologies, Sidi Mohamed Ben Abdellah University, Fez, Morocco
mohamed.elbakkali@usmba.ac.ma
[3] School of Electrical, Computer and Telecommunications Engineering,
University of Wollongong, Wollongong, NSW 2522, Australia
faisel@uow.edu.au
[4] School of Computing, Engineering and Mathematics, Western Sydney
University, Sydney, NSW 2522, Australia
[5] Technological Projects Department, The Libyan Centre for Remote Sensing
and Space Science, Tripoli, Libya

Abstract. Diverse methodologies of Diversity combining schemes are used for performance improvements of Filter Bank Multicarrier (FBMC) by using Additive White Gaussian Noise and Rayleigh channels. These diversity combining schemes are Maximum Ratio combining and Selection Combining. The proposed schemes are implemented by using different channels of MIMO methodology, which results in high order diversity. This system simulation includes varying number of receiving antennas to analyzes the performance over AWGN and Rayleigh channel. The aim of the proposed schemes is to improve bit error rate (BER) performance with using two different diversity combining schemes. It observed through MATLAB simulations that the proposed schemes provides evident performance improvements.

Keywords: FBMC · OFDM · ICI · ISI · SNR · MRC · SC

1 Introduction

Multicarrier modulation is an efficient transmission technique. In multicarrier modulation, bandwidth of channel is divided into many parallel sub channels. Each subchannel has own carrier. FBMC refers as Filter Bank Multicarrier. The first multicarrier schemes were based on filter bank developed in early 1960s [1]. In filter bank multicarrier modulation techniques, in which two types of filters are used. A Synthesis filter

© Springer Nature Singapore Pte Ltd. 2019
A. K. Luhach et al. (Eds.): ICAICR 2018, CCIS 956, pp. 138–152, 2019.
https://doi.org/10.1007/978-981-13-3143-5_13

bank is used all parallel transmit filters and the analysis filter bank includes the matched received filters. These filters are used to overcome the interference from system. The main disadvantage of OFDM is high PAPR (peak to average ratio). To overcome this problem FBMC is introduced. Interference is one of the important factors that can be identified in any communication system or in medium of transmission. To perform in an error-free manner under perfect conditions and without AWGN some communication systems are designed. Moreover, they are tested through transmission mediums or channels under different fading, synchronization and propagation conditions. Performance is checked in terms of Bit Error Rate for an FBMC system operated in different multipath channels under different synchronization conditions.

2 Literature Review

Being multicarrier techniques, FBMC suffer with high peak to average paper ratio. Kaiming et al. [2] proposed an efficient Peak to Average Ratio reduction method that is depends on a two steps optimal configuration. It is known as pretreated partial transmit sequence. A various overlapping symbols with optimization methods are used first and after that according to previous overlapped symbols, the current symbol is determined and optimized with phase rotation sequences. Another operation, it employs segment Peak to Average Ratio reduction scheme depends on PTS technique. Due to this, pretreated partial transmit sequence technique can achieve better Peak to Average Ratio reduction results than previous schemes with less complexity. The lower complexity can be made system more flexible with Peak to Average Ratio reduction performance. To overcome the overlap problem system become more effective, the overlapping structure of Filter Bank Multicarrier Orthogonal Quadrature Amplitude Modulation symbols are taken fully into account and two step optimization structure are used. It gives better BER then conventional methods.

OFDM/OQAM is a modulation techniques used for reduced the interference from the system. Bodinier et al. [3] show the new methods to generate new waveforms. These waveforms are gives efficient spectral localization and less sensitivity. Due to this asynchronism effects less than the Cyclic Prefix Orthogonal Frequency Division Multiplexing. By using Orthogonal Frequency Division Multiplexing over Orthogonal Quadrature Amplitude Modulation in other systems is beneficial. It brings limited gain in the context of coexistence with present Cyclic Prefix Orthogonal Frequency Division Multiplexing systems. PSD based model is highly flawed and fails to give a better approximation of the interference seen by each user in heterogeneous scenarios. The second method, it utilizes OFDM/OQAM, the actual values of interference are higher than those considered by the PSD based model by more than 50 dB.

The first multicarrier technique was OFDM. It was proposed for Long Term Evolution-Advanced (4th Generation). Two major challenges of OFDM are cyclic prefix and the high PAPR, by this Orthogonal Frequency Division Multiplexing communication system cannot be suitable for 5th Generation. FBMC techniques are used to increase the data bit rate, instead of guard interval and cyclic prefix digital filters are used, but in OFDM cyclic prefix and guard intervals are used. Chettri et al. [4] designed FBMC and proved that FBMC is an efficient waveform selected upcoming generation wireless communication that is upcoming generation (5G) communication system. The OQAM processing, the synthesis filter bank and the transform decomposition schemes are used in the transmitter side. The polyphase network, Analysis filter bank and the OQAM post processing methods are used in reception side. To minimize the complexity, multiple stage filter banks are used. FBMC solves the problems of OFDM. To provide out of band spectrum character FBMC applies filter methods on a per-subcarrier. By using poly phase network or an extended IFFT the baseband filter process is done. Filter can use different overlapping factors to provide different varying levels of out of band rejected.

The prototype filters are designed for Quadrature Amplitude Modulation based filter bank multicarrier. Jeon et al. [5] proposed two different types of prototype filters such as OQAM-processing for even or odd. It consists of a Generalized Nyquist criterion for closed perfect reconstruction and meeting the stop-band condition for a small side-lobe. By using small side-lobe higher spectral efficiency is achieved, it is an essential factor to minimizing the size of the guard band with channels. Moreover, previous generalized Nyquist criterion is derived under the assumed ideal channel. In practical multipath channel, it can be easily broken. After that undisturbed NPR that considers in the frequency domain the multipath delay using a $2L$-oversampled discrete Fourier transform. In addition Quadrature Amplitude Modulation based filter bank multicarrier prototype filters are designed and proposed a prototype filter with a small side lobe and gives better bit error rate performance. The advantages of the side lobe condition allow the planned prototype filter, the undisturbed nearly perfect reconstruction-F, by minimizing the guard band in the frequency domain to improve spectral efficiency.

Two prototype filters are used in Filter Bank Multicarrier Quadrature Amplitude Modulation system. For transmitting Quadrature Amplitude Modulation symbol is planned and derived orthogonality conditions for the Filter Bank Multicarrier Quadrature Amplitude Modulation system without the any interference. Nam et al. [6] show that transmitter used for filtering the Even and odd numbered associated carrier symbols, respectively. To satisfied orthogonality conditions, it performs a sub block wise reverse ordering procedure for the outputs of the odd numbered sub-carrier filter [7]. After that conventional orthogonal frequency division multiplexing used with MIMO schemes [9–11]. By this analyzed results of bit error rate and Signal to interference power ratio. Practically results indicate that the previous FBMC-OQAM and OFDM systems outcomes are almost same as compared to new FBMC-QAM system.

An Alamouti's scheme used for Filter bank multicarrier (FBMC) to overcomes the problem of intersymbol interference (ISI). By using Alamouti's methods with FBMC modulation there are some application issues are being discussed. Due to error propagation only interference are not effectively removes with receiver schemes. Zakaria et al. [12] shares own views regarding some arrangements such as space time block coding and space frequency block coding. These are used to cancelling the effect of interference. After that Alamouti's decoding are used by interference canceller. In which basic 2×1 Alamouti's coding methods are used. The performance is observed on basis of the bit error rate and the signal to noise ratio. It will show that this new arrangement gives the optimal results [13, 14]. Filter-bank multicarrier gives the solution to overcome the problems of orthogonal frequency division multiplexing.

In FBMC filters are used so no need to insert guard intervals. FBMC gives the high spectral efficiency [1]. During the decoding process self- interference is not removed automatically.

The performance of OSTBC-MIMO with different channels Dholakia et al. [15] are proposed. Nowadays technology is burgeoning day by day, with increasing the usage of this new wireless technology some environment effects will occurs. One problem in wireless communication is data rate and range. So, one solution is there to overcome this kind of problem is MIMO. Multiple no. of antennas is used to solve this particular problem. These multiple antennas perform space time coding and spatial multiplexing. By using the beam forming techniques, same signal transmit with different gain and phase on all transmit signals and through receiver antennas maximum signals are received. In spatial multiplexing, high data rate signals are divided into large no. of lower rate streams and these signals are transmitted through different antennas [12]. MIMO is the best techniques to transmit multiple signals on same channels without using additional antennas, bandwidth and transmit power [20, 21]. An introduction to Space-Time coding was given by showing Alamouti's arrangement. After that examined block codes plans with diverse code rates of ½ and ¾. The encoding and interpreting calculations for each were exhibited. It is attractive over usage low idol gathering with high code rate in Orthogonal Space Time Block Code Multiple Input Multiple Output with 4 × 4 setup.

3 FBMC

FBMC defines as Filter Bank Multicarrier. It introduced by Chang in 1960. In FBMC two types of filters are used Synthesis filter bank and Analysis filter bank. At the transmitter side used Inverse fast Fourier transform as a modulator [1] (Fig. 1).

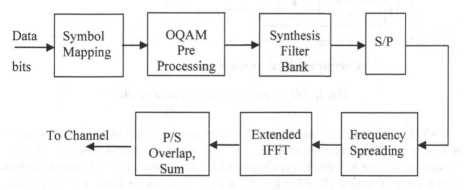

Fig. 1. FBMC transmitter

Data Bits: The data bits are used as an input of the transmitter.

Symbol Mapping: The modulation symbol map is used to generate 16QAM modulated electrical signals, and then the modulation symbol de-mapper demodulates the signals according to that which type of modulation is used. The symbol mapper's modulation type matches the mapper's modulation type; the original transmitted signal should be matched.

OQAM Processing: OQAM processing has two techniques. One is OQAM-pre-processing and second is OQAM-post-processing. The offset of M/2 samples are used for QAM mapping in time domain between the in phase and Quadrature components of complexes signal. The offset defines to the time change of 1/2 of the sub channel/sub carrier (Fig. 2).

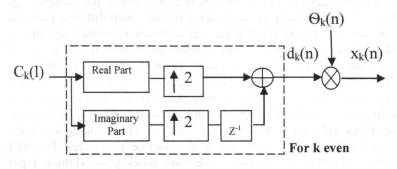

Complex to Real Conversion

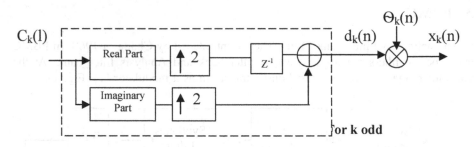

Complex to Real Conversion

Fig. 2. OQAM pre-processing for even or odd

OQAM post processing have two different operations. The θ pattern is reproduction in first stage. The operation of taking the real part θ pattern is followed. R to C conversion is done in second operation, in which two successive real valued symbols form a complex valued [2]. After that the R to C conversion reduces the sample rate. Signals at the input of the filter bank are indeed first oversampled by a factor of N/2, and then filtered by the impulse response of Gk[n] the kth filter and is defined by:

$$Gk[n] = G[n].\exp(j * 2\pi k/N(n - Tp - 1/2)) \tag{1}$$

Where s[n] is a low pass filter called the prototype filter, and is of duration T_p. It is common practice to impose that L_p is a multiple or almost a multiple of N ($T_p = kN$, $T_p = kN - 1$, $T_p = kN + 1$ are possible choices).

Serial to Parallel (S/P) Conversion: After that Serial to Parallel conversion is done [6]. At the output of the OQAM-preprocessing a serial to parallel conversion done and the samples data show in parallel form.

Frequency Spreading: In Frequency Spreading gives accurate equalization. Spread range is a type of remote interchanges in which the frequency of the transmitted signal is intentionally changed.

P/S, Overlap and Sum: Parallel to serial conversion Contrast of Serial to Parallel. At the block of data at the Extended- Inverse Fast Fourier Transform transmitter is improved at the output of the Fast Fourier Transform at the receiver. The overlap defined as when two singles are mixed with each other, but in FBMC signals are not overlap with each other.

At the receiver side, output of transmitter used as an input of receiver and preceded further. The FBMC receiver blocks are explained below (Fig. 3):

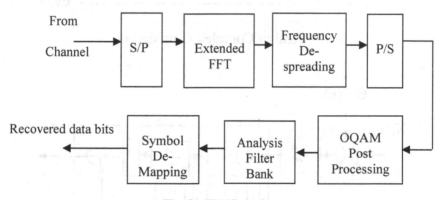

Fig. 3. FBMC receiver

Serial to Parallel Conversion: ASerial to Parallel converter is introduced at the output of the IFFT and the samples data appear in parallel form. At the receiver side serial to parallel conversion is done, in which data sequences changes from serial to parallel.

Extended FFT: It can be modified to implement the filter bank, it is sufficient to extend the Inverse Fast Fourier Transform and the Fast Fourier Transform. For each arrangement of information, the yield of the Inverse Fast Fourier Transform is a piece of KM tests and, since the image rate is 1/M, K sequential IFFT yields cover in the time space. The usage of the recipient depends on an augmented FFT, of size KM. The implementation of the reception is based on an extended Fast Fourier Transform, of size KM. The FFT input blocks are overlap, this situation is known as the classical sliding window situation.

Frequency De-spreading: It is opposite of frequency spreading. Gotten baseband waveform is the mix of the transmitted waveform and commotion in the channel.

OQAM Post Processing: The Synthesis Filter Bank (SFB) is used in modulator part [6]. The information sources to the SFB are the Offset QAM. In OQAM-post-processing, uses two minor different structures that structures are depending on the sub channel index. At the initial stage, multiplication by $\Theta_{k,n}$ sequence that is follow by the process of taking the real part (Fig. 4).

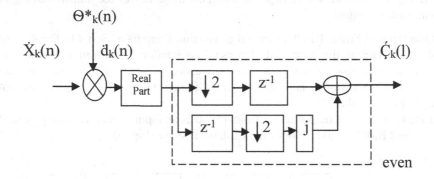

Real to Complex Conversion

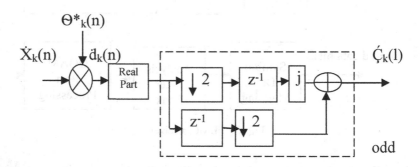

Real to Complex Conversion

Fig. 4. OQAM post processing in FBMC for k even & odd

In OQAM-post processing in FBMC convert real to complex conversion for even and odd. The two successive real value symbols i.e. multiplied by j and form a complex valued symbol $c_{k,n}$. In OQAM-post-processing the R to C conversion reduces the sample rate by a factor 2.

Symbol De-mapping: The de-mapper modulation type matches the mapper's modulation types, where the original transmitted signal should be recovered. In the end, at the receiver data bits are recovered.

4 MIMO

MIMO is defined as Multiple Input Multiple Output. In which multiple number of antennas are used at transmitter side and at receiver side [18]. It provides gains in channel robustness and throughput by using multiple antennas. It has the capacity to interact with various antennas at a same time which are 2×2, 3×3, and 4×4 (Fig. 5).

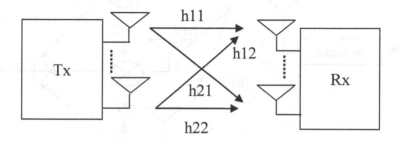

Fig. 5. Basic Diagram of MIMO

MIMO methods are utilized today in advances like Wi-Fi and LTE, and new strategies are under review for future benchmarks like LTE Advanced. The primary element of MIMO frameworks is space-time preparing. Space-Time Codes (STCs) are the codes intended for the utilization in MIMO frameworks [19]. In STCs, signs are coded in both transient and spatial areas. Here encoder and decoders are used at the transmitter side and the receiver side respectively.

Nowadays technology is burgeoning day by day, due to this increasing demand of multimedia services, web related services and high data rate. To fulfill the demand, MIMO is combined with FBMC. MIMO is defined as Multiple Input Multiple Output. In which N no. transmitter signals are transfer through the different channels and received at receiver side. To reduce fading effect between multiple data streams different MIMO channels are used. Another method is to minimize the effect of fading is diversity combining schemes. In this technique the same information passes through different channels because the same information received if any data stream is lost [16]. To obtain improvement through different channels the MIMO diversity combining scheme provided different types of combining schemes that are MRC and SC. In these combining schemes, N no. of transmitter and receiving antennas send information through different channels. Diversity combining technique used to merge the multiple received signals on diversity receiver device into a single enhanced signal [17]. Different schemes are used in diversity combining are:

1. Maximum ratio combining
2. Selection combining or switching combining
3. Equal gain combining

These are explained below:

Maximum Ratio Combining (MRC): Maximum ratio combining defines as it mostly used as a phased array systems (Fig. 6).

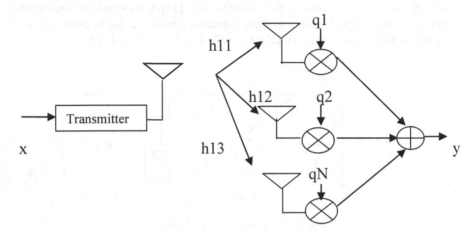

Fig. 6. Maximum Ratio combining

With respect to SNR the received signals are weighted and summed. FBMC-Maximum ratio combining (MRC) diversity technique is used with varying number of receiving antennas N over AWGN and Rayleigh channel. Here, the number of receiving antennas are varied from 1 to 4 i.e. N = 1, 2, 3 and 4. By using different antennas at receiver side, BER performance of FBMC is varying. When the number of receiving antenna are increasing, the Bit Error Rate keeps on decreasing and thus this system would provide better Bit Error Rate performance with respect to a specified value of Signal to Noise Ratio. The outcomes of SNR yields are:

$$\sum_{k=1}^{N} SNR_k \tag{2}$$

Selection Combining: Selection combining is from the N no. of signals, stronger signal is selected [17]. Selection combining is used to select the best signal from N no. of signals. The performance of system is improved and it gives better results.

In Diversity system, SC is the simple and common method that is used for combining signals. SC is based on choosing the branch with the most favorable SNR. The Fig. 7 shows that SC receiver estimates the new value of SNR in all branches and selects the one with the most favorable SNR. With selection diversity, the receiver side

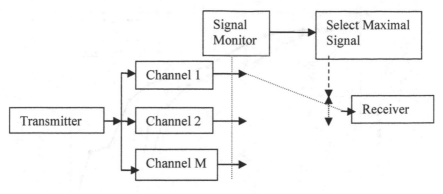

Fig. 7. Selection combining

the highest received signal power antenna is selected and neglect observations from the other antennas.

The expected diversity gain has been shown to be expressed as power ratio:

$$\sum_{k=1}^{N} \frac{1}{k} \tag{3}$$

5 Simulation Results

The simulation results for illustrating the impact of using MIMO systems on the BER vs SNR performance of FBMC system are presented in this session. In the simulation work AWGN and Rayleigh channels are used for analyzing the performance of FBMC system augmented with MIMO system [18]. In MIMO-FBMC, different diversity combining techniques are used to analyze the performance of system.

A. AWGN Augmented FBMC:

In Figs. 8 and 9 FBMC- Maximum ratio combining (MRC) and FBMC-Selection combining diversity technique are used with varying number of receiving antennas N over AWGN channel. Here, the number of receiving antennas are varied from 1 to 4 i.e. N = 1, 2, 3 and 4. By using different antennas at receiver side, BER performance of FBMC is varying. When number of receiving antenna are increasing, the Bit Error Rate keeps on decreasing and thus this system would provide better bit error rate performance with respect to a specified value of SNR [22] (Table 1).

The performance of FBMC-MRC is better in case of AWGN channel in comparison to FBMC-SC, as in case of AWGN channel no LOS path is available in between the transmitter and receiver, moreover the effect of multipath fading also comes in to play in case of AWGN fading channel.

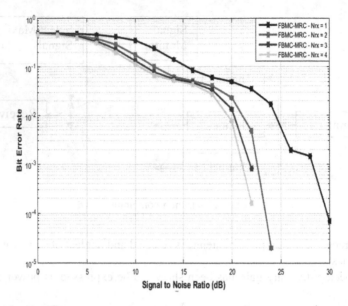

Fig. 8. SNR vs BER performance of FBMC-MRC in AWGN channel

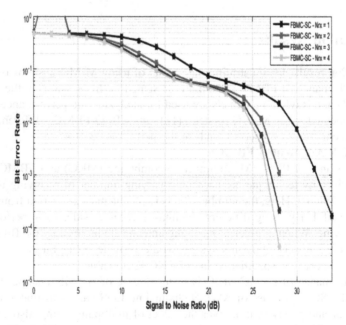

Fig. 9. SNR vs BER performance of FBMC-SC in AWGN channel

Table 1. Variation in BER values for different receiving antennas using AWGN channels

Diversity techniques	SNR (dB) required to achieve a BER of 10^{-3} for different receiving antennas			
	$N_{rx} = 1$	$N_{rx} = 2$	$N_{rx} = 3$	$N_{rx} = 4$
MRC	28	23	22	21
SC	33	28	27.5	27

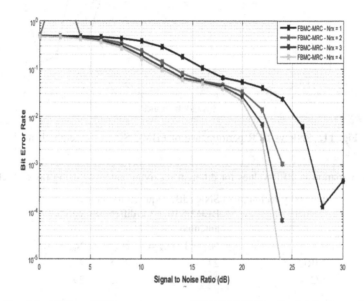

Fig. 10. SNR vs BER performance of FBMC-MRC in Rayleigh channel

B. Rayleigh Augmented FBMC:

In Figs. 10 and 11 FBMC-Selection combining (SC) diversity technique is used with varying number of receiving antennas N over AWGN and Rayleigh channel [8]. In Selection combining number of signals are present but stronger signal is selected. Here, the number of receiving antennas are varried from 1 to 4 i.e. N = 1, 2, 3 and 4. By using different antennas at receiver side, BER performance of FBMC varies (Table 2).

When number of receiving antennas are increasing, the Bit Error Rate keeps on decreasing and thus this system would provide better Bit Error Rate performance with respect to a specified value of SNR. The performance of AWGN is better in case of FBMC-SC in comparison to FBMC-MRC, as in case of Rayleigh channel no line of sight path is available in between the transmitter and receiver, moreover the effect of multipath fading also comes in to play in case of rayleigh fading channel.

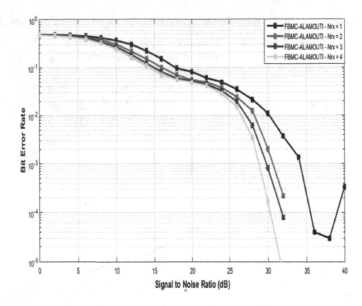

Fig. 11. SNR vs BER performance of FBMC-SC in Rayleigh channel

Table 2. Variation in BER values for different receiving antennas using rayleigh channels

Diversity techniques	SNR (dB) required to achieve a BER of 10^{-3} for different receiving antennas			
	$N_{rx} = 1$	$N_{rx} = 2$	$N_{rx} = 3$	$N_{rx} = 4$
MRC	27	24	23.5	23
SC	34.5	29	29.5	29

Here, from Figs. 8, 9, 10 and 11 observed that using MRC and SC diversity techniques, MRC gives better performance than SC in case of AWGN and Rayleigh channels [23, 24].

6 Conclusion

In this paper, better Bit Error Rate (BER) which have been obtained by combining FBMC with Diversity combining scheme, have been analyzed using MIMO-FBMC system. In order to be able to better comparison the above results with other available BER results, the following observations can be given: if the N no. of antenna are increased system give better results. The two different Diversity combining scheme such as Maximum Ratio combining and Selection combining. In all the graphs different N values are used that are 1, 2, 3 and 4 to the compare the performance for different receiving antennas. Through different antenna two different channels are used for the comparison of SNR with BER using different values of N receiving antenna, BER performance of FBMC is varying. In the comparison of FBMC-MRC and FBMC-SC over AWGN and Rayleigh the BER is greater in case of Rayleigh as compared to AWGN channel.

References

1. Viholainen, A., Ihlainen, T., Stitz, T.H., Renfors, M., Bellanger, M.: Prototype filter design for filter bank based multicarrier transmission. In: 17th European Signal Processing Conference, Glasgow, pp. 1359–1363 (2009)
2. Kaiming, L., Jundan, H., Peng, Z., Yuan, L.: PAPR reduction for FBMC-OQAM systems using P-PTS scheme. J. China Univ. Posts Telecommun. 22(6), 78–85 (2015). https://doi. org/10.1016/s1005-8885(15)60698-7
3. Bodinier, Q., Bader, F., Palicot, J.: Modeling interference between OFDM/OQAM and CP-OFDM: limitations of the PSD-based model. In: 23rd International Conference on Telecommunications, France, vol. 1, pp. 1–7 (2016) https://doi.org/10.1109/ict.2016. 7500462
4. Chettri, L., Bera, R., Bhaskar, D.: Design and simulation of OQAM based filter bank multicarrier (FBMC) for 5G wireless communication systems. In: 24th IRF International Conference, Bengaluru, pp. 1–6 (2016)
5. Jeon, D., Kim, S., Kwon, B., Lee, H., Lee, S.: Prototype filter design for QAM-based filter bank multicarrier system. Digit. Signal Process. 57, 66–78 (2016). https://doi.org/10.1016/j. dsp.2016.05.002
6. Nam, H., Choi, M., Han, S., Kim, C., Choi, S., Hong, D.: A new filter-bank multicarrier system with two prototype filters for QAM symbols transmission and reception. IEEE Trans. Wirel. Commun. 15(9), 5998–6009 (2016). https://doi.org/10.1109/twc.2016.2575839
7. Wang, H., Wang, X., Xu, L., Du, W.: Hybrid PAPR reduction scheme for FBMC/OQAM systems based on multi data block PTS and TR methods. IEEE Access: Green Commun. Netw. 5G Wirel. 4, 4761–4768 (2016). https://doi.org/10.1109/access.2016.2605008
8. Gerzaguet, R., et al.: The 5G candidate waveform race: a comparison of complexity and performance. EURASIP J. Wirel. Commun. Netw., 1–6 (2017) https://doi.org/10.1186/ s13638-016-0792-0
9. Gesbert, D., Shafi, M., Shiu, D., Smith, P.J., Naguib, A.: From theory to practice: an overview of MIMO space-time coded wireless systems. IEEE J. Sel. Areas Commun. 21(3), 281–302 (2003). https://doi.org/10.1109/JSAC.2003.809458
10. Bolcskei, H., Zurich, E.: MIMO-OFDM wireless systems: basics, perspectives, and challenges. IEEE Wirel. Commun. 13(4), 31–37 (2008). https://doi.org/10.1109/MWC.2006. 1678163
11. Jadhav, S.P., Hendre, V.S.: Performance of maximum ratio combining (MRC) MIMO systems for rayleigh fading channel. Int. J. Sci. Res. Publ. 3(2), 1–4 (2013)
12. Zakaria, R., Ruyet, D.L.: On interference cancellation in Alamouti coding scheme for filter bank based multicarrier systems. The Tenth International Symposium on Wireless Communication Systems, Germany, pp. 1–5 (2013)
13. Caus, M., Neira, A.I.P.: Multi-stream transmission in MIMO-FBMC systems. In: IEEE International Conference on Acoustics, Speech Signal processing (ICASSP), Canada, pp. 5041–5045 (2013). https://doi.org/10.1109/icassp.2013.6638621

14. Ruyet, L., Zakaria, R., Ozbek, B.: On precoding MIMO-FBMC with imperfect channel state information at the transmitter. In: 11th International Symposium on Wireless Communications Systems (ISWCS), Barcelona, Spain, pp. 808–812 (2014). https://doi.org/10.1109/iswcs.2014.6933464
15. Dholakia, P.M., Kumar, S., Vithlani, C.H., Solanki, M.: On performance analysis of OSTBC-MIMO systems for audio [mp3] transmission in Rayleigh fading environments. In: IEEE International Conference on Advances in Communication and Computing Technologies, Mumbai, India, pp. 1–7 (2014). https://doi.org/10.1109/eic.2015.7230700
16. Winn, K.C., Han, P., Sewaiwar, A., Chung, Y.H.: Quasi-orthogonal space-time block code (QOSTBC) for full-rate massive MIMO with up to 32 antennas. In: IEEE Conference U-GIT, South Korea, pp. 1–6 (2014)
17. Ho, Z., Kim, K., Kim, C., Yun, Y.H., Cho, Y.H., Seol, J.Y.: A QAM-FBMC space-time block code system with linear equalizers. In: IEEE Globecom Workshops (GC Wkshps), San Diego, CA, pp. 1–5 (2015). https://doi.org/10.1109/glocomw.2015.7414208
18. Abdullahi, B.: Performance evaluation of MIMO system using LTE downlink physical layer. In: IEEE SAI Computing Conference, London UK, vol. 978, pp. 4673–8460 (2016). https://doi.org/10.1109/sai.2016.7556053
19. Arti, M.K.: OSTBC transmission in large MIMO systems. IEEE Commun. Lett. 20(11), 2308–2311 (2016). https://doi.org/10.1109/LCOMM.2016.2597229
20. Nissel, R., Rupp, M.: Enabling low-complexity MIMO in FBMC-OQAM. In: IEEE Globecom Workshops (GC Wkshps), Washington (2016). https://doi.org/10.1109/glocomw.2016.7848888
21. Bellanger, M., Mattera, D., Tanda, M.: MIMO techniques in the frequency domain with FBMC-PAM. In: European Conference on Networks and Communications (EuCNC), Athens, pp. 345–349 (2016). https://doi.org/10.1109/eucnc.2016.7561060
22. Nissel, R., Rupp, M.: Pruned DFT spread FBMC: low PAPR, low latency, high spectral efficiency. IEEE Trans. Commun. (99), 1–15 (2018). https://doi.org/10.1109/tcomm.2018.2837130
23. Mesleh, R., Alhassi, A.: MIMO system and channel models. In: Space Modulation Techniques, p. 288 (2018) https://doi.org/10.1002/9781119375692.ch2
24. Li, S., Liu, N., Zhang, L., Zhang, J., Tang, S., Huang, X.: Transmit beampattern synthesis for MIMO radar using extended circulating code. IET Radar Sonar Navig. 12(6), 610–616 (2018). https://doi.org/10.1049/iet-rsn.2017.0386
25. Zhao, X., Zhang, X., Li, S., Jiang, F., Peng, J.: A cooperative interference eliminated mechanism in MIMO systems. In: IEEE International Conference on Big Data and Smart Computing (BigComp), China, pp. 569–572 (2018). https://doi.org/10.1109/bigcomp.2018.00098

Information Systems

Comprehensive Analysis of Personalized Web Search Engines Through Information Retrieval Feedback System and User Profiling

Kamlesh Makvana[✉], Jay Patel, Parth Shah, and Amit Thakkar

Charusat University, Changa, Gujarat, India
{kamleshmakvana.it,jaypatel.it,parthshah.ce,
amitthakkar.it}@charusat.ac.in

Abstract. Information retrieval with its feedback feature provides the way to bridge gap between user's search queries and the documents returned by search engines. Recently, there has been a drift of personalization in Web search by many commercial and prominent search engines, where users receive different search results without considering relevancy of search query. Though many of the search engines are facilitating the features of personalized search results to provide the best user experiences of their search context. This paper provides composite review of research done for the personalization the web search as well as notified efforts has been done by web search engines to provide personalized results to users without compromising their privacy of search queries. Through the comparative analysis it has been identified the performance of key parameters like accuracy, efficiency and diversity of retrieved search result w.r.t. various user profiling and retrieval model techniques.

Keywords: Personalized web search · Search engines · Information filtering
Information retrieval · User profiling · Re-ranking algorithms

1 Introduction

Search engines try to retrieve personalized result from the web. However, the web results fetched might not be relevant to the user, due to lack of interpretation of search context of the query. A specific word may have different information in dissimilar contexts. Hence, the requirement arises to design the system that outputs results to the user as ranked pages. When queries for different intention are inserted to a search engine, similar results may return to different users. User's search query input is the vital source of assessing information need. Shortness, incomplete and ambiguousness nature of queries control the user information requirements. The result of the fetching web results relies exclusively on the query words. Without considering information's needs and preferences, Search engine presents the similar search results for different users. As a matter of fact many of the commercial search engines are trying to provide the personalized results without processing the search history of their search queries. As shown in Fig. 1, Commercial search engines like Google treats the user queries as bags of word representation.

© Springer Nature Singapore Pte Ltd. 2019
A. K. Luhach et al. (Eds.): ICAICR 2018, CCIS 956, pp. 155–164, 2019.
https://doi.org/10.1007/978-981-13-3143-5_14

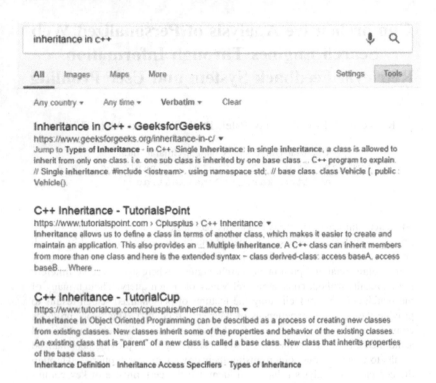

Fig. 1. Results of search query on Google

Meaning, when different users enters the same query, his request will be processed by search engine as similar to former user. Many of the research papers [1, 3, 4, 11, 12, 18, 19] have proposed a techniques of personalized web search results to user through processing click through information i.e. storing their search histories and process the same or through providing the recommendation of some query terms [1] to users by analyzing their previous search histories. But the reality is that to personalize search results through click through data or recommendation of search terms or search results requires a lot of process to perform. As per the recent censes around 40,000 searches are being performed by the users across the globe in every second and to store and process the search history of millions of users in a fractions of second is not a feasible solution even though prominence of the latest technologies like Big Data. But as commercial search engines are tried to provide best contextual search results to the user as given in Fig. 2.

Search engine tried to recommend personalized search terms instead of search result based on user's previous search results. Apart from personalized search terms many of the commercial search engines like Google have started to analyze search histories of users through many activities like location history, YouTube not interested feedback analysis, YouTube survey answers, Google word coach, and Google place answers. But efficiency of providing personalized search results is very less than the techniques proposed by a lots of researchers to provide personalized search results [1,

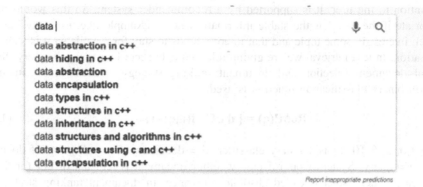

Fig. 2. Search term recommendation

3–12, 19]. Lots of researches have carried out their research to improve the ranking of the retrieved search results through improving areas of feedback system like Query Reformulation, Ontological user profile storage and processing, Web log processing, Knowledge Base generation, Semantic relationship between different quires etc. The structure of the paper is as follows: Sect. 2 describes some background knowledge about the information retrieval, ranking models, web mining, semantic web Mining and personalized web search. Section 3 describes some related works done in ranking model, personalize web and search engines. Section 4 describes comparative study of existing frameworks finally Sect. 5 concludes paper.

2 Background

Information retrieval is finding information according to user's need from large collection of various types of data. Text data are in natural language and computers have to understand this natural language to use this data [2]. For preprocessing of data Natural Language Processing (NLP) is used. There are many NLP systems which consider words as atomic units which are represented as indices in vocabulary. An example is n-gram model used for statistical language model. N-Gram model is limited to few hundreds of millions of words only. N- Gram model is statistical and language independent approach. N-gram model is useful in speech recognition, handwriting recognition, and information retrieval. Limitation of n-gram model is text categorization and machine translation [2]. To retrieve text NLP technique must be robust and efficient. The stat of art NLP techniques are not good enough to process a lot of unrestricted text data in a robust manner. So many search engine uses bags of words representation and it doesn't care about order of words and duplication of words. It is important to convert big data in to small relevant data to give access of relevant text data to user. Pull and push method is useful to give access of relevant text to user. In pull method user takes initiative for text access. Like user may type a query and browse results to find the relevant information. So this is usually appropriate for satisfying user's ad-hoc information. And in push mode system will take initiative to push the information to the user. It is supported by a recommender system. So this would be appropriate if the user has the stable information need. Example like user may have research interest in some topic and that interest tends to stay for a while so it is stable information. In text retrieval we are giving relevant data according to user's query. So for that document selection and document ranking strategy is used. In document selection binary classification function is used.

$$RoM'(q) = \{ d \in C \mid f(d,q)=1\} \tag{1}$$

Where f(d, q) $\in$ {0, 1} is a binary classifier, d = document, C = collection of documents, q = query. System would decide whether document is relevant or not for the users search query so it is called absolute relevance. In document ranking strategy system is not going to decide about document's relevance but some real value is assigned to every document and by this value system will give result. So it is called ranking of documents according to user's query.

$$RoM'(q) = \{ d \in C \mid f(d,q)>\mu\} \tag{2}$$

Where μ is a cut-off determined by user, d = document, C = collection of documents, q = query. System only decides if one document is more relevant than other document so it is called relative relevance. Document ranking is generally preferred. The progressions in web technologies have personalized services & information by integration of various existing technologies. By developing a standard, intelligent, adaptive and distributed framework is essential for the support of heterogeneous is obvious. The basic purpose is to make semantic personalization mining. The key process of Personalization include (i) Preprocessing web data (ii) Modeling user data (iii) Page Ranking Strategies. Every step requires adaptability due the change in the user's interest. Personalized web search broadly categorized as two types: (i) user's click-through-based methods and (ii) profile-based ones. The click through based simply imposes bias to clicked pages in the user's query log. Profile based improves user's search with data generated from user profiling techniques. Due to upsurge in competition, commercial search engines for instance, Google's Personalized Search allows to specify the interest in form of categories while some use relevance feedback. As these approaches need users to specify their preferences manually further than search, approaches that are capable of implicitly recognizing users' information needs should be developed. The process is as follows: whenever user enter a query, it is first pass on to query expansion agent that identifies ambiguity in query and pass this expanded. Query to retrieval agent. Then system get backs result on expanded query and move into the system which re-orders the fetched result by interpreting user interest stored in Vector Space Model (VSM) containing the user interest of specific user on clicked link is calculated by frequency of clicks, dwell time, actions performed on the link and actual rank of link given by the commercial search engine. If a link has Higher interest value it means that user has more interest in this link than other links. Personalizing the Web is to generate individual views based on the interests, access-context and many more. More precisely it is a process of filtering web (World Wide Web) data based on individual needs of each user. The personalized systems based on Web mining are often called recommender systems, which are in focus of research [13]. The Semantic Personalization presents framework which allows data to be shared, reused across applications. Ontologies are semantic data models to process information [35]. This process involves data preprocessing in which the information of user interests pre-processed from where user models are built. Data merging without requiring all the data consumers to be changed if the schemas differ and supports their evolution, RDF is used [24]. The linking structure of the Web can be extended by RDF to use URIs to name the relationship between the two ends of the link. Structured and semi structured data are exposed and shared across application.

3 Related Works

In [2], First feedforward neural net language model proposed. But this model has some limitation. Like time complexity will be higher on large data set. Because dominating term in this model is n * d * h. It also consists hidden layer which is dominating term in time complexity. Another model is recurrent neural net language mode which does not consist projection layer. In this model dominating term is h * h. To overcome the limitation of time complexity which is dominated by non-hidden layer. We use non log linear model. Continuous bag of words model in which non-linear hidden 3 layer is not present. In this model words from history does not influence the projection and they use words from future. In continuous skip gram model they predict words within range before and after the current word which causes improve quality in word vector but also increases the time complexity. In [32], another technique in vector space model to represent documents in terms of the Index terms. In this method vector t in space s, it has assumed that t_i is vector of unit length. It is sufficient to restrict our scope of discussion to the subspace spanned by term vectors, the t_i can be thought to be the generating set. In [33], another technique used in vector space model is matrices. In which data are modeled as a matrix and user's query as vector. Relevant documents in the database are then identified via simple vector operations. Personalized recommendation in e-commerce [34] as service for recommending online pages to the user based on user's clustering features is proposed. It analyzes Web log. Garofalakis [3] generated the Cluster of User profile by analyzing web log of users. Open Directory Project (ODP) is used as reference to identify semantic of the key words. It uses Google Search API and retrieves the result based on user interest which semantically annotate in user profile. In [4] web snippets were used to identify Short-term query context. Thakur [5] proposed a novel technique to process the web content and store the information in ontology and analyze the web log file to generate the navigational patterns of user by applying association rule algorithm (C log) and additionally it generate the cluster of documents. Yilmaz [6] represented a technique which incorporates semantic knowledge and sequence information to generate navigational patterns. In [7] user navigational pattern is generated in two phase offline phase in which first web log data is analyzed and converted it into a knowledge base passed to online phase which provide the recommendation list by applying LCS Algorithm to find out frequent products. [8] The author clustered and applied algorithms to organize the web results based on user interest that are clustered using suffix tree clustering algorithm, to enhance the performance. Page ReRank algorithm was used which uses hyperlink and link structure to retrieve result. In [9] this framework has generated the ontology from content of web data. It analyzed web log data and constructed reference for mapping to the ontology that was created from content of web data and refined the conceptual relations to provide more personalized view to user. [10] Proposed a RankBox, an adaptive ranking system. This algorithm learns from user's relevance feedback and re-rank the retrieved results using current ranking algorithm with new machine learning based ranking technique. Through analyzing user feedback system, RankBox learns to determine preferences of user's information need. Daoud in [25] proposed personalized search using ontological user Profile based on search session build using a score propagation that activates a set of semantically related concepts. Session boundary recognition based on tracking changes in the concepts by the user profile relatively to a query using the correlation measure of Kendall. Dou [26] proposed an algorithm to learn ranking system through training. The problem of exploiting click-through data was investigated for training web search rankings. In [26] it extracted pair wise preferences from an aggregated click-through dataset, compared with human judgments, to learn ranking functions. In [27], Shen has developed a re-ranking model (UCAIR) that analyze implicit feedback and perform ranking of user's search term. It is a browser plug-in that act as proxy for search engine to capture user data. Agichtein [28] proposed a method to provide an implicit feedback from user and by integrating implicit feedback directly to ranking algorithm. This could be achieved by analyzing click through and other user interaction on query in previous search session [29]. Personalized web search based on browsing history by artificial immune system (AIS). AIS was defined by de Castro and Timmis as adaptive systems, inspired by theoretical immunology and observed immune functions, principles and models, which was applied to problem solving [30]. AIS was works as follows;

- It processes the users' search activities and represented as log files stored on web servers.
- Then it pre-process the log to eliminate any irrelevant data.
- After pre-processing, it discovers the usage patterns using various web usage mining algorithm. [31] Improved rank of retrieved results through result diversification as diversification is also essential part of personalized web search. They have proposed three methods to improve the diversity of the top search results and evaluate the effectiveness of these methods through Most Frequent (MF) method Maximum Result Variety (MRV) method Most Satisfied (MS) method.

4 Analysis of Existing System

State of the art techniques have been employed by the various researchers for the personalization of web search results or recommendation of search terms/results according to user's context. There are many retrieval models used by the various researchers using user profile given in Fig. 3. To analyze usage of the user profile techniques to be used across the research community, we have implemented a simple term frequency retrieval model as shown in Fig. 3.

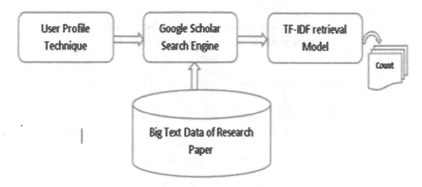

Fig. 3. Count of research papers for user profiling techniques.

User profiling techniques will searched into google scholar search engine to analyzing usage of those specific techniques. System will use TF-IDF vector space retrieval model [2] to count total research papers using searched user profiling techniques from top 50 retrieved results. In addition to that we have also included 20 commercial search engines and analysis of their user profiling techniques. Description of techniques, knowledge base and its usage w.r.t. to commercial search engine and Google scholar's research papers has been identified. Apart from that we have also analyzed performance of various search engines through three parameters named accuracy, efficiency and diversity of retrieved results. Based on the characteristics of different retrieval model, knowledge base and user profiling techniques, we have observed changes in [1, 3, 4, 6, 8, 16–21, 25–35]. Below table gives the comprehensive analysis of the various methods, their usage by commercial search engines as well as research community and performance of various parameters w.r.t usage of the user profiling techniques.

It is clear from Fig. 4 that majorities of the search engines are focusing to personalized search results without processing user's search history or query log though search engine like Google stores the user's search terms but not process it while another side of story is completely reverse. Research communities are more focusing to user profile at was even not feasible to design efficient re-ranking model because of huge amount of data being used in real time search engine applications. Accuracy, Efficiency and diversity are the key parameter to measure the performance of the any ranking model intended for personalized web search results. As shown in Fig. 5 and Table 1, Commercial search engines give best performance in terms of efficiency and diversity of retrieved results than a models that have used user profile.

But accuracy of search term with user's context may very as such search engine may process any user's requests as a general. Click through information that has been used in many research papers are giving the best accuracy w.r.t. to user's search context but very low in efficiency and diversity of search result as it takes much time in computation of user's intent on specific search query by analyzing user profile and once user's context is identified there will be no scope for other similar search result to be on top of retrieved results leads to lower the diversity.

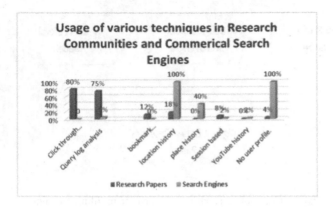

Fig. 4. Analysis of user profiling usage

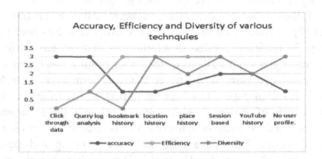

Fig. 5. Performance evaluation of accuracy, efficiency and diversity of search results.

5 Conclusion

Due of large growing of information, it is very crucial to design a retrieval model that ranked the retrieved search results according to the user's context on specific term. Analyzing the user's search profile may lead to higher the accuracy but it may also leads to lower the efficiency and diversity of the system. Efficiency and diversity are also an important factor to consider while designing a retrieval model as user's wants accurate results based on his context but also in minimum time(efficiency) and with some diversity in result in case of change in context. It is hard for any commercial search engine to analyze web log files of every users to identify their context on query, they are not adopting user profiling techniques. From the analysis it is also been covered that some hybrid mode of techniques i.e. minimal usage of user profile may balance all the factors (accuracy, efficiency and diversity) of the system.

References

1. Makvana, K., Shah, P., Shah,P.: A novel approach to personalize web search through user profiling and query reformulation. In: 2014 International Conference on Data Mining and Intelligent Computing (ICDMIC). IEEE (2014)
2. Majumder, P., Mitra, M., Chaudhari, B.: N-gram: a language independent approach to ir and natural language processing. Lecture Notes
3. Garofalakis, J., Giannakoudi, T., Vopi, A.: Personalized web search by constructing semantic clusters of user profiles. In: Lovrek, I., Howlett, Robert J., Jain, Lakhmi C. (eds.) KES 2008. LNCS (LNAI), vol. 5178, pp. 238–247. Springer, Heidelberg (2008). https://doi.org/10.1007/978-3-540-85565-1_30
4. Yu, J., Liu, F.: Mining user context based on interactive computing for personalized Web search. In: 2010 2nd International Conference on Computer Engineering and Technology (ICCET), vol. 2. IEEE (2010)
5. Thakur, M., Pandey, G.S.: Performance based novel techniques for semantic web mining. Int. J. Comput. Sci. Issues (IJCSI) 9(1), 317 (2012)
6. Yilmaz, H., Senkul, P.: Using ontology and sequence information for extracting behavior patterns from web navigation logs. In: 2010 IEEE International Conference on Data Mining Workshops (ICDMW). IEEE (2010)
7. Madia, N., Thakkar, A., Makvana, K.: Survey on recommendation system using semantic web mining
8. Annadurai, A.: Architecture of personalized web search engine using suffix tree clustering. In: 2011 International Conference on Signal Processing, Communication, Computing and Networking Technologies (ICSCCN). IEEE (2011)
9. Jayatilaka, A.D.S., Wimalarathne, G.D.S.P.: Knowledge extraction for semantic web using web mining. In: 2011 International Conference on Advances in ICT for Emerging Regions (ICTer). IEEE (2011)
10. Chen, N., Prasanna, V.K.: Rankbox: an adaptive ranking system for mining complex semantic relationships using user feedback. In: 2012 IEEE 13th International Conference on Information Reuse and Integration (IRI). IEEE (2012)
11. Tao, Z., et al.: Modeling user's preference in folksonomy for personalized search. In: 2011 International Conference on Cloud and Service Computing (CSC). IEEE (2011)
12. Oemarjadi, C.S., Maulidevi, N.U.: Web personalization in used cars ecommerce site. In: 2011 International Conference on Electrical Engineering and Informatics (ICEEI). IEEE (2011)
13. Linden, G., Smith, B., York, J.: Amazon.com recommendations: item-to-item collaborative filtering. Internet Comput. IEEE 7(1), 76–80 (2003)
14. Stumme, G., Hotho, A., Berendt, B.: Semantic web mining: state of the art and future directions. Web Semant.: Sci. Serv. Agents World Wide Web 4(2), 124–143 (2006)
15. Singh, A.: Agent based framework for semantic web content mining. Int. J. Adv. Technol. 3(2), 108–113 (2012)
16. Annappa, B., Chandrasekaran, K., Shet, K.C.: Meta-level constructs in content personalization of a web application. In: 2010 International Conference on Computer and Communication Technology (ICCCT). IEEE (2010)
17. Malik, S.K., Prakash, N., Rizvi, S.A.M.: Ontology and web usage mining towards an intelligent web focusing web logs. In: 2010 International Conference on Computational Intelligence and Communication Networks (CICN). IEEE (2010)
18. Makvana, K.: An approach to identify semantic relations between user's queries in text retrieval. In: ICTCS 2016 (2016)

19. Liu, F., Yu, C., Meng, W.: Personalized web search for improving retrieval effectiveness. IEEE Trans. Knowl. Data Eng. **16**(1), 28–40 (2004). https://doi.org/10.1109/TKDE.2004.1264820
20. Allan, J.: Incremental relevance feedback for information filtering. In: Proceedings of the 19th Annual International ACM SIGIR Conference on Research and Development in Information Retrieval, pp. 270–278 (1996)
21. de Campos, L.M., Fernández-Luna, J.M., Huete, J.F., Vicente-López, E.: Using personalization to improve XML retrieval. IEEE Trans. Knowl. Data Eng. **26**, 1280–1292 (2014). ISSN 1041-4347
22. Malik, S.K., Rizvi, S.A.M.: Information extraction using web usage mining, web scrapping and semantic annotation. In: 2011 International Conference on Computational Intelligence and Communication Networks (CICN). IEEE (2011)
23. http://www.businessinsider.com/how-manyweb-sites-are-are-there-2012-3
24. RDF (1999). http://www.w3c.org/tr/1999/rec-rdfsyntax-19990222/
25. Daoud, M., et al.: A session based personalized search using an ontological user profile. In: Proceedings of the 2009 ACM Symposium on Applied Computing. ACM (2009)
26. Dou, Z., et al.: Are click-through data adequate for learning web search rankings?. In: Proceedings of the 17th ACM Conference on Information and Knowledge Management. ACM (2008)
27. Shen, X., Tan, B., Zhai, C.X.: Implicit user modeling for personalized search. In: Proceedings of the 14th ACM International Conference on Information and Knowledge Management. ACM (2005)
28. Agichtein, E., Brill, E., Dumais, S.: Improving web search ranking by incorporating user behavior information. In: Proceedings of the 29th Annual International ACM SIGIR Conference on Research and Development in Information Retrieval. ACM (2006)
29. Rastegari, H., Shamsuddin, S.M.: Web search personalization based on browsing history by artificial immune system. Int. J. Adv. Soft Comput. Appl. **2**(3), 282–301 (2010)
30. Dasgupta, D., Ji, Z., Gonzalez, F.: Artificial immune system (AIS) research in the last five years. In: The 2003 Congress on Evolutionary Computation, CEC 2003, vol. 1. IEEE (2003)
31. Radlinski, F., Dumais, S.: Improving personalized web search using result diversification. In: Proceedings of the 29th Annual International ACM SIGIR Conference on Research and Development in Information Retrieval. ACM (2006)
32. Raghavan, V.V., Wong, S.K.M.: A critical analysis of vector space model for information retrieval. J. Am. Soc. Inf. Sci. **37**(5), 279–287 (1986)
33. Berry, M.W., Drmac, Z., Jessup, E.R.: Matrices, vector spaces, and information retrieval. SIAM Rev. **41**, 335–362 (1999)
34. Chirita, P.-A., Firan, C.S., Nejdl, W.: Personalized query expansion for the web. In: Proceedings of the 30th Annual International ACM SIGIR Conference on Research and Development in Information Retrieval. ACM (2007)
35. Sharma, S., Rana, V.: Web personalization through semantic annotation system. Adv. Comput. Sci. Technol. **10**(6), 1683–1690 (2017)

A Survey of Semantic Multi Agent System to Retrieve and Exchange Information in Healthcare

Shah Pinal[✉] and Thakkar Amit

Chandubhai S Patel Institute of Technology, Changa 388421, Gujarat, India
{pinalshah.it,amitthakkar.it}@charusat.ac.in

Abstract. Medical web and Life Science are the leading research area to apply advanced information technology for congruous data management and cognizance revelation purpose. Utilization of biomedical engineering with bio informatics can engender a Health Information System (HIS) for any hospital or medical institution which keep the record of patient's personal data and anterior medical history. Although modern medical equipment and sensors can generate substantial amount of data, utilization of data through HIS is very impecunious due to data integration and interoperability problem. Semantic web is utilized to share, link and integrate the generated data from various contrivances while data mining techniques can be acclimated to take automated decision predicated on accumulated quality data. So this paper provides a conception for applying semantic web along with data mining technique on medical data to solve the issue of heterogeneous platform by discussing semantic framework and multi agent system.

Keywords: Semantic · Ontology · Linked data · HIS · Interoperability
Multi agent

1 Introduction

This In the era of digitization, everything is stored in a digital format (i.e. computer) and same is applicable to healthcare also. Prodigious amount of data engendered by the medical institution and Hospitals but due to lack of proper data management and knowledge discovery tool sometimes not able to find hidden and important data of patients. Proper management of data will help to uncover valuable information regarding patient's life and that valuable knowledge leads to improve healthcare practices because even Doctors can take right decisions based on the data they got from the various tools and products. The reason for selecting this topic is to connect medical field with latest technology and bring some automation because it is the high time for this field to connect with world and generate eHealth solution as this field has remain traditional for a long time. Combining Semantic web with mining in eHealth is even more justified in terms of searching medical related data because mining techniques are purely depended on quality of data [1]. Quality of data matters a lot in medical field because poor, incomplete and inaccurate data can lead to wrong inference. Therefore,

© Springer Nature Singapore Pte Ltd. 2019
A. K. Luhach et al. (Eds.): ICAICR 2018, CCIS 956, pp. 165–174, 2019.
https://doi.org/10.1007/978-981-13-3143-5_15

the Semantic Web will take a lead to improve the quality of data by including intelligence into existing eHealth solutions around the world. Healthcare and Life Sciences Interest Group (HCLSIG) has been established by W3C consortium to provide extensive support for research in semantic web tools and technologies particularly for Healthcare and clinical field [2].

This paper is organized as follows. Section 1.1 covers the research problem followed by related work in Sect. 1.2. The various architecture of the framework is described in Sect. 1.3. Section 1.4 covers the comparison of existing frameworks and gives idea to select the best one. Section 2 covers the major challenges in Healthcare using semantic web technologies and Sect. 3 concludes the paper.

1.1 A Research Problem

Designing the semantic framework using semantic search techniques which allows us to retrieve and exchange information between hospitals for providing preventive and personalized healthcare services to society (specially for chronically ill people) (Fig. 1).

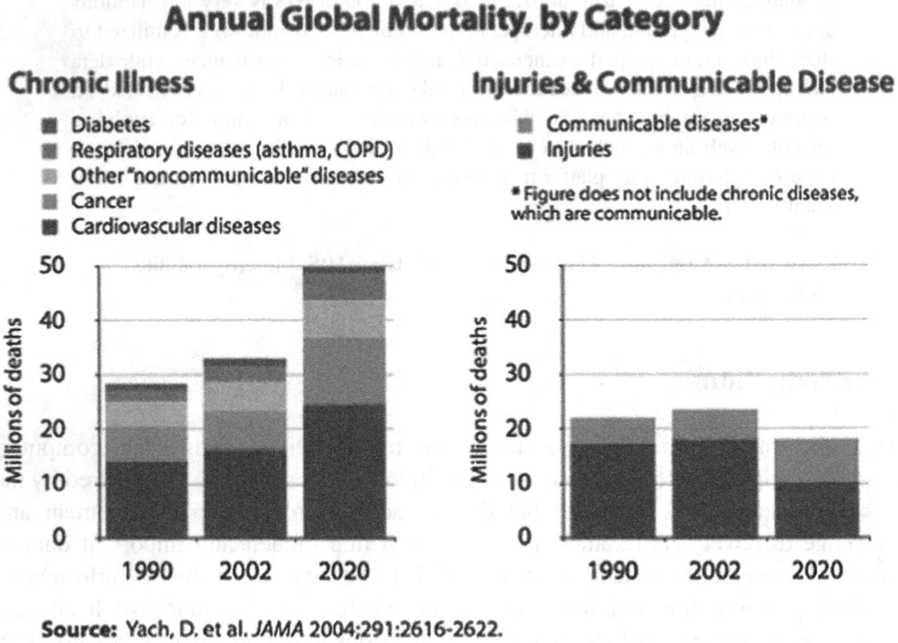

Source: Yach, D. et al. *JAMA* 2004;291:2616-2622.

Fig. 1. Annual global mortality report

Today in healthcare, chronic disease is the most immensely colossal challenge to tackle for any country. Major chronic disease are diabetes, stroke, breast cancer and heart disease. According to the World Health Organization, among 58 million deaths in 2017; majority of them are caused by cardiac disease and cancer. Chronic disease are incurable after some stage and it requires continuous remedies and proper treatment.

Popular reason for chronic disease are lacks of physical activity, poor pabulum, and exorbitant use tobacco and of alcohol [3]. The designing of semantic framework is always challenging task because coordination between different components is required for effective data processing and data transmission. Unlike other domain, Healthcare is having many inherent complexities to resolve. There are many challenges in Healthcare domain arise and solved but the communication and interpretation of data correctly is the main research problem among the researchers since last many years [4, 5]. Here in this paper we addressed some research challenges found in the existing semantic framework and provide the scope for improvement [6].

1.2 Related Work

This section gives brief about various recent semantic framework, semantic searching methods and ontology building. It also discusses various multi agent systems for exchanging and retrieving information between the hospitals and medical institutions.

Different application have been successfully deployed for monitoring the patient remotely, which are suffering by chronic disease like diabetes stroke and cardiac disease [7–9] but the main issue with these systems are, it focuses particularly on one or more diseases.

Recently, some of the semantic frameworks for the continuous health services incorporates the concept of artificial intelligence, machine learning, and data mining over bio sensors data to assist health professionals in the interpretation of medical data and decision making [10, 11]. Various web services have also been developed in order to integrate and exchange the information between hospitals but again the main limitation is they need to evolve their system with SOA (Service Oriented Architecture) [12, 13].

AIOS is an ontology based multi-agent system implemented in JADE development which connect the users through Internet. Each time when users made any changes to existing ontology or system, remaining all the users will get notification regarding updates so all the time users will get the updated information. AIOS system has been implemented using Nutch Plugin [14].

SCKE (Statistics and Collaborative Knowledge Exchange) is a light weight multi agent system which assumes each hospital as a separate agent and they can share or exchange information via secure connection. System has been implemented using JADE environment with Protégé as main component for ontology development and Nutch plugin for connecting each hospital with secure connection [15].

When data are coming from heterogeneous origins like medicine, biology, geography and sociology, complexity has led to a challenge in developing the decision support system. MASE is a semantic multi agent system which solves the above issue. System has used Protégé software for ontology development and JADE framework to build the system [16].

MET4 is another multi-agent system that allows interdisciplinary Healthcare team (IHT) to manage patients according to specific clinical work flows. It also allows patient to choose best professional practitioners in nearby area. This system has been implemented WADE environment and protégé tool for ontology development.

In all the cases one thing is common and that is ontology. Ontologies play vital role in achieving semantic interoperability across hospitals by provide a standard vocabulary and grammar for publishing data. It can be consider as the back-bone of Semantic Web [18].

1.3 Issues in Existing Framework/Multi Agent System

Authors have proposed the semantic framework in Fig. 2 to deal with u-healthcare services. This framework is used to measure the patient risk level whether patient is at low risk, moderate risk or high risk. Authors have mainly focuses on three parts of the framework.

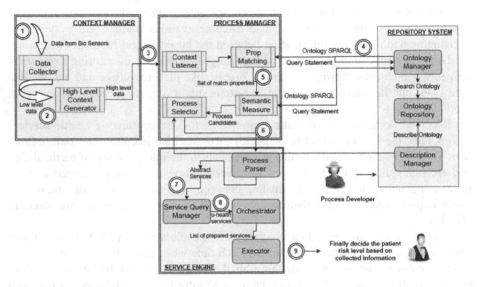

Fig. 2. Existing semantic framework for U health services

Context Manager: Context manager will receive the low level raw data from the various sensors like bio sensors or temperature sensors. Then it is the responsibility of context manager to convert low level data into high level context by matching low level data with predictive semantic ontologies. So the role of context manager is to decide the patient risk level based on raw data which it has received as an input.

Process Manager: This module is used to select the appropriate u health care services from the repository system based on the patient risk level. Once the service has been identified executor executes it for the patient.

Repository System: It contain the complete information regarding process such as input and output variables, preconditions and effects variables, functional definition, URIs, and QoS parameters.

Authors have used low level data set (captured from bio sensors) for the experiments in above case but they have not used any high level context information coming from the different hospitals as an input to this system. So accuracy may differ or there is a problem of interoperability when you select input parameters from different system.

This paper introduces a multi agent system so called SCKE (Fig. 3) which allows to exchanges patient information between hospitals. This system uses semantic search method to make searching results more accurate and meaningful. The implemented framework treats each hospital as a separate agent and the communication between two hospitals is accomplished by message passing system using Java runtime environment [16]. Hospital agents are responsible for performing mainly three functions like:

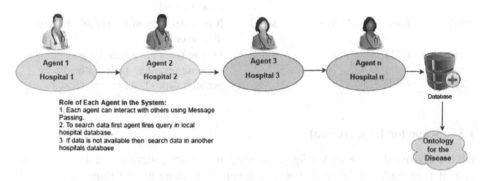

Fig. 3. SCKE multi agent system

- Each agent can interact with other agent using message passing system.
- Each agent is capable enough to accept user query and forward to the particular location in the database.
- If the information is not available in local database or hospital than it looks into the other hospital database.

Semantic search method has been introduced in above multi agent system which helps to provide more meaningful and relevant information from the database. Major drawback for this system is it supports only sharing of patient information among all the hospitals in specific format but if doctor wants to share patient x-ray image or MRI images then file sharing is not possible because this system is capable to transfer messages only in asynchronous manner.

1.4 Comparative Study of Existing Framework

Table 1 shows the summary of existing framework with major issues and challenges. Majority of the frameworks uses JADE and WADE environment for communication purpose and protégé for developing ontologies. [15–18].

Table 1. Comparison of existing multi agent system

System	Platform	Framework	Single-multi	Issues
AIOS	Java	JADE	Multi	Use of bit torrent platform for the communication which is now illegal in most of the country
SCKE	Java	JADE	Multi	System does not support file sharing it supports only message passing among the agents
MASE	Java	JADE	Multi	System focuses mostly on geographical data for taking decision regarding patient's health
MET4	Java	WADE	Multi	It provides support for chronic kidney disease only
Cancer search engine	HTML	RDF	Single	System takes more time for generating response regarding patient's health as decision depends on neural network

1.5   Scope for Improvement

Above discussed framework (Fig. 2) is used to decide patient's risk level whether patient is at high, moderate or low risk level. Remaining all the things are manual means after deciding risk level, to select particular services from repository system is the manual process. So we can add automation at this phase by adding data mining expert judgment system. This technique can be used to categorize patient data in different zone like family history of patients, symptoms and conditions to identify the cause of disease and it also provide cost effective solution to the patient. Below we discusses various data mining techniques used in Healthcare for the solution of interoperability and data integration [1]. In computer science these two terms are used interchangeably but there is slight difference between these two. Integration refers to the sharing and exchange of data with the help of interpreter while interoperability refers the real time exchange of data without any interpreter.

- K-NN Classification. Used to diagnosis heart disease.
- Improved fuzzy k-nearest classifier. For diagnosing thyroid diseases.
- Integrated decision tree model. Used for skin disease and it also helps to predict the breast cancer in patients.
- Neural Network Classification. Used for asthma, chest disease and lung cancer.

Data Mining along with semantic web brings various tools and techniques that can be applied on large ontologies available in Healthcare domain to extract and discover valuable information regarding patients such as cause of diseases, identification of appropriate medical treatment and approximate cost for treatments.

2   Research Challenges

Semantic data can provide benefit to health organizations, clinic, medical institutions and society people but the survey reveals certain loopholes and challenges on the use of semantic web technologies in Healthcare domain. In order to achieve maximum productivity in Healthcare domain from the semantic web technologies, a number of barriers need to be addressed:

- Large amount of data has been produced by health organizations daily and all that data continue to be generated in proprietary format which may be accurate and complete or inaccurate and inconsistent. There are some strong mapping tools required to convert such data from local format to standard format to get the best and relevant result.
- Biggest problem in Healthcare domain is availability of multiple ontologies for the same domain. Reaching to common and standard ontology is the challenge for any developer. For example, several ontologies are available for the cancer domain but very difficult to choose the standard and accurate one. So efforts are required to standardize vocabularies in specific domain.
- The data will be updated and described continuously using different vocabularies. No single ontology is enough to describe heterogeneous data. Various strategies and tools are required to integrate different ontologies.
- Integration of data mining technique with semantic web technologies will bring lots of opportunities for the researcher and developer to extract unknown patterns and knowledge in large Healthcare ontologies. Performance of mining technique is depended on format of underlying data generated from semantic framework therefore quality of data is challenge because it is the issue of patient's life or death.

Many Researchers have tried to overcome all barrier discussed above at some extent by achieving interoperability in Healthcare standard.

2.1   Interoperability in Healthcare

Interoperability can be of two types. Standard Interoperability and Translation Interoperability. There exist many different standards in healthcare; each is developed to fulfill different purposes [19–21]. In [22], the authors express the challenges in implementing universal standards, the complexity of the standards, diverse use cases and evolution of the standards. These hurdles cause the standardization efforts to take significant amounts of time and the systems relying on the standards also need to be updated along with the standardization. Consequently a proficient route for translation between different data models is more practical for information interoperability. Given the fact that it is unrealistic to have one universal standard that fits all the use cases [23, 24], is it conceivable to implement standard information translation? We think the answer is \yes." Our work is based on the technical side of healthcare information translation. We propose translation oriented methods, metrics, algorithms and frameworks that assist in healthcare information interoperability.

2.2 Healthcare Data Interoperability Initiatives

The Yosemite Project [25] suggests an ambitious roadmap for health care information interoperability on a global scale, by using RDF as a universal information representation and creating a hub for crowd-sourcing translation rules. They provide general translation rules, metadata including source and target data models, translation rules language (such as SPARQL/SPIN N3, Java, Python, etc.), dependencies, test data with validation, license, maintainer and usage metrics. They envision a translation hub that allows downloading the translation rules as needed.

3M Health Information Systems [26] created a public use version of the 3M Health care Data Dictionary (HDD), a medical terminology server that has been in operational use at the US Department of Defense (DoD) and other health care organizations. The project is named as HDD Access [27]. It is an application that contains a controlled medical vocabulary stored in a relational database with application programming interface (API) run-time services that other applications can call. In this sense their work is a standardization effort.

In [28], the authors presented FURTHeR, a semantic framework intended to run federated queries across disparate sources. The infrastructure incorporates a terminology server, a metadata repository and translation services for translating the semantic queries to run on disparate data sources. The infrastructure enables semantic interoperability via semantic search.

SemanticDB is a semi-structured patient data repository system developed within the Cleveland Clinic that leverages several advances in XML processing and Semantic Web technology standards for the purpose of outcomes research [29]. The SemanticDB patient data registry stores the current and historical data for a patient population which is specifically selected for clinical research in cardiology domain. SemanticDB contains a data production pipeline that translates the pertinent patient data to generate customized views of the repository content for statistical analysis and reporting.

3 Conclusion

Enormous amount of data has been generated from the heterogeneous devices and the amount of information is consistently increasing day by day in medical field. Sometimes it becomes very hard to move from traditional method to new method because this field requires precise and efficacious information and they don't want to take any peril regarding patient's life. In order to achieve a solution, different semantic framework has been discussed in this paper and out of all this framework and system, SCKE, the multi agent system, perform best on medical cognate data to provide more precise and germane results.

References

1. Zenunia, X., Raufia, B., Ismailia, F., Ajdaria, J.: State of the art of semantic web for healthcare. Procedia - Soc. Behav. Sci. **195**, 1990–1998 (2015)
2. Ye, J., et al.: Semantic web technologies in pervasive computing: a survey and research roadmap. Pervasive Mob. Comput. **23**, 1–25 (2015)
3. Echeverriaa, M., Jimenez-Molina, A., Riosa, S.: A semantic framework for continuous u-health services provisioning. Procedia Computer Science **60**, 603–612 (2015)
4. Eysenbach, G.: The semantic web and healthcare consumers: a new challenge and opportunity on the horizon. Int. J. Healthc. Technol. Manag. (2016)
5. Kolias, Vassileios D., Stoitsis, J., Golemati, S., Nikita, Konstantina S.: Utilizing semantic web technologies in healthcare. In: Koutsouris, D.-D., Lazakidou, A.A. (eds.) Concepts and Trends in Healthcare Information Systems. AIS, vol. 16, pp. 9–19. Springer, Cham (2014). https://doi.org/10.1007/978-3-319-06844-2_2
6. Dumontier, M.: Building effective semantic web for healthcare and life science. IEEE Trans. (2015)
7. Fortier, P., Viall, B.: Development of a mobile cardiac wellness application and integrated wearable sensor suite. In: The Fifth International Conference on Sensor Technologies and Applications, p. 301–306 (2011)
8. Gao, R.: A phone-based e-health system for OSAS and its energy issue. In: 2012 International Symposium on Information Technology in Medicine and Education, pp. 682–686 (2012)
9. Miao, F., Miao, X., Shangguan, W., Li, Y.: Mobihealthcare system: body sensor network based m-health system for healthcare application. E-Health Telecommun. Syst. Netw. **1**(1), 12–18 (2012)
10. Fotiadis, D., Likas, A., Protopappas, V.: Intelligent Patient Monitoring, 1st edn. Wiley, Hoboken (2006)
11. Patil, D., Wadhai, V., Gund, M., Biyani, R., Andhalkar, S., Agrawal, B.: An adaptive parameter free data mining approach for healthcare application. Int. J. Adv. Comput. Sci. Appl. **3**(1), (2012)
12. Omar, W., Ahmad, B., Taleb-Bendiab, A., Karam, Y.: A software framework for open standard self-managing sensor overlay for web services. In: Proceedings of the Seventh International Conference on Enterprise Information Systems, p. 72–81 (2005)
13. Serhani, M.A., Benharref, A., Badidi, E.: Towards dynamic non-obtrusive health monitoring based on SOA and cloud. In: Huang, G., Liu, X., He, J., Klawonn, F., Yao, G. (eds.) HIS 2013. LNCS, vol. 7798, pp. 125–136. Springer, Heidelberg (2013). https://doi.org/10.1007/978-3-642-37899-7_11
14. Poggi, A., Tomaiuolo, M.: A DHT-based multi-agent system for semantic information sharing. In: Lai, C., Semeraro, G., Vargiu, E. (eds.) New Challenges in Distributed Information Filtering and Retrieval. SCI, vol. 439, pp. 197–213. Springer, Heidelberg (2013). https://doi.org/10.1007/978-3-642-31546-6_12
15. Alkahtani, N., Almohsen, S., Alkahtani, N., Meshref, S., Kurdi, H.: A semantic multi-agent system to exchange information between hospitals. Procedia Comput. Sci. **109**, 704–709 (2017)
16. Li, S., Mackaness, W.: A multi-agent-based, semantic-driven system for decision support in epidemic management. Health Inform. J. **21**(3), 195–208 (2014)
17. Raj, S., Sarumathi, S.: Ontology based semantic search engine for cancer. Int. J. Comput. Appl. **95**(5), 39–43 (2014)

18. Lance, P.: The role big data ontology and semantic search will play to improve healthcare (2015)
19. Greenhalgh, T., Howick, J., Maskrey, N.: Evidence based medicine: a movement in crisis? BMJ **348**, g3725 (2014)
20. Djulbegovic, B., Guyatt, G.H., Ashcroft, R.E.: Epistemologic inquiries in evidence-based medicine. Cancer Control **16**(2), 158–168 (2009)
21. McGinnis, J.M., Aisner, D., Olsen, L. (eds.): The Learning Healthcare System: Workshop Summary. National Academies Press, Washington, D.C. (2007)
22. Friedman, C.P., Wong, A.K., Blumenthal, D.: Achieving a nationwide learning health system. Sci. Transl. Med. **2**(57), 57cm29 (2010)
23. Stroetman, V., et al.: Semantic interoperability for better health and safer healthcare, 34 p. (2009)
24. Martínez-Costa, C., Cornet, R., Karlsson, D., Schulz, S., Kalra, D.: Semantic enrichment of clinical models towards semantic interoperability. The heart failure summary use case. J. Am. Med. Inform. Assoc. **22**(3), 565–576 (2015)
25. Booth, D., Dowling, C., Fry, E., Huff, S., Mandel, J.: RDF as a universal healthcare exchange language. SEMTECH Panel (2013)
26. 3M: 3M Health Information Systems. Accessed 26 July 2015
27. Lau, L., et al.: U.S. Patent Application No. 09/755,966 (2002)
28. Matney, S.A., et al.: Developing a semantic framework for clinical and translational research. AMIA Summit Translational Bioinform., 7–9 (2011)
29. Pierce, C.D., Booth, D., Ogbuji, C., Deaton, C., Blackstone, E., Lenat, D.: SemanticDB: a semantic web infrastructure for clinical research and quality reporting. Curr. Bioinform. **7**(3), 267–277 (2012)

Integration of ICT in Curriculum - A Case Study of Botswana Junior Secondary Schools

Peggy Siamisang, Rajiv Kumar[✉], Sreekumar Narayanan,
and Neelamegam Chandirakasan

Botho University, Gaborone, Botswana
psiamisang@gmail.com, dhiman.rajiv@gmail.com,
{sreekumar.narayanan,
neelamegam.chandirakasan}@bothouniversity.ac.bw

Abstract. Information and Communication Technology (ICT) has been growing so fast for the past 20 years in most of sectors, but still a lot of done in the education sector. Teachers are still relying on the old traditional way of teaching methods. Botswana are still far behind in benefiting from ICT usage in classroom. This study reviews various technology adoption frameworks such as Technology Pedagogy and Content knowledge, Teacher Development model, and Conceptual framework. This study assess the ICT infrastructure found in Botswana public junior secondary schools, assess teachers' skills, knowledge, confidence, and the perception on the integration of ICT in teaching and learning. A quantitative research design is used to collect data from teachers in Botswana Junior Secondary Schools. The major findings show that integration of ICT in Botswana Junior secondary schools is very low or not yet started. This has been influenced by factors such as lack of skill, lack of confidence in the use of technology by teachers, and lack ICT equipment in schools. The study recommends that schools should be equipped with education ICT supporting infrastructure, and teachers should be trained on the pedagogy of ICT in teaching. Furthermore, the curriculum should be designed in such a way that it includes ICT integration in subject areas.

Keywords: ICT · Content knowledge · Pedagogy · TPCK · TDM

1 Introduction

1.1 Background Information

Botswana is one of the countries in the world with fast growing economy. The country is putting more emphases on integrating ICT in education sector to ensure that all ministries are equipped with computer infrastructures. Policies and strategies are put in place e.g. Education and Training Strategic Sector Plan (ETSSP), Nteletsa project, Maitlamo, Thuto Net and other sectors such as Botswana Fibre Network Ltd (Bofinet), Botswana Communication Regulatory Authority (BOCRA) are playing a major role in the country by partnering with the government to ensure that ICT literacy is realized. Botswana is spending millions of Pulas' in order to improve the education system and currently there are more than 215 Junior Secondary Schools in Botswana.

© Springer Nature Singapore Pte Ltd. 2019
A. K. Luhach et al. (Eds.): ICAICR 2018, CCIS 956, pp. 175–192, 2019.
https://doi.org/10.1007/978-981-13-3143-5_16

In 2002, Botswana made it a point that all secondary schools are equipped with computer infrastructures and internet connectivity, to ensure students learns basic computer skills. The introduction of ICT in education was made possible through national ICT policy called Maitlamo National ICT policies (2004) which is in line with the United Nations to provide a road map to socio economic, cultural, and political transformation through the use of ICT. Maitlamo's aim is to provide communication network of high international standard to ensure that ICT industry grows and to provide the ICT training to the teacher. The Revised National Policy on Education (2004) came up with the policy framework for the education system in Botswana called Education Training Strategic Sector Plan (ETSSP) which was formed in order to transform education from pre-primary to tertiary school, which is a five-year strategy for (2015–2020).

1.2   Problem Statement

ICT has the potential to improve students' performance in schools but it is a challenge to integrate ICT in teaching and learning in schools. Currently ICT is offered as a subject to enhance students' computer basic skills. But, most subjects are still relying on traditional methods to teach the content.

1.3   The Goal of the Study

The aim of the study is to investigate various factors that influence the use of ICT in Botswana public Junior Secondary Schools.

1.4   The Significance of the Study

The research is useful to identify the importance of ICT in school education; curriculum designers. Maitlamo National ICT policy designed a framework that addressed four stages (emerging, applying, infusion and transformation) teacher development in relation to ICT usage in classroom and to ensure that the strategy is implemented and monitored.

1.5   Research Objectives

The following research objectives are:

- To assess the skill and knowledge that teachers can integrate technology in a teaching and learning.
- To identify ICT equipment available to support teacher in delivering the content of the subject.
- To assess the level of ICT application.
- To assess the perception of teachers in the use of technology in their subject expertise.
- To investigate the influence of gender on the use technology in delivering the content of the subject.
- To investigate the influence of qualification on ICT integration in teaching and learning.

1.6   Research Questions

The following research questions are:

- What are the skills and knowledge that teachers possess in the use of computer aided instructional tools in junior secondary schools?
- What are the ICT tools available to support delivering of the content of the subject matter?
- To what extend are ICT facilities used to support teaching and learning?
- What are teachers' views on the use of technology in their subject areas?
- Does gender influence the intention to use computer aided instructional tools?
- Does qualification influence the intention to use computer aided instructional tools?

1.7   Scope of the Study

The survey focused on Junior Secondary School teachers in Botswana who are employed by Ministry of Education Skills and Development for Basic Education. The study is useful for the effective use of computer aided instructional tools in a classroom environment.

2   Literature Review

2.1   The Importance of ICT in *Schools*

The computer aided instructional tools can support teachers to ensure that students stay focused throughout the lesson. Students can learn by doing, they can also receive feedback and continuously, refine their understanding and build new knowledge and provide self-paced learning. Computer assistant instructional packages can be developed in order to assist and inspire teachers to prepare for subject areas [3]. They carried research on e-reader project in rural Tanzania which addressed lack of books in rural schools and found that students showed a lot of improvement in reading skills when e-reader was introduced, both the teacher and student were motivated and engaged in learning.

Botswana Inter-Governmental Information for All Programme (IFAP) established in 2001 as successor to the General Information Programme (PGI) [1] and International Informatics Programme (IIP) under UNESCO conducted the desktop survey on ICT in education at all levels primary, Junior and secondary schools and tertiary education. The committee followed a framework by the UNESCO-UIS (2009) when analyzing the effective use of the ICT in Botswana schools. The Botswana IFAP literacy report (2016) indicated that ICT policies relevant to ICT are available but they focus on availability of computers and internet connectivity in school but lacking in integrating ICT in curriculum [1]. The report also revealed that computer awareness course is offered at Junior Secondary School, which is not compulsory to some schools and also not examinable.

The IFAP policy framework has recommended that the Ministry of Skill and Education development (MOESD) should develop an ICT pedagogy framework in education, provide schools with high speed internet connection, integrate ICT in other subjects, identify teachers skills and qualification in ICT and train teachers to boost their confidence on the use of ICT in schools, increase computer-based learning resources that are of high quality in schools and establish a centre for excellence for ICT that will support research and the ICT pedagogy in education [1]. They investigated the "ICT usage and perceptions of public primary school teachers, Gaborone" in Botswana. The survey indicated that ICT can add value to teaching and learning, even though there are some challenges which hinder the integration of ICT in education [3, 4].

The use of ICT in classrooms does not mean that traditional method will be faced out technology is introduced to support the teaching methods and to make learning more interactive. Researchers have proposed various models that could help in adopting integrating ICT in classroom environment for any subject. This study reviews various models which were proposed for adoption of technology in classroom.

3   Technology Integration Models

To adopt technology in classroom, various models have been used;

- Technology Pedagogy and Content Knowledge (TPCK)
- Teacher Development model (TDM)
- Conceptual framework

3.1   The Implication of Technology Pedagogy and Content Knowledge (TPCK)

Teachers' knowledge has been focusing on the content and the pedagogy (how to teach) with model called Pedagogy Content Knowledge (PCK) for effective teaching and learning in classroom. A teacher should must familiar with Content Knowledge (CK) and various approaches e.g. lesson plan, assessment, and alternative methods: recap of the previous knowledge by students or strategies on how to deliver the content of Pedagogy Knowledge (PK). This approach has been adopted by Botswana education system: there are training institutes for teachers in Botswana, which provide teachers with the content and pedagogy.

Due to the increase usage of technology, this model was later developed by introducing Technology knowledge; the 21st generation could benefit a lot from technology if it can be integration in education [6].

3.1.1   TPCK (Technology Pedagogy and Content Knowledge)

According to Mishra et al. [6], the ability to connect Technology Knowledge (TK), Content Knowledge (CK) and Pedagogy Knowledge (PK) together, Technology Knowledge (TK) refers to understanding the computer hardware and software, the internet and use the hardware and software in a classroom environment [6]. The aim of technology is to support teachers in delivering the content of the subject in such a manner that will be easily understood by learners. In this situation, technology will be used as a pedagogy tool. "The Content Knowledge (CK) is the knowledge about the subject to be learned, Pedagogy Knowledge (PK) refers to knowledge about processes, strategies and methods to be used in delivering a subject". The Pedagogical Content Knowledge (PCK) that can be used to address an objective for a specific method. PCK covers teaching strategies, lesson plan, assessment and curriculum (Fig. 1).

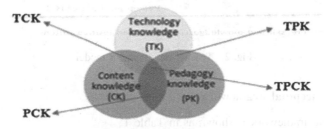

Fig. 1. TPCK model

3.1.2   Technology Content Knowledge (TCK)
Different technologies are available, the teacher need to understand the impact of technology in their subjects. They need to know how the introduction of technology is going to change, support or enhance the subject.

3.1.3   Technological Pedagogical Knowledge (TPK)
Technology Pedagogy Knowledge (TPK) is vital because teachers are the drivers of the lesson that they need to develop a skill that can reconfigure the technology to suit the pedagogy approach. This requires teachers' creativity, being able to customize the tools in such way that will suit the strategies.

3.2   Teacher Development Model (TDM)

Teacher Development model (TDM) addressed four steps (emerging, applying, infusing and transforming) that can be adopted in order to integrate technology in teaching processes. *Emerging Stage* is the initial stage of the model to ensure that computers and other tools are in place. Teachers familiarize themselves with the ICT tools and develop the ICT literacy skill. The *Applying stage* is where the teacher decides what, where, when and how-to ICT tools will contribute to subject objective and choose the appropriate tool. The *infusion stage* enables teachers to infuse technology in all aspect of learning. At this stage teachers are more creative, active, and plan for the lesson with technology. The *transformation stage* where the whole school is transformed. Teaching is transformed from teacher centered to learner centered and new uses of technology are discovered (Fig. 2).

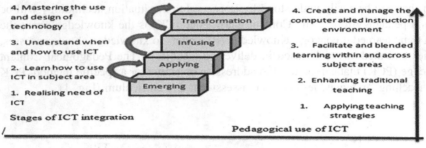

Fig. 2. Teacher development model

3.3   The Conceptual Framework

The conceptual framework is shown as in Table 1.

Table 1. Conceptual framework

Variables	Enabling factors
ICT infrastructure	-Presence of ICT correct and enough infrastructure (hardware and software) -Internet connectivity
Teacher and learner's ICT skill	-Teachers and learners need necessary ICT training -Understand when, where, and how to use the tools
Technical and financial support	-Without technical support, integration will lead to failure -The infrastructure will continuously need to repaired funds required for technical support)
Perception of teachers, school management towards ICT integration	-Positive attitude and perception about integration of ICT supporting the content of the subject matter -Teachers and learners need confidence in using the ICT tools -School management should be willing to fund the technical support

4   The Research Framework

The study has been based on the TPACK and the Teacher Development Model. The models were chosen because they cover all the aspects that are necessary when using computer aided instructional tools in delivering the content of the subject.

4.1 The Framework for Map/Processes to use ICT to Support Teaching Methods Using TDM Model and TPCK Framework

Adoption of Computer aided instructional tools stages; the first thing is to ensure that ICT tools are available. The next step will provide training to teachers how to use the tools in the subject by integrating ICT in lesson plans to enhance the traditional teaching. We need to understand when and how to use ICT for pedagogical transformation through specializing in the use/design of ICT e.g. creating learning multimedia software, interactive tools and gaming etc.

4.2 Implication of TPCK and the TDM Models for ICT Integration in Teaching and Learning

Implementation of the TPCK and TDM Model is shown in Table 2.

Table 2. Implementation of the TPCK and TDM model

TPCK	TDM	Subject content and professional competencies	ICT competency that can be learned by teachers
Mastering learning through ICT	Transforming	Developed professional skills	Creation of interactive tools and gaming; creation of 3D animation in education
Facilitating student learning with or through ICT	Infusing	Designing ICT enabled lessons	Specific learning tools; web quests
ICT integrated in the subject teaching	Applying	Integrating ICT in lesson plans	Multimedia tools: graphic design of educational media
Teachers learning about ICT	Infusing	Enhance traditional teaching management using ICT	Productivity tools and internet: email

4.3 TPCK in a Classroom

Firstly, a teacher must know about the content knowledge (CK). Secondly, the pedagogy knowledge how the student learns the content. Thirdly, the technology knowledge (TK), teacher need to understand a wide range of tools available and knowledge about the tools. Technology Pedagogy Knowledge (TPK), is useful to select the technology tools for a specific subject. TCK is the understanding of the relationship between content and tools, the ability to modify and manipulate content with the tools and PCK is how to teach what you are teaching to specific students [6].

Technology Pedagogy and Content Knowledge (TPCK) is used to connect pedagogy, content and technology knowledge. Computer awareness subject was introduced in Botswana Junior Secondary schools in order to equip learners and teachers with technological skill on the use of computers e.g. Microsoft word, PowerPoint, graphics, excel such that students are familiar with technology, it is going to be easy for teachers to use technology to support learning in their subject areas.

Table 3. How ICT is offered to classes in schools

	Responses	Percentage
ICT is taught as a subject	Yes 52	98%
	No 1	2%
I choose to incorporate ICT in my subject	Yes 16	30%
	No 37	70%
ICT is integrated in my subject area (syllabus)	Yes 30	57%
	No 23	43%

5 Research Methodology

The study uses the survey method to investigate the objectives of research work that is based on the quantitative research design.

5.1 Instrumentation and Sampling

The research methods consist of self-administered and online questionnaire, the first section covered background information (age, sex, years in service and subject taught by the teacher and training in ICT and indicate how ICT is offered in their schools), the second part is response category which assess the available technical resources. the third section was about teacher's skill and knowledge on ICT forth part will look at teacher's ICT application looking at how often do they use technology the last section included teacher's perception in integrating of ICT in subject areas. The survey is distributed to the participants at Makhubu J S S teaching staff. To increase the number of participant, an online questionnaire sends to specific teachers through various media. The questionnaire has taken from three researchers, which are "on teacher's attitude" about "the level ICT usage" on Malaysian Online journal of Educational technology (MOJET) and Teacher questionnaire on the use of ICT (2015)-Agrupamento de Escolas de Atouguia da Baleia – Portugal [6].

5.2 Data Collection Procedure

The researcher started by consulting schools to ask for permission to do research. Then the researcher asked for permission from relevant authorities Once granted the researcher sent the letter to Makhubu J S S and specific individuals who are teachers. The Cochran formula used to determine the sample size.

$$\text{The Cochran formula}: \qquad n = \frac{N}{1 + N(\delta)^2} \qquad (1)$$

Where, n is the sample size, N is Target population and δ is the Significance level". 5% significance level is used to select number of teachers.

Data is collected using simple random sampling. All the names of teachers in Makhubu Secondary school is collected. The researcher randomly selects the list, 38 teachers from a total of 42 staff members from Makhubu secondary school.

5.3   Data Analysis Process

The application provides a summary sheet for all the responses analyzed in different formats like pie charts, tables and bar charts. This study follows a descriptive statistic where by numerical counts, percentages, tables, measure of central tendency (mode) and measure of variability is used to analyses the data.

5.4   Questionnaire Return Rate

The questionnaire was administered to sample size of 66 teachers, of which 80% were filled.

6   Findings

6.1   Background of Teachers

6.1.1   Gender

The participants were asked to state their gender. The study shows that 42% males compared to 58% females (Fig. 3).

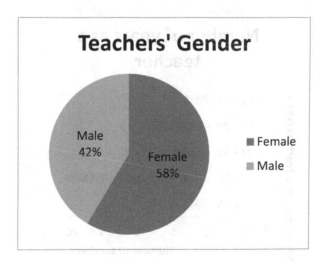

Fig. 3. Gender for the participants

6.1.2   Ages

The study involved teachers of varies ages ranges with most teachers interviewed being at 36–45 years, followed by age between 26 and 35, then 45 and above. The least were 18–25 years and above (Fig. 4).

6.1.3   Number of Years of Teaching

The study also wanted to find out work experience for the participants, the majority were having working experience which is between 6 and 10, followed by 11–15 years and 16–20 years by 24.5%, 1–5 years and lastly 1–5 years and those 21 at 5.7% (Fig. 5).

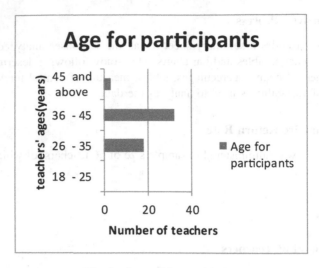

Fig. 4. Ages of the participants

Fig. 5. Number of years as teachers

6.1.4   Qualification

The modal qualification from the participants' responses is Diploma with 50% followed by Degree with 48% and others by 2% (Fig. 6).

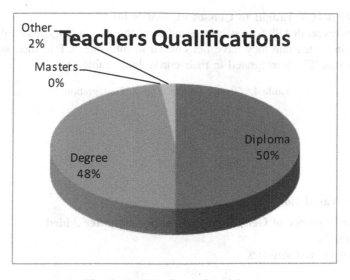

Fig. 6. Qualifications of participants

6.1.5   Training on the Pedagogical use of ICT in Supporting Content Delivery

According to the pie chart the majority of teachers have not been trained on the pedagogy use of computer aided instructional tools, this was shown by 94% rate of No's followed by 6% of Yes (Fig. 7).

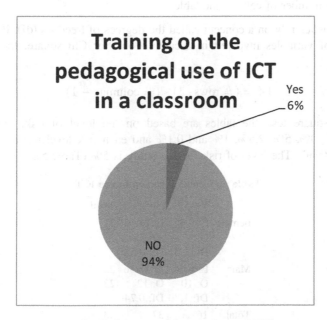

Fig. 7. Training on pedagogical use of ICT

6.1.6   How is ICT Taught to Classes in your School?

The findings reveal that 98% of responses indicated that ICT is taught as a subject, 70% of teachers indicated that they have not chosen to integrate ICT in their subject and 57% shows that ICT is integrated in their curriculum (Table 4).

Table 4. Gender influence on ICT integration

	Yes	No	Total
Female	6	25	31
Male	10	12	22
Total	16	37	53

6.2   Cross Tabulation

6.2.1   The Influence of Gender on the use of Computer Aided Instructional Tools

The value of the test statistics

$$x^2 = \sum_{i=1}^{n} \frac{(O_i - E_i)^2}{E} \text{(Cochran formula)} \tag{2}$$

Where

x^2 = Pearson cumulative test statistics, chi square value
i = is the ith position in the contingency table
O_i = observed frequency
E_i = expected frequency
N = is the number of cells in the table

Many statistics rely on a concept called the degrees of freedom (df). It is based on the number of variables involved in a calculation. For Chi square, the degrees of freedom are:

$$Df = (\# \text{ rows} - 1) * (\# \text{ columns} - 1) \tag{3}$$

For Chi square test, the tables are based on the level of risk, with common thresholds of 10%, 5%, 2.5%, 1% and 0.1% and each risk level has a critical value associated with it". The level of risk for this study is 5% (Table 5).

Table 5. Gender intention to use ICT

	Yes	No	Total
Female	E: 9.36	E: 21.64	31
	O: 6	\O: 25	31
	Df: 1.21	Df: 0.52	
Male	E: 6.64	E: 15.36	22
	O: 10	O: 12	22
	Df: 1.70	Df: 0.74	
Total	16	37	53

Expected value for yes' (E) = (Total Yes * Total female)/Total Table
Observed value (O) = observed frequency from the Table 3.

A low value for chi square means there is high correlation between the set of data, if the expected and observed value are equal it means there is no difference.

$$\text{Cochran Formula} \quad x^2 = \sum_{i=1}^{n} \frac{(O_i - E_i)^2}{E} = 1.21 + 0.52 + 1.70 + 0.74 \tag{4}$$
$$= 4.17$$

After adding all the differences, the total Chi square value was 4.17.
For this analysis, the degrees of freedom (df) will be:

$$Df = (\# \text{ rows}-1) * (\# \text{ columns} - 1)$$
$$= (2 - 1) * (2 - 1) = 1 \tag{5}$$
$$\text{Total Chi square} = 4.17$$

According to Cochran formula, the calculated Chi square 4.17 is greater than the tabulated Chi square value of 3.84 at 5% significant level with 1 degree of freedom. The chi square value (4.17) lies between 3.841 and 5.142 of the chi square distribution table of with 1 degree of freedom and the corresponding probability is between 0.05 and 0.02 of probability levels. The p value is of $0.04 < 0.05$. Because calculated value exceeds the critical value, the difference is significant. Therefore, it means the male use of ICT is significant compared to female counter part.

6.2.2 The Influence of Qualification on Intend to use ICT in Subject Areas

The study found out teacher's responses towards behavior to choose ICT in teaching and learning (Table 6).

$$x^2 = \sum_{i=1}^{n} \frac{(O_i - E_i)^2}{E} = 4.2 + 1.82 + 4.36 + 1.89 = 12.27 \tag{6}$$

After adding all the differences, the total Chi square value was 12.27
In this case, the Degrees of freedom will be:

$$Df = (\#r - 1) * (\#c - 1) :$$
$$= (2 - 1) * (2 - 1) = 1$$

r represents rows and c represent columns.

The Chi square statistics ($x^2 = 12.27$), at a level risk of (0.05) and degrees of freedom (df = 1). The calculated value is more than the critical value; therefore, the difference is statistically significant. The p-value of 0.00046 is less 0.05. According to the study 52% of degree holders shown that they integrate ICT in their subject area because they chose to do so as compared to only 8% of the Diploma holders.

6.3   Infrastructure

This question was designed to identify the type of technical and instructional support available to teachers to use in schools. The findings as indicated by the Table 7 shows that learners have computers and computers are connected to the internet as this was indicted by the high percentages rate in the table (98% and 100%), followed by projection system by 77%, digital audio.

Table 6. The critical value of qualification influence

	Yes	No	Total
Degree, Honors Degree,	Observed 14	Observed 13	27
	Expected 8.15	Expected 18.85	27
	Df: 4.2	Df: 1.82	
Diploma	Observed 2	Observed 24	26
	Expected 7.85	Expected 18.15	26
	Df: 4.36	Df: 1.89	13.02
Total	16	37	53

6.4   Teachers ICT Usage

Findings provided in Table 7 about teacher's skill and knowledge on ICT equipment shows that most teachers have a less skill in using most of the ICT facilities available in their schools. The responses rate increases towards the left side of the table (the sometimes, rarely and never) which indicate that teachers rarely use the hardware and software available (Table 8).

6.5   Teachers Skill and Knowledge

The findings show that the participant lacked skill and knowledge in using the hardware and software as indicated by Table 10. The purpose of the question was to identify the level in which teachers use this technology to support teaching in class. What most teachers are conversant with is using word processing document as it was at 81%, followed by the use of emails to communicate. Other computer instructions teachers showed that they have little knowledge in using tools as the sum of none and little were more than half of the total of the participants.

6.6   Teachers Perception

The last question was designed to assess teachers' perception on the integration ICT in subject areas. Teachers were asked to indicate how they feel about the use of technology in order to support the old traditional style of teaching. Table 11 illustrates the

Table 7. Availability of ICT equipment (hardware and software)

Infrastructure availability	Responses	Percentage
Computers for learners	Yes 52	Yes 98%
	No 1	No 2%
Interactive white boards	Yes 49	Yes 8%
	No 4	No 92%
Video conferencing systems	Yes 48	Yes 91%
	No 5	No 9%
Audio equipment	Yes 21	Yes 40%
	No 32	No 60%
Digital photo camera	Yes 37	Yes 70%
	No 16	No 30%
Digital video camera	Yes 35	Yes 66%
	No 18	No 34%
Projection system	Yes 41	Yes 77%
	No 12	No 23%
Educational software for my subject	Yes 3	Yes 6%
	No 50	No 94%
Internet connectivity	Yes 53	Yes 100%
	No 0	No 0%
Online prescribed textbooks for my subject	Yes 51	Yes 96%
	No 2	No 4%
Website for the school	Yes 3	Yes 6%
	No 50	No 94%

Table 8. The extend in which the participants use the ICT equipment (hardware and software)

Items	Never	Rarely	Sometimes	Often	All time	Never	Rarely	Sometimes	Often	All time
	Frequency					Percentage (%)				
Browse/search the internet to collect information to prepare lessons		7	1			7	2	0		
Browse/search the internet to collect resources to be used during lessons	3	3	2			5	5	2		
Use applications to prepare presentation for lessons	3	1	4			3	1	6		
Create your own digital material for students	0					5		5		
Use ICT to prepare exercises and tasks for students	1	1	5			7	3			
Use ICT to provide feedback and/or assess students' learning	1	1	5			0	1	8		
Evaluate digital learning resources in the subject you teach	1					7	3			
Download/upload/browse material from learning platform	2		1			0	1	1		
Look for online professional development opportunities	2	1				2	1	3	1	3
Prepare lesson plans using computer applications like word processing	5					9				

results that shows how to use computer aided instructional tools in supporting my subject (81%), Use of Technology tools can increase the interest of students toward learning (79%), Use of technologies can improve the quality of education (74%), ICT supported teaching can make learning more effective (70%), Use of computer aided instructional tools is very important (70%), Using instructional technologies can make teachers more productive (66%) and Students can easily understand concepts if ICT is integrated in the curriculum (62%) (Table 9).

Table 9. The participants' knowledge on the hardware and software

Item	None	Alittle	Somewhat	Alot
	Frequency and percentage (%)			
Capture and edit digital photos movies or other images	42	6	1	4
	79%	11%	2%	8%
Use email to communicate with others	9	8	6	30
	17%	15%	11%	57%
Produce a text using a word processing document	3	4	3	43
	6%	8%	6%	81%
Edit text online containing internet links and images	42	6	0	5
	79%	11%	0%	9%
Create database	38	9	2	4
	72%	17%	4%	8%
Use a spreadsheet (e.g. excel)	18	17	6	12
	34%	32%	11%	23%
Use spreadsheet to create graphs	18	19	4	12
	34%	36%	8%	23%
Create presentations with video or audio clips	37	5	6	5
	70%	9%	11%	9%
Download and install software on computer	19	20	7	7
	36%	38%	13%	13%
Participate in discussion forum on the internet	43	3	4	3
	81%	6%	8%	6%
Prepare material to use with an interactive whiteboard	46	4	1	2
	87%	8%	2%	4%
Download curriculum resources from the internet or learning platforms for student use	34	12	4	3
	64%	23%	8%	6%
Use students response systems (e.g. ActiVote, ActvExpression or other)	47	3	1	2
	89%	6%	2%	4%

Table 10. Teachers' perception on the use of computer aided instructional tools

Item	Strongly disagree	Disagree	Neutral	Agree	Strongly agree
	Frequency and percentage (%)				
Use of ICT for instructional purposes is very important	1 2%	1 2%	2 23%	12 23%	37 70%
Use of technology tools can increase the interest of students toward learning	2 4%	2 4%	1 2%	6 11%	42 79%
ICT supported teaching can make learning more effective	1 2%	1 2%	2 4%	12 23%	37 70%
I would like to be trained on how to use computer aided instructional tools in supporting my subject	1 2%	2 4%	1 2%	7 13%	43 81%
Use of technologies can improve the quality of education	1 2%	5 9%		9 17%	38 72%
Students can easily understand concepts if ICT is integrated in the curriculum	1 2%	6 11%	4 8%	8 15%	34 64%
Using instructional technologies can make teachers more productive	2	5	1	10	35

Table 11. Comparative analysis between TPCK and TDM

TPCK	TDM	Status	ICT competency that can be learned by teachers
Mastering learning through ICT	Transformation Mastering the use and design of technology	Not there	Teachers cannot create interactive tools and gaming; creation of 3D animation in education
Facilitating student learning with or through ICT	Infusion Understand when and how to use ICT	Designing ICT enabled lessons is not yet enhanced. Teachers lack the skill	Teachers still rely on chalk and board, manila to draw charts
ICT integrated in the subject teaching	Applying Learn how to use ICT in subject area	No Integrating ICT in lesson plans	No multimedia tools: graphic design of educational media is being used
Teachers learning about ICT	Emerging Realising need of ICT	Schools are equipped with computers and slow internet connectivity. Little is being done to enhance traditional teaching management using ICT	Computers are there for computer awareness lesson not for other subject areas. The school set up does not have an ICT policy that can be give other subject areas opportunity to use the computer lab

7 Conclusion and Future Scope of the Study

Base on the data analysis, most of Botswana Junior Secondary schools are at the following stages of TPACK and TDM model as shown in Table 11.

The study assessed the training of pedagogy use of computer aided instructional tools and it is clear from the teachers' responses that more than 90% teachers have not received any training. So, it is necessary to teach teachers how to incorporate technology in their teaching subject areas. The study revealed that ICT is offered as a subject in school meaning that students are taught computer basics like word processing, spreadsheet, and paint leaving out teacher development. Teachers' professional development should focus on pedagogy, content and technology. Unfortunately, most of the Botswana training institutes for teachers do not focus on the pedagogy principles which facilitate the use of ICT in supporting the delivery of the subject content. For this, model need monitoring and evaluation for it to work.

Infrastructure is one of the key elements that need to be in place for effective integration of ICT teaching and learning. Using hardware and software such as emails; web sites; digital audio, digital video, computer conferencing, interactive boards, developed educational software and individual learning environment can enable a learner to learn any time anywhere and empower the learner. It is also clear that teachers see the benefits of using computer aided instructional tools to support their traditional method of teaching and they are willing to be trained.

In the future, we will cover the study over the large population. We have performed the research in the Botswana region, we are planning to conduct the research in the neighboring countries as well. We only focused on the junior secondary schools in Botswana, we would like to conduct the study in higher level also.

Acknowledgement. The authors are thankful to management of Botho University, Gaborone to provide their support. We also grateful to management of Makhubu Secondary Schools to conduct the research in their organization.

References

1. Botswana IFAP Report: ICT Literacy Policy-Botswana Paris, 9th Session (2016)
2. Maitlamo: Botswana's National ICT policy legislative framework and change report. Botswana Government, Final Report 2004 (2014)
3. Bhatt, J.M.: Integrating information and communication technology in teacher Education, Vol 6, India (2016)
4. Adomi, E.E., Kpangban, E.: Application of ICT in Nigerian secondary schools. Library Philosophy and Practice 2010, Abraka, Delta State University (2010)
5. Mishra, P., Koehler, M.J.: Technological pedagogy knowledge content knowledge: the framework for teachers knowledge. Teach. Coll. Rec. **108**(6), 1017–1054 (2006)
6. Albirini, A.: Teachers attitude towards information and communication technologies. The case of Syrian EFL teachers. Comput. Educ. **47**(4), 373–378 (2006)
7. Esleem, M.B.: Relationship of selected factors and the level of computer use for instructional purposes by technology education teachers in Ohio public schools. A statewide survey (2003)
8. http://math.hws.edu/javamath/ryan/ChiSquare.html. Accessed 04 June 2017

Mining on the Basis of Similarity in Graph and Image Data

Vishal Srivastava$^{(\boxtimes)}$ and Bhaskar Biswas

IIT (BHU), Varanasi, India
vishalismdhanbad@gmail.com

Abstract. Data sets emanating from number of engineering and physical world realm can be depicted as the mutual or one way interaction within a graph like connected structure, in a quite common, robust and relevant way. This is precisely a real context in social graphs, notably the accustomed current advances in navigation in map based technologies, vision on biometrics and various web based application advances towards a disparate range of emerging social graphs and other networks. Careful scrutiny of such networks precisely results in diagnosis of potentially useful and interesting pattern in networks as well as their relative and combined growth. Some social structures of graphs and networks displays the robust commutable behaviour for any community,represented as graph. That is why an precise research plan is exits to describe and analyse the communities within the graph in the domain of community detection. Vast majority of graph based application also resilient in image and vision based application and mining in the field of geoinformation engineering and neural computation. In this paper we studied the graph based approaches for classification and clustering in graph based datasets subsequently we applied the approach in coloured images and identified the clustering trends in both types of data. Our study is completely uncovering the complex nature of graph based trend detection.

Keywords: Graph mining · Node classification
Dimension reduction · Kernal dimensionality reduction

1 Introduction

from past few year we have seen an overwhelming research and development in graph data from a variety of technical, social, medicine, and engineering domains. In the basic level, graph is collection of nodes an edges, converted from any real world problem. Examples are pipelines connecting oil stations across geographic locations, or an epidemic spreading across a population,random walk in particle swarm, business or work place relation by trust, weak or strong entities, and banking transactions. Graph data mining extract the valuable and robust knowledge from set of graph data and analyses our daily life problems and their possible outcomes. Often we analyse the data in graphical format when its huge

© Springer Nature Singapore Pte Ltd. 2019
A. K. Luhach et al. (Eds.); ICAICR 2018, CCIS 956, pp. 193–203, 2019.
https://doi.org/10.1007/978-981-13-0143-5_17

in nature and we want diffusion of any information across the graph. A failure in a transaction for a node can cause a series of failures in mandatory parts of whole banking system infrastructure. In the same way a computer virus can disrupt the working in organization at random places if we do not know the behaviour of spreading. In present work we have studied different type of method to simulate information in graph. Some graph clustering and classification methods are also discussed to apply machine learning methods in graph based mining.

2   Kernel Methods for Graph

in Kernel Method, The transformation of data in a problem's input data into a high-dimensional feature data space, allowing the performing of analysis algorithms on the transformed space. Consider the following feature space transformation for two-dimensional vectors $x = (x1; x2)$:

$$\phi(x) = (x_1^2, \sqrt{2}x_1x_2, x_2^2)$$

2.1   Some Common Kernel Functions

Polynomial:
$$(xy + \theta)^d$$

Gaussian RBF:
$$e^{\frac{(x-y)^2}{c}}$$

Sigmoidal:
$$tanh(\alpha(xy) + \theta)$$

$x.y = x_1y_1 + x_2y_2 + ...$ Consider the inner product of vectors in this new space:

$$\phi(u); \phi(v)i = (u_1^2v_1^2 + 2u_1u_2v_1v_2 + u_2^2v_2^2)$$
$$= (u_1v_1 + u_2v_2)^2$$
$$= (u.v)^2$$

3   Clustering in Graphs

classification in graphical data is a method, in which we assign different class labels to a large collection of data. However, if we do not know about labelling of data in graphical mode then finding similar nodes is always a problem? In such cases, we try to collect input data together by measurement of diffused value similarity. when we divide the data into small sub groups, each element in group has some informative similarity, is known as clustering, hence the method to find label in such kind of data is called unsupervised clustering.

Unsupervised Learning. The process of finding relationships in sets of unlabeled or unclassified data.

Clustering. The method of categorise a collection of input data into some over-lapping subsets, where data in each collection are somehow related to each other by some similarity measurement.

Clustering on graphs can take two forms, similar to graph classification: within-graph clustering and between-graph clustering. Within-graph clustering clusters the vertices within an individual graph, while between-graph clustering clusters sets of graphs, each based on some measure of similarity appropriate to the problem at hand. Graphical clustering methods are very useful and robust for different real world problems, where they can represented by a natural graph. network or graph data is one such example, where each vertex represents a user within the network, and relationships between users (such as being friends) are represented by edges. Clustering social networks can help identify people that are not related at present but have common characteristics, such as having a similar set of relations, or edges. This information can then be used to recommend new relationships to a person. Another example of within-graph clustering is in the field of bio-informatics, where the interaction of proteins of an organism can be represented as a network. Each vertex is a protein and an edge is placed between a pair of vertices if there is evidence that suggests an interaction between them.

3.1 Shared Nearest Neighbor Clustering

MST-based clustering defines similarity between vertices by the existence of high-weight edges and paths between vertex pairs. Removal of a possibly large number of edges results in loss of information in the resulting clusters. There-fore, a more general notion of similarity of vertex-vertex pairs can be captured through shared nearest neighbor (SNN) clustering, based on proximity measures of vertex pairs. Jarvis-Patrick clustering is a popular within-graph, shared near-est neighbor clustering algorithm. The algorithm has three main steps

1. If graph G is weighted, then preprocess G in two successive steps. In the first step all edges that fall below an input threshold ϕ are removed from G. In the second step, for each vertex only the k edges with the highest weight are retained. The new graph obtained after the two preprocessing steps is called the "nearest neighbor graph" GNN. If G is unweighted, call it GNN.
2. Transform GNN into GSNN, the shared "nearest neighbor" graph. GSNN is the weighted version of the GNN, where each edge weight represents the number of neighbors an adjacent vertex pair have in common.
3. Obtain the clusters by applying the threshold τ to GSNN, removing all edges in GSNN whose weight is $< \tau$. Then, the connected components from the resulting graph form the clusters.

4   Classification for Graph

Graphical data have numerous applications in domain of machine learning based classification. For example, DNA or nucleolus pattern can be represented as network, and various classification methods can be applied to predict properties, behaviour and DNA orientation. Images can also be represented in graphical form, and we have shown similarity based spectral and Laplace clustering in image data from Laplace graph. The information provided by graph can be used as diffusion in image grids, minimum energy based method for efficient clustering.

4.1 Classification Graphs and Vertices

Graph classification can be studied via from two kind of relations in graph, by graphical classification which measures between the graph relations or grouping in one part of complete graph also known as vertex classification or within the graph. Suitability depends upon the need of application.

Graph Classication. The classification of individual graphs.

Vertex Classification. The classification of individual vertices within a graph.

4.1.1 Graph Classification: The Direct Product Kernel

The derivation of a direct product kernel out turns in four steps:

1. Compute the direct product of the pair of input graphs.
2. Compute the decay constant using the maximum indegree and outdegree of the direct product graph.
3. Compute the geometric series of weighted walks.
4. Sum each value in the matrix and return the resulting value. First, the direct product of the two graphs is computed, denoted by $G1 \otimes G2$. As a reminder, the direct product of adjacency matrices $A_{M \times N}$ and $B_{P \times Q}$ is computed as follows:

$$\left\| \begin{matrix} a_{11}B & ... & a_{1n}B \\ .... & ... & .... \\ a_{m1}B & ..... & a_{mn}B \end{matrix} \right\|$$

where aB represents the multiplication between an element of matrix A, a, by the entire matrix B. If the graphs are unweighted, you can think of it as a copy of B everywhere there is a 1 in A, and a zero-matrix, otherwise. Next, we want to compute the decay constant, using direct product adjacency matrix A:

$$\gamma < \frac{1}{min((\delta + A), (\delta - A))} \tag{1}$$

the kernel value, given the direct product adjacency matrix A and decay constant:

$$k = \sum_{i,j}(I - \gamma(j))^{-}1 \tag{2}$$

Input: Ai and Aj : the adjacency matrices for graphs Gi and Gj
Output: Kernel function value k 1

$$A_{ij} = Ai \oplus Aj$$

2 Compute decay constant using Algorithm, with A_{ij}

3 $k = \sum_{i,j}(I - \gamma(j))^{-1}$

4 return k

Input D is a $p \times p$ direct product matrix of two graphs.
Output is γ Decay constant

$$maxIndegree = 0$$

$$maxOutdegree = 0$$

for each vertex $v_i \epsilon$ direct product matrix D do

$$outdegree = \Sigma_{j=1}^{p}D_{i,j}$$

$$indegree = \Sigma_{j=1}^{p}D_{j,i}$$

$$maxIndegree = max(indegree, maxIndegree)$$

$$maxOutdegree = max(outdegree, maxOutdegree)$$

$$end$$

return

5 Dimensionality Reduction Based on Multi Dimensional Scaling (MDS)

Visualization is an important requirement for graph mining applications in different disciplines, including biology, computer science, and chemistry, as well as several application domains such as social network analysis, computer network analysis, chemical bonding analysis, etc. For most of these applications, the datasets are huge, and the graph representations are non-planar in nature. The dataset may contain a set of graphs, where each network or sub graph represents a single data value, or one graph, where each node in the graph depict an isolate data value. Multidimensional scaling (MDS) can be used to visualize graphs by labelling the dataset in a two- or three-dimensional vector data in a way that the dwells away from (similar or dissimilar) between the graphs or node-edges, that are perpetuate. MDS can be thought of as a way to reduce the amount of data to the point where one can visually see the relationships between the different data objects in the set. The objective of MDS is to minimize the stress function.

stress: "Stress can be loosely defined as a function that represents the differences between the pairwise relationships of the objects in the transformed space relative to the original data".

The following sections describe the steps of MDS in detail.

Input: D is the distance matrix
Input: p is the dimensions in the projected space
Output: Y is the transformed matrix
1 Compute S by squaring D
2 compute GR by double centering $\frac{S}{2}$
3 Compute the eigenvalues $\wedge$ and eigenvectors Z^T from the eigenvalue decomposition of GR
4 Let $\wedge'$ be the p largest eigenvalues of $\wedge$
5 Let $\wedge'$ be the p largest eigenvalues of $\wedge$
6 Assign Z_p^T to be the corresponding p eigenvectors from Z^T
7 Compute $Y = \wedge_p^{\frac{1}{2}} . Z^T$
8 Return Y

5.1   Spectral Clustering

The algorithm uses the normalized graph Laplacian L, which is why we refer to this algorithm as the normalized spectral clustering algorithm. In simple words, the algorithm is:

Let $S \epsilon R^{n \times n}$ be the similarity index in the n data values $x1, x2.....xn$ where $s^{i,j}$ describes the spectral similarity between x_i and x_j. consider k to be the expected cluster count.
1. Derive a similarity graph having adjacency matrix W .
2. Find the unnormalized graph Laplacian $L = D - W$.
3. Find the principle k eigenvectors for $u1....uk$ of L.
4. suppose $U \epsilon R^{n \times k}$ is the data matrix having the data vectors $u1....uk$ as columns
5. For $i = 1......n$ consider $yi \epsilon R^k$ as the vector regarding the i-th row of U.
6. Group the points $(y_i)_{i=1}^n$ into clusters $C1.....Ck$ by k-means algorithm.   7. Find the clusters $A1....Ak$ by $Ai = (j|y_j \epsilon C_i)$.

6   Experimental Result

6.1   N-cut Based Spectral Clustering

Shi and malik has proposed a N-cut graph based spectral clustering algorithm for grouping of data. He treated the image based segmentation as a robust graph clustering problem and proposed a the normalized cut, for segmenting the graph. The normalized cut or N-cut criterion derives both the complete dissimilarity between the association of clusters as well as the total similarity within the clusters. shi-malik shown that an robust estimation technique based on a principle component based computation, can be used to solve the problem. We have bestowed this method to cluster the static data, hence found this method very

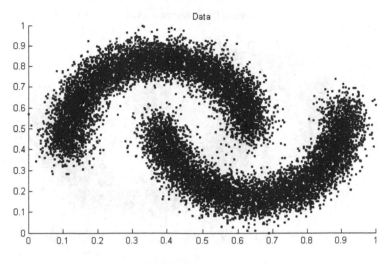

Fig. 1. Two moon

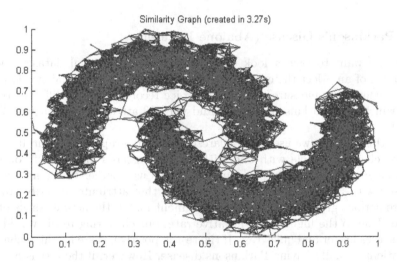

Fig. 2. Similarity graph of two moon data

encouraging for such problem solving. We have applied spectral clustering shi-malik algorithm on examples like toy, half moon, to see how well spectral clustering works on them.

6.2   The Half Moon Dataset

The half-moons toy example consists of two to the human eye obvious clusters which are in the shape of semi-circles. This is an useful example to test clustering algorithms on, as it will test their ability to separate clusters with geometrically non-trivial shapes that are not completely separated through a higher dimension. In our case, each half-moon consists of roughly 7:500 points.

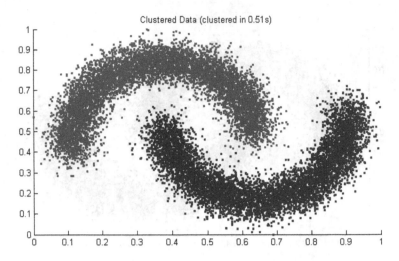

Fig. 3. Clustering in two clusters of two moon data

6.3   Parkinson's Disease (Abalone Dataset)

Lastly, we want to take a look on a more high-dimensional dataset and see how much of an eUect the curse of dimensionality takes. For that, we look at a dataset containing measurements of 195 voice recordings of 31 different people, 23 of which with Parkinson's disease and with 23 attributes per datum (Figs. 1 and 2).

For this dataset, we used a 12-nearest neighbors graph and naturally looked for two clusters: people with and without Parkinsons's disease. Of course we didn't take the attribute into account that tells us whether the sample is from a person with Parkinson's or not, but we used that attribute to verify how well our predictions given by the cluster assignment match the actual status of that person. Due to the higher false negative rate, our clustering result would most likely serves better and quick test. If the test is positive, there is a high chance of the patient actually having Parkinsons disease. However, if the test is negative, we shouldn't conclude that the patient probably is healthy, but rather go on with a maybe more complicated test.

Parkinson dataset is collection of voice samples of 31 people of whom 23 infected with Parkinson's disease (PD). Every column in the dataset is a different kind of voice sample, and each row depicts the, one of 195 voice samples from these sets. The motto of dataset is to discriminate the non-infected persons to infected one's, which is a value of 0 for non PD and 1 for PD one's. We also performed Unsupervised clustering of the two-moon dataset. Each moon has 1,000 data values in respective space. Figure 3 is the result given by the spectral clustering method of Shi and Malik. Graphs Laplacians is mainly used in both clustering and image mining. In clustering, the most popular algorithm we have used is spectral clustering, which first does a spectral embedding of the original data, and then applies k-means to the transform domain. In image mining, the

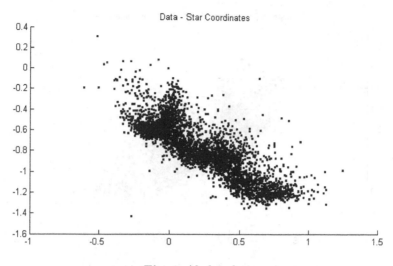

Fig. 4. Abalon data

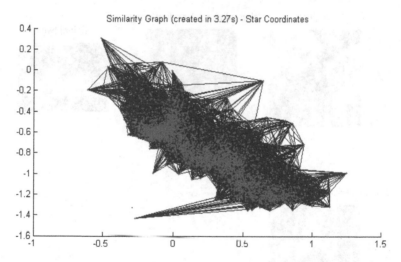

Fig. 5. Similarity graph of two set of nodes in parkinson data

Graph Laplacian is mainly used as a non-local smoothing term $X^T LX$ to boost the performance in images with lots of self-similarities. Recently, several new algorithms using the graph Laplacian has been proposed by number of authors. Unlike methods before, these algorithms aims to approximately minimize the full Graph-Cut energy, and have showned to outperform the standard algorithms mentioned here. These methods also have their origins in the area of PDE's and material science, and can be seen as an elegant connection between the world of machine learning and differential equation (Figs. 4 and 5).

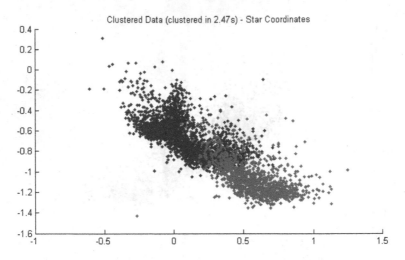

Fig. 6. Clustering of two sets in parkinson data

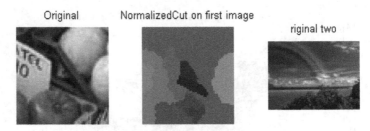

Original   NormalizedCut on first image   riginal two

NormalizedCut on second image

Fig. 7. Images after N-cut spectral clustering

6.4 N-Cut Based Spectral Clustering on Image Data

Spectral clustering based algorithm is applied for image segmentation based on spatial and spectral color values. In the monocular case, we derived the graph$G\epsilon(V, E)$ y considering each spectral value as a node and allocate the edge weight w_{ij} between node i and j with Laplace beltway operator as the product of a pixel similarity term and spatial contiguity term (Fig. 6). Results are depicting completely the normalized cut notion of segmentation in graph and images. Normalized cut is an impartial allotment of separation among the sub graphs in a complete network. It persist the unbiased property that minimum N-cut edges precisely to maximize the normal cooperation, which is a fair allowance for cumulative association within the sub graphs. We have shown that a generalized eigenvalue environment caters the optimum solution for N-cut based problem and finds the efficient algorithm for computation of minimum N-cut (Fig. 7).

7 Conclusion

In this paper, we studied the clustering algorithm based on local similarity of pixels, that are preprocess in such a way to represent the global features of graph and image. By considering the clustering problem as a graph partitioning set, we reproduced normalized cut criteria proposed by shi and malik for clustering the Laplace graph. Normalized cut is an impartial measurement of similarity between sub graphs of a complete graph. It contains the robust quality that minimizes the N-cut undergoes precisely by maximizing the generated associations, which is an impartial allotment for clustering within the sub graphs. For finding out an robust method of calculating the minimized normalized cut, we have generalised that a common eigenvalue solution provides real valued solution to our problem. A derivation based method on this idea is developed and bestowed the segmentation of spatial, and spectral value of images. Results of experiments on graph and images are very promising and explaining the normalized cut assumption completely satisfy our initial study objective.

References

1. Atkinson, M.D., Sack, J.-R., Santoro, N., Strothotte, T.: Minmax heaps and generalized priority queues. Commun. ACM **29**(10), 9961000 (1986)
2. Bach, F.R., Jordan, M.I.: Spectral clustering for speech separation. In: Automatic Speech and Speaker Recognition: Large Margin and Kernel Methods. Wiley, Chichester (2009)
3. Blake, C., Keogh, E., Merz, C.J.: UCI repository of machine learning databases. University of California, Department of Information and Computer Science, Irvine, CA (1998)
4. Golub, G.H., Van Loan, C.F.: Matrix Computations. JHU Press, Baltimore (1996)
5. Horn, R.A., Johnson, C.R.: Topics in Matrix Analysis. Cambridge University Press, Cambridge (1985)
6. Kandogan, E.: Visualizing multi-dimensional clusters, trends, and outliers using star coordinates. In: The proceedings of ACM SIGKDD2001, pp. 107–116 (2001)
7. Rousseeuw, P.J.: Silhouettes: a graphical aid to the interpretation and validation of cluster analysis. Comput. Appl. Math. **20**, 5365 (1987)
8. Saad, Y.: Numerical Methods for Large Eigenvalue Problems, 2nd edn. Manchester University Press, Manchester (2011)
9. Shi, J., Malik, J.: Normalized cuts and image segmentation. IEEE Trans. Pattern Anal. Mach. Intell. **22**(8), 888–905 (2000)
10. Song, Y., Chen, W.-Y., Bai, H., Lin, C.-J., Chang, E.Y.: Parallel spectral clustering. IEEE Trans. Pattern Anal. Mach. Intell. **33**(3), 568–586 (2011)
11. Yan, D., Huang, L., Jordan, M.I.: Fast approximate spectral clustering. In: 15th ACM Conference on Knowledge Discovery and Data Mining (SIGKDD) (2009)

HESSIS: Hybrid Encryption Scheme for Secure Image Sharing in a Cloud Environment

Jaspreet Kaur$^{(\boxtimes)}$ and Sumit Sharma

Department of Computer Science and Engineering, Chandigarh University,
Gharuan, Mohali, India
jaspreetkaurpaul@gmail.com, cu.sumitsharma@gmail.com

Abstract. Cloud computing has appeared as a new computing paradigm that offers a great possibility of storing information remotely. Advancements in this new technology have reduced computational cost, the expense for requisition hosting, computation, content delivery, and storage. Cloud has many advantages but has issues or threats also. Alongside that mobile devices are making major changes in the world. Users share their confidential information on an unsecured channel which is vulnerable to attack. Security is fundamental concern over cloud computing and Cryptography is one of the best techniques for protection. The main focus of this research work is to provide the high-level security to data while storing on the cloud. In existing work, security is provided to images but that security is not high level and encryption/ decryption time also increased. In this research work, a hybrid algorithm 'HESSIS' is proposed to secure data while sharing. In this proposed scheme Secure hashing algorithm-3, Elliptic Curve and Advanced encryption algorithm are combined to enhance the security. Parameters calculated are index building time, candidate selection time, and accuracy.

Keywords: Cryptography · Cloud computing · AES · SHA-3
ECC · Security

1 Introduction

Cloud computing (CC) [1] is a large pool of computing paradigms in which a number of services are provided according to the user requirements. Systems are connected in different networks such as private & public for providing the infrastructure for user applications, files, and data storage, and these infrastructures are dynamically scalable [2]. Advancements in this new technology have reduced computational cost, the cost of application hosting, computation, content delivery, and storage. This is just a platform for the economical, simple storage & computing power [3]. It became a central hub and responsible for extensive and fast data analytics/processing [4], on-demand data dissemination, and massive new data generation [5].

As compared to a distributed server in cloud server all the facilities presented by the cloud are handled by the CSP (cloud service providers) [1, 6]. Cloud provides the various features to their clients or users such as high performance, data flexibility, security of data, cost savings, disaster recovery etc. [7]. But the security which is

© Springer Nature Singapore Pte Ltd. 2019
A. K. Luhach et al. (Eds.): ICAICR 2018, CCIS 956, pp. 204–216, 2019.
https://doi.org/10.1007/978-981-13-3143-5_18

provided by the cloud is not sufficient (semi-trusted) to protect personal as well as confidential information from unauthorized access. Hackers can hack the user's cloud account and view or access their confidential information. To the users or clients, the cloud is naturally not secure or reliable furthermore this postures new challenges to the integrity, confidentiality, and availability [8] of users data over cloud computing. For providing the high security to the user data superlative approach is to store all the data in an encrypted form or unreadable form.

1.1 Cryptography

Cryptography [9, 10] is the superlative approach for the protection of user's data from any unauthorized access. It ensures the confidentiality of the data, the integrity of data, availability of data, authentication. There are number of algorithms available which can help users or organizations to protect their confidential data. Basically, cryptographic algorithms translate the real form data into encrypted (ciphertext) form. This transformation by cryptography is performing on some mathematical calculations.

In cryptography, 2-types of encryption methods are used such as encryption and hashing algorithms. Encryption type further has two types i.e. encryption algorithms symmetric (private) key and asymmetric (public) key. Symmetric (private) key processes are AES (Advance encryption standard) [11, 12], Blowfish, DES (distributed encryption standard), 3DES, RSA (Rivest Shamir Adleman) [13–16], BRA (Byte Rotation Algorithm) [17], RC4 (Rivest Cipher), RC5 [18] etc. Asymmetric (public) key algorithms are Elliptic curve (EC) cryptography [19], PKCS (Public-key Cryptography Standards), DH (Diffie-Hillman) [20], DSA (digital signature algorithm) [20] etc.

Hashing algorithms transform the data into a numeric string (fixed length). Hash value is small digest of the original data. The difference among the hashing and encryption algorithms are just encryption converts the coded data into its real form but the hash doesn't. Hashing algorithms are SHA-1(Secure hash algorithm), MD-5 (Message Digest) [21], SHA-2, SHA-3 [22] etc. A hash function (HF) uses some mathematical transformations to encrypt the user data. HF uses a hash value instead of any key. HF is used to check the integrity of our message. It ensures that message which is shared with other client isn't altered or infected with the virus.

For secure sharing, encoding algorithms convert the real user image or data using encryption algorithms and encryption key, and at the client side, [23] it converts the cipher image or data into real form by using decryption algorithms and decryption key (Fig. 1).

For maintaining the security level of a confidential data conventional techniques of encryptions are not sufficient. In this way, it is paramount to apply an effective and powerful encoding/decoding technique on data to enhance its security level so that no unauthorized person can use data for any malicious purpose. Steganography is also another way to hide the information, this technique hides the secret into an envelope and the only authorized person knows that secret. The huge amount of data is stored in the cloud by different users and that data is highly correlated. This is a time when everyone has their own mobile phones and they like to click pictures of different locations, building, hills, different sites etc. and then upload it to the cloud. It generates the correlated pictures in the cloud because multiple users upload same place image with different views and angles. When users want to share any image with other users they first upload the full-size image in the cloud and then share it. But it can increase the uploading time, transmission

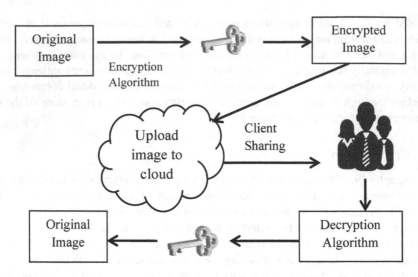

Fig. 1. Secure image sharing

time and cost while image selection and then sharing. So for sharing the original large size image just find the correlated images in the cloud and shared that image with other. For finding the correlated images just upload the small portion of the large-sized image and apply feature matching algorithm i.e. SURF algorithm [24] and extract the features, if features of that small image are matched with more than one image then all the correlated images are decrypted at the user end. With upload the small portion of the large size image, save the time and cost of uploading image.

In the existing system, AES is utilized for encoding and decoding purpose with a SHA-1 hashing algorithm. But this algorithm is not provided the high security for storing the images in the cloud. In the existing system, bandwidth consumption is saving up to 90% but the encryption and decoding time is increased. In proposed work, hybrid algorithms are used to enhance the security level of image store and increase the performance of downloading from the cloud. For hybrid algorithms, AES, SHA-3 and ECC algorithms are used.

2   Related Work

Cloud service providers provide cloud space for the multimedia data storage. Various traditional security algorithms are proposed by many authors for securing data while sharing. Cryptographic algorithms are best used by researchers and they improve the performance of the single algorithm with the use of some other cryptography algorithm. In this section, we provide the different improve versions of cryptographic algorithms.

Cui et al., proposed a secure and mobile-friendly design for mobile clients. In this paper, the author uses hybrid mechanisms [25] of AES and SHA to provide the security to the multimedia data store in the cloud. The author proposed a system in which multiples images of a same place or site can be stored in cloud server and when the user wants to share any new image with other users they first search the relevant images which are correlated and then shared. By using this system users can save data transmission as well as bandwidth, and energy consumption. Parameters calculated such as index building time, candidate selection time, saving bandwidth. The main focus of author is only on the security guarantees of candidate selection time.

Bala and Kamboj proposed a hybrid algorithm [26] for high-level security to data. They used cryptography with steganography because both the techniques are very popular in security point of view. In this hybrid algorithm provide the security to every block or part of the data. In this paper symmetric algorithms AES, BRA, RC6, and blowfish are hybrid for secure block-wise information. In this multithreading, a method is used for the different part to encrypt and used a different algorithm. Steganography used to insert the encryption keys into the cover image and that cover image (stego) is sent via email to validate the user. Data integrity is ensured using SHA-1 algorithm. At the end parameters which are accomplished are high security, the integrity of data, authentication, low delay, and confidentiality.

Mahalle and Shahade presented a hybrid cryptography method. In this, they used AES and RSA symmetric/asymmetric key algorithms for building hybrid algorithm [27]. For securing the data proposed system used 3 keys for the data encode and decode purpose. AES key and RSA public keys are used to upload the encrypted form on cloud and RSA private and AES key used for downloading the cipher form and convert that into real one.

Three algorithms are used by Gora et al. for hybrid algorithm implementation [28]. Authors used digital signature, blowfish and SHA algorithms for achieving a level of security to data in the cloud. For authentication purpose digital signature used, for the integrity of data SHA used and for confidentiality blowfish used. Blowfish has used a single key for encoding and decoding the data with least amount of time. The objective of this technique is for achieving high security to upload and downloads data to/from the cloud. This resolves the authentication, security, confidentiality concerns.

Mitri et al. presented an approach which ensures the security in the cloud. Whenever utilize makes an exertion will transfer information for the cloud that files saved onto directory for short duration of the time [29]. After applying keys files are converted into the encoded structure and saved with respect to a cloud server. Merits of this algorithm need aid information integrity, security, secrecy what's more accessibility. Disadvantages for RSA calculation is huge amount time vital for data encrypt and decode.

There are various challenges in media data sharing which is address by Wang [30] and proposed a secure sharing framework and watermarking schemes for protecting user data in the cloud. Challenges like large-sized data, upload/download multi-resolution images/videos, failure in authentication security due to error-prone (EP) wireless environment. Proposed secure sharing framework enables the user to share multiple images on different clouds. Using watermarking scheme authentication of the data is ensuring while sharing data between users and cloud.

From this survey, we concluded that each cryptographic algorithm has different properties and functionalities. To ensure the security SHA algorithm is best for integrity, for confidentiality and AES, blowfish is best.

3 Proposed Methodology

This section provides the framework setup that empowers the cloud to provide security guaranteed what's more versatile and image sharing services. In this point, the users outsourced the encrypted data in the cloud which containing the encrypted pictures, related title, and key. This allows the users to access the user choice data with valid id. Users upload all the encrypted images in the cloud and at client side authorized users can access the choice images. They first upload the small part of the chosen image and the system will search the correlated images in the database. If the features of choice image will be matched with more than one image then all the correlated images will be displayed at client window. The proposed system is developed in MATLAB [31] and for storing and sharing the images in cloud dropbox cloud is used. Dropbox works across heterogeneous platforms including Linux, iOS, Microsoft Windows, Mac OS, Blackberry, and Android. Dropbox permits sharing stored images with others, and file revisions. For comparing the images we use dataset "INRIA Holiday" [32]. In this dataset, high-resolution images are stored with different views and scale of the same scene and place.

3.1 Secure Hash Algorithm

SHA-3 is hashing algorithm which is used to generate a small message digest of the large data. It supports four hash function such as SHA-3 224, 256, 384, and 512. For the security reasons, these hash functions are used for the authentication purpose of the data. The hash value or message digest is generated by a hash function are of fixed sized and short from the original one. Every algorithm needs some hashing techniques to find the unique properties and design a key pair for uploaded data. In proposed architecture is using a SHA3 hashing technique to enhance the working of ECC algorithm and secure key pair generation process.

3.2 Elliptic Curve Cryptography

ECC algorithm is utilized for the generation of two keys one is for encryption and other is for decryption. Key generation is fast in ECC. While maintaining the performance this algorithm ensures the highest security level. The ECC algorithm generates a pair of keys and system exchange the keys with AES encryption process. This process makes the encryption process more secure as compare to other techniques and decrease the probability of decryption at the time of un-authorization. The system extracts all bytes of an uploaded image and generates keys for the uploaded data. Also generated the key is shared with the destination end for decryption process to complete the transmission process.

3.3 Advanced Encryption Algorithm

AES algorithm uses a single key for encrypt and decrypt the data. AES key length is 128, 192, and 256. As AES is utilized broadly nowadays, for security purpose of the cloud. A number of rounds of AES are depending upon the key length 10 for 128, 12 for 192, and 14 for 256. System designs a block-wise encryption process and AES algorithm encrypts a file with the help of exchanged keys to transmit over the cloud environment. At the destination end system accessed the secure key and decrypt user choice of file to complete the transmission (Fig. 2).

This is a security model which combines the symmetric and asymmetric functionalities and security of image sharing will be improved. Also a time of encryption and decryption the images improved. SHA-1 hash is very long and a number of rounds

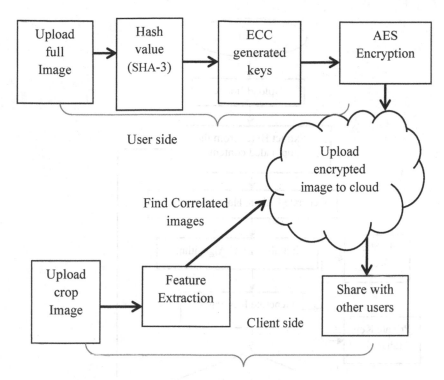

Fig. 2. Security model

to generate that hash value are also very large but SHA-3 (256) hash value is small and rounds also less as compared to SHA-1. The key generation time of ECC also very fast. In proposed system hashing is perform first to generate the hash value to compute the distinctive secret key, after that using ECC algorithm generate the key pair which then passed to AES to encoding and decoding time. Encrypted images will be uploading in the cloud with their secret key and user choice images will be downloaded by only authorized users. Various steps

Step 1: Upload full size image
Step 2: Apply SHA algorithm and generate hash value
Step 3: Generate key pair using ECC algorithm
Step 4: Apply AES encryption algorithm
Step 5: Upload encrypted images on cloud
Step 6: Upload cropped image
Step 7: Apply feature extraction
Step 8: Find correlated images out of uploaded images
Step 9: Share with client

3.4 Proposed Flowchart

(See Fig. 3)

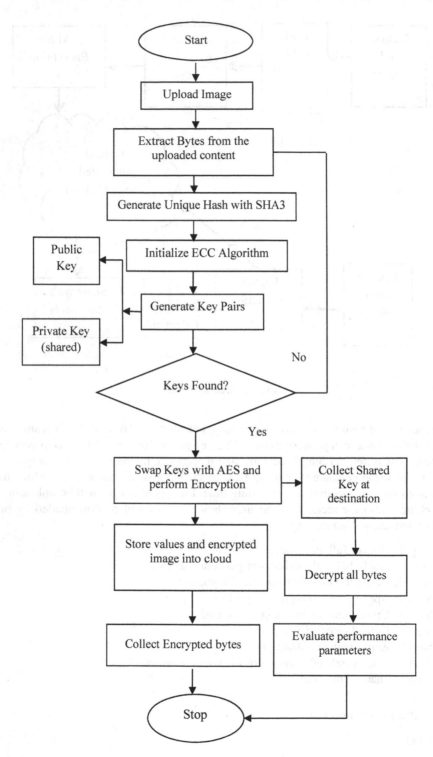

Fig. 3. Proposed flowchart

4   Experimental Setup

To perform the encryption/decryption task, data set which contains high resolution and high quality images are used. Simulation tool 'MATLAB' is used to build the hybrid algorithm. Researchers investigates that cryptography is one of the best way for providing the security to confidential data. Cryptography is important technique to ensure the security measurements such as integrity, reliability, availability and authorization of the data. Commonly used cryptography technique is AES for encryption and for hashing MD5 and SHA techniques are used. 'INRIA Holiday' data set is used by various researchers in their research work. In this data set images of different locations and with different-different views with high quality and resolution are stored.

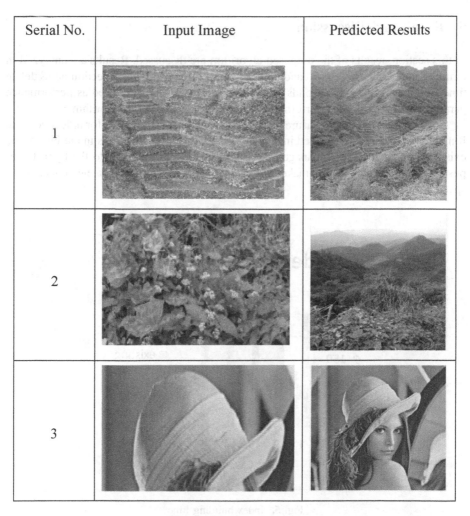

Fig. 4. Various test cases

4.1 Dataset

In proposed research work INRIA Holidays data set is used. This data set will be a set about pictures which mostly contains personal holiday's photographs. The remaining photos were tackled motivation to test the different attacks robustness: blurring, viewpoint, rotations and illumination changes, etc. In this dataset incorporates a vast mixture for scene types (man-made scenes, natural scenes, forest scenes, hills, fire and water effects, etc.) and all of these photographs are in good and high resolution. 500 images group are present in this dataset, and each of them represents different object or scenes. Size of Dataset is 1.1 GB and 1.6 GB (Fig. 4).

This figure shows the different test cases apply on different images. Input image is a cropped image and output is full image finds from the database of cloud highly correlated image.

5 Result and Discussion

In this section, results of the proposed algorithm are discussed. Results are analyzed in terms of index building time, candidate selection time, candidate selection add&delete time in term of ms (milli seconds) and accuracy. These four are used as performance parameters to measure the performance of the proposed hybrid algorithm.

Secure index building measurement is used to build secure index for uploaded data. It manages clusters of encrypted image and their extracted feature. As in the Fig. 5, the existing approach for this management is time taking as compare to the hybrid proposed algorithm. This feature makes the storage and extraction of data elements in high speed.

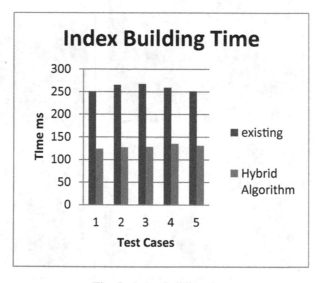

Fig. 5. Index building time

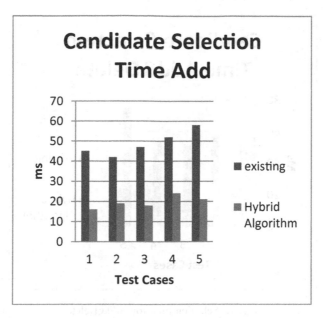

Fig. 6. Selection time for Add

The candidate selection time is used to find the image interest with stored database. This feature is measured with the help of add operation which provides also high speed as compared to the existing algorithms. This section compares the features and provides high-speed matching in very short span of time. When a user uploads an image and system find a various related image from the database. Now selection of a highly matched image and measurement of that section become high speed with the use of proposed architecture (Fig. 6).

The candidate selection time for various operations with stored database is one of the important factors in this research. This factor provides test cases facility for verification of all the phases of the proposed architecture. Here the time consumption of the proposed architecture to perform this operation is less time consuming as compare to the existing one (Fig. 7).

Accuracy factor is used to check the working of the proposed architecture with various users and images dataset. Here the proposed architecture shows high accuracy factor for retrieve images as per the user interests. Proposed architecture shows stable accuracy for all the test cases (Fig. 8).

In this chapter the various results and their comparison shows difference between the performance of proposed hybrid algorithm and existing technique. With the use of hybrid approach the image sharing process in mobile cloud become more accurate and high in security with better management of backend processes. Various parameters like index building, candidate selection time and accuracy show the enhancement of hybrid technique provide highly accurate image sharing in less time consumption.

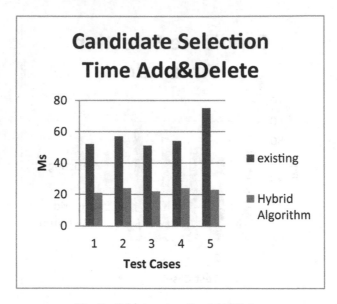

Fig. 7. Selection time for Add&Delete

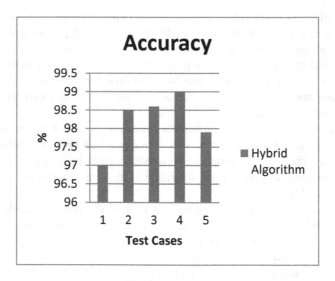

Fig. 8. Accuracy

6 Conclusion

The proposed hybrid algorithm in this paper is suitable for image store and downloads to/from cloud storage with high security and provided integrity, confidentiality, and authentication of data. For hybrid algorithm AES, SHA-3, and ECC cryptographic algorithms are used, all of three are very popular in term of security. Images are encrypted using a hybrid algorithm and then upload on the cloud. Before uploading first hashing is performing which ensure integrity, encryption using ECC and AES ensure confidentiality and at client side decrypted images are download ensure data authenticity. In this paper, we enhance the security and time for encrypt/decrypt data. For future work, feature extraction time can be improved. From the proposed hybrid algorithm for secure image sharing, clearly understood that this hybrid algorithm provide the high security for image sharing and time for encryption and decryption the image also decreases. Highly correlated images found from the cloud database and this can save the transmission cost and time. Results prove that proposed algorithm is more secure, efficient.

References

1. Mell, P., Grance, T.: SP 800-145. The NIST definition of cloud computing. NIST Special Publication (2011)
2. Armbrust, M., et al.: A view of cloud computing. Commun. ACM, **53**(4), 50 (2010)
3. CLOUD COMPUTING – An Overview. Torry Harris. http://www.thbs.com/downloads/Cloud-Computing-Overview.pdf
4. Sunyaev, A., Schneider, S.: Cloud services certification. Commun. ACM **56**(2), 33 (2013)
5. Cui, H., Yuan, X., Wang, C.: Harnessing encrypted data in cloud for secure and efficient image sharing from mobile devices. In: IEEE International Conference on Computer Communication, pp. 2659–2667 (2015)
6. Alhanahnah, M., Bertok, P., Tari, Z.: Trusting cloud service providers: trust phases and a taxonomy of trust factors. IEEE Cloud Comput. **4**(1), 44–54 (2017)
7. Singh, S., Jeong, Y.S., Park, J.: A survey on cloud computing security: Issues, threats, and solutions. J. Netw. Comput. Appl. **75**, 200–222 (2016)
8. Devi, T., San, R.G.: Data security frameworks in cloud. In: IEEE International Conference on Science, Engineering and Management Research (2014)
9. Kessler, G.C.: An Overview of Cryptography. Auerbach (2018)
10. Sharma, S., Gupta, Y.: Study on cryptography and techniques. Int. J. Sci. Res. Comput. Sci. Eng. Inf. Technol. **2**(1), 249–252 (2017)
11. Kumar, P., Rana, S.: Development of modified AES algorithm for data security. Opt.-Int. J. Light. Electron Opt. **127**(4), 2341–2345 (2016)
12. Kakade, V., Kirve, A., Bhoir, A., Kadam, S.: Enhancing distributed data storage security for cloud computing using AES algorithm. IJARCCE **6**(3), 752–755 (2017)
13. Mathur, N., Bansode, R.: AES based text encryption using 12 rounds with dynamic key selection. Procedia Comput. Sci. **79**, 1036–1043 (2016)
14. Kaur, J., Bagga, S.: Hybrid model of RSA, AES and blowfish to enhance cloud security. Int. J. Comput. Technol. **14**(9), 6059–6066 (2015)
15. Arora, R., Parashar, A.: Secure user data in cloud computing using encryption algorithms. Int. J. Eng. Res. Appl. **3**(4), 1922–1926 (2013)
16. Patil, P., Narayankar, P., Narayan, D.G., Meena, S.M.: A comprehensive evaluation of cryptographic algorithms: DES, 3DES, AES RSA and Blowfish. Procedia Comput. Sci. **78**, 617–624 (2016)
17. Gulhane, K.V., Dalvi, G.D.: Low latency for file encryption and decryption using BRA algorithm for secure transmission of data. Int. J. Sci. Res. **5**(12), 1531–1535 (2016)

18. Rivest, R.L.: The RC5 encryption algorithm. In: Preneel, B. (ed.) FSE 1994. LNCS, vol. 1008, pp. 86–96. Springer, Heidelberg (1995). https://doi.org/10.1007/3-540-60590-8_7
19. Thompson, D.: Elliptic Curve Cryptography (2016)
20. Gajra, N., Khan, S.S., Rane, P.: Private cloud security: secured user authentication by using enhanced hybrid algorithm. In: Advances in Communication and Computing Technologies (2014)
21. Ora, P., Pal, P.: Data security and integrity in cloud computing based on RSA partial homomorphic and MD5 cryptography. In: 2015 International Conference on Computer, Communication and Control (IC4) (2015)
22. Debnath, S., Chattopadhyay, A., Dutta, S.: Brief review on journey of secured hash algorithms. In: 2017 4th International Conference on Opto-Electronics and Applied Optics (Optronix) (2017)
23. Kaur, J., Sharma, S.: Secure image sharing on cloud using cryptographic algorithms: survey. Int. J. Future Revolut. Comput. Sci. Commun. Eng. 4(2), 319–325 (2018)
24. Pang, Y., Li, W., Yuan, Y., Pan, J.: Fully affine invariant SURF for image matching. Neurocomputing 85, 6–10 (2012)
25. Cui, H., Yuan, X., Wang, C.: Harnessing encrypted data in cloud for secure and efficient mobile image sharing. IEEE Trans. Mob. Comput. 16(5), 1315–1329 (2017)
26. Bala, B., Kamboj, L.: Secure file storage in cloud computing using hybrid cryptography algorithm. Int. J. Adv. Res. Comput. Sci. 9(2), 773–776 (2018)
27. Mahalle, V.S., Shahade, A.K.: Enhancing the data security in cloud by implementing hybrid (RSA & AES) encryption algorithm. In: International Conference on IEEE Power, Automation and Communication (INPAC), pp. 146–149 (2014)
28. Gore, A., Meena, S.S., Purohit, P.: Hybrid cryptosystem using modified blowfish algorithm and SHA algorithm on public cloud. Int. J. Comput. Appl. 155(3) (2016)
29. Maitri, P.V., Verma, A.: Secure file storage in cloud computing using hybrid cryptography algorithm. In: 2016 International Conference on Wireless Communications, Signal Processing and Networking (WiSPNET) (2016)
30. Wang, H., Wu, S., Chen, M., Wang, W.: Security protection between users and the mobile media cloud. IEEE Commun. Mag. 52(3), 73–79 (2014)
31. Higham, D.J., Higham, N.J.: MATLAB Guide, vol. 150. SIAM (2016)
32. Jegou, H., Douze, M., Schmid, C.: Inria holiday dataset (2008). http://lear.inrialpes.fr/people/jegou/data.php

Decision Support System for Plant Disease Identification

Sachin Prabhu Thandapani[1,2], Subikshaa Senthilkumar[1,2],
and S. Shanmuga Priya[1,2(✉)]

[1] Department of Computer Science and Engineering,
Amrita School of Engineering, Coimbatore, India
{cb.en.u4cse14441,
cb.en.u4cse14451}@cb.students.amrita.edu,
ss_priya@cb.amrita.edu
[2] Amrita Vishwa Vidyapeetham, Coimbatore, India

Abstract. The significance of agriculture in India and the amount of damage to the sector due to plant diseases, calls for a system which can identify plant diseases accurately. Improper identification of diseases and taking wrong measures to prevent the disease will be cost inefficient and time consuming. There are highly accurate existing techniques to identify plant diseases but they are specific to a particular crop. In this project, a generic system is developed to identify plant diseases accurately based on textual description of plant diseases. Dataset containing description of diseases is created using the concept of web scraping. The dataset is preprocessed where, keywords are extracted, categorized and grouped to obtain the list of symptoms from the disease description. Based on the symptoms provided by the user to the system, plant disease is identified and the output is the identified disease along with preventive measures.

Keywords: Decision support system · Plant disease identification
Grouping keywords · Rice disease

1 Introduction

Agricultural sector plays a vital role in contributing towards country's health and economy. Major variation in the climatic conditions which is not expected for a seasonal plant, has led to the arrival of pest and diseases. One of the major challenge faced by the farmers in the current scenario is that the proper care at the earlier stage will not affect the quantity and quality of the plant. Naked eye observation is common and an easy method to identify the diseases. But, these observations require continuous monitoring and high expertise in that field thereby failing to produce accurate results. Hence, identification of plant diseases is important as well as difficult. The proposed system focuses on addressing this issue. The advantage of using automatic detection technique is the significant reduction in cost as well as achieving high level of accuracy.

© Springer Nature Singapore Pte Ltd. 2019
A. K. Luhach et al. (Eds.): ICAICR 2018, CCIS 956, pp. 217–229, 2019.
https://doi.org/10.1007/978-981-13-3143-5_19

We intend to create a system that helps farmer identify plant diseases based on textual description and obtain relevant measures for treatment. Various symptoms of a plant disease is obtained from the user. These symptoms are compared with the existing dataset containing plant diseases and their corresponding symptoms. Identified disease is provided to the user along with various preventive measures and methods for treatment.

The project uses web scraping technique to create dataset containing textual descriptions of plant diseases. Keywords are extracted from this dataset based on NLP techniques and various features. To increase the frequency of keywords in the document, textual description of plant diseases are scrapped from multiple websites. Extracted keywords are classified based on various predefined categories. Keywords are then grouped using distance and frequency measures. List of symptoms for each disease are generated and a novel approach is used to identify the plant disease or possible plant diseases. Users are provided with preventive measures scrapped from websites and based on user's requirements, they are connected to a website elaborating the symptoms of the disease.

The paper is organized as follows. Section 2 gives the reason for why the system has been developed. Section 3 examines various existing techniques and the limitations of them. Section 4 discusses the architecture of the system. Section 5 contains background information required to achieve the goals of this work and an overview of the system. In Sect. 6 screenshots of the system describing its functions are provided. Section 7 discusses of future work and Sect. 8 concludes the work.

2 Motivation

Identifying plant diseases is very crucial as it causes great deal of damage to the crops and thus affecting the agricultural sector. Identifying the plant diseases at the right time accurately is essential because, failing to identify the plant disease at the right time will lead to damaging crops beyond repair. Also wrongly identifying the plant disease will cause improper treatment of the disease which is both waste of crops and money. There are many existing tools to identify the plant's disease using image processing techniques [1, 2] or developing a knowledge base for rule based approach [3–5]. These systems have their limitations and thus requires development of a system without requirement for a camera or need to develop a knowledge base specific to certain plant disease. Hence, a technique is devised in this work that can identify the plant's disease accurately with just textual descriptions of the disease.

3 Related Works

Plant disease identification is a task of finding the right plant disease using the given symptoms. Earlier plant disease identification or classification techniques are mostly image based where the user is asked to provide the image of the affected plant to the system.

In the work by Singh and Misra [1], plant leaf diseases are identified using image segmentation and soft computing techniques. Plant disease is identified using image processing technique. The image of the plant is taken, quality improved by increasing the contrast and preprocessing techniques are applied to segment the affected parts. Green colored pixels are masked, threshold values are set and features are identified. But increasing the quality of the image alters the image, thus providing inaccurate results. Also, using only the green colored pixels is a drawback since other major symptoms contributing to the plant's disease are ignored. Johannes et al. [2] proposed a system for diagnosing plant disease using mobile capture devices, applied on a wheat use case. This method uses image processing techniques to identify the plant disease. Images of plant during early stages of disease is taken. Leaf is clipped from the image, segmented and analyzed. The features obtained from the process is then compared with the disease detection inference model, processed by meta-classifier and the result is provided. Only leaf of the plant is observed for identifying the disease. When the stem or any other part is affected by the disease, this technique fails. In these two works, there is a requirement of an additional hardware, a camera to capture the image of the plant. Hence, even if these techniques provide accurate results, they are not cost effective. Our tool does not require an additional hardware as it requires only textual descriptions and provides accurate results based on them.

Khan et al. [3] have developed a web based expert system- Dr. Wheat, for Diagnosis of Diseases and Pests in Pakistani Wheat. A database for wheat diseases is created, a survey was conducted to identify the problems in wheat. Finally, rule based technique is used to identify the wheat plant's disease. Shikar et al. [4] have created an expert system for diagnosis of diseases of rice plants. This is a rule based approach with a knowledge base of simple if-then rules. People with experience in the domain reviewed the rules. These rules are the basis of the internal logic of the inference engine. Forward and backward chaining techniques are used in this technique. In the techniques mentioned, the rule-based approach was used and this requires the creation of knowledge base specific to each disease. This requires a lot of human effort and thus leading to the possibility of human errors. In our proposed work, we have introduced a novel approach to solve this issue thus avoiding human errors entirely. Our method requires a database containing plant disease description which is automated using web scraping techniques, therefore requires less human effort. In our work, we extract keywords from the created database.

Matsuo and Ishizuka [6] extracted keywords from a single document using word co-occurrence statistical information and uses frequency to identify the keywords and the probability of them occurring. A co-occurrence matrix is constructed for the same. $\chi 2$ values are calculated and the terms with the highest $\chi 2$ value are then selected as the keyword. Terms that are not frequent but relevant are not identified by this technique and thus becomes a major drawback. Claude [7] performed single document keyphrase extraction using sentence clustering and latent dirichlet allocation. This technique uses the brown corpus to identify the potential words. A matrix is created and co-occurrence is computed. Dimensionality reduction and data clustering are then performed. Latent Dirichlet algorithm is then used to identify the keywords. However, this approach requires a corpus of similar documents, which is not always readily available and it is a major drawback. There are many existing techniques for keyphrase extraction [8–12] but most of them require the keyphrases to have a high frequency. This problem is solved during the creation of the database by scraping content from multiple websites thus increasing the frequency of the keywords. The above mentioned techniques for keyword extraction are successful but are less accurate. Thus the work by Balasubramanian et al. [13] is adopted in this system and it is explained in detail in later sections of the paper.

4 System Architecture

The scope of this project is to meet the needs of a farmer with symptoms of plant diseases but is clueless about the plant's disease and needs help with identification of the same to treat the disease accordingly. In this work, a system is developed to get symptoms from researchers and provide them with the respective plant disease and method of treatment. The working of the system is as follows:

Since there is no existing dataset with textual descriptions for plant diseases to work on, a dataset containing symptoms of plant diseases is created using the method of web scraping. For every disease, keyword extraction is performed by using NLP techniques and various text-related features. These keywords are categorized and a novel approach is used to group keywords into symptoms. Symptoms of plant diseases are obtained from the user, compared with the grouped keywords and identified plant disease or possible plant diseases are provided to the user. Also, the system provides the user with an option to visit a website containing symptoms and various techniques to prevent and treat the disease based on their requirements.

In order to meet the goals of this project, a system is developed. The architecture of the system is shown in Fig. 1. Major components of the system include –Web scraper, Keyword Extractor, Keyword Classifier, Disease Classifier, Database and User Interface. The working of the system and the functionalities of each component is explained in detail subsequently.

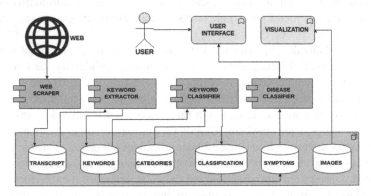

PLANT DISEASE CLASSIFICATION

Fig. 1. System architecture

1. *Web Scraper*: Extracts relevant information related to plant disease description from the websites using web scraping techniques. Uses HTMLParser and BeautifulSoup packages to meet the needs of the work. Creates a dataset containing Description of plant diseases from multiple websites.
2. *Keyword Extractor*: Using the dataset created by web scraper, applying the techniques mention in Sect. 3, keywords are extracted from documents and stored in the database.
3. *Keyword Classifier*: This module uses certain predefined characteristics with keywords associated with them and uses the keywords generated by keyword extractor to categorize the keywords based on characteristics.
4. *Disease Identifier*: Major component of the system which groups keywords and generates scores for them. Interacts with the user interface to obtain symptoms from the user and processes them to obtain the required result.
5. *Database*: Stores all the results from intermediate steps involved in identifying the plant's disease. Information stored in the database include:
    i. Description of plant disease
    ii. Keywords and categories
    iii. Categorized and grouped keywords
    iv. Various scores generate
6. *User Interface*: Serves as a medium for interaction between the user and the system. Obtains symptoms from the user and displays the results.

5 Methodology

In this section, the background information required to meet the goals of the work and the working of the system is explained in detail.

5.1 Dataset Creation (Web Scraping)

Web scraping is a software technique used to extract information from websites. There are many python libraries such as BeautifulSoup, Scrapy, lxml, etc. for web scraping. In this project, to extract the HTML content from websites, the following libraries have been used:

  (i) HTML Parser
 (ii) BeautifulSoup

Many websites offer information related to plant diseases but not all of these websites are well organized. Some of the websites provide little information for only a few diseases and others have repetitive information. Considering these problems, four websites have been identified which contain enough information about the majority of the diseases. The websites are as follows: TNAU Agritech Portal [14], Plantwise [15] and KnowledgeBank [16]. URLs of all diseases from the list of websites taken and categorized based on diseases. Using the URLs imported, the goal is to extract symptoms of plant diseases from the website. It is essential to understand the way in which HTML documents from different websites are structured. The HTML content, in different web pages, were structured in a way specific to that particular domain. Hence a pattern common to all the diseases belonging to the same website is identified to extract the information related to the symptoms of the disease. Tags associated with the symptoms are analyzed and also regular expression matching is performed since some web pages are poorly structured. Using these identified patterns, we retrieve the symptoms of the diseases. For every plant disease, symptoms of the disease from multiple websites are exported to a document and dataset is created.

5.2   Keyword Extraction and Categorization

Web Keyword extraction helps in identifying words that relate best to the subject of the document. Various approaches to keyword extraction include rule-based linguistic approaches, statistical approaches, machine learning approaches and domain-specific approaches. For this project, we use a supervised machine learning approach, defined from previous works on keyword extraction [1]. This method uses multiple features of keywords such as dispersion, C-value, and TF-IDF.

(i) Dispersion is the measure of the spread of keywords in the document. This helps us to identify the words that have high spread and high frequency. Dispersion of a keyword, with occurrences I_a, length of occurrences |I_a| and variance as var(I_a) is mathematically defined as

$$dispersion(a) = \frac{|I_a|}{var(I_a)} \tag{1}$$

(ii) C-value identifies the significance of a term to a document. It combines both linguistic approach and statistical approach, thereby, improving accuracy. It is calculated as

$$C - value(a) = \begin{cases} \log_2|a| * freq(a), & \text{if } a \text{ not nested} \\ \log_2|a| * \left\{ \frac{1}{T_a} * \sum b \text{ in } T_a * freq(b) \right\}, & \text{otherwise} \end{cases} \tag{2}$$

(iii) TF-IDF, frequency-inverse document frequency, is a common measure to identify the importance of a term to the document. It is a frequency based measure and thus higher occurrence of the keyword, higher is its TF-IDF value.

For every document containing plant disease descriptions, stop words are removed, stemming is performed and keywords are extracted. Now the extracted keywords are categorized into characteristics specific to plant diseases such as part affected, visible symptom, shape and size of the symptom, weather condition, etc. To do so, a dataset containing these characteristics and all the keywords related to these categories was created. Each keyword from the extracted keyword list is compared with different characteristics and if it belongs to a particular category it is tagged with that category.

Categorizing the keyword involves a lot of search operations. In order to improve the efficiency of search operations and to reduce the search complexity, trie data structure is used. Multiple trie data structures corresponding to multiple characteristics are created and the keywords specific to a particular characteristic are added to the respective trie. Searching for keywords is performed by prefix matching which reduces the search complexity to O (log(n)). Keywords along with their categories are obtained from this process. Table 1 displays various keywords, their feature scores and corresponding categories.

Table 1. Keyword feature scores and categories

Keyword	tfidf	Dispersion	c-score	Category
Panicle	0.002323	0.5000	0.0	Part
Powdery	0.014785	0.8571	0.0	Symptom
Brown	0.006902	0.8000	1.0	Color
Long	0.001221	0.0000	4.0	Size

5.3 Grouping of Keywords

From the extracted keywords, it is essential to combine these keywords in order to identify the symptoms explicit to the disease. For this purpose, keywords are grouped in pairs of two based on a novel approach. Considering keywords Key1and Key2, the algorithm for grouping the keywords is as follows:

(i) Key1 and Key2 are compared and various positions of the keywords in the document are obtained.

(ii) Positions of Key1 and Key2 are subtracted to find the distance between occurrences between the key pair. Only the keywords occurring close to each other, within 50 characters distance limit and their distance values in list DistVal are taken into consideration. Also, the keyword pairs belonging to same categories are excluded since there are no two same characteristics will together describe a symptom.

(iii) Length of DistVal is decided to be the *frequency* of occurrence of the keywords together in the document. Mean and Standard Deviation of values in the list are also considered to make sure that the distances between Key1 and Key2 are similar throughout the document.

(iv) Key1 and Key2 pair is given a score that will help determine the closeness and frequency of occurrence of keywords in the document. The score for the group is determined as follows:

$$combscore(key1, key2) = \frac{closeness(key1, key2)}{frequency(key1, key2)} \qquad (3)$$

$$closeness(key1, key2) = (mean(DistList) * standard\ deviation(DistList)) \qquad (4)$$

(v) Keywords with lower combscore are given higher priority because lower mean value suggests that the keywords occur close to each other; lower standard deviation implies that they are close to each other throughout the document; higher frequency shows that they occur together more frequently in the document.

(vi) The combscore of all keyword pairs specific to a document are then normalized with respect to other scores in the document to minimize the impact of uncertainties in multiple documents.

Thus keywords are grouped based on their closeness and frequency of occurrence together in the document and combination scores are generated. Table 2 shows the sample of keyword pairs and their generated scores.

Table 2. Keywords combination score

Keyword 1	Keyword 2	Combscore
Leaf	Fungal	270.998
Leaf	Sheath	11.322
Powdery	Whitish	1.031
Panicle	Brown	61.967
Leaf	Lesion	103.681

5.4   User Input and Identification of Plant Disease

In order to identify the plant disease, symptoms of the plant disease for which the user needs identification if obtained from them. The user is given an option to enter a group of symptoms in the order "part affected, symptom, the color of the part affected or the symptom, size of the symptom" for more accurate results. The input for this kind of symptom will be like "leaf, spot, yellow, large". The user is also provided with an option to enter unique factors individually.

Using the symptoms provided by the user, plant disease/possible plant diseases are identified using the following steps

(i) Since the keywords are grouped into pairs, the symptoms provided the by the user are also grouped into pairs of two. Hence from the list of symptoms provided by the user as a group of 4 elements, keywords are converted into groups of two and one. This does not apply to the unique factors as they are entered individually.

(ii) Two scores are generated for the list of symptoms entered by the user.
  i. Hitscore
  ii. Keyscore

(iii) For every disease, using the symptoms provided by the user, hitscore is determined as the ratio of the number of keywords in symptom present in the document to the total number of keywords in the symptom. For the keywords Ks entered as a symptom by the user:

$$Hitscore(doc) = \frac{N(Ks)\,in\,doc}{N(Ks)} \tag{5}$$

(iv) For every disease, keyscore is determined as the sum of all inverted combscore of keyword groups generated from symptoms list entered by the user. For the keyword group Kg entered as symptoms by the user:

$$Keyscore(doc) = \sum(1 - combscore(Kg)) \tag{6}$$

(v) A weighted sum of these scores is calculated and keyword combination scores are given higher weight.

$$Finalscore(doc) = 0.25 * Hitscore(doc) + 0.75 * Keyscore(doc) \tag{7}$$

Table 3 contains the hitscore, combscore and finalscore generated for various diseases. Based on the generated finalscore for each document, results are provided to the user based on conditions explained in the following subsection.

Table 3. Final score for different diseases

Disease name	Hit score	Combination score	Final score
Brown spot	0.89	5.50	3.96
False smut	0.11	0.0	0.04
Blast	0.78	7.02	4.94

5.5 Output

Identified plant diseases are provided to the user based on their input and their requirements. When the user provides less number of symptoms, the system cannot pinpoint the plant disease. Thereby, instead of providing the user with one plant disease, he is provided with a set of possible plant diseases. The diseases provided are chosen based on the criteria where Hitscore == 1. The user is also notified that the symptoms provided are not sufficient and given an option to include more symptoms.

When the user provides enough symptoms, the plant disease containing the highest generated finalscore is provided to the user as the "Identified Plant Disease". The user is also provided with a link to a website containing details of the plant's disease, its symptoms, preventive measure and methods for treatment of the identified disease in an elaborate manner.

6 Results

This section contains a set of images representing various kinds of inputs and different types of outputs provided to the user, step-by-step. Figures 2 and 3 display the first set of symptoms entered by the user and the corresponding result generated with the list of possible diseases. Figure 4 shows the additional symptom entered and Fig. 5 displays the result generated. Then the user is redirected to a website containing the detailed description of the disease and method to prevent and treat them.

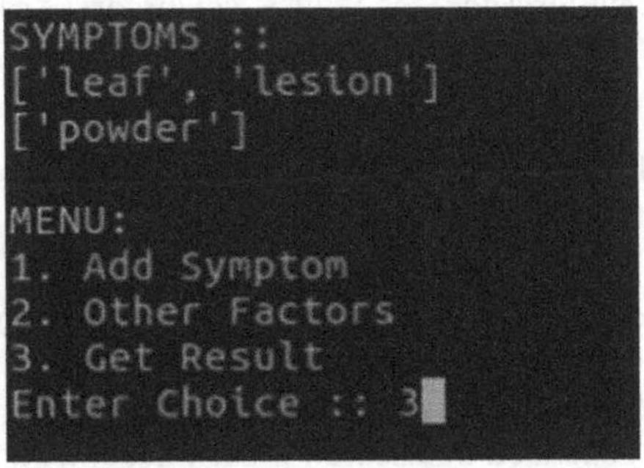

```
SYMPTOMS ::
['leaf', 'lesion']
['powder']

MENU:
1. Add Symptom
2. Other Factors
3. Get Result
Enter Choice :: 3
```

Fig. 2. First set of symptoms

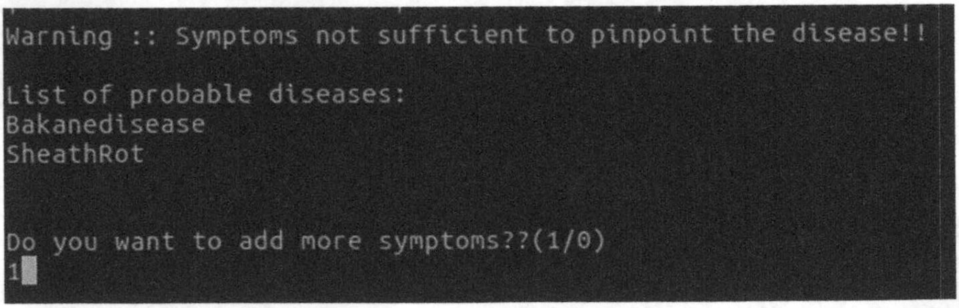

```
Warning :: Symptoms not sufficient to pinpoint the disease!!

List of probable diseases:
Bakanedisease
SheathRot


Do you want to add more symptoms??(1/0)
1
```

Fig. 3. List of possible diseases

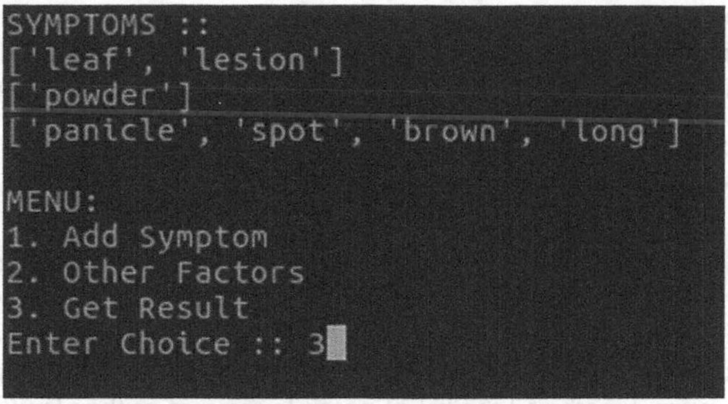

```
SYMPTOMS ::
['leaf', 'lesion']
['powder']
['panicle', 'spot', 'brown', 'long']

MENU:
1. Add Symptom
2. Other Factors
3. Get Result
Enter Choice :: 3
```

Fig. 4. Second set of symptoms

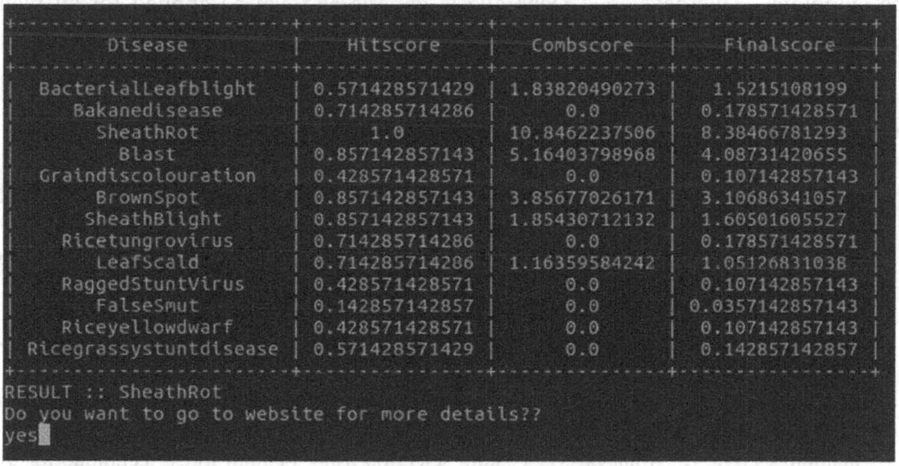

```
+------------------------+----------------+----------------+----------------+
|        Disease         |    Hitscore    |    Combscore   |   Finalscore   |
+------------------------+----------------+----------------+----------------+
|   BacterialLeafblight  | 0.571428571429 | 1.83820490273  |  1.5215108199  |
|      Bakanedisease     | 0.714285714286 |      0.0        | 0.178571428571 |
|       SheathRot        |      1.0       | 10.8462237506  | 8.38466781293  |
|         Blast          | 0.857142857143 | 5.16403798968  | 4.08731420655  |
|   Graindiscolouration  | 0.428571428571 |      0.0        | 0.107142857143 |
|       BrownSpot        | 0.857142857143 | 3.85677026171  | 3.10686341057  |
|      SheathBlight      | 0.857142857143 | 1.85430712132  | 1.60501605527  |
|     Ricetungrovirus    | 0.714285714286 |      0.0        | 0.178571428571 |
|       LeafScald        | 0.714285714286 | 1.16359584242  | 1.05126831038  |
|    RaggedStuntVirus    | 0.428571428571 |      0.0        | 0.107142857143 |
|       FalseSmut        | 0.142857142857 |      0.0        | 0.0357142857143|
|    Riceyellowdwarf     | 0.428571428571 |      0.0        | 0.107142857143 |
| Ricegrassystuntdisease | 0.571428571429 |      0.0        | 0.142857142857 |
+------------------------+----------------+----------------+----------------+
RESULT :: SheathRot
Do you want to go to website for more details??
yes
```

Fig. 5. Result with generated scores

7 Future Work and Limitations

The system can further be developed to identify the diseases of various other crops. In this project, rice diseases was taken into consideration. Similarly, this system can be expanded to identify the plant diseases of agricultural and horticultural plants. This can be done by scraping the textual description of agricultural and horticultural plants and then performing the algorithm used in this project. In the proposed system, user has to specify symptoms in English. The system can be developed wherein users can specify symptoms in any language in order to identify the plant disease. For further development of the system, an application can be created where users can select from the options in drop down menu rather than typing the symptoms.

The system identifies the right disease when the correct symptoms are provided by the user. In case the user provides the wrong symptom, system will not be able to produce accurate results. In this system, dataset has been created only for all the diseases of rice plant. Using this dataset, the diseases are identified. The proposed system can further be extended to identify disease of all the plants by creating datasets.

8 Conclusion

A technique that identifies the plant disease based on the textual descriptions of symptoms provided by the user is developed. A dataset containing plant disease descriptions is developed. The system extracts keywords using supervised machine learning algorithm, categorizes and groups them. Finally based on user input scores are generated for every disease and the list of possible diseases or the identified disease is provided to the user as output. Also user is allowed to visit a website containing more details on the disease. This technique does not require any additional hardware to achieve its goal. The system is flexible as it provides user with different options to enter the symptoms. This developed technique is generic and can be applied for all plant diseases.

References

1. Singh, V., Misra, A.K.: Detection of plant leaf diseases using image segmentation and soft computing techniques. Inf. Process. Agric. **4**(1), 41–49 (2017)
2. Johannes, A., et al.: Automatic plant disease diagnosis using mobile capture devices, applied on a wheat use case. Comput. Electron. Agric. **138**, 200–209 (2017)
3. Khan, F.S., et al.: Dr. Wheat: a web-based expert system for diagnosis of diseases and pests in Pakistani wheat. In: Proceedings of the World Congress on Engineering, vol. 1, pp. 2–4 (2008)
4. Sarma, S.K., Singh, K.R., Singh, A.: An expert system for diagnosis of diseases in rice plant. Int. J. Artif. Intell. **1**(1), 26–31 (2010)
5. Shanmuga Priya, S., Abinaya, M.: Feature selection using random forest technique for the prediction of pest attack in cotton crops. Int. J. Pure Appl. Math. **118**, 2899–2903
6. Matsuo, Y., Ishizuka, M.: Keyword extraction from a single document using word co-occurrence statistical information. Int. J. Artif. Intell. Tools **13**(01), 157–169 (2004)
7. Pasquier, C.: Task 5: single document keyphrase extraction using sentence clustering and latent Dirichlet allocation. In: Proceedings of the 5th International Workshop on Semantic Evaluation. Association for Computational Linguistics, pp. 154–157 (2010)
8. El-Beltagy, S.R.: KP-miner: a simple system for effective keyphrase extraction. In: 2006 Innovations in Information Technology. IEEE, pp. 1–5 (2006)
9. Wan, X. Xiao, J.: Single document keyphrase extraction using neighborhood knowledge. In: AAAI, vol. 8, pp. 855–860 (2008)
10. Emu, I.H., et al.: An efficient approach for keyphrase extraction from english document. Int. J. Intell. Syst. Appl. **9**(12), 59 (2017)
11. D'Avanzo, E., Magnini, B.: A keyphrase-based approach to summarization: the lake system at duc-2005. In: Proceedings of DUC (2005)
12. Hulth, A.: Improved automatic keyword extraction given more linguistic knowledge. In: Proceedings of the 2003 Conference on Empirical Methods in Natural Language Processing. Association for Computational Linguistics, pp. 216–223 (2003)

13. Balagopalan, A., et al.: Automatic keyphrase extraction and segmentation of video lectures. In: 2012 IEEE International Conference on Technology Enhanced Education (ICTEE). IEEE, pp. 1–10 (2012)
14. TNAU Agritech Portal. http://agritech.tnau.ac.in
15. CABI Plantwise. http://www.plantwise.org
16. IRRI Rice Knowledge Bank. http://www.knowledgebank.irri.org

Optimizing Performance of User Web Browsing Search

Sunita[1(✉)] and Vijay Rana[2(✉)]

[1] Arni University, Kangra, India
sunitamahajan2603@gmail.com
[2] SBBS University, Khiala, India
vijayrana93@gmail.com

Abstract. Web crawling and word sensing are critical nowadays. In case of web browsing, searching consume time in case proposer requirements from user is not extracted. In earlier work on web browsers word correction was missing which is a main inclusion in the proposed work. The problem with existing literature is time complexity in fetching the correct keyword from user query string. We propose character shuffle pre-processing searching mechanism. Using the proposed method, time complexity is reduced since clustering is used for searching the keywords. The searching don't required entire database to be searched over rather only particular cluster is searched. To fetch meaningful keywords database is maintained. The keywords within the database increases as more and more user interact with this search engine. The worth of this study is proved using parameters execution time and number of meaningful keywords.

Keywords: Preprocessing · Clustering · Time complexity · Word sensing

1 Introduction

The detecting word sensing is critical and complicated task. The techniques following as under category is known as Word Sense Disambiguation (WSD). Is follow with NLP with reduced the energy consumption. The phases with natural language processing (NLP) is include with preprocessing, feature extraction, segmentation and classification. Preprocessing indicate removing any abnormal present in the data. The feature ext is next phase, which is used in order to fetch the critical necessary feature out of the available information. The segmentation is a phase which is used to divide the information into critical and non-critical words. Classification is the last phase which is used to divide the information into correct phase all of these phases area critical in general data mining. NLP (Natural language processing) uses this specific field to extract the meaningful information out of the user query.

The problem associated with word sensing for all under NP hard, NP hard problem is complex problem since a same word has contain different meaning associated from user query. They consider the two sentences underneath

© Springer Nature Singapore Pte Ltd. 2019
A. K. Luhach et al. (Eds.): ICAICR 2018, CCIS 956, pp. 230–239, 2019.
https://doi.org/10.1007/978-981-13-3143-5_20

E.g.

(1) "I am sit near the bank".
(2) "What is interest of the SBI bank".

The word bank obviously has different meanings in the two contexts above [13]. In the primary first context it implies the bank of the river and in the second it implies the money of bank. The machine can't to find the actual meaning of the words. In this case to be need a trained the system to extract the sense of the words. There are four regular ways to deal with Word Sense Disambiguation

- **Unsupervised methods:** Unsupervised [1] models concentrate on taking in an example in the information with no outside input. Clustering is an exemplary case of unsupervised learning model.
- **Semi-supervised methods:** Semi-Supervised learning [2] uses a set of curated, labelled data and tries to infer new labels/attributes on new data sets. Semi-Supervised learning models are a solid middle ground between supervised and unsupervised models.
- **Supervised methods:** Supervised learning [3] models use external feedback to learning functions that map inputs to output observations. In those models the external environment acts as a "teacher" of the AI algorithms. These use word sensing methods to learn from labelled preparation sets. A number of the general techniques used are "decision-lists", "decision trees", "naïve-Bayes", "neural-networks", "support vector machines" (SVM).
- **Knowledge-based methods:** Reinforcement learning models use opposite dynamics such as rewards and punishment to "reinforce" different types of knowledge. This type of learning technique is becoming really popular in modern AI solutions. Knowledge-based methods rely on "dictionaries-based", "thesauri" and "lexical-resources" for knowledge bases.

In unsupervised learning dictionary maintains is not possible since customization is not possible. Semi-supervised this mechanism could be time consuming is expensive and it could be parsley customized. This is mechanism historical data plays a part the proposed work uses present and future work associated searching. Hence it can't be used along with proposed system. Supervised learning it is customizable and can be used along with proposed.

The learning mechanisms greatly influence the pattern by which discovery of normal and abnormal phrase is made. For this purpose, supervised learning mechanism is proposed in this research. The word correction and searching take into consideration application program interface (API) from online source JOC. Survey of the article is organised as below: part 2 gives the literature review, part 3 illustrated the gaps, part 4 recently the proposed system, part 5 gives the results and last details are gives in the conclusion and future scope.

2 Literature Survey

The literature is conducted to look for optimal technique used for browsing websites with minimum amount of time consumed.

[4] proposed model suggested a social content unfolding along the line of semantics and time. Clustering [5] mechanism is imposed reducing the overall search time required. [6, 7] proposed a challenging task of surveying through the mechanism used for sentiment analysis. Sentiment analysis techniques suggested in the literature used to accurately predict the desire of the user by looking at the search query. [8] In this article highlights many searching techniques with various searching algorithms like fast string search algorithm with vector approach & bi linear search. [9] The proposed method beats different baselines and before proposed web-construct semantic closeness measures in light of three benchmark datasets demonstrating a high relationship with human appraisals. Proposed strategy fundamentally enhances the precision in a network mining assignment. [10, 11] Proposed framework a lexical example extraction algorithm to extricate various semantic relations that exist between two words. Work is led on datasets of vague questions, demonstrate that our approach enhances query output clustering as far as both clustering quality and level of expansion. [12] Proposed a portion based KNN clustering algorithm which enhanced exactness of KNN clustering algorithm. The proposed algorithm KKNNC utilizing the six UCI data sets, and contrasted it and KNNC algorithm in the tests. The exploratory outcomes demonstrate that KKNNC algorithm outflank KNNC algorithm in precision fundamentally. [13] Proposed model to distinguish some ease of use related issues in Semantic Web. Ease of use of some catchphrase and shape based instruments and their restrictions are being talked about. Results and discoveries of an ease of use study of the device are exhibited. [3] Proposed framework examines different systems for client driven relationship of inquiry and thinking. Human critical thinking in psychological science, a client inquiry in view of connected client interests. The multi-level technique from the human critical thinking to vast scale look was proposed through [3]. [14] proposed exponential law-based intrigue's safeguarding demonstrating, arrange statistics– based data gathering, and philosophy managed various leveled thinking were created to execute client question parsing and seeking criteria. Talked about methods utilized for question expectation recognition, exploiting client conduct to comprehend their interests and inclinations on web based business. Technique was intended for utilizing the substance of internet searcher result pages (SERPs), alongside the data acquired from question strings, to examine qualities of inquiry aim, with a specific spotlight on supported pursuit.

In the studied literature, execution time is sufficiently high due to lack of clustering and redundant information search and retrieval. The proposed system utilizes the tokenization and keyword searching mechanism for effectively finding the resources required for user query.

3 Research Gap

The existing literature provides content based searching however does not eliminate redundant keywords. Also dissimilar keyword searching and elimination is missing causing higher execution time and least efficient URL retrieval. This system will require large amount of information in order to make correct decision. The information which is provided to the recommender system must be consistent in nature. For the information some sort of information system is required. The recommender system will take the information and formulate the decision in one of the following two ways- either by the use of collaborative filtering or by the use of content filtering. The collaborative filtering is the mechanism of filtering for information among the multi agents, viewpoints, data sources etc. The content filtering on the other hand is the mechanism of using the program in order to filter the information which is going to be used within the system. People now days are more and more concerned with the environment. For this purpose concise information retrieval system is required.

For this purpose, efficient parsing and correction system along with clustering for reducing execution time is designed. The proposed model is described in next section as.

4 Proposed Model

Proposed model combination of multiple phases and Parsing is one of the critical phases.

- **Parsing**

Extracting the meaningful information out of the particular string is the main objective of the parsing. In order to do this, space is act as the separator. Example "My name is Sunita Mahajan". Suppose we have a dict.mdb database.

Since the specified words matched with dictionary hence successful tokenization & as well as parsing is done. "my", "name", "is", "Sunita", "Mahajan". After performing parsing successfully extract the meaningful keywords from the given string.

Table 1. Showing the dictionary containing words along with meaning

Words	Meanings
My	Personal
Name	Title, label
Is	Am, are
Sunita	Daughter of Dharma, good behaviour
Mahajan	Castes, communities

- **Finding meaningful keywords**

Another dictionary with the co-related words is maintained order to determined meaning of the sentence. The match is counted as hit and no match is indicated with missed. The main task of our approach is to increase hit and missed occur words replaced with corrected words. The equation is used to calculate hit to miss ratio.

$$TS\_hit\,ratio = \frac{Hits_i}{TS_i} \tag{1}$$

Equation 1: Total hit ratio
This equation indicates the total number of keywords fetched by the proposed system to the total keywords present within the dictionary. The result is presented in the form of percentages.

In the word sensing model which is proposed the hit ratio is given by considering the total words count of 100 in a dictionary.

Table 2. Comparison in terms of ratio

String searched	Hit ratio with existing system (ontology based model)	Hit ratio with proposed system (user perception based)
Live cricket score today	0.03	0.04
I am sit near the bank of the river	0.08	0.09
What is the interest of the current in SBI bank	0.08	0.10
SBI saving account interest rate per month	0.06	0.07
Fashion is a popular style, especially in clothing, footwear on Amazon	0.10	0.11

The hit ration ex and pro indicated that the result of pro model is better since the words which does not exists in the dictionary are added to the dictionary with user permission. This procedure of higher hit ratio as compared to existing model (Fig. 1).

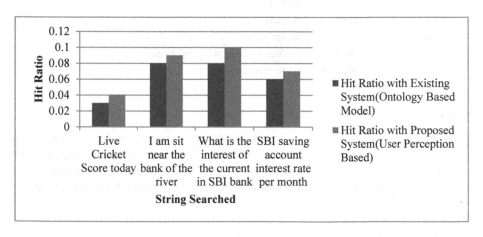

Fig. 1. Comparison of hit ration of existing system & proposed system

4.1 Proposed Algorithm

The algorithm which will describes the creation of Recommender system for the promotion of Selected Websites is describes through the following steps.

Algorithm-Auto Query Resolving system
a. Receive the parameters of the user query to be tested(Pi)
b. Divide the string into meaningful tokens (t) is also known as parsing.
• In the parsing space is act as the separator.
• The (t) are matched within dict.mdb (db) database.
• Extract the meaningful keywords (k).
c. Find the sense(s) of the k.
• The meaning of the words are found using hit ratio
• hit ratio $= \frac{Hits_i}{TS_i}$
d. check for availability
• if(t==db) is rejected
• then
• Otherwise it will be added into (db).
• Results as present into percentage
e. Stop

In the proposed algorithm first step receive the parameters of the user query to be tested (Pi). In the second step preprocessing, divide the string into tokens, this process is also known as parsing. Parsing act as a separator after the parsing extract the keywords are matched within a dict.mdb database. Find the meaningful keywords. The actual keywords the fetched from the user query. In the next step find the ambiguous words, and find the actual sense the keywords.

The success of the system will be determined using Hit Ratio.

$$hit\, ratio = \frac{Hits_i}{TS_i} \tag{2}$$

Higher the hit ratio more successful will be the given system.

The existing approach doesn't consider the identification of similar words & also the token matching process is slow in the proposed literature the explanations variation of keyword fetch and matching consider. The complexity of the search is reducing greatly by the use of proposed system.

5 Performance and Result Evaluation

In this section performance can be evaluate on number of websites compare along with execution time. It is total time consumed to relevant websites.

- **Recall**

$$Recall = \frac{Number\ of\ RW}{RW + NRW} \times 100 \qquad (3)$$

The overall performance is described in Tables 1 and 2 highlights list of four keywords with their recall measurer that describes the relevant and non-relevant result.

- **Single-keyword based query**

(See Figs. 2, 3 and Table 3).

Table 3. Study of quantitative analysis

Keywords	Total no. of websites retrieved	Time consumed (milli seconds)
University	9	3
Online	11	4
Computer	10	3
School	7	4

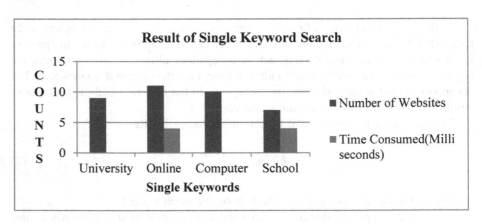

Fig. 2. Plot of frequency vs keywords

Table 4. Confusion matrix for single-keyword

Search query	No. of sites retrieved	RW (related websites)	LRW (less related websites)	NRW (non-related websites)
University	9	7	1	1
Online	11	8	3	0
Computer	10	7	2	1
School	7	5	1	1

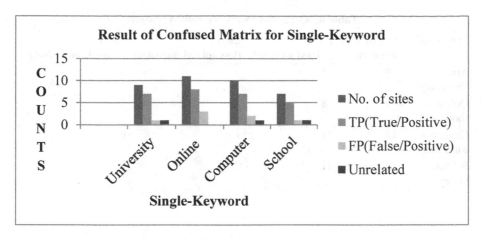

Fig. 3. Confused matrix for single keyword

- **Multi-keyword based query**

  (See Figs. 4, 5, Tables 4, 5 and 6).

Table 5. Study of quantitative analysis

Multi-keywords	Total of no. of websites retrieved	Time consumed (milli seconds)
Arni University	12	5
Online shopping	11	4
Computer education	12	3
School library	11	4

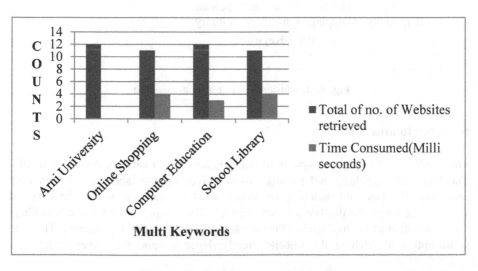

Fig. 4. Plot of frequency vs keywords

Table 6. Confusion matrix for multi-keywords

Search query	No. of sites retrieved	RW (related websites)	LRW (less related websites)	NRW (non-related websites)
Arni University	9	5	3	1
Online shopping	11	8	2	1
Computer education	12	11	1	0
School library	11	11	0	0

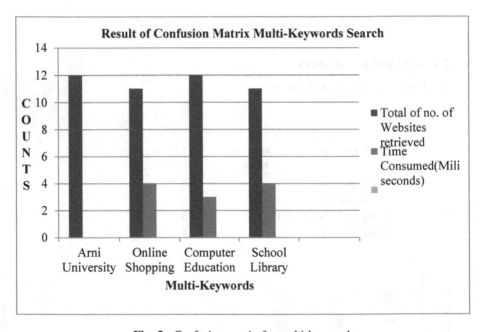

Fig. 5. Confusion matrix for multi-keywords

6 Conclusion

The result from the proposed system indicates betterment in terms of confusion matrix. The keywords matching and parsing process gives unique labels along with high precision. The keyword matching frequency yield the order at which the obtained website is going to be displayed at the browser. The pre-processing phase also filters the information to be displayed to the user keeping in mind the user interest. The time consumption in fetching the website greatly depends upon the server caches and processor speed. The proposed system is tested on single CPU but may perform better on GPU. In the future work, clustering along with sense annotation and location sensitive along with proposed system.

References

1. Che, W., Liu, T.: Using word sense disambiguation for semantic role labeling. In: 2010 4th International Universal Communication Symposium, pp. 167–174 (2010)
2. Features, S.: A method for word sense disambiguation combining context semantic features, pp. 283–287 (2016)
3. Zeng, Y., et al.: User-centric query refinement and processing using granularity-based strategies. Knowl. Inf. Syst. **27**(3), 419–450 (2011)
4. De Maio, C., Fenza, G., Loia, V., Orciuoli, F.: Unfolding social content evolution along time and semantics. Future Gener. Comput. Syst. **66**, 146–159 (2017)
5. Shekarpour, S., Marx, E.: RQUERY : rewriting natural language queries on knowledge graphs to alleviate the vocabulary mismatch problem (2017)
6. Mohey, D., Hussein, E.M.: A survey on sentiment analysis challenges. J. King Saud Univ. - Eng. Sci. **30**, 330–338 (2016)
7. Mahajan, S., Sharma, S., Rana, V.: Design a perception based semantics model for knowledge extraction. Int. J. Comput. Intell. Res. **13**(6), 1547–1556 (2017)
8. Chandra, S.: A brief study and analysis of different searching algorithms (2017)
9. Bollegala, D., Matsuo, Y., Ishizuka, M.: A web search engine-based approach to measure semantic similarity between words. IEEE Trans. Knowl. Data Eng. **23**(7), 977–990 (2011)
10. Navigli, R., Crisafulli, G.: Inducing word senses to improve web search result clustering. Computational Linguistics, pp. 116–126 (2010)
11. Rana, V.: An approaches & comprehensive survey for measuring semantic relatedness with knowledge resources, vol. 6, no. 1, pp. 398–403 (2018)
12. Wang, Y.: K-nearest neighbor clustering algorithm based on kernel methods, pp. 0–3 (2010)
13. Haider, A., Raza, A.: Keyword and form based semantic search tools and their usability. In: 8th International Conference on Digital Information Management ICDIM 2013, pp. 85–89 (2013)
14. Ashkan, A., Clarke, C.L.A.: Impact of query intent and search context on clickthrough behavior in sponsored search. Knowl. Inf. Syst. **34**(2), 425–452 (2013)

Networks

A Distributed Key Management Protocol for Wireless Sensor Network

Vishal Choudhary[1](✉) and S. Taruna[2]

[1] Banasthali University, Vanasthali, Rajasthan, India
vishalhim@yahoo.com
[2] Computer Science, JK Lakshmipat University, Jaipur, India
staruna71@yahoo.com

Abstract. In sensor network where large group of nodes share the information, in such scenario it's difficult to scale the application, in addition security in wireless sensor network often vary with purpose and context, but in broadspectrum, security for wireless sensor networks should centered on the protection of the data itself and the network communications between the nodes. Privacy, reliability and validation are the most important data security concerns. Traditional cryptographic methods are not promising on resource limited sensor nodes. Node initiated key management is a novel idea where rather than base station or key distribution center initiate the security algorithm. We can give control to sensor nodes or cluster head for securing communicating nodes with in a sensor network. It is a non centralized key management method which is more robust than other methods. in this paper we proposed the proactive key management which guarantee efficiency, robustness, and dynamic clustering.

Keywords: Cryptography · Random graph theory
Key distribution and management · Intrusion detection system
Sensor network

1 Introduction

There are certain problem pre-exist with key distribution, like private-key cryptography requires shared, secret between each communicating parties. So how to exchange the keys first time securely is a difficult task. In sensor network where large group of nodes share the information, in such scenario it's difficult to scale the application. Another problem is related to storage if there are n numbers of nodes and each node need to store up to n − 1 keys. Here storage requirement are directly related to amount of nodes participating in communication. In order to deal with storage problem there is a need for central authority that can distribute the keys a per requirements of sensor nodes. Such that each node can directly correspond with central authority which is known as key distribution center, each node should have to store only one secret key for communication with key distribution center and then key distribution center provides the secure link in between the communicating nodes. This is an indirect authentication scheme. But here deadlock like situation can occur, this scheme unable to provide the complete distributed environment of computing and communication.

© Springer Nature Singapore Pte Ltd. 2019
A. K. Luhach et al. (Eds.): ICAICR 2018, CCIS 956, pp. 243–256, 2019.
https://doi.org/10.1007/978-981-13-3143-5_21

Only single point of failure can make the entire system halt. In order to reduce the problem associate with private key cryptography, the public key encryption scheme was developed; where the sender will encrypt the information with receiver's public key. The message cannot be decrypted by anybody who doesn't have the corresponding private key. Public-key distribution and deployment is easy. Also public-key reduces the need to store many different secret keys. if there are large numbers of pairs want to communicate secretly all need to store only one key and its most suitable technique for open environment. We have discussed various key distribution techniques in order to device the efficient algorithm for key distribution.

2 Background: Overview of Basic Key Pre-distribution Scheme

There are different key distribution and management scheme discussed in literature few of them are discussed here.

2.1 Single Network Distributed Key

In single network distributed or master key approach same key is loaded in all sensor nodes prior to deployment. After that same key is applied for encryption and decryption for data [1]. The main advantages in this approach are that, it is simple and need minimum storage requirement. But the security resistance throughout network can be damaged while attackers crack any sensor in the network.

2.2 Key Distribution by Trusted Base Station Scheme

The trusted secure base station is essential component of WSN. The sensor nodes validate itself to base station [1]. The base station produces a connection key and transmits to both communication nodes. It is similar to Kerberos [2] before deployment a distinct symmetric key is induced for every node in the WSN. This key is saved in the sensor memory and will acts as authentication entity for the node and assist encrypted transmission in between the sensor and base station. But this protocol needs consistent communication in between both entities.

2.3 Elliptical Curve Cryptography

The main problem with public key cryptography is complexity in key generation and exchange. ECC was invented by Victor Miller and Neal Koblitz [3]. The benefit of ECC over other public key cryptography technique is that the hard mathematical equation in ECC takes exponential time. Whereas best public key algorithm (RSA, Diffie-Hellman) takes sub exponential time. Elliptical curve cryptography is promising key generation technique where key size is drastically reduced without negotiating with the security of the network. The smaller key size makes the encryption and decryption more efficient and fast.

2.4   Random Key Pre-distribution

Sensor nodes are placed in hostile environment and some time they are scattered randomly and thus key-setup methods may not presume prior knowledge of the deployment. Eschenauer and Gligor projected [4, 5] in this technique each node gets an arbitrary set of keys from key pool to form key ring afore deployment, to make communication prosperous the communicating nodes find one mundane key within their subset to share secret data. "This method was developed on the theoretical foundation of random graph [22]. A random graph is formed by a group of n vertices as initial nodes and subsequently adding edges as joint between them randomly. a arbitrary graph is specified by notation G(n, p) in which every possible edge occurs freely with possibility p. To obtain complete connected graph, each pair of node should have comparatively minimum probability P_0 for making a straightforward channel. During operation of sensor network in real environment, a key-setup operation is implemented. In this stage entire set of nodes determine their acquaintance and use the common key. Key exploration procedure is followed by handing over a small identity to every key afore making operational in field. The nodes which recognizes the shared key ring can authenticate their acquaintance by transmitting a challenging question and verifying the result. For that link mutual key is the key for particular link" [22].

2.5   q-Composite Keys Scheme

In this scheme sub set of P desultory keys are culled out of immensely colossal key pool, further for every sensor m arbitrary keys are culled from P and stored in the sensor nodes' key ring. During the opening phase, each sensor node must agnize mutual keys with each of its acquaintance. This is done by local broadcasting a key identifier. every node can discover each acquaintance n with whom it uses at most q keys [4, 12]. In order to engender the transmission link key k, it uses hashing of all common keys. The keys hashing predicated on the order in which its occurs in the pristine key group P. key initialization is not done between nodes that have common keys fewer than q keys. It is found from analysis as the number of needed key overlap grow, it turns aggressively harder for an assailant to break a association. But, in order to optimize the given feasibility p of two nodes will share adequate keys to make a secure association, it is essential to decrease the key pool size |P|.it is found that the q synthesized keys scheme provides enough resistance counter to node capture when the number of nodes snatching is diminutive.

2.6   Polynomial Strategies of Key Pool in Key Distribution

Polynomial predicated key distribution is an efficacious technique in order to minimize the amount of data sharing and each pair of node can efficiently compute the shared key. Polynomial predicated key distribution is λ collision resistance, which denotes that as possible as less than λ nodes are conciliate rest part of network is protected [10, 11, 15]. Polynomial strategies utilizes a symmetric binary polynomial over finite field GF (q). A sensor that have ID i reserve a portion in P containing the uni-variate polynomial $f_i(y)$ equals to P(i, y). In case to exchanging the message with node j, it calculate the prevalent key k_{ij} equal to $f_i(j)$ that further equals to $f_j(i)$ this procedure "enable two communicating entities to apportion a prevalent key.

2.7   Grid-Based Key Sharing and Distribution

In grid-predicated key sharing consists of identical sensors arranged in such a way that it composes a grid. Within maximum communication radius r. a sensor node can converse precisely among all entities inside the circle of range r that circumvents it [13]. Let k be predetermined group whose numbers we reference as keys to a group G of wireless sensors, and each have enough memory to contain m keys, subsequent deployment the nodes from G to form a wireless sensor network. A key pre-distribution scheme for wireless sensor network w is a mapping $G \rightarrow K^m$ that designate up to m keys from K to every node in G. Every node stocks the keys designated to it in its recollection afore deployment. After the nodes are deployment two communicating nodes contribute one or more prevalent elements of k that can be acclimated to engender a prevalent key. The nodes that do not apportion a prevalent key may depend on intermediary nodes with whom they both disseminate a key in order to converse securely.

2.8   Hypercube Based Key Distribution and Management Scheme

It is an elongated version of polynomial predicated key distribution. In this method afore deployment, the entities are arranged in three dimensional hypercube like structure. The fundamental pool of key spaces is engendered like multi space polynomial scheme [9]. There after the nodes within a given dimension are nominated with a polynomial structure from the ditto key space and hence are capable to compose shared pair sagacious key directly. If both nodes X and Y wish to establish a dyad sapient key, all indicators of nodes within all dimensional are correlated and if at minimum one index is matched then a key can be precisely ingrained. Otherwise rest entities are requested for alliance such that virtual link from x to y can be composed (X; k1;k2;k3;;;;;;Kn;Y), where X is able to establish direct pair sagacious key with K_1, K_i with K_{i+1} and K_n with Y, key is engendered at X and conveyed with re-encryptions over intermediate nodes K_i to node Y with incrementing dimension of hypercube number such path withal increases and if minimal one non-negotiate path subsists, and a secure pair of key can be established.

2.9   Deployment Knowledge in Key Management

In deployment cognizance scheme, it is supposed that sensor entities are immobile after deployment. The sensor nodes can reside at points around "positioning point as the point location where a sensor entities are operational [7]. It is postulated that target opeartional area is two dimensional rectangular regions with size X.Y and the inception point is the upper left rectangular corner. The probability density functions for the target of entity I for i = 1...... N, over the bi- dimensional space is represented by fi(x, y), where $x \in [0, X]$ and $y \in [0, Y]$.

2.10   Location Aware Key Dissemination

In location dependent key dissemination scheme sensor entities can be integrated at any time. Afore deployment a master key is embedded in all sensors. After setup in operational field each sensor node utilizes this key to achieve a group of subset-keys predicated on the nonce acknowledged from pairing nodes [9]. Utilizing the set of prevalent subset-keys with each acquaintance, a sensor will engenders distinctive keys for each and every communicating path with others nodes. After this the nodes expunges the prevalent key in order to evade capturing from adversaries. In the time of starting phase each sensor node transmit a periodic signal at dissimilar energy level, each periodic signal enclose a dissimilar nonce encapsulated utilizing the prevalent key k fragmented in between all entities. Each entity receives a set of periodic signal predicated on the comparative position of the sensor node from sundry nodes. The sensor entity then drives sub-keys utilizing an amalgamation of the mundane key set k and the received set of nonce's. The key updation is carry out by each sensor entity predicated on location this is due to sensors that are not in the same position, receives different set of nonces. Thus final sub-keys must be unique.

2.11   Combinatorial Key Management Using Location

It is a lightweight combinatorial design for key administration for clustered sensor network which is additionally kenned as SHELL. In SHELL, here the probability of node capture is reduced as physical location is utilized in computing the keys of a node [14]. Here any node with in a cluster can directly communicate through the doorway nodes which are central ascendancy of individual cluster. The gateway nodes are puissant enough to converse with the individual node with in a cluster and invoke the key management functions. Each switch node can communicate with at minimum two other switch entities in the network. The gateway uses three different kinds of keys. The first category of key is a prior loaded key that sanctions the switch node to directly communicate with key distribution node. The second type of keys sanctions the different bypass and hub nodes to communicate. The third key type sanctions the bridge to communicate with all of the sensor entities in the cluster. The key distribution node is surmised that it is unable to be compromised it acts a key repository, authenticate bridge node and sensor nodes, distribute keys to all other nodes, and it perform key updation when needed. If any node get compromised. A key revocation is initialized and the gateway node watches the node in its cluster for failure and key distribution node do same thing for bridge nodes.

3   Distributed Key Management

3.1   Key Management Techniques

Key administration in WSN is a complicated process due to nature of sensor nodes and its deployment in the multifarious environment [18]. Some of key management techniques are highlighted as:

(a) **Universal key:** In this scheme, only "single key is publically shared by the whole network. To transmit a packet, it is encrypted with this shared key. Once the information is received, it is decoded with the same key. It is an energy proficient way" of key distribution. Here data is encrypted only one time by the sender and decrypted only one time by the receiver. However, it provides limited security. Here only hacking of single key leads to compromise of whole network which converse with this unique key. Intruder can also insert duplicate node in network.

(b) **Pair wise key node:** Each node store an separate key for correspondence with its neighboring node [6, 8, 19]. On the off chance that there are k neighbors for a sensor node, at that point it has k exceptional key in memory to speak with its neighbors. In this arrangement, a node that communicates something specific needs to encode the message with a key neighbor who gets the data. The neighboring node unscrambles data and re-encode with the key comparing to the accompanying beneficiary. This procedure gives sufficient security because of localization of keys. In any case, it's not vitality productive as encryption and decoding at every node increment computation overhead and consume more energy additionally require more storage at every node.

(c) **Combine insightful key gathering:** here each bunch of node speak with unique keys inside its cluster [17]. In this method there is pacification between security and energy proficiency. It confines the quantity of encryption in correspondences. Anyway it enhances computation of cluster head, which need to decode and encode the information. To be viable, we need to" progressively change the CHs keeping in mind the end goal to limiting the energy consumption.

(d) **Singular key:** In this technique, each node has its own particular key to scramble the data [16]. Here each node sends the encrypted data that can only be decrypted by sink node. it can provide the robust security but main problem here is the overhead faced by sink node to decrypt as separate packet need separate decryption key. That is key decryption algorithm is quite complicated at sink node. Also key revocation and distribution is problem.

3.2 Key Generation

Key generation and distribution plays major role in protecting the sensor network. For each round if key distribution center insert new keys in the sensor nodes then computations and communication is high. In order to optimize the performance of sensor network we have to set the protocol when and where to updates the keys. We need an intelligent system which can take the decisions to update the keys based on suspicious behavior of node. Also there is problem for delay in updating the keys due to certain communication problems with in network. The main advantages of dynamic regeneration keys are that it keeps the sensor network secure.

3.3 Localization

Sensor network localization calculates approximately the location of sensor node with initially unknown location. Localization based key distribution needs exact position of sensor node that can be augmented with the help of GPS. The distance of each node can be calculated with received signal strength from base station. Location aware sensor can improve the energy efficiency. Here nodes can be optimized with distance from base station. The nodes near base station can be switched to low power as compared to node that is very far from base station.

4 Interruption Discovery Framework (IDS)

An interruption discovery framework (IDS) screens suspicious exercises beyond ordinary and unsurprising behaviour, "It depends on the presumption that there exists a reasonable separation in the activities of an intruder and approved client in the system to such an extent that an IDS can coordinate it with pre-chosen or conceivable learned strategy [20]. In view of the examination IDS can distinguish unauthorized activities. Intrusion is an unapproved action inside a system. On the off chance that intrusion goes undetected from beginning state i.e. the time when an intruder endeavor to break the system then it might be unsafe and enemy can take control over the whole system. Once the assault is recognized in the system then IDS raise the flag to advise the base station to make the move for securing the framework (Fig. 1) [22].

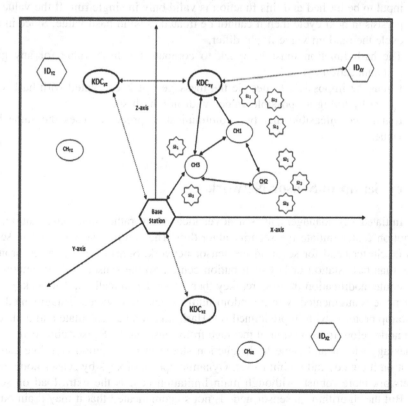

Fig. 1. Interruption discovery framework (IDS) consists of following steps: regular checks on intrusion in network, on detecting suspicious activity inform the key distribution center (KDC), KDC updates key, registering the updated key status in base station.

5 Hashing

We can use the interesting properties of hashing technique. The hash function is one way and hash function is without crash to keep the dynamic attack that changes and retransmits the message. Key updates in light of key chains where each key is gotten by applying a hash formula on next key in chain". Here all keys require not be put in sensor nodes rather that a counter will produce the keys by simply picking an arbitrary number with in a predefined set. Verification of keys id done by checking the hash result. Unapproved client or assailants unfit to ascertain hash values.

5.1 Dynamic Hash Function

The values that are stored in hash table is calculated with a hash function. During the communication process the hash table needs to be expanded or shrink. Such a function is known as dynamic hash function. The ideal cryptographic hash function has following main properties.

I. It is deterministic in context of reuse of same function. That is hash function uses the randomized number that is generated once when a process starts also the input to be hashed and this function is valid only in single run. If the value still persists in next cycle then it cannot be treated as valid hash value. Since in next cycle the random value might differ.

II. The hash function must be quick to compute the hash value for any given communication cycle.

III. It must be impossible to decode the message that is encrypted with hash value except by trying all possible values with in a hash set.

IV. It must be infeasible that two communication processes uses the same hash value.

6 Key Set up in Sensor Network

Node Initiated key management is a novel idea where rather than base station, key distribution center initiate the security algorithm. The control can be given to sensor nodes or cluster head for securing the sensor network. Sensor node is more prone to attacks than base station or key distribution center. So the sensor node if empowered with minute modification in its stored key then it can dynamically update its key. Here sensor node is augmented with a random number generator which is augmented with time stamp protocol with in predefined set. Hash function can calculate and update the key in node before transmission of message from sensor node. Sensor node can encrypt the message with it and same hash function stored in base station can take care for decryption if the key fall within its set. Dynamic update of keys by sensor node makes the network more robust. Although main limitation here is the extra load on sensor node. But the algorithm on sensor node is not so complicated that it may drain out the battery life faster (Fig. 2).

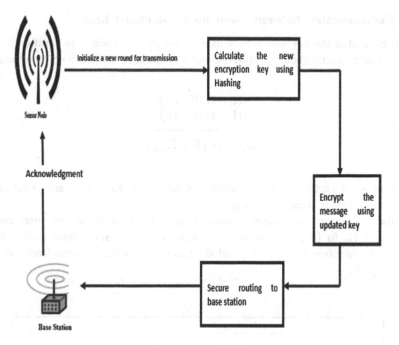

Fig. 2. Proactive key update

During network boot up the following key management process will be initiated.

I. Communication between base station and key distribution center

During boot up process base station transmits a key ring with in the specified hash function to key distribution center (KDC). The key distribution center authenticates and acknowledges the key ring with base station.

$$B(K_i \| KDC_{key}) <\text{-----------------------}> KDC(Ki \| B)$$

Here base station (B) encrypted the key ring (K_i) with key distribution center master key (KDC_{key}).

II. Communication in between KDC and cluster head

Key distribution center encrypt the key ring with cluster head identification number Ksj. i.e. secret key of cluster head and broadcast in network. Cluster head send acknowledgement to key distribution center.

$$KDC (Ki \| K_{sj}) <\text{-------------------}> CH(K_{sj} \| KDC_{key})$$

III. Communication between sensor node and cluster head

Cluster head allot the key values to sensor nodes by processing the certification code for itself and its group nodes by utilizing one way hashing method with its n members" as follows.

$$H_1 = H (K_1, K_{sj})$$
$$H_2 = H (K_2, H_1)$$

$$H_n = H (K_i, H_{n-1})$$

Where K_{sj} is cluster head own secret key and K_{i-1}, K_{i-2}, K_{i-n} are secret keys of sensor nodes with in a cluster group.

In the next phase cluster head transmit its member identification numbers and their hash values H_n to base station by encrypting with K_{sj}. Since base station has all identification numbers and their key values it can decrypt the message from the sensor nodes (Fig. 3).

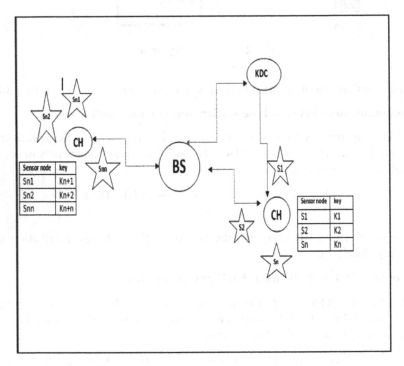

Fig. 3. The figure depicts the mapping in between base station, cluster head and key distribution center. Cluster head have their member table which stores the private key of each sensor node. The member table is updated periodically.

7 Real Time Key Updates in Sensor Network

In order to create a secure transmission" it is necessary to revise the "session key Ksi. Session key is associated with time period for each transmission" cycle. There is a need to update the session key periodically. To updates the keys in sensor nodes cluster head CH broadcast a random number Rt at time t before node capturing time T_{cap} i.e. $(t \ll T_{cap})$ here random number Rt is a function of time period. All nodes under the cluster head updates their key using one way hash method and get rid of the old keys.

The sensor node S scans the time interval t.

$$for \quad S\text{<--------}CH\,(R_t)$$
$$do$$
$$S \text{<--------}F(S,H[t_j])$$

i.e. update in sensor is a function of time cycle. The updated keys now in sensor nodes will be

$$Ks_i\text{-}t1 = H(K_{si},Rt_1)$$
$$Ks_i\text{-}t2 = H(Ks_i\text{--}t1,Rt_2)$$
$$\text{----------------------------}$$
$$Ks_i\text{-}tn = H(Ks_i\text{-}tn\text{-}1,Rt_n)$$

8 Data Transmission Phase

The sensor node with in a cluster head encode the information packet by utilizing its own private key Ksi. Ksi became the session key to exchange message with cluster head. As cluster head node gets all undisclosed key of its nodes, it can decode data from any node i if it is a component of the cluster. The data packet format as" follows:

ID_i	$E_{KSi}(M)$	$M_{ACKSi}(M)$

Where M is sensed data for sensor node, $E_{KSi}(M)$ is the encoded information and $M_{ACKSi}(M)$ is the message validation code. When cluster head (CH) transmits data packets to base station (BS) for execution. It encrypts the packet using its own session key along with insertion of its identification number. If the distance in between cluster head and base station is multihop, then intermediate node just relay the data packets to base station.

If a sensor node would not obtain the broadcasted arbitrary number due to defective wireless channel then it cannot encrypt the message using the latest key and this node can be understood as a intruder node or may be a hacked node to cluster head. Then the proposed method manages this condition as follows.

Each sensor node starts its counter to count the transmission cycle. If a node does not receive any broadcast acknowledgement from base station with in time T_{cap}, it without delay sends a message to its cluster head using previous updated key and last received broadcast number Rt. Cluster head updates the old key Ksi-n-1 with new update key Ksi-n and register this update in base station.

In order to balance the energy consumption re-clustering will take place within the sensor network. After definite time period old cluster will breaks down and new cluster will be formed.re-clustering is done by base station here base station sends a special broadcast message to all its cluster heads to erase its member table. After that a node with energy greater than thrash hold energy is selected as a cluster head and a new member table is formed. All key distribution and management process restarts.

9   Accomplishing Security Goals

Secure key administration and calculation must accomplish the security objectives [21] i.e. honesty, privacy, Availability and freshness to moderate assaults and intimidation as much as expected. These objectives can be outlined as the accompanying:

- Integrity: Data must not be adjusted in transmission way, and insurances must be taken to ensure that information can't be changed by unapproved party. To guarantee that information scopes to the proposed recipient with no modification, a method like hash capacity can be utilized.
- Confidentiality: Confidentiality stays away from vulnerable data from achieving the wrong goal, while ensuring that exclusive the correct collector can in certainty get it. Along these lines, while transmission the information in the system, nobody can comprehend with the exception of" proposed beneficiary.
- Availability: Availability requires that information are accessible to approved gatherings. It is a "necessity proposed to guarantee that WSN work at the named time and administration isn't denied to approve hubs when they ask for them. Along these lines, with accessibility system ought to be accessible even within the sight of assaults.
- Freshness: replay assault abuses the freshness in which assailant retransmits an old message to possess framework assets or befuddling the" collector. Freshness protect that no old message have been replayed.

10   Conclusion

Security in wireless sensor network often vary with purpose and context, but in broad-spectrum, security for wireless sensor networks should centered on the protection of the data itself and the network communications between the nodes. Privacy, reliability and validation are the most important data security concerns. Key management is major concern for security in wireless sensor network. The nodes in sensor network cannot rely on centralized security system like Kerberos. Also tradition cryptographic methods are not promising on resource limited sensor nodes. Node initiated key management is a novel idea where rather than base station or key distribution center initiate the security algorithm. We can give control to sensor nodes or cluster head for securing communicating nodes with in a sensor network. It is a non centralized key management method which is more robust than other methods. Proactive key management must guarantee efficiency, robustness, and dynamic clustering.

References

1. Chan, H., Perrig, A., Song, D.: Key distribution techniques for sensor networks. In: Znati, T., et al. (eds.) Wireless Sensor Networks (2004)
2. Miller, S.P., Neuman, C., Schiller, J.I., Saltzer, J.H.: Kerberos authentication and authorization system. In: Project Athena Technical Plan (1987). Page section E.2.1
3. Huang, X., Shah, P., Sharma, D.: Fast algorithm in ECC for wireless sensor network. In: Proceeding of the International Multiconference of Engineers and Computer Scientist, vol. 2 (2010)
4. Chan, H., Perrig, A., Song, D.: Random key predistribution schemes for sensor networks. In: Proceedings of Symposium on Security and Privacy (2003)
5. Eschenauer, L., Gligor, V.D.: A key-management scheme for distributed sensor networks. In: Proceedings of the 9th ACM Conference on Computer and Communication Security, November 2002
6. Du, W., Deng, J., Han, Y., Varsney, P.: A pairwise key pre distribution system for wireless sensor networks. In: Proceedings of the Tenth ACM Conference on Computer and Communications Security (CCS 2003), pp. 42–51, October 2003
7. Du, W., Deng, J., Han, Y.S., Chen, S., Varshney, P.K.: A key management scheme for wireless sensor networks using deployment knowledge. In: INFOCOM, 2004, April 2004
8. Du, W., Deng, J., Han, Y.S., Varshney, P.K.: A pairwise key pre-distribution for wireless sensor networks. In: Proceedings of the 10th ACM Conference on Computer and Communications Security (CCS 2003), Washington, DC, USA, pp. 42–51 (2003)
9. Faghani, M.R., Motahari, S.M.: Sectorized location dependent key management. In: IEEE International Conference on Wireless and Mobile Computing, Networking and Communications, 12–14 October 2009
10. Boneh, D., Corrigan-Gibbs, H.: Bivariate polynomials modulo composites and their applications. In: Sarkar, P., Iwata, T. (eds.) ASIACRYPT 2014. LNCS, vol. 8873, pp. 42–62. Springer, Heidelberg (2014). https://doi.org/10.1007/978-3-662-45611-8_3
11. Sen, J.: A survey on wireless sensor network security. Int. J. Commun. Netw. Secur. (IJCNIS) 1(2), 55–78 (2009)
12. Azarderakhsh, R., et al.: A key management scheme for cluster base wireless sensor networks. In: IEEE International Conference on Embedded and Ubiquitous Computing (2008)
13. Blackburn, S.R., Etzion, T., Martin, K.M., Paterson, M.B.: Efficient key predistribution for grid-based wireless sensor networks. In: Safavi-Naini, R. (ed.) ICITS 2008. LNCS, vol. 5155, pp. 54–69. Springer, Heidelberg (2008). https://doi.org/10.1007/978-3-540-85093-9_6
14. Younis, M.F., et al.: Location-aware combinatorial key management scheme for clustered sensor networks. IEEE Trans. Parallel Distrib. Syst. 17(8), 865–882 (2006)
15. Magar, A.A.: A Survey about key pre-distribution scheme in wireless sensor networks. Int. J. Eng. Res. General Sci. 2(6) (2014). ISSN 2091-2730

16. Cui, B., Wang, Z., Zhao, B., Liang, X., Ding, Y.: Enhanced key management protocols for wireless sensor networks. Mob. Inf. Syst. **2015**, 10 p. https://doi.org/10.1155/2015/627548. Article ID 627548
17. Kun, M., Li, L.: An efficient pair wise key predistribution scheme for wireless sensor networks. J. Netw. **9**(2), 277 (2014)
18. Lee, J., et al.: Key management issues in wireless sensor networks: current proposals and future developments. IEEE Wirel. Commun. Mag. **14**(5), 76-85 (2007)
19. Diop, A., Qi, Y., Wang, Q., Hussain, S.: An efficient and secure key management scheme for hierarchical wireless sensor networks. Int. J. Comput. Commun. Eng. **1**(4), 365 (2012)
20. Alrajeh, N., Khan, S., Shams, B.: Intrusion detection systems in wireless sensor networks: a review. Int. J. Distrib. Sens. Netw. **9**, 167575 (2013)
21. Gaubatz, G., Kaps, J.-P. Sunar, B.: Public key cryptography in sensor networks. Revisited in 1st European Workshop on Security in Ad-Hoc and Sensor Networks (ESAS 2004) (2004)
22. Choudhary, V., Taruna, S.: Improved key distribution and management in wireless sensor network. J. Wirel. Commun. **1**(1), 16–22 (2016)

Internal Network Penetration Testing Using Free/Open Source Tools: Network and System Administration Approach

Rajiv Kumar[(✉)] and Katlego Tlhagadikgora

Botho University, Gaborone, Botswana
dhiman.rajiv@gmail.com,
katlego.tlhagadikgora@bothouniversity.ac.bw

Abstract. Network security is a growing concern in a modern world, irrespective of the size or volume of the organization. Penetration testing is one of the techniques that are used for network and systems security assessment. It involves legally attempting to break into the network to check available vulnerability and exploits, simulating what a real hacker might do. It can enhance the security of the network as it looks for exploits and vulnerability present in the system, then come up with ways to mitigate the risks. In this paper, a virtual network laboratory is designed and setup to conduct the penetration test by demonstrating attacks and intrusion into the network infrastructure. Kali Linux operating system is used to perform penetration testing. Information gathering, vulnerability analysis, exploitation, reporting also presented as part of penetration testing followed by a penetration testing methodology. Theoretical background on penetration testing has also been discussed. Information gathering tools (Dmitry, Nmap and zenmap), vulnerability scanning tools (Nexpose community, Nessus, GFI Languard and OpenVAS) and exploitation tools (Armitage, Metasploit framework) are used to simulate possible attacks.

Keywords: Kali Linux · Information gathering tools · Network security
Penetration testing · Vulnerability

1 Introduction

1.1 Background Information

Nowadays, Information Technology systems have become an inseparable part of many organization and companies, for easy operations including administration, procurement, teaching, research and sharing information. Even though, IT systems have great advantages, but companies that are using it may suffer a lot if the network is exposed to hackers. Some of the common treats are Denial of Services (DoS), Computer viruses and hackers. The open access nature and many network users in a network makes it difficult for the network administrator to secure the network. But still there is a need for the network to be secured. As a result, the best defense mechanisms need to be implemented to help in securing the network from intruders. To be effectiveness of security measures, there will be a need to conduct penetration testing for assessing

© Springer Nature Singapore Pte Ltd. 2019
A. K. Luhach et al. (Eds.): ICAICR 2018, CCIS 956, pp. 257–269, 2019.
https://doi.org/10.1007/978-981-13-3143-5_22

network security. Penetration testing is a simulation of actions that a real hacker performs to intrude computer network. However, penetration testing and hacking are different. The aim of hacking is more on to causing loss and harm whereas, the main goal of penetration testing is to conduct the test for potential security loopholes that may exist in a computer network. Penetration testing will allow the organization to come up with best solutions for tackling weaknesses, hence increasing network security.

1.2   Objective

The objective of this work is to:

- Setup and design a virtual penetration testing laboratory.
- Identify the appropriate methodology of penetration testing.
- Investigate suitable penetration testing tools based on their performance.
- Explore how penetration testing can help network and systems administrator in improving network security.

2   Literature Review

2.1   Penetration Testing Concepts and Definitions

There are many definitions of penetration testing. Penetration testing is some sequences of tasks or activities that are carried to find out and exploit loop holes. It is researching and studying methods to exploit and counter measures to protect network infrastructures for intruders [1]. Pen testing is not only on information technology infrastructure, but it may also involve a combination of building and users [2]. Penetration testing is defined as "a proactive and authorized attempt to evaluate the security of an IT infrastructure by safely attempting to exploit network and system vulnerabilities, including OS, service and application flaws, improper configurations, and even risky end-user behavior" [3]. Penetration testing is analyzing IT infrastructure and searching for vulnerabilities that might be present and attempt to fix it before intruders can exploit them [4]. "Penetration testing uses the same principles as crackers or hackers to penetrate computer network infrastructure and there by verify the presence of flaws and vulnerabilities and help to confirm the security measures" [5].

2.2   Penetration Tester Tool Box

There are many open source tools available for penetration testing which can perform various task in any phases of pen testing.

2.2.1   Information Gathering Tools

Information gathering tools are used for scanning port, perform operating system and services fingerprinting. Following tools are as:

2.2.1.1 Nmap

Nmap is a open source software licensed under the GNU General Public License. This is used for network administration and penetration testers as it can help in discovering, monitoring and troubleshooting TCP/IP systems [6].

2.2.1.2 Zenmap

Zenmap is an official Nmap graphical user interface (GUI) software. Just like Nmap, it is supported by many operating systems like Linux, Mac OS X Windows operating systems etc. The advantage of Zenmap over Nmap is that it is user-friendly.

2.2.1.3 Dmitry

DMitry is one of the information gathering tools that are pre-installed in Kali Linux [7]. It also called as DeepMagic Information Gathering tool, the application is written in C programing language. It is a Linux command line application. Dmitry is used in gathering information about the targeted host. It is mostly used to gather information like port scan, subdomains associated with the host, email addresses.

2.2.2 Vulnerability Analysis Tools

These tools are used to identify the vulnerability in targeted host.

2.2.2.1 The Open Vulnerability Assessments System

The Open Vulnerability Assessment System commonly known as OpenVAS. This framework offers a complete and one of the powerful scanning and management of vulnerability. It was first called GNessUs. OpenVAS is part of the Greenbone Networks since 2009 which is a commercial solution for managing vulnerability. The development from GreenBone network given to Open Source community [8].

2.2.3 Exploitation Tools

Exploitation tools are used to exploits that has been discovered during scanning phase of penetration testing.

2.2.3.1 Metasploit Framework

Metasploit framework used in the penetration testing. It is developed by Metasploit LLC, the framework was firstly developed using Perl programming language but later re-written in ruby programing language. Metasploit can help user with the following; developing an exploit, penetration testing, fuzzing, creating payloads to attack clients and active exploitation.

2.2.4   Penetration Testing Operating Systems

There are various operating systems designed for conducting the pen testing. Many of these operating systems comes with pre-installed free and open sources tools to perform penetration testing.

2.2.4.1 Kali Linux

Kali Linux is an operating system developed for penetration testing. It is the most popular and powerful penetration testing platform. It is used to perform various security assessments work including penetrating testing and computer forensics [9]. Figure 1 shows the modules available in the operating system.

Fig. 1. Kali Linux menu

3   Research Methodology

3.1   Research Questions

The following research questions are:

- What are the requirements and tools used in setting up of a virtual penetration testing environment?
- What are the free and open source information gathering tools?
- Which methodology is suitable for internal penetration testing?

3.2   Proposed Methodology of Penetration Testing

The proposed methodology for penetration testing are shown in Fig. 2:

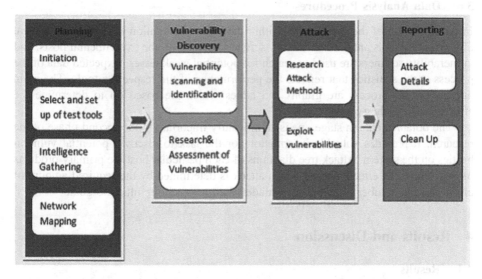

Fig. 2. Proposed methodology of penetration testing

Conducting penetration testing on the production environment can be risky, therefore, virtual penetration laboratory is setup to simulate the environment.

3.3   Virtual Machine Host

Virtual penetration testing laboratory can be achieved by having a computer which has Virtual Machine installed in it. VMware Workstation 12 Player (available at http://www.vmware.com/downloads/) is installed on Windows 10 operating system.

3.4   Kali Linux 2017.3

The virtual machine is installed on Kali Linux operating system. Kali Linux is the most popular penetration testing operating system with more than 600 pre-installed penetration testing tools. Kali Linux 2017.3 ISO file was downloaded free from http://www.kali.org/ website. Kali Linux requires at least 8 GB of disk space and at least 512 MB of RAM.

3.5   PenTester's Tools Installations and Configurations

Kali Linux has already some pre-installed penetration tools, but some tools have installed which are not preinstalled. Information gathering tools (Nmap, Dmitry and zenmap), vulnerability scanning tools (Nessus, OpenVAS and GFI Languard) and exploitation tools (Armitage, Metasploit framework) are used to simulate possible attacks [10].

3.6   Data Analysis Procedures

In the first stage of the experiment, within the virtual simulation environment, several fingerprinting tools are used to identify services running on the experimental hosts, and vulnerability scanners are used to search for potential weaknesses. Expected data of the process is the statistics that reflects the performance of the respective tools. The main outputs of this process are graphs and tables which are based on to determine the effectiveness of the selected tools.

The obtained data in stage one is significantly important to the second phase of the research. It provides valuable information for the task to discover potential vulnerabilities on the system. Attack tree diagrams of each particular host are primary products of this stage. The effectiveness of each attack is determined by the required amount of effort and the number of steps/stages undertaken to reach the ultimate goal.

4   Results and Discussion

4.1   Results

4.1.1   Intelligence Gathering

The intelligence gathering is used to surveying of the network, scanning of ports and operating system fingerprinting. Nmap, Zenmap are used to survey the network, scan for open ports and to find out the operating system running on the targeted host.

4.1.1.1 Intelligence Gathering Results
The intelligence gathering results include surveying of the network, scanning of ports and operating system fingerprinting.

4.1.1.2 Network Surveying
Nmap, Zenmap aree used to identify all live hosts in virtual network segment (Figs. 3 and 4). Network surveying is achieved in Nmap by executing the following command:
    nmap -sP 192.168.100.0/24
    Network surveying was achieved in Zenmap by executing the following command:
    nmap -sn 192.168.100.0/24
    In the above results, nine live host are identified which responded to the ICMP packet. The host on 192.168.100.147 is a Kali Linux machine which is the pen tester's machine. The host on 192.168.100.1 is the host operating system which VMware workstation is installed. The VMware workstation has the IP address 192.168.100.2. Also, there is host 192.168.100.254 which is identified. Therefore, host 192.168.100.2 and 192.168. 100.254 are not part of the targeted host but the remaining six live host being

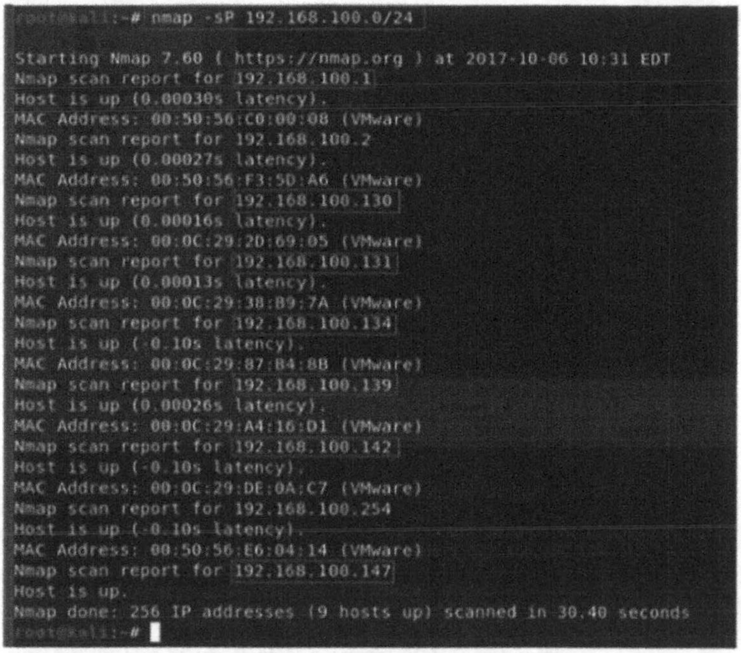

Fig. 3. Nmap's ICMP ping-sweep scan of a network segment

192.168.100.1, 192.168.100.142, 192.168.100.147, 192.168.100.130, 192.168.100.131, 192.168.100.134 and 92.168.100.139 are scanned and enumerated further as they are the targeted hosts.

4.1.1.3 Network Scanning

Identifying live host and their IP addresses are followed by port scanning together with operating system and services fingerprinting. The main purpose of network scanning is to find open ports and provide the services which are running. Two live host 192.168.100.131 and 192.168.100.147 do not have any ports open so they are not used during the next stage of operating system and service fingerprinting (Fig. 5).

4.1.1.4 OS and Services Fingerprinting

Only host which has open port, are used for OS and Services fingerprinting. Host 192.168.100.1, 192.168.100.142, 192.168.100.130, 192.168.100.134 and 192.168.100. 139 are used (Figs. 6, 7, 8 and 9). It is achieved by executing the following command:
nmap -T4 -A -v 192.168.100.0/24.

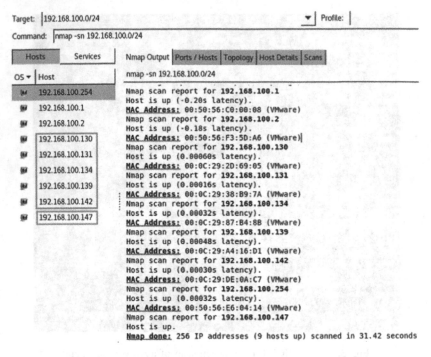

Fig. 4. Zenmap host Scan results

Nmap scan report for 192.168.100.130		
PORT	STATE	SERVICE
25/tcp	open	smtp
80/tcp	open	http
135/tcp	open	msrpc
445/tcp	open	microsoft-ds
3389/tcp	open	ms-wbt-server
49153/tcp	open	unknown
49155/tcp	open	unknown
49156/tcp	open	unknown

Nmap scan report for 192.168.100.142		
PORT	STATE	SERVICE
135/tcp	open	msrpc
139/tcp	open	netbios-ssn
445/tcp	open	microsoft-ds
49156/tcp	open	unknown

Nmap scan report for 192.168.100.139		
PORT	STATE	SERVICE
21/tcp	open	ftp
22/tcp	open	ssh
23/tcp	open	telnet
25/tcp	open	smtp
53/tcp	open	domain
80/tcp	open	http
111/tcp	open	rpcbind
139/tcp	open	netbios-ssn
445/tcp	open	microsoft-ds
513/tcp	open	login
514/tcp	open	shell
2049/tcp	open	nfs
2121/tcp	open	ccproxy-ftp
3306/tcp	open	mysql
5432/tcp	open	postgresql
5900/tcp	open	vnc
6000/tcp	open	X11
8009/tcp	open	ajp13

Nmap scan report for 192.168.100.1		
PORT	STATE	SERVICE
135/tcp	open	msrpc
139/tcp	open	netbios-ssn
445/tcp	open	microsoft-ds

Nmap scan report for 192.168.100.131		
PORT	STATE	SERVICE

Nmap scan report for 192.168.100.147		
PORT	STATE	SERVICE

Fig. 5. Nmap and Zenmap scan results

4.1.1.5 Conclusion

Intelligence gathering is used during vulnerability scanning and analysis. Nine live host are identified during network surveying but only the following are used during network scanning as they are the targeted host. The host went through network scanning are

IP Address	192.168.100.1	
OS	Windows 10 Enterprise 10240 (Windows 10 Enterprise 6.3)	
Name	USER-PC	

PORT	STATE	SERVICE	VERSION
135/tcp	open	msrpc	Microsoft Windows RPC
139/tcp	open	netbios-ssn	Microsoft Windows netbios-ssn
445/tcp	open	microsoft-ds	Windows 10 Enterprise 10240 microsoft-ds (workgroup: WORKGROUP)
1801/tcp	open	msmq?	
2103/tcp	open	msrpc	Microsoft Windows RPC
2105/tcp	open	msrpc	Microsoft Windows RPC
2107/tcp	open	msrpc	Microsoft Windows RPC

Fig. 6. Services Enumerating on host 192.168.100.1 results for Nmap and Zenmap

IP Address	192.168.100.130	
OS	Windows Server (R) 2008 Enterprise 6002 Service Pack 2 (Windows Server (R) 2008 Enterprise 6.0)	
Name	WIN-OL9D5CIXLV7	

PORT	STATE	SERVICE	VERSION
25/tcp	open	smtp	Microsoft ESMTP 7.0.6001.18000
80/tcp	open	http	Microsoft IIS httpd 7.0
135/tcp	open	msrpc	Microsoft Windows RPC
445/tcp	open	microsoft-ds	Windows Server (R) 2008 Enterprise 6002 Service Pack 2 microsoft-ds (workgroup: WORKGROUP)
1801/tcp	open	msmq?	
2103/tcp	open	msrpc	Microsoft Windows RPC
2105/tcp	open	msrpc	Microsoft Windows RPC
2107/tcp	open	msrpc	Microsoft Windows RPC
3389/tcp	open	ssl/ms-wbt-server?	
49153/tcp	open	msrpc	Microsoft Windows RPC
49155/tcp	open	msrpc	Microsoft Windows RPC
49156/tcp	open	msrpc	Microsoft Windows RPC
49158/tcp	open	msrpc	Microsoft Windows RPC

Fig. 7. Services Enumerating on host 192.168.100.130 results for Nmap and Zenmap

192.168.100.1, 192.168.100.142, 192.168.100.147, 192.168.100.130, 192.168.100. 131, 192.168.100.134 and 192.168.100.139. On which are 192.168.100.147 is a Kali Linux machine which is the pen tester's machine. The host on 192.168.100.1 is the host operating system which VMware workstation is installed. The VMware workstation has the IP address 192.168.100.2. Also, there is host 192.168.100.254 which is identified and unknown. OS and service fingerprinting results show that host 192.168.100.1 operating system is Windows 10 Enterprise 10240 (Windows 10 Enterprise 6.3) and has the following services running msrpc, netbios-ssn, microsoft-ds, msmq?, msrpc, msrpc, msrpc. Host 192.168.100.130 operating system is Windows Server (R) 2008 Enterprise 6002 Service Pack 2 (Windows Server (R) 2008 Enterprise 6.0) has the following services were identified smtp, http, msrpc, microsoft-ds, msmq?, ssl/ms-wbt-server?.

IP Address	192.168.100.139
OS	Linux 2.6.9 - 2.6.33
Name	metasploitable

PORT	STATE	SERVICE	VERSION
21/tcp	open	ftp	vsftpd 2.3.4
22/tcp	open	ssh	OpenSSH 4.7p1 Debian 8ubuntu1 (protocol 2.0)
23/tcp	open	telnet	Linux telnetd
25/tcp	open	smtp	Postfix smtpd
53/tcp	open	domain	ISC BIND 9.4.2
80/tcp	open	http	Apache httpd 2.2.8 ((Ubuntu) DAV/2)
111/tcp	open	rpcbind	2 (RPC #100000)
139/tcp	open	netbios-ssn	Samba smbd 3.X - 4.X (workgroup: WORKGROUP)
445/tcp	open	netbios-ssn	Samba smbd 3.0.20-Debian (workgroup: WORKGROUP)
512/tcp	open	exec	netkit-rsh rexecd
513/tcp	open	login?	
514/tcp	open	shell	Netkit rshd
1099/tcp	open	java-rmi	Java RMI Registry
1524/tcp	open	shell	Metasploitable root shell
2049/tcp	open	nfs	2-4 (RPC #100003)
2121/tcp	open	ftp	ProFTPD 1.3.1
3306/tcp	open	mysql	MySQL 5.0.51a-3ubuntu5
5432/tcp	open	postgresql	PostgreSQL DB 8.3.0 - 8.3.7
5900/tcp	open	vnc	VNC (protocol 3.3)
6000/tcp	open	X11	(access denied)
6667/tcp	open	irc	UnrealIRCd
8009/tcp	open	ajp13	Apache Jserv (Protocol v1.3)
8180/tcp	open	http	Apache Tomcat/Coyote JSP engine 1.1

Fig. 8. Services Enumerating on host 192.168.100.139 results for Nmap and Zenmap

IP Address	192.168.100.142
OS	Windows 8.1 Enterprise 9600 (Windows 8.1 Enterprise 6.3)
Name	WIN-1O38MSKB5Q6

PORT	STATE	SERVICE	VERSION
135/tcp	open	msrpc	Microsoft Windows RPC
139/tcp	open	netbios-ssn	Microsoft Windows netbios-ssn
445/tcp	open	microsoft-ds	Windows 8.1 Enterprise 9600 microsoft-ds (workgroup: WORKGROUP)
49156/tcp	open	msrpc	Microsoft Windows RPC

Fig. 9. Services Enumerating on host 192.168.100.142 results for Nmap and Zenmap

4.1.2 Results from Nessus

Nessus is used for vulnerability scanning and analysis against the already identified target host. The report of the scan is generated listing vulnerabilities against each host. The vulnerability results of the scan using Nessus on the targeted host is shown in Table 1:

Table 1. Vulnerability results of the scan using Nessus

Target host	Critical	High	Medium	Low
192.168.100.130	1	2	0	5
192.168.100.1	1	5	2	4
192.168.100.139	14	109	27	1
192.168.100.142	1	29	23	98

4.1.3 Results from OpenVAS

OpenVAS is also used together with Nessus under similar configuration. The report of the scan is generated that list vulnerabilities against each host. From both the scanners, shows that the host were vulnerable to Buffer overflow, spoofing, remote execution of code, Denial of services and privilege elevation. Further investigation is performed to see if the vulnerable identified are exploitable in the next phase that is shown in Table 2:

Table 2. Efficiency of the scanners

Scanner	Plug-ins Count	Total Discovered	CVE's Identified	% (all CVEs Vulnerabilities)
Nessus	48,296	915	473	51%
OpenVAS	25,563	803	493	61%

4.2 Discussion

In each penetration testing phase, information is obtained to successfully test the network. Intelligence gathering phase used to identify host that are reachable in the network, open ports, guessing the operating system and its services running. Nmap and Zenmap are used to perform different scans including ping scam, port scan, operating system and services fingerprinting.

The -sP flag is initially used in nmap to find out all host that are available in the network. The -sn flag is used in zenmap to find available host. Nine live host are identified which responded to the ICMP packet. To check if the network has any device that filter the intruders the -sA flag was used and was successful which means there were not firewalls in the network. The -T4, -A -v flags are used to find out which operating system, open ports, services and service version are running on the identified host. Nmap has proved to be the best penetration tools for intelligence gathering phase. Network vulnerability scanning, and analysis are performed using OpenVAS and Nessus vulnerability scanners. Both the scanners performed the scan on the virtual penetration testing network. Vulnerabilities detected by Nessus are higher than that of OpenVAS, but the effectiveness of the tool is not based on higher detection rate because there are possibilities that they are affected by false negative and false positive. So, it is important for network and system administrator come out with a reliable way to compare effectiveness of the scanner. It is hard to find whether the scanners refer to the same vulnerability because both the scanner has their own matrices for ranking the vulnerability.

For common evaluation, the CVE's identifiers are used for providing a standardized platform for evaluation. OpenVAS vulnerability scanner is effective than Nessus based on the CVE's vulnerabilities percentages. Though OpenVAS had misses some vulnerabilities on some hosts e.g. it misses to address the Microsoft Bulleting 11-020 but Nessus is able to address it. Both the tools are good at discovering the vulnerabilities. OpenVAS has performed satisfactorily even though Nessus has many plugins. While performing network scanning and vulnerability assessments, Nessus discovered that 192.168.100.130 has vulnerabilities that are exploitable and critical. The vulnerabilities are addressed by Microsoft in 2009 bulletin MS09-050. The host has installed Microsoft Windows Server 2008 and the vulnerability are exploited by Metasploit Framework. The results have shown the importance of penetration testing in identifying network weaknesses.

5 Conclusion

Penetration testing is very important in information systems security. It provides the security posture of the organization's Information technology infrastructure. It is useful in data breach investigation to find out the loop holes exploited to even the attackers. It is useful to find and learn as much as possible information about the tested network or host which used to find the active hacker on the network. Penetration testing is used to find flaws both on hardware or software either known or unknown and attempt to exploit the vulnerabilities before they are being exploited by hackers. Penetration testing access the network defense mechanisms far much better then vulnerability assessment and able to identify whether the weakness are technical issues or human errors. Penetration testing used to test Information technology (IT) policies and procedure and help in testing employee's awareness on IT security by conducting phishing and social engineering.

References

1. Almubairik, N.A., Wills, G.: Automated penetration testing based on a threat model. In: International Conference for Internet Technology and Secured Transactions (ICITST-2016), vol. 11, pp. 413–414 (2016)
2. Ami, P., Hasan, A.: Seven phrase penetration testing model. Int. J. Comput. Appl. **59**(5), 16–20 (2012)
3. Cardwell, K.: Building Virtual Pentesting Labs for Advanced Penetration Testing, 1st edn. Packt Publishing, Birmingham (2014)
4. Concise, A.C.: Hacker tools top ten (2017). https://www.concise-courses.com/hacking-tools/ . Accessed 2 Nov 2017
5. Denis, M., Zena, C., Hayajneh, T.: Penetration testing: concepts, attack methods, and defense strategies. IEEE (2014)
6. Infosec Institute: Pros and cons in penetration testing services: the debate continues (2016). http://resources.infosecinstitute.com/pros-and-cons-in-penetration-testing-servicesthe-debate-continues/#gref. Accessed 6 Oct 2017
7. InfoSec Institute: The types of penetration testing (2016). http://resources.infosecinstitute.com/the-types-of-penetration-testing/#gref. Accessed 4 Oct 2017
8. Kennedy, D., O'Gorman, J., Kearns, D., Aharoni, M.: METASPLOIT - The Penetration Tester's Guide. No Starch Press, San Francisco (2011)
9. Kim, P.: The Hacker Playbook - Practical Guide to Penetration Testing. Secure Planet LLC, South Carolina (2014)
10. Liu, L., Xu, J., Cuo, C.: Exposing SQL injection vulnerability through penetration test based on finite state machine. In: IEEE International Conference on Computer and Communications, vol. 2, pp. 1171–1175 (2016)

Performance Analysis of Receiver Diversity Incorporated WiMAX Systems

Akanksha Sharma[1], Lavish Kansal[1], Gurjot Singh Gaba[1($\boxtimes$)],
Mohamed El Bakkali[2], and Faisel Em Tubbal[3,4,5]

[1] School of Electronics and Electrical Engineering, Lovely Professional
University, Phagwara, Punjab, India
akkugood.sharma@gmail.com, lavish.15911@lpu.co.in,
er.gurjotgaba@gmail.com
[2] Signals, Systems and Components Laboratory, Faculty of Sciences
and Technologies, Sidi Mohamed Ben Abdellah University, Fez, Morocco
mohamed.elbakkali@usmba.ac.ma
[3] School of Electrical, Computer and Telecommunications Engineering,
University of Wollongong, Wollongong, NSW 2522, Australia
faisel@uow.edu.au
[4] School of Computing, Engineering and Mathematics,
Western Sydney University, Sydney, NSW 2522, Australia
[5] Technological Projects Department, The Libyan Centre for Remote Sensing
and Space Science, Tripoli, Libya

Abstract. Orthogonal Frequency Division Multiplexing (OFDM) being used as two layers specifically in wireless interoperability for microwave access (WiMAX) i.e. Physical layer (PHY) and MAC layer and we considered PHY layer having scalable OFDM based Multiple access (OFDMA) due to empowering achievable usage of multiple antenna systems, for example, Multiple input multiple output (MIMO) with sensible intricacy. This paper includes a simulation analysis of the hybrid combination of receiver diversity (MIMO) and WiMAX system. The receiver diversity techniques studied in this paper are maximal ratio combining (MRC) and selection combining (SC). The analysis is done for diverse diversity techniques, modulation levels and cyclic prefix rates. Simulated results clearly depict the effect on increasing the number of receiving antenna on the bit error rate (BER) of every modulation level.

Keywords: OFDM · WiMAX · MIMO · MRC · SC

1 Introduction

In June 2001, the WiMAX Forum described a standardized form IEEE 802.16 for the purpose of ensuring the coherence and reliability that is popularly known as Wireless MAN [1]. WiMAX is a get to innovation that grants higher information rates of about 1Gbps over long separations, proficient transmission bandwidth and diminishes obstructions. IEEE 802.16 viable organization started creating innovations for wireless urban connections in 2000 [2–4]; in 2002 they distributed their first standard for observable pathway availability in 10–66 GHz frequency band (IEEE 802.16c). The

© Springer Nature Singapore Pte Ltd. 2019
A. K. Luhach et al. (Eds.): ICAICR 2018, CCIS 956, pp. 270–281, 2019.
https://doi.org/10.1007/978-981-13-3143-5_23

interconnection between remote users, point to multi-point (PMP) and point to point (PPP) microwave communications uses IEEE 802.16c standard [5–7]. For non-line-of-sight (NLOS) connectivity, IEEE 802.16a was proposed by IEEE which operated in the lower frequency range of 2–11 GHz. This was redesigned in 2004 (IEEE 802.16d) for smaller frequencies of 2–11 GHz range, focused to give a wideband associations to indoor clients [8–11].

The organization of the paper is as: Sect. 2 presents a detail idea about the functioning of the physical layer of WiMAX under the principle of orthogonal frequency division multiplexing. Section 3 depicts diverse classifications of the MIMO, whereas Sect. 4 briefly presents an idea about the methodology of MIMO-WiMAX system. Section 5 elaborated the Receiver Diversity techniques and Sect. 6 comprises of simulation results and their discussions. The conclusions inferred from the simulation results are presented in Sect. 7.

2 OFDM: PHY Layer of WiMAX

The fundamental part of WiMAX physical layer is to cipher the binary digits that serve as MAC outlines and furthermore, to transmit and get these signals over the correspondence media [12]. This errand is finished by the accompanying procedure as demonstrated as follows. The block diagram for WiMAX system (802.16e standard) is shown in Fig. 1.

(a) Randomization

The first assignment is given to randomization to remove copied arrangement of ones and nulls by improving coding performance

Equation (1) determines the generator of the Randomizer

$$1 + x^{14} + x^{15} = out \tag{1}$$

(b) Forward Error Correction (FEC)

Forward error correction (FEC) is used to encode the data which in turn enables the detection and correction of the errors at the receiver side. Diverse FEC encoding schemes are: RS codes, TURBO codes, convolution codes etc.

RS codes

They are effective straight non-binary block codes equipped for remedying numerous irregular errors, as well as 'burst-error' correction; that is, they are successful for channels that have consciousness.

Convolution Codes

Convolutional codes provide a way to deal with error control coding generously unique about that of block codes. They encode/work on serial data code streams as opposed to on data hinders, as done by Block error adjusting codes. Convolution codes contain memory that uses past bits information to encode or decode (Block codes are memoryless). Its execution is less delicate to Signal-to-Noise Ratio variations than that of Block codes. In circumstances of constrained power where SNR would be a worry, the favored strategy for accomplishing FEC depends on convolutional codes.

(c) Interleaving

Interleaving is a procedure or philosophy to make a framework more effective, quick and dependable by arranging information in a noncontiguous manner. A block interleaver acknowledges an arrangement of symbols and revises them, without rehashing or excluding any of the symbols from the set. The quantity of images in every set is settled for a given interleaver.

(d) Modulation

The output of the interleaver is forwarded to the digital modulation system which maps the bits onto the constellation points. The serially input data bits in the digital modulator are mapped onto the constellation points based on the level of modulation being utilized in the modulator i.e. M-QAM & M-PSK, where M is a number constellation of points in the constellation diagram.

(e) Inverse FFT

Inverse FFT is being utilized in OFDM to assign diverse orthogonal sub carriers to the symbols being generated by the digital modulator. Inverse FFT is being implemented in discrete domain having N point input and output. By utilizing N no. of subcarriers then IFFT gets N no. of sinusoidal symbols.

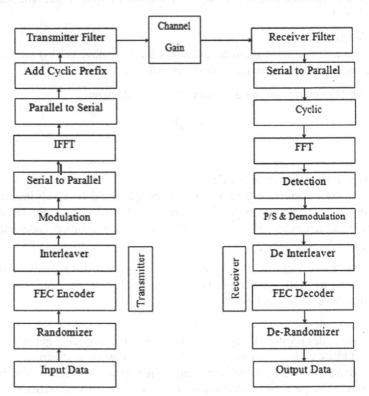

Fig. 1. WiMAX physical layer model

(f) Cyclic Prefix

It copies a few specimens from the end of the symbols and puts them in front to add some redundancy. These cloned samples are called Cyclic Prefix. Principle reason for existing is to avert inter-symbol interference brought about by multi path spread.

(g) Reciever

Principle intention is to acquire unique information bits. The cyclic prefix is expelled as guard interval. At that point, FFT is performed and changed in the frequency domain. Then demodulation, de-interleaving and de-randomization are performed easily.

As observed from Fig. 1, it is shown that how the Physical WiMAX flow works and the various terms associated with it. This model tells how the data is processed from Input to output and in between what process is used and how to be implemented to make it work successfully. Behavior of transmitter and receiver is well explained and we can get to know from this Physical layer model.

3 MIMO Systems

Multiple antennas are placed at transmitter and receiver, and this collection of arrangement can be called as MIMO as shown in Fig. 2. MIMO systems specially take the advantage of spatial diversity which is obtained by spatially detached antennas in multipath dispersed surroundings. MIMO systems can be resolved using numerous ways that can be either diversity gain or coding gain and both play an important role in MIMO [13, 14]. The requirement of better SNR in MIMO is needed and advances the data rate by providing better capacity being proportional to antennas. Broadly classified into three categories [15, 16], first one is directing the beam in focused & needed direction. Second is sending same copies of data from the transmitter to receiver to experience different fading and better reliability. The third one is spatial multiplexing for sending different data from transmitter to receiver to get maximum throughput.

(a) Spatial diversity (SD)

A technique that gives at least two contributions at the recipient to such an extent that contributions of the blurring phenomena are not associated. On the off chance that one radio way experiences extreme blur at a certain time, another independent way may have a stable signal at that information.

Successful implementation of the diversity requires that all the diverse branches must be having low degree of correlation between them. All the diverse aspects of the radio channel are being utilized to ensure that the multiple replicas of the signal will be received at the receiver end. Expecting two radio wires at the transmitter side and we utilize them to send same information. Since these two antennas are set sufficiently far from each other, similar information is transmitted to the beneficiary using various ways that are encountering distinctive signals called as spatial diversity or transmit diversity [3]. It battles channel fading and reliable communication.

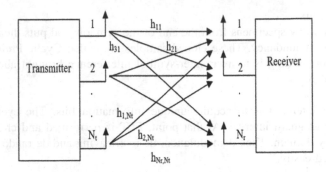

Fig. 2. Block diagram of MIMO system

The main idea behind this technique is that, when two or more independent signals are taken, these signals fade in such a manner such that some signals are less attenuated. This diversity technique receives multiple replicas of the transmitted signal at the receiver as same information is transmitted through different antennas such that the received signal is the coherent combination of the transmitted signals but with small correlation in fading statistics.

(b) Spatial multiplexing (SM)

The spatial multiplexing technique includes layered architectures that improve the capacity of the MIMO system. One such technique is known as V-BLAST which was developed by Bell Laboratories [6]. The number of receiving antennas must be equal to or greater than the number of transmit antennas such that data can be transmitted over different antennas [14].

(c) Beamforming

Beamforming, a third technique in MIMO systems, exploits the knowledge of channel at the transmitter end. Mainly to focus energy towards one receiver, we

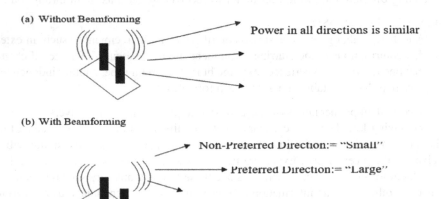

Fig. 3. Beamforming (with & without)

prefer beamforming as shown in Fig. 3. It provides the gain which is in between diversity and multiplexing. Main benefits of beamforming technique are increased receive signal gain, by making signals add up constructively that are emitted from different antennas and reducing the multipath fading effect which is caused when the transmitted signal passes through the channel.

4 MIMO-WiMAX

The MIMO-WiMAX stage is computationally effective and fit for reproducing space-specific, time-specific and frequency specific fading conditions [15]. The test system can re-enact any subjective power-delay profile without expanding the recipients sampling frequency. The test system has the capacity of simulating semi static fading conditions and block fading conditions [17, 18]. The stage was utilized to simulate current coding advances which comprise of Space-Time codes, Space-Frequency codes and Space-Time-Frequency codes [8]. To enhance information rate and spectral efficiency, WIMAX includes Matrix A and Matrix B MIMO as shown in Fig. 4.

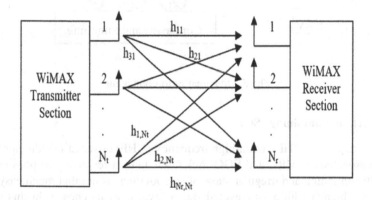

Fig. 4. MIMO-WiMAX system communication

5 Diversity Combining Techniques

It is vital to consolidate the uncorrelated blurred signs which were acquired from the diversity branches to get legitimate diversity advantage. The brushing framework ought to be in such a way, to the point that enhances the execution of the communication systems. Diversity combining likewise expands the signal-to-noise ratio (SNR) or the power of received signal [13]. For the most part, the combining ought to be connected in receiver part; in any case, it is likewise conceivable to apply in transmission.

5.1   Maximal Ratio Combining (MRC)

This is an extremely valuable procedure to affray channel fading. It is a matchless combining process which accomplishes the finest execution change contrasting with different strategies. In the MRC combining technique, before summing or joining, the signals from various diversity branches are co-phased and weighted. The connected weighting to the diversity branches must be balanced bestowing to the SNR [16]. In MRC, all the branches are utilized at the same time. Each of the branch signals is weighted with a pickup element about its particular SNR. We have points of interest over other combining methods. Like, MRC combining can be substantial regardless of the possibility that individual SNRs are little. For two recipients, MRC gives almost 10 dB improvement at 1% BER, while selection diversity 2–3 dB. MRC is an ideal arrangement as shown in Fig. 5.

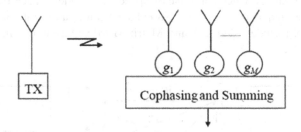

Fig. 5. Maximal ratio combining

5.2   Selection Combining (SC)

Very high frequency (VHF), Ultra-high frequency (UHF) or versatile radio applications are not reasonable for MRC and EGC. Acknowledgment regarding co-phasing circuit with multipath fading and irregular stage of surroundings is not that much easy. In SC, the diversity branch with most elevated signal level must be chosen. In this way, the primary calculation of this technique is on the basis of rule to choose the best signal amongst all signals at receiver side. Accordingly the SC is the most utilized diversity technique in wireless communication [17].

The general type of choice joining needs screening of every diversity branch and choose the finest one (the one which has the highest SNR) for revelation. So, we can say that SC is not a consolidating strategy rather a determination methodology at the applicable diversity. However, as system has to select the best antenna in a very short time, so measuring the signal is difficult. By choosing the connection with the highest SNR is directly related to choose the connection with highest received power when average noise power is similar in every branch. Along these lines, it is commonsense to choose the branch which has the biggest signal structure, noise and impedance (Fig. 6).

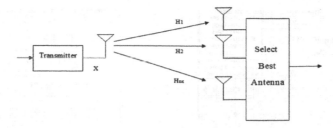

Fig. 6. Selection combining

6   Results Discussion

6.1   Selection Combining – WiMAX vs. Conventional WiMAX

Analysis of Selection Combining-WiMAX vs. conventional WiMAX is being shown in Fig. 7. Simulations are carried by varying Modulation rates i.e. BPSK1/2, QPSK1/2, QPSK1/4, 16-QAM1/2, 16-QAM3/4, 64-QAM2/3 & 64-QAM 3/4, cyclic prefix values i.e. 1/4, 1/8, 1/16 and taking Rayleigh channel into consideration, means there is no a direct LOS communication between each transmitting and receiving end. Taking two receiver antennas i.e. Nrx = 2 and Nrx = 3 of SC and WiMAX and compared these three and overall results showed that BER (Bit Error Rate) decreases in all cases which is the biggest advantage. So, these all analysis are in case of selection combining, where it has to choose best antenna and BER also decreases at a sufficient rate for CP = 1/4, 1/8, 1/16. While comparing with conventional WiMAX, there is much decrease in BER which provides the better system.

6.2   Maximal Ratio Combining –WiMAX vs Conventional WiMAX

Analysis of Maximal Ratio Combining-WiMAX vs. conventional WiMAX is being shown in Fig. 8. Simulation is being carried over various Modulation rates i.e. BPSK1/2, QPSK1/2, QPSK1/4, 16-QAM1/2, 16-QAM3/4, 64-QAM2/3 & 64-QAM 3/4, cyclic prefix values i.e. 1/4, 1/8, 1/16 and taking Rayleigh channel into consideration, means there is no direct LOS communication between each transmitting and receiving end. Taking two receiver antennas i.e. Nrx = 2 and Nrx = 3 of MRC and WiMAX and compared these three and overall results showed that BER (Bit Error Rate) decreases in all cases which is the biggest advantage.

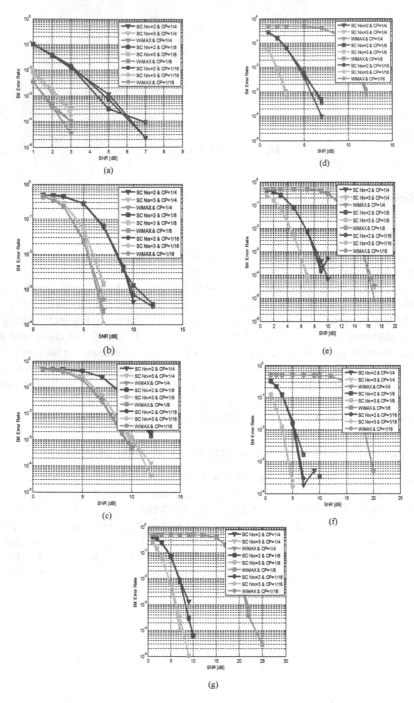

Fig. 7. (a–g): BER versus SNR comparison of Selection Combining-WiMAX vs Conventional WiMAX for (a) BPSK1/2 (b) QPSK1/2 (c) QPSK1/4 (d) 16-QAM1/2 (e) 16-QAM3/4 (f) 64-QAM2/3 (g) 64-QAM3/4

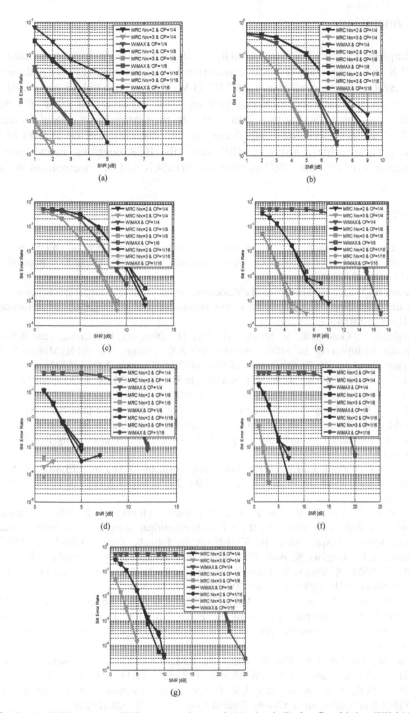

Fig. 8. (a–g): BER versus SNR comparison of Maximal Ratio Combining-WiMAX vs Conventional WiMAX for (a) BPSK1/2 (b) QPSK1/2 (c) QPSK1/4 (d) 16-QAM1/2 (e) 16-QAM3/4 (f) 64-QAM2/3 (g) 64-QAM3/4

7 Conclusion

The implementation of various techniques of receiver diversity incorporated with WiMAX and comparison of it with conventional WiMAX schemes clearly depicts the better BER performance in case of MIMO-WiMAX. This hybrid combination of receiver diversity and WiMAX can give an SNR advantage of 10–20 dB with a number of antennas varying from 2 to 3. The detailed comparison clearly depicts that the MRC diversity technique outperforms the SC diversity scheme in term of SNR requirements to achieve a desired BER. Also, the BER degrades on increasing the modulation level for both MRC incorporated WiMAX and SC incorporated WiMAX.

References

1. Banelli, P., Cacopardi, S.: Theoretical analysis and performance of OFDM signals in nonlinear AWGN channels. IEEE Trans. Commun. **48**(3), 430–441 (2000). https://doi.org/10.1109/26.837046
2. Chen, B., Wang, H.: Maximum likelihood estimation of OFDM carrier frequency offset. In: IEEE International Conference on Communications, pp. 49–53 (2002). https://doi.org/10.1109/97.1001648
3. Bighieri, E., Goldsmith, A., Muquet, B., Sari, H.: Diversity, interference cancellation and spatial multiplexing in MIMO mobile WiMAX systems. In: IEEE Mobile WiMAX Symposium, pp. 74–79 (2007). https://doi.org/10.1109/wimax.2007.348702
4. Li, Q., Lin, X.E., Zhang, J.: MIMO precoding in 802.16e WiMAX. J. Commun. Netw. **9**(2), 141–149 (2007). https://doi.org/10.1109/JCN.2007.6182833
5. Maré, K.P., Maharaj, B.T.: Performance analysis of modern space-time codes on a MIMO-WiMAX platform. In: IEEE International Conference on Wireless and Mobile Computing, Networking and Communications, pp. 139–144 (2008). https://doi.org/10.1109/wimob.2008.84
6. Alex, S.P., Jalloul, L.M.A.: Performance evaluation of MIMO in IEEE802.16e/WiMAX. IEEE J. Sel. Topics Sig. Process. **2**(2), 181–190 (2008). https://doi.org/10.1109/JSTSP.2008.922508
7. Sezginer, S., Sari, H., Biglieri, E.: A comparison of full-rate full-diversity 2x2 space-time codes for WiMAX systems. In: IEEE 10th International Symposium on Spread Spectrum Techniques and Applications, pp. 97–102 (2008). https://doi.org/10.1109/isssta.2008.24
8. Kobeissi, R., Sezginer, S., Buda, F.: Downlink performance analysis of full-rate STCs in 2x2 MIMO WiMAX systems. In: IEEE 69th Vehicular Technology Conference, pp. 1–5 (2009). https://doi.org/10.1109/vetecs.2009.5073513
9. Mehlführer, C., Caban, S., García-Naya, J.A., Rupp, M.: Throughput and capacity of MIMO WiMAX. In: Conference Record of the Forty-Third Asilomar Conference on Signals, Systems and Computers, pp. 1426–1430 (2009). https://doi.org/10.1109/acssc.2009.5469848
10. Tan, K., Andrian, J.H., Zhu, H., Candocia, F.M., Zhou, C.: A novel spectrum encoding MIMO communication system. Wirel. Pers. Commun. **52**(1), 147–163 (2010)
11. Murty, M.S., Veeraiah, D., Rao, A.S.: Performance evaluation of Wi-Fi comparison with WiMAX networks. Int. J. Distrib. Parallel Syst. **3**(1), 321–328 (2012)

12. Tilwari, V., Kushwah, A.S.: Performance analysis of Wi-Max 802.16 e physical layer using digital modulation techniques and code rates. Int. J. Eng. Res. Appl. **3**(4), 2248–9622 (2013). https://doi.org/10.1109/WOCN.2012.6335540
13. Hemalatha, M., Prithviraj, V., Jayalalitha, S., Thenmozhi, K.: Space diversity knotted with WiMAX-a way for undistorted and anti-corruptive channel. Wirel. Pers. Commun. **71**(4), 3023–3032 (2013)
14. Zerrouki, H., Feham, M.: A physical layer simulation for WiMAX MIMO-OFDM system: throughput comparison between 2×2 STBC and 2×2 V-BLAST in Rayleigh fading channel. In: International Conference on Multimedia Computing and Systems, pp. 757–764 (2014). https://doi.org/10.1109/ICMCS.2014.6911358
15. Divya, S., Kumar, H.A., Vishalakshi, A.: An improved spectral efficiency of WiMAX using 802.16G based technology. In: International Conference on Advanced Computing and Communication Systems, pp. 1–4 (2015). https://doi.org/10.1109/icaccs.2015.7324098
16. Yang, K., Yang, N., Xing, C., Wu, J., An, J.: Space–time network coding with antenna selection. IEEE Trans. Veh. Technol. **65**, 5264–5274 (2016). https://doi.org/10.1109/tvt.2015.2455233
17. Khedhiri, R., Hajri, N., Youssef, N.: On the performance analysis of binary non-coherent modulations with selection combining in double rice fading channels. In: IEEE 27th Annual International Symposium on Personal, Indoor, and Mobile Radio Communications (PIMRC), Valencia, Spain, pp. 1–5 (2016). https://doi.org/10.1109/pimrc.2016.7794644
18. Fang, C., Makki, B., Xu, X., Svensson, T.: Equal gain combining in Poisson networks with spatially correlated interference signals. IEEE Wirel. Commun. Lett. **5**(6), 628–631 (2016). https://doi.org/10.1109/lwc.2016.2608960

Multi-source Energy Harvesting System for Sensor Nodes

Neha Garg$^{(\boxtimes)}$ and Ritu Garg

Computer Engineering Department, National Institute of Technology,
Kurukshetra, Kurukshetra, India
Nehagarg702@gmail.com, Ritu.59@nitkkr.ac.in

Abstract. To prolong the lifetime of sensor nodes, energy harvesting systems are installed with sensor nodes for harvesting energy from environmental sources like sunlight, wind speed and so on and recharge their batteries. Widely utilized energy harvesting systems depend on sunlight and wind speed, which are predictable. However, the energy produced by the solar light is not continuous during the daytime and null at night. Energy produced by wind speed is not sufficient for powering the sensor nodes all the time. To resolve this problem, we have proposed a multi-source energy harvesting system which harvests energy from both solar light and wind speed. We also discuss how energy is produced by our proposed multi-source energy harvesting system. Our proposed multi-source energy harvesting system comprises of the real-world sensor node platform, solar panel and wind turbine. Results from simulation analysis clearly manifests that our proposed multi-source energy harvesting system extracts more energy as compared to energy produced by a single solar panel or a wind turbine.

Keywords: IoT · Sensor node · Solar energy · Wind energy
Multi-source energy harvesting system

1 Introduction

An IoT network is composed of wired and wireless devices such as sensor nodes and actuators. Sensor nodes have the capability of monitoring environmental phenomena and transmitting the measured data. Sensor nodes are the front end of the IoT devices as they connect the world's physical objects with the internet [1]. An actuator is a device which uses data collected and analyzed by sensor nodes to control the IoT system [1]. For simplification, in this paper, we have considered IoT systems comprising of sensor nodes only. Sensor nodes are powered by the fixed capacity batteries, due to which sensor nodes operate for the limited duration as long as the battery lasts. The lifetime of a sensor is calculated as the time taken to discharge the battery below the threshold which is required by sensor for performing their operations. Energy harvesting is one of the most promising techniques used for extending the lifetime of sensor nodes.

Energy harvesting system extracts energy from the environmental sources (like solar, water, wind, etc.) and human body sources (like footfall, walking, etc.) and converts this energy into usable electrical energy to power the sensor nodes. Batteries

© Springer Nature Singapore Pte Ltd. 2019
A. K. Luhach et al. (Eds.): ICAICR 2018, CCIS 956, pp. 282–293, 2019.
https://doi.org/10.1007/978-981-13-3143-5_24

are still necessary for sensor nodes as electrical energy produced by harvesting systems is uncontrollable and insufficient to continuously power them. When the energy harvesting system extracts more energy as compared to required energy then, remaining energy recharges the battery for later use. When energy produced by energy harvesting systems is insufficient then, sensor nodes are powered by the batteries. Sensor node remains unavailable temporarily if the battery level is below the lowest threshold or energy produced by energy harvesting system is insufficient for powering the sensor node. To avoid this period, we need to manage the battery recharge and energy production cycles.

In literature, several solar and wind energy harvesting systems are used such as Heliomote [2], Prometheus [3], Everlast [3] and micro horizontal and vertical scale wind turbines [4] respectively. A large number of sensor nodes use this type of harvesting systems. A drawback of these systems is that they support only one form of energy and can be used in locations where this energy source is available. To ensure the energy availability, a number of research works proposed the use of multi-source energy harvesters such as Smart Power Unit [5], Ambimax [6] and Plug and Play [5]. By using a wind turbine with a photovoltaic cell, more amount of energy is harvested then a single photovoltaic cell or a wind turbine. In Ambimax [6], authors compare the performance of Ambimax (multi-source) with Prometheus (Single source-solar) and shows that Ambimax generates more amounts of energy then Prometheus that too in less time. Ambimax [6] is not a feasible solution in real-world IoT systems because author uses a fan in place of wind turbine and fixed its speed at approximately 8.3 m/s.

Thus in this paper, we proposed a multi-source energy harvesting system which consists of a real world sensor node platform, photovoltaic cell and wind turbine. The rest of the paper is organized as follows: Firstly in Sect. 2, we discuss our proposed multi-source energy harvesting system which consists of a real sensor node, photovoltaic cell and proposed wind turbine for IoT system. In Sect. 3 we discuss, how usable energy is produced by proposed multi-source energy harvesting system. In Sect. 4 we discuss the energy consumption model and finally in Sect. 5 we discuss the conclusion.

2 Energy Harvesting System

We proposed a real world multi-source energy harvesting system comprises of a real sensor node platform, photovoltaic cells and wind turbine. The system comprises super capacitor and rechargeable batteries for powering the sensor nodes in situations when there is no or very less solar light and no wind. The main aim of our system is to extract energy from the sun light and wind speed and transform it into usable electrical energy for recharging the batteries. Battery and super capacitor is charged in following ways: by default, harvested energy is stored in the super capacitor. Secondly, when super capacitor charge is above the threshold value, then harvested energy is transmitted into rechargeable batteries. Sensor nodes are powered in following ways: by default, during day time when there is solar light, sensor nodes are powered by the solar energy. Secondly, during night time or cloudy days when there is no solar light, sensor nodes are powered by super capacitors connected to the multi-source energy harvesting system. Thirdly, when there is no solar light and no energy in super capacitor, then sensor nodes are powered by the rechargeable batteries.

In our work, we consider MSX-005F photovoltaic cell, a polycrystalline cell manufactured by BP-SOLAR. MSX-00SF photovoltaic cell is made up of semiconductor material silicon, with the property of transforming photon energy to electricity with the help of photovoltaic effect. Photovoltaic cell acquires small space because total surface area of this solar module is 36 cm^2 only. The maximum output power (P$_m$) produced by the MSX-00SF photovoltaic cell is 500 mW. The maximum power voltage (V$_{ld}$) and the current at which photovoltaic cell operate is 3.3 V and 150 mA respectively. The open circuit voltage and short circuit current of the photovoltaic cell is 4.6 V and 160 mA.

The efficiency of photovoltaic cell is the percentage of the amount of solar light transmitted by photovoltaic cells into usable electric power. The efficiency (η) of photovoltaic cells is calculated by using Eq. (1) where P$_m$ is the peak power produced by the MSX-005f photovoltaic cell (in watts), D is the solar radiance incident on the surface of the photovoltaic cell (in W/m^2) and A is the total surface area of the photovoltaic cell (in m^2). The efficiency of the photovoltaic cells depends upon the solar radiance and size of the photovoltaic cell. Solar radiance depends upon the various factors like geographical location where photovoltaic cell is placed, sun angle, solar time. According to the manufacturers, efficiency of MSX-005F solar module is 11.38%.

$$\eta = \frac{P_m}{D \times A} \qquad (1)$$

The micro scale wind energy harvester PIMWEH [7] is considered as promising option for our multi-source energy harvesting system. Firstly, wind speed is converted into mechanical wind turbine power by using wind turbine of diameter 9 cm and efficiency 34.1%. Then PZT converts mechanical wind turbine power to AC electrical power with efficiency of 26.1%. LTC3588-1 converts the AC electrical power into DC electrical power, with efficiency of 35.7%. As per [7], a 3.3 V pure DC voltage is generated at 11 KΩ resistive loads. The overall experimental efficiency of the wind energy harvester is 3.2%.

Both solar and wind energy harvester are connected to Waspmote [8], an open source low power wireless sensor platform. Note, however, we can also use any other sensor platform in place of Waspmote and similarly solar and wind energy harvester according to our needs. Waspmote 9 is based on ATmega1281 microcontroller and operates at 14.74 MHz frequency. Waspmote contains: built in 8 KB SRAM, 4 KB EEPROM, 128 KB Flash memory and 2 GB SD card slot. Dimensions of Waspmote are 73.5 × 51 × 13 mm. Waspmote is powered by a single battery of voltage 3.3–4.2 V and operates in four operational modes: Normal, Sleep, Deep Sleep and Hibernate. The energy requirement of Waspmote platform is shown in Table 1.

Table 1. Waspmote energy requirement [8].

Parameter	Value			
Battery Voltage				$3.3 - 4.2$ V
Consumption	ON	Sleep	Deep Sleep	Hibernate
	9 mA	62 μA	62 μA	0.7 μA
GPS Module	ON			OFF
	36 mA			0 μA
SD Card	ON			OFF
	14 mA			0 μA
XBEE	ON	Sleep		OFF
	37-64 mA	1-93 mA		0 μA
Accelerometer	ON			Hibernate
	65 mA			O μA
GPRS Module	ON	Sleep		Hibernate
	10-400 mA	1-2 mA		56 μA

3   Proposed System Model

This section presents the system model used for production of total energy that is harvested from solar cell and wind turbine. Total amount of harvested energy is calculated by adding the amount of energy separately harvested from sunlight and wind energy respectively. Mathematically, we can compute the power output produced by MSX-00F by using Eq. (2). The power output produced by MSX-00F depends on the various factors like location where it is placed and climatic condition. For example, if we consider daily averaged solar irradiance $D = 4.29$ KWh/m^2 then the amount of power produced by MSX-00Fby using Eq. (2) is 49.90 Wh. Figure1 show the monthly averaged solar power output generated by MSX-005F solar cell (by using Eq. (2)) corresponding to data of solar irradiance in Thanesar (Haryana, India) for all months of the year. Value of the monthly solar radiance is taken from the NASA Program: RETScreen [9] i.e., solar irradiance (D) is: 3.58, 4.39, 5.59, 6.1, 6.4, 6.2, 5.5, 5.14, 5.23, 4.71, 4.02, 3.36 KWh/m^2/day. We can clearly see from the Fig. 1 the amount of energy harvested by MSX-00F depends on the solar irradiance i.e., greater the solar irradiance, larger amount of energy is harvested by MSX-00F solar panel.

$$P_{so} = D \times \eta \times A \tag{2}$$

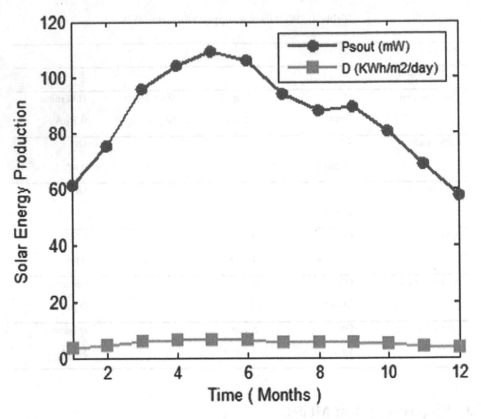

Fig. 1. Monthly averaged solar power produced by MSX-00F and monthly averaged solar irradiance in Thanesar (Haryana, India)

Like sunlight, the amount of power harvested by PIMWEH [7] from wind speed is calculated by using Eq. (3) where, ρ is the air mass density in Kgm^{-3}, A is the turbine rotor area in m^2 and v is wind speed in m/s. The air mass density is calculated at 1 atmospheric pressure with the help of an online calculator [10]. Area of wind turbine is calculated by using Eq. (4) which depends on rotor radius R (in m). The amount of power output produced by wind energy harvester depends on the climatic conditions like wind speed. For example, if we consider daily averaged solar irradiance $v = 3.70$ m/s then the amount of power produced by PIMWEH by using Eqs. (3) and (4) is 6.13 mW. Figure 2 shows the monthly averaged wind power generated by PIMWEH [7] (by using Eq. (3)) corresponding to the data of monthly average wind speed in Thanesar (Haryana, India) for all month of the year. Value of the monthly wind speed is taken from the NASA Program: RETScreen [9] i.e., wind speed is: 2.87, 3.37, 3.70, 3.69, 2.98, 3.18, 2.61, 2.55, 2.31, 1.99, 2.58, 2.76 m/s. We can clearly see from the Fig. 2 the amount of energy harvested by PIMWEH depends on the wind speed and rotor diameter.

$$P_{wo} = \frac{1}{2} \times \rho \times A \times v^3 \tag{3}$$

$$A = \pi R^2 \tag{4}$$

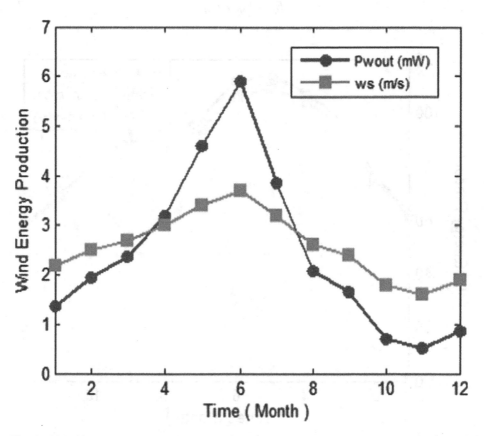

Fig. 2. Monthly averaged wind power produced by PIMWEH and monthly averaged wind speed in Thanesar (Haryana, India)

The energy produced by the solar panel is calculated by using Eq. (5). Like solar energy, wind energy (E_{wo}) is calculated. Total Energy Power Output (P_o) is calculated by combining power separately generated by solar panel and wind turbine. Total Energy Production (E_P) is calculated by combining energy produced by solar panel and wind turbine as shown in Eq. (7). Total power output we get after adding the amount of energy harvested by MSX-00SF and PIMWEH is shown in Fig. 3. As shown in Figs. 1, 2 and 3, more amount of energy is harvested after combining solar and wind energy harvester as compared to a single solar panel or a wind energy harvester.

$$Esp = \frac{P_{so}}{V_{ld}} \tag{5}$$

$$P_o = P_{so} + P_{wo} \tag{6}$$

$$E_p = E_{sp} + E_{wp} \tag{7}$$

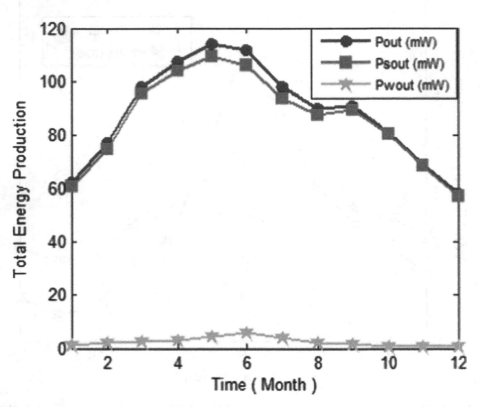

Fig. 3. Monthly averaged total power, solar power and wind power produced by our proposed multi-source energy harvesting system, MSX-00F and PIMWEH in Thanesar (Haryana, India)

   Mathematically we can also calculate the amount of energy produced by photovoltaic cell at any time t by using the zenith angle. For calculating the solar power at any instance of time, firstly we need to calculate the instantaneous solar irradiance at that time. The instantaneous solar irradiance at any time t in a day varies according to the climate changes at that time and zenith angle (θ_z) between vertical axes of earth surface and the sun. Solar radiance at time t is calculated [11] by using Eq. (8). Zenithangle θ_z [11] is computed by using Eq. (9) where γ is the latitude of geographical location where photovoltaic cell is placed β is solar declination angle and h is time of day. β is calculated by using Eq. (10) where d represents the specific day of the year, d $\in [1, 365]$. h is calculated by using Eq. (11) where t is the solar time and $t \in [0, 23]$.

Finally the hourly averaged solar power output is computed by using Eq. (12). Figure 4 shows the hourly averaged solar power generated corresponding to some specificday of January, May, July, September and November, i.e., 26th January, 27th may, 16[th]july, 24th September and 4th November, in Thanesar (Haryana, India) by using Eqs. (8–12). As shown in Fig. 4, the solar irradiance is approximately zero before sunrise and after sunset that's why the power output produced by MSX-00F is approximately zero before 6:00 am (sunrise) and after 6:00 pm (sunset). Figure 4 clearly shows that power produced by MSX-00F in a day make a parabola curve and maximum power output is produced at 12:00 h for all days of the year.

$$D(t) = D\cos(\theta z) \tag{8}$$

$$\theta_z = \cos^{-1}(\sin\gamma\sin\beta + \cos\gamma\cos\beta\cos h) \tag{9}$$

$$\beta = 23.45^o \times \left(360^o\left(\frac{284+d}{366}\right)\right) \tag{10}$$

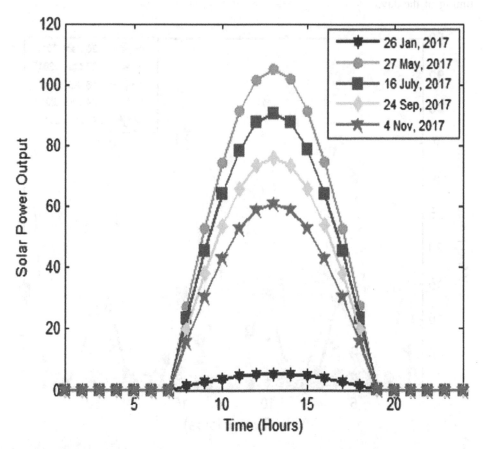

Fig. 4. Hourly averaged solar power output produced by MSX-00F for some specific days of the year

$$h = 15^{o}(t - 12) \qquad (11)$$

$$E_{so}(t) = \frac{(D(t) \times \eta \times A)}{V_{ld}} \qquad (12)$$

Similar to solar power, for calculating the wind power at any instance of time, firstly, we need to calculate wind speed at that time. The instantaneous wind speed at any time t depends upon the climatic conditions and daily averaged wind speed. Wind speed at any time t is calculated by using Eq. (13) [12] where h is the hour, $h \in [0, 23]$ at which wind speed is calculated, W_h represent wind speed at any hour h and W_a represent the daily averaged wind speed. Figure 5 shows the hourly averaged wind power output generated corresponding to some specific day of January, May, July, September and November, i.e., 26th January, 27th may, 16th july, 24th September and 4th November, in Thanesar (Haryana, India) by using Eq. (13). As shown in Fig. 5, like solar power there is no fixed time when amount of energy harvested by wind speed is zero. Figure 5 clearly shows that power produced by PIMWEH is not depends on the timing of the day.

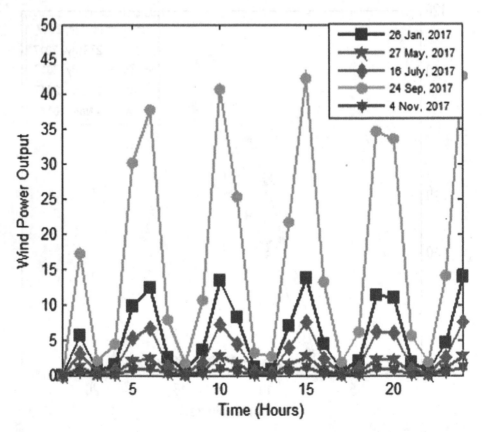

Fig. 5. Hourly averaged wind power outputs produced by PIMWEH for some specific days of the year

$$W_h = W_a + \frac{1}{2} W_a \times cos\left(\frac{h.\pi}{12}\right) \tag{13}$$

By Comparing Figs. 4 and 5 we can easily see that the amount of energy harvested from wind speed is very less as compare to amount of energy harvested from sunlight for same five days of a year. But Figs. 4 and 5 also shows that wind energy harvester also produces power for those hours when solar power output is zero, for example before sunrise and after sunset. If we combine the power output produced by theMSX-00F and PIMWEH, more amount of energy is harvestedas compare to single MSX-00F and PIMWEH. Figure 6 clearly shows more amount of energy is harvested by our multi-source energy harvesting system as compare to single solar cell and wind energy har-vester. Figure 6 also shows that our proposed energy harvesting system produce energy for those hours when the amount of energy harvested by single solar cell is zero. With the increase in output power, definitely the lifetime of the sensor node will also increase.

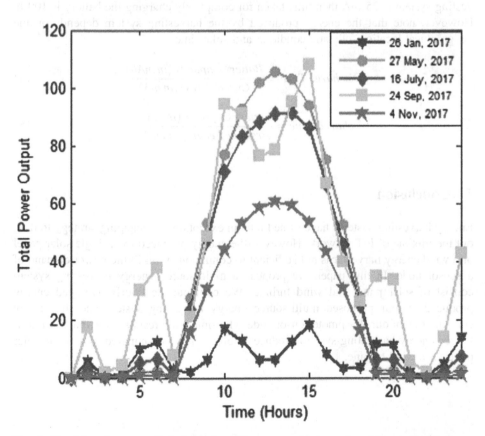

Fig. 6. Total hourly averaged (solar and wind) power outputs produced by our multi-source energy harvesting system for some specific days of the year

4 Energy Consumption Model

In this section, we present the energy consumption model of Waspmote. In our work battery is charged by energy produced by multiple source energy harvesting system and battery discharging depends on the energy consumption of component of waspmote. Discharging time of battery depends on two factors: first is the battery capacity and second is the amount of current draw required for working of sensor node. For example, consider Zero energy is produced by harvesting system then the discharge time of the battery is computed by using Eq. (14). For example, if capacity of the battery is 2500 mAh, and required current draw is 200 mA then total time taken to completely discharge the battery is 12.5 h. Note however the current draw required by any application is not constant, it depends on the requirement of the system. Similarly, charging time of battery depends upon two factors: first the capacity of the battery and second is the energy produced by the harvesting system. For example consider energy consumption is zero and battery is recharged by the energy harvested by energy harvesting system, then battery charging time is calculated by using Eq. (15). For example, capacity of the battery is 2500 mAh and the energy produced by the harvesting system is 25 mA then time taken for completely charging the battery is 100 h. However, note that the energy produced by the harvesting system depends on the geographical location, climatic condition and solar time.

$$Discharge\ Time = \frac{Battery\ Capacity\ (in\ mAh)}{Curent\ Draw\ (in\ mA)} \tag{14}$$

$$charge\ Time = \frac{Battery\ Capacity\ (in\ mAh)}{Produced\ energy\ (in\ mA)} \tag{15}$$

5 Conclusion

Energy harvesting systems have turned into an exceptionally engaging strategy to drag out the lifetime of IoT network. However, the energy produced by a single solar panel or a wind energy harvester is not sufficient to continuously fulfill the power demand of a sensor node. In this paper, we propose a multi-source energy harvesting system consist of solar panel and wind turbine. We compute the hourly averaged energy produced by our proposed multi-source energy harvesting system and the energy consumption of our Waspmote sensor node. The simulation results show that our multi-source energy harvesting system produces more energy as compared to a single solar panel or a wind turbine.

References

1. Rayes, A., Salam, S.: The things in IoT: sensors and actuators. In: Rayes, A., Salam, S. (eds.) Internet of Things From Hype to Reality, pp. 57–77. Springer, Cham (2017). https://doi.org/10.1007/978-3-319-44860-2_3
2. Raghunathan, V., Kansal, A., Hsu, J., Friedman, J., Srivastava, M.: Design considerations for solar energy harvesting wireless embedded systems. In: Fourth International Symposium on Information Processing in Sensor Networks, IPSN 2005, pp. 457–462. IEEE, April 2005. https://doi.org/10.1109/ipsn.2005.1440973
3. Panatik, K.Z., et al.: Energy harvesting in wireless sensor networks: a survey. In: 2016 IEEE 3rd International Symposium on Telecommunication Technologies (ISTT), pp. 53–58, November 2016. IEEE. https://doi.org/10.1109/istt.2016.7918084
4. El-Sayed, A.R., Tai, K., Biglarbegian, M., Mahmud, S.: A survey on recent energy harvesting mechanisms. In: 2016 IEEE Canadian Conference on Electrical and Computer Engineering (CCECE), pp. 1–5. IEEE, May 2016. https://doi.org/10.1109/ccece.2016.7726698
5. Weddell, A.S., Magno, M., Merrett, G.V., Brunelli, D., Al-Hashimi, B.M., Benini, L.: A survey of multi-source energy harvesting systems. In: Proceedings of the Conference on Design, Automation and Test in Europe, pp. 905–908. EDA Consortium, March 2013
6. Park, C., Chou, P.H.: Ambimax: autonomous energy harvesting platform for multi-supply wireless sensor nodes. In: 2006 3rd Annual IEEE Communications Society on Sensor and Ad Hoc Communications and Networks, SECON 2006, vol. 1, pp. 168–177. IEEE, September 2006. https://doi.org/10.1109/sahcn.2006.288421
7. Jung, H.J., et al.: Design and optimization of piezoelectric impact-based micro wind energy harvester for wireless sensor network. Sens. Actuators A: Phys. **222**, 314–321 (2015). https://doi.org/10.1016/j.sna.2014.12.010
8. https://www.libelium.com/v11-files/documentation/waspmote/waspmote-power-programming_guide.pdf
9. https://eosweb.larc.nasa.gov/sse/RETScreen
10. https://www.engineeringtoolbox.com/air-density-specific-weight-d_600.html
11. Escolar, S., Chessa, S., Carretero, J.: Quality of service optimization in photovoltaic cells-based energy harvesting wireless sensor networks. Energ. Effi. **10**(2), 331–357 (2017). https://doi.org/10.1007/s12053-016-9458-3
12. Guo, Z., Chang, C., Wang, R.: A novel method to downscale daily wind statistics to hourly wind data for wind erosion modelling. In: Bian, F., Xie, Y. (eds.) GRMSE 2015. CCIS, vol. 569, pp. 611–619. Springer, Heidelberg (2016). https://doi.org/10.1007/978-3-662-49155-3_64

Analysis and Comparison of Localization Approaches in WSN: A Review

Bhupinder Kaur[✉] and Deepak Prashar

School of Computer Science Engineering, Lovely Professional University,
Phagwara, Punjab, India
bhupinder.kaur.bhatia786@gmail.com,
deepak.prashar@lpu.co.in

Abstract. Wireless Sensor Network (WSN) is made up of huge no. of sensing nodes those are known as sensor nodes. In WSN Localization for the unknown nodes, is significant task. Various techniques are available to solve this problem. Two main categories are rough and excellent. Rough categories require less detail to determine the position of unknown node, easy to implement and less complex and the excellent technique require more detail to determine the position and provide the accuracy about position of the node. In this review paper we are presenting the analysis of various localization algorithms and providing the comparison of performances and approaches.

Keywords: WSN · Localization · Anchor node · Unknown node
Accuracy

1 Introduction

Wireless Sensor Networks (WSNs) is model of huge amount of sensing nodes. These nodes are known as Sensors. WSN is technique in which all the sensors sense activities in target area to check and control the activities [1]. All of the sensor nodes in WSNs works together to achieve one common goal as in military for target tracking. In WSNs, there can be one or few sink nodes, all the sensor nodes gather the data from target area and transfer it to sink node, sink node contain more energy, strong calculations and transmission capabilities [2]. Sensor node is essential part of the WSNs; hardware of sensor is consisting of four parts: power and power management module, sensor, microcontroller and transceiver [3]. Sensors collect the data from target area in form of signal such as light, vibration, chemical signal, temperature and change them into electrical signal then sent it to microcontroller, after that microcontroller process this data then transceiver sent this data, so that physical realization of communication can be achieved [3]. WSNs include five categories: terrestrial WSN, underground WSN, underwater WSN, multimedia WSN, and mobile WSN [4].

Terrestrial WSN: In this network nodes are placed in target area in ad hoc or pre-planned way. In ad-hoc, nodes are dropped into the target area randomly via plane and in pre-planned, placement models are used to place the nodes [4].

© Springer Nature Singapore Pte Ltd. 2019
A. K. Luhach et al. (Eds.): ICAICR 2018, CCIS 956, pp. 294–309, 2019.
https://doi.org/10.1007/978-981-13-3143-5_25

Underground WSN: In this network nodes are buried in underground, mines, caves to check the activities and sink node is placed above the ground to transfer the information to base station [4].

Underwater WSN: In this network less number of nodes are used as compare to terrestrial WSN. These sensing nodes are costly and instead of using dense placement of nodes in terrestrial WSN, underwater WSN uses sparse placement of nodes [4].

Multimedia WSN: In this network particular area's activities are monitored and tracked by sensor nodes in the form of audio, video, images. These sensor networks are consists of less cost sensing nodes and in this sensing nodes are placed in target area in pre-planned way [4].

Mobile WSN: In this network sensor nodes moves in target area. As static nodes sense the target area, perform computations similarly mobile nodes also perform these functions. The difference is, in Mobile WSN data is transferred with dynamic routing while static nodes uses fixed routing. There are various issues that mobile WSN faces:- localization, energy, maintenance, self-organization [4]. WSNs are becoming more popular because these are used in various areas as in:- military, health, environmental, agricultural, domestic, industries [5]. In WSNs sensor nodes plays a vital role. So, in WSN some technical and design challenges are there in ad hoc deployment as typical calculations, less battery, fault tolerance, hardware constraints, network topology, production cost [1].

1.1 Applications of Wireless Sensor Networks

WSN performs a vital job in different areas. Some of the areas are military, environmental area, medical field, home and in others are also.

1. **Military Applications:** In military WSN is used for battlefield surveillance and in targeting system.
2. **Environmental Applications:** In Environmental WSN is used for forest fire detection, flood detection, earthquake detection, in air and water pollution.
3. **Medical Applications:** Wireless Sensor nodes are mostly useable now a day for the removal of cables and physical links in the middle of the patient and monitoring equipment.
4. **Home-related Applications:** WSNs applications are now reaches to the home users as technologies in the form of intelligent appliances.

1.2 Localization in Wireless Sensor Network

In WSN sensing nodes sense the particular area and transfer the details to the main station, but details received by sensor nodes is not useful if the location of sensor node is not known in case of ad-hoc deployment. As in forest area sensor nodes are dropped into forest via airplane, so after that when these node start to send the information, this information would not be meaningful if the exact position of node is not known. So after deployment of the sensor nodes, nodes have to find out its location in the network is known as localization [1]. Localization means determine the exact position of an event or activity where it is occurring. In WSNs the sensor nodes who know there position are known as anchor node (Beacon nodes or Landmarks) and the nodes who have to find out its position are known as unknown nodes (Free or Dumb nodes) [5]. To solve the problem of localization one method is to place all the sensor nodes manually, but this method will not work in case of large areas, dense forest, volcanoes areas. Another method is, connect all the sensors with GPS (Global Positioning System) this method is very costly when more sensing nodes are there in network [6].

2 Localization Process

In localization we are considering three topics those are shown below:

2.1 Position Determination Steps

The exact position of the sensing nodes is determined with following three steps [5].

1. **Distance or Angle Estimation:** In this node determine the distance or angle with anchor nodes.
2. **Position Computation:** From above step with the help of the distance or angle calculate position.
3. **Localization Algorithm:** This will help to determine the position of other sensors by using available information.

2.2 Location Measurement Technique

Three categories of location measurement are [1].

1. **Triangulation:** In this AOA (Angle of Arrival) calculations are collected at unknown node from three anchor nodes and trigonometric laws are applied on calculated data.
2. **Trilateration:** In this distance calculation are used at unknown node from three anchor nodes. Unknown node will receive (x, y, d) where (x, y) is detail of coordinates for anchor and d is distance in the middle of the anchor and unknown sensor. After that geometric calculations are performed to determine the position of unknown sensor.
3. **Multilateration:** In this more than 3 anchor nodes are used for the position calculation of the unknown sensor.

Figure 1 shows the three measurement techniques in which a, b, c, d are anchors and u is the unknown node.

2.3 Localization Schemes

Localization Algorithm are categorised into four part [7].

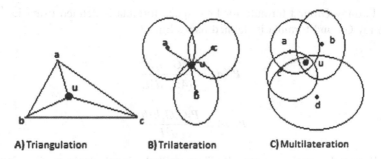

A) Triangulation   B) Trilateration   C) Multilateration

Fig. 1. Measurement techniques

GPS Basis/GPS Free: In GPS basis scheme all the sensor nodes are connected with GPS, this scheme provide the accurate position of all the nodes. But to connect all the sensor nodes with GPS is not possible, reason is GPS communicate in line of sight so due to the obstacles in the path if take the density of plants the GPS will not work and the another reason is GPS increases the cost of network. To solve this problem other scheme GPS free introduced in which instead of connecting all the nodes with the GPS only few sensors are getting connected with GPS those are considered as anchor node. In GPS free unknown nodes who have to find out there position will use the anchor nodes to find their position in the network [1].

Anchor Basis/Anchor Free: In anchor based scheme few of the nodes already knows its position because these nodes are placed by hand or connected with GPS [7]. Anchor nodes start the localization process to determine the location of another unknown node. Accuracy in anchor based scheme based on the amount of anchors. On the another hand anchor free scheme use neighbor distance information to find out the location of unknown nodes when there is no any anchor node [7].

Centralized/Distributed: In centralized scheme all the nodes depends on the sink node, another nodes no need to perform any calculations because all the communications are performed via sink node that perform all the calculations for the nodes. The advantage is it provides the more accuracy [7]. In distributed scheme all the nodes perform the calculations all the nodes perform localization algorithm and error increases [7].

Range Basis/Range Free: Different types of method are available to determine estimate of the distance or the angle in the middle of the nodes, to find the position of nodes. These estimates should be accurate because this information is used to calculate the position of the nodes and in the localization algorithm [5]. Various methods to find out the estimate of distance/angle are:- (i) RSSI (Received Signal Strength Indication) (ii) ToA (Time of Arrival) (iii) TDoA (Time Difference-of Arrival) (iv) AoA (Angle of Arrival).

- **RSSI:** In RSSI distance in the middle of the 2 nodes is calculated on the basis of the strength of the signal, which is reached to one of the node [5]. When the signal propagates its strength gets reduced. Two radio propagation models are Free space and Two-ray Ground formula for Free space formula is defined using Eq. (1) and Two-ray Ground formula is defined using Eq. (2).

$$P_r(d) = \frac{P_t G_t G_r \lambda^2}{(4\pi)^2 d^2 L} \tag{1}$$

$$P_r(d) = \frac{P_t G_t G_r h_t^2 h_r^2}{d^4 L} \tag{2}$$

P_t: Received signal strength, P_r: Transmitted Signal strength, G_t: Transmitter Antenna gain, G_r: Receiver Antenna gain, λ: Wavelength.

This method has some advantages and disadvantages also, advantage is this method requires less cost because the receivers are proficient to estimate the strength of the received signal and the disadvantage is noise and interference in communication provide less accurate results of localized node [5]. First time this technique is used by RADAR system [1].

- **ToA:** Another method to find out the distance in the middle of nodes is ToA that calculate the distance on the basis of the time [5]. Distance is directly proportionate to the time require by signal to transfer from one place to another point. ToA method requires synchronized nodes [5]. Distance is calculated using Eq. (3).

$$Dis = Sr(Tr - Ts) \tag{3}$$

In Fig. 2. Receiver estimate the distance by multiply the speed of the radio signal with time difference arrival of the radio signal.

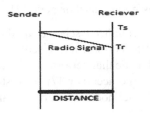

Fig. 2. Time of Arrival (ToA)

Ts: signal transmitted at time, Tr: signal received at time, Sr: Speed of the radio signal, Dis: Distance.

- **TDoA:** In TDoA use the hardware ranging scheme the sensor node is provide with speaker and microphones [8]. In this method transmitter sends a radio message and wait for some time ($T.de$) that can be equal to zero and then generate the pattern of chirp on the speaker [8]. When the receiver receives radio signal, receiver will record the time ($T.ra$) and switch on the microphone, after that microphone will detect the chirp pattern and the receiver will note the time ($T.so$). When the receiver have all the time $T.de$, $T.ra$, $T.so$ the receiver calculate the distance (Dis) with Eq. (4). Where $S.radio$ is speed of radio signal and $S.sound$ is speed of the sound [8].

$$Dis = (S.radio - S.sound) * (T.so - T.ra - T.de) \tag{4}$$

In Fig. 3. Sensor A (Sender) sends radio signal then after some delay sends sound signal now the Sensor B (Receiver) calculate the distance with arrival Time Difference-of two radio and sound signal [8].

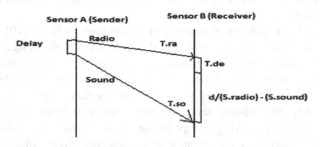

Fig. 3. Time Difference-of Arrival (TDoA)

- **AoA:** Some localizations method uses the data of AOA to calculate the position of the sensor. Detail of AoA is gathered using microphones/radio arrays those allow the receiving node to find out the orientation of the transmitting node [8].

In Fig. 4 Time Difference-of arrival of the signal to every receiver as well as the difference in the positions of the all recipient; allow the sensor node to determine the AoA of the signal.

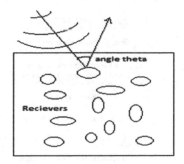

Fig. 4. Angle of Arrival (AoA)

- **Range Free:** The range free method do not use any measurement equipment so this method require less cost as compare to range basis method. Range free localization algorithm uses distance approximate algorithm to determine the location of node.

Range free method uses some anchor nodes to determine the position of the node [9]. Although the range free method yield less accurate result as compare to range based even then range based methods are used due to the less cost and these are appropriate for large network [9]. Various Range free algorithms are Centroid, DV-hop, APIT etc.

3 Literature Review

In related work we are going to review the basic localization and various improvement in localization approaches.

Sharma et al. has published Issues and Challenges in WSN [10], this paper is defining a various difficulties and problems that comes under the design of the WSN. These difficulties and problems have more effect on the WSN. This paper has defined difficulties and problems with following Fig. 5. Here few issues would be defined. As Energy in sensors for WSN is very important because more energy is consumed by sensors when they continuously sense the environment of target area, for data collection. Batteries that are giving energy to the sensors need to be replaced or again charged after the batteries of sensors have been consumed. So the major challenge for the researcher is to propose an energy efficient hardware and software or algorithm those works efficiently in WSN. Another issue is security that is also very important as WSN is used in battle fields, for surveillance. So the confidentiality of data, during the transmission in the middle of sensors or in the middle of sensor and base station is required. Because if there is no security then any third person can read the confidential data, can change the data that would not be good. So the researcher should take care of this issue also, to provide the security.

Fig. 5. Issues and challenges

Pal Singh et al. has published paper **Critical Analysis of Distributed Localization Algorithms in WSNs** [11] that defines the categories of localization method in WSN like GPS Based, Anchor Based, Computational based, and on range basis as mentioned in following Fig. 6. Computational has further two categories centralized and distributed. These all approaches have own advantages and disadvantages. Advantages come in form of more accuracy, less cost.

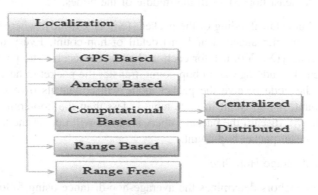

Fig. 6. Localizations

Bulusu et al. has proposed Centroid Localization Algorithm [12], that was consist of two phases. In the initial phase all the anchors broadcast their position data as packet to other unknown nodes that comes under the area of threshold. In the second phase unknown node determines the mean of co-ordinates of all the anchor who comes in area of threshold using following Eqs. (5) and (6).

$$X_u = \frac{\sum_{i=1}^{n} X_i}{n},$$ (5)

$$Y_u = \frac{\sum_{i=1}^{n} Y_i}{n}$$ (6)

(X_i, Y_i) is co-ordinates of anchor node i and total number of anchors are n those comes under the area of threshold. This algorithm is easy to implement but it does not provides the best result and it requires complex method to set the threshold value.

Niculescu et al. Has published Ad Hoc Positioning System (APS) [13], this paper defines distributed and hop to hop positioning algorithm that uses DV routing and GPS positioning to give approximate position of the nodes, where few number of anchor nodes are available. The areas which are inaccessible uses plane for deployment of the node and distances to the anchors is transmitted with hop by hop propagation method, when node find out the distances up to equal or greater than 3 anchor nodes, then unknown node can calculate its position using GPS method. In this the nearest node of the anchor estimates the distance to anchor using direct signal strength measurement. The nodes those are not immediate neighbors of anchor would be able to calculate the distance to the anchor using these three ways, hop by hop-distance transfer methods are:- DV -hop, DV -Distance, Euclidean -Distance.

DV -hop and DV-distance Method:- Both methods use the basic distance vector exchange to transmit the distance information. DV -hop works in following three steps.

1. Calculate the least hop-count in the middle of the nodes.

In this anchors start flooding of the packet {(Xi, Yi,), hi, id}, where (Xi, Yi) detail of co-ordinates for the anchor i and (hi) detail of hop-count. Every unknown node preserve the table {(Xi, Yi), hi} for each anchor i, and receive the packet from least hop-count then after adding one in hop-count, transfer the packet to neighboring node. In this when the node receive the packet, node will collate its own hop-count with packet hop-count, if hop-count in node table is less than the hop-count for packet of anchor i, node will discard the packet, otherwise node will update the table hop-count and will add one in packet hop-count.

2. Determine Average Hop Size

In this step anchors determines the average-hop-distance using following Eq. (7).

$$AverageHop \quad Size_i = \frac{\sum \sqrt{(X_i - X_j)^2 + (Y_i - Y_j)^2}}{\sum h_i} \tag{7}$$

Now every anchor broadcasts the average hop size in network and node i which is unknown node calculate the distance (dis) from anchor i using Eq. (8).

$$dist_i = AverageHopSize_i \times h_i \tag{8}$$

Now calculate the co-ordinates of unknown node by using the estimated distances into triangulation method. Here assume (Xu, Yu) are the co-ordinates of unknown node, (Xa, Ya) are the co-ordinates of anchor a nodes and tn is total no of anchor nodes. dist is defined as distance and get the co-ordinates using Eq. (9).

$$\begin{bmatrix} (X_u - X_1)^2 + (Y_u - Y_1)^2 = dist_1^2 \\ (X_u - X_2)^2 + (Y_u - Y_2)^2 = dist_2^2 \\ \vdots \\ (X_u - X_{tn})^2 + (Y_u - Y_{tn})^2 = dist_{tn}^2 \end{bmatrix}, \begin{bmatrix} X_1^2 - X_{tn}^2 + Y_1^2 - Y_{tn}^2 - dist_1^2 - dist_{tn}^2 \\ = 2 \times X_u \times (X_1 - X_{tn}) + 2 \times Y_u \times (Y_1 - Y_u) \\ X_2^2 - X_{tn}^2 + Y_2^2 - Y_{tn}^2 - dist_2^2 - dist_{tn}^2 \\ = 2 \times X_u \times (X_2 - X_{tn}) + 2 \times Y_u \times (Y_2 - Y_u) \\ \vdots \\ X_{m-1}^2 - X_{tn}^2 + Y_{m-1}^2 - Y_{tn}^2 - dist_{m-1}^2 - dist_{tn}^2 \\ = 2 \times X_u \times (X_{m-1} - X_{tn}) + 2 \times Y_u \times (Y_{tn-1} - Y_u) \end{bmatrix}$$

The above Equations can be modified as Following Equation in form of A and b.

$$A = 2 \times \begin{bmatrix} (X_1 - X_{tm})(Y_1 - Y_{tm}) \\ (X_2 - X_{tm})(Y_2 - Y_{tm}) \\ \vdots \\ (X_{tm-1} - X_{tm})(Y_{tm-1} - Y_{tm}) \end{bmatrix}, \quad X_u = \begin{bmatrix} X_u \\ Y_u \end{bmatrix},$$

$$b = \begin{bmatrix} X_1^2 - X_{tm}^2 + Y_1^2 - Y_{tm}^2 - dist_1^2 - dist_{tm}^2 \\ X_2^2 - X_{tm}^2 + Y_2^2 - Y_{tm}^2 - dist_2^2 - dist_{tm}^2 \\ \vdots \\ X_{tm-1}^2 - X_{tm}^2 + Y_{tm-1}^2 - Y_{tm}^2 - dist_{tm-1}^2 - dist_{tm}^2 \end{bmatrix}$$

$$X_u = (A^T A)^{-1} A^T b \tag{9}$$

Advantage of DV -hop is, it is cost effective and it is simplicity make its more useable. Disadvantage is, it can only work in identical network. Where as in **DV-distance,** distance in the middle of neighboring node is calculated using radio signal strength and is transmitted in the meter instead of hops. **Euclidian** method, transmit the true Euclidian distance instead of hop-count or distance in meter.

Zhang et al. has proposed Weighted Centroid Localization (WCL) Algorithm based on DV-Hop for WSN [14], a new algorithm that boosts the complexity of the algorithm as compare to DV-Hop algorithm. WCL algorithm calculates the position of the unknown sensor in the following two steps:

1. Determine the least hop-count in the middle of unknown and the anchor nodes, like DV-Hop.
2. In second step unknown node finds the co-ordinates with the following Eqs. (10) and (11).

$$x = \frac{\sum_{i=1}^{n} w_i X_i}{\sum_{i=1}^{n} w_i} \tag{10}$$

$$y = \frac{\sum_{i=1}^{n} w_i Y_i}{\sum_{i=1}^{n} w_i} \tag{11}$$

$$w_i = \frac{1}{hop_i} \tag{12}$$

Where w_i in Eq. (12) is weight of anchor i, and hop i is less hop-count in the middle of anchor i and unknown node. Weight factor is more when there is less number of hops in the middle of unknown and the anchor node. As in the second steps there is no any broadcast of packets that is the reason of less complexity and less consumption of power.

Zhang et al. has proposed An Improved Weighted Centroid Localization Algorithm Based on DV-Hop Algorithm for WSN [14], to provide greater exactness than the DV-Hop. This algorithm works in two steps:-

1. Calculate the least hop-count in the middle of unknown and the anchors.

In this phase each unknown node find out less no. of hop to every anchor and preserve the hop-count table, arrange the table according to less to more no. of hop-counts required to reach the every anchor node then choose the anchor whose hop-count is less.

2. Determine the position of unknown node

In this phase every anchor node using Eq. (7) will calculate the Average Hop Size, now unknown will calculate the Average of all Average Hop Sizes of anchors selected in step 1. Using Eq. (13). This algorithm will calculate the weight of node using Eq. (14). Now unknown will find out the location with Eqs. (10) and (11).

$$HopSize_{av} = \frac{\sum_{i=1}^{N} AverageHop \;\; Size_i}{N} \tag{13}$$

$$w_i = \left(\frac{1}{h_i}\right)^{\frac{1}{n}} \tag{14}$$

w_i is the weight factor, h_i is hop-count and $n = \frac{HopSize_{av}}{r}$, where r is the interchange radius of node.

Fu et al. has proposed FDV -hop Localization Algorithm for WSN [15], algorithm in which second and 3rd step of basic DV-Hop algorithm is changed. It works in following three steps:

1. Calculate the least hop-count in the middle of unknown and the anchors, like DV-Hop.
2. In this step anchor i determines error of average hop size of anchor i, then with error and the hop-count, all anchors average hop size is weighted by unknown node. Average Hop size for anchor i is determines using Eq. (7). Now the actual distance D_{rij} in the middle of the anchor node i and j is calculated using Eq. (15).

$$D_{rij} = \sqrt{(X_i - X_j)^2 + (Y_i - Y_j)^2} \tag{15}$$

The measured distance in the middle of anchor i and the j is calculated using following Eq. (16)

$$D_{eij} = AverageHopSize_i * h_{ij} \qquad (16)$$

Now the anchor i calculates the error for Average Hop Size i using following Eq. (17) where M is total anchor.

$$ER_i = \frac{\sum\limits_{\substack{i \neq j}}^{M} |D_{rij} - D_{eij}| \Big/ h_{ij}}{M - 1} \qquad (17)$$

Now find out the weight (w_i) for each anchor using following Eq. (18), and calculate the Average hop-distance for unknown node using Eq. (19).

$$w_i = \frac{\frac{1}{ER_i} + \frac{1}{N_i}}{\sum\limits_{j=1}^{M} \left(\frac{1}{ER_j} + \frac{1}{N_j}\right)} \qquad (18)$$

$$AverageHop \quad Size = \sum\limits_{i=1}^{M} w_i * AverageHop \quad Size_i \qquad (19)$$

3. In the third step, it uses triangulation method with validation formulas to determine the co-ordinates for the unknown node.

This algorithm reduces the positioning error as compare to DV -hop and improves the accuracy.

Liu et al. has proposed Multi-Dimensional Scaling method for WSN [16], in this all the sensors in the network find out the far away matrix. When the matrix consists of distances in the middle of couple of nodes is obtained, give that matrix as input to Multi-Dimensional Scaling method in order to get respective position of the unknown node. Once respective position is obtained apply the shift, rotation, reflection on relative position according to anchor nodes to yield exact location for the nodes. The most interesting advantage of this method is it can determine the location of all unknown nodes at identical time rather than at discrete time. On another hand it calculates the respective position in the absence of the anchors. It is easy in implementation, less complex and provides exact solution.

Son et al. has proposed Hyperbolic DV-Hop Localization Algorithm [17], that defines a one new algorithm to make better correctness of the traditional DV- Hop. This algorithm changes the second and 3rd step of the DV-Hop.

1. Calculate the least hop-count in the middle of unknown and the anchor nodes, same as DV- Hop.
2. Determine Average Hop Size.

In this step instead of taking Average hop-distance of nearest anchor to the unknown node, this algorithm uses the average of Average hop-distances of all anchor nodes as Average hop-distance of unknown node using Eq. (20).

$$AverageHop \quad Size = \frac{\sum_{i=1}^{N} AverageHop \quad Size_i}{N} \tag{20}$$

Now calculate the distance using Eq. (8).

3. In third step to find out the co-ordinates of unknown node this algorithm uses the hyperbolic localization algorithm instead of using trilateration method.

This algorithm is much accurate as compare to traditional DV- Hop. Hyperbolic DV-Hop results 9.3% more accurate than the traditional DV- Hop.

Liu et al. has proposed The Performance Evaluation of Hybrid Localization Algorithm in WSNs [18], that works on the improvement of approximate point in triangle (APIT) and DV-hop Algorithm. In APIT new angle based method is used to find out, the unknown lies within the triangle of three anchors or not. In this if the unknown node is making a total of 360 degree angle with all the anchors, and then unknown node would be considered as lies in three anchors. This method to know the point in triangle or not is more accurate than previous methods. On the other side this paper has improved the DV -hop also. Both improved APIT and DV -hop helps to determine the position of unknown. In this Hybrid Localization Algorithm, all the unknown nodes would be localized with improved APIT, those lies in triangle of the anchors means making angle of 360 with three anchors and remaining unknown node who does not lies within the triangle of three anchors will be localized with improved DV -hop algorithm. This paper ensures this algorithm has less localization error as compare to basic APIT and DV -hop.

Mohamed et al. has proposed An Improved DV-Hop Localization Algorithm [19], in this two algorithms were proposed the first is equal zone based DV-Hop and Equal zone based DV –Hop with RSSI. The first one split the network area into sub areas, and unknown nodes in that sub area will find out there position using only the anchors who comes in that sub area. In the second algorithm again the network is divided into sub areas, and the unknown node will use the hop-count to find out the distance in the middle of itself and the anchor if they are not neighbouring node, but if they are neighbouring nodes then node will use RSSI method to find the distance. This algorithm improves the more accuracy as compare to basic DV-Hop algorithm.

Ma et al. has proposed Node localization of WSN Based on Secondary Correction Error [20], new algorithm for node localization Algorithm. In this orthogonal polynomial fitting is used to precise the distance error. After calculating the corrected distance with orthogonal polynomial it use least square method to find the location of the node and it creates the weight matrix. Now it processes the co-ordinates of unknown node. Simulation result shows that, this algorithm is decreasing the localization error and increasing the position accuracy.

Table 1. Comparison

Algorithm	Computational complexity	Accuracy	Energy consumption	Computational	Range based/range free
Centroid	Less	Less	Less	Distributed	Range free
Traditional DV-Hop	Medium	Less	More	Distributed	Range free
WCL	Less	Less	Medium	Distributed	Range free
IWCL-DV-Hop	Less	More	Medium	Distributed	Range free
Fixed DV-Hop	Medium	Improved	Medium	Distributed	Range free
MDS Based	Less	More	Medium	Centralized	Range free
Hyperbolic DV-Hop	Medium	Medium	More	Distributed	Range free
Hybrid (APIT and DV-Hop)	More	Improved	Medium	Distributed	Range free
IDV-HOP	Medium	Improved	Medium	Distributed	1st Algorithm (Range free) 2nd Algorithm (Range based/range free)
Secondary correction error	More	More	More	Distributed	Range free

4 Comparison of Algorithms

In this we are going to compare the different algorithm on the basis of the some parameters in tabular form with Table 1.

5 Issues and Challenges

In this review paper we defined various proposed localization algorithms for WSNs. In this part we are going to define the various research issues for the improvement of the node localization methods and challenges in WSNs. Above defined algorithms have advantages and disadvantages in form of accuracy, computational cost, energy consumption, computational, those become issues. Accuracy of node position is most challenging task in WSNs, and as well as localization of the node in 3D area is also a challenging phase. One more interesting challenge in WSNs is localization of node in Mobile Networks.

6 Conclusion

In this review paper we have given the basic introduction of WSNs, Localization Process, Localization Schemes, and review of the various node localization algorithms. We have given the review of research papers those are containing the localization algorithms from centroid algorithm and comparison is defined using some parameter in the above table. Some of the algorithms have more accuracy less computational cost and some of the algorithms are consuming more energy. After analysing these algorithms we identified no algorithm is too good because when one parameter gets improved the other parameter becomes an issue. So there is a further need of improvement in localization algorithms that can provide the more accuracy and should be able to meet the requirements of the localization as less energy consumption, less computational cost.

References

1. Priya, Malik, A.: A review on localization algorithms in wireless sensor networks. Int. J. Comput. Sci. Eng. Technol. **5**, 677–682 (2014). ISSN: 2229-3345
2. Du, T., Qu, S., Guo, Q., Zhu, L.: A simple efficient anchor-free node localization algorithm for wireless sensor networks. Int. J. Distrib. Sens. Netw. **13**(4) (2017). https://doi.org/10.1177/1550147717705784
3. IEC: Internet of Things: Wireless Sensor Networks Executive summary, p. 78 (2014)
4. Yick, J., Mukherjee, B., Ghosal, D.: Wireless sensor network survey. Comput. Netw. **52**(12), 2292–2330 (2008)
5. Protocols for Wireless Sensor (2009)
6. Alrajeh, N.A., Bashir, M., Shams, B.: Localization techniques in wireless sensor networks. Int. J. Distrib. Sens. Netw. **9**, Article ID 304628 (2013)
7. Bal, M., Liu, M., Shen, W., Ghenniwa, H.: Localization in cooperative wireless sensor networks: a review. In: 2009 13th International Conference Computer Supported Cooperative Work in Design, pp. 438–443 (2009)
8. Stojmenović, I.: Handbook of Sensor Networks: Algorithms and Architectures. Wiley, Hoboken (2005)
9. Kaur, A., Kumar, P., Gupta, G.P.: A weighted centroid localization algorithm for randomly deployed wireless sensor networks. J. King Saud Univ. – Comput. Inf. Sci. 1–10 (2016)
10. Sharma, S., Bansal, R.K., Bansal, S.: Issues and challenges in wireless sensor networks. In: International Conference on Machine Intelligence and Research Advancement, pp. 58–62 (2013)
11. Pal Singh, S., Sharma, S.C.: Critical Analysis of Distributed Localization Algorithms for Wireless Sensor Networks. Int. J. Wirel. Microw. Technol. **6**(4), 72–83 (2016)
12. Bulusu, N., Heidemann, J., Estrin, D.: GPS-less low cost outdoor localization for very small devices. IEEE Pers. Commun. **7**(5), 28–34 (2000)
13. Niculescu, D., Nath, B.: Ad hoc positioning system (APS) using AOA. In: IEEE INFOCOM 2003. Twenty-second Annual Joint Conference of the IEEE Computer Communications (IEEE Cat. No.03CH37428), vol. 3, pp. 1734–1743 (2001)
14. Zhang, B., Ji, M., Shan, L.: A weighted centroid localization algorithm based on DV-hop for wireless sensor network (2012)

15. Fu, C., Wang, X.: An improved DV-hop localization algorithm in wireless sensor network (2013)
16. Liu, L., Guntaka, K.K.: A non-iterative localization approach based on multi-dimensional scaling method for wireless, pp. 328–333 (2014)
17. Song, G., Tam, D.: Two novel DV-hop localization algorithms for randomly deployed wireless sensor networks (2015)
18. Liu, C., Liu, S., Zhang, W., Zhao, D.: The performance evaluation of hybrid localization algorithm in wireless sensor networks. Mob. Netw. Appl. 21(6), 994–1001 (2016)
19. Mohamed, E., Zakaria, H., Abdelhalim, M.B.: Proceedings of the International Conference on Advanced Intelligent Systems and Informatics 2016, vol. 533. Springer, Heidelberg (2017). https://doi.org/10.1007/978-3-319-48308-5
20. Ma, X., Liu, W., Wang, Z.: Node localization of wireless sensor network based on secondary correction error. In: Chen, G., Shen, H., Chen, M. (eds.) PAAP 2017. CCIS, vol. 729, pp. 142–151. Springer, Singapore (2017). https://doi.org/10.1007/978-981-10-6442-5_13
21. Khamparia, A., Pandey, B.: A novel method of case representation and retrieval in CBR for e-learning. Educ. Inf. Technol. 22(1), 337–354 (2017). https://doi.org/10.1007/s10639-015-9447-8
22. Khamparia, A., Pandey, B.: Knowledge and intelligent computing methods in e-learning. Int. J. Technol. Enhanc. Learn. 7(3), 221–242 (2015). https://doi.org/10.1504/IJTEL.2015.072810
23. Khamparia, A., Pandey, B.: SpringerPlus 5, 446 (2016). https://doi.org/10.1186/s40064-016-2101-0

Inferring Causal Gene Regulatory Networks Using Time-Delay Association Rules

Syed Sazzad Ahmed[1,2](✉), Swarup Roy[1,3], and Pabitra Pal Choudhury[4]

[1] Department of Information Technology, North Eastern Hill University,
Shillong, India
sazzad.tezu@gmail.com, swarup@nehu.ac.in
[2] Assam Don Bosco University, Guwahati, India
[3] Department of Computer Applications, Sikkim University, Gangtok, Sikkim, India
sroy01@cus.ac.in
[4] Applied Statistics Unit, Indian Statistical Institute, Kolkata, West Bengal, India
pabitra@isical.ac.in

Abstract. Inferring cause and effect relationship in Gene Regulatory Networks (GRNs) is a vital and a challenging topic. In this paper, we generate association rules between a pair of genes to reconstruct GRN from expression data. While computing confidence of a rule, we emphasize on the fact of time delay involved during the process of regulation between a target factor gene and any target gene.

We, generate strong binary rules to infer GRN from expression data. We use in-silico DREAM challenge data for experimentation and assessments, due to the availability of ground truth networks. We compare our results with few well known causality inference methods and outcomes are satisfactory. Our results confirm the fact that inference of causality in GRN is a time delay activity and should be taken care during inference process.

Keywords: Causality · Gene regulatory networks · Inference
Association rule mining · Discretization

1 Introduction

Often complex biological systems are represented as networks. Gene Regulatory Network (GRN) models the regulatory or cause-effect relationships between a pair of genes in terms of their expressions [1]. Tremendous growth of high density DNA micro array technology allows to monitor thousand of genes expression simultaneously. With the availability of abundance of genomic expression data, it imposes an additional challenge to the informatics community to reverse engineering the true biological network. Especially, discovering complete causal relationships among the various genes of a GRN is one of the unresolved open problems. Such a discovery would give a blue print on how a gene operates and

© Springer Nature Singapore Pte Ltd. 2019
A. K. Luhach et al. (Eds.): ICAICR 2018, CCIS 956, pp. 310–321, 2019.
https://doi.org/10.1007/978-981-13-3143-5_26

helps to understand better the working principle of genes during any critical diseases. It may also throw lights on some of the probable causes of some of the terminal diseases like Cancer, AIDS, etc.

Gene regulation among various genes in a cell can be depicted using GRN. GRN is a group of genes within a cell which communicate among themselves and with other materials like metabolites or proteins in the cell, thereby controlling the rates at which genes in the cell are transcribed into mRNA [1]. Mathematically, a GRN can be defined as follows.

Definition 1 (Gene Regulatory Network). *GRN is a mixed graph and is defined by three tuples $T := (V, U, D)$, where V represents the nodes or the genes, the unordered pairs U represents the undirected links among the genes, and the ordered pairs D represents the directed links among the genes. A directed link d_{ij} from v_i to v_j portrays that a causal inference is from node v_i to v_j. An undirected link u_{ij} between the nodes v_i and v_j depicts only an association between v_i and v_j and does not give any information regarding the causal relationship between the nodes.*

Thus, GRNs consist of nodes and edges where the nodes signifies genes and the edges represents relationship among the genes. Such a relationship could be represented by a directed edge $(G_i \rightarrow G_j)$ or an undirected edge $(G_i - G_j)$. If only undirected edges are present in a network it is known as Gene Co-Expression Network and if only directed edges are present it is known as Gene Regulatory Network, otherwise a mixed graph. The undirected edges in a Gene Co-Expression Network signifies only an association between the corresponding genes whereas the directed edges in a Gene Regulatory Network signifies that a causal effect runs from the originating gene to the target gene. There can be many possible edges in a GRN such as one-to-one, one-to-many, many-to-one, self-loop, etc.

Number of causality inference methods are available in the literature. Few of them are applied in GRN for inferringcause-effect relationships. However, they are not very effective considering the input expression data and gold networks. They are either computationally expensive or unable to handle large networks. Moreover, most of the cases look for immediate effect on variable due to the cause of factor variable.

Biologically, it is unrealistic to assume that the effect happens immediately. Over expression of one gene may require time to give influence in the expression level of another target gene during regulation process. Hence, observing regulation effect on another target gene, one must wait for certain time gap.

In our work, we generate association rules, which is a vital concept in data mining in generating the rules among item sets in transactional or market-basket data [2], to infer cause-effect relationship between a pair of genes. While computing the rules, we consider a time delay as regulation does not happen immediately. In our work, the inferred GRN is constructed by using in-silico DREAM challenge datasets.

Organization of the rest of the paper is as follows. A brief literature review is described in Sect. 2. In Sect. 3, we describe how Association Rule Mining is used to reconstruct the causal structure in GRN. In Sect. 4, we report empirical findings on synthetic expression data. Finally, we give our concluding remarks in Sect. 5.

2 Prior Research

Finding causality among the various component of the genes is a daunting task. Researchers have tried to establish the causal interaction among the genes by proposing various techniques like Granger Causality [3–5], bayesian networks [6–8], boolean networks [9–12], Relevance network and Information Theory Based Techniques - Mutual Information Based Techniques and Entropy based Techniques [13–17], Causation Entropy [18,19] etc. Majority of these techniques have been applied successfully in domains like Economics, Statistics and other such fields. But when applied to detecting causality in Gene network it does not yield satisfactory results. Reasons behind it are many. First, Gene network consist of large to medium size network and the causality finding techniques are mostly applicable to small datasets. Second, majority of these techniques require discrete data as input but gene expression data is continuous in nature and hence it has to go through a pre-processing stage called discretization which results in loss of information. Finally, there is a limit in the availability of real GRN and hence the validation process is not straightforward. Thus inference and analysis of GRN from time series expression data is still an open research issue. More elaborate discussions on the above methods can be found in one of our recent works [20].

Next, we attempt to use well known association rules to reconstruct causal regulatory networks.

3 Time Lagged Association Rules for Causal Inference

Association rule mining is a widely discussed domain in the field of data mining that have received quite prominence, especially in the field of marketing, retail communities as well as in reconstructing co-expression networks [21]. It is initially introduced keeping in view market-basket databases consists of transactions and itemsets.

Agrawal et al. [22] gave a formal definition of the association rule-mining problem as follows.

Definition 2 (Association Rule). *Consider a transaction database, $D = T \times I$ of T transactions and I items, then a association rule is described in the form of $A \Rightarrow B$, where $A, B \subset I$ are known as itemsets and are subsets of items, and $A \cap B = \phi$. A is known as the antecedent and B the consequent. The rule simply denotes that A implies B.*

Two basic quantities namely *confidence* and *support* and their corresponding thresholds, *minimum confidence* and *minimum support*, are used to compute the authenticity of an association rule.

Definition 3 (Support). *An association rule's support is given by the fraction of records that have $A \cup B$ to the total number of records in the database. The count for each item is incremented by one each time the item is encountered in a different transaction T in database D during the scanning process. Computation of support is done by using Eq. 1.*

$$Support(A, B) = \frac{|A \cup B|}{|D|}. \tag{1}$$

The minimum support threshold value is usually specified by the user before the start of the mining process, meaning that the user is concerned with only those rules whose support is greater than that threshold.

Definition 4 (Confidence). *An association rule's confidence is given by the fraction of the number of transactions that consist of both $A \cup B$ to the overall records that have only A. Computation of confidence is done by using Eq. 2.*

$$Confidence(A \Rightarrow B) = \frac{Support(A, B)}{Support(A)}. \tag{2}$$

A strong association rule $A \Rightarrow B$ is produced, if the confidence value exceeds the minimum confidence threshold value. Confidence is an estimate of how strong an association rule is. Association rule mining's main goal is to uncover those rules whose confidence and support is greater than its predefined threshold value. A rule which is greater than both its minimum confidence threshold and minimum support threshold is known as *Strong Rule*.

To model causal relationship among a pair of genes we treat genes as items and time points as transactions. Unlike association which infer rules involving any arbitrary numbers of items, we use here only binary rules between any two genes. It is inappropriate to assume that cause and effect happens immediately during regulation. Motivated from the fact of delay in the affect of regulation we use time lag association rule. Accordingly, we redefine support and confidence for gene expression data (time series) as follows.

Let $T = \{t_1, t_2, \cdots, t_M\}$ be the set of M time points and $G = \{G_1, G_2, \cdots, G_N\}$ be the set of N genes from microarray experiments. The gene expression dataset D is a representation of the matrix $D_{N \times M}$ where each cell of the matrix $d_{i,j}$ is a measure of the logarithm of the relative abundance of $mRNA$ of a gene.

Time delay support is the fraction of the number of time points for which genes G_i and G_j are identical to the total number of time points, M and is given by Eq. 3.

$$Support(G_i, G_j) = \frac{\sum_{i,j=1}^{M} \varphi(G_i(t), G_j(t+k))}{M}, \tag{3}$$

where, φ is the similarity of expression values for t and $t+k$ time intervals. We consider a delay in k time points while computing the expression similarity. We calculate similarity, (φ), between a pair genes with respect to M time points as follows.

$$\varphi(G_i(t), G_j(t+k)) = \begin{cases} 1, \text{ if } G_i(t) = G_j(t+k) \\ 0, \text{ otherwise,} \end{cases} \tag{4}$$

Two genes are co-expressed if their expression values either inhibit or exhibit for a specific observations. A possible co-expressed gene pairs with respect to time delay of one unit is shown in Fig. 1. We use only two values 0 and 1 to represent inhibition and exhibition respectively after using any thresholding or discretization method.

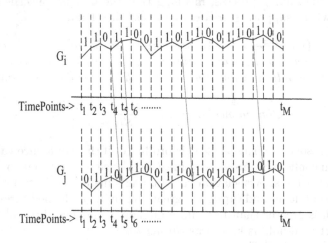

Fig. 1. Expression profiles of two genes with M time points exhibiting a coregulation in one unit time delay (shown in red arrow). Up-regulations and down-regulations in expression is indicated using the value 1 and 0 respectively. (Color figure online)

Similarly, the confidence of a causal edge between G_i and G_j can be given as follows.

$$Confidence(G_i \Rightarrow G_j) = \frac{Support(G_i, G_j)}{Support(G_i)}. \tag{5}$$

The support of G_i or G_j is equal to the total number of time point i.e. M as we take into account both inhibition and exhibition for capturing co-expression. It needless to say that time delay support of G_i and G_j is non symmetric (unlike traditional support) in nature. Hence, we calculate support between G_i and G_j, as well as G_j and G_i both.

We use following steps to construct the inferred network. First, we discretize the expression profile to convert them into market basket form containing only 0 and 1. Next, the support value is calculated for each pair of nodes in both the directions. We defined a minimum support threshold and retain only those pairs whose support value is larger than the minimum threshold support. We compute confidence for those pairs retained in second step. We calculate a minimum confidence threshold and retain only those rules whose confidence value is larger than the minimum threshold confidence value. Finally, an adjacency matrix is created between all the pairs retained in fourth step as described in Eq. 6, where a value of 1 signifies a directed edge exist from G_i to G_j and a value of 0 signifies no edges between them.

$$A(G_i, G_j) = \begin{cases} 1 & \text{if } Support(G_i, G_j) \geq min\_supp \text{ and} \\ & Confidence(G_i \Rightarrow G_j) \geq min\_conf \\ 0 & \text{otherwise} \end{cases} \tag{6}$$

3.1   Computing the Minimum Thresholds

Association rules are sensitive towards selection of minimum support (min_supp) and minimum confidence (min_conf) thresholds. The min_supp and the min_conf threshold plays a crucial role in determining inferred network as we retain only those rule (or directed edges) whose value is greater then the threshold (Eq. 6). A very low threshold value may lead to many false positive edges and high value produce sparse network by ignoring important edges. We try to set the threshold values automatically by looking into the distribution of all pairs support and confidence scores. While selecting the thresholds we choose mid value in the range of all pairs support scores (or confidence scores). To ensure that the mid value should not fall below the minimum boundary of the range, we add the minimum boundary value with the mid value.

Given a vector of all support values $\mathcal{S} = \{Support(G_i, G_j) | \forall G_i, G_j \in G \wedge i \neq j\}$, the minimum support value, can be calculated by using Eq. 7.

$$min\_supp = \min(\mathcal{S}) + \frac{\max(\mathcal{S}) - \min(\mathcal{S})}{2} \tag{7}$$

Similarly we can calculate the minimum confidence (min_conf) threshold by using Eq. 8.

$$min\_conf = \min(\mathcal{C}) + \frac{\max(\mathcal{C}) - \min(\mathcal{C})}{2}, \tag{8}$$

where, $\mathcal{C} = \{Confidence(G_i, G_j) | \forall G_i, G_j \in G \wedge i \neq j\}$.

4   Experimental Evaluation

In this section a comparison of inferred networks and the gold-standard networks is done to determine the quality of the inferred networks.

4.1   Dataset Generation

The gene regulatory networks are constructed using In-silico DREAM challenge datasets. We generate four datasets each of size 10, 15, 20 and 50 from *E coli* using the *Gene Net Weaver (GNW)* tool, developed by Marbach and his team [23]. GNW generates benchmark *in-silico* time-series expression data by reverse engineering the gold networks. To analyze the time complexity, datasets of size 10, 15, 50, 100, 200, 500 and 1000 are used. For all datasets we use 21 time-points uniformly. Each time stamp is of 50 ms duration. In Table 1 the various datasets used for our experiments is listed.

Table 1. Abstract of the various datasets used

Challenges	Dataset	In-silico network	Network size	Number of timepoints
Dream 3	1	Ecoli1	10	21
	2	Ecoli1	15	21
	3	Ecoli1	20	21
	4	Ecoli1	50	21
	5	Ecoli2	10	21
	6	Ecoli2	15	21
	7	Ecoli2	20	21
	8	Ecoli2	50	21
Dream 4	9	Ecoli9	10	21
	10	Ecoli9	15	21
	11	Ecoli9	50	21
	12	Ecoli9	100	21
	13	Ecoli9	200	21
	14	Ecoli9	500	21
	15	Ecoli9	1000	21

4.2   Assessment

Three assessment parameters, viz, Accuracy, Precision and F_β Score are used to make a relative study of the method proposed by varying discretization methods and bin sizes. Four variables namely - the number of true positives (tp), the number of false positives (fp), the number of true negatives (tn) and the number of false negatives (fn) are used to compute the assessment parameters.

The quality of the proposed inference method is first measured by Accuracy. Accuracy is the measure of how closely the true network is similar to the inferred network and gives the gross effectiveness of a classifier [24]. Accuracy is calculated by using Eq. 9.

$$\frac{tp + tn}{tp + tn + fp + fn}. \tag{9}$$

We perform experiment with three discretization techniques - Equal Width [25], Equal Frequency [25] and Global Equal Width [25] which are unsupervised learning techniques based on binning and splitting of the continuous data into varying bin sizes. The sizes of bins used in our experiment are 2, 3, 4 and 5. The various accuracy scores are presented in Table 2 for network size of 10 and 15 and in Table 3 for network size of 20 and 50.

Table 2. Computation of the assessment parameters of the proposed method with different discretization techniques for network size of 10 and 15

Discretization Method	No of bins	Precision	F-Score	Accuracy	Discretization Method	No of bins	Precision	F-Score	Accuracy
	2	0.209	0.246	0.64		2	0.048	0.058	0.516
Equal Width	3	0.242	0.28	0.72	Equal Width	3	0.065	0.078	0.578
	4	0.067	0.07	0.76		4	0.083	0.099	0.671
	5	0.053	0.057	0.72		5	0.079	0.09	0.796
	2	0.163	0.191	0.6		2	0.045	0.055	0.512
Equal Frequency	3	0.125	0.144	0.65	Equal Frequency	3	0.065	0.078	0.64
	4	0.192	0.217	0.73		4	0.066	0.079	0.587
	5	0.179	0.203	0.71		5	0.073	0.084	0.782
	2	0.111	0.12	0.75		2	0.055	0.065	0.649
Global Equal Width	3	0.259	0.294	0.76	Global Equal Width	3	0.064	0.074	0.756
	4	0.067	0.07	0.76		4	0.031	0.035	0.804
	5	0.111	0.106	0.82		5	0.033	0.029	0.787

Network Size 10   Network Size 15

Table 3. Computation of the assessment parameters of the proposed method with different discretization techniques for network size of 20 and 50

Discretization Method	No of bins	Precision	F-Score	Accuracy	Discretization Method	No of bins	Precision	F-Score	Accuracy
	2	0.045	0.054	0.548		2	0.032	0.04	0.536
Equal Width	3	0.062	0.076	0.64	Equal Width	3	0.04	0.049	0.701
	4	0.033	0.04	0.675		4	0.018	0.022	0.786
	5	0.035	0.042	0.758		5	0.008	0.01	0.838
	2	0.054	0.066	0.542		2	0.029	0.036	0.512
Equal Frequency	3	0.055	0.067	0.552	Equal Frequency	3	0.022	0.028	0.62
	4	0.07	0.085	0.588		4	0.022	0.027	0.592
	5	0.043	0.052	0.69		5	0.02	0.025	0.752
	2	0.079	0.097	0.558		2	0.032	0.04	0.642
Global Equal Width	3	0.036	0.044	0.7	Global Equal Width	3	0.03	0.036	0.799
	4	0.0036	0.022	0.721		4	0.0036	0.004	0.866
	5	0.053	0.061	0.742		5	0.008	0.009	0.927

A. Network Size 20   B. Network Size 50

From the accuracy result it can be observed in general that higher accuracy value is obtained when the number of bins is high. It is also observed that accuracy result is comparatively insensitive to the size of the network.

F-score measures how effective a technique is, assuming recall to be β times more crucial than precision and can be calculated as given in Eq. 10.

$$F_\beta = (1 + \beta^2) \frac{precision.recall}{(\beta^2.precision) + recall}. \tag{10}$$

In our experiments, we use $\beta = 0.5$ which indicates that recall is half as important as precision. The β value of 0.5 also suggests that higher weight is given to precision compared to recall.

We also performed experiments by varying the discretization methods and the number of bins and computed the precision (in Tables 2 and 3) which is the fraction of correctly classified positive examples to the number of examples labeled by the system as positive [24] and is measured as the ratio of $\frac{tp}{tp+fp}$.

Whereas, recall is the fraction of correctly classified positive examples to the number of positive examples in the data [24] and is measured as the ratio of $\frac{tp}{tp+fn}$.

4.3 Performance Comparison

We also make a comparative analysis by plotting the accuracy value of some of the causality finding techniques. Table 4 shows the bar diagram for dataset size 10 and 15 which shows that the accuracy value is better in the association rule mining technique compared to the other techniques in almost all the scenarios.

Table 4. Efficiency of various causality finding techniques for dataset size of 10 and 15

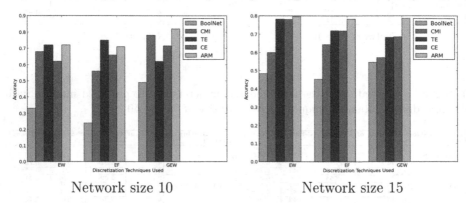

Network size 10   Network size 15

4.4 Scalability Test

Real world networks contain large number of nodes in the order of thousands. It is of utmost importance that along with the inference quality, the inference methods have fine scalability. Hence, we performed experiments and made an analysis of the time taken for computation by each of the techniques with increasing network size.

Figure 2 depicts the plotting of the time taken in seconds of the different techniques for network of varied sizes. From the graph it is clearly observed that time complexity of ARM technique is comparatively better to most of the other techniques. However, for dataset sizes of 100 and 200, Transfer Entropy's time complexity is slightly better.

4.5 Assessing the Inference Quality with Varying Time Lags

We perform additional experiments to see the impact in accuracy by varying time lags. Table 5 show the accuracy variation with the variation of time delay of up to 3 time units for network of size 10 and 15. Value 0 indicates no time lag, whereas rest of the values corresponds to unit time lags while calculating the

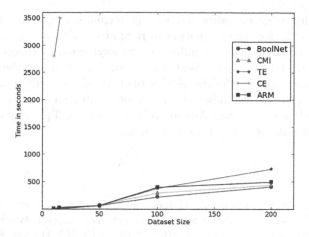

Fig. 2. Computational time taken by various techniques on varied dataset size

causation. Results further confirm the fact that regulation is a time delay activity and happens after a gap of certain time durations. For all the experiments we observe a very good accuracy for the delay of one time point. However, results are not uniform with respect to different discretization methods. Hence, we may conclude that inference of causation also depends on quality of discretization.

Table 5. Effect of varying time lags and discretization methods applied during causal inference for network of size 10 and 15

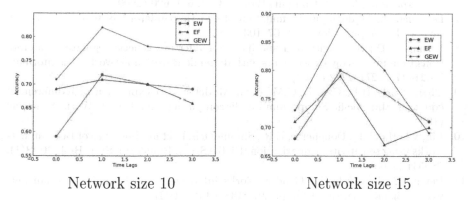

Network size 10   Network size 15

5   Conclusion

We proposed a new way of inferring causal gene regulatory network with the help of time delay association rule generation. The inferred network is evaluated using various assessment parameters like Accuracy, Precision and $F_{0.5}$ score. Proposed technique is basic in nature, yet produce better outcomes compared to other cutting edge causality discovering techniques. Our experiments further confirmed the fact the regulation in regulatory networks is not happening immediately and needs time to influence the expression of target gene by the regulator or target factor gene. Next, the research is on to see the mutual relationship (with regards to the chemical properties of the individual nucleotides such as purine (A, G)/pyrimidine (C, T), strong hydrogen bonding (C, G)/weak hydrogen bonding (A, T) and Amino (A, C)/Kyto (G, T)) between the target gene and the regulator or the target factor gene.

References

1. Roy, S., Das, D., Choudhury, D., Gohain, G.G., Sharma, R., Bhattacharyya, D.K.: Causality inference techniques for *In-Silico* gene regulatory network. In: Prasath, R., Kathirvalavakumar, T. (eds.) MIKE 2013. LNCS (LNAI), vol. 8284, pp. 432–443. Springer, Cham (2013). https://doi.org/10.1007/978-3-319-03844-5_44
2. Roy, S., Bhattacharyya, D.K.: OPAM: an efficient one pass association mining technique without candidate generation. J. Converg. Inf. Technol. **3**(3), 32–38 (2008)
3. Granger, C.W.J.: Investigating causal relations by econometric models and cross-spectral methods. Econom.: J. Econom. Soc. **37**, 424–438 (1969)
4. Tam, G.H.F., Chang, C., Hung, Y.S.: Application of granger causality to gene regulatory network discovery. In: 2012 IEEE 6th International Conference on Systems Biology (ISB), pp. 232–239. IEEE (2012)
5. Tam, G.H.F., Hung, Y.S., Chang, C.: Meta-analysis on gene regulatory networks discovered by pairwise Granger causality. In: 2013 7th International Conference on Systems Biology (ISB), pp. 123–128. IEEE (2013)
6. Friedman, N., Linial, M., Nachman, I., Pe'er, D.: Using Bayesian networks to analyze expression data. J. Comput. Biol. **7**(3–4), 601–620 (2000)
7. De Jong, H.: Modeling and simulation of genetic regulatory systems: a literature review. J. Comput. Biol. **9**(1), 67–103 (2002)
8. Husmeier, D.: Sensitivity and specificity of inferring genetic regulatory interactions from microarray experiments with dynamic Bayesian networks. Bioinformatics **19**(17), 2271–2282 (2003)
9. Chen, T., He, H.L., Church, G.M., et al.: Modeling gene expression with differential equations. In: Pacific Symposium on Biocomputing, vol. 4, p. 4. World Scientific (1999)
10. Liu, W., Harri, L., Dougherty, E.R., Shmulevich, I., et al.: Inference of Boolean networks using sensitivity regularization. EURASIP J. Bioinform. Syst. Biol. **2008**(1), 780541 (2008)
11. Perrin, B., Ralaivola, L.: Gene networks inference using dynamic Bayesian networks. Bioinformatics **19**(Suppl. 2), ii138–ii148 (2003)
12. Zou, M., Conzen, S.D.: A new dynamic Bayesian network (DBN) approach for identifying gene regulatory networks from time course microarray data. Bioinformatics **21**(1), 71–79 (2005)
13. Butte, A.J., Kohane, I.S.: Mutual information relevance networks: functional genomic clustering using pairwise entropy measurements. In: Pacific Symposium on Biocomputing, vol. 5, pp. 415–426 (2000)
14. Margolin, A.A., et al.: ARACNE: an algorithm for the reconstruction of gene regulatory networks in a mammalian cellular context. BMC Bioinform. **7**, S7 (2006)

15. Dougherty, J., Tabus, I., Astola, J.: Inference of gene regulatory networks based on a universal minimum description length. EURASIP J. Bioinform. Syst. Biol. **2008**, 5 (2008)
16. Meyer, P.E., Lafitte, F., Bontempi,G.: MINET: an open source R/Bioconductor package for mutual information based network inference. BMC Bioinform. **9**(article 461) (2008)
17. Liang, K.-C., Wang, X.: Gene regulatory network reconstruction using conditional mutual information. URASIP J. Bioinform. Syst. Biol. **2008**(1), 253894 (2008)
18. Sun, J., Taylor, D., Bollt, E.M.: Causal network inference by optimal causation entropy. SIAM J. Appl. Dyn. Syst. **14**(1), 73–106 (2015)
19. Sun, J., Bollt, E.M.: Causation entropy identifies indirect influences, dominance of neighbors and anticipatory couplings. Phys. D: Nonlinear Phenom. **267**, 49–57 (2014)
20. Ahmed, S.S., Roy, S., Kalita,J.K.: Assessing the effectiveness of causality inference methods for gene regulatory networks. IEEE/ACM Trans. Comput. Biol. Bioinform. (2018)
21. Roy, S., Bhattacharyya, D.K., Kalita, J.K.: Reconstruction of gene co-expression network from microarray data using local expression patterns. BMC Bioinform. **15**(7), S10 (2014)
22. Agrawal, R., Imieliński, T., Swami, A.: Mining association rules between sets of items in large databases. ACM SIGMOD Rec. **22**, 207–216 (1993)
23. Schaffter, T., Marbach, D., Floreano, D.: Genenetweaver: in silico benchmark generation and performance profiling of network inference methods. Bioinformatics **27**(16), 2263–2270 (2011)
24. Sokolova, M., Lapalme, G.: A systematic analysis of performance measures for classification tasks. Inf. Process. Manag. **45**(4), 427–437 (2009)
25. Dougherty, J., Kohavi, R., Sahami, M., et al.: Supervised and unsupervised discretization of continuous features. In: Machine learning: Proceedings of the Twelfth International Conference, vol. 12, pp. 194–202 (1995)

Assessment of Different Security Issues, Threats with Their Detection and Prevention Security Models in Mobile Cloud Computing (MCC)

Vishal[1](✉), Bikrampal Kaur[2], and Surender Jangra[3]

[1] Department of Computer Science & Engineering, IKGPTU, Kapurthala, India
vishalgarg.9@gmail.com
[2] Department of Computer Science & Engineering, CGC,
Landran, Punjab, India
mca.bikrampal@gmail.com
[3] Department of Computer Science, GTBC, Bhawanigarh, Punjab, India
jangra.surender@gmail.com

Abstract. MCC integrates cloud computing services into the mobile environment that helps users to improve performance by utilizing battery life and storage of devices. When mobile data is stored on cloud rather than in mobile phone storage then less memory and less battery will be consumed by mobile phone and it will helps to increases the performance of data transmission but at same time it violates security of data. As data is transmitted from mobile to cloud at the mean time there are lots of attackers presented in open environment that may access or harm the data. To overcome this kind of hazards it is necessary to propose a mechanism that provides secure data transmission in MCC. In this paper an attempt has been made to perform assessment on different security threats and their prevention models with different scenarios. This paper is divided into six sections. Section 1 presents introduction of mobile cloud computing (mcc), Sect. 2 covers deployment models of mcc, in Sect. 3 service models of mcc has been discussed, Sect. 4 presents different kinds of attacks in mcc environment, in Sect. 5 covers related work of different research papers that presents security issues and detection techniques in mcc, in Sect. 6 conclusion of paper has been discussed.

Keywords: Mobile cloud computing MCC mobile computing
Cloud computing · Security issues · Security models
Threats and security techniques

1 Introduction

To group routinely varying commerce desires, affiliations require to give instance and use intend to extent up IT establishment, in favor of instance, gear, training, as well as organizations. Anyway through on-premises IT system the extent methodology be able to direct and affiliations are a great part of the time unfit to achieve perfect utilization of the IT establishment [1]. Cloud computing is a standard move which gives computing

© Springer Nature Singapore Pte Ltd. 2019
A. K. Luhach et al. (Eds.): ICAICR 2018, CCIS 956, pp. 322–333, 2019.
https://doi.org/10.1007/978-981-13-3143-5_27

through web. A mobile cloud computing organization contains particularly upgraded simulated server develops so as to provide exacting programming, Mobile computing is sorting out with cloud computing as a result of the focal qualities of cloud illustrate, for example, on-request self-advantage, wide system get to, asset pooling, fast versatility, and evaluated organizations. Likewise, the cloud computing is being perceptible to the mobile customers as it can give cloud like organizations [3]. Regardless, the mobile contraptions are going up against different difficulties in their advantages (e.g., battery life, accumulating, and trade speed) and exchanges (e.g., portability and security). The obliged assets all things considered square the distinction in advantage attributes. Underneath specified Fig. 1 is speaking to Mobile Cloud Computing Architecture and as indicated by that Storage, processor and even application offices are accessible with reasonable middleware and correspondence protocol [4].

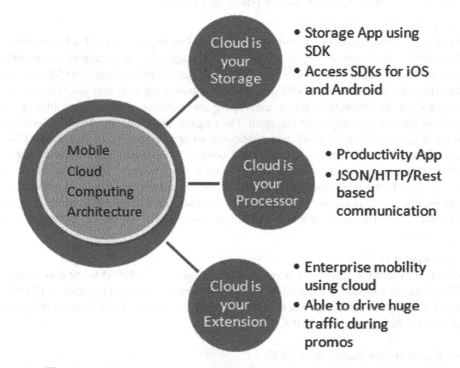

Fig. 1. Mobile cloud computing architecture [5], mobile cloud applications

The capacity of MCC to enable the gadget to run cloud-based web-applications not at all like other local applications separates it from the idea of 'Mobile Computing'. Here the clients can remotely get to the store applications and their related information whenever on the Internet by buying in to the cloud administrations. Albeit most gadgets as of now run a blend of electronic and local applications, the pattern nowa-days is by all accounts moving more toward the administrations and comfort that are offered by a mobile cloud. Associations and organizations have changed their approach towards outlining and conceptualizing new items in the wake of incorporating cloud-figuring in their estimations.

Clients and designers' recently earned capacity to get to the monstrously adaptable and financially savvy energy of cloud registering has created administrations that more likely than not appeared to be basically infeasible only a couple of years back. An ideal case of this is Voice Search by Google for mobile gadgets. 'Voice Search' has empowered clients to pass on a voice inquiry and have it deciphered precisely on their gadgets continuously. The credit for this goes to Google's capacity to utilize the immense measure of pursuit information to refine and characterize such voice questions with cloud foundation. As far back as its presentation, brilliant voice look administrations have. Today, very nearly 25% of inquiries on Android gadgets are utilizing it. Mechanical technology and cloud figuring can be an awesome blend which might include more capacities and may likewise help in sparing the battery life of the gadget. What's more, by adding mobile network to this gives mechanical technology new abilities while utilizing lesser battery power and memory.

MCC Working Principle

MCC is an improvement of mobile computing and an expansion to cloud computing. In mobile cloud computing, the past mobile gadget based escalated computing, information stockpiling and mass data preparing have been exchanged to 'cloud' and therefore the necessities of mobile gadgets in computing capacity and assets have been lessened, so the creating, running, conveying and utilizing method of mobile applications have been completely changed. Then again, the terminals which individuals used to get to and secure cloud administrations are appropriate for mobile gadgets like cell phone, PDA, Tablet, and iPad yet not confined to settled gadgets, (for example, PC), which mirrors the favorable circumstances and unique expectation of cloud computing. In this way, from the two parts of mobile computing and cloud computing, the mobile cloud computing is a blend of the two innovations, an advancement of circulated, matrix and unified calculations, and have expansive prospects for application.

Advantages of MCC

Cloud computing is considered as one of the best solution for MC (Mobile computing). This is due to various factors such as mobility, communication and portability. Here we are discussing the advantage that how to overcome the barrier of mobile computing and discussed the advantages of MCC [2].

- Business save money with MCC.
- MCC enables the clients to share apps and sources with less hardware and software investment and thus decrease the economic expenditure.
- It requires less technical devices that reduce the cost.
- Consumers can use more features on their smart phones.
- The features such as position based social networks; home security, mobile security etc. are provided.
- The addition of features in the mobile phone is continuously growing [3].
- Designer reach a larger market through mobile cloud.

It occurs since the cloud application carries similar browser that is executed effortlessly of mobile OS (Operating system) in destination mobile phone of users or some another devices.

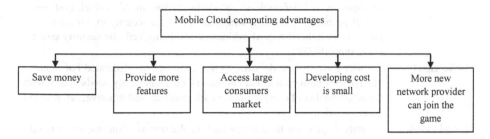

Fig. 2. MCC advantages

- Developers reduce costs and increase revenue through mobile computing
- They can also reduce expenses while retaining greater profits
- More novel mobile network providers may join the game
- The providers of mobile network have extended and now have become equivalent equal area of competition.

Various novel providers have used MCC service offerings. The sense of competition is fine for users as it helps in precise and accurate price and is considered good for the advertisers as it enhances the innovation.

Although in the past great issues have been encountered in designing applications for all mobile operating systems, the latest mobile browsers, such as Google and Apple, have been able to enter the larger consumer market.

2 Mobile Cloud Computing Deployment Models

It's definitely not hard to pass on a cloud computing organization by using three interesting models public, private and crossover cloud. The private cloud works only for one relationship on a private framework and is extremely secure.

An open cloud is controlled by the cloud pro center and offers the most unusual measure of profitability and shared resources. A half and half cloud is a arrangement of private and public game plan models, in a hybrid cloud specific resources are run or used as a piece of an public cloud more over rest are run or used on-premises [6, 7].

These computing models have some security concerns which are talked about in Table 1.

Table 1. Security concerns related with mobile cloud computing deployment model [8]

Deployment model	Security disputes
Private cloud	Security confront integrate high cost of execution and Management, prerequisite, and defenselessness administration. In this model, cost and rate of profitability are key components and the security execution is normally in light of hazard evaluation and henceforth the security cover isn't complete [8]
Public cloud	Security concerns are delicate, as the assets are not dedicated but rather utilized over numerous cloud purchasers Yet additionally needs to deal with the large number of outside impacts, for example, authoritative, information security and so on [9]
Hybrid cloud	Security dispute are moderately high as the organization display is mind boggling with heterogeneous environment, various coordination, and computerization apparatuses. This will require extra regulatory overhead with any oversight bringing about critical hazard presentation [10]

3   Mobile Cloud Service Models

In this section different services model of MCC has been covered. These models are discussed below:

MCC has following administration models to give cloud administrations to mobile clients.

a. MNaaS: The administration show, the administration providers offer a framework establishment with the objective that the clients can influence their own specific frameworks, to control the traffics, and connect with the servers. Delineation: Open Stack Networking Service.

b. MIaaS: The administration demonstrate, the administration users deal cloud system and ability to mobile clients.

c. MDaaS: The administration display, the administration users give database-linked organizers all together that mobile clients can do their data organization, trade and other data linked jobs.

d. MAppaaS: The administration show, the clients can use, get to and accomplish cloud based mobile applications through remote framework in wherever and at whatever point.

e. MMaaS: The administration demonstrate, the clients can run and manage the blended media administrations, for instance, playing movies or preoccupations through the remote framework in rich hardware outfit.

f. MCaaS: The administration show, a get-together of mobile clients can create and manage a mobile casual association or gathering where the clients can get gave relational association or gathering services [12].

Table 2. List of offered services related to service models of the cloud computing [13].

Sr. No.	Services offered	MNaaS service model	MCaaS service model	MIaaS service model
1.	Application	✓	Client's responsibility	Client's responsibility
2.	Data	✓	Client's responsibility	Client's responsibility
3.	Runtime	✓	✓	Client's responsibility
4.	Middleware	✓	✓	Client's responsibility
5.	Operating system	✓	✓	Client's responsibility
6.	Virtualization	✓	✓	✓
7.	Storage	✓	✓	✓
8.	Server	✓	✓	✓
9.	Networking	✓	✓	✓

4 Security Attacks in Mobile Cloud Computing

To get a profound plunge into security worries of the cloud computing, underneath segment has been exhibiting different security issues and dangers in cloud. Some most prominent danger of the present time where cloud wellbeing falls little, are [14–16]:

a. Information breaks

A data crack is a security scene in which sensitive, guaranteed or private data is copied, transmitted, seen, stolen or used by an individual unapproved to do as such [17].

b. Weak characters, accreditation and access administration

A nonattendance of suitable affirmation and identity organization is accountable for data breaks inside affiliations. Associations much of the time fight with identity organization as they attempt to administer approvals legitimate to every customer's action part. Two-factor/Multi-factor check systems, like one-time passwords and phone based affirmation, guarantee cloud benefits by making it harder for aggressors to sign in using stolen passwords [18].

c. Uncertain interfaces and APIs

Most cloud organizations and applications use APIs to talk with other cloud organizations. In this way, the security of the APIs themselves specifically influences the security of the cloud organizations. The shot of getting hacked increases when associations give outcasts access to the APIs [19].

d. Account seizing

Record catch sounds too much essential, making it difficult to be a stress in the cloud, yet Cloud Security Alliance says it is an issue. Phishing, manhandle of programming vulnerabilities, for instance, bolster surge strikes, and loss of passwords and accreditations would all have the capacity to incite the loss of control over a customer account. Associations that don't weight the hugeness of secure affirmations are at a more genuine threat of being exchanged off. Despite using strong passwords, associations can in like manner secure themselves by setting the right customer parts and rolling out structures for recognizing essential improvements made by various customers [20].

e. Denial of administration assault

DoS attacks every now and again impact the openness and for endeavors that run essential system in the cloud. This kind of strike can be debilitating, and systems may direct or time out. Driving forward dissent of organization strikes may make it "too much expensive for you, making it difficult to run [your service] and you'll be constrained to cut it down yourself," DoS attacks have harmed PC frameworks for a long time. The most exceedingly terrible part is that there is nothing you can do once it happens however to sit and delay [16]. Examining hazard elements of the previously mentioned security dangers based on universes surely understood standard i.e. Cloud Security Alliance (CSA) positioning on the size of 1–7, albeit any assault isn't useful for framework yet to comprehend hazard factor the scale setting resembles, profoundly unsafe assault will be depend on scale 1 and slightest will get scale position 7.

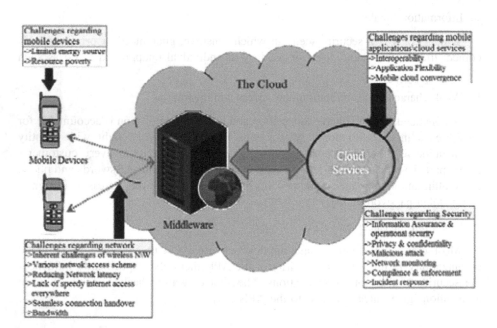

Fig. 3. Cloud computing implementation challenges calculate in mobile app

f. Mobile gadgets security challenges

It is possible to hardship, spillage, get to or accidentally unveil of the information or applications to unapproved clients, if the mobile gadgets are lost, lost or burglary. In spite of the fact that there are secret key or example based darted highlights; numerous mobile clients do not use these highlights. What's more, the character module card inside the mobile gadget likewise can be approached from gadget and got to by unapproved individuals. In addition, most of mobile gadgets are absence of security component against dangers. The assailants can assault by using unmistakable accessibility assault strategies, for instance, by sending high malignant activity stream, tremendous messages to focusing on mobile gadgets to make unused or diminishing the capacity.

Table 3. CSA based scaling of cloud computing security threats with quick guidelines [21]

Sr. No.	Security Threats	CSA ranking (Scale 1–7)	Quick look up references for the supervision
1.	Information breaks	1	Data administration and information security, application security, encryption and key administration, personality and access administration, virtualization
2.	Weak identities, accreditation and access management	2	Encryption and key administration, identity and access administration
3.	Uncertain interfaces and APIs	3	Data administration and information security, interoperability and portability, event reaction, application security, encryption and key administration, access administration
4.	Account seizing	4	supremacy and venture Risk Management, Data Management and information Security, conventional Security, Business stability and failure Recovery, Incident Response, Key Management, Identity and Access Management
5.	Malevolent insiders	5	supremacy and venture Risk Management, Data Management and information Security, Key Management, Identity and Access Management

Below mentioned Table 4. Analyses the loss of the above mentioned security threats and take a deep dive to get the clear vision of these cloud attacks.

Table 4. Estimation of the losses from various security threats in cloud [21]

Losses	Cloud security threats						
	Information breaks	Weak identities, accreditation and access management	Uncertain interfaces and APIs	Account seizing	Malevolent insiders	Information loss	Denial of service attack
Parodying personality	N	Y	Y	Y	Y	N	N
Tempering with data	N	Y	N	Y	Y	N	N
Disavowal	N	Y	N	Y	N	Y	N
Data divulgence	Y	Y	N	Y	Y	N	N
Disavowal of Service	N	Y	Y	Y	N	Y	Y
Rise of benefit	N	Y	N	Y	N	N	N

5   Related Work

Till now different strategies has been proposed keeping in mind the end goal to accomplish better security in cloud. Specialists gave their best push to give answers for previously mentioned dangers like in [22] proposed a secure model in which private key was used to encrypt the message in order to send it to the cloud environment. Here author discussed different security threats and issues occurred in MCC environment. [23] Author proposed proactive unique secure data plot (P2DS) to confirm the mobile client's data security from unapproved access in cloud. In [24, 25] creator proposes a capable multi-catchphrase situated look for (EMRS) approach. This approach grants multi-watchword look for over encoded mobile client's data on cloud and besides achieves significance based result situating. This approach relied upon importance score, secures k-nearest neighbor technique, a gainful record and outwardly hindered limit system. The congruity score and k-nearest neighbor techniques in available encryption enable beneficial multi-watchword situated chase, and benefit inquiry things based for precision. The gainful rundown was used to redesign the chase viability. Moreover, the outwardly debilitated limit system was used to conceal the passageway case of the chase client inside the cloud server. In [26] have given thorough data with respect to the cloud security issues. The creators examined the security issue from cloud design perspective, the cloud partners' perspective and toward the end from cloud benefit conveyance models perspective. From design imminent, the cloud specialist co-ops need to give multitenancy and versatility as both these attributes assume a noteworthy part in cloud security. From partner forthcoming, the security setups should be composed thus, each administration ought to be kept up a level and at runtime. From benefit conveyance show forthcoming, the IaaS, PaaS and SaaS models have security issues. The cloud administration security issues and cloud get to strategy security issues are additionally featured. In [27] have displayed an outline of MCC security engineering. Protection and honesty of the information is imperative part of MCC security. The creator ordered the clients' in term of security into two classes: mobile system security and cloud security. In first classification the security for mobile applications and protection are clarified. The second classification is tied in with anchoring the data on the cloud or essentially anchoring the cloud. In cloud security the creators feature essential concerns related with information honesty, confirmation and computerized rights. The creators in [28] have featured MCC design. After the nitty gritty MCC engineering, the utilizations of MCC are clarified extending from mobile business, mobile learning, mobile human services and mobile gaming.

The current arrangements are additionally introduced in detail. The creator likewise examined open issues connected with low transmission capacity, arrange get to administration, nature of administration, evaluating, and standard interface.

The study displayed in [29] clarifies MCC extremely well. The creators clarify the current arrangement proposed to anchor MCC framework and furthermore feature the uprising issues in MCC. The paper presents MCC engineering alongside the diagram of the distinctive security administrations at various layers of the cloud computing conveyance benefit display. At spine layer, the safe cloud physical administrations are accessible. At the framework and administrator layers, secure cloud process facilitating administrations are accessible. Secure cloud application administrations are accessible at the application, stage and framework layer of the cloud conveyance benefit show. The Paper likewise portrays the criteria previously assessing the current structures for MCC. Based on the assessment criteria a points of interest overview has been delivered of existing systems. The current structures sanctuary been isolated into two systems, the application security system and information security structure. In [30] the creators have recognized the genuine dangers and dangers identified with protection and security for the mass and corporate clients when they will incorporate their mobile hand held gadgets with the cloud foundation. The paper focuses towards the diverse motivational variables which are compelling mobile cloud administrators to move their administrations and activities to cloud. A portion of the key motivational elements are business intrigue, client request, planning of system specialist organization, QoS and develop innovations. The creators directed a study that how remote mobile gadgets incorporates with the cloud. The general population focused for the review are mobile gadget clients, cloud designers, IT supervisor or officials and remote system executives. These individuals are focused with a specific end goal to get appropriate outcomes whether the security and protection worries of the clients have expanded or not in the event that they are intending to move for the cloud. In [31] planned an information benefit instrument (SDSM). The SDSM gives best information get to control and privacy of information put away in the cloud. In SDSM, the information and security administration is outsourced to the mobile cloud trustedly. The framework show is isolated into two classifications, the system demonstrate and the security display. In arrange display the information proprietors, information servers and information sharers are included. Security demonstrate clarifies that the calculation utilized as a part of it guarantees that exclusive approved information sharers can get to the information. The proposed SDSM gives benefits like, solid access control, adaptability and low overhead. The calculation utilized as a part of model speaks to in five stages. The principal stage contract with setup, information encryption is in second, information partaking in third, get to information in fourth and arrangement refreshing in fifth stage.

6 Conclusion

MCC is a technology that integrates features of cloud and mobile computing and provides ideal facilities to mobile customers. In this paper we present services and deployment models of MCC after that security and privacy concerns related with MC have also been highlighted with brief introduction. Apart from that we have analyzed threats scaling also for regular cloud by getting reference from standard security alliance. This paper assessed the riskiest level security threats of cloud and also provides some quick references to deal with those. Moreover, this exploration is as yet youthful and unexplored inside and out, numerous security and protection related difficulties are under progress, but then to be explained.

References

1. Voorsluys, W., Broberg, J., Buyya, R.: Introduction to cloud computing. In: Cloud Computing: Principles and Paradigms, Chap. 1, pp. 1–41. Wiley (2011)
2. Buyya, R., Ranjan, R., Calheiros, R.N.: Modeling and simulation of scalable cloud computing environments and the cloudsim toolkit: challenges and opportunities. In: 2009 International Conference on High Performance Computing and Simulation, HPCS 2009, pp. 1–11. IEEE, June 2009
3. Zissis, D., Lekkas, D.: Addressing cloud computing security issues. Future Gener. Comput. Syst. 28(3), 583–592 (2012)
4. Krutz, R.L., Vines, R.D.: Cloud Security: A Comprehensive Guide to Secure Cloud Computing. Wiley Publishing, Hoboken (2010)
5. Popović, K., Hocenski, Ž.: Cloud computing security issues and challenges. In: MIPRO, 2010 Proceedings of the 33rd International Convention, pp. 344–349. IEEE, May 2010
6. Rimal, B.P., Choi, E., Lumb, I.: A taxonomy and survey of cloud computing systems. NCM 9, 44–51 (2009)
7. Grover, J., Katiyar, S.: Agent based dynamic load balancing in Cloud Computing. In: 2013 International Conference on Human Computer Interactions (ICHCI), pp. 1–6. IEEE, August 2013
8. Jensen, M., Schwenk, J., Gruschka, N., Iacono, L.L.: On technical security issues in cloud computing. In: 2009 IEEE International Conference on Cloud Computing, CLOUD 2009, pp. 109–116. IEEE, September (2009)
9. Hashizume, K., Rosado, D.G., Fernández-Medina, E., Fernandez, E.B.: An analysis of security issues for cloud computing. J. Internet Serv. Appl. 4(1), 5 (2013)
10. Hamlen, K., Kantarcioglu, M., Khan, L., Thuraisingham, B.: Security Issues for Cloud Computing. Optimizing Information Security and Advancing Privacy Assurance: New Technologies, vol. 150 (2012)
11. Almorsy, M., Grundy, J., Müller, I.: An analysis of the cloud computing security problem. arXiv preprint arXiv:1609.01107 (2016)
12. Pearson, S.: Privacy, security and trust in cloud computing. In: Pearson, S., Yee, G. (eds.) Privacy and Security for Cloud Computing. CCN, pp. 3–42. Springer, London (2013). https://doi.org/10.1007/978-1-4471-4189-1_1
13. Che, J., Duan, Y., Zhang, T., Fan, J.: Study on the security models and strategies of cloud computing. Proc. Eng. 23, 586–593 (2011)

14. AlZain, M.A., Soh, B., Pardede, E.: A new approach using redundancy technique to improve security in cloud computing. In: 2012 International Conference on Cyber Security, Cyber Warfare and Digital Forensic (CyberSec), pp. 230–235. IEEE, June 2012

15. Kalaiprasath, R., Elankavi, R., Udayakumar, D.R.: Cloud security and compliance - a semantic approach in end to end security. Int. J. Mech. Eng. Technol. (IJMET) 8(5), 987–994 (2017)

16. Ficco, M., Palmieri, F.: Introducing fraudulent energy consumption in cloud infrastructures: a new generation of denial-of-service attacks. IEEE Syst. J. 11(2), 460–470 (2017)

17. Yin, Z., Yu, F.R., Bu, S., Han, Z.: Joint cloud and wireless networks operations in mobile cloud computing environments with telecom operator cloud. Wirel. Commun. IEEE Trans. 14, 4020–4033 (2015)

18. Yu, Y., Mu, Y., Ni, J., Deng, J., Huang, K.: Identity privacy-preserving public auditing with dynamic group for secure mobile cloud storage. In: Au, M.H., Carminati, B., Kuo, C.-C.Jay (eds.) NSS 2014. LNCS, vol. 8792, pp. 28–40. Springer, Cham (2014). https://doi.org/10.1007/978-3-319-11698-3_3

19. Yang, Y., Zhu, H., Lu, H., Weng, J., Zhang, Y., Choo, K.-K.R.: Cloud based data sharing with fine-grained proxy re-encryption. Pervasive Mob. Comput. 28, 122–134 (2016)

20. Zhang, Y., Zheng, D., Chen, X., Li, J., Li, H.: Efficient attribute-based data sharing in mobile clouds. Pervasive Mob. Comput. 28, 135–149 (2016)

21. Dubey, A.K., Dubey, A.K., Namdev, M., Shrivastava, S.S.: Cloud-user security based on RSA and MD5 algorithm for resource attestation and sharing in Java environment. In: 2012 CSI Sixth International Conference on Software Engineering (CONSEG), pp. 1–8. IEEE, September 2012

22. Qiu, M., Gai, K., Thuraisingham, B., Tao, L., Zhao, H.: Proactive user-centric secure data scheme using attribute-based semantic access controls for mobile clouds in financial industry. Future Gener. Comput. Syst. 80, 421–429 (2016)

23. Li, H., Liu, D., Dai, Y., Luan, T.H., Shen, X.: Enabling efficient multi-keyword ranked search over encrypted mobile cloud data through blind storage. Emerg. Top. Comput. IEEE Trans. 3, 127–138 (2015)

24. Guo, C., Zhuang, R., Jie, Y., Ren, Y., Wu, T., Choo, K.-K.R.: Fine-grained database field search using attribute-based encryption for e-healthcare clouds. J. Med. Syst. 40, 235 (2016)

25. Sookhak, M., Gani, A., Khan, M.K., Buyya, R.: Dynamic remote data auditing for securing big data storage in cloud computing. Inf. Sci. 380, 101–116 (2017)

26. Al Morsy, M., Grundy, J., Müller, I.: An analysis of the cloud computing security problem. In: Proceedings of APSEC 2010 Cloud Workshop, Sydney, Australia, 30 November 2010

27. Ko, S.K.V., Lee, J.-H., Kim, S.W.: Mobile cloud computing security considerations. J. Secur. Eng. 9, 143–150 (2012)

28. Dinh, H.T., Lee, C., Niyato, D., Wang, P.: A survey of mobile cloud computing: architecture, applications, and approaches. Wirel. Commun. Mob. Comput. 13(18), 1587–1611 (2011)

29. Khana, A.N., Kiaha, M.L.M., Khanb, S.U., Madanic, S.A.: Towards secure mobile cloud computing: a survey. Future Gener. Comput. Syst. 29(5), 1278–1299 (2013)

30. Morshed, M.S.J., Islam, M.M., Huq, M.K., Hossain, M.S., Basher, M.A.: Integration of wireless hand-held devices with the cloud architecture: security and privacy issues. In: International Conference on P2P, Parallel, Grid, Cloud and Internet Computing (3PGCIC), October 2011

31. Jia, W., Zhu, H., Cao, Z., Wei, L., Lin, X.: SDSM: a secure data service mechanism in mobile cloud computing. In: IEEE Conference on Computer Communications Workshops (INFOCOM WKSHPS), 10–15 April 2011

Neural Network Based Test Case Prioritization in Software Engineering

Akshit Thakur[(✉)] and Gitika Sharma

Department of Computer Science and Engineering, Chandigarh University,
Chandigarh, India
akshitthakur9999@gmail.com, gitikasharma4l@gmail.com

Abstract. The test case prioritization is the technique of Regression testing in which test cases are prioritized according to the changes which are done in the project. This work is based on manual slicing and automated slicing for test case prioritization to detect maximum number of faults from the project in which some changes are done for the new version release. The slicing is the technique which will divide the whole project function wise and detect associated functions. To increase the fault detection rate the automated technique is being applied in which multi-objective algorithm is been applied which calculates the function importance in the automated manner. In the simulation it is being analyzed that fault detection rate is increased and execution time is reduced with the implementation of automated test case prioritization as compared to manual test case prioritization in regression testing.

Keywords: Regression testing · Prioritization · Function importance
Fault rate

1 Introduction

Software is defined as the combination of process in which only program coding is not sufficient. It performs various computational purposes as it is known for the execution of codes [1]. Hence, it is considered as the program using which numbers of programming codes are executed. It is the collection of programming code, associated libraries and documentations. A software product is termed as software which serves the specific requirement.

Engineering is defined as the technique using which products are developed using well-defined, scientific principles and methods in effective and efficient manner.

The development of large programs becomes difficult task if the principal of software engineering is not utilized. For the execution of multiple functions, it is required to develop a large program using which all the requirements can be fulfilled. The development of large programs increase the issue of complexity and difficulty as their size is increase with increase in program coding [2]. Hence, programming complexity can be easily reduced using principal of software engineering. In order to reduce the complexity of the programs, it utilizes the two important techniques such as abstraction and decomposition. Abstraction is the process in which all the irrelevant data is removed or simplified. In this process all the required data utilized for the given

© Springer Nature Singapore Pte Ltd. 2019
A. K. Luhach et al. (Eds.): ICAICR 2018, CCIS 956, pp. 334–345, 2019.
https://doi.org/10.1007/978-981-13-3143-5_28

purpose is utilized at that certain period and suppress all the irrelevant data that is not required for the given purpose. The suppressed data is regained again after solving the issues in order to solve the next lower level abstraction. Hence, the complexity of the program is reduced using the powerful tool of abstraction. Decomposition also minimizes the issue of complexity in which the major issues divides into simpler one after which issues having low complexity is solver. Hence, this decomposition is done in order to solve the problem of each component so that at the end all the solutions can be combined together to obtain complete result.

1.1   Testing in Software Engineering

Software Testing is the process in which software is examined whether they are working accurately according to system specification and fulfilling the requirements of the users [3]. In the software development life cycle, testing is performed at the phase level. Validation and verification are the two processes using which testing in the software is done.

a. Software Validation

(i)   It is process in which functioning of the software is checked whether it satisfies the user requirement or not. and it is performed at the end of the SDLC (Software development life cycle). It is validated if the requirement of the software is fulfilled by the software.

(ii) It ensures that development of product is done on the basis of user requirement.

(iii) Its main objective is to fulfill the requirements of user.

b. Software Verification

(i)   It is the process in which it is confirmed whether all the business requirements are fulfilled or not by software [4]. This is done in order to ensure that all the specification is working properly.

(ii) It is done to verify that all the design specification is made on the basis of requirements.

(iii) It mainly concentrates on the design and system specifications.

1.2   Testing Approaches

On the basis of two approaches testing can be conducted:
    Tests can be conducted based on two approaches –

1. Functionality testing
2. Implementation testing

Black-box testing is the testing technique in which functionality of the software is tested without considering the actual implementation of the software product. In case of white box testing, functionality as well as its implementation is tested [5]. For the perfect testing exhaustive tests has been considered. It tests the every possible value lies within the range of the input and output. If this range of value is large, then it is not possible to measure each and every value.

1.2.1   Black-Box Testing

Black-box testing is a technique in which there is no information about the internal part or the applications used to execute any program [6]. Therefore, in first step a tester uses input to interact with user interface and then examined the desired output without having any knowledge about the task performed internally. The tester does not have any access to the given source code and its system architecture. The following figure depicts the process of Black-Box Testing (Fig. 1).

Fig. 1. Black box testing

In this testing, tester and testing engineers knows nothing about the design and structure of the code while end users conduct this test on the software.

1.2.2   White-Box Testing

White box testing technique is also known as open-box testing or glass testing [7]. It is different from black box testing as tester needs to perform functions internally which is based on the detailed examination of structure of code and internal-logic [8]. In order to find the error in the source code a proper investigation is required to find out which unit is not behaving appropriately. For the improvement in the code efficiency or structure, test program and its implementation is conducted. Tester knows all about the design and structure of the code (Fig. 2).

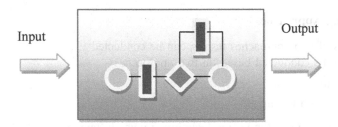

Fig. 2. White box testing

1.3 Mutation Analysis for Software Fault Prediction

In order to assess test effectiveness, mutation testing was introduced. In mutation testing mutant creation of the alternative of program is known as mutant done with the help of mutation testing. Mutation operators create the mutants in which faults are seeded for the particular class by which one relational operator is replaced with another [9]. A test case killed the mutant, if the original program and its mutant behave differently due to the cause of test case. The generation of test cases has been guided by using this technique and it also utilized to improve test oracles. Hypothesis is known as the basis of the mutation testing in which at least some of the mutants will turn out to be coupled to real faults.

1.4 Test Case Prioritization

It is beneficial to prioritize the test cases present within a test suite such that the time and cost being spent on testing can be optimized. The test cases are executed in a specific order through the explicit planning of Test case prioritization (TCP). Thus, within the software process, the rate of fault detection is enhanced through the increase in effectiveness of software testing activities. Primarily, the regression testing efforts were improved using TCP. In order to assure that no unintended effects have been made to the system code and the system works as per the specified requirements by the modifications, the system of component is retested within regression testing. The test cases are saved by the software engineers and in the form of regression tests, these test cases are re run by them. It would be costly to run the complete set of test cases on new or similar version of an application. The test cases are chosen on the basis of structural coverage criteria by the regression TCP techniques [10]. At the code level, the structural coverage techniques are applied. For maximizing the objective function, the test cases are prioritized and scheduled using test case prioritization techniques. The test cases are scheduled and run as per the highest priority such that the faults can be detected earlier within these techniques. It is important to perform software testing through the test case prioritization process as there is large amount of time and cost consumed when running the regression testing phase. Also, for running the entire test suite again, enough time or resources are not available. It is also seen that the order in which the test cases are made to run is not decided here.

2 Literature Review

Meiliana and Karim et al. presented faults in the software are detected and removed using software testing techniques widely utilized in the software development life cycle model [11]. Further, this detected error is removed from the software. More time is consumed by the testing process in order to plan good way and resources. Hence, predication of the optimal testing before the testing process is the essential step by which there is increase in time, effort and cost in efficient manner. The quality of the software is measured using the software metrics in order to determine the present faults in the software. Prediction of faults becomes more effective using machine learning techniques. This is the first survey conducted on the PROMISE repository dataset usage as per author review. They performed various experiments in order to compared software metrics and machine learning method using PROMISE repository dataset used for the prediction of faults.

Yohannese et al. presented with the development in the software fault prediction, there is reduction in the cost, resources enhancement and on time delivery of the products along with the quality [12]. The classification issue in the SFP has been removed using machine learning. The performance of the single learning algorithms is improved when ensemble learning algorithms is utilized. The main objective of this paper is to evaluate the ELA methods and to improve their performance. This can be done by combining the feature selection and data balancing techniques using which there is improvement in the prediction of the software faults more efficiently. They proposed an effective method in this paper that alone handles all the issues faced by the other methods.

Owhadi-Kareshk et al. presented in the process of the testing software, fault prediction is considered as the most essential stage. This stage measure the probability of occurring faults on the basis of the information obtained from the previously tested software's [13]. The classification issue can be easily resolved using the machine learning method. They proposed a pre-training technique in this paper using artificial neural network having fewer hidden layers. With the help of this method the issues of the over fitting in the deep ANN can be easily removed even in a shallow network by removing the local minima to increase the accuracy. Comparison made between proposed and other methods

Kaur et al. presented performance of machine leaning techniques degraded due to the highly imbalanced nature of software that predicts less faults in the software [14]. The main objective of this paper is to minimize the issue of imbalanced data by examining the sampling techniques and Meta-Cost learning. In the metrics or in codes, they evaluated the four sampling techniques in this paper on the basis of fault data sets of two open source systems ANT and POI. On the basis of the obtained results, it is predicted that for the metrics based faults Resample technique is optimal while for code smells based faults, synthetic minority oversampling is best. They evaluated the Meta-Cost learning and demonstrate that sampling techniques outperform Meta-Cost learning.

Altinger et al. presented due to the low bug rate fault prediction suffers from the strong imbalanced class distribution when it is predicted on the high quality industry grade software. It is required to have tuning parameters as the low performance is predicted from the previous work [15]. They analyze the effects on the training data when processed under seven different classification algorithms. On the basis of the performed experiments, it is concluded that classifiers are influenced by the different parameters.

Sultan et al. presented an essential role is played by the software testing in the prediction of the quality of any software system. Sometimes, the methods of software engineering are not implemented accurately as per done observation in many cases [16]. The same predefined development path is followed all the time by many of the development methodologies due to which changes in the results are very less. Regression testing is considered as the essential type of software testing in the whole process. This testing is taking place, if there is any change occur in the software using this it is checked whether it influence other parts of the software or not. In order to utilize the previously used test cases and the newer ones, they prioritized the test cases in the regression testing. Various techniques have been utilized in order to perform the test case prioritization. The different test case prioritization techniques were reviewed in this paper.

Vescan et al. presented the regression testing in this paper which is widely used in the process of testing as this process ensure the software quality which is not affected by doing changes. In the initial step, TCP has been utilized in this process, which is further divided into three steps. They implemented the TCS and TCP individually after that same procedure is followed for the same set of test cases [17]. Therefore, in the structural code, fault detection to execution cost, they implemented various approaches in this paper.

OZTURK et al. presented there are various issues faced while developing software some of the issues are time and budget constraints due to which a test case prioritization technique in introduced in this paper. Inadequate maintenance and test processes are some effects created while performing these test processes as it create burden on the person [18]. The researchers investigated the complexity correlation between some code maintainability in which WMC, LCOM, and Coupling and cyclomatic are included. On the basis of performed experiments and comparisons it is concluded that performance of proposed method is superior to other methods. The obtained results from APFD become high and stable, if the factors affecting code maintenance are considered while developing test case prioritization techniques.

Ding et al. presented the two adaptive Test Case Prioritization (TCP) approaches in this paper using which desired results are obtained. The names of these two approaches are the Adaptive Random Testing (ART) and the Dynamic Random Testing (DRT). They concluded that Both ART and DRT are extensions of RT [19]. There are some attributes which are not similar in both approaches such as different heuristics, distinct attitudes and revealing test cases. Due to the dependency on the current executed test cases, DRT is more adaptive as compared to ART. With the help of ART, failure detection is determined easily as it covers the entire input domain and used the similar algorithm of binary search. The pattern of the failure domain is described efficiently using the DRT as it has the good understanding of faults.

Chen et al. presented that allocation of the faulty modules in software testing is an easy process by utilizing the fault prediction software. This leads to improvement in the software quality as well as save the time and cost [20]. They proposed a one-class SFP model in this paper in which non-faulty samples has been utilized which is based on one-class SVM. They performed the experiments on the collected imbalanced datasets from real-world software in which small amount of fault is present. In terms of G-mean measure proposed model performs better as compared to existing methods and over-come all the issues reside with the SFP.

Rathore et al. presented for the prediction of the faults in the software system an efficient approach is proposed in this paper. With the help of neural network and genetic programming, they develop a fault prediction model [21]. They obtained fault datasets from the PROMISE data repository in order to compare the effectiveness of the proposed techniques. On the basis of the error rate, recall and parameters, the obtained results were evaluated in this paper. It is concluded that better performance is achieved by the neural network for the small datasets and genetic programming for the large datasets. Neural network has better performance than genetic programming in terms of error values and lack of performance than genetic programming in terms of recall and completeness analysis.

3 Research Methodology

The Regression testing is the testing which is applied to test the software when some changes are done in the already developed project. The test case prioritization is the technique of regression testing which prioritizes the test cases according to the changes which are done in the developed project. This work is based on automated and manual test case prioritization techniques. In the existing technique the manual test case prioritization is been implemented to detect faults from the project. In the manual test case prioritization two parameters are considered which are, number of times function encountered and number of functions associated with the particular function. On the basis of these two parameters the importance of each function is calculated which are prioritized by calculating FTV value. The FTV value is calculated according to the changes which are defined in the developed project. To increase the fault detection rate of the test case prioritization, automated test case prioritization is being implemented in this work (Fig. 3).

In the first step of the algorithm, the population values are taken as input which is the number of times function encountered and number of functions associated with a particular function. In the second step, the algorithm will start traversing the population values and error is calculated after every iteration. The iteration at which the error is maximum at that point the mutation value is calculated as the best mutation value of the function. The function mutation value will be the function importance from where the test cases are prioritized according to the defined changes. In the last step of the algorithm the function importance values are accessed according to the defined changes and best fitness value is calculated which will be the final percentage of faults detected from the project after the particular change. To increase the fault detection rate of the test case prioritization, automated test case prioritization is being implemented in this work. In the first step of the algorithm, the population values are taken as input which is the number of times function encountered and number of functions associated with a particular function. The population is set of input values on this basis of which functional importance need to calculate. In the second step, the algorithm will start traversing the population values and error is calculated after each iteration. The iteration at which the error is maximum at that point the mutation value is calculated as the best mutation value of the function. The function mutation value will be the function importance from where the test cases are prioritized according to the defined changes. In the last step of the algorithm the function importance values are accessed according to the defined changes and best fitness value is calculated which will be the final percentage of faults detected from the project after the particular change.

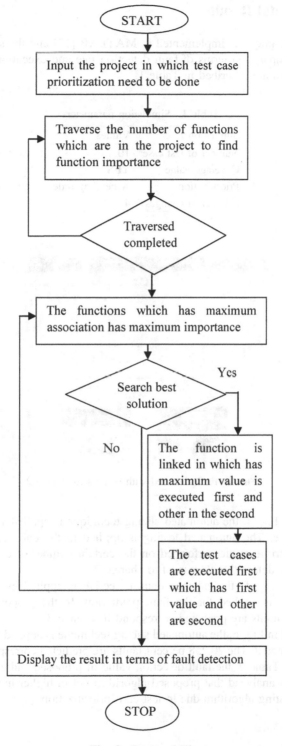

Fig. 3. Proposed Ff

4 Experimental Results

The proposed technique is implemented in MATLAB [12] and the simulation results achieved are compared in terms of fault detection rate and execution time. The simulation parameters are described in Table 1.

Table 1. Simulation parameters

Simulation	Values
Number of test cases	10
Coverage value	YES
Prioritization	Ascending order
Number of changes	4

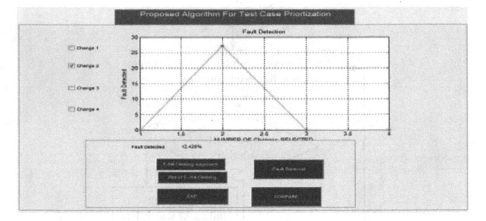

Fig. 4. Fault detected with respect to change 2.

As shown in Fig. 4, the automated slicing technique is applied which detect fault from the software. The automated testing is applied in the enhance multi-objective model. The experiments are performed on the certain number of changes and 12.42 percent faults are detected with respect to change 2

As shown in Fig. 5, the enhance multi-objective is applied in which automated slicing technique is applied for the fault prediction. In the proposed approach the 14.4892 percent faults are predicted correspond to change 3.

As illustrated in Fig. 6, the automated slicing technique is applied which is enhance multi-objective model. The 20.258 percent faults are predicted correspond to change 4.

As shown in Table 2, the fault detection value of proposed and existing algorithm is compared It is analyzed that proposed algorithm detect higher number of faults as compared to existing algorithm due to test case prioritization.

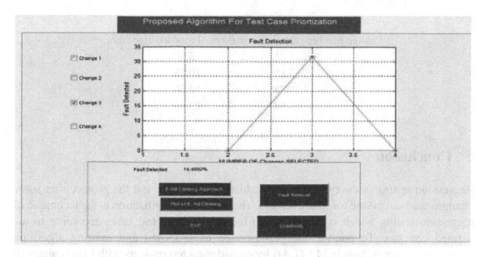

Fig. 5. Fault detected with respect to change 3.

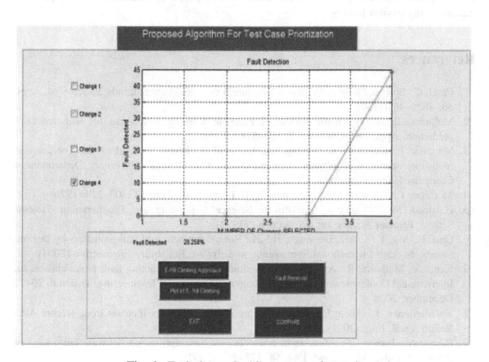

Fig. 6. Fault detected with respect to change 4

Table 2. Compression

Change number	Existing algorithm	Proposed algorithm
1	5.45	8.90
2	7.89	10.23
3	10.78	12.56
4	19.98	23.45

5 Conclusion

Regression testing is the type of testing which is applied to test the project after some changes are being done for future release. The test case prioritization is the technique of regression testing which is being applied to prioritize the test cases according to the defined changes. To analyze the performance of proposed and existing algorithm simulation is being done in MATLAB by considering ten projects with four changes. It has been analyzed that fault detection rate is increased and execution time is reduced by applying automated test case prioritization as compared to manual test case prioritization in regression testing.

References

1. Catal, C.: Software fault prediction: a literature review and current trends. Expert Syst. Appl. **38**, 4626–4636 (2011)
2. Malhotra, R.: A systematic review of machine learning techniques for software fault prediction. Appl. Soft Comput. **27**, 504–518 (2015)
3. Menzies, T., Caglayan, B., Kocaguneli, E., Krall, J., Peters, F., Turhan, B.: The promise repository of empirical software engineering data. West Virginia University, Department of Computer Science (2012)
4. McCabe, T.J.: A complexity measure. IEEE Trans. Softw. Eng. **2**, 308–320 (1976)
5. Halstead, M.H.: Elements of Software Science (Operating and Programming Systems Series). Elsevier Science Inc., Amsterdam (1977)
6. Guo, L., Ma, Y., Cukic, B., Singh, H.S.H.: Robust prediction of faultproneness by random forests. In: 15th International Symposium on Software Reliability Engineering (2004)
7. Kaur, A., Malhotra, R.: Application of random forest for predicting fault prone classes. In: International Conference on Advanced Computer Theory and Engineering, Thailand, 20–22 December, 2008
8. Khoshgoftaar, T., Allen, E.: Model software quality with classification trees. Recent Adv. Reliab. Qual. Eng. (2001)
9. Bener, A., Turhan, B.: Analysis of Naive Bayes' assumptions on software fault data: an empirical study. Data Knowl. Eng. **68**, 278–290 (2009)
10. Meiliana, Karim, S., Warnars, H.L.H.S., Soewito, B.: Software Metrics for fault prediction using machine learning approaches. IEEE 2017
11. Elbaum, S., Malishevsky, A.G., Rothermel, G.: Test case prioritization: a family of empirical studies. IEEE Trans. Softw. Eng. **28**(2), 159–182 (2002)

12. Yohannese, C.W., Li, T., Simfukwe, M., Khurshid, F.: Ensembles based combined learning for improved software fault prediction: a comparative study. In: 2017 12th International Conference on Intelligent Systems and Knowledge Engineering (2017)
13. Owhadi-Kareshk, M., Sedaghat, Y., Akbarzadeh, T.M.R.: Pre-training of an artificial neural network for software fault prediction. In: 7th International Conference on Computer and Knowledge Engineering (ICCKE 2017), 26–27 October 2017
14. Kaur, K., Kaur, P.: Evaluation of sampling techniques in software fault prediction using metrics and code smells. IEEE (2017)
15. Altinger, H., Herboldy, S., Schneemann, F., Grabowskiy, J., Wotawa, F.: Performance tuning for automotive software fault prediction. IEEE (2017)
16. Sultan, Z., Bhatti, S.N., Abbas, R., Asim Ali Shah, S.: Analytical review on test cases prioritization techniques: an empirical study. Int. J. Adv. Comput. Sci. Appl. **8**(2) (2017)
17. Vescan, A., serban, C., Chisalita Creu, C., Dioan, L.: Requirement dependencies–based formal approach for test case prioritization in regression testing. IEEE (2017)
18. Ozturk, M.M.: Adapting code maintainability to bat-inspired test case prioritization. IEEE (2017)
19. Ding, J., Zhang, X.Y.: Comparison analysis of two test case prioritization approaches with the core idea of adaptive. IEEE (2017)
20. Chen, L., Fang, B., Shang, Z.: software fault prediction based on one class SVM. IEEE (2016)
21. Rathore, S.S., Kuamr, S.: Comparative analysis of neural network and genetic programming for number of software faults prediction. In: National Conference on Recent Advances in Electronics & Computer Engineering, RAECE-2015, 13–15 February 2015

Blockchain-Based Security Aspects in Internet of Things Network

Fabiola Hazel Pohrmen$^{(\boxtimes)}$, Rohit Kumar Das, Wanbanker Khongbuh,
and Goutam Saha

North-Eastern Hill University, Shillong, Meghalaya, India
fhpohrmen@gmail.com, rohitdas.it.13@gmail.com,
wnbnkr.khongbuh@gmail.com, dr.goutamsaha@gmail.com

Abstract. The Internet of Things (IoT) is an upcoming technology in our present day network scenario. IoT consists of resource constrained devices which communicate with each other to deliver the required services to the users. As more and more devices are connected to the existing IoT network, security and privacy aspects in IoT have become prominent. Limitations of IoT devices are resource and energy constraints, which restrict its computational capability. Thus, it becomes a challenge for scientists to design suitable security systems for IoT. The Blockchain is a proven distributed and secure system for financial transactions. This paper outlines security and privacy problems in IoT. It also explores the convergence of IoT and Blockchain technology and explores how the underlying technologies of Blockchain can be improved to address the various security problems associated with IoT.

Keywords: Internet of Things · Blockchain · Security
Lightweight hash functions

1 Introduction

The Internet of Things (IoT) applications such as Agriculture, Transport, HealthCare, Smart Cities, etc. are growing rapidly. Use of IoT in day-to-day life is going to increase within a few years of its standardization. The researchers from both academia and industries are taking huge interests in this field. Due to the rise in the number of applications, the number of devices is also increasing. There will be a need for better IoT security, privacy and scalability for those devices as well as its generated data. IoT devices do not have high processing capability and memory to implement strong security solutions [1]. The use of existing security policies for IoT domain can greatly affect the performance of the overall system. Some of the challenges that can be faced by IoT are [2]:

i. **Resource constraints:** IoT devices are restricted by battery, computation power, and memory constraints. This makes implementation of complex security solutions on IoT devices very challenging or sometimes impossible.

© Springer Nature Singapore Pte Ltd. 2019
A. K. Luhach et al. (Eds.): ICAICR 2018, CCIS 956, pp. 346–357, 2019.
https://doi.org/10.1007/978-981-13-3143-5_29

ii. **Centralization:** The identification and authentication of IoT devices are performed from a centralized point. If this centralized point (maybe a sink or gateway or server) malfunctions, the whole system can go down. This can also induce bottleneck problem and increase the load balancing issue.

iii. **Privacy Issues:** IoT applications can track and monitor a user's personal data in order to provide personalized services. Without proper access control, this becomes a privacy nightmare where users have no control over their data.

These issues make it very challenging to secure the IoT. IoT can, however, be combined with other technologies like Blockchain and Software Defined Networking (SDN) to improve its overall security and privacy as shown in Fig. 1.

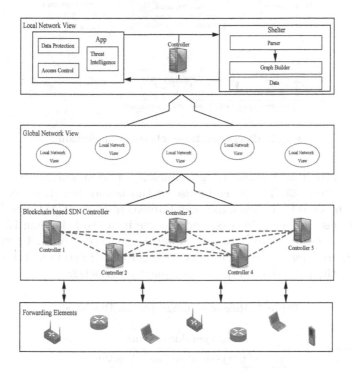

Fig. 1. Blockchain-based SDN IoT [3]

As shown in Fig. 1, Blockchain can be introduced in different levels of IoT. The IoT gateway/controller can be connected together in a distributed manner using the Blockchain approach. This can provide a collection of local network view from where different network services can be carried out.

In this paper, a discussion has been carried out on the convergence of Blockchain and IoT technologies. This paper also provides a brief overview on the challenges in IoT-Blockchain implementation and potential solutions.

2 Blockchain

In a distributed network, transactions are stored in a secure ledger database which is shared by all participants/nodes/members, in a peer-to-peer network. This secure, digital ledger is known as Blockchain. As shown in Fig. 2, transactions are grouped into "blocks" and the blocks are linked together through Cryptographic Hash Functions forming a chain of blocks, hence the name Blockchain [4].

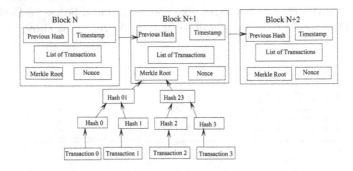

Fig. 2. Blocks and transactions in blockchain

The Blockchain is the underlying technology of cryptocurrencies like Bitcoin [5] and Ethereum [6]. The potential use of Blockchain has increased endlessly with the Ethereum Blockchain, as it can implement Smart Contracts. The users write programs (Smart Contracts) and execute it in the Ethereum Blockchain.

Blockchain core technologies are: Public Key Cryptography, Cryptographic Hash functions, Merkle trees and a Peer-to-Peer (P2P) network. Table 1 gives a summary of the roles that Cryptography plays on Blockchain.

Table 1. Role of cryptography on Blockchain

Role	Cryptographic scheme
Integrity	Cryptographic hash functions
Authenticity	Elliptic curve digital signature algorithm [7]
Transaction confidentiality	Homomorphic encryption [8], Secure multi-party computation (MPC) [9], Zero knowledge proofs [10]
Identity of participants	Pseudonymous address derived from User's public key [11]
Auditability	Merkle tree
Availability	Blockchain maintains multiple copies of the ledger

The underlying technologies in current implementations of Blockchain are discussed in detail below.

i. **Public Key Cryptography Used in Blockchain:** Public Key Cryptography consists of algorithms which use a pair of keys: public key and private key. Among public-key algorithms, there are two established families of practical relevance: Elliptic Curve Cryptography (ECC) [12] and RSA [13]. Bitcoin and Ethereum use Elliptic Curve Digital Signature Algorithm (ECDSA) for authorization and authentication of transactions. They both work with the elliptic curve secp256k1 [7]. It also provides identity for participants as the addresses are derived from the public key.

ii. **Cryptographic Hash Functions used in Blockchain:** Cryptographic Hash Function are one-way functions in which data of any length can be taken and a fixed size hash can be generated. The Hash Function currently being used by Bitcoin is SHA-256 and Ethereum uses Keccak-256 [4]. The traditional hash functions cannot be used with IoT, as they are configured with low power and memory resource. This is where Lightweight Hash Functions can improve the security in IoT domains.

   (a) Types of Lightweight hash functions available: There are many Lightweight Hash Functions available. Some of them are Photon [14], Quark [15] and Spongent [16]. Lightweight implementations of Keccak have also been done [17]. They are all based on sponge constructions. Among them, Spongent has been used as the lightweight cryptographic hash function in LSB, a Lightweight Scalable Blockchain for IoT [18].

iii. **Merkle Tree:** The integrity of data can be verified and summarized by using Merkle Trees or Binary Hash Tree [4]. This is a data structure which is used in Bitcoin and Ethereum as shown in Fig. 2.

iv. **Peer-to-Peer (P2P) network:** Peer-to-peer (P2P) network is a distributed, interconnected network in which the computers that participate in the network are peers to each other. There is no server, no centralized service, and no hierarchy within the network. Nodes in a peer-to-peer network both provide and consume services at the same time. P2P networks are decentralized and open. In Cryptocurrencies like Bitcoin, the shared ledger is maintained by these nodes. These nodes are also called miners [19].

The following schemes are used for providing privacy to improved privacy-preserving versions of the Blockchain.

i. **Homomorphic Encryption:** It is an encryption algorithm in which computations can be done over encrypted data. The privacy of the data/ transactions is preserved while computations are performed on it. Fully Homomorphic Encryption is computationally intensive. Bao-Kun Zheng et. al used a partial homomorphic encryption scheme called Paillier Encryption to preserve the privacy of the data. The BeeKeeper system [20] also allow homomorphic computation on encrypted data.

ii. **Secure Multi-party Computation (MPC):** MPC is another scheme in which computation over encrypted data can be performed. MPC can be implemented in two ways: Secret Sharing and Garbled Circuits. The Enigma platform use the Secret Sharing Scheme to keep the data private.

iii. **Zero Knowledge proofs (ZKP):** Zero Knowledge Proofs are methods which focus on two parties: a prover and a verifier. The prover has to prove to the verifier that he/she knows some information without revealing the information. zk-SNARK (Zero-Knowledge Succinct Non-Interactive Arguments of Knowledge) is a variant of ZKP in which there is no interaction between the prover and verifier. The cryptocurrency, ZCash and the Hawk Smart Contract system use zk-SNARKs.

Although Symmetric Cryptography is not an inherent part of Blockchain, it can be used for securing IoT devices as well. Blockchain-based IoT will require the use of lightweight symmetric cryptography at the device level. Symmetric key cryptography is divided into two categories: Block ciphers and Stream cipher. Some of the existing ciphers with lightweight properties are discussed below:

i. **Block Ciphers:** Among the existing block ciphers with lightweight properties, security and implementation of CLEFIA (128 bits) [21] and PRESENT (64 bits) [22] are considered more robust.
ii. **Stream Ciphers:** Some of the existing stream ciphers that have lightweight properties are Grain v1, MICKEY v2, and Trivium.

3   IoT-Blockchain Security Solutions

Blockchain architecture can enhance IoT security due to its distributed, transparent, incorruptible and decentralized nature. In this section, discussions have been made on the various IoT problems and how Blockchain and its underlying technologies can be tailored to suit the needs of IoT.

3.1   IoT Problems and Potential Blockchain Solution

– **Addressing Schemes:** IoT protocols (6LoWPAN, ZigBee, MQTT, etc.,) use IPv6 addressing scheme. These are generally 128-bit in hexadecimal format, with fixed 40-bytes of the packet header. Blockchain deals with 20-bytes packet header with ECDSA-160 bit (Elliptic Curve Digital Signature Algorithm) [4] enhancing the security of the packet.
– **Identity and Access Management:** The huge number of IoT devices require proper identification which is a major challenge. Identification of devices is needed in most of the security applications, so that they can be trusted and proper access control can be granted. Blockchain can help in solving these issues in a more efficient manner through the use of pseudonymous addresses similar to Bitcoin addresses.
– **Authentication, Authorization, and Privacy:** Authentication, authorization and privacy in IoT are very challenging tasks. Blockchain can provide simple and effective authentication and authorization solutions to IoT with the help of smart contracts and digital signatures.
– **Integrity of Data:** In Blockchain, Cryptographic Hash Functions are used ensure the authenticity and integrity of the data transmitted by IoT devices.

- **Secure Communications:** Protocols (MQTT, CoAP or XMPP) with standard DTLS or TLS are used in IoT communication. These protocols require more computation power. Using Blockchain technology, these protocols can be simplified with more or less alteration/modification. The use of PKI (Public Key Infrastructure) in IoT with Blockchain can further increase the security level of the existing protocol.

4 Literature Review

In recent years, researchers from academia and industries are working together on the improvement of IoT with Blockchain technology. Some of the notable works have been summarized below:

BCTrust [23] is a Blockchain-based authentication protocol. In this protocol, device trust is established when one device is authenticated in one cluster, it becomes trustful and accepted by all other clusters. The Blockchain ensures that information is available for all participating nodes.

Gaoqi Liang et al. [24] proposed a consensus-based framework in which geographically distributed nodes (meters/sensors) form a distributed network. Their framework eliminated the need for block reward as the behaviour of the miners are pre-programmed and the nodes are driven by consensus.

Ali Dorri et al. [18] proposed Lightweight Scalable Blockchain (LSB). Their Consensus Algorithm eliminates the need for Proof-Of-Work (POW), in which miners need to solve a puzzle before adding a block to the Blockchain.

Blockchain Connected Gateway (BC Gateway) [25] prevents users' personal data from being accessed by intruders. In the Blockchain network, user's personal preferences are maintain by the BC Gateway.

A New Blockchain cloud architecture model was proposed by PK Sharma et al. [26]. Their distributed cloud manages the data produced by IoT devices. It is based on three technologies: fog computing, SDN, and Blockchain.

Lijing Zhou et al. [20] proposed BeeKeeper, a Blockchain-based IoT system with privacy-preserving homomorphic computation. Their system consists of record nodes and light nodes. The record nodes maintain the Blockchain and verify transactions. Consensus is achieved by using a Practical Byzantine Fault Tolerant (PBFT) consensus scheme.

Yogachandran Rahulamathavan et al. [27] also proposed a privacy-preserving Blockchain-based IoT architecture. They have used Attribute-Based Encryption (ABE) to maintain privacy with minimal computational overhead.

Oscar Novo's paper [28] introduces a decentralized, Blockchain-based Access Management system for IoT. The proposed system eliminated the need for a centralized access control server.

Seyoung Huh et al. [29] proposed Smart Contracts to control and configure IoT devices in Ethereum Blockchain Computing Platform. Using smart contracts, the data coming from meter and smartphone can be stored.

Kamanashis Biswas et al. [30] proposed Layer-wise security framework that integrates the Blockchain technology with smart devices with Telehash and Bit-Torrent for peer to peer communication and Ethereum for smart contracts.

O. J. A. Pinno et al. [31] proposed ControlChain for managing access control in the Blockchain network. This architecture can help in making the network more scalable and fault-tolerant with wide range access control to IoT devices. The ControlChain also provides attributes assignment and relationship management in a secure manner.

Block4Forensic [32] is a permissioned Blockchain framework for managing the collected vehicle related data. This can address the issues regarding the overhead of storage and membership management.

5   Blockchain-Based IoT Architecture

We have developed a Blockchain-based IoT architecture where Blockchain security can be effectively implemented. The architecture has been depicted in Fig. 3. It consists of Infrastructure, Control and Application layers.

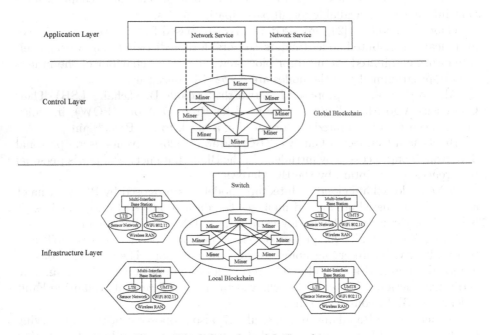

Fig. 3. Blockchain-based IoT architecture

The Infrastructure layer consists of different networking elements (switches, routers, interface, sensor nodes, fog, etc.) and networks (WSN, WAN, RAN, LAN, IoT, LTE, UMTS). The Network Element (NE) will forward the collected data from the network to the upper Control layer using Local Blockchain (LB). During the transaction process, proper security mechanisms should be provided to ensure that the delivered packets cannot be tampered by an external intruder. As NEs are mostly resource constrained, Lightweight Cryptographic Hash Functions can be used in this level.

The Control layer is a collection of miners (mining nodes) with high computing resources, connected with each other in a distributed manner. Hence, more sophisticated security mechanisms like Asymmetric Cryptography can be applied in this level (Global Blockchain). The distributed nature of the miners can further increase the level of security in terms of data integrity.

The Application Layer consists of application specific services that are provided to the user. The proposed architecture is application-agnostic. In this layer, numerous Internet of Things applications can be deployed, for example, smart campus, smart railways, and smart grids, etc.

Table 2. Layer-wise security issues and requirements

Layer	Level	Type of cryptography	Potential solution
Infrastructure layer	Fog level	Symmetric cryptography	PRESENT CLEFIA Block Ciphers
	Local Blockchain	Lightweight cryptographic hash functions	Spongent, Keccak-200 Keccak-400
Control layer	Global Blockchain	Asymmetric cryptography	Elliptic Curve Cryptography (ECC)

The various Cryptographic schemes mentioned in Sect. 2 can be incorporated into the Blockchain-based IoT architecture. These schemes can provide maximum security at every layer of the architecture. Table 2 provides information of how different cryptographic schemes can be applied at different levels of the proposed Blockchain-based IoT architecture.

The Infrastructure layer security can be divided into two levels: Fog Level Security and Local Blockchain Level Security.

i. Fog Level Security: At this level, security can be provided by using existing symmetric cryptographic schemes like PRESENT, CLEFIA, etc.
ii. Local Blockchain Level Security: At this level, security can be improved by the use of existing Lightweight Cryptographic Hash functions like Photon, Quark, Spongent, lightweight implementations of Keccak etc. The data collected by the sensors is sent to the Local Blockchain. Using these lightweight hash functions, blocks of data can be hashed together to form the local Blockchain.

The Control layer Security can be provided by using Asymmetric Cryptography like ECC as this layer consists of devices with high computation power with no resource constraints.

6 Potential Research Scope

The existing IoT system on its own comprises of different challenges. Incorporating a new technology (Blockchain) will make it more complex and difficult to implement. Blockchain for IoT needs to be modified to meet the security requirement of IoT domain. This opens opportunities to further improve the current system. The following are the research areas which require more focus:

- **Consensus algorithms:** Current implementations of Blockchain implement consensus algorithms like POW. POW is energy-consuming and requires significant computational resources which is not possible for most IoT devices.
- **Scalability and Processing Overheads:** In Blockchain, an increase in the number of nodes in the network leads to scalability issues. This is because all blocks are verified by all nodes.
- **Latency and Throughput:** IoT applications have strict delay requirements. In current Blockchain implementations, there is a delay in transaction confirmation by nodes participating in the Blockchain. This leads to increase in latency and decrease in throughput.
- **Security overheads:** In Digital Cash, Double spending is a problem in which the same digital token is spent twice. Cryptocurrencies have security mechanisms that prevent Double spending. However, these mechanisms are not necessary for IoT Blockchain.
- **Transactional Privacy:** Transactional privacy is difficult to attain on the Blockchain as transparency is one of its main features. In IoT environment, however, transactional privacy is required due to the nature of transactions involved. This problem might be solved by using Homomorphic Encryption, Obfuscation and Zero Knowledge Proofs. However, application of these methods on IoT devices might be challenging as they are resource intensive.
- **User Identity:** Current Blockchains use pseudonyms as user identity. This method does not ensure complete privacy. The transactions are public and the identity of the user can be revealed by analyzing the transactions.
- **Authentication, Authorization and Accounting(AAA):** Smart Contracts can be used for specifying authentication and authorization access rules for IoT devices. In current IoT scenario, access management is based on centralized models. A Blockchain-based access control architecture could help manage the millions of distributed devices in an efficient and decentralized manner.
- **Energy Efficiency:** Blockchain uses schemes like Consensus protocols, P2P communication and Asymmetric Cryptographic Schemes which consume very high energy in IoT devices. Proper energy-efficient consensus protocols are required for IoT Blockchain. Lightweight cryptographic solutions need to be

investigated to ensure that these devices have an acceptable level of security without draining the devices' energy. Researchers have proposed improvements to existing P2P protocols in order to make them more energy efficient.

– **Lightweight Blockchain for Resource Constrained Devices:** The resource-constrained nature of IoT necessitates the need to explore lightweight cryptographic schemes to implement IoT Blockchain efficiently. These schemes can greatly improve the efficiency of IoT Blockchain without compromising on security.

These challenges in IoT Blockchain convergence have opened new research questions. Blockchain for IoT needs to be tailored specifically for IoT needs. This would require finding the solutions to the challenges mentioned above.

7 Conclusion

Implementation of Blockchain technology in IoT security system is still in its nascent stages and research on its convergence with different technologies is very limited. In this paper, a study on the convergence of Blockchain with IoT was done. Discussions in detail about the underlying Cryptographic techniques involved in current implementations of the Blockchain are provided. It also suggests the use of Lightweight Cryptography to enhance the security aspects of resource constrained IoT devices. The convergence of Blockchain and IoT has opened up various research issues which are discussed in this paper as well. This paper provides an idea of how Blockchain can be merged with IoT so that it can provide a better secure network.

References

1. Zhou, J., Cao, Z., Dong, X., Vasilakos, A.V.: Security and privacy for cloud-based IoT: challenges. IEEE Commun. Mag. **55**(1), 26–33 (2017)
2. Banafa, A.: IoT and blockchain convergence: benefits and challenges. IEEE Internet Things Newsl. (2017). https://iot.ieee.org/newsletter/january-2017/iot-and-blockchain-convergence-benefits-and-challenges.html. Accessed 25 May 2018
3. Sharma, P.K., Singh, S., Jeong, Y.S., Park, J.H.: DistBlockNet: a distributed blockchains-based secure SDN architecture for IoT networks. IEEE Commun. Mag. **55**(9), 78–85 (2017)
4. Antonopoulos, A.M.: Mastering Bitcoin: Unlocking Digital Crypto-Currencies, 1st edn. O'Reilly Media Inc., Sebastopol (2014)
5. Nakamoto, S.: Bitcoin: a peer-to-peer electronic cash system, pp. 1–9 (2008)
6. Buterin, V.: Ethereum white paper. GitHub repository (2013)
7. Mayer, H.: ECDSA security in bitcoin and ethereum: a research survey. Coin-Faabrik **28**, 1–10 (2016)
8. Zheng, B.K., et al.: Scalable and privacy-preserving data sharing based on Blockchain. J. Comput. Sci. Technol. **33**(3), 557–567 (2018)
9. Zyskind, G., Nathan, O., Pentland, A.: Enigma: decentralized computation platform with guaranteed privacy. arXiv preprint arXiv:1506.03471 (2015)

10. Lee, C.H., Kim, K.H.: Implementation of IoT system using block chain with authentication and data protection. In: 2018 International Conference on Information Networking (ICOIN), pp. 936–940. IEEE (2018)
11. Zyskind, G., Nathan, O.: Decentralizing privacy: using blockchain to protect personal data. In: Security and Privacy Workshops (SPW), pp. 180–184. IEEE (2015)
12. Bruen, A.A., Forcinito, M.A.: Elliptic Curve Cryptography (ECC). Cryptography, Information Theory, and Error-Correction: A Handbook for the 21st Century, vol. 68, pp. 113–129. Wiley, Hoboken (2005)
13. Rivest, R.L., Shamir, A., Adleman, L.: A method for obtaining digital signatures and public-key cryptosystems. Commun. ACM **21**(2), 120–126 (1978)
14. Guo, J., Peyrin, T., Poschmann, A.: The PHOTON family of lightweight hash functions. In: Rogaway, P. (ed.) CRYPTO 2011. LNCS, vol. 6841, pp. 222–239. Springer, Heidelberg (2011). https://doi.org/10.1007/978-3-642-22792-9_13
15. Aumasson, J.-P., Henzen, L., Meier, W., Naya-Plasencia, M.: QUARK: a lightweight hash. In: Mangard, S., Standaert, F.-X. (eds.) CHES 2010. LNCS, vol. 6225, pp. 1–15. Springer, Heidelberg (2010). https://doi.org/10.1007/978-3-642-15031-9_1
16. Bogdanov, A., Knežević, M., Leander, G., Toz, D., Varıcı, K., Verbauwhede, I.: SPONGENT: a lightweight hash function. In: Preneel, B., Takagi, T. (eds.) CHES 2011. LNCS, vol. 6917, pp. 312–325. Springer, Heidelberg (2011). https://doi.org/10.1007/978-3-642-23951-9_21
17. Kavun, E.B., Yalcin, T.: A lightweight implementation of keccak hash function for radio-frequency identification applications. In: Ors Yalcin, S.B. (ed.) RFIDSec 2010. LNCS, vol. 6370, pp. 258–269. Springer, Heidelberg (2010). https://doi.org/10.1007/978-3-642-16822-2_20
18. Dorri, A., Kanhere, S.S., Jurdak, R., Gauravaram, P.: LSB: a lightweight scalable blockchain for IoT security and privacy. arXiv preprint arXiv:1712.02969, pp. 1–17 (2017)
19. Fernández-Caramés, T.M., Fraga-Lamas, P.: A review on the use of Blockchain for the Internet of Things. IEEE Access **6**, 32979–33001 (2018)
20. Zhou, L., Wang, L., Sun, Y., Lv, P.: BeeKeeper: a Blockchain-based IoT system with secure storage and homomorphic computation. IEEE Access **6**, 43472–43488 (2018)
21. Shirai, T., Shibutani, K., Akishita, T., Moriai, S., Iwata, T.: The 128-bit blockcipher CLEFIA (extended abstract). In: Biryukov, A. (ed.) FSE 2007. LNCS, vol. 4593, pp. 181–195. Springer, Heidelberg (2007). https://doi.org/10.1007/978-3-540-74619-5_12
22. Bogdanov, A., Knudsen, L.R., Leander, G., Paar, C., Poschmann, A., Robshaw, M.J.B., Seurin, Y., Vikkelsoe, C.: PRESENT: an ultra-lightweight block cipher. In: Paillier, P., Verbauwhede, I. (eds.) CHES 2007. LNCS, vol. 4727, pp. 450–466. Springer, Heidelberg (2007). https://doi.org/10.1007/978-3-540-74735-2_31
23. Hammi, M.T., Bellot, P., Serhrouchni, A.: BCTrust: a decentralized authentication blockchain-based mechanism. In: Wireless Communications and Networking Conference (WCNC), pp. 1–6. IEEE (2018)
24. Liang, G., Weller, S.R., Luo, F., Zhao, J., Dong, Z.Y.: Distributed blockchain-based data protection framework for modern power systems against cyber attacks. IEEE Trans. Smart Grid, 1 (2018)
25. Cha, S.C., Chen, J.F., Su, C., Yeh, K.H.: A Blockchain connected gateway for BLE-based devices in the Internet of Things. IEEE Access **6**, 1–10 (2018)
26. Sharma, P.K., Chen, M.Y., Park, J.H.: A software defined fog node based distributed Blockchain cloud architecture for IoT. IEEE Access **6**, 115–124 (2018)

27. Rahulamathavan, Y., Phan, R.C.W., Rajarajan, M., Misra, S., Kondoz, A.: Privacy-preserving blockchain based IoT ecosystem using attribute-based encryption. In: 2017 IEEE International Conference on Advanced Networks and Telecommunications Systems (ANTS), pp. 1–6. IEEE (2017)
28. Novo, O.: Blockchain meets IoT: an architecture for scalable access management in IoT. IEEE Internet Things J. 5(2), 1184–1195 (2018)
29. Huh, S., Cho, S., Kim, S.: Managing IoT devices using blockchain platform. In: 19th International Conference on Advanced Communication Technology (ICACT), pp. 464–467. IEEE (2017)
30. Biswas, K., Muthukkumarasamy, V.: Securing smart cities using blockchain technology. In: High Performance Computing and Communications, IEEE 18th International Conference on High Performance Computing and Communications (HPCC/SmartCity/DSS), pp. 1392–1393. IEEE (2016)
31. Pinno, O.J.A., Gregio, A.R.A., De Bona, L.C.: ControlChain: blockchain as a central enabler for access control authorizations in the IoT. In: GLOBECOM 2017–2017 IEEE Global Communications Conference, pp. 1–6. IEEE (2017)
32. Cebe, M., Erdin, E., Akkaya, K., Aksu, H., Uluagac, S.: Block4Forensic: an integrated lightweight blockchain framework for forensics applications of connected vehicles. arXiv preprint arXiv:1802.00561 (2018)

A Comparative Analysis of Different Intrusion Detection Techniques in Cloud Computing

Aditya Bakshi[1(✉)] and Sunanda[2]

[1] Lovely Professional University, Phagwara, India
addybakshi@gmail.com
[2] Shri Mata Vaishno Devi University, Katra, India

Abstract. Nowadays, the foremost optimal choice of every IT organization is cloud computing. Cloud computing technology is very flexible and scalable in nature. The prime concern in cloud computing is its security and privacy, because intruders are trying to breach it. The main reason for breaching is its open and distributed architecture. For detection of various attacks on cloud, the most common mechanism used is Intrusion Detection System (IDS). We have presented a comparative analysis of some existing cloud based intrusion detection systems and different methods of deploying the IDS are used for overcoming the security challenges. In spite of the fact that there are various existing literatures in this area of study, we endeavor to give more intricate picture of a thorough analysis. This paper shares an overview of different intrusions in cloud. The metrics, which are used for comparative analysis, are of various types like positioning, detection time, detection techniques, data source and attacks. The comparative analysis also shows the limitations of each technique that tells whether the cloud-computing environment is secure or not.

Keywords: Cloud computing · Firewall · Detection techniques
Data sources · Intrusion detection system

1 Introduction

Cloud computing is the latest computing technology which provides various services on demand and pay per use basis. Fundamental idea behind the evolution of this technology is diversity of computing relative to users. Every user has his own needs and expectations about the services. To fulfil their need, various features from computing components i.e. software, hardware and network are required. It is almost impossible to have distinguish computing environment for every user. Each client or user requirements are diverse i.e. on demand services or highly paid services from network; software development organizations cannot purchase every development environment for clients. As the technological advancements are increasing at a very fast rate, this lead to the evolution of cloud computing environment where all the services can be provided to the client in virtual environment. There are cloud servers created and maintained by computing giant firms, which provide numerous services required by users. Basically, cloud services are categorized in three broad categories. First one is Software as a Service (SaaS) which provides various applications especially bounded

© Springer Nature Singapore Pte Ltd. 2019
A. K. Luhach et al. (Eds.): ICAICR 2018, CCIS 956, pp. 358–378, 2019.
https://doi.org/10.1007/978-981-13-3143-5_30

to software to users. Second one is Infrastructure as a Service (IaaS) which provides various infrastructure environments to users and last one is Platform as a Service (PaaS) which deals with various platforms like OSs, etc. [4, 5]. All these services are available to users on pay per use and on demand basis, which helps the users to get the services at minimum cost that is impossible to get at affordable price in the past. Users have to just pay the rent for the time to which they are using services. Apart from this unique feature, cloud computing provides various other features like availability, maintainability, scalability, interoperability, etc. Not these all facilities can be achieved anyhow by standalone users in their local infrastructure due to various unavoidable conditions whereas cloud providers support them due to devoted services.

2 Common Attacks in Cloud

Cloud computing is the next generation technology, which is suitable for varied users having different resource and operating requirements [1]. The platforms for the cloud, computing are attractive because they are different from the traditional physical infrastructure on the basis of on-demand resources such as purchase, installation, configuration and deployment etc. Moreover, due to the openness behavior (i.e. data privacy for individuals) of the cloud, there are various security issues architecture that involves network as Internet and intranets Some of the major intrusions are described as follows:

Insider Attack: This attack is performed by insider cloud users i.e. It enters to the system by legitimate authorization. As, this attack is performed by some insider, the prediction and lethality of an attack is very difficult to find. Users may try to breach the security of cloud by gaining unprivileged access by using their credentials. Such attack covers the data tempering, deletion of critical assets and spreading of falsified information to hamper the system etc. This is one of the most disastrous threat to cloud because once the internal security architecture will be breached then overall system can be compromised easily.

Flooding Attack: For providing stability to the internet service, the flooding attack is considered to be the major challenge in cloud computing environment. In this attack, attacker frequently flood the huge amount of data packets to choke the network system. The data may include the ICMP, TCP, UDP packets etc. which are sent to just flood the system and gain access to other resources [2]. The two major techniques used for the flooding attack are DoS (Denial of service) and DDoS (Distributed denial of service) attack. Flooding of packets on server by one computer is called as denial of service attack whereas the same process to be done from many computers is called distributed denial of service attack.

User to Root Access: In this attack, those users are compromised which are having root access to the cloud system. In this attack, attacker can perform administrator level work for accessing the root level permissions and compromising the user credentials [3]. However it is not a single attack based on paradigm that will be applied on the cloud system. User to root access attack also involves many techniques like eavesdropping etc. The main motto behind this attack is to gain credentials to reach to the root level of the cloud server which can be further compromised by using the same.

Port Scanning: Port scanning is the technique to scan all ports of any system. Although it is a manual process to check for each and every port and their status as open or close. There are various automated tools such as nmap, wireshark and tcpdump which provide detailed description about the port numbers that can be incorporated with IP address [3]. These tools are sometimes used to attack on the cloud environment. If not all open ports are being used by any specific service, that ports can be used as a back door. In backdoor, the attacker inserted the malicious code for gaining access the network system.

Attacks on Virtual Machine (VM) or Hypervisor: Cloud environment is completely based on virtual architecture. It virtualizes both the environments either internal or external. Virtual machine is a dedicated machine that works virtually on behalf of real environment. The most popular technique for clubbing and splitting VMs is based on hypervisor. A hypervisor is a virtual machine manager that allows multiple operating system runs on a single host system at a same time. There are various known attacks which try to compromise either VMs or target hypervisor to completely choke the system. The attacker always target the middle layer that works between the upper and lower layer in VMs. If the attackers can compromise any one of these three layers then he would result compromise the whole system very easily.

Apart from the above discussed attacks there are various other attacks which lead to severe security problems. The common solution to the problem is firewall implementation. However it does not solve the problems at all which forces the intrusion detection system (IDS) or sometimes intrusion detection and prevention system (IDPS) implementation. First of all we see the features of firewall and various other firewalls which can be implemented and then after various other IDPSs and their comparison in cloud environment [7].

3 Firewall

Firewall comprises various set of rules which act as the first line defence mechanism involved in the system. It protects and filters all the incoming and outgoing requests from the system. However, it is completely static in nature working on the pre-defined rules of network. It is unable to protect the system in cases where requests are evasion in nature and here IDPSs play crucial role for the system [8, 9]. Some of the major firewall techniques that are used in cloud environment are Static Packet Filtering Firewall, Stateful Packet Filtering Firewall, Stateful Inspection Firewall and Proxy Firewalls [10].

Firewalls restrict to some extent in security attacks but not as an overall solution. For sustaining more security in different types of attacks, IDS or IPS can be served as solution that could be incorporate in cloud. However, the different parameters and techniques are required for improving the efficacy of an IDS/IPS in cloud computing. The parameters comprises of different techniques used in IDS and its configuration within the network. Some traditional IDS/IPS techniques such signature based detection, anomaly detection, state protocol analysis etc. can also be incorporated in cloud. The next section covers the common IDS/IPS techniques.

4 Cloud Based IDS Techniques

4.1 Signature Based Detection

This technique incorporates signatures of various known attacks. These signatures are stored in database server of IDS and any incoming or outgoing requests are matched with them. Any matching signature request is discarded immediately from the network or other consequences may be applied like changing the contents, modifying the target, etc. However, it is the best technique for known attacks but proves to be very ineffective in case of unknown attacks. Any attack or security breach, which is attempted by modifying the content, is unable to be detected by this technique. One of the key reason for using signature-based detection is because its rules can be easily reconfigured. Reconfiguration of rules is required for updating the signatures of unknown attacks. These signatures are helpful for detecting the network traffic [11].

In cloud, the known attack can be easily detected by using signature based intrusion detection technique. The signature-based technique is applied on the front end of cloud for detecting the external intrusion or at back end of cloud for detecting internal intrusions. If signatures are not updated, it cannot be used to detect unknown attacks in cloud. Different signature based detection approaches along with the methodology adopted and salient features are shown in Table 1. All approaches in tables tells about the methodologies that have been used to provide the security in cloud environment. Jia et al. [14] proposed an efficient revocable ID-Based Signature scheme that is performed on cloud revocation server. In this approach, large prime numbers are used to provide the greater security. The main advantage of this approach is that it uses less time consumption for detection of unknown attacks than other traditional techniques. Arjunan et al. [15] proposed an enhanced intrusion detection approach for securing of networks by incorporating correlation module (CM) and management module (MM). This technique is used for both anomaly based and signature based detection attacks. Hamdi et al. proposed cloud based signature learning service approach using inductive logic programming.

The results for this technique is better than previous technique as it automatically generates the signature for SNORT IDS [16]. Table 1 shows different Signature based detection approaches along with their methodologies and salient features.

4.2 Anomaly Detection

Anomaly detection technique tries to detect intrusions that are anomalous to the actual definition. This technique involves various profiles that are used to filter the traffic as genuine or malicious activity.

All such profiles are stored in advance as well as dynamically updated based on the uses and traffic pattern. Some of the known products based on this technique are working very well in real life scenarios [12].

Apart from the normal computing, it is also very useful in case of cloud computing. It involves data collection related to the behavior of legitimate users over training period, and then applies various test, which are statistical in nature, are used to observe behavior and determines genuine user. It is very useful in cases of unknown attacks

Table 1. Signature based detection approaches and their comparison

Reference	Methodology adopted	Salient features
[14] Efficient revocable ID-based signature with cloud revocation server	The proposed model uses RIBS scheme which is composed of 4 phases namely I. Setup: used for generating master key and master time key II. InitKeyExt: for sending the initial key to the user through a secured channel III. TimeKeyUpd: the cloud based server will computes the time update key and send it back to the user IV. Sign: the signer will finally sign the message with the given user key and time update key	- A revocable IBS scheme is proposed in which the revocation functionality is done on a Cloud Revocation Server (CRS) - To ensure appropriate security level, large prime numbers (512 & 160 bits) have been used - The proposed model is less time consuming compared to the traditional techniques - Hash functions used are much more efficient and have shorter signature size than the previous models - Suitable for resource constrained devices such as wireless sensors
[15] An enhanced intrusion detection framework for securing network layer of cloud computing	The proposed system consists of different security modules like *management module, correlation module* and NIDS Correlation Module (CM) is used to detect distributed attacks at each cluster node Management Module (MM) is used to gather the distributed attack evidences from cluster nodes The NIDS is used to monitor the physical as well as virtual network traffic A network traffic profile will be generated from the capture packets	- Combines signature based and anomaly based detection techniques - Snort is used for Signature based detection, and different classifiers such as decision tree, naïve bayes, random forest, linear discriminant analysis and random forest are used for anomaly based detection - Uses Dempster Shafer Theory (DST) for making final decision on collected intrusion evidences from the cloud
[16] A cloud-based architecture for network attack signature learning	- The Learning Nodes (LN) provides the signature learning service - It will record the network traffic in a PCAP format which will be translated using prolog rules	- Cloud based signature learning service using inductive logic programming is proposed - Predicates were formed in order to describe signature of different attack vectors in the system

(continued)

Table 1. (*continued*)

Reference	Methodology adopted	Salient features
	- The Inductive Logic Programming (ILP) engine is present inside the learning node along with the Background Knowledge (BK) database and a Grammar Translator Proxy - The existing prolog signature rules are transformed into SNORT signature rules - Finally the signature is sent to the user and gets feed into its signature database	- Results have shown that the proposed framework has successfully been able to automatically generate signatures of SNORT IDS
[17] Event pattern discovery on IDS traces of cloud services	- Authors have applied Growing Hierarchical Self Organizing Maps (GHSOM) technique - Initially, the network data traffic is collected using IDS/Honeypot traces - Data is clustered using GHSOM and a series of visualization; feature observation and even pattern discovery are performed	- Unsupervised learning techniques are used for classifying network data more efficiently - GHSOM technique helps in efficient data analysis - Effectively discovers different critical attack vectors and efficiently reduces the trace log size

where definitions or any specific signatures are unknown in advance. The main idea behind use of this detection technique is to decrease the false alarm rate and work either perfectly either with known or unknown attacks [13]. Anomaly detection techniques detects unknown and known attacks, which are segregated at different levels. In cloud, by using anomaly based detection, large number of events that can (network level or system level) occur, which makes difficult to monitor or control intrusion [1].

Capability of soft computing to deal with uncertain and data that is partially true, makes them very useful technique in intrusion detection. There are various techniques from this computing like Fuzzy Logic, Association rule mining, Artificial Neural Network (ANN), Genetic Algorithm (GA), Support Vector Machine (SVM), etc. that can be incorporated to improve the accuracy of detection and efficiency of anomaly detection based IDS and signature based IDS. Sunita et al. [19] uses k-learning classification over cloud to improve detection accuracy of anomaly based IDS. It uses Bayesian classifier, which converges quicker than other discriminative models and requires less model training time.

Suaad et al. [20] proposed a unique model of detecting anomalies in IaaS environments by monitoring the VM in cloud system. Their detection system proved very

Table 2. Anomaly based detection approaches and their comparison

Reference	Methodology adopted	Salient features
[18] Intrusion detection and prevention system using K-learning classification in cloud	- The proposed model uses cloud based hybrid architecture to improve the intrusion detection accuracy - Data packets are logged and checked against the rules over the cloud platform - Log files are divided into two datasets for testing and training purpose - K2 learning algorithm is applied on the obtained datasets and Bayesian algorithm is used for creating a junction tree - Finally check the new connections are checked against the given threshold value are datasets will be updated accordingly	- Snort is used as an intrusion detection tool - Filtering rules are logged onto the cloud server - log files are used as training data set in weka - K2 learning algorithm is used for training the data - Junction tree is created using Bayesian algorithm - Results thus obtained are categorized into two types, namely: users and services - Graphs are plotted for showing anomalous users as well as services used
[19] Detecting anomalies in IaaS environments through virtual machine host system call analysis	The IaaS environment is monitored using the following setup - A single cluster setup is used which consists of 3 servers as well as a network infrastructure of switches and routers - Server 1 contains all the cloud components and acts as the gateway of cloud network; server 2 hosts the entire client VMs and acts as a node controller - Server 3 is used for management and initiation VMs - All the system calls issued by clients are recorded using Linux strace mechanism - Normal behavior profile for each VM is maintained using collected data and classifier is trained	- System calls are monitored at the VM level without any arrangement within VMs - Level of granularity is higher and sufficient to detect a relevant number of attack vectors - Linux KVM-based references are used for conducting experiments and statistical analysis - Unlike the previous research studies, the proposed system does not require any knowledge about the VM or the underlying OS - System is successfully able to categorize normal and anomalous system calls

(*continued*)

Table 2. (*continued*)

Reference	Methodology adopted	Salient features
	- Finally, the system is tested by generating some anomalous system calls	
[20] Preventing mistraining of anomaly-based IDSs through ensemble systems	- Proposed an ensemble classifier for preventing the mistraining of a classifier - One classifier is trained online with the incoming data and other is trained offline with its initial decision rules - Experiment is performed on distributed IDS EMERALD that uses Bayesian inference for its decision making process - System is tested by generating multiple mistraining attacks and measured according to the amount if false positives and negatives	- Anomaly based IDS is trained online according to the nature of incoming data traffic - Ensemble classifier is proposed which contains multiple copies of a single classifier - EMERALD IDS is used for conduction the experiment - Mistraining attacks includes target integrity attacks and red herring attacks
[22] Machine learning for anomaly detection and categorization in multi-cloud environments	Their work comprises of four different stages: - Detection of anomalous packets from normal traffic - Test whether the detected attack is generic to avoid any misclassification of attack vectors - Attacks are categorized as Shellcode, Reconnaissance and Backdoor attacks - Classification algorithm further distinguishes Reconnaissance attacks from rest of the network traffic	- Detection as well as categorization of anomalies is done - Machine learning techniques utilized by their learning model are Random Forest (RF) and Linear Regression (LR) - Achieved detection accuracy of 99% and accuracy for categorization of anomalies is 93.6% respectively - The proposed technique can be applied in multi-cloud environments - Dataset used was of UNSW, which is publicly available for comprehensive study

successful in classifying normal and anomalous behavior than other cloud-based approaches. Pan et al. [22] gives a beautiful categorization of several different attacks which was absent in many of the past researches. In addition, they further segregates the attacks and prevents any misclassification of attack vectors. Different anomaly based detection approaches are shown in Table 2. The table shows the comparison and methodologies of all the anomaly based detection approaches along with salient features.

4.3 Artificial Neural Networks (ANN) Based IDS

ANNs generalizes data from incomplete data for intrusion detection classifier as normal or intrusive behavior. Types of ANN are used in IDS are: Back Propagation (BP), Multi-Layer Feed-Forward (MLFF) nets and Multi-Layer Perceptron (MLP). Distributed Time Delay Neural Network (DTDNN) has been claimed as the best detection technique in this category until now. It contains capability of classifying and fast conversion rates of data and proves to be a very simple and efficient solution. Its

Table 3. ANN based detection approaches and their comparison

Reference	Methodology adopted	Salient features
[23] An efficient approach of trigger mechanism through IDS in cloud computing	- Information Theoretic Model (ITM) is used to detect any intrusion over cloud network - Data stream is marked as intrusive or normal using state transition diagrams - Misuse detection is used to detect anomalies by comparing with existing obtrusion signature - In case any intrusion is detected, alarm is raised - The action engine is responsible for taking valid action	- Efficient triggering mechanism that uses Artificial Neural Networks (ANN) and Information Theoretic Model (ITM) - Uses State transition diagrams and Misuse detection engine to identify any unapproved event over cloud network - Gives better execution results over other triggering mechanisms in cloud computing environment
[24] A neural network based distributed intrusion detection system on cloud platform	- Firstly, the neural network is trained using KDD dataset - The IDS then receives instruction signals for making intrusion detection tasks for the given 5-node architecture - After the training phase, ANN performance is tested using KDD no-label dataset and corrected dataset - The output thus obtained will help in determining whether there is any malicious actions as well as what kind of attack vector is captured	- ANN based distributed IDS to make full utilization of available resources - Capable of detecting new kinds of attack vectors with genuinely precise results within acceptable time limits - Accuracy for classifying whether activities are normal or malicious in nature is 100% - Promising way for identifying new attack vectors in cloud platforms

accuracy can be improved by combining various other techniques related to soft computing.

ANN based solutions of IDS proves a better solution over other techniques for network data which are unstructured in nature. Accuracy of intrusion detection involved with these techniques is completely dependent on training profile and layers that are hidden. Gupta et al. [23] proposed an efficient triggering mechanism that uses ANN and ITM model to detect any intrusion over the cloud. It gives better results over other triggering mechanisms in cloud environment. However, their system lacks the capability of attack categorization. ANN based detection approaches and their comparison is shown in Table 3. Li et al. [24] proposed a distributed IDS for cloud platforms that performed better than ITM model when comes to detection of new kinds of attack vectors.

4.4 Fuzzy Logic Based IDS

FIDS are used for detecting and inspecting various network traffic related to SYN and UDP floods, Ping of Death, E-mail Bomb, FTP/Telnet password guessing and port scanning. Some evolving techniques under Fuzzy Neural Network (FuNN) collaborates both type of learning as supervised and unsupervised learning [1]. EuFNN has better accuracy in intrusion detection than normal ANN techniques and experimental results shown in [1] prove accuracy. Real time intrusions can be also detected in real time environment by involving association rules of Fuzzy System. The experimental results generate two result sets that are mined online from training data. It is very suitable for DoS or DDoS attacks that are implemented on large scale. Alqahtani et al. [26] have examined popular IDS framework using different classifiers against each other to identify the most effective classifier in detecting various attacks. Their results shows that SuricataIDS when used with decision-based classifier gives the highest accuracy among other classification mechanisms. Mary et al. [27] have used fuzzy logic control for building multi-layer trust security model, which unlike previous fuzzy based systems is capable of faster classification with higher degree of accuracy. Fuzzy based detection approaches and comparison is shown in Table 4.

4.5 Association Rule Based IDS

There are various intrusions that are formed based on known or variants of known attacks. Apriori algorithm for determining the signatures of such attacks are used and they are also capable to determine the variants of such attacks can be determined and detected by frequent item sets. Data mining technique used in Network based intrusion detection with signature-based algorithm generates signatures for misuse detection.

However, drawback of the proposed algorithm is involved time consumption, which is more than considerable for generating signatures. Scanning reduction algorithm solved this problem, which reduces the number of database scans for effectively generating signatures from previously known attacks. However, there are very high false positive rates occur which generate due to unwanted and unknown patterns.

Table 4. Fuzzy based detection approaches and their comparison

Reference	Methodology adopted	Salient features
[25] A comparative analysis of different classification techniques for cloud intrusion detection systems' alerts and fuzzy classifiers	- The main aim of this research is to compare different IDS using certain number of classifier algorithms to check which one is better - They have tested different IDS like Snort, Suricata, FL-Snort and FL-Suricata using different classifiers such as Naïve Bayes, Decision Tree, K-NN and OneR - First step is to rank every class of attack and compare them based upon following metrics: 1. Accuracy 2. Precision 3. Sensitivity 4. Specificity 5. F-measure - The second step was to compare the given IDS one by one against each other and conclude that which IDS works better in identifying attack vectors with each classifier	- Popular IDS framework are examined extensively using different classifiers - Classifiers taken were: Naïve Bayes Decision Tree K-Nearest Neighbor OneR - IDS frameworks used are: Snort Suricata FL-Snort FL-Suricata - Experiments were carried upon ISCX dataset on WEKA platform - Decision Tree classifier gives the highest accuracy of 99.5% among all the four classification mechanisms
[26] A comparative study of different fuzzy classifiers for cloud intrusion detection systems' alerts	- Firstly, they have categorized the ISCX dataset into different categories like, Normal, Infiltrated, HTTP DOS, DDOS, and Brute Force - They run this dataset on Snort as well as Suricata IDS in offline mode - After obtaining the results, to get more accuracy in categorizing different attack vectors they have built IDS fuzzy classifiers - Finally the attack vectors were categorized more	- Their main goal was to identify unique sorts of network attacks inside MyCloud network using two most popular IDS frameworks namely, Snort and Suricata - A Fuzzy logic system is proposed to better classify different attack vectors - Different performance metrics were chosen like accuracy, sensitivity, specificity and false alarm rate

(continued)

Table 4. (*continued*)

Reference	Methodology adopted	Salient features
	accurately based on the analyzed alert files	- In depth comparison between different classifier based IDS is given
[27] Fuzzy logic approach to modelling trust in cloud computing	- Proposed a multi-layer trust security model (MLTSM) based on fuzzy logic control - Trust evaluation across three layers namely IaaS, PaaS and SaaS is done - Trust value is obtained through data center policy (DCP), Secure Shell (SSH) and intrusion detection/prevention ID. - Fuzzy logic control is used to evaluate the degree of membership whose value lies between 0 and 1, where 0 signifies low security and 1 signifies high security	- Their model MLTSM is capable of enhancing the protected deployment of cloud framework in mission critical applications such as military, threat management etc. - Its experimental results confirms coordinate assurance and verification of trust condition of any given distributed computing administration - Proved valuable for correlation, arrangement and enhancing end-client trust in choosing or devouring distributed cloud based computing resources

4.6   Support Vector Machine Based IDS

SVM is better than other artificial intelligence techniques used with IDS. There are various available experiments, which shows its efficiency over other techniques. It uses limited sample data to detect intrusions where accuracy does not get affected due to dimensions of data. False positives rate is also very less than other techniques as experimented in [6].

This is because that various other techniques require large sample dataset whereas it works on a limited sample dataset. It uses limited sample data to detect intrusions where accuracy does not get affected due to dimensions of data. False positives rate is also very less than other techniques as experimented in [6]. This is because that various other techniques require large sample dataset whereas it works on a limited sample dataset. SVM works on binary data so for better accuracy, it can be combined with other techniques which can improve its accuracy in detection. SVM is combined with SNORT and some basic rule sets of firewall, which allows it to generate a new and effective technique for intrusion detection.

The SVM- classifier is also used with SNORT to reduce false alarm rate and improve accuracy of IPS. SVM IDS techniques can prove the best techniques for intrusion detection in cloud, which can enhance its current feature and extends its security level up to a considerable level. Raneel et al. [28] proposed a similar study [19] for the protection of VMs over Infrastructure-as-a-Service (IaaS) environments but uses

SVM classifiers. They presented a thorough study of different classes of DoS attacks and were capable of detecting these attacks in cloud platforms. Mukkavilli et al. [29] proposed a theoretical model for detecting anomalous changes in network traffic by

Table 5. SVM based detection approaches and their comparison

References	Methodology adopted	Salient features
[28] Detecting denial of service attacks in the cloud	The proposed approach is implemented in the following manner: - First an IaaS (Infrastructure as-a Service) cloud is created - A testbed is selected for this cloud platform consisting of VMs. Of those VMs, some are normal and some are furnished with DoS attack tools - This framework will monitor all the outgoing and incoming network traffic and generates an alert to the cloud admin in case if denial of service attack is detected	- Novel approach for the protection of virtual machines (VMs) against DoS attacks - Eucalyptus is the open source cloud platform used for carrying out this experiment - A novel IDS is proposed which contains different features such as: feature extraction, packet sniffing and SVM classification - Different DoS attacks detected includes: - Ping of Death - ICMP flooding attack - TCP SYN flooding attack - TCP LAND - UDP flooding attack - DNS flooding attack
[29] Mining concept drifting network in cloud computing environments	- A test environment is made for processing data and converting it into LIBSVM (SVM library) format - Dataset used is KDDSUBSET, LBNL and DARPA - Manual dataset is also created using "tcpdump" -Cloud environment is set up for getting real time data using Amazon Web Services (AWS) - Captured data is classified as attacks based on certain behaviors	- Theoretical model for integrated supervised machine learning and control over cloud platform for detection of drift in network traffic pattern is presented - Different components in the proposed model includes: Kullback Leibler, divergence based relative entropy scheme, an online SVM classifier, anomaly based IDS and feedback control engine - Proposed model will report any alert only, if there is a significant changes in the traffic pattern, and does not report any minor changes

(continued)

Table 5. (*continued*)

References	Methodology adopted	Salient features
[30] Combined analysis of support vector machine and principle component analysis for IDS	- Firstly data is collected and normalized and passed through the PCA (Principle Component Analysis) - PCA further categorize the data into normal or attack vector using a predefined threshold value - The selected dataset (KDD99) is used for training and testing purpose - Finally the data is saved and used for detecting future attack vectors with similar attacking patterns	- A controlling mechanism is proposed for wireless data using IDS - Concept of Principle Component Analysis (PCA) is used for detecting attack vectors and intrusion detection in smart grid - Multiple factors considered are: rate of increase in network efficiency, response time, rate of increase in system error and differences in usage of PCA respectively - PCA technique gives better results than most of the conventional schemes and usage of SVM enhances the overall performance of IDS and decreases the overall analysis time

using supervised machine learning and SCM classifier over cloud environment. Their system is susceptible to higher false positive rates. Raja et al. [30] proposed a novel approach of using Principle Component Analysis (PCA) for detecting attack vectors over cloud platforms. Their approach gives better results than most of the conventional SVM based classifiers and decreases overall analysis time. Different SVM based detection approaches and their comparison is shown in Table 5.

4.7   Genetic Algorithm Based IDS

Genetic Algorithms (GA) use confidence based fitness functions for intrusion detection, which classifies network in a very efficient manner. These values can be used and determined for the profile generation as well. These services are very much useful in cases where intrusion behaviors are very dynamic in nature. These techniques can be collaborated with other techniques, which are resource intensive and prioritize the overall performance of the system. These techniques use training period and determine the fitness value based on the trained profiles. However, GA can be integrated with other such techniques for better results in cloud technology.

This feature is more important than any other techniques involved for intrusion detection. It is also suitable in scenarios wherever there is a need of mutual authentication in cloud among users. Most of the genetic algorithms uses techniques, which are derived from biological concepts like mutation, inheritance, crossover and selection. Fan, Yu et al. [31] proposed a cloud-based platform called T-DNA Tagged Rice

Table 6. Genetics based detection approaches and their comparison

References	Methodology adopted	Salient features
[31] TTRSIS: a cloud computing platform for rice functional genomics research through a reverse genetics approach	The Genomic analysis is carried out using the following procedure: i. BLASTN (Basic Local Alignment Search Tool) is used for the identification of T-DNA and binary vector procedures ii. Rice GAAS (Genome Automated Annotation System) is utilized to obtain Rice genomic sequences iii. Align module utilized BLASTN search to find sequences match to RB region iv. Search module is used for providing search options for gene id, gene name, and mutant line number v. Rice gene functional characterization module makes the functional characteristics of rice genome as current as possible vi. Physical distribution module provides rice seed distribution and inventory for academic research	- TTRSC is established in Asia University to with the administration, protection and circulation of mutant rice seeds stock - It is used for handling the genomic information produced from Taiwan Rice Insertional Mutagenesis (TRIM) - TTRSC consists of four modules: i. Align module ii. Rice quality module iii. Physical distribution module iv. Search module - TTRSC helps academicians and scientists to query intrigued genes stored 21 Kb downstream or upstream of T-DNA addition sites
[32] Genetic algorithm based feature selection algorithm for effective intrusion detection in cloud networks	- A new genetics based feature selection algorithm is proposed using Fuzzy SVM (Support Vector Machines) - The GA find and eliminates any redundant features which ultimately reduces the training time and ambiguousness - Next the feature selection search is used to add and/or remove unwanted features into the framework - Then a search strategy is decided like complete, random and sequential	- Novel IDS which uses genetics based feature detection and Fuzzy SVM based classification mechanism - Overall runtime is reduced by selecting only important features using the feature selection module - Reduction in runtime improves the accuracy of the classification mechanism done through SVM classifier - Final execution outcomes when tested with KDD Cup 99 dataset, using the

(continued)

Table 6. (*continued*)

References	Methodology adopted	Salient features
	- Finally a subset is generated, which is evaluated using certain evaluation criteria. These criteria could be information, distance, dependency etc. - A stopping condition is used when any of the given condition is met. Like when the maximum number of iterations are completed etc.	proposed classification and feature detection mechanism results in higher detection rate and a reduced false alarm rate
[33] A classification algorithm based on ensemble feature selections for imbalanced-class dataset	The following algorithm (IESF) has been adopted by the authors: - A subset of random feature is generated along with a classifier L - Ensemble prediction results are gained from the testing example - Initial objective function is calculated and classifier i is flipped over its jth index - New ensemble is gained from the testing example and value of the objective function is re-calculated - Search will be stopped when all the features are over or it reaches the number of configured loops	- Novel classification mechanism for solving imbalanced class dataset called Ensemble Feature Selection (EFS) - Proposed system uses the predominance of EFS in precision, at that point considers the decent variety and unevenness in the outlining proper component subset target capacity to make it fit for the imbalanced dataset - To compute accuracy of the system, it picks the class oriented F-measurement and ingresses a punishment-reward algorithm into KW diversity estimations

Service Information System (TTRSIS) for research based on rice genomics using Genome Annotation System (GAAS). Their system helps researchers and scientists to query genes stored 21 Kb downstream or upstream of T-DNA addition sites. Kannan et al. [32] proposed a novel mechanism that uses genetics based feature detection and SVM based classifier, which improves the classification accuracy when compared to other techniques by selecting only important features. The running time is reduced by removing unnecessary features with the help of feature selection module. The proposed system has a higher detection rate and reduced false alarm rate. Yin et al. [33] proposed a novel classification mechanism for solving imbalanced class dataset and shows a higher accuracy when compared to other conventional algorithms. Different Genetic based detection approaches along with their comparison is shown in Table 6.

Table 7. Analysis of intrusion detection techniques in cloud computing

References	Features					
	Detection technique	IDS type	Positioning	Detection time	Data source	Attacks covered
[14]	Signature based	Revocable identity based (RBS)	Cloud server	Real time	Network traffic, Signature of known attack	Existential forgery on adaptively chosen messages and identity attacks in the random oracle model
[15]	Signature based	Network based	Each cloud region	Real time	Virtual network layer of cloud	Distributed attacks at cluster or cloud layer
[16]	Signature based	Network based	At each node of cloud	Real time	Network Traffic, cloud-based signature learning service	Signature attack on cloud
[17]	Signature based	Network based	Each cluster of cloud	Real time	Network Traffic, real-world IDS traces	Detection of zero day attack
[18]	Signature based	Network based, host based	Different parts of the cloud	Real time	Network traffic	Detection of distributed attacks
[19]	Anomaly based detection	Network based, host based	Different parts of the cloud	Real time	Network traffic	Random attack in networks
[20]	Anomaly based detection	Host based	Public cloud environments	Real time	Host traffic	Dos attack on IAAS
[21]	Anomaly based detection	Network based	Different parts of the cloud	Real time	Network traffic	Mis-training of an IDS trained online
[22]	Anomaly based detection	Network based, host based	Intrusion detection system	Real time	Network Traffic, context awareness and cyber DNA	Cyber attack
[23]	Artificial based detection	Network based	Cloud region	Real time	Network communication	Trigger attacks
[24]	Artificial based detection	Neural network based	Cloud platform	Real time	Network traffic, KDD dataset	ANN based attacks
[25]	Fuzzy based detection	Network based	On cloud system	Real time	Normal and abnormal network traffic	Detection of zero day attack

(continued)

Table 7. (*continued*)

References	Features					
	Detection technique	IDS type	Positioning	Detection time	Data source	Attacks covered
[26]	Fuzzy based detection	Network based	Fuzzy-Logic engine based on IDSs	Real time	Network traffic	Cyber attacks
[27]	Fuzzy based detection	Network based	Different cloud computing platform	Real time	Cloud traffic	Cloud computing attacks
[28]	Genetic based detection	Network based	Cloud computing platform	Real time	Network traffic	Management, conservation and distribution of mutant rice seeds inventory
[30]	Genetic based detection	Cloud networks	Cloud computing platform	Real time	Cloud traffic	Different types of attacks on IDS
[31]	SVM based detection	Cloud networks	Different parts of the cloud network	Real time	Cloud traffic	ICMP Flood, Ping-of-Death, UDP Flood, TCP SYN Flood
[32]	SVM based detection	Network based	Cloud computing environment	Real time	Network Traffic	False positive rates

4.8 Hybrid Techniques

Hybrid techniques combine various such technologies together for a better result in sense of intrusion detection. This is such a kind of technology, which contains various flavours related to other techniques. NeGPAIM is based on hybrid technique combining two low level components including fuzzy logic for misuse detection and neural networks for anomaly detection, and one high level component which is a central engine analyzing outcome of two low level components. This is an effective model and does not require dynamic update of rules. It is more suitable to be integrated with soft computing techniques, which are traditional ones or focused towards intrusion detection.

With pros and cons of every technique, this is also not an exception. Some of the limitations under this technique are mainly oriented towards training profiles, period and rules. The lead role in this technique is of algorithm, which makes it stand clear form other techniques. Justin et al. [34] proposed a hybrid IDS model that uses SVM classifier for getting highly accurate results and anomaly-based detection is used for detecting DoS attacks in Mobile Ad-Hoc Networks (MANETs). Now, the analytical study of all techniques are shown in tabular format i.e. in Table 7. The table covers the comparison between different detection techniques based on certain silent features such as IDS type, Positioning, detection time, data source and attacks covered etc. Each detection technique has different positioning, detection time, data source and attack that effects the cloud-computing environment because network traffic, signatures, servers and cloud regions are different for each detection technique.

5 Conclusion

In this paper, different types of intrusion detection systems have shown that are useful in the cloud-computing environment. In the first section, we talk about different attacks on cloud platforms like Insider attack, Flooding attack, Port Scanning and attacks on VMs. After that a little description about firewall is given. Then we described different cloud based IDS techniques. The paper also covers different researches in tabular form that are helpful for understanding the cloud-computing scenario in efficient way. Furthermore, the analysis of different IDS techniques such as signature based, anomaly based, artificial based and genetic based detection etc. have been shown in the paper. The confidentiality, integrity, and availability of data in cloud that are affected by the intrusions are also presented here. Finally, the analytical study of all cloud based IDS techniques is done on the basis of salient features such as IDS type, positioning, detection time, data source and attacks covered. Each detection technique has different positioning, detection time, data source and attack that effects the cloud computing environment because network traffic, signatures, server positioning and cloud regions are different for each technique. With this analytical study, we presented a detailed analysis on how different IDS techniques have been used over the cloud platform and how we can better select the IDS based on our requirements.

References

1. Modi, C., Patel, D., Borisaniya, B., Patel, H.: A survey of intrusion detection techniques in cloud. J. Netw. Comput. Appl. **36**, 42–57 (2013)
2. Almorsy, M., Grundy, J., Ibrahim, A.S.: Adaptable, model-driven security engineering for SaaS cloud-based applications. Automated Software Engineering **21**(2), 187–224 (2014)
3. Du, Y., Zhang, R., Li, M.: Research on a security mechanism for cloud computing based on virtualization. Telecommun. Syst. **53**, 19–24 (2013)
4. Edurado, F.B., Monge, R., Hashizume, K.: Building a security reference architecture for cloud systems. Requir. Eng. **21**, 1–25 (2015)
5. He, J., Dong, M., Ota, K., Fan, M., Wang, G.: NetSecCC: a scalable and fault tolerant architecture for cloud computing security. Peer-to-Peer Netw. Appl. **9**, 1–15 (2014)
6. Hu, P., Sung, C.W., Ho, S., Chan, T.H.: Optimal coding and allocation for perfect secrecy in multiple clouds. Inf. Forensics Secur. **11**, 388–399 (2014)
7. Lee, J., Cho, J., Seo, J., Shon, T., Won, D.: A novel approach to analyzing for detecting malicious network activity using a cloud computing testbed. Mob. Netw. Appl. **18**, 122–128 (2012)
8. Li, J., Li, Y.K., Chen, X., Lee, P.P.C., Lou, W.: A hybrid cloud approach for secure authorized deduplication. IEEE Trans. Parallel Distrib. Syst. **26**, 1206–1216 (2014)

9. Rahat, M., Shibli, M.A., Niazi, M.A.: Cloud identity management security issues and solutions: a taxonomy. Complex Adapt. Syst. Model. **2**, 1–37 (2014)

10. Rho, S., Chang, H., Kim, S., Lee, Y.S.: An efficient peer-to-peer distributed scheduling for cloud and grid computing. Peer-to-Peer Netw. Appl. **8**, 863–871 (2014)

11. Li, Q., Han, Q., Sun, L.: Collaborative recognition of queuing behavior on mobile phones. Mob. Comput. **15**, 60–73 (2014)

12. Tak, G.K., Badge, N., Manwatkar, P., Rangnathan, A., Tapaswi, S.: Asynchronous anti phishing image captcha approach towards phishing. In: International Conference on Future Computer and Communication, vol. 3, pp. 694–698. IEEE (2010)

13. Malhotra, K., Gardner, S., Patz, R.: Implementation of elliptic-curve cryptography on mobile healthcare devices. IEEE (2007)

14. Jia, X., et al.: Efficient revocable id-based signature with cloud revocation server. IEEE Access **5**, 2945–2954 (2017)

15. Arjunan, K., Modi, C.N.: An enhanced intrusion detection framework for securing network layer of cloud computing. In: Asia Security and Privacy (ISEASP), 2017 ISEA. IEEE (2017)

16. Hamdi, O., Mbaye, M., Krief, F.: A cloud-based architecture for network attack signature learning. In: 2015 7th International Conference on New Technologies, Mobility and Security (NTMS). IEEE (2015)

17. Huang, S.-Y., Huang, Y., Suri, N.: Event pattern discovery on IDS traces of cloud services. In: 2014 IEEE Fourth International Conference on Big Data and Cloud Computing (BdCloud). IEEE (2014)

18. Mehmood, Y., et al.: Intrusion detection system in cloud computing: challenges and opportunities. In: 2013 2nd National Conference on Information Assurance (NCIA). IEEE (2013)

19. Kumawat, S., Sharma, A.K., Kumawat, A.: Intrusion detection and prevention system using K-learning classification in cloud. In: 2016 3rd International Conference on Computing for Sustainable Global Development (INDIACom). IEEE (2016)

20. Alarifi, S.S., Wolthusen, S.D.: Detecting anomalies in IaaS environments through virtual machine host system call analysis. In: 2012 International Conference for Internet Technology and Secured Transactions. IEEE (2012)

21. Fellin, C., Haney, M.: Preventing the mistraining of anomaly-based IDSs through ensemble systems. In: 2014 IEEE World Congress on Services (SERVICES). IEEE (2014)

22. Pan, Z., Pacheco, J., Hariri, S.: Anomaly behavior analysis for building automation systems. In: 2016 IEEE/ACS 13th International Conference of Computer Systems and Applications (AICCSA). IEEE (2016)

23. Gupta, D., Gupta, S.: An efficient approach of trigger mechanism through IDS in cloud computing. In: 2017 4th IEEE Uttar Pradesh Section International Conference on Electrical, Computer and Electronics (UPCON). IEEE (2017)

24. Li, Z., Sun, W., Wang, L.: A neural network based distributed intrusion detection system on cloud platform. In: 2012 IEEE 2nd International Conference on Cloud Computing and Intelligent Systems (CCIS), vol. 1. IEEE (2012)

25. Alqahtani, S.M., John, R.: A comparative analysis of different classification techniques for cloud intrusion detection systems' alerts and fuzzy classifiers. In: 2017 Computing Conference. IEEE (2017)

26. Alqahtani, S.M., John, R.: A comparative study of different fuzzy classifiers for cloud intrusion detection systems' alerts. In: 2016 IEEE Symposium Series on Computational Intelligence (SSCI). IEEE (2016)

27. Sule, M.-J., et al.: Fuzzy logic approach to modelling trust in cloud computing. IET Cyber-Phys. Syst. Theory Appl. **2**(2), 84–89 (2017)

28. Kumar, R., Lal, S.P., Sharma, A.: Detecting denial of service attacks in the cloud. In: 2016 IEEE 14th International Conference on Dependable, Autonomic and Secure Computing, 14th International Conference on Pervasive Intelligence and Computing, 2nd International Conference on Big Data Intelligence and Computing and Cyber Science and Technology Congress (DASC/PiCom/DataCom/CyberSciTech). IEEE (2016)

29. Mukkavilli, S.K., Shetty, S.: Mining concept drifting network traffic in cloud computing environments. In: Proceedings of the 2012 12th IEEE/ACM International Symposium on Cluster, Cloud and Grid Computing (CCGrid 2012). IEEE Computer Society (2012)

30. Raja, M.C., Rabbani, M.M.A.: Combined analysis of support vector machine and principle component analysis for IDS. In: International Conference on Communication and Electronics Systems (ICCES). IEEE (2016)

31. Fan, M.-J., et al.: TTRSIS: a cloud computing platform for rice functional genomics research through a reverse genetics approach. In: 2011 IEEE 11th International Conference on Bioinformatics and Bioengineering (BIBE). IEEE (2011)

32. Kannan, A., et al.: Genetic algorithm based feature selection algorithm for effective intrusion detection in cloud networks. In: Data Mining Workshops (ICDMW). IEEE (2012)

33. Yin, H., Gai, K., Wang, Z.: A classification algorithm based on ensemble feature selections for imbalanced-class dataset. In: IEEE International Conference on High Performance and Smart Computing (HPSC), 2016 IEEE 2nd International Conference on Big Data Security on Cloud (BigDataSecurity), and IEEE International Conference on Intelligent Data and Security (IDS). IEEE (2016)

34. Justin, V., Marathe, N., Dongre, N.: Hybrid IDS using SVM classifier for detecting DoS attack in MANET application. In: 2017 International Conference on I-SMAC (IoT in Social, Mobile, Analytics and Cloud) (I-SMAC), pp. 775–778. IEEE (2017)

An Intrusion Detection Method Using Artificial Immune System Approach

Juniorika Lyngdoh, Md. Iftekhar Hussain, Suktilang Majaw,
and Hemanta Kumar Kalita[✉]

North-Eastern Hill University, Shillong, Meghalaya, India
rikalyngdoh@gmail.com, ifteeh@gmail.com, smajaw.nehu@gmail.com,
kalita.hemanta@gmail.com

Abstract. Artificial Immune System (AIS) motivated from the immune systems work to defend against abnormal behaviors has inspired the computer systems to defend against the intruders. One of the ability of the AIS is distinguishing insiders and outsiders i.e. what is self and non self. With an increase rise and speedy usage of internet, the requirements of securities are increasing. Detection of intruders an any system is the vital role and we can do so by the technique of Intrusion Detection for reduction of intruders. We have suggested in our the use of artificial immune system approach based intrusion detection to check that only authorized users are entitled to connect into the network. Many research efforts encouraged by biological systems have rapidly risen up that out perform traditional methods. The immune system of human body safeguards against any diseases as it has its own special scheme to recognize pathogens.

Keywords: Artificial immune system
Intrusion detection systems (IDS) · Specific immune defense

1 Introduction

Biologically inspired algorithms (BIAs) offer a number of aspects for future networks that require scalability, adaptive and robust design to address potential failures caused by large scale networks. A variety of biological algorithms convey new networks design and applications compared to the old ones [1]. Artificial Immune System is a technique for pattern recognition algorithm applied for information security. The immune systems characteristics of self learning and memorization are exploited to facilitate the development of communication networks and intrusion detection. The detection of viruses and network intrusions has been considered as one of anomaly detection task in communication networks [2]. The key goal of AIS which is inspired by the immune systems is to be capable to identify changes in the surrounding from the regular behaviors. The old approach and their techniques are static. AIS seem to be one of the potential solutions for networking security. An immune system is a biological process that

© Springer Nature Singapore Pte Ltd. 2019
A. K. Luhach et al. (Eds.): ICAICR 2018, CCIS 956, pp. 379–387, 2019.
https://doi.org/10.1007/978-981-13-3143-5_31

identifies and kills pathogens. The adaptive immune system has specialized cells called T cells and B cells [3]. The cells of the immune system are the ones that should identify the pathogens. The immune system needs to detect and eliminate the pathogens as soon as possible so the cells should learn and adapt with the pathogens. Among the cells of the immune system there are memory cells that will respond much more vigorously to antigens it has previously encountered [4]. AIS can be an artificial approach after genetic algorithms neural networks and evolutionary computation in the artificial intelligence. Natures footprint hosts an astounding number of bio-inspired methods which include genetic algorithms, neural networks, and ant algorithms also some technologies such as swarm intelligence and artificial immune systems [5].

2   Human Immune System

The Human defense mechanism deals with defense system of the body. The human immune system is a complex giant system with a collection of cells and proteins to protect the body from pathogens. Pathogens can be a virus, a bacteria or a fungus that can cause an infection. Pathogens are made up of a bunch of components they are mostly proteins, carbohydrates, and lipids. The proteins that make up a pathogen are different compared to the proteins that make up the human immune system. So our body is able to recognize them as foreign. The specific peptides to which our body generates an immune are antigens. Antigens are molecules that are found on the surface of pathogens and are specific to that pathogen [6]. Any foreign molecule or foreign substance that can trigger a specific immune response against it is term as an antigen. The human immune system is divided into two types of defenses. They are the Non Specific immune defenses and the Specific immune defenses. The Non Specific immune defenses also referred as innate immune take part immediately within hours of an antigen appearance in the body. This defense mechanism recognizes some of the general property marking the invader as foreign. The innate immune system comprises of cells and proteins that are always alert and ready to kill and engulf pathogens [7]. The Specific immune system also known as the adaptive immune system or the acquired immune system employs even more highly specialized immune cells to get rid the pathogens. The components of adaptive immunity are usually silent but when activated, launch a ferocious attack by activating other immune cells and releasing special proteins to neutralize the microbes. The Specific immune defenses depend upon specific recognition by the lymphocyte cell. Lymphocytes are essential cells in the Specific immune defense. The lymphocytes contain two important cells which are B cells and T cells Adaptive immunity also plays an important role in creating immunological memory enabling the immune system to remember any pathogen it has encountered and fought before. This memory allows the immune system to respond much more quickly and efficiently the next time it faces the attack [8] (Fig. 1).

The lymphocytes of the adaptive immune system have evolved to recognize different antigens from bacteria, viruses and other disease causing organisms.

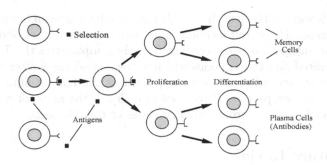

Fig. 1. Clonal selection

The antigenic property of the immune system allows it to distinguish subtle differences among antigens. Antibodies can differentiate between two proteins molecules that differ in a single amino acid. When the body encounters the pathogen the immune system is able to recognize it as an antigen because the molecules on the surface of the pathogen differ from those found in the body [9] (Fig. 2).

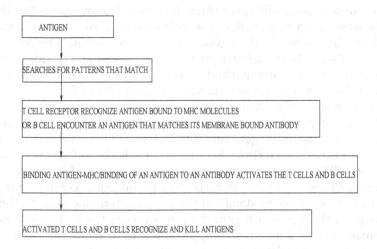

Fig. 2. Recognition of antigen

The acquired immune system needs to have seen the pathogen because the way the acquired immune system attacks is very specific and takes time to prepare. All foreign agents to our body have unique patterns on their surfaces that allow the cells of the immune system to detect them. When the cells of the acquired immune system detect these patterns, the agents are recognized as foreign, and the immune system can therefore mount an attack.

An effective immune response involves two major groups of cells: T lymphocytes and antigen-presenting cells. The two major populations of lymphocytes are the T cells and the B cells. The B cells have a unique antigen binding receptor on its membrane. The B cell receptor is a membrane bound antibody molecule [10]. Once the antigen has been recognized by the lymphocytes the T cells and B cells get activated and forms clones which is the second stage after recognition. In this paper we are using the same approach as the human immune system. The model which we propose is to develop nodes in the network which should recognize malicious nodes from ordinary nodes or the self node.

3   Literature Review

Negative selection algorithms tries to make an effort to model the negative selection process by self training, searching, identification, and elimination. The surviving and self cells circulate through the body in search of pathogens. On identifying the pathogens, which means that those pathogens that matched are identified and marked as non self foreign bodies and destroyed by the immune system.

In [11] a network with N nodes is created having Master agent Communication agent and Mobile agent at each node. Mobile agent sends signal with the communication agent on any incoming new node. Master agent passes information to the foreign mobile agent through communication agent. Mobile agent stores the information on its buffer. The mobile agent on reaching the home node and delivers the gathered information to the master agent. The set collected called the self set. Master agent runs the negative clonal selection algorithm. The signatures of both abnormal and normal are stored in the database. In this experiment different node density changes the probability of loss delay between nodes so the chances of misdetection are quite high.

In [12] the proposed model consist of four groups of agents the presenter agent the helper, memory agent and killer agent. This model has self healing and self protection characteristics because it defends the self agents against non self intruders. The system recognizes and records audit defects such as faults and failures. Presenter agent plays the role of antigen presenter cells in this model. This agent moves randomly in the network from one node to the other. When auditing the logs which gained via monitoring the node operations and finding audit trails if a defect occurs, presenter agent sends the audit trail for eliminating the cause of defect occurrence and to remove these causes. T memory agent generates a pattern based on the killing way and stores it in its memory. However the role of centralized node could not be ignored or eliminated. The management is decentralized partly.

The proposed IDS design in [13] consists of two main components IDS central engine and detection sensors. IDS central engine is located in the gateway of each LAN and detection sensors are located in each host in the network. Each of these components is composed of some software agent who perform special task. The training module composed of converter agent and trainer agent which have responsibility of primary detectors. After training, all detectors must be sent to all hosts in the network. There are two types of detectors that will be present in each host. Detector agents and Memory cell agents. The detector agents are composed of a set of trained detectors which have the ability to discriminate between self and non self packets. All increasing packets match with these detectors. If any detector match with any packets with effective affinity then an anomaly will report to IDS center to be investigated.

In [14] the paper explains concerning about both Negative selection and Clonal Selection Algorithm which are is used for pattern recognition problem domain. At the beginning the self-strings and randomly generated strings are matched. The strings that are matched are treated as malicious and destroyed. The strings that do not get matched are moved to the detector set. In the second step, protected strings are matched with those in the detector set. The strings that get matched are identified as nonself and the rest are matched again. The Clonal selection algorithm is an algorithm inspired by the clonal selection theory of acquired immunity that explains how B and T lymphocytes improve their response to antigens. The theory specifies that the organism have a pre-existing pool of heterogeneous antibodies. These antibodies can recognize all antigens with some level of specificity. The cells can replicate and produce more cells when an antigen is matched with an antibody. During the cell proliferation stage, genetic mutations occur in the clone of cells. This allows the binding ability of the cells to improve with time and exposure to the antigen.

In [15] it is a new combination of each of the Negative selection and Positive selection. In the negative selection the component that match any element of the self set are destroyed and the rest are hold on and within among the detector set. In the detection phase if any incoming data instance matches any detector, it is claimed as non self or anomaly. In the Positive selection the candidates that do not match any elements of the self set are eliminated and the rest are kept and stored in the detector set. In the detection phase the collection of detectors are used to distinguish self and non self. The collection of both the theories was theoretically shown to achieve better detector storage complexity in comparison to single Negative or Positive Selection.

In [16] describes protection of the human immune system against antigens. There are modules that pre-processes the training dataset. At the time of pre-processing the dataset is normalized between 0 and 1. Detector generation would generate real valued random detectors of dissimilar value using detector generation engine. The set that is pre-processed is denoted as self. The generated detectors are matched with all the instances of training dataset. The Detectors use binary representation, r-contiguous bit, r-chunks and hamming distance as matching rules. Detector set is the output of Detector set Generation Module.

In [17] briefly explain the AIS methods and algorithms. The algorithm used here is the negative selection algorithm. This algorithm generates a set of sensors and compares the affinity or the similarity with the self. Once an element is detected as non self it is eliminated. The negative selection algorithm is used in many areas such as anomaly detection, image processing and fault tolerance. The other algorithm of AIS is Clonal selection. The algorithm works to produce more number of B cells. The B cells have antigen receptors which will recognize the antigens. On encountering with an antigen the cells will reproduce, the selected cells will undergo a mutation process. After deactivating the cells which are antigens some of the cells become memory cells to remember in case the system meets the same antigen and the time to create antibodies will be faster.

In [18] the main goal of using AIS is to find the misbehaviour in wireless networks. Misbehaviour detection is a mechanism to remove harmful attacks. The AIS works like the Human system and we will map the Human Immune System parameters to the things that considered in a wireless Network. The Body is considered as the entire network, Self cells are the well behaving nodes. The nodes that do not actually behave well are the suspicious nodes. Generating number of patterns is a sequence of protocol events. Antibody generation function and mapping function are created. This mechanism allows the detection of system to have a relatively smaller misbehaving nodes. Antibodies are generated randomly. After creation of antibodies it is passed to the negative selection. In Antigen mapping, antigen is represented as a pattern of observed protocol events. During the process of execution the nodes are created and matched with the antibodies and any suspicious act during an event describes the behavior of a node as misbehaving nodes such as loss of a packet and such occurrence is considered as damage to the system.

4 Proposed Work

Our proposed work is to create a network of nodes which should recognize foreign or malicious nodes from normal nodes. First we have defined the self nodes or the existing nodes. The self nodes are like the self cells which pre exist in the body. They represent the safe cells. We defined antibodies of various types that will recognize the malicious nodes. We created the antibodies in such a way that they do not match the self nodes. Both the antibodies and the self defined nodes are represented in bits. When any new node enters into the network which are generated randomly in bits pattern, there will be a matching of the newly generated bits with the antibodies. If those random bits pattern match with the antibodies, they are detected as the malicious ones. A counter is enabled that counts how many antibodies have detected that particular bit pattern as malicious. A threshold minimum value is set. If the number of antibodies matching the bit pattern exceeds the minimum threshold value then the bit string generated is considered as Malicious. Below is the algorithm and output of the detection (Fig. 3).

The output shows the detection of malicious nodes. Here we can see a set of self nodes and antibodies in bits pattern. When a new node is generated it is generated with some random bit patterns. The newly generated bit is matched with all the antibodies bit patterns. If we set detection say for 4 bits it will check if any 4 bits of the newly generated incoming pattern match or not with any of the antibodies. If there is a match of four digits of bits pattern with any antibodies it is considered as a malicious node. A counter is set to check how many number of antibodies match with the new incoming pattern. In our

1.Prepare a pool of antibodies D of fixed sized

2.Define a self set S

3.Generate incoming patterns P in bits

4.Define a counter count to keep track of the stimulation threshold value T

5.For each form of P do

6.If (P==D)

    Mark as malicious

    Increment count

7. If (count>=T)

    Mark as crossed the stimulated threshold

    End if

    End if

8.Calculate the fitness of P with D.

9.Update the antibodies

10.End for

Fig. 3. Algorithm for intrusion detection

program we have set a counter 3 which means if the number of antibodies that match the new incoming pattern has reached 3 and more we alarm the network that the incoming pattern is malicious. This is our recognition approach. The updation of antibodies and removal of the malicious node will be done in future. We will try to refine better our algorithm and give better efficient results (Fig. 4).

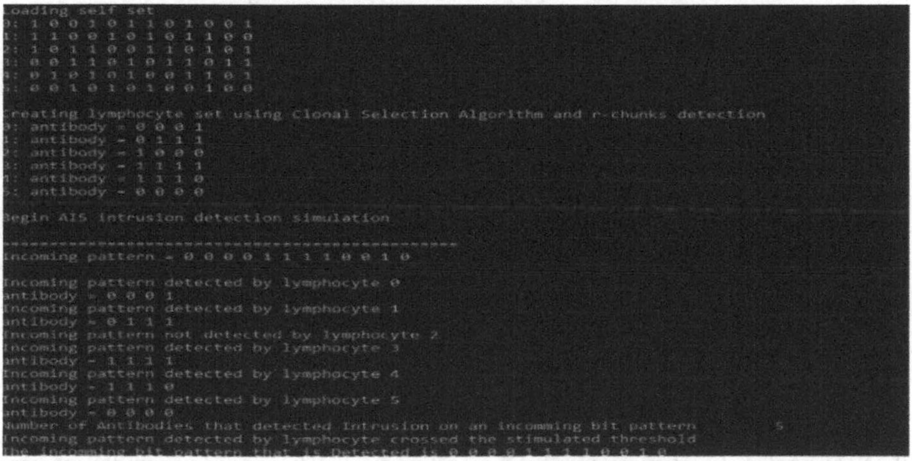

Fig. 4. Intrusion detection

5   Conclusion

This paper depicts a defense mechanism inspired from the human immune system. Our human body consist of many cells. The cells interact with one another. When a virus enters our body it is the antibodies that detect the virus. In the same manner we have created a network of existing nodes and antibodies which should detect any malicious node that enters the network. We have only detected the suspicious ones but in our future work, we planned to refine the proposed algorithm with a better and efficient output to make a network that can be much secured and which can be used for implementing proactive prevention security mechanisms, based on the identification.

References

1. EshghiShargh, A.: Using artificial immune system on implementation of intrusion detection systems. In: Third UKSim European Symposium on Computer Modeling and Simulation, pp. 164–168 (2009)
2. Mazurczyk, W., Rzeszutko, E.: Security -a perpetual war: lessons from nature. IT Professional, vol. 17, pp. 16–22 (2015)
3. Kermanshahi, S.K., Salleh, M.: Towards the security issues in mobile ad hoc networks. Int. J. Innov. Res. Inf. Secur. (IJIRIS) **2**, 22–27 (2015)
4. Abdelhadi, A., Mous, L.M.: The use of artificial immune system algorithms in monitoring industrial. In: 6th International Conference on Sciences of Electronics, Technologies of Information and Telecommunications, SETIT. IEEE, pp. 50–55 (2012)
5. Alberts, B., Johnson, A., Lewis, J., Raff, M.: Immunobiology: The Immune System in Health and Disease, 5th edn (2008). ISBN 978-0815341055
6. Widmaier, E.P., Hershel, R., Strang, K.T.: Mechanisms of Body, 9th edn. McGraw-Hill Global Education Holdings, pp. 701–7011. ISBN 978-0072437935 (2014)
7. Molnar, C., Gair, J.: Concepts of Biology. 1st Canadian edn. OpenStax College (2015)
8. Owen, J.A., Punt, J., Stranford, S.A., Jones, P.P., Kuby, J.: Kuby Immunology, 7th edn. W H Freeman Co (Sd) (2013). ISBN 1464119910
9. Sankar, S.A.: Review of Microbiology and Immunology. McGraw-Hill Education/Medical (2014). ISBN 0071818111
10. Sompayrac, L.: How the Immune System Works, 4th edn. Wiley Blackwell (1999). ISBN 13: 978-1118997772
11. Kumar, G.V.P., Reddy, D.K.: An agent based intrusion detection system for wireless network with Artificial Immune System (AIS) and negative clone selection. In: 2014 International Conference on Electronic Systems, Signal Processing and Computing Technologies, pp. 429–433 (2014)
12. Noeparast, E.B., Banirostam, T.: A cognitive model of immune system for increasing security in distributed systems. In: 2012 UKSim 14th International Conference on Computer Modelling and Simulation, pp. 181–186 (2012)
13. Hosseinpour, F., Bakar, K.A., Hardoroudi, A.H., Dareshur, A.F.: Design of a new distributed model for Intrusion Detection System based on Artificial Immune System. In: 2010 6th International Conference on Advanced Information Management and Service (IMS), pp. 378–383 (2010)

14. Johny, D.C., Haripriya, P.V., Anju, J.S.: Negative selection algorithm: a survey. Int. J. Sci. Eng. Technol. Res. (IJSETR) **6**(4) (2017)

15. Nguyen, V.T., Nguyen, X.H., Luong, C.M.: A novel combination of negative and positive selection in Artificial Immune Systems. In: The 2013 RIVF International Conference on Computing Communication Technologies - Research, Innovation, and Vision for Future (RIVF), pp. 6–11 (2013)

16. Haripriya, P.V., Anju, J.S.: An AIS based anomaly detection system. In: 2017 International Conference on Computing Methodologies and Communication (ICCMC), pp. 708–711 (2017)

17. Seresht, N.A., Azmi, R., Pishgoo, B.: A new clonal selection algorithm based on radius regularization of anomaly detectors. In: The 16th CSI International Symposium on Artificial Intelligence and Signal Processing (AISP 2012), pp. 497–502 (2012)

18. Ansari, M.S.A., Inamullah, M.: Misbehavior detection in mobile adhoc networks using artificial immune system approach. In: 2011 Fifth IEEE International Conference on Advanced Telecommunication Systems and Networks (ANTS), pp. 1–6 (2011)

Fault Aware Improved Clustering Algorithm to Improve Execution Time of the Cloudlets

Jasleen Kaur[✉] and Kamaljit Kaur

Computer Engineering and Technology, Guru Nanak Dev University,
Amritsar, India
Kaurjasleen93@yahoo.com, Kamal.aujla86@gmail.com

Abstract. With the development of web and its clients, Cloud computing, with its Quality of service and on-interest administrations, incredible possibilities in ease, has transformed into an ensuring figuring stage for both business and non-business computation clients. It is an interactive innovation as it gives combination of programming and resources which are powerfully adaptable. The dynamic condition of cloud brings about different faults and failures. The ability of the system to respond unexpected problems is known as fault tolerance. Various fault detection techniques are proposed to avoid and enhance failure tolerance in cloud with end goal to make it power efficient. In our proposed work DCLCA (Dynamic clustering league championship algorithm) is used for failure aware task scheduling that reduces faults but less energy efficient. To make it energy efficient VM consolidation operation is performed. The proposed mechanism enhances the performance in terms of fault tolerance rate and Makespan.

Keywords: Fault tolerance · DCLCA · Consolidation · Energy efficient

1 Introduction

Cloud is a critical and remarkable achievement of grid, web 2.0 and service oriented architecture. It provides extendibility to the devices having limited resources on pay per use basis. Heavy dependency on cloud leads to dramatic situations such as failures that must be tackled to provide reliable services. Failure aware scheduling strategies are devised to tackle faulty environment within cloud computing. These fault aware scheduling schemes are described in this paper. Load driven environment is presented over the virtual machines. In case load exceeded the threshold values then migration of task to other VM takes place and rest of the job is executed at the fittest virtual machine. Scheduling schemes considered in this approach consider Datacenter oriented application. To better understand fault and failure oriented environments description is also presented. Overall objective is to achieve the mechanism to enhance fault tolerance rate and reduce execution time in future endeavors.

Cloud computing provides solution to resource sharing through broker aware environment is provided. As more and more users interact with cloud, problem of reliability creeps in. Reliability in terms of resource availability and task allocation is specified in this literature. Reliability enhancement can be ensured using the

© Springer Nature Singapore Pte Ltd. 2019
A. K. Luhach et al. (Eds.): ICAICR 2018, CCIS 956, pp. 388–400, 2019.
https://doi.org/10.1007/978-981-13-3143-5_32

mechanisms of fault tolerance. Fault tolerance and energy efficiency has been researched upon issues that are still under consideration. Cloud computing provides mechanism to provide resources to the clients on pay per use basis. As the resources are utilized, energy is consumed. Most of the work research is oriented towards minimization of energy consumption while resources are utilized. Services with cloud computing is provided on the basis of service level agreement [7]. The layers division indicates the level of services required by the client [6]. Cloud computing provide concurrent access of resources on shared basis. But by allowing the users to access the resources, energy consumption significantly increases. To tackle the issue, monitors were established to check the usage of resources [12]. In most of the cases broker acts as a monitoring mechanism for resources. Task of broker is to map the cloudlet towards the VM [19]. The load allocation however considers resource available with the virtual machine along with load the current VM has. The load allocation and diversification is the main task of broker. Our contribution is to provide fault resistant resource utilization mechanism by the use of LCA with maximum resource first algorithm. In the faulty environment if the VM fails then live VM migration approach using pre copy approach is used. The main purpose of using this approach is that migration time and downtime is improved as memory states are saved initially to destination VM from source VM when fault is occurred.

Rest of the paper is organized as under: Sect. 2 gives the literature survey of techniques used to conserve energy within cloud, Sect. 3 gives the proposed system, Sect. 4 gives the experimental setup, Sect. 5 gives the performance analysis, Sect. 6 gives the conclusion and future scope.

2 Literature Survey

As of late, numerous techniques are divided to achieve energy efficiency. Primarily stress is given towards dynamic scheduling which forms clusters and allocate load league championship algorithm. It is the most appropriate strategy to allot load to most fit virtual machine and achieve optimization [13]. In addition to LCA, shortest seek time associated with the jobs can also be considered to allot the load to the virtual machines [8]. Load allocation can significantly affects the performance in terms of latency or delay in execution of job. For this, load balancing strategies can be used.

Cloud computing is dynamic in nature. In other words, load allotment and distribution prediction is uncertain [14]. This literature considers the dynamic mechanism to check for faults occurring due to the application or load over the virtual machine because of the contrasts between the typical and real conduct of the framework [10]. It defers the administration and affects parameters like execution, transmission capacity, preparing time, unwavering quality and so on. The impacts of faults are adverse to the point that the conservative condition of the specialist organization is damaged [15]. Indeed, even subsequent to cloud computing has not yet achieved the level of trust expected by clients and fault taking care of cloud is viewed as an open test in cloud computing [10]. The number of faults that can occur in cloud are given below:

1. *Parametric faults*: The faults happened because of the different nature of the parameters that mismatch while invoking the virtual machine or cloudlets and parametric faults appear.
2. *System faults*: System faults occur due to inappropriate information available about the logic of the development system.
3. *Configuration faults*: Faults related to the mismatch associated with the platform required by the application is termed as configuration faults.
4. *Software faults*: Problems within the logic of the program or bugs are termed as software faults.
5. *Hardware faults*: Faults appearing because of hardware crash are known as hardware faults.
6. *Resource dispute faults*: These faults are the resultants of the contention when an asset is being shared for the execution.
7. *Stochastic faults*: Due to inadequate factual data to survey the framework are called stochastic faults.
8. *Participant faults*: These faults happen because of the contention between cloud members like buyer, supplier, administrator, and so on.
9. *Constraint faults*: When a fault condition occurs & disregarded by the dependable specialist, the faults are called constraint faults.
10. *Retrospective faults*: The faults happened because of the absence of data about the past conduct of the framework are called review faults.

Among all extraordinary sort of failures or faults, for example, hub failures and connection failures, the faults that are extremely exorbitant and set asides longer opportunity to relieve are Hardware Failures [11]. In addition to the above said faults which have covered almost all types, one more type of fault that can harm the complete system adversely includes storage fault [1]. Storage fault can occur out of the failure of hard disk drive or any other media used in the cloud for fast storage and retrieval. In the event of cloud computing, a few VMs are running on a solitary physical machine. In such a domain, if an equipment failure happens, at that point all the VMs must be moved that bring about longer downtime when contrasted with a product or application failure [17]. In addition, the equipment gadget may require to be supplanted, bringing about longer repair times. The equipment failures have huge influence on execution time and the solution of which may include (a) gadget substitution, and (b) movements, including VM relocations, which causes the recuperation time to increment [16]. Cloud computing frameworks keep on growing in their scale and multifaceted nature, it is of basic significance to guarantee the dependability and accessibility [3, 18]. The uproarious situations are vulnerable to failure in light of fluctuating execution conditions, expansion and expulsion of framework parts, visit updates and redesigns, online repairs, escalated workload. The unwavering quality of such frameworks can be easily bargained if the proactive measures are not taken to handle the conceivable failures developing in the noisy subsystems [4].

Reliability in Cloud. Fault resistance, dependability and strength in Cloud Computing are of fundamental significance to guarantee persistent activity and right outcomes, even within the sight of a given greatest measure of faulty segments [20]. Most existing examination and executions centre around engineering particular answers for present fault resistance. This infers clients must tailor their applications by considering condition particular fault tolerant highlights. Such a need brings about non straightforward and rigid Cloud situations, requiring excessively push to engineers and clients. This paper presents an inventive point of view on making and overseeing fault tolerance that covers the execution elements of the dependability. This enables clients to determine and apply the coveted level of fault resistance without requiring any information about its execution.

Energy Optimization. Energy optimization is achieved in cloud computing by reducing the amount of workload present over the virtual machine [16]. Dynamic scheduling algorithm required to tackle the needs of every virtual machines within the datacenter. The energy optimization can also be achieved by selecting the high power datacenter for processing of job. Makepsan and flowtime considerably reduced using the said literature.

Virtualization and Resource Scheduling. Virtualization innovation has been generally used to virtualize single server into different servers, enhances its productivity [10]. Li, Chen present a Greedy Particle Swarm Optimization (G&PSO) based calculation to take care of the undertaking planning issue. It utilizes a ravenous calculation to rapidly understand the underlying molecule estimation of a molecule swarm enhancement calculation got from a virtual machine-based cloud stage. G&PSO calculation exhibits enhanced virtual machine productivity and asset use contrasted and the conventional molecule swarm advancement calculation.

Dynamic Power Management. Zhong examines an incorporated approach for accomplishing fault resistance and vitality reserve funds progressively m-slept with frameworks. Fault resistance is accomplished by means of checkpointing, and vitality is spared utilizing Dynamic Voltage Scaling (DVS) [2]. The creators show an attainability investigation for checkpointing plans for a consistent processor speed and also for variable processor speeds. DVS is then done based on the practicality examination.

Resource Utilization. Present-days, cloud makes an accomplishment in different fields, for example, monetary exchange, logical computing etc. [5]. Unwavering Quality and Availability are most imperative between cloud supplier and client. Fault resilience assumes a noteworthy part to use cloud administrations for industry and logical particular purposes. In the current framework, Primary Backup (PB) show is utilized, however it doesn't contain any unique asset apportioning component. Zhou, Wang propose a dynamic asset assigning component with fault resistance to enhance asset use. They join a reinforcement covering component and proficient VM movement technique for planning novel Dynamic Fault Tolerant Scheduling Mechanism for Real Time Tasks in cloud computing. The proposed demonstration goes for accomplishing both fault resilience and high asset use in the cloud. The investigations are assessed utilizing arbitrary engineered workload and Google cloud & follow logs to test the productivity of the proposed show.

By surveying the above research we reviewed the number of problems like energy consumption, resource utilization and reliability in cloud etc. These all problems slow down the system or decrease the efficiency of system due to those faults that are occurring in the system. To get rid of this, we migrate our tasks to virtual machines using pre copy approach and complete its work. In our proposed methodology, in the case of fault occurring, we migrate our tasks to virtual machine by knowing its resource utilization or resource requirements. We compare the execution time of each task that how much time a particular VM take for completion of its job. This job migration will be done by migrating the job to a fittest machine that can complete our job in less time. This process will work for all the tasks till all the jobs finished.

The League Championship Algorithm [9] employed selects only the optimal virtual machine having optimal or best possible virtual machine for operation. The problem, however, arises when there are more cloudlets as compared to virtual machines in the system. The starvation will cause the performance of the system goes down considerably. To overcome this problem, the proposed system uses LCA with proportionate virtual machine selections along with live VM migration using pre copy approach. In case of faulty environment as VM fail, VM migration becomes critical. VM migration help saving the progress to some other VM and execution can begin from the place where it is left off, hence saving considerable amount of time while executing a current job.

3 Proposed System

The dynamic clustering algorithm uses the mechanism to incorporate tasks dynamically that means at run time. VM list contains list of virtual machines based on league championship algorithm. In LCA resource consideration is made without establishing the compatibility of cloudlet with virtual machine [9]. It will find optimized VM while allocation of the resources which means dynamic allocation has to be done. In proposed literature cloudlet sorting along with virtual machine sorting for compatibility establishment is made. In this we arrange the VM and cloudlets according to resources. Resources requirements is checked against the virtual machine resources which if not matched, then next VM for resources is checked. The main reason of sorting them is to make them compatible to each other. League championship algorithm is also used to determine optimal virtual machine obtained after comparing the resources of VM and assigning probability in terms of heavy resource availability. In case same VM is selected again and again for job allocation fault and failure may appear within the system. Every VM has certain capacity associated with it. As jobs are allotted to virtual machine its capacity exhausted after certain number of jobs causing faults to appear within the system. To tackle the issue, live VM migration is associated within the proposed system. For VM migration the pre copy approach is utilized. In this approach first of all initial and destination VM is selected and then memory state of VM is pre copied. After that migration is performed and all transfer from initial state to destination is to be done. The main advantage of this approach is that migration time is improved as initial memory states are saved and down time is also improved. As the faults appear within the system, VM migration is initiated and hence current failed machines put to halt state. As long as VM is not restored to stable state, no more load is dispersed on the VM allowing degradation of faults.

Existing algorithms not taking fault management as a factor while scheduling tasks. In general, same virtual machine selection may cause cloudlet loss along with high energy consumption. These problems are formulated as under

- The time when server is down becomes a problem if job cannot successfully execute on current machine and other tasks required wait indefinitely causing starvation.
- Fault tolerance rate is not considered or no significant proof is given about fault tolerance rate of LCA.

3.1   Objectives of Study

The objectives achieved through proposed system is given as under

- Using compatibility establishment with the Virtual machine and cloudlets in terms of probability. For migration the pre copy approach is utilized. Higher the probability associated with the VM corresponding to cloudlet, more chances of VM selection ispresent. In other words, optimized VM will be selected.
- Compatibility causes optimal VM selection, hence cloudlet execution rate improvement is achieved. VM resources are checked according to cloudlet requirements. The requirements of cloudlet if matched with the resources then allocation is achieved.
- Higher fault tolerance rate achievement through the proposed system. As and when faults appear within the system, migration is initiated causing resilient network to be formed.

3.2   Methodology

The flow of proposed system is given through algorithm as under

    Input: Task List (Cloudlets)

    Output: Makespan, Fault tolerance rate

1. Gather the information about the VM_list

    Broker aware monitoring is used to check status of virtual machine resources.

2. Compute Execution time of each task (burst Time)
3. Exchange the information about VM to each Cluster.

    Cluster consists of cloudlets with specific need. This need is on the basis of resources (CPU, RAM, Bandwidth). Cloudlets with minimum resource requirements are given one cluster, Cloudlet with intermediate requirements form another cluster. This process continues until all the jobs are classified into appropriate clusters.

    For j = 1: N

    For i = 1: size (Cloudlets)

    If (Cloudlet_req$_i$ <= Cluster$_j$)

    Cluster$_j$ = Cloudlet$_i$

    End of if

    End of for

End of for
The information to the cluster is conveyed using VM allocation method.
If alloc == 1
Go to next VM
Else
Add to a list compatible VM
End of
4. Perform task allocation to fittest VM on the basis of parameters(RAM, CPU, Bandwidth)
Fitness_Function = max (*VM* (*RAM, PES, BW*))
where PES is number of processing elements and BW is bandwidth.
5. If (VM_Fail)
   a. Add VM to failed List
   b. Discover another VM from VM_LIST on the basis of RAM, CPU, Bandwidth.
   c. Migrate the task to that VM (Resource Provisioning Strategy for VM selection is on the basis of number of CPU, Bandwidth and RAM VMs possess)
   d. Perform LIVEVM migration using Pre Copy Approach
   e. Check for Task_Failure if yes goto step a.
      Else
   a. Add to fittest_machine
   b. Task Execution Finish
      End of if
6. Perform step 5 continuously for every cloudlet

4   Experimental Setup

The experiment is conducted in cloudsim 4.0. Total of 50 virtual machines are employed within 2 datacenters. 2 hosts are configured within each datacenter. Time shared policy is implemented to share the virtual machines among the jobs or task. 512 MB RAM is used with each Virtual machine. Image size is of 20,000 BM, Number of processing elements with each VM is 1. Total of 100 cloudlets with 40000 image size are created to demonstrate the simulation process.

There are two scenarios which are used to evaluate the proposed system. There are two scenarios which are used to evaluate the proposed system. First scenario takes the workload in two forms without considering faults and failures. This workload includes uniform and bursty distribution. The results are obtained in terms of fault tolerance rate and makespan.

In the second scenario, faults are injected manually within the proposed system to check the resilient nature of the proposed system. In cloudsim, we have created a bug method. This bug method causes the resource preemption from the VM causing it to fail. A result does not show much deviation hence fault tolerance rate is improved.

This setup is used to evaluate the validity of the proposed system.

5 Performance Analysis and Results

The results are obtained in terms of makespan and total fault tolerance rate achieved through the system.

Result in terms of makespan is obtained indicating total time required to execute current set of cloudlets. Makespan is calculated using the following formula:

$$Makespan = \sum_{i=1}^{n} Job\_Finish\_time_i$$

Here 'i' indicates jobs and 'n' indicates total number of jobs

Fault tolerance rate indicates total jobs that are successfully completed even with the occurrence of faults within the system. Fault tolerance rate is given in terms of total cloudlet submitted to the total number of successfully finished cloudlets. The overall execution obtained should be divided with total faults incurred in order to obtained fault tolerance. Fault tolerance rate is evaluated as:

$$Fault_{tolerance_{rate}} = \sum_{i=1}^{n} \left(\frac{Jobs_{Executed_i}}{Total_{Jobs_{Submitted_i}}} \right) \Big/ Total\_Faults_i$$

'Total' indicates cloudlets which are submitted and 'finished' indicates cloudlets that are successfully finished.

Scenario 1
Distribution of Cloudlets without considering faults and failures
Figures 1, 2, 3 and 4 indicate the parameter deviation with the size of the cloudlets. Performance shows degradation as the number of cloudlets increases in terms of makespan. The prime reason is the schedule required to complete the job increases and hence execution time increases. Fault tolerance rate also reduced since jobs may not be able to finish in time as fault appear within the system. The workload can be uniform or bursty.

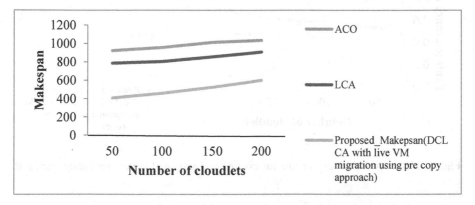

Fig. 1. Describes makespan for existing and proposed system for uniform workload

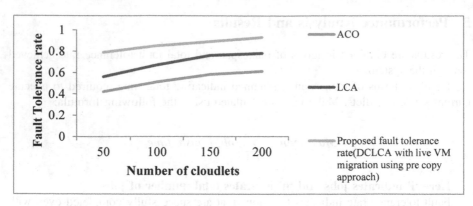

Fig. 2. Describes fault tolerance rate for existing and proposed system for uniform workload

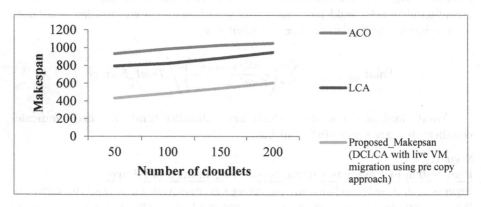

Fig. 3. Describes makespan for existing and proposed system for bursty workload

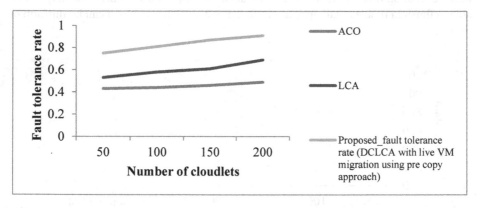

Fig. 4. Describes fault tolerance rate for existing and proposed system for bursty workload

Figures 1 and 2 describe the workload distribution which is uniform in nature. Performance evolution is done in terms of makespan and fault tolerance degree.

Figures 3 and 4 describe the workload distribution which is bursty in nature. Random faults introduce problems in terms of job execution and also load on single VM may become high due to the arrival of faults. Evolution show great deviation in result as workload encountered is heavy in this case. Fault tolerance rate decreases and makespan increases in this case.

Scenario 2

Figures 5 and 6 give the performance degradation when **manually fault is introduced** within the system. Proposed system shows deviation however small in terms of makespan and fault tolerance degree. As the migration initiates because of failure of VM, overhead in terms of makespan increases. In proposed system, this overhead is negligible and does not affect overall system performance. The VM migration is initiated using the following mechanism.

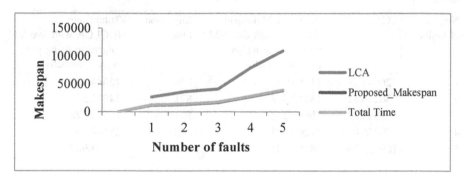

Fig. 5. Describes makespan for existing and proposed system when random faults are introduced

    If (VM is instantiated ())// if this statement is true then migration is required. Select VM from VM list for migration

I = i+1

VM_i = $VMList_i$

End of if

    This method initiates migration to next VM from within VM list. After performing the migration task starts from where it is left over hence negligible overhead is encountered and reliability enhances (Table 1).

    Makespan = Job_Burst_Time*Number_Jobs

    Total time = Makespan +Migration_Time

    In case random faults are introduced within the system, result degradation or performance deviation is given collaboratively as:

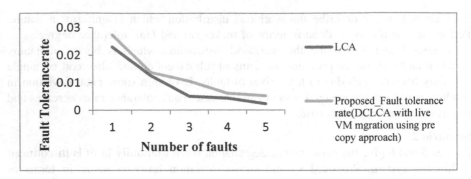

Fig. 6. Describes fault tolerance rate for existing and proposed system when random faults are introduced

Table 1. Describes makespan for existing and proposed system when random faults are introduced.

Number of faults	LCA	Proposed_Makespan (DCLCA with live VM migration using pre copy approach)	Migration time	Total time (DCLCA with live VM migration using pre copy approach)
1	26644.69	11856.955	828	12684.955
2	36236.81	13132.517	871	14003.517
3	41083.72	16683.272	891	17574.272
4	79256.072	27267.104	922	28189.104
5	109523.76	38154.902	949	39103.902

6 Conclusion and Future Scope

Dynamic clustering and league championship algorithms collaborated with VM migration using pre-copy approach enhanced the performance in terms of Makespan. Makespan is reduced considerably using the proposed mechanism. In case of fault and failure, VM migration is used as a backup. Migration is performed on fittest machine. The viability of the proposed approach is tested using faulty and fault free environments. The result section demonstrated the worth of the study as results shows improvement.

The proposed approach with dynamic clustering and pre-copy approach however does not tackle the issues present within datacenters and in future datacenter migration along with dynamic clustering can be used for enhancing degree of fault tolerance.

References

1. Kaur, K., Kaur, N., Kaur, K.: A novel context and load-aware family genetic algorithm based task scheduling in cloud computing. In: Satapathy, S.C., Bhateja, V., Raju, K., Janakiramaiah, B. (eds.) Data Engineering and Intelligent Computing. AISC, vol. 542, pp. 521–531. Springer, Singapore (2018). https://doi.org/10.1007/978-981-10-3223-3_51
2. Zhong, Z., Chen, K., Zhai, X., Zhou, S.: Virtual machine-based task scheduling algorithm in a cloud computing environment. Tsinghua Sci. Technol. **21**, 660–667 (2016)
3. Soniya, J., Sujana, J.A.J., Revathi, T.: Dynamic fault tolerant scheduling mechanism for real time tasks in cloud computing. In: International Conference on Electrical Electronics and Optimization Techniques ICEEOT 2016, pp. 124–129 (2016)
4. Zhang, Y., Chakrabarty, K.: A unified approach for fault tolerance and dynamic power management in fixed-priority real-time embedded systems. IEEE Trans. Comput. Des. Integr. Circuits Syst. **25**, 111–125 (2006)
5. Zhou, A., et al.: Cloud service reliability enhancement via virtual machine placement optimization. IEEE Trans. Serv. Comput. **10**, 902–913 (2017)
6. Boru, D., Kliazovich, D., Granelli, F., Bouvry, P., Zomaya, A.Y.: Energy-efficient data replication in cloud computing datacenters. Cluster Comput. **18**, 385–402 (2015)
7. Abbas, N., Zhang, Y., Taherkordi, A., Skeie, T.: Mobile edge computing: a survey. IEEE Internet Things J. **5**, 450–465 (2018)
8. Kaur, K., Garg, S., Aujla, G.S., Kumar, N., Rodrigues, J.J.P.C., Guizani, M.: Edge computing in the industrial Internet of things environment: software-defined- networks-based edge-cloud interplay. IEEE Commun. Mag. **56**, 44–51 (2018)
9. Abdulhamid, S.M., AbdLatiff, M.S., Madni, S.H.H., Abdullahi, M.: Fault tolerance aware scheduling technique for cloud computing environment using dynamic clustering algorithm. Neural Comput. Appl. **29**, 279–293 (2018)
10. Li, Y., Chen, M., Dai, W., Qiu, M.: Energy optimization with dynamic task scheduling mobile cloud computing. IEEE Syst. J. **11**, 1–10 (2015)
11. Nadu, T.: Fault tolerant workflow scheduling based on replication and resubmission of tasks in cloud computing. Int. J. Comput. Sci. Eng. **4**, 996–1006 (2012)
12. Gokhroo, M.K., Govil, M.C., Pilli, E.S.: Detecting and mitigating faults in cloud computing environment. In: 3rd IEEE International Conference (2017)
13. Kaur, J., Kinger, S.: Efficient algorithm for fault tolerance in cloud computing. Int. J. Comput. Sci. Inf. Technol. **5**, 6278–6281 (2014)
14. Nguyen, K.K., Cheriet, M.: Environment-aware virtual slice provisioning in green cloud environment. IEEE Trans. Serv. Comput. **8**, 507–519 (2015)
15. Lin, X., Wang, Y., Xie, Q., Pedram, M.: Task scheduling with dynamic voltage and frequency scaling for energy minimization in the mobile cloud computing environment. IEEE Trans. Serv. Comput. **8**, 175–186 (2015)
16. Prathiba, S., Sowvarnica, S.: Survey of failures and fault tolerance in cloud. In: Proceedings of 2017 2nd International Conference on Computing and Communicaions Technologies ICCCT 2017, pp. 169–172 (2017)
17. Ping, F., Li, X., McConnell, C., Vabbalareddy, R., Hwang, J.: Towards optimal data replication across data centers. In: 2011 31st International Conference on Distributed Computing Systems Workshop, pp. 66–71 (2011)
18. Wu, K., Lu, P., Zhu, Z.: Distributed online scheduling and routing of multicast-oriented tasks for profit-driven cloud computing. IEEE Commun. Lett. **20**, 684–687 (2016)

19. Jhawar, R., Piuri, V., Santambrogio, M.: A comprehensive conceptual system-level approach to fault tolerance in cloud computing. In: Proceedings of 2012 IEEE International System Conference on SysCon 2012, pp. 601–605 (2012)
20. Zhang, Y., Zheng, Z., Lyu, M.R.: BFTCloud: a byzantine fault tolerance framework for voluntary-resource cloud computing. In: Proceedings of 2011 IEEE 4th International Conference on Cloud Computing CLOUD 2011, pp. 444–451 (2011)

Cooperative Mitigation of DDoS Attacks Using an Optimized Auction Scheme on Cache Servers

Prachi Gulihar and B. B. Gupta[✉]

National Institute of Technology, Kurukshetra, Kurukshetra, India
prachigulihar2@gmail.com, gupta.brij@gmail.com

Abstract. Distributed Denial of Service (DDoS) attack is one of the most prevalent attacks on the internet today which attacks the availability of the server by resource and bandwidth depletion exhaustion. Many mechanisms exist to fight against DDoS attack, a set of which are the cooperative defense mechanisms which work in a distributed manner and are more robust. This work makes use of one of the latest meta-heuristic optimization techniques, Whale Optimization Algorithm (WOA) to find underutilized internet cache servers which are in best position to absorb DDoS flood. These multiple caches will absorb a part of the attack flood thus preventing the victim's network from getting congested. For effective allocation of these cache resources a Continuous Double Auction (CDA) mechanism is applied. It is more flexible and efficient as it allows simultaneous bidding by sellers and buyers. The cache servers are selected through multi-objective WOA in MATLAB and then the auction platform is set-up using Actor Model. In cooperative defense, selection of a pricing strategy which maximizes collateral profit is very important so a round-wise bidding strategy is implemented which promotes long-term participation. For evaluation of the scheme, the workload traces of distributed servers are used to generate three scenarios under different attack load conditions. Depending on the supply-demand of free cache resources, the results show that the proposed algorithm has high detection rate of close optimum solutions. This leads to increased throughput because the attack traffic is not only shared, but is shared in a balanced way.

Keywords: Flooding distributed denial of service attack · Cooperative defense DDoS mitigation · Resource allocation

1 Introduction

Distributed denial of service (DDoS) attack [1] is one of the biggest challenges faced by the internet community today. They are performed by the slave machines which are a part of botnet army and act on the commands of the master machine whose motive is to exhaust network and server resources like bandwidth and storage so that its services become unavailable to the legitimate clients. The largest reported DDoS attack was of volume 400 Gpbs in year 2014 [2]. Since then the DDoS attacks are growing in volume. Their efficiency and implementation techniques have become more

© Springer Nature Singapore Pte Ltd. 2019
A. K. Luhach et al. (Eds.): ICAICR 2018, CCIS 956, pp. 401–412, 2019.
https://doi.org/10.1007/978-981-13-3143-5_33

sophisticated day by day making it a big challenge for the security professionals. Figure 1 shows the distribution of various kinds of DDoS attacks the systems are prone to, with 65% of the attacks being the volumetric attacks which are mainly caused by floods of User Datagram Protocol and Internet Control Message Protocol packets. This work focuses on defending this volumetric DDoS attack flood.

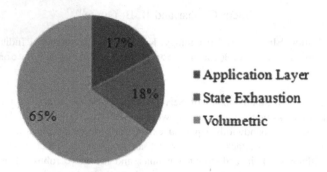

Fig. 1. Types of DDoS attacks

The DDoS attack scenario can be divided into attack phase, detection phase and response phase. The difference between a DoS attack and a DDoS attack is that a DDoS attack is launched from different machines whereas the DoS attack involves only single attacking machine which makes it difficult to fight against DDoS attack. When the attacker machines perform in cooperation then for the defense mechanism to be strong it should also be in cooperation. In a cooperative mechanism the defense mechanism is performed in cooperation with other nodes which may lie on the victim-end, source-end or in the network. This overcomes the major drawback of the centralised defense mechanism where there is single point of failure when the central kingpin point of defense itself comes under attack. Although many cooperative techniques have been developed, but they are rarely deployed in the real world because the researchers have long ignored the economic incentive part in the working of cooperatives DDoS mechanisms. Due to lack of incremental payment structures the cooperation between the nodes fails. Sometimes the payment structures are non-existent and in some cases the payment structure is in place but the incentives are not lucrative enough for the nodes to share their resources. Figure 2 shows the timeline depicting the evolution of DDoS exploits and their counter defenses starting from software bugs to traffic flood. The recent defense mechanism involves cooperative traffic control.

Internet comprises of several cache servers which may not be fully utilized. These unused cache capacities can be utilized in cooperative DDoS defense. The traffic flood can be diverted to these multiple servers each handling only a fraction of attack traffic thus preventing congestion from the attack flood. This resource is already existing and will incur meagre costs to the parties involved but management of network resources is one of the most essential issues of Internet. The heuristic techniques of optimization have always been the backbone in solving economic engineering problems and so the main task of the double auction mechanism used in this work is not only to increase the

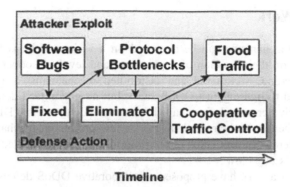

Fig. 2. Evolution of DDoS attacks

utility of free cache resources but also promote sustainable individual profits in the long-run. For any cooperative DDoS defense mechanism to be efficient, the resource allocation scheme should be fair any must incentivize the participants to collaborate. The proposed model meets the following design goals [3]:

- *Combination of services:* The marketplace mechanism should allow the users to express complementary requirements like does the victim machine only wants the excess traffic to be diverted and absorbed or it also wants the server to analyze the traffic and report the feedback. Such a combination of services increases the usability of the scheme.
- *Flexibility and predictability:* Depending on the size of the traffic flood at any server, the supply and demand of the free caches in the internet will change dynamically over time. So the buyer will desire an anticipated deal which can be modified and adjusted with changing needs.
- *Economic efficiency:* The provider of the resource and the buyer of the resource both of them desire effective allocation of resources. The policy design should maximize the gains of the participating parties and should minimize the wastage of the resource. So adopting an optimized approach is beneficial.
- *Double-sided competition:* Fair exchange of services should be encouraged between the service providers and the user, the victim machine in this case. The prices should solely depend on the condition of supply and demand and should neither be biased to seller nor to buyer. The market mechanism proposed here is based on double-sided auction model in which the buyers and sellers compete with one another.
- *Functional constraints:* In designing any economic incentive policy, socio-economic objective function needs to be combined with constraints of the network. For optimal results, it is important that the objective function is multi-objective like the basis for the objective functions should depend on multiple attributes like bandwidth, latency, utilization and storage constraints considered while designing the proposed approach.

2 Related Work

DDoS defense mechanisms can be classified on a variety of basis like they can be classified based on their location of deployment and level of cooperation from other nodes as source-end, victim-end and distributed mechanisms. Many methods are already proposed to fight against DDoS attack but no guaranteed defense mechanism exists till now. Numerous solutions have been developed to combat DDoS attack using collaborative schemes in their mechanisms. A few prominent mechanisms suggested till 2018 that catered to formulation of our proposed scheme presented in the following section are discussed below.

Steinberger et al. [4], have proposed a collaborative DDoS defense strategy using flow based event exchange format (FLEX) to exchange event information related to security. They have tried to shift the defense mechanism from victim side to the network of Internet Service Providers (ISP) and their trusted partners. Among several available formats like Incident Object Description Exchange Format, Abuse Reporting Format etc., they have made use of FLEX exchange format in ISPs which makes it possible to deploy this strategy without making any major modifications in the current network infrastructure of network operators.

Rashidi et al. [5], have proposed a collaborative DDoS defense scheme using network function virtualization. Many DDoS defense mechanisms are not hardware compatible with the existing network infrastructure. To overcome this drawback they have made use of emerging technology of network function virtualization by making a domain to domain collaborative network which filters the excessive incoming traffic. For optimal resource allocation they have made use of stakelberg game model. The CoFence framework developed facilitates the resource sharing but it itself may become a target of betrayal, tamper and collusion attacks.

Devi and Yogesh [6], have proposed a hybrid defense mechanism for DDoS attacks at application layer. They have made use of trust information metrics based on information theory. Filtering is done on the basis of the score of the trust value. The rate is further limited based on the user browsing behavior like webpage request order and viewing time elapsed. This two level filtering mechanism gives low false rejection rate and it not only checks the illegitimate traffic but also prevents flooding of legitimate traffic that is flash crowd.

Rodrigues et al. [7], have proposed a cooperative DDOS defense which expands to multiple domains using the signaling process of blockchain. They have overcome a prevalent drawback of existing coordinated DDoS defense mechanism which is signaling of attack information in a distributed environment. The blockchain technology is used for the same which not only signals the information at reduced costs but can also provide financial incentives to cooperate. This happens because of there is no central point management in the system which makes it suitable for collaborative defense. The major drawback of this scheme is absence of any security mechanism to curb misuse.

Kalkan and Alagöz [8], have developed a collaborative filtering based defense mechanism to prevent DDoS attacks. They have proposed a statistical mechanism which filters the traffic based on the current set of attributes like IP address, packet size, destination port number, TTL value, type of protocol and TCP flag. This mechanism called ScoreForCore filters a large volume of the attack packets at the source-end. The score of the packets is calculated based on these attributes and a threshold value is calculated for selective discarding. This cumulative mechanism of scoring is not bound to give accurate results because of dependency on selection of attributes, irrelevant selection may mislead the analysis.

Shuai et al. [9], have used bloom filters to develop a cooperative DDoS defense scheme which is lightweight. They have deployed two counting bloom filters, the first one differentiates among different network topologies by tracing options field of internet packet. The second filter queries the data collected by filter one to identify the suspicious packets and send alert messages to the victim-end. All the connection topologies possible by the router are analyzed by the first bloom filter and the time complexity of querying is O(1). This method has low processing and memory costs.

3 Proposed Approach

In this section, we describe the different components of the proposed cooperative approach to protect the victim machine from DDoS attack. Figure 3 illustrates the architecture of the proposed defense scheme that can be explained by the following modules.

A. **Broker Node:** The broker node acts as the first step of defense. All the traffic destined to the victim server cannot directly reach there, it has to pass through the broker node which comprises of the following sub-module.

- *Fetching Module:* The responsibility of this module is to fetch details from the incoming traffic packets. It fetches information like source IP and Destination IP and forwards this information to the analyzing module.
- *Analyzing Module:* This module gets the information of source IP of the packet as input and compares these IP addresses from the IP addresses stored in the log files of the blacklist server. If the address matches, then the packets are not sent to forwarding module. The payload data is also analysed for similarity in packets.
- *Forwarding Module:* This module decides whether to transfer the packets to victim machine or to the optimal resource allocator (ORA) depending upon the congestion levels of the victim machine link. If the threshold level has reached, then the packets are diverted to ORA module instead of victim machine.

B. **Blacklist Server:** The blacklist server stores the list of IP addresses which have sent malicious packets in the past. This record is regularly updated and stored in the log files as the traffic arrives at the broker node.

C. **Optimal Resource Allocator:** When the traffic overflow occurs then the forwarding module sends the incoming packets to the ORA module which is responsible to divert this traffic flood to helping cache servers using the following sub-modules.

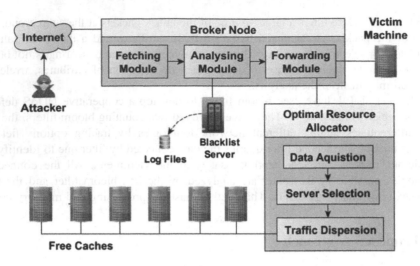

Fig. 3. Architecture of defense scheme

- *Data Acquisition:* This is the premier step of the allocation mechanism. In this step the configuration of the cache server like their utilization, latency, capacity and throughput are collected. The initial bid by the victim is set up according to these parameters.
- *Server Selection:* This module is the policy administrator component [10] of the double auction scheme. Its purpose is to select the server in best position to cooperate among the participating cache servers using whale optimization algorithm.
- *Traffic Dispersion:* This module is the policy deployment component which is diverts the traffic to the cooperative cache servers according to the double auction mechanism implemented on the cache servers selected by the administrator component.

D. **Free Caches:** These are the internet cache servers which are not under full utilization and hence choose to offer their free caches for the cooperative DDoS defense against benefits and economic incentives.

The resource allocation policy used by ORA module can be explained by the following three phases which are executed in a consecutive manner of execution (Fig. 4).

A. **Cache server selection phase:** Undertaking minimization fitness function, the operation of optimal selection of cache servers is done between different participating servers. The WOA algorithm which is used for optimal selection is based on hunting strategy of baleen whale. They use the technique of bubble-net feeding in a circular path to hunt the fishes swimming on the surface. This can be mathematically explained by two stages- exploitation and investigation. Firstly, a best candidate is selected which is close optimum and then other operators accordingly

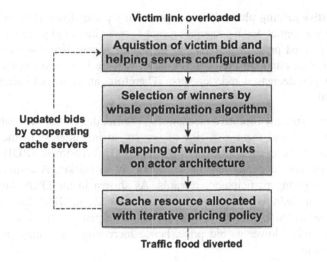

Fig. 4. Flowchart of the proposed algorithm

modify their location to find a better solution from the available data set. Its working can be explained by the following mathematical equations [11]:

$$D = |C.X'[t] - X[t]| \tag{1}$$

$$X[t+1] = X'[t] - A * D \tag{2}$$

Where t is the current iteration, A and C denote the coefficient vectors, X denotes location vector, X' denotes modified location vector. Further, these vectors A and C are described by the following mathematical equations,

$$A = 2 * a * r - a \tag{3}$$

$$C - 2 * r \tag{4}$$

Where r ranges from [0, 1] and a ranges from [2, 0] depicting shrinking of the encircling system in both exploitation and investigation stage.

B. **Resource allocation phase:** For allocation of free cache memory the decision can be made problem using two different approaches dynamic and greedy. The policy administrator component stores the values of the costs offered by different servers and the utility function needs to be maximized for maximum benefit. In this policy we have used greedy approach over dynamic because the greedy approach finds the best local solution at every stage leading to a global solution in the end.

C. **Iterative pricing phase:** The analysis of any policy from a brokering point of view is very essential. Each cooperating cache server has a bid price which is higher than the incurred price of maintaining the cache server. If the server increases its bid price, then although the expected profit will be increased but the winning probability gets decreased and vice-versa. Therefore, an adaptive bidding strategy will be useful.

In designing any incentive mechanism scheme, there exist the problem of incentive cost explosion and there is a risk of servers losing interest in the long run if the incentives received are not at par with Return On Investment (ROI). The dissatisfied servers will not cooperate leading to monopoly in market. A countermeasure of this problem is giving participatory rewards. As shown in the ORA Algorithm, P is the participation credit which is rewarded to the cache server which fails to get a deal. This keeps it motivated to pool the resource. This participation credit is also used by helping server to further lower its bid price, hence increasing its wining probability in next auction round.

Algorithm 1: Broker Module

Input: Incoming traffic X_{in} havingpackets Pk

V[t]: Traffic volume at current instant,

V_{max}: Maximum capacity of channel

Start

Fetch (Pk header, V[t])

If(Source_address[Pk_i]∈blacklist_log

&&payload[Pk_i]==payload[Pk_j])

{   Alert();   //malicious behavior

                          Drop();

                          Update_log();}

Else Fwd_module(){   **If** (V[t] <V_{max})   //normal flow

                          {Fwd_server()

                                {Send[X_{in}] -> server;}}

                          Else Fwd_ORA();   //overflow

Stop

Algorithm 2: ORA Module

```
Input: Cache servers Cs_i, configuration(u,m,t)
        Where, u= server utilization
               m= free cache, t= throughput
Start   WOA(u, m, t);
        fitness = u + (-m) + (-b); // objective function
             If m_reqd> m
                m = -infinity;
                   Else    m = absolute(m_reqd - m);
             If t_reqd> t
                   t = -infinity;
                      Else    t = absolute(t_reqd - t);
Add Cs_i ->winnerlist;                      //optimal servers
Send[winnerlist] ->Auction();
Auction(){Fetch(Rank, winnerlist);
 //utility function at policy administrator component
Utility= (bid_price - incurred_price) * 1/Rank;
Disperse_traffic[X_in] -> Max(Utility[Cs_i])
For all Cs_i
        //iterative pricing at policy deployment component
        If (Cache_NotAllocated)
{P[next_round]=P[previousround]+Incentive[current_round];
           Send(Participation_Credit P)->Cs_i;
           Update_bid()
                   {    New_bid= old_bid - P;
                        Proceed(new_bid);}}
        Else If (Cache_Allocated)
        {    Incentive[current_round]=NULL;
             Proceed(old_bid); }
Stop
```

4 Results and Discussion

We build a prototype of continuous double-auction mechanism using Actor Architecture (AA) [12] and extensive analysis of the double auction mechanism of cache trading is done with key objectives to provide crucial insights on mitigation of the traffic flood. The design of the simulation analysis comprises of Bitbrains dataset [13] of 1250 server machines whose configuration is used for optimal allocation. To select the optimal caches, the MATLAB R2013a version is used in the laptop of Intel COR i3 processor, RAM 4 GB, operating system-64 bit. The schedule of workflows is preprocessed and is fed to the whale algorithm and the results are stored in a CSV file which is inputted to the AA using Engine API.

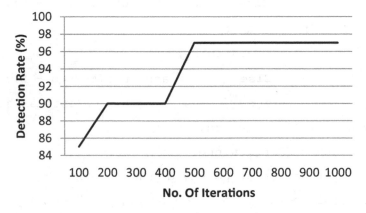

Fig. 5. Detection rate vs. Number if iterations

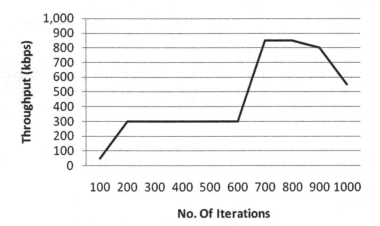

Fig. 6. Throughput vs. Number of iterations

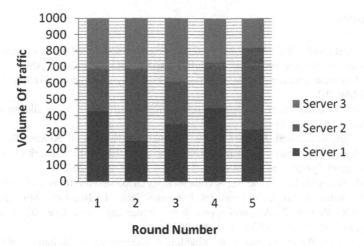

Fig. 7. Distribution of attack traffic among helping servers

The above results illustrate a significant convergence in the detection rate of the optimal cache servers. The detection rate of optimal servers in locality is shown in Fig. 5. The throughput variation of WOA with simulation time of about 3.6 s for 1000 iterations is shown in Fig. 6. Different volumes of cache are traded under different load conditions and an instance of the round wise distribution of attack traffic among different helping cache servers is shown in Fig. 7. This graph shows that the attack traffic is not only diverted to the cache servers but the diversion is done in a proportional and balanced manner.

5   Conclusion and Future Work

The DDoS attacks are evolving with time and the attackers are creating new ways to exhaust the resources. In this paper we have proposed a cooperative DDoS defense scheme where the victim network redirects the excessive traffic flood to other collaborative internet cache servers with partially filled caches. We have specifically focused on resource allocation mechanism which determines how much cache should the cache servers offer to the victim servers so that free cache resource is distributed fairly, efficiently and with incentives to participate in collaborative defense mechanism. In order to make the allocation of resources optimal we used whale optimization algorithm which finds out the cache servers in best position to help on the basis of attributes like bandwidth, latency, memory and server utilization. To make the collaboration fair, we propose a continuous double auction scheme which allows the both victim server and helping servers to offers bids for the free caches at any moment. The simulation results demonstrate that cooperative DDoS defense effectively mitigates the traffic and reduces the impact of the attack and the proposed resource allocation mechanism meets the design goal. Long term participation of the helping servers is ensured by offering incentives in the form of participation credit which improves the collateral profit and this mechanism is easily deployable since the cache servers already exist in the internet network.

References

1. Gupta, B.B., Joshi, R.C., Misra, M.: Defending against distributed denial of service attacks: issues and challenges. Inf. Secur. J.: Glob. Perspect. **18**(5), 224–247 (2009)
2. https://www.calyptix.com/top-threats/ddos-attacks-101-types-targets-motivations/.   Access on 21 Mar 2018
3. Fujiwara, I.: Study on combinatorial auction mechanism for resource allocation in cloud computing environment (2012)
4. Steinberger, J., Kuhnert, B., Sperotto, A., Baier, H., Pras, A.: Collaborative DDoS defense using flow-based security event information. In: 2016 IEEE/IFIP Network Operations and Management Symposium (NOMS), pp. 516–522. IEEE, April 2016
5. Rashidi, B., Fung, C., Bertino, E.: A collaborative DDoS defense framework using network function virtualization. IEEE Trans. Inf. Forensics Secur. **12**(10), 2483–2497 (2017)
6. Devi, S.R., Yogesh, P.: A hybrid approach to counter application layer DDoS attacks. Int. J. Cryptogr. Inf. Secur. (IJCIS) **2**(2), 45 (2012)
7. Rodrigues, B., Bocek, T., Stiller, B.: Enabling a cooperative, multi-domain DDoS defense by a blockchain signaling system (BloSS). Semantic Scholar (2017)
8. Kalkan, K., Alagöz, F.: A distributed filtering mechanism against DDoS attacks: scoreForCore. Comput. Netw. **108**, 199–209 (2016)
9. Shuai, C., Jiang, J., Ouyang, X.: A lightweight cooperative detection framework odfDDoS/DoS attacks based on counting bloom filter. J. Theor. Appl. Inf. Technol. **45**(1), 160–167 (2012)
10. Fortier, D., Spradlin, J.C., Sigroha, P., Fulton, A.: U.S. Patent No. 8,909,751. U.S. Patent and Trademark Office, Washington, D.C. (2014)
11. Mirjalili, S., Lewis, A.: The whale optimization algorithm. Adv. Eng. Softw. **95**, 51–67 (2016)
12. Jang, M.W.: The actor architecture manual. Department of Computer Science, University of Illinois at Urbana-Champaign (2004)
13. Iosup, A., et al.: The grid workloads archive. FGCS **24**(7), 672–686 (2008)

A Comprehensive Study of Mobile Computing in Telemedicine

Atta-ur-Rahman[1], Sujata Dash[2($\boxtimes$)], Mahi Kamaleldin[1], Areej Abed[1], Atheer Alshaikhhussain[1], Heba Motawei[1], Nadeen Al. Amoudi[1], Wejdan Abahussain[1], and Kiran Sultan[3]

[1] College of Computer Science and Information Technology (CCSIT), Department of Computer Science, Imam Abdulrahman Bin Faisal University, P.O. Box 1982, Dammam, Kingdom of Saudi Arabia
aaurrahman@iau.edu.sa, mahi.kamaleldin@gmail.com,
areej.h.abed@gmail.com, atheer.alsh55@gmail.com,
hebamotawei@gmail.com, nadeensaleh94@gmail.com,
wejdan_011@hotmail.com
[2] Department of Computer Science, North Orissa University, Baripada, India
sujata238dash@gmail.com
[3] Department of CIT, JCC, King AbdulAziz University, Jeddah, Kingdom of Saudi Arabia
Kkhan2@kau.edu.sa

Abstract. *Telemedicine* is the concept coined by the use of telecommunication and information technology to cater healthcare facilities to patients from a far-off place. Telemedicine has exhibited an efficient mechanism to face the hurdles of helthcare to provide superior quality medical services from specialized doctors situated in urban areas to communities particularly located in rural or remote areas. This research paper will introduce several telemedicine applications that helped easier access to specialist doctors, improved satisfaction level of patients, and better clinical outcomes. The first section will define the architecture of telemedicine. Secondly, the second section will represent different telemedicine applications. Lastly, the study will also depict opposing views on the technology of telemedicine and possible solutions.

Keywords: Cloud computing · Mobile computing · Telecommunications
Telediagnosis · Telemedicine · Telepharmacy

1 Introduction

Nowadays, medical fields use a lot of technologies that aim to improve patient care quality and interaction between medical professions.

A remote delivery of healthcare services, such as health consultations over the telecommunications infrastructure, can be defined as Telemedicine. Telemedicine is a new concept that is developing rapidly and allows healthcare providers to diagnose, treat, and evaluate patients without the need for in-person visits [1]. The primary advantage of Telemedicine is to help the patients living in remote areas, who are far from local health facilities or are in areas with shortage of medical professionals.

© Springer Nature Singapore Pte Ltd. 2019
A. K. Luhach et al. (Eds.): ICAICR 2018, CCIS 956, pp. 413–425, 2019.
https://doi.org/10.1007/978-981-13-3143-5_34

To uncover more about the concept of Telemedicine, many recent published papers were researched. The aim of this paper is to convey the model of telemedicine to the reader. Furthermore, the target is also to illustrate how the field of mobile computing contributes to and enhances telemedicine services. '

This study introduces Telemedicine and its architecture first. Then it provides the reader with different applications of Telemedicine such as Tele-diagnosis, Cardiac Tele-rehabilitation, Tablet PC, and mobile cloud computing.

2 Telemedicine System Architecture

Telemedicine, a terminology coined in the 70s, involves the use of Information and Communications Technology, ICT, to enhance patients' outcomes by increasing access to healthcare services and medical information [2]. Literally, Telemedicine is "healing at a distance". Moreover, according to the American Telemedicine Association, ATA, it could be defined as "use of medical information exchanged from one site to another via electronic communication for health and education of the patient or healthcare providers [3] for the purpose of improving patient care". The main focus of telemedicine is to provide high-quality medical services from specialized doctors situated in urban areas to individuals living in isolated communities and remote regions [3].

The notion of telemedicine started with the evolution of telecommunications, telecom, technologies that allowed the transmission of information in the form of electromagnetic signals over a distance [2]. In 1910, the trans-telephonic, electrical stethoscope, was introduced. The trans-telephonic was one of the initial applications of telemedicine. It was used to amplify the sounds from a stethoscope and transfer them over a telephonic network. Over time and with the recent technological advances, the field of telemedicine has transformed into a more complex integrated system used in most of the healthcare facilities [3].

According to the published paper 'Telemedicine and e-health: Today and Tomorrow' [3] the architecture of the existing telemedicine system consists of two main units; mobile and rural telemedicine units, Fig. 1. The mobile unit can either be a fixed or a portable unit. The fixed unit is located at the patient's site. On the other hand, the portable unit includes doctor's unit and base unit, located in a hospital having the facility of medical monitoring system. These hospitals are connected through wireless or wired communication links to a hospital located in urban area which comprises of several workstations and is reserved to a specialized doctor.

Telemedicine workstations use a network interface card, NIC. Thus, enabling the telemedicine system to transmit and receive medical images, videos, and audios on a high speed. For low-bandwidth links, the workstation encodes the videos using the International Telecommunication Union (ITU), H.320 standard for video conferencing (VC). Conversely, for high-bandwidth applications, the workstation uses the Motion Picture Experts Group, MPEG, standard [3]. The telemedicine system employs a image processing unit to perform basic computation of images. These activities include, 90° rotations, zooming and panning. Other functions are necessitated by the need to simulate the VCR environment regularly used in ultrasound consultation in the case of diagnostic video [3].

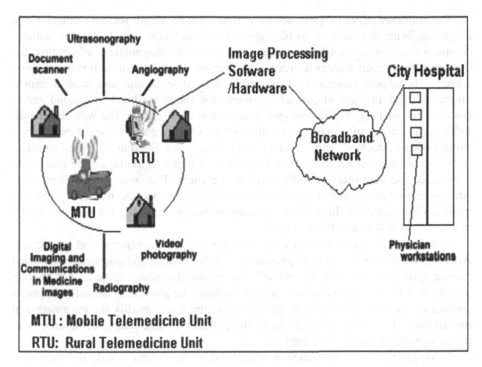

Fig. 1. Architecture of telemedicine

VC, life transmission of image and voice over distance, is one of the technologies that has significantly influenced several types of telemedicine, e.g. tele-psychiatry consultation. Nevertheless, in VC a real time consultation is carried out with all participants available. However, this is not always possible. This limitation led to the birth of a new telemedicine architecture, called store and forward. In contrast to the VC, in this architecture the participants work in an asynchronous way. The patient, will prepare his/her questions and any necessary materials (store). Then, these materials are transmitted to the specialized doctor for his expert comment. The specialized doctor reviews the material later and send a report back to the patient [3].

In conclusion, this revolutionary concept 'telemedicine' can be retained to provide high-quality medical facilities and information to individuals located in areas constrained by lack of finance and physical distance. In addition, the architecture of the telemedicine system establishes a convenience and reliable communication link between the patient and the medical staff [3].

3   Applications of Telemedicine

A. Tele-diagnosis

Mobile tele-diagnosis system is an application of telemedicine that is used nowadays to help the doctors diagnose people living in remote areas at any time [4].

The published paper [4] proposes a cloud based software for remote medical image diagnosis. With the help of mobile internet and different mobile phones, tablets, computers, and other mobile terminals used as remote diagnostic workstations, the system enables expert doctors to access and establish a wireless connection to the cloud servers. The remote diagnostics workstation is used to handle and browse remote diagnostics and medical images of a patient. On the other hand, the cloud server contains the database, medical images storage, and web servers. The web server provides maintenance and management to the system. On the contrary, the database server stores patients', doctors', and hospitals' information, and different diagnosis reports.

As mentioned before, the system is partitioned into two modules: one deals with server side and the other one with smart device client. The smart device client side, Android is used as the operating system for mobile system, because it suits the mobile's medical client perfectly. In addition, to easily exchange and share the data, the HTTP protocol is used between these two [4].

The system is designed with three user roles; patients, experts, and physicians. After logging into the system, the patients can choose doctors and hospitals, upload and browse their own information, and ask for remote diagnosis. Experts can provide patients with the remote diagnosis report. In addition, the physicians can offer diagnosis application. Both of them have the privilege to submit and modify the information in the database. To guarantee reliability of the patient's remote diagnosis reports, electronic signature technology is used [4].

Some image processing functions were used in the system to help the experts in diagnosing the patients. Some of these functions are edge detection, magnification, and image gray-scale inversion. To process medical images, the system follows the DICOM 3 standard and supports DICOM3 transport protocol [4].

Developers of the system also added a feature that enable real-time interaction between smart devices and remote diagnostics i.e. patients and experts to help experts check up on their patients at any time during the diagnosis period via SMS messaging [4].

As a result, the proposed system offers several activities that can be done by users. For example, appointment registrations, expert- patient interaction, diagnostics, management functions, etc. The medical image remote diagnosis is a developing technology and as long as there are signals in a phone, experts can access the remote diagnosis server anytime and anywhere [4].

B. Cardiac Telerehabilitaion Application for Mobile Devices

Consistent check-ups and cardiac rehabilitation are essential for patients recovering from cardiac or heart surgeries to minimize the risk of further cardiac diseases. The length of time for rehabilitation is divided into two phases; inpatient and outpatient. The patient need to be hospitalized roughly for 12 weeks in the first phase. The second phase takes more time than the first phase [5] and can be carried out either in a rehabilitation center or at home.

The rapid growth of electronic and communication technologies paved the way for a new turn in remote medical rehabilitation, the cardiac telerehabilitation. The main target of cardiac telerehabilitation is to observe patients out of the hospital and upsurge the number of patients participating in the cardiac rehabilitation [5].

A personal system and software architecture for cardiac telerehabilitation have been recommended by a released paper 'A Cardiac Telerehabilitaition Application for Mobile Devices' [5]. The anticipated system requires a ECG signal recorder in a Bluetooth-based body surface network, BSN and a mobile device. The architecture of the system is divided into 5 modules, Fig. 2.

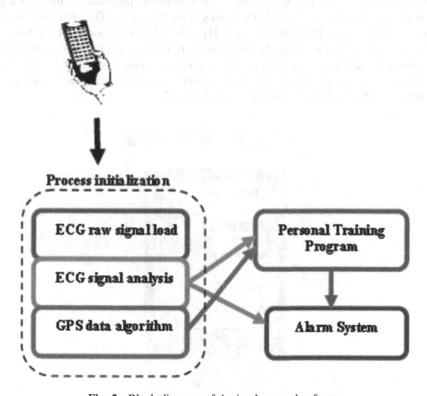

Fig. 2. Block diagram of the implemented software

The first module exchanges data among the ECG signal recorder and the mobile communication device available over the Internet [5]. Next, the second module consists of a QRS detection algorithm. The algorithm designed by Pan and Tompkins [16], is an optimal and efficient algorithm, easy to implement, was employed in this module. The framework of the algorithm is designed by employing digital analysis of amplitude, slope, and width. The algorithm first uses a bandpass filter, a combination of high and low pass filters. The filter improves components inside a frequency range of 5 to 17 Hz and reduces noise in the signal [5]. Next, a derivative operator is employed to differentiate the P and T waves by its sharp slope from the QRS detection algorithm. Then, to highlight large characteristic differences for QRS and to make the results positive, squaring operation is used. Then a moving-window integrator is used to identify a QRS complex in each ECG cycle as a unique point. Lastly, the adaptive thresholding operation is performed and QRS complex is validated only if it exceeds the given threshold value and then RR interval is evaluated as a time difference from the previous detection point [5].

The third module deals with the Geographical Positioning System (GPS) algorithm. This process computes speed of the motion and inclination which is based on location and elevation. The fourth module deals with indivisual training program, which is the most important part for the rehabilitation. This helps the physician to develop a personal training programme without intervening with the patient. The physician also has access to the list of programs through Hypertext Preprocessor which allows the selection of the patient to change his/her training program. The physician could also set the values for speed, altitude, and minimum and maximum heart rate [5]. Afterward, the data is stored on the server. The patient could access the data when he/she pushes the button START on the mobile application, Fig. 3.

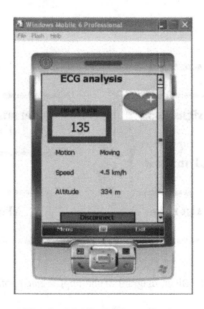

Fig. 3. Mobile ECG application

Lastly the module designed for Alarm ensures a safe and comfortable rehabilitation. This module provides two main services for patient's safety [5]. First, whenever an abnormal situation occurs, the system sends a SMS message to the physicians and to the family members. The message delivers information about the location and heart rate of the patient. This feature eliminates risks of very high/low heart rate and collapsing and not getting any help from anyone. Secondly, the module is connected to the training program, so it could inform the current status of patient i.e., about his/her speed, altitude, distance and heart rate. When the threshold values are surpass, messages inverbal form is shown up. The proposed application is designed to appeal to patients from different age groups. The application was developed with .NET 3.5 using C# programming language [5].

To validate the application of the proposed algorithm, a test was carried out on the records from the MIT-BIH Arrhythmia Dataset [17, 18]. The results of the test detected only less than 2% of the beats which is satisfactory [5].

C. Tablet PC Enabled Body Sensor System

Elderly adults who need more health care services are quickly increasing, and the ratio is higher in rural areas than in urban area [6]. Interventions may be needed for older rural adults to maintain physical and mental health [6], but the current tele-medicine solutions for conserving health focus on diagnosis, treatment and expert consultation [7]. There are two rising public health problems that need to be detected are hypertension and accidental falls which need to control in order to reduce the risk and save lives [7].

Hypertension is higher or lower blood pressure than what it should be. Also, this is considered as a "silent killer" because it does not show any signs or symptoms and many people do not realise that they already have it [8]. Eventually, the constant pressure burden causes serious health problems such as heart failure, heart stroke, and kidney failure [7]. However, constant-monitoring of hypertension is advisable, and it leads to better blood pressure control [7]. A fall is an accidental event whereby a person unintentionally and without control moves to the ground. Injury can result from a fall [9]. Peoples' health who experience a fall is important to get timely assistance to avoid getting affected with this health problem. Therefore, timely detection of the fall is important to receive timely assistance and get help to improve the chance of survival [7].

The latest developments in the field of cloud computing and wireless technology can be utilized for developing healthcare monitoring systems. The growth of mobile communication technology increases the efficiency of Telehealth systems for evaluating the physiological parameters [7]. The use of mobile applications for healthcare can help in handling patient's information remotely by a medical practitioner. The paper 'Tablet PC Enabled Body Sensor for Rural Telehealth Applications' [7] introduces a health monitoring system that measures and collects accidental fall, hypertension, pulse rate, and temperature information. Subsequently, by using a body sensor unit the acquired biological information is transmitted via Bluetooth to the patient's tablet PC. Afterwards, this information is transferred to the mobile device of a medical staff of a primary healthcare center [7].

The developed body sensor system consists of body sensor unit and a tablet PC. The body sensor unit consists of sensors, an embedded system, and a Bluetooth module, Fig. 4. A wearable wrist sensor is worn by the patient. This unit is an integration of the sensors used to collect blood pressure/pulse rate, temperature, and accelerometer. The sensor for blood pressure/pulse rate is used to measure systolic and diastolic blood pressure. Whereas, the accelerometer sensor is used to detect falls. After the sensor unit gathers the necessary biological information, they are acquired by the embedded system. The embedded platform is linked with the Bluetooth module for seamless transmission. The Bluetooth module is used because Bluetooth wireless communication has high data rate and could easily interface with the tablet PC. After that, the acquired information by the embedded system will be transmitted to the tablet PC for real-time acquisition of data, comparison with a threshold value, storage in SQL

database, and alert facility. The alert facility in the form of SMS [7] sends the information of the hypertensive patient to the medical officer.

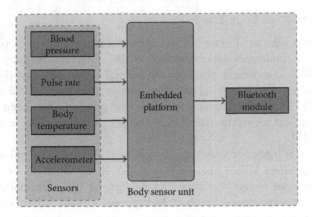

Fig. 4. Block diagram of the developed body sensor unit

Validation of the wrist sensor is carried out to approve the reliability of the data
obtained. According to [7], 291 of the subjects suspected to have hypertension were
first measured by the sphygmomanometric method and then by the wrist sensor that is
based on the oscillo1metric method. The comparison was done by using Bland-Altman
plot or a difference plot and then a graphical method was used to compare two measurement techniques [10]. The results of Bland-Altman analysis showed very good
understanding between the two methods. Thus, wrist sensor under proper supervision
can be used instead of the sphygmomanometric method for hypertension monitoring
[7]. Also, the system was tested in a practical environment. The information was
transmitted successfully to the tablet PC and stored in the SQL database. Patients with
hypertension were correctly identified and automatic SMSs were generated and sent to
the medical officer. This facility helps elderly care in out-of-hospital or home environment where the SMS contains the patient's physiological information. In addition, it
also contains the latitude and longitude information to precisely locate the patient in
case of abnormal conditions that need immediate help.

To conclude, modern approaches of health monitoring can significantly reduce the
workload of the medical officer, manage an enormous number of patients with the
shortfall of doctors, and monitor elderly people's health in rural areas. Such proposed
system is less expensive and causes less inconvenience for the patients [7].

D. Mobile Cloud Computing for Telemedicne Solutions

The Mobile Cloud Computing technology was introduced as an upgradation of
Cloud Computing for mobile users. It is described as "the availability of cloud computing services in a mobile ecosystem that incorporates many elements, including
consumer, enterprise, femtocells, transcoding, end-to-end security, home gateways and
mobile broadband-enabled services" [11]. According to the released journal, 'Mobile

Cloud Computing in Telemedicine Solutions,' one of the primary rewards of mobile cloud computing is that it is inferred from cloud computing proficiencies and potentials [12]. Hence, a theoretical typical architecture of Mobile Cloud Computing is depicted in Fig. 5.

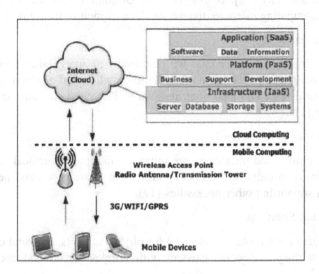

Fig. 5. Mobile cloud computing architecture

Based on the above architecture, two universal technologies are taken into consideration:

- Mobile Computing

Mobile devices can be characterized by smartphones or laptops that can be linked to a network through 3G, WIFI or GPRS. Mobile handlers can direct cloud requests through a variety of mobile resources and they will be allocated to the connections which were established. After the web application has been loaded and started, particular system functions will be deployed to guarantee that the quality of service will be preserved until the connection ends [12].

- Cloud Computing

Cloud computing is a universal term for everything that comprises the transfer of technology across the Internet. It is an example for permitting suitable, on-demand network access to a public blend of configurable computing resources that can be quickly supplied and discharged with minimal management or service provider collaboration [12].

Due to the power of this technology, the healthcare industry can take the benefit of mobile cloud computing to develop telemedicine solutions that can aid in the process of refining the excellence and productivity of medical services [12].

Mobile Cloud Computing proposes important gains to the healthcare industry, specifically to clinics and hospitals that demand an almost instant access to computing services. In addition, healthcare information is desired throughout numerous geographical locations to avoid some noteworthy interruptions through patients' treatments. This new technological tactic offers a chance to advance medical facilities, to share data more conveniently between patients and medics, and also to enhance operational productivity [12]. Below, is a list of some of the main advantages that mobile cloud computing offers to diverse services explicit to the field of telemedicine.

- Clinical Research

Many pharmacology merchants are beginning to merge the cloud to expand research and drug creation. Profitmaking cloud suppliers have created specific pharmacology clinical research cloud contributions to lower the cost and development of new medicine [12].

- Electronic Medical Records

Hospitals, clinics and physicians are initiating the use of medical records on the cloud. The aim is to unburden the heavy task from IT divisions and permit them to emphasize on supporting other necessities [12].

- Collaboration Solutions

Remote video conference is under trial for physician visits. For rural environments, telehealth is starting to become existent with wireless broadband and smartphone acceptance [12].

- Real-time Monitoring

The field of telemedicine has grown to embrace tele-consultations tele surgeries, health record exchange, video-conferencing, and home monitoring [12].

- Health Information Exchange

Health information exchanges assists healthcare entities share data stored in exclusive systems [12].

Mobile cloud computing combined with telemedicine concentrates towards attaining two explicit targets: the accessibility of health applications and medical data anywhere and anytime and the invisibility of computing. In addition, it permits patients to be observed at anytime and anywhere using wireless technologies [12].

In conclusion, mobile cloud computing keys for telemedicine have a major influence in the process of lessening the boundaries and restrictions of traditional medical treatment. These constraints and challenges are beating by integrating advanced technologies to increase patient outcomes via quality facilities. For example, monitoring, assessment, diagnosis, treatments, and rehabilitation within healthcare providers and consumers.

4 Opposing Views on Telemedicine

Telemedicine is a new concept that is developing rapidly, thus creating controversy between individuals. This section portrays a small debate or the opposing views on one of the primary fields of telemedicine, telepharmacy.

A. Telepharmacy: Controversy and Promise

Telepharmacy has become the latest trend in the pharmacy community. According to the released journal 'Telepharmacy: Controversy and Promise', it covers pharmaceutical services available at distance places and often contains information on electronic health records (EHR), multimedia, static images, and audio-video connections. Telepharmacy has become one of the most popular telemedicine applications and it increases the accessibility of patients to health care services, such as patient and medication counselling. By connecting to the Internet any patient could receive the services from anywhere. Another major advantage of telepharmacy is that it helps the remote pharmacists to dispense more clinical services [13] than the on-site pharmacist.

It is believed that telepharmacy is the best way to provide health services to the communities located far-off and other regions deprived of medical facilities. Since, it is difficult to attract pharmacists to these areas. Other possible benefits of telepharmacy include improving the economic development in the rural areas and improving the relationship between the rural physician and pharmacist. On the other hand, the oppositions worry that this new trend may ruin or dilute the profession of the pharmacists and the business of running a pharmacy. In addition, the critics are worried about the additional work burden placed on the technical people of the pharmacy [13].

Patient acceptance and variable local and global laws are two of the largest hurdles the opposition thinks that telepharmacy should overcome to truly flourish. Another point of controversy relates to patient counselling. The system of telepharmacy allows the patient to decline counselling easily by just pressing the (NO) button. Whereas, in traditional pharmacies the patient will have to give the consent or decline counselling. The patients may assume that the pharmacist is busy with other duties, which makes pressing the (YES) button for counselling like an interruption to him/her. Therefore, they are more likely to press (NO). Nonetheless, it is unacceptable to let any patient leave the telepharmacy with a new prescription without any interaction with the pharmacist [13].

Another hurdle that needs to be addressed is the responsibility of the pharmacy technicians. The amount of trust that is entrusted to telepharmacy technicians is a matter of concern for the pharmacists and owners. Technicians dispense the job of pharmacist in his absence and are accountable for maintain the sanctity of the profession. In response to the above need, the technicians need to be cetified by competent certification board. This will ensure that technicians will be more confident and skilled than ever [13].

Finally, this is a new opportunity for pharmacies to grow and collaborate with modern technology to extend benefits to patients, especially to those who must travel long distances and lack quality of pharmaceutical assistances. In addition, it allows pharmacists to grow and increase their role in aiding the patients. So, when people are ready and willing to accept telepharmacy technology, it is poised to spread throughout [13]. It can incorporate various standards like HL7 [14]. Similar work has been proposed in [15].

5 Conclusion

The field of telemedicine is rapidly growing and advancing to provide healthcare for patients without the need for in-person visits. In this comprehensive study, many different journals and papers have been researched to discuss the different areas of telemedicine. This study is divided into two main sections. First, telemedicine was introduced along with and architecture. Second, the different applications used in the telemedicine was presented. Four different applications were discussed and how the field of mobile computing contributed to enhancing these applications. Lastly, the fourth section shows that telemedicine is still under examination and that many individuals may not widely accept telemedicine technologies because of the different threats they may face. Yet, telemedicine is still developing and is the near future.

References

1. Rouse, M., Holman, T.: Telemedicine. http://searchhealthit.techtarget.com/definition/telemedicine. Accessed 16 Dec 2017
2. World Health Organization Global Observatory for eHealth: Telemedicine: opportunities and developments in member states. Observatory, vol. 2, p. 96 (2010)
3. Singhroha, M.: Telemedicine and e-health: today and tomorrow. Compusoft **3**, 1228 (2014)
4. Xing-Hua, S., Xiao, Z., Xiaoling, G., Wei, P.: Design and development of tele-diagnosis system of medical image based on mobile terminal. In: 2014 7th International Conference on Intelligent Computation Technology and Automation, pp. 149–153 (2014)
5. Jaworek, J., Augustyniak, P.: A cardiac telerehabilitation application for mobile devices. In: 2011 Computing in Cardiology, pp. 241–244 (2011)
6. Baernholdt, M., Yan, G., Hinton, I., Rose, K., Mattos, M.: Quality of life in rural and urban adults 65 years and older: findings from the national health and nutrition examination survey. J. Rural Heal. **28**(4), 339–347 (2012)
7. Panicker, N.V., Kumar, A.S.: Tablet PC enabled body sensor system for rural telehealth applications. Int. J. Telemed. Appl. **2016**, 9 (2016)
8. KhanAcademy: What is hypertension? (2017). https://www.khanacademy.org/. Accessed 16 Dec 2017
9. Digital For Me: patientslikeme. https://www.patientslikeme.com/. Accessed 16 Dec 2017
10. Schoonjans, F.: Easy-to-use statistical software. MedCalc (2017). https://www.medcalc.org/. Accessed 16 Dec 2017
11. Cox, P.: Mobile cloud computing: devices, trends, issues, and the enabling technologies. In: Developer Works (2011). http://www.ibm.com/developerworks/cloud/library/cl-mobilecloud computing/. Accessed 16 Dec 2017
12. Gheorghe, M.: Mobile cloud computing for telemedicine solutions. Inform. Econ. **18**(4), 50–61 (2014)
13. Steckler, T.: Telepharmacy: controversy and promise. J. Pharm. Technol. **32**, 227–229 (2016)

14. Atta-ur-Rahman, Alhiyafi, J.: Health level seven generic web interface. J. Comput. Theor. Nanosci. **15**, 1261–1274 (2018)
15. Atta-ur-Rahman, Salam, M.H., Jamil, S.: Virtual clinic: a telemedicine proposal for remote areas of Pakistan. In: 3rd World Congress on Information and Communication Technologies (WICT 2013), pp. 46–50, 15–18 December 2013
16. Pan, J., Tompkins, W.: A real-time QRS detection algorithm. IEEE Trans. Eng. Biomed. Eng. **32**(3), 230–236 (1985)
17. Moody, G.B., Mark, R.G.: The impact of the MIT-BIH arrhythmia database. IEEE Eng. Med. Biol. Mag. **20**(3), 45–50 (2001). (PMID: 11446209)
18. Goldberger, A.L., et al.: PhysioBank, PhysioToolkit, and PhysioNet: components of a new research resource for complex physiologic signals. Circulation **101**(23), e215–e220 (2000)

A Survey on Information Diffusion Models in Social Networks

Shashank Sheshar Singh[✉], Kuldeep Singh, Ajay Kumar,
Harish Kumar Shakya, and Bhaskar Biswas

Department of Computer Science and Engineering,
Indian Institute of Technology (BHU), Varanasi 221 005, India
{shashankss.rs.cse16,kuldeep.rs.cse13,ajayk.rs.cse16,
hkshakya.rs.cse,bhaskar.cse}@iitbhu.ac.in

Abstract. Nowadays, social influence plays an important role in every-
day life because peoples are spending too much time in social the networks. Social influence is the change in a people behaviors, thoughts,
attitudes, and feeling by interacting other peoples in the social networks.
Thus, analysis of social influence spreading has emerged as an important
topic of interest in areas of computer science, economics, and sociology.
In 1940s, only empirical studies of diffusion process have been done. In
1970s, some theoretical propagation models were proposed. Later, motivated by marketing strategy influence maximization problem is emerges.
The main objective of influence maximization (IM) problem is to maximize the social influence spreading with fixed predetermined budget k
in online social networks such as twitter, Epinions, Facebook, HEP-PH
and Google+ etc.

Keywords: Information diffusion · Social networks · Social influence
Influence maximization

1 Introduction

Nowadays, Social Networks such as Facebook, Twitter, Weibo, Epinions etc. are
playing vital role in understanding of user's behavior and opinions in viral marketing, online advertising and influential blog discovery. Social Network analysis
is important for finding social influence when some new information are spreading within network. This analysis gives us the information about social influence
such as initial opinions of users, user opinion after social influence, maximum
social influence. Social influence stands for individual's behavioral change based
on other network users. Social influence strength depends on various factors
such as similarity and dissimilarity between users, relationship strength and
trust between users, characteristics of individuals in the network like age, background, religion, educational qualification etc. In this paper, we discussed various
measures and approaches to analysis of social influence and its diffusion models.

First, we discussed various concepts and measures of social network such
as degree, betweenness and closeness centrality, density, degree distribution etc.

© Springer Nature Singapore Pte Ltd. 2019
A. K. Luhach et al. (Eds.): ICAICR 2018, CCIS 956, pp. 426–439, 2019.
https://doi.org/10.1007/978-981-13-3143-5_35

These concepts and measures are important in analyzing edges and nodes influence in social network. Further, we discussed quantitative and qualitative analysis of social influence. Finally, We discussed various information diffusion models such as threshold model, cascading model, epidemic model and so on with their special variants.

2 Social Influence Analysis Statistics

A Social network is molded as a graph which consists a set of nodes and edges and represented as $G = (V, E)$, where V is known as nodes (actors or users in social network) and E is known as edges (social relationship between users). Edges can be directed or undirected. Edges can be labeled, weighted or valued. Locally, we can measure social influence of nodes using their edge strength from one node to other. Globally, depending on network structure, some nodes of network have more influence than other nodes. Local measures are frequently allied with network edges while global measure are allied with nodes. We next discussed the local as well as global measures of networks respectively.

2.1 Local Measures: Edge Measures

Edge measures such as Tie Strength, Weak Ties, Edge Betweenness etc. measures on a pair of nodes (connects by edge) of network. These measures explain the influence of one to another based on network topology and interactions between them. Basically they measure the importance of an edge.

Tie Strength. According to Granovetter et al. [14], Tie strength is a measure of relationship strength between users. Basically Ties are strong and weak in nature. Generally strong ties are exist between family members or very close friends and these ties are rare while weak are much more common. In social network, tie strength measure depends on how much common neighbor nodes exist between pair of nodes u and v. If more common neighbors exists between node u and v then strength of tie is strong between else weak. Tie strength can be calculated based on following Jaccard Coefficient formula.

$$Strength(u, v) = \frac{N(u) \cap N(v)}{N(u) \cup N(v)} \tag{1}$$

where $N(u)$ and $N(v)$ are neighbors of A and B respectively. There is no single factor exist that is able to define strength of relationship but combination of some predictors can find the relationship is weak or strong. Granovetter et al. gives four instinctive factors that may participate in calculation of tie strength. He states that *"Tie strength is probably linear combination of the emotional intensity, the mutual confiding (intimacy), the amount of time and the reciprocal services which characterize the tie"*. The tie strength also refer as embeddedness. Edge embeddedness is high if connecting nodes of edge are having more common neighbors. It is easy to develop trust and reliability to one another, if connecting node pair have an embedded edge. If edge embeddedness is zero, no common neighbors exists between them. Thus, trusting each other is risky because no one exists for behavioral verification.

Weak Tie. When common neighbors of pair u and v is small then relationship (u, v) is weak in nature. If no common node exist between them then edge (u, v) works as a local bridge of network that means removal of edge, may increase the no. of connected component in network [14]. In such cases, local bridge may be work as a global bridge. Although, in real world occurrence of global bridge is rare. The effect of local as well as global bridges is similar. Nowadays, weak ties are much more important because they are able to provide access to a more diverse set of resources and information.

Edge Betweenness Centrality. Freeman et al. [10,11] introduced betweenness centrality concept first time in the context of sociology. Edge betweenness centrality measures the flow across the edge. Betweenness centrality of an edge (u, v) is defined as the number of shortest paths that go through edge (u, v) in the network. Here, he assume that the information flow between any pair of nodes are spread through shortest paths between them.

2.2 Global Measures: Node Measures

Node based centrality measures how central a node in network i.e. it estimate the importance of a node in social network [2,11]. A node is highly influential if it contains higher centrality score. Various node centrality measures such as degree centrality, closeness centrality and betweenness centrality have been proposed. These centrality measures can be divided into two group's radial and medial measures. Random walk start from or end on a given node when assess radial measure while random walk going through a given node when assess medial measure. Based on random walks type, radial measure categorized into length measures and volume measures. Length measures set the target nodes volume and try to find out the length of walk to achieve target volume while volume measure just vice versa. Now we discussed popular node centrality measures.

Degree Centrality. Degree centrality is a type of radial volume based centrality measures. It is easiest centrality measure because degree centrality is simply node degree i.e. $C_D(U) = deg(U)$. It is a good measure for calculating total no of connection of node bit it is not necessary that degree centrality always indicate its importance. We can use adjacency matrix of network for degree centrality calculation because it adds all length 1 path that start from node. Similarly, we can calculate K-path length centrality that count all the path of length at most K.

Closeness Centrality. Closeness centrality is a type of radial length based centrality measure. Closeness centrality find closeness of a node from all other nodes. Closeness centrality of a node is the average of all the shortest paths from given node to all other nodes. If this centrality value is less i.e. node is more central. Closeness centrality can be calculated as follows.

$$C_C(u) = \frac{\sum_{v \in (V \setminus v)} d(u, v)}{|V| - 1} \tag{2}$$

where $d(u, v)$ is the shortest distance between u and v.

Node Betweenness Centrality. This centrality measure is a type of medial centrality measure. As discussed in edge betweenness, high betweenness value indicate edge conquer critical position. Similarly, High node betweenness value indicate node conquers precarious position i.e. it permitted high amount of information spreading. Calculation of node betweenness centrality is based on existence of node in the shortest paths of any pair nodes, similar as edge betweenness centrality. It compute the importance of a node in the network in context of information spreading. Betweenness centrality of a node u is given as follows.

$$C_B(u) = \sum_{u \neq v \neg w} \frac{SP_{w,v}(v)}{SP_{w,v}} \tag{3}$$

where $SP_{w,v}$ is total number of shortest paths between w and v and and $SP_{w,v}(v)$ is total number of shortest paths between w and v that goes through u.

Structural Holes. Burt et al. [20] defined structural node as a connecting node that connect multiple local bridges of the network. Removal of that node create a "empty space" in the network, these space are structural holes. The node that generate structural hole can interconnect information initiating from many non-interacting nodes. Thus, that node play an important role to connecting diverse areas of network.

3 Social Influence and Influence Maximization

3.1 Social Influence

According to Rashotte et al. [19] the change in a user behaviors, thoughts, attitudes and feeling by interacting other users in the social network is referred as social influence. Various application in big data analysis and data mining field such as recommendation system, viral marketing, online advertising, influential blog discovery, information diffusion etc. are involved with social influence. Social influence is frequently reproduced in change in user behavior or pattern of social action.

3.2   Influence Maximization

In social influence study one major problem arises, that is influence maximization. For the reason that users opinions or behaviors are affected by their neighbors, colleagues, friends, family members, relatives, researchers decisions as well as word of mouth about new product. Thus, for making profitable marketing strategies influence maximization is important. Suppose that we want to promote a product in a way that product is adopted by users as much as possible using knowledge of users preferences and their influence on each other. For this purpose, viral marketing strategy for information diffusion is to find a small amount of users within network and try to convince them to adopt product and use social influence effect to recommend others in network such that maximize the adoption of product. Thus we try to maximize only positive influence rather than negative influence. Therefore, influence maximization problem is stated as targeting small amount of seed users for information diffusion in order to maximizing influence in network [15,16].

Given a social network, represented by directed graph $G = (V, E)$ such that V represents users as nodes and E represent relationship between users as edges with a seed set size k. Our goal is to find out k users set as seed value such that targeting on these users initially and expected maximum influence gain (in terms of adopted users count).

4   Information Diffusion Models in Social Network

Information propagation among the users through various intermediate users over time in social network is called information diffusion. Formal mathematical model for information diffusion is firstly introduced by Granovetter et al. [13]. Nowadays, various information diffusion models are developed from sociology and economics communities. Independent Cascading model and Linear Threshold model are most popular models of information diffusion. Many extensions and variation of these two popular models are also used to tackle more complex real world problem. For example, Chen et al. [7] proposed IC-N model, is an independent cascade model with considering negative sentiments of users which is more accurate in understanding people behaviors. Table 1 shows various extensions of information diffusion models with their activation condition and application.

A Social network is molded as a graph which consists a set of nodes and edges and represented as $G = V, E$, where V is known as nodes (actors or users in social network) and E is known as edges (social relationship between users). Edges can be directed or undirected based on the application. An edge $(x, y) \in E$ in directed graph G shows that x influence on y while an edge $(x, y) \in E$ in undirected graph G shows mutual influence. Undirected graph can be used as a directed graph considering every edge as bidirectional. Let us assume that $N(u)$ represents neighbors of u in undirected network while $N_{in}(u)$ and $N_{out}(u)$ are in-neighbors and out-neighbors respectively in directed network.

4.1 Threshold Model

A threshold model is a mathematical model which has some threshold values to differentiate behavior prediction of users. The very first model was introduced by [13] to simulate collective behavior of users over voting trend, spreading rumors, diffusion of innovations etc. According to Granovetter threshold model, threshold value is the number of user who make a decision before given user make such decision. It is important to focus on threshold determinants. Threshold values are varies from user to user based on some factor such as age, education, background, economic condition etc. Granovetter et al. also describe relation between threshold values and utility function. Based on that utility function, each user will calculate benefit and cost of each action. It might be possible that cost and benefit of action are change based on situation. The output of aggregate opinion of users depends on distribution of threshold. In threshold models, every edge (x, y) is allied with a W_{xy} weight and every node x has a threshold value T_x which is responsible for activeness of user x such that at least T_x neighbor users must be active before x is active.

Linear Threshold Model. Linear threshold model is a basic threshold model which is broadly used in analyzing the information diffusion among the users. Every node y has a threshold value T_y and every edge (x, y) for each $x \in N(y)$ has a positive weight such that sum of all W_{xy} must be less than or equal to 1 i.e. $\sum_{x \in N(y)} W_{xy} \leq 1$. Initially, start with a set of active nodes and threshold values. After time t, a node y is active iff at least T_y neighbor users must be active.

$$\sum_{x \in N^a(y)} W_{xy} \geq T_y \tag{4}$$

where $N^a(y)$ represents active neighbors of node y. If no further possibility of activation of new node, process simply terminate without changing state of active node. The threshold used by linear threshold model is linear check of edge weights that's the name suggested. One important point is we need prior knowledge of threshold values. Although this model is deterministic in nature but we can introduce randomness using threshold value randomization. For the purpose of information diffusion and influence maximization, Kempe et al. [15,16] used linear model with uniform randomness in interval [0,1] in complex social network. For linear threshold model Kempe et al. [15] proved that:

Theorem 1. *In linear threshold model at any time instance t, influence function $\sigma(.)$ must be submodular.*

Theorem 2. *In linear threshold model, problem of influence maximization is NP-hard in nature.*

There is some another class of models where threshold values are fixed, known and node specific in nature are given by [13]. These models are generally used in application such that virus propagation, voting and so on. In this class of models, $d(y)$ and T_y represent node y degree and threshold respectively where $y \in V$ and $T_y \in [1, d(y)]$. Following three models uses this definitions.

The Majority Threshold Model. In majority based threshold model, a vertex $y \in V$ is activated iff majority of its neighbors are activated i.e. threshold value of node y is $T_y = \frac{1}{2}d(y)$. Most popular applications of this model is voting system, distributing computing etc. In majority based threshold model, Chen et al. [5] proved that influence maximization problem has the same hardness of approximation as the general model and provides following result.

Theorem 3. *Suppose that solving influence maximization problem is NP-hard with arbitrary threshold value. Maximization problem is not solvable in polynomial time function $\sigma(n)$ i.e. not approximated within ratio of $\sigma(n)$. Then influence maximization problem also can not be approximated within $O(\sigma(n))$ for majority threshold values.*

The Small Threshold Model. The other variant of linear threshold model is small threshold model. In this model threshold values of nodes are small constant. Suppose that the threshold value of node y, $T_y = 1$, then solving influence maximization problem is easy by choosing any node in every connected components. For threshold value $T_y = 2$, Chen et al. [6] proved that solving influence maximization problem have the same approximation results as threshold value $T_y = 1$. For threshold value $T_y \geq 3$, Dreyer et al. [8] proved that solving influence maximization problem is *NP-hard* in nature as well.

Theorem 4. *Suppose that solving influence maximization problem is NP-hard with arbitrary threshold value. Maximization problem is not solvable in polynomial time function $\sigma(n)$ i.e. not approximated within ratio of $\sigma(n)$. Then influence maximization problem also can not be approximated within $O(\sigma(n))$ for all $y \in V, T_y \leq 2$.*

The Unanimous Threshold Model. The most influence resistant threshold model is unanimous threshold model among all threshold models. In this model, threshold value of a node is its node degree i.e. $T_y = d(y)$ for each node $y \in V$. This model is mostly used in more complex network security. Suppose when the computer virus is spread in virus resistant network then a node may be affected while its all neighbors are infected. Influence maximization problem in this case is similar to Vertex Cover problem. Chen et al. [6] proposed hardness of influence maximization under unanimous threshold model as follows.

Theorem 5. *If all nodes $y \in V$ in the network have unanimous thresholds $T_y = d(y)$, then Influence Maximization problem is NP-hard in nature.*

Other Extensions. We can generalized the threshold models using some change in activation function or threshold limit. This can be done using an arbitrary function in place of activation function in relation with activated neighbors. Bhagat et al. [1] proposed a model with linear threshold model and color that capture product adoption explicitly, not the influence using three status of users activities. One more extension of threshold model is given by Banerjee et al. [18] in which he allowed a node to switch between its active and inactive state. This model is a combination of Markov chain model and their corresponding steady state distribution with assumption that nodes are participating in various social networks simultaneously.

4.2   Cascading Model

In the viral marketing, cascade models are firstly studied by Goldenberg et al. [12]. Cascade models work in iterative manner. When node x is activated at time t, then at time $t + 1$, active node x has only chance to influence other inactive neighbor y. This activation is happens with probability P_{xy}. Suppose multiple nodes are active at time t and they have the common neighbor y then their attempts to y activation is in arbitrary order. Let us assume that node z at time t succeeds in activating node y at time t. Although node w succeeds or not, in activating y. It not allowed by this model to activate node y further. Termination of this model is same as threshold model, when no nodes are activated at any time instance.

Independent Cascading Model. Before discussing cascading models, we need to define the activation probability of a inactive node y by active node x where y is the neighbors of x. The first and very simple case is Cascading Models where activation probability $P_y(x)$ is constant, doesn't depend on history of information diffusion so far. For the betterment of model we need to define order-independence. Suppose that set S represent the nodes that was tried to activate inactive node y and failed. $P_y(x|S)$ represent the activation probability of inactive node y by active node x after S attempt. Let us assume that M_i and M_i' are represent two permutations of S such that $M_i = (v_1, v_2, v_3, \ldots, v_i)$ and $M_i = (v_1', v_2', v_3', \ldots, v_i')$. The order-independence states that attempt order of set S nodes doesn't effect the activation probability for y to active at the end. i.e.

$$\prod_{i=1}^{k}(1 - P_y(v_i|S \cup M_i)) = \prod_{i=1}^{k}(1 - P_y(v_i'|S \cup M_i')) \tag{5}$$

where $S \cap M = \Phi$.

Decreasing Cascading Model. In comparison to Independent Cascading Model this model is more practical [16]. In addition to Independent Cascading Model this model has a restriction that $P_y(x|S)$ function is non-decreasing in nature in S i.e. we can say that it satisfies $P_y(x|S) \leq P_y(x|M)$ for $S \subset M$. If high no. of nodes are already attempt to activate node y, then successful activation probability decreases in furthers attempts. This model is special case of Independent Cascading Model.

Independent Cascading Model with Negative Opinion. This model is developed by Chen et al. [7] which consider negative opinion also in information propagation process. In addition to cascade model, this model introduced a new factor called quality factor, q. Quality factor is the measure like quality of product. This factor consider the natural behavior of users considering negative for defective product. We can say that new active user adopt positive opinion with probability $(1 - q)$ and negative opinion with probability q. If a node y is activated negatively then node y becomes negative with 1 probability and it remains negative in further iteration. That makes it bias towards negativity.

Generalized Cascade Model. We can generalize the specific cascade models by updating their activation probability. Activation probability P_{xy} of activating node y by node x in cascade model not only depend on u but also depend on already unsuccessfully attempted users S where set S and u are disjoint subset of $N(y)$. So we need to change activation probability from P_{xy} to $P_y(x|S) \in [0, 1]$. Thus, at each time instance, when a newly active node y try to activate inactive node y then it activate node y with probability $P_y(x|S)$.

4.3   Epidemic Model

This model had a powerful impact on life of people and country politics as well because in 19th century, propagation of infectious diseases became a topic of general interest. This model describes how to propagate infectious diseases from one people to another. Nowadays, this model is useful to model various news and rumors transmission and virus infections in computers. Let us assume that $S(t)$ contains the no. of people who are susceptible at any time instance t; $I(t)$ contains the no. of infected people and able to infect susceptible people at any time instance t; $R(t)$ contains the no. of recovered people who are infected in past and have a chance to be infected in future.

SIR Model. Susceptible Infectious Recovered model is firstly introduced by Kermack and McKendrick et al. [17]. SIR model consider population as a fixed entity and it divides population into three groups which are susceptible, infectious and recovered. Any individual people goes through these consecutive states i.e. the flow of model is $S \rightarrow I \rightarrow R$. Kermack and McKendrick derived following equations with the help of contact rate (β) and average infectious period $(1/\gamma)$ are:

$$\frac{dS}{dt} = -\beta SI \tag{6}$$

$$\frac{dI}{dt} = \beta SI - \gamma I \tag{7}$$

$$\frac{dR}{dt} = \gamma I \tag{8}$$

The parameter R_0 is called basic reproduction number which is defined as $R_0 = \beta S_0/\gamma$. Value of R is defined the chances of epidemic i.e. $R < 1$ indicate no possibility of epidemic, $R > 1$ indicate possibility of epidemic while $R = 1$ indicate critical value.

SIS Model. Susceptible Infectious Susceptible model consider population as a fixed entity and it divides population into two groups which are susceptible and infectious. This model doesn't consider recover state i.e. the flow of model is $S \rightarrow I \rightarrow S$. This model is generated from SIR model by taking an assumption that people recovered with zero immunity i.e. peoples are immediately go through recover to susceptible state. Thus we can update SIR differential equations by eliminating recovery state equation and adding these effect into appropriate equation. So SIS differential equations are:

$$\frac{dS}{dt} = -\beta SI + \gamma I \tag{9}$$

$$\frac{dI}{dt} = \beta SI - \gamma I \tag{10}$$

SIRS Model. Another variant of SIR model is called SIRS models. As SIR model, in this model also people can go from one state to another consecutively. Only difference is an individual can leave R state and rejoin S state i.e. the flow of model is $S \rightarrow I \rightarrow R \rightarrow S$. we can update SIR differential equations by removing and adding those effect that are generated from state R to state S flow with considering loss in immunity rate f. So SIS differential equations are:

$$\frac{dS}{dt} = -\beta SI + fI \tag{11}$$

$$\frac{dI}{dt} = \beta SI - \gamma I \tag{12}$$

$$\frac{dR}{dt} = \gamma I - fR \tag{13}$$

4.4 Competitive Influence Diffusion Models

All above discussed information diffusion models are primarily concentrate on only single cascade, but multiple cascade competition within network is much interesting. Carnes et al. [4] taking in consideration a problem of an organization which are interested in introducing a new product, but problem is that one another competing product already introduced in market. Carnes et al. also consider two assumption, first is an individual using only one product and influences friends also and second is that follower has a fixed amount to target set of users. For this scenario Carnes et al. introduced two technique that diffuse information simultaneously.

Distance-Based Model. The distance-based Model is used in competitive scenario in network [9]. Adoption of an individual is highly depend on its location in network i.e. distances from influential node and connectivity from those nodes. Core idea behind this model is that a node y had more chances to adopt the behavior of node x if distance between x and y is relatively small in network. The number of nodes that are expected (calculation done using only on active edges) to adopt the behavior of node A is:

$$\rho(I_A|I_B) = E[\sum_{y \in V} \frac{V_y(I_A, d_y(I, E_a))}{V_y(I_A, d_y(I, E_a)) + V_y(I_B, d_y(I, E_a))}] \tag{14}$$

Initial set of nodes that adopted influence from technology A and B are denoted by I_A and I_B respectively and I is union of both sets. $d_y(I, E_a)$ represent smallest distance from y to I with E_a edges. Now try to find out I_A so that no. of expected nodes are maximized, after fixing I_B is:

$$max[\rho(I_A|I_B) : I_A \subseteq (V - I_B), |I_A| = n] \tag{15}$$

Wave Propagation Model. In wave propagation model information propagates in discrete steps $\{1, 2, \ldots, (t-1), t\}$. All nodes that have distance less than t from initially active set, adopt a technology A or B in step t. Those nodes who have more distance than t, not adopt any technology in time instance t. Similar to above model this model also find out I_A so that no. of expected nodes are maximized, after fixing I_B is:

$$max[\pi(I_A|I_B) : I_A \subseteq (V - I_B), |I_A| = n] \tag{16}$$

where

$$\pi(I_A|I_B) = E[\sum_{x \in V} P(x|(I_A, I_B, E_a))] \tag{17}$$

Weight-Proportional Threshold Model. This model is focused on real world situation like different kinds of products competed. Borodin et al. [3] introduced this type of threshold models where various products are competing. Objective of this model is to propagate the single cascade over many competitors presence. Let us assume that φ^t represent the active nodes at time instance t. While φ_A^t and φ_B^t denotes A-active and B-active nodes respectively. Suppose initially A-active and B-active nodes are S_A and S_B respectively. Each inactive node y becomes active if it satisfies $\sum_{x \in \varphi^t} w_{x,y} \geq T_y$. Node y becomes active with A influence i.e. A-active with probability:

$$P[y \in \varphi_A^t | y \in \varphi^t \setminus \varphi^{t-1}] = \frac{\sum_{x \in \varphi_A^t} w_{x,y}}{\sum_{x \in \varphi^t} w_{x,y}} \tag{18}$$

Node y becomes active with A influence i.e. A-active, otherwise. The problem maximization of propagating A influence is converted in original maximization problem by simply setting value of $S_B = \phi$.

Table 1. Listing of diffusion models and comparisons

Listing of diffusion models			
Model name	Activation condition	Properties	Applications
LT	$\sum_{x \in N^a(y)} W_{xy} \geq T_y$	$\sigma(.)$ is submodular; IM is NP-hard	Collective behavior, spreading rumors and diseases
MT	$T_y = \frac{1}{2}d(y)$	IM is NP-hard	Voting system, distributed computing
ST	$\sum_{x \in N^a(y)} W_{xy} \geq T_y$; T_y is a small constant	$T_y = 1$, select an arbitrary node in each connected component; For $T_y \geq 2$, IM is NP-hard	
UT	$\sum_{x \in N^a(y)} W_{xy} \geq T_y$; $T_y = d(v)$	IM is NP-hard, 2-approximation algorithm	Network security and vulnerability
WT	$P[y \in \varphi_A^t \mid y \in \varphi^t \setminus \varphi^{t-1}]$ $= \frac{\sum_{x \in \varphi_A^t} w_{x,y}}{\sum_{x \in \varphi^t} w_{x,y}}$	$\sigma(.)$ is neither submodular nor monotonic; IM is NP-hard	Deal with two competitive influence
SepT	$\sum_{x \in N^a(y) \cap \varphi_A^{t-1}} w_{x,y}^A \geq T_y^A$	$\sigma(.)$ is monotonic but not submodular; IM is NP-hard	Network with competitive sources
OC	$\sum_{x \in N^a(y)} W_{xy} \geq T_y$	$\sigma(.)$ is neither submodular nor monotonic; IM is NP-hard	Incorporate user opinions
IC	$\prod_{i=1}^{k}(1 - P_y(v_i \mid S \cup M_i)) =$ $\prod_{i=1}^{k}(1 - P_y(v_i' \mid S \cup M_i'))$	$\sigma(.)$ is submodular; IM is NP-hard	Collective behavior, promote new products
DC	$P_y(x \mid S) \leq P_y(x \mid M)$	$\sigma(.)$ is submodular, and IM is NP-hard	Collective behavior, spreading information
IC-N	$\prod_{i=1}^{k}(1 - P_y(v_i \mid S \cup M_i)) =$ $\prod_{i=1}^{k}(1 - P_y(v_i' \mid S \cup M_i'))$	With probability P, each newly active node become positive and with probability 1−P	Incorporate negative opinions
SIR		$\frac{dS}{dt} = -\beta SI$, $\frac{dI}{dt} = \beta SI - \gamma I$, $\frac{dR}{dt} = \gamma I$	Transmission of contagious disease

Separated Threshold Model. This model consider the assumption that it is not necessary to have the same threshold for each cascade, node may have different threshold for different cascade. In Weight-proportional Threshold Model, a node y become active if its neighbors influence reaches its threshold T_y but in this model threshold values are change based on respective cascade. So every node y have threshold values T_y^A and T_y^B for A-cascade and B-cascade respectively. Similarly, weight corresponding to each edge (x, y) have to values $w_{x,y}^A$ and

$w_{x,y}^B$ for A-cascade and B-cascade respectively. In time instance t, every node y goes from inactive to active state with A and B influences. Node y becomes A-Active and B-Active if it satisfies conditions $\sum_{x \in N^a(y) \cap \varphi_A^{t-1}} w_{x,y}^A \geq T_y^A$ and $\sum_{x \in N^a(y) \cap \varphi_B^{t-1}} w_{x,y}^B \geq T_y^B$ respectively.

5   Conclusion and Future Directions

Social networks can be represented in graph $G = (V, E)$ where users of networks are denoted by nodes $x \in V$ in graph and relationship between users x and y is denoted by edge $(x, y) \in E$. Social network play an important role to understands users views for any new product, technology, etc. This review paper gives a framework to analyzing how information spreading is done through network and how people influence each other. This survey covers the various information spread models. Although, these models are basic techniques to analysis social networks, still many questions remains to cover. In future, we can relax some assumption in above models and try to develop better technique for influence diffusion.

References

1. Bhagat, S., Goyal, A., Lakshmanan, L.V.: Maximizing product adoption in social networks. In: Proceedings of the Fifth ACM International Conference on Web Search and Data Mining, WSDM 2012, pp. 603–612. ACM, New York (2012). https://doi.org/10.1145/2124295.2124368
2. Borgatti, S.P., Everett, M.G.: A graph-theoretic perspective on centrality. Soc. Netw. **28**(4), 466–484 (2006). http://www.sciencedirect.com/science/article/pii/S0378873305000833
3. Borodin, A., Filmus, Y., Oren, J.: Threshold models for competitive influence in social networks. In: Saberi, A. (ed.) WINE 2010. LNCS, vol. 6484, pp. 539–550. Springer, Heidelberg (2010). https://doi.org/10.1007/978-3-642-17572-5_48
4. Carnes, T., Nagarajan, C., Wild, S.M., van Zuylen, A.: Maximizing influence in a competitive social network: a follower's perspective. In: Proceedings of the Ninth International Conference on Electronic Commerce, ICEC 2007, pp. 351–360. ACM, New York (2007)
5. Chen, N.: On the approximability of influence in social networks. In: Proceedings of the Nineteenth Annual ACM-SIAM Symposium on Discrete Algorithms, SODA 2008, pp. 1029–1037. Society for Industrial and Applied Mathematics, Philadelphia (2008)
6. Chen, N.: On the approximability of influence in social networks. SIAM J. Discret. Math. **23**(3), 1400–1415 (2009)
7. Chen, W., et al.: Influence maximization in social networks when negative opinions may emerge and propagate. In: Proceedings of the 2011 SIAM International Conference on Data Mining (SDM 2011), April 2011
8. Dreyer, P.: Applications and variations of domination in graphs, January 2000
9. Eiselt, H., Laporte, G.: Competitive spatial models. Eur. J. Oper. Res. **39**(3), 231–242 (1989)

10. Freeman, L.C.: A set of measures of centrality based on betweenness. Sociometry **40**(1), 35–41 (1977). http://www.jstor.org/stable/3033543
11. Freeman, L.C.: Centrality in social networks conceptual clarification. Soc. Netw. **1**(3), 215–239 (1978). http://www.sciencedirect.com/science/article/pii/0378873378900217
12. Goldenberg, J., Libai, B., Muller, E.: Talk of the network: a complex systems look at the underlying process of word-of-mouth. Mark. Lett. **12**(3), 211–223 (2001)
13. Granovetter, M.: Threshold models of collective behavior. Am. J. Sociol. **83**(6), 1420–1443 (1978)
14. Granovetter, M.S.: The strength of weak ties. American Journal of Sociology **78**(6), 1360–1380 (1973). http://www.jstor.org/stable/2776392
15. Kempe, D., Kleinberg, J., Tardos, E.: Maximizing the spread of influence through a social network. In: Proceedings of the Ninth ACM SIGKDD International Conference on Knowledge Discovery and Data Mining, KDD 2003, pp. 137–146. ACM, New York (2003)
16. Kempe, D., Kleinberg, J., Tardos, É.: Influential nodes in a diffusion model for social networks. In: Caires, L., Italiano, G.F., Monteiro, L., Palamidessi, C., Yung, M. (eds.) ICALP 2005. LNCS, vol. 3580, pp. 1127–1138. Springer, Heidelberg (2005). https://doi.org/10.1007/11523468_91
17. Kermack, W.O., McKendrick, A.G.: A contribution to the mathematical theory of epidemics. Proc. R. Soc. Lond. A: Math. Phys. **115**(772), 700–721 (1927)
18. Pathak, N., Banerjee, A., Srivastava, J.: A generalized linear threshold model for multiple cascades, December 2010
19. Rashotte, L.: Social influence, pp. 4426–4429, January 2007
20. Swedberg, R.: Acta Sociologica **37**(4), 426–428 (1994). http://www.jstor.org/stable/4200925

CoIM: Community-Based Influence Maximization in Social Networks

Shashank Sheshar Singh$^{(\boxtimes)}$, Kuldeep Singh, Ajay Kumar, and Bhaskar Biswas

Department of Computer Science and Engineering,
Indian Institute of Technology (BHU), Varanasi 221 005, India
{shashankss.rs.cse16,kuldeep.rs.cse13,
ajayk.rs.cse16,bhaskar.cse}@iitbhu.ac.in

Abstract. *Influence maximization* (IM) is the problem of identifying k most influential users *(seed)* in social networks to maximize influence spread. Despite some recent development achieved by the state-of-the-art *greedy* IM techniques, these works are not time-efficient for large-scale networks. To solve time-efficiency issue, we propose *Community-based Influence Maximization* (CoIM) algorithm. CoIM first partitions the network into sub-networks. Then it selects influential users from sub-networks based on their local influence. The experimental results on both synthetic and real datasets show that proposed algorithm performs better than *greedy* regarding time with the almost same level of memory-consumption and influence spread.

Keywords: Influence maximization · Information diffusion
Social networks · Community detection

1 Introduction

Influence Maximization (IM) is the problem of identifying k most influential users in social network. Recently, IM has gain considerable attention in viral marketing [3], rumor control [24], network monitoring [11], revenue maximization [21], and social recommendation [25]. Domingos and Richardson [3] and Kempe et al. [9] were first to studied IM problem. IM problem is to identify k most influential users known as seed nodes, whose aggregate influence is maximized, i.e.

$$S^* = arg_S max\{\sigma(S)\} \tag{1}$$

where $\sigma(S)$ is an objective function to find expected influence in the network. Kempe et al. proved that $\sigma(S)$ is sub-modular. In order to solve IM problem, there is a need of diffusion model to propagate information in social network [18]. Kempe et al. proposed greedy algorithm and incorporated two basic diffusion models *linear threshold* (*LT*) and *independent Cascade* (*IC*) for information diffusion. IM problem is *NP-hard* under both *LT* and *IC* models proved by [9]. The author also proved that greedy solution is approximated to within a factor of $(1 - 1/e - \epsilon)$.

© Springer Nature Singapore Pte Ltd. 2019
A. K. Luhach et al. (Eds.): ICAICR 2018, CCIS 956, pp. 440–453, 2019.
https://doi.org/10.1007/978-981-13-3143-5_36

Svirdenko et al. [20] proposed a sub-modularity based algorithm named *knapsack greedy* by adding node price constraint. Some other sub-modularity based approaches are introduced in [7,12] to improve efficiency of greedy algorithm. To improve scalability of IM problem many centrality based algorithms are introduced such as *degree discount* [2], *targeted wise greedy* [22], and *diffusion degree* [10]. Wang et al. [23] proposed *community based algorithm (CGA)* to maximize influence in the network. *CGA* first partition the mobile network into sub-networks and it finds seed across sub-networks. Li et al. [14] proposed a community based algorithm viz. *CINEMA*. *CINEMA* introduces conformity first time in IM problem. Recently, context-aware influence maximization techniques are introduced to improve the effectiveness of seed. Some research work has been proposed considering contextual features such as spatial [8,13], competitive [16,26], temporal [5,6], and topical features [1,15] etc.

Contribution. In the era of big data, most of the influence maximization approaches are not time-efficient. We propose a time-efficient community-based framework CoIM. The major contributions of proposed work are as follows.

- We present a community-based framework to identify most influential users in the network.
- We devise a hierarchical clustering approach based on *Jaccard similarity* to identify community structure of influence graph G.
- The experimental results on synthetic and real-world datasets show that CoIM is faster than the state-of-the-art *greedy* algorithms.

Organization. Section 2 defines the problem statement and explains some background information for better understanding of concepts. Section 3 describes CoIM framework. Section 4 explains the algorithm in detail. Section 5 discusses dataset and result analysis. Finally, Sect. 6 is devoted to our conclusion and directions for future work.

2 Preliminaries

2.1 Notations and Definitions

Notations that will be needed for problem formulations in the paper are given in the Table 1 and definitions related our research work are given as follows.

Definition 1 *(Influence graph). An influence graph is an undirected graph $G(V, E)$ that shows the relationship between users. Here V and E represent a set of users and a set of edges respectively.*

Definition 2 *(Neighbors). Neighbors $N(u)$ of node u is defined as the set of users v such that $v \in N(u)$ iff $\exists (u, v) \in E$, $v \in V$.*

Definition 3 *(Influential users). Influential users S refers to k users set that have most influence spread in the network.*

Definition 4 *(Community structure).* *Community structure of an influence graph* $G(V, E)$ *is the set of sub-graph* $C = \{C_1, C_2, C_3, \ldots, C_m\}$ *in such that,* $V(C_i) \cap V(C_j) = \phi$ *and* $\cup_{i=1}^{i=m} V(C_i) = V$ *where* $V(C_i)$ *denotes the set of nodes in community* C_i.

Definition 5 *(Closeness centrality).* *Closeness centrality* $C_C(V_i)$ *measures how a node* v_i *close to all other nodes in the network. It is estimated as the average of shortest path length* D_{SP} *from a node to all other nodes, as follows.*

$$C_C(V_i) = \frac{\sum_{l \in V} D_{SP}(i \to l)}{|V| - 1} \tag{2}$$

Table 1. Notations

$G = (V, E) \triangleq$ A undirected social network with vertex set V and edge set E
$S \triangleq$ Seed Set
$k \triangleq$ The number of nodes in seed set ($|S|$)
$\sigma(S) \triangleq$ The expected influence of seed set in the network
$C \triangleq$ Community structure of influence graph G.
$Sim(u, v) \triangleq$ Jaccard similarity score between node u and v.
$D(V_i) \triangleq$ Degree of node V_i.
$D_{SP}(i \to l) \triangleq$ Shortest path length between node i to l.

2.2   Diffusion Model

We incorporated the use of traditional diffusion models *linear threshold* (*LT*), *independent Cascade* (*IC*), and *weighted Cascade* (*WC*) model for information diffusion [9]. In all of these models, each node at any time t belongs to one of the two-state (inactive or active). Nodes that are not influenced by their neighbors are known as inactive nodes. Initially at time ($t = 0$), all nodes are inactive. Active nodes are influenced by their neighbors and only such nodes can propagate influence to their neighbors.

– In *LT* model, every node u has an activation threshold θ_u and a node v becomes active only if $\Sigma_{u \in N^A(v)} w(u, v) \geq \theta_u$ where $N^A(v)$ and $w(u, v)$ are set of active neighbors of v and edge weight of (u, v) respectively.
– In *IC* and *WC* model, when a node u becomes active at time t, it has a only chance to activate its inactive neighbors v with activation probability p_{uv} at the time ($t + 1$). If node v becomes active at the time ($t + 1$) then it will never be inactive in future.

For each edge $(u, v) \in E$, we assign edge weight $w(u, v)$ under these diffusion models, as follows.

$$w(u,v) = \begin{cases} (0,1) & \text{LT Diffusion Model} \\ [0.01, 0.1] & \text{IC Diffusion Model} \\ \frac{1}{indegree(v)} & \text{WC Diffusion Model} \end{cases} \tag{3}$$

2.3 Problem Statement

Given an influence graph $G = (V, E)$, a diffusion model M, an integer k then influence maximization process selects a seed set S^* from V to maximize influence spread in G, i.e.

$$\sigma(S^*) = argmax_{S \subseteq V \wedge |S|=k} \sigma(S) \tag{4}$$

3 Proposed Work

In this section, we present a novel algorithm named CoIM. The proposed algorithm uses a community-based framework to maximize influence spread in the network. Figure 1 presents the proposed framework of our algorithm. CoIM works in three phases. Each phase of CoIM discusses in the following section.

3.1 Preprocessing

CoIM finds crisp community structure of the network as a preprocessing step. It uses hierarchical clustering to identify community structure of graph G. CoIM uses *Jaccard Index* [19] to calculate similarity between u and v for each edge $e_{(}u, v) \in E$. Similarity score $Sim(u, v)$, $e_{(}u, v) \in E$ is estimated as follows.

$$Sim(u, v) = \frac{|N(u) \cap N(v)|}{|N(u) \cup N(v)|} \tag{5}$$

where $N(u)$ represents neighbors of node u. Initially, CoIM begin by making every nodes as an individual community. After that, it merges two nodes if similarity between these two is highest among others. Now, we consider merged community as a node and continue process until a termination condition satisfied. we use *modularity gain* [4] as termination condition. Suppose that an influence graph $G(V, E)$ with community structure $C = \{C_1, C_2, \ldots, C_m\}$. We can estimate *modularity gain* using following *modularity function*.

$$Q(C) = \sum_{j=1}^{m} \left[\left(\frac{\sum_{v,w \in C_j} Sim(v, w)}{\sum_{v,w \in V} Sim(v, w)} \right) - \left(\frac{\sum_{v \in C_j, w \in V} Sim(v, w)}{\sum_{v,w \in V} Sim(v, w)} \right)^2 \right] \tag{6}$$

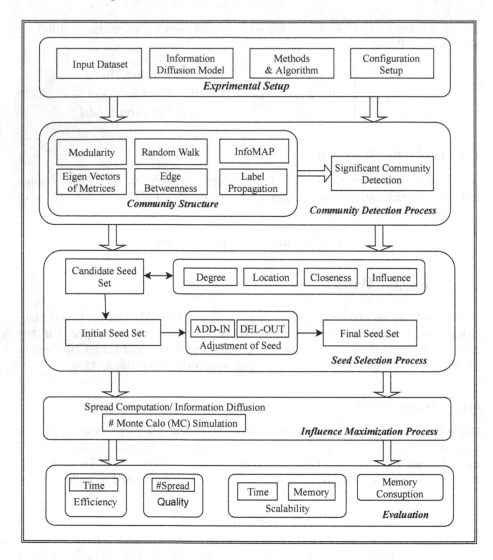

Fig. 1. The proposed CoIM framework

Suppose that we have two community structure C and C' for graph $G(V, E)$ at time t and $(t+1)$ respectively. The *modularity gain* from C to C' is calculated as $\Delta Q_{C \rightarrow C'} = Q_{C'} - Q_C$. After that, we identify *significant communities* in $C = \{C_1, C_2, \ldots, C_m\}$. *Significant communities* are those whose size is more than the *AvgInf(seed)*. *AvgInf(seed)* is the expected influence per seed, as follows.

$$AvgInf(seed) = \frac{|V|}{k} \tag{7}$$

3.2   Seed Selection

In this phase CoIM finds seed nodes. Seed selection process divided into following steps.

- *Candidate seed selection:* CoIM identifies top $p\%$ ($p = 20$) potential centroid nodes to find small set of seed candidates. We finds centroid nodes based on degree centrality, closeness centrality, and influence weight. Candidate seed set is the set of top $p\%$ centroid nodes and hub nodes. We can estimate centroid value of node $V_i \in C_j$ as $AggW(V_i)$.

$$AggW(V_i) = \frac{1}{3}\left[\frac{D(V_i)}{|V|} + \frac{\sum_{l \in C_j} D_{SP}(i \rightarrow l)}{|C_j|^2} + \frac{\sum_{l \in N(V_i)} Inf(i \rightarrow l)}{D(V_i)}\right] \tag{8}$$

  where $D(V_i)$, $D_{SP}(i \rightarrow l)$ and $Inf(i \rightarrow l)$ represent degree of V_i, shortest path distance from node i to l, and influence weight from node i to l respectively.
- *Initial seed selection:* CoIM selects $SeedQ(C_i)$ number of nodes as initial seed nodes for each community $C_i \in \{C_1, C_2, \ldots, C_m\}$ based on priority (using centroid value). $SeedQ(C_i)$ is estimated as follows.

$$SeedQ(C_i) = \frac{k * |C_i|}{\sum_{j=1}^{j=m} |C_j|} \tag{9}$$

- *Adjustment of seed:* CoIM stabilizes the seed set based on *coverage gain*. *Coverage* $C(V_i)$ is define as the number of nodes influenced by V_i after diffusion process. We can estimate the *coverage gain* of node $V_i \in C_i$ using *Coverage* and *Expected Coverage* of V_i, as follows.

$$CG(V_i) = CG_L(V_i) + CG_L(V_i) \tag{10}$$

$$CG_L(V_i) = \frac{C_L(V_i) - EC_L(V_i)}{|C_i|} \tag{11}$$

$$CG_G(V_i) = \frac{C_G(V_i) - EC_G(V_i)}{|C_i|} \tag{12}$$

where $EC_L(V_i)$ and $EC_G(V_i)$ are *local expected coverage* and *global expected coverage* of V_i respectively. $C_L(V_i)$ and $C_G(V_i)$ represent local and global coverage of V_i respectively. Similarly, we estimate *Coverage gain* (CG) for a community C_i, as follows.

$$CG(C_i) = \frac{1}{|C_i|} \sum_{V_i \in C_i} CG(V_i) \tag{13}$$

3.3   Influence Spreading

Finally, CoIM estimates influence spread in the network from seed set S under diffusion models (IC, WC, and LT). Influence diffusion process is dependent on the community structure of the network. It maximize influence spread based on local influence of nodes.

4   Algorithm

The main Algorithm 1 takes two input, an influence graph G and size of seed set k. Lines 1-3 initialize S, IS, and C_S with an empty set. Line 4 considers every node as a community and place it to community structure C. The **for** loop in lines 5–6 calculates similarity score of each edge $e_{uv} \in E$. The **while** loop in lines 7–9 merges most similar communities C_i and C_j repeatedly, until modularity gain $\Delta_{C \rightarrow C'}$ is positive. Line 10 gives community structure C of G. The **for** loop in lines 11–13 identifies significant communities in C. The **for** loop in lines 14–22 finds candidate seed nodes for seed selection. The **for** loop in lines 15–19 calculates centroid value $AggW$ of each node V_i based on degree centrality, closeness centrality, and influence weight. Line 20 selects $p\%$ nodes as candidate seed based on $AggW(V_i)$. Line 21 selects hub nodes and add these nodes to seed set. Line 22 gives final candidate set for significant community C_i. The **for** loop in lines 23–28 selects seed set from candidate set. The **for** loop in lines 29–30 finds initial seed set. The **for** loop in lines 32–41 performs tunning of seed to maximize influence spread. Line 42 gives final seed. Line 43 returns desired outcome seed set S.

4.1   Running Example

Figure 2 presents an overview of proposed algorithm CoIM. There are seven steps perform to find seed set as shown in Fig. 2. Initially, given an influence graph G with $V = \{A, B, C, D, E, F, G\}$ with unknown community structure. Now, we explain working of running example in detail.

1. CoIM considers each node as an individual community, i.e., initially community structure $C = \{A, B, C, D, E, F, G\}$. After that, it merges most similar communities until $\Delta Q_{C \rightarrow C'} \geq 0$, i.e., $C' = \{\{A, D\}, B, \{C, F\}, E, G\}$.
2. $C = \{\{A, D\}, B, \{C, F\}, E, G\}$, $C' = \{\{A, B, D\}, \{C, F\}, \{E, G\}\}$.
3. $C = \{\{A, B, D\}, \{C, F\}, \{E, G\}\}$, $C' = \{\{A, B, D\}, \{C, E, F, G\}\}$.
4. Now, CoIM does not able to merge communities because of $\Delta Q_{C \rightarrow C'} < 0$. So final significant community structure $C' = \{\{A, B, D\}, \{C, E, F, G\}\}$.
5. It selects candidate seed based on centroid values and hubs, i.e., $Candidate_{Set}(C') = \{\{A, D\}, \{E, G\}\}$.
6. Next, it identifies seed nodes, i.e., $S = \{A, G\}$.
7. Finally, it finds influenced nodes, i.e., $Inf_{Nodes} = \{B, C, D, E, F\}$.

Algorithm 1. *CoIM* : Proposed Algorithm

Input: Graph $G(V, E)$, Number of seed k
Output: Seed set S

1: $S \leftarrow \phi$;   ▷ Initialization
2: $IS \leftarrow \phi$
3: $C_S \leftarrow \phi$;
4: $C \leftarrow \{V_1, V_2, ..., V_N\}$;
5: **for each edge** $e_{u,v} \in E$ **do** ▷ Identification of Community Structure in Graph G
6:      Calculate $Sim(u, v)$;
7: **while** $(\Delta Q_{C \rightarrow C'} \geq 0$) **do**
8:      **if** $\{(Sim(C_i, C_j) \geq Sim(C_i, C_k)) \wedge (Sim(C_i, C_j) \geq Sim(C_l, C_j)\}$ **then**
9:          $C' \leftarrow$ merge communities C_i and C_j of C, $k \neq j, l \neq i, \forall k, l$;
10: $C \leftarrow C'$;
11: **for** $(\forall C_i \in C)$ **do**   ▷ Identification of Significant Communities
12:     **if** $\{|C_i| \geq AvgInf(seed)\}$ **then**
13:         $C_S \leftarrow C_S \cup C_i$;
14: **for** $(\forall C'_i \in C_S)$ **do**   ▷ Candidate seed selection
15:     **for each node** $V_i \in C'_i$ **do**
16:         Calculate $DegreeC(V_i)$;
17:         Calculate $CloseC(V_i)$;
18:         Calculate $Inf(V_i)$;
19:         Calculate $AggW(V_i)$;
20:     $S_1 \leftarrow$ select top p% nodes $V'_i s$ in C'_i based on $AggW(V_i)$;
21:     $S_2 \leftarrow$ Hub nodes $H'_i s$ connecting to community C'_i ;
22:     $Candidate_{Set}(C'_i) \leftarrow S_1 \cup S_2$;
23: **for** $(\forall C'_i \in C_S)$ **do**   ▷ Seed selection
24:     $K_i \leftarrow SeedQ(C'_i)$;
25:     $Seed(C'_i) \leftarrow$ select K_i top priority node from $Candidate_{Set}(C'_i)$;
26:     **if** (any hub node $H_i \in Seed(C'_i)$) **then**
27:         **for** $(\forall C'_j \in C_S$ **which have edges** $(H_i, C'_j))$ **do**
28:             $Seed(C'_j) \leftarrow Seed(C'_j) \setminus V_i(C'_j, H_i)$;
29: **for** ($\forall C'_i \in C_S$) **do**   ▷ Initial seed
30:     $IS \leftarrow IS \cup Seed(C'_i)$;
31: Coverage $\leftarrow$ Set of influenced node in C_S with seed set IS ;
32: **for** (l= 1 to 2k) **do**   ▷ Adjustment of seed
33:     TS $\leftarrow$ IS ;
34:     DEL-OUT $\leftarrow$ Select lowest Coverage Gain node $V_i \in Coverage$;
35:     $C_j \leftarrow$ Select Highest Coverage Gain Community $C_j \in C_S$;
36:     ADD-IN $\leftarrow$ Select Highest priority node from Community C_j ;
37:     Replace node DEL-OUT $\in$ TS with node ADD-IN $\in C_j$;
38:     TCoverage $\leftarrow$ Set of influenced node in C_S with seed set TS ;
39:     **if** ($|TCoverage| > |Coverage|$) **then**
40:         IS $\leftarrow$ TS;
41:         Coverage $\leftarrow$ TCoverage;
42: S $\leftarrow$ IS;
43: **return** S;

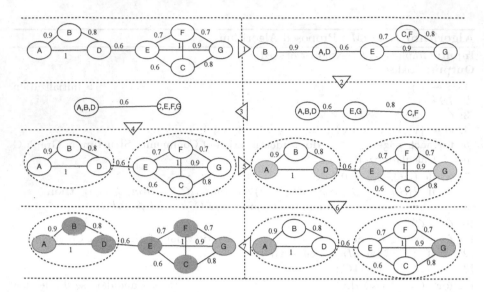

Fig. 2. CoIM overview using a running example

5   Evaluation

5.1   Dataset

The synthetic networks are produced using *erdos-renyi* model in *R* language with parameters to control the nature of graph. *Dolphin*[1] network is a social network of frequent associations between 62 dolphins in a community living off Doubtful Sound, New Zealand, as compiled by [17]. All the networks used in the experiment are undirected (Table 2).

Table 2. Statistical information of datasets.

Dataset	$|V|$	$|E|$	P	Type
SN1000	1000	2519	0.05	Synthetic (gnp)
SN1200	1200	2485	0.02	Synthetic (gnp)
Dolphin	62	159	-	Real Network

5.2   Algorithm to Compare

- *Random*: This algorithm randomly selects k users as influential users.
- *MaxDegree*: This algorithm selects k highest degree users.

---

[1] http://www-personal.umich.edu/~mejn/netdata/dolphins.zip.

- *Greedy*: This algorithm obtains approximate solution of IM problem [9].
- *CoIM*: This is our proposed work which takes into account the nature of the network to form communities. Therefore, it reduces search space of IM.

5.3   Experimental Result

Quality: Quality in IM problem equates influence spread in the network from given seed users. Figure 3 shows that comparison of influence spread of proposed algorithm with the state-of-the-art algorithms under traditional diffusion models (*IC*, *WC*, and *LT*). Figure 3 shows that proposed algorithm outperforms the

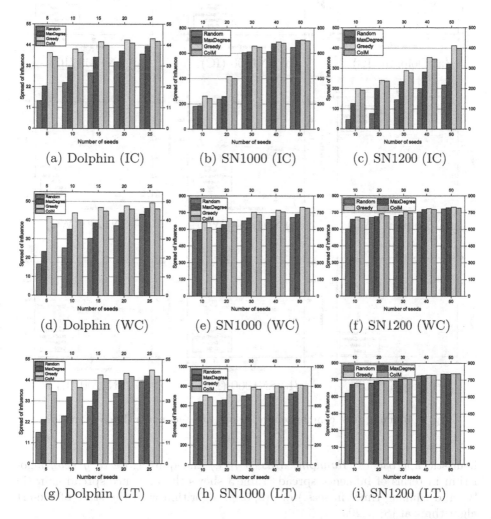

(a) Dolphin (IC)   (b) SN1000 (IC)   (c) SN1200 (IC)

(d) Dolphin (WC)   (e) SN1000 (WC)   (f) SN1200 (WC)

(g) Dolphin (LT)   (h) SN1000 (LT)   (i) SN1200 (LT)

Fig. 3. Influence spread comparison in various datasets under different models.

Table 3. Performance of our proposed algorithm CoIM at $|S| = 20$ under different diffusion models. Spread (%) shows speedup of CoIM from baseline methods in terms of influence spread. Time (sec.) represents running time of corresponding technique.

Dataset	IC Spread (%)			IC Time (sec.)				WC Spread (%)			WC Time (sec.)				LT Spread (%)			LT Time (sec.)			
	Random	MaxDegree	Greedy	Random	MaxDegree	Greedy	CoIM	Random	MaxDegree	Greedy	Random	MaxDegree	Greedy	CoIM	Random	MaxDegree	Greedy	Random	MaxDegree	Greedy	CoIM
SN1000	68.91	55.21	-3.60	16.48	25.19	668.96	8.36	9.34	3.73	-4.30	46.35	29.70	874.26	14.36	8.56	7.41	-494626.00	43.47	30.19	768.96	11.36
SN1200	34.66	17.91	-1.25	24.48	28.19	768.96	9.69	21.16	2.66	-0.95	32.48	43.19	974.26	22.69	19.45	0.41	-0.27	27.48	37.19	874.26	12.69
Dolphin	28.22	10.16	-3.43	3.04	3.86	21.45	1.12	24.01	4.91	-3.36	4.01	4.93	54.94	1.32	46.34	27.66	-1.64	3.64	1.84	51.68	0.22

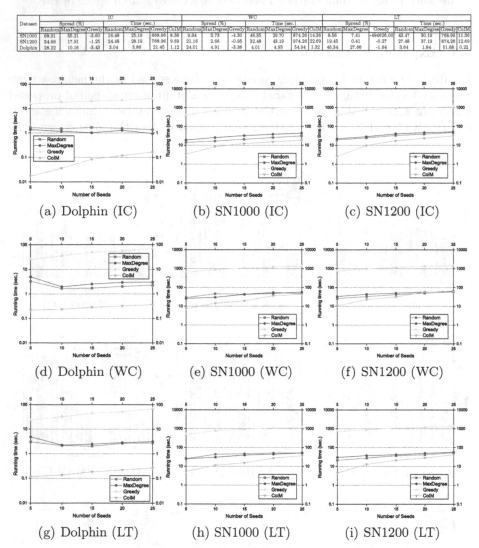

(a) Dolphin (IC)   (b) SN1000 (IC)   (c) SN1200 (IC)

(d) Dolphin (WC)   (e) SN1000 (WC)   (f) SN1200 (WC)

(g) Dolphin (LT)   (h) SN1000 (LT)   (i) SN1200 (LT)

Fig. 4. Running time comparison in various datasets under different models.

heuristic approaches (*Random, MaxDegree*) and quite close to *greedy* algorithm in terms of influence spread. Table 3 shows the influence spread gain (in %) and running time (in secs.) of proposed algorithm with the state-of-the-art algorithms at $|S| = 20$.

Efficiency: Figure 4 shows that proposed algorithm outperforms *greedy* algorithm in terms of efficiency. CoIM considers only local influence of nodes in seed selection while *greedy* uses marginal gain of nodes globally. Heuristic approaches (*Random, MaxDegree*) are much faster than CoIM. Though these approaches generate poor quality seed. Thus proposed algorithm is more efficient than *greedy* with almost no compromising in spread.

Memory Consumption: Figure 5 shows that heuristic approaches take very less memory. *Random* does not consider any feature of node in seed selection process while *MaxDegree* considers only node degree. Thus memory consumption is very less in heuristic approaches because no need to maintain features of nodes. *Greedy* needs marginal gain of each node so it takes more memory to

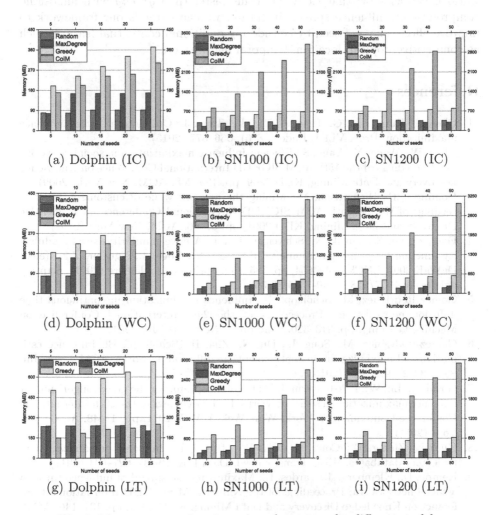

(a) Dolphin (IC)	(b) SN1000 (IC)	(c) SN1200 (IC)
(d) Dolphin (WC)	(e) SN1000 (WC)	(f) SN1200 (WC)
(g) Dolphin (LT)	(h) SN1000 (LT)	(i) SN1200 (LT)

Fig. 5. Memory comparison in various datasets under different models.

store marginal gain of each node. Proposed algorithm CoIM needs comparatively more memory to store nodes with their community information.

6   Conclusion and Future Directions

In this work, we propose a community-based influence maximization algorithm CoIM under traditional diffusion models (IC, WC, LT). CoIM focuses on the time-efficiency without much compromising on quality of seed. In the era of big data, time-efficiency is a critical issue on network mining problems. CoIM first partitions the network into sub-networks using hierarchical clustering based on *Jaccard similarity*. Then it finds seed nodes from sub-networks based on their local importance. The experimental results on both synthetic and real-world networks show that CoIM performs faster than *greedy* with almost no compromise on influence spread. In future, we can extends our framework to improve effectiveness of seed by considering additional contextual features such as competitive, topical, location, temporal features, etc.

References

1. Chen, S., Fan, J., Li, G., Feng, J., Tan, K., Tang, J.: Online topic-aware influence maximization. Proc. VLDB Endow. **8**(6), 666–677 (2015)
2. Chen, W., Wang, Y., Yang, S.: Efficient influence maximization in social networks. In: Proceedings of the 15th ACM SIGKDD International Conference on Knowledge Discovery and Data Mining, KDD 2009, pp. 199–208. ACM, New York (2009)
3. Domingos, P., Richardson, M.: Mining the network value of customers. In: Proceedings of the Seventh ACM SIGKDD International Conference on Knowledge Discovery and Data Mining, KDD 2001, pp. 57–66. ACM, New York (2001)
4. Feng, Z., Xu, X., Yuruk, N., Schweiger, T.A.J.: A novel similarity-based modularity function for graph partitioning. In: Song, I.Y., Eder, J., Nguyen, T.M. (eds.) DaWaK 2007. LNCS, vol. 4654, pp. 385–396. Springer, Heidelberg (2007). https://doi.org/10.1007/978-3-540-74553-2_36
5. Gomez Rodriguez, M., Schölkopf, B.: Influence maximization in continuous time diffusion networks. In: Proceedings of the 29th International Conference on Machine Learning, pp. 313–320. Omnipress, New York, July 2012
6. Gomez-Rodriguez, M., Song, L., Du, N., Zha, H., Schölkopf, B.: Influence estimation and maximization in continuous-time diffusion networks. ACM Trans. Inf. Syst. **34**(2), 9:1–9:33 (2016)
7. Goyal, A., Lu, W., Lakshmanan, L.V.: Celf++: optimizing the greedy algorithm for influence maximization in social networks. In: Proceedings of the 20th International Conference Companion on World Wide Web, WWW 2011, pp. 47–48. ACM, New York (2011)
8. Guo, L., Zhang, D., Cong, G., Wu, W., Tan, K.L.: Influence maximization in trajectory databases. IEEE Trans. Knowl. Data Eng. **29**(3), 627–641 (2017)
9. Kempe, D., Kleinberg, J., Tardos, E.: Maximizing the spread of influence through a social network. In: Proceedings of the Ninth ACM SIGKDD International Conference on Knowledge Discovery and Data Mining, KDD 2003, pp. 137–146. ACM, New York (2003)

10. Kundu, S., Murthy, C.A., Pal, S.K.: A new centrality measure for influence maximization in social networks. In: Kuznetsov, S.O., Mandal, D.P., Kundu, M.K., Pal, S.K. (eds.) PReMI 2011. LNCS, vol. 6744, pp. 242–247. Springer, Heidelberg (2011). https://doi.org/10.1007/978-3-642-21786-9_40

11. Leskovec, J., Adamic, L.A., Huberman, B.A.: The dynamics of viral marketing. ACM Trans. Web **1**(1) (2007)

12. Leskovec, J., Krause, A., Guestrin, C., Faloutsos, C., VanBriesen, J., Glance, N.: Cost-effective outbreak detection in networks. In: Proceedings of the 13th ACM SIGKDD International Conference on Knowledge Discovery and Data Mining, KDD 2007, pp. 420–429. ACM, New York (2007)

13. Li, G., Chen, S., Feng, J., Tan, K., Li, W.: Efficient location-aware influence maximization. In: Proceedings of the 2014 ACM SIGMOD International Conference on Management of Data, SIGMOD 2014, pp. 87–98. ACM, New York (2014)

14. Li, H., Bhowmick, S.S., Sun, A., Cui, J.: Conformity-aware influence maximization in online social networks. VLDB J. **24**(1), 117–141 (2015)

15. Li, Y., Zhang, D., Tan, K.L.: Real-time targeted influence maximization for online advertisements. Proc. VLDB Endow. **8**(10), 1070–1081 (2015)

16. Lin, S.C., Lin, S.D., Chen, M.S.: A learning-based framework to handle multi-round multi-party influence maximization on social networks. In: Proceedings of the 21th ACM SIGKDD International Conference on Knowledge Discovery and Data Mining, KDD 2015, pp. 695–704. ACM, New York (2015)

17. Lusseau, D., Schneider, K., Boisseau, O.J., Haase, P., Slooten, E., Dawson, S.M.: The bottlenose dolphin community of doubtful sound features a large proportion of long-lasting associations. Behav. Ecol. Sociobiol. **54**(4), 396–405 (2003)

18. Mahajan, V., Muller, E., Bass, F.M.: New product diffusion models in marketing: a review and directions for research. J. Mark. **54**(1), 1–26 (1990)

19. Paul, J.: The distribution of the flora in the alpine zone.1. New Phytol. **11**(2), 37–50 (1912)

20. Sviridenko, M.: A note on maximizing a submodular set function subject to a knapsack constraint. Oper. Res. Lett. **32**(1), 41–43 (2004)

21. Teng, Y.W., Tai, C.H., Yu, P.S., Chen, M.S.: Revenue maximization on the multi-grade product, pp. 576–584 (2018)

22. Wang, Y., Feng, X.: A potential-based node selection strategy for influence maximization in a social network. In: Huang, R., Yang, Q., Pei, J., Gama, J., Meng, X., Li, X. (eds.) ADMA 2009. LNCS (LNAI), vol. 5678, pp. 350–361. Springer, Heidelberg (2009). https://doi.org/10.1007/978-3-642-03348-3_34

23. Wang, Y., Cong, G., Song, G., Xie, K.: Community-based greedy algorithm for mining top-k influential nodes in mobile social networks. In: KDD (2010)

24. Wu, P., Pan, L.: Scalable influence blocking maximization in social networks under competitive independent cascade models. Comput. Netw. **123**, 38–50 (2017)

25. Ye, M., Liu, X., Lee, W.C.: Exploring social influence for recommendation: a generative model approach. In: Proceedings of the 35th International ACM SIGIR Conference on Research and Development in Information Retrieval, SIGIR 2012, pp. 671–680. ACM, New York (2012)

26. Zhu, Y., Li, D., Zhang, Z.: Minimum cost seed set for competitive social influence. In: IEEE INFOCOM 2016 - The 35th Annual IEEE International Conference on Computer Communications, pp. 1–9, April 2016

Anomaly Detection in MANET Using Zone Based AODV Routing Protocol

G. S. Prasanna Lakshmi$^{(\boxtimes)}$, Shantakumar B. Patil,
and Premjyothi Patil

Department of Computer Science and Engineering,
Nagarjuna College of Engineering and Technology, VTU, Belgavi, India
prasannalakshmigs@gmail.com

Abstract. Intrusion Detection System (IDS) is a famous approach for finding attacks in anomalies. This system is used for monitoring the attacks happening in mesh or computers. The anomaly intrusion detection technique plays the significant part in the intrusion detection systems to recognize the recent or a novel attacks by identifying any variation from common profile. This research provides the proof for enhancement of anomaly intrusion detection. The introduced method improves the security by using anomaly based intrusion detection process and zone based AODV routing protocol to discover shortest path. First it contains selection of the features for anomaly IDS. Next is essential to identify the novel or recent attacks by achieved decision rules from database.

Keywords: Anomaly based intrusion detection technique
Security mobile Ad-hoc network (MANET) zone based AODV routing protocol

1 Introduction

Mobile Ad-hoc Networks (MANETs) contains mobile node interrelated by wireless links in communication-less atmospheres with no relying on any federalized power like base station as shown in Fig. 1. The nodes which will not be inside the communication range of one another, will converse by intermediate nodes known as the relay nodes. The Mobile Ad-hoc Networks are organized in the regions or such conditions where communications is not accessible or when operation of communication is not possible or costly, like environmental disasters, emergency operations etc. Because of the distributed architecture, dynamic mesh topology and the nonappearance of the centralized authority, the MANETs are helpless to the packet routing attack [13].

The MANET is a self structured grouping of mobile nodes which will converse with each other without the assist of any permanent infrastructure or central coordinator. A node is any mobile device with capability to converse with another device. The node acts as router and also host in MANET. A node planning to converse with other node that is not within conversion range, then it will take the help of intermediate nodes to send out its message. Network topology is robustly modified over time as nodes travel about. Several novel nodes link the network or some nodes separate themselves from network [13].

© Springer Nature Singapore Pte Ltd. 2019
A. K. Luhach et al. (Eds.): ICAICR 2018, CCIS 956, pp. 454–468, 2019.
https://doi.org/10.1007/978-981-13-3143-5_37

Mobile Ad-hoc Network may be a multi hop wireless network, whenever nodes converse with each other without previously organized infrastructure. With nonexistence of previously recognized infrastructure, (for example no access purpose, no router etc.) 2 nodes converse with one another in an extremely peer to peer manner. When 2 nodes converse straightly inside transmission, it differs from all dissimilar nodes. Or else, nodes converse through multi-hop route with assistance of dissimilar nodes. In the MANET, it contains self organizing, self-administrating and self creating capacity. For example disaster relief, embrace field of honor condition and shortest conditions like public events. Limited information measure, frequent vary in topology, process capability and restricted storage of MANETs have increased a lot of challenges for researchers of network. In every required challenge is to create a support for time period multicast communication [11]. Ad-hoc networking is a promising technology that permits every node to join by wireless communication links, without any base station. These networking have some features; energy, bandwidth and physical security are limited to topology dynamics. Hence the routing protocols utilized in wired network are not matched for the MANET.

The IDS is a practice of examining the events happening in the computer or mesh and examining them for the signals of the intrusion. The IDS is intended to care the availability, confidentiality and integrity of significant networked information system. The IDS is the method that combines and evaluates information from the different regions contained by the mesh or computer to recognize the attacks prepared against these components. Intrusion detection system utilizes number of general processes for examining the utilizations of vulnerabilities.

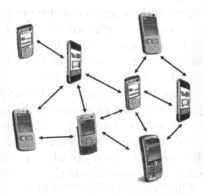

Fig. 1. Mobile ad-hoc network

The IDS is mainly a security system of network system which identifies any harmful behaviors and raise an alarm so that protecting measures are taken to avoid attack. The IDS is categorized into 2 categories, which are signature detection and anomaly detection. Signature detection method is dependable in nature since it is deterministic. It utilizes patterns of well known attack to recognize identical intrusions. Although this technique has some disadvantages, that it is impossible to detect unknown attacks, a dataset is necessary for it which makes it complicated to maintain and also time consuming. Alternatively, anomaly based IDS can evaluate among anomalous and regular behavior of a network scheme. Thus unlike signature detection, this anomaly detection technique works well for known as well unknown or new attacks. But drawback of this detection method is that, it excludes identifying the actual attacks; it can also raise few fake alarms where the intrusions are not occurred. In this paper we are detecting the attacks on MANET by using zone based AODV protocol. From the AODV we are finding the shortest path for communicating the source and destination. There are many types in anomaly intrusion detection system, in this proposed system the buffer overflow is detected using suitable techniques.

2   Literature Survey

Lin et al. [1] introduced a technique with the feature collection and decision rules used for anomaly IDS. The aim is to obtain advantage of the Decision Tree (DT), Simulated Annealing (SA) and SVM. In introduced algorithm, the SA and SVM can discover top selected characteristics to promote the accurateness of anomaly ID. With analyzing information from utilizing the KDD'99 dataset, the SA and DT will get decision rules for recent attack and be able to develop the accuracy of the categorization. The good parameter settings for support vector machine and DT are routinely adjusted by the SA. The result of simulations shows that introduced technique is victorious in identifying the anomaly IDS.

Mingqiang et al. [5] proposed graph-based IDS by utilizing the outlier detection system based on the (LDCGB) Local Deviation Coefficient. Evaluated with the other intrusion detection techniques of clustering, this technique is needless to early cluster number. For now, it is strong in outlier's affection and capable to identify any figure of the cluster somewhat that the circle one only. Furthermore, it still contains the steady rate of recognition on muted or strange attacks. The LDCGB utilizes the graph based cluster technique to achieve the primary division of the dataset. This will be based on cluster precision parameter quite than the primary cluster number. Alternatively, due to these, IDS is depending on dataset of mixed training, hence it should contain high accuracy to warranty its presentation. Thus in phrase labeling, the algorithm forces outlier detection technique of local variation coefficient to tag the GB algorithm result. This calculation is capable to develop accuracy of labeling. After the algorithm is tested by the KDDCup99 dataset, the false positive rate (2.24%) and detection rate (93.30%) are achieved. The result of the experiment expresses that the introduced algorithm can achieve a reasonable performance.

Al-Janabi et al. [3] has taken the behavior of packet as parameter in the anomaly intrusion detection for the research. There are some techniques to help IDSs to study behavior of the system. The introduced IDS utilize a back propagation ANN to study behavior of method. They have utilized KDD'99 data set in their research and achieved results satisfy the work intention.

Sommer et al. [2] studied the differentiations among the system intrusion detection issue and different regions where machine learning frequently finds great achievement. Their important state is the duty of discovering attacks is essentially dissimilar from other applications, making it considerably difficult for intrusion detection area to make use of machine learning successfully. They maintain this state by recognizing challenges exacting to network intrusion detection and give a set of instructions aimed to make stronger future research on the anomaly detection.

Hu [4] introduced the essentials of HIDS and the famous HIDS were examined. Some performance aspects were given and talented HIDS technologies were examined. A novel framework is introduced to add the multiple detection engines. Some systems under this frame work are advised. They consider that in addition to scheming novel individual detection engines and getting better presently active detection engines, much effort is essential to improve novel schemes or architectures like a verity of benefits of individual detection engines can employed successfully.

Meng [6] executes and evaluates machine learning systems of neural network, the SVM and decision tree in same atmosphere with the reason of discovering the practice and problems of utilizing these approaches in recognizing irregular behaviors. By the examination of investigational results, they maintain that the actual presentation of machine learning algorithm based greatly on practical situations. Hence, machine learning approach is believed to be used in a suitable way in terms of actual settings. Researchers in [12, 14] and [15] also proposed an efficient approach.

Lalli et al. [11] says that the traditional IDS contain a problem dealing with lack of protected boundaries, threats from compromised nodes, lack of centralized organization service, restricted scalability and power supply. Because of these problems, they are encouraged to introduce well-organized intrusion detection system, which contains a novel method to recognize the anomalous behaviors in MANETs. They introduced a genetic based feature selection and rule valuation procedure for the detection of anomaly. This procedure is efficiently categorized with novel rules and as well enlarges with higher positive rate alarm. A novel discovery of their introduced work is efficiently observe anomalies with higher detection rate, lower false positive rate and achieves upper detection accuracy.

Bhuyan et al. [16] proved a comprehensive and structured overview of different features of network anomaly detection so that a researcher can become rapidly familiar with each portion of network anomaly detection. They present attacks usually encountered by network IDS. They classify existing network anomaly recognition systems and methods based on fundamental computational techniques utilized. Inside this frame work, they shortly explain and compare a large number of network anomaly detection systems and methods. Additionally, they as well discuss tools that may be utilized by network protectors and datasets that researchers in network anomaly detection will utilized. They as well as emphasize research directions in the network anomaly detection.

Sen et al. [17] introduced and implemented BPNN (Back Propagation Neural Network) technique as a standard, robust supervised learning neural network. Utilizing dissimilar testing and training database, they tried to improve an anomaly based IDS that will assist them to discover detection rate and false positive rate of dissimilar kinds of dataset. A better model is improved which may increase effectiveness of BPNN technique for enhanced recognition of anomaly attacks and as well is capable to converge more quickly to ultimate outcome.

3 Methodology

The Fig. 2 depicts block diagram of proposed scheme. Here the first step is initialize network that is selection of source node and destination node to find some node parameters. A zone based AODV protocol is utilized to choose path among source node and destination node or for communicating source and destination node.

The source node will transmit RREQ (Route Request) message to destination node. When RREQ message is reached to destination node, the path will establish among source and destination. The node at destination will transmits RREP to source node and then source node will transfer data packet to destination. This zone based protocol partitions complete network into zones. It makes use of any reactive or proactive protocols inside and among zones. Intra-zone routing is presented generally by proactive protocol, thereby decreases delay to communicate to nodes inside network. Inter-zone routing protocol utilizes reactive protocol; this ignores the need to keep proactive fresh state of the whole network. By using the FSM (Finite State Machine) verifying the RREQ and RREP messages then the anomaly IDSs check that the nodes are anomaly behavioral or not. Here the buffer over flow attack is detected. The buffer overflow attack is a kind of anomaly. If the anomaly behavioral nodes or buffer overflow attacks are present in network, an alarm will be generating. If not it will forward data packet to next node or destination.

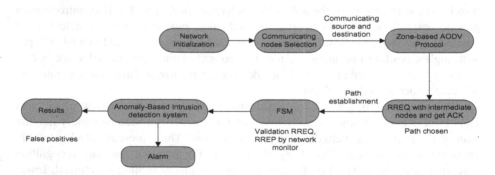

Fig. 2. Block diagram of proposed technique

3.1 AODV Routing Protocol

For the wireless Ad-hoc network the AODV (Ad-hoc On Demand Distance Vector) is a routing protocol. It's a reactive protocol that will find out a route to destination only when it is necessary. In AODV the knob that wants an association sends out a route request message that is RREQ. Every nearest node can achieve one of below given two actions:

- Send the RREP that is route replay message to source node suppose it is previously contain the route.

- Make the way inside its routing chart regards the source node, increase the hop count in route request message and retransmit route request message to its neighbours.

The RREQ arrive at destination or several intermediate nodes, which contain fresh route to destination and robotically generates the repeal path. The route replay message follow reverse path and sets up forward pointer for data packet to the destination. Once source gets a route replay message it will begin to sending the data packets. Suppose later on source receive the route replay message containing a higher series number or the similar sequence number with the fewer number of hops, it will modernize its routing chart and begins utilizing best route to destination. Suppose a link break happen the upstream node transfer a route error message that is RERR to source node and discovery of route is reinitiated at source suppose needed.

The RREQ, RREP, and RERR etc. messages are concluded by the series numbers employed in the messages. The node increases the series number of the message, before sending the any kind of routing control message. The highest series number specifies much fresh information. When a node obtains multiple control messages, one with the highest series number is measured more up to date and it is utilized in route organization by the other nodes.

3.2   RREQ Message and RREP Message

a. **Route request:** Suppose there is no route for destination, a Route Request message (RREQ) is sent throughout the network. The route request contains the following phases which is depicted in Table 1:

Table 1. Phases in route request message

Source address	Request ID	Source sequence no.	Destination address	Destination sequence No.	Hop count

Request ID is incremented all time the source node transmits a novel route request, thus the pair (request ID, source address) recognize a RREQ individually. On getting a route request message every node verifies ID of request and address of source. Suppose node is previously received the route request message with similar set of parameters the novel RREQ packet can be unused. Or else the RREQ is either broadcasted or responded with a Route REPlay message (RREP). Suppose, for the destination, the node will not has route entry or it contain one but this is no more an up to date route, the RREQ is again broadcasted with incremented hop count and also suppose node contain a route along with sequence number larger than or equivalent to that of route request, a route replay message is created and transferred back to source. Number of route request message that a node can transferred per second is restricted. There is an optimization of AODV utilizing an expanding ring (ESR) method when flooding route request message. Each RREQ contains a TTL (Time To Live) value that indicates number of times this message will be rebroadcasted. This value is fixed to the previously defined value at first broadcast and enlarged at the retransmission. Retransmission arises suppose no replies are received. Previously such flooding utilized a TTL larger enough-larger than diameter of network to attain every node in network, and hence to promise successful route finding in only one round of the flooding. Though, this lower delay time system causes higher overhead and needless broadcast messages. Afterwards, it was revealed that least cost flooding search issue will be resolved through a sequence of flooding with an optimally selected group of TTLs.

b. **Route replay**: Suppose a node is destination or has a suitable route to the destination, it sends a route replay message back to source. This RREP contain below format which is depicted in Table 2.

Table 2. Format of route replay message

Source address	Destination address	Destination sequence no.	Hop count	Life time

The cause one can unicast route replay back is that. Each node transferring a route request message caches a route back to source. The route request message and route replay message are shown in Figs. 3 and 4.

c. **Route error**: Every node observes its own neighborhood node. When a node in an active route gets lost, a Route ERRor (RERR) message is produced to inform other nodes on both the sides of the link about loss of this link.

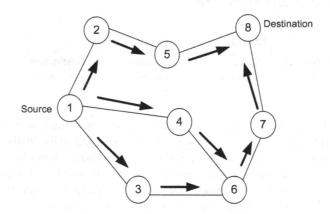

Fig. 3. The RREQ message

Zone Routing Protocol

Zone Routing Protocol (ZRP) joins the benefits of reactive and proactive approaches by preserving an up to date topological map of the zone centered on every node. Inside the zone, the routes will be instantly obtainable. Outside the zone, the ZRP utilizes the route detection processes, which can profit from local routing information of zone.

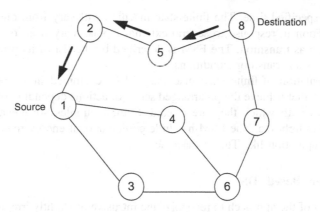

Fig. 4. The RREP message

Reactive and proactive routing contains particular advantage and disadvantage that create them suitable for definite types of scenarios. Because reactive protocol should initially resolve the route, which might be the result in the significant delay, suppose the information will not obtainable in the cache. On the opposite the proactive routing preserves information that is instantly obtainable and the wait before transmitting a packet is minimum.

The proactive routing utilizes extra bandwidth to maintain information of routing, where as reactive routing includes lengthy route request delay. The reactive routing in addition wastefully overflows the total network for the determination of route. The ZRP intended to address issues by adding the better properties of together approaches. Zone Routing Protocol is classified as hybrid reactive or proactive routing protocol. In the ad-hoc network, it is believed that the biggest part of traffic is fixed to nearer nodes. Hence, ZRP decreases proactive range to the zone centered on every nodes. The protection of routing information is simple in limited zone. Furthermore the routing information amount that is not utilized is reduced. Still nodes further can arrived with reactive routing. Because every node proactively store information of local route, the route request can be most powerfully executed without enquiring every network nodes. Even with the use of zone, the zone routing protocol has a plane view over network. Like this manner, the directorial overhead connected to the hierarchical protocols can be ignored. The hierarchical routing protocols depends on planned assignment of landmarks or gateways, hence every nodes can contact every levels, mainly the top level. The nodes related to altered subnets should transmit their communication to a subnet that is general to both nodes. This might block the network parts. The ZRP is considered as flat protocol because the zone overlaps. Therefore, finest routes can be recognized and network jamming can be decreased. The behavior of ZRP depends on the present configuration of network and users behavior [8].

3.3   FSM

A Finite State Machine or simply state machine, is the mathematical replica of computation. It is a theoretical machine that will be accurately one of the finite numbers of states at any specified time. The finite state machine will vary from one condition to another condition in response to several external inputs. Vary from one condition to other is known as transition. The FSM is described by the list of its primary state, its state and the every transition conditions.

The presentation of finite state machine will be examined in various devices in present society that achieve the prearranged series of actions depending on sequence of the procedures with which they are offered. Some examples are elevators, vending machine, traffic light etc. The FSM has little computational energy than several other replica of computation like Turing machine.

3.4   Anomaly Based IDS

The capability of the approach to recognize the intrusive or slightly irregular behaviour is a foundation of anomaly based intrusion systems. Initial problem in this position is the meaning of the anomaly. The regular understanding of anomaly as activity dissimilar from the common brings many challenges in the practical settings. The intellectual research largely describes anomaly as an irregular behavior, for example outlier.

The anomaly based detection depends on statistical behavior modeling. Common operations of the members are profiled and some quantity of variation from the common activities is ensign as an anomaly. The weakness of this anomaly IDS is that the common profiles should be modernized regularly, because the presentation of network may change quickly. This might increase the load on the resource controlled sensor nodes. This system will recognize the intrusions in a more ideal and steady way under the situation that the network being monitored follows statistic behavioural patterns. The benefit of this anomaly intrusion detection technique is that it is much suited to recognize the unfamiliar or attacks which are not encountered before.

Anomaly detection technique generates a common base line profile of common behaviors of mesh traffic activity. After that, the behavior that moves away from the base line is considered as a possible intrusion. Major cause is to assemble set of helpful characteristics from traffic to decide the decision that sampled traffic is abnormal or normal. Few benefits of anomaly recognition technique are it will recognize insider attacks, it is tougher for attackers to carry attacks without fixing off an alarm and it can detect unknown or new attacks [7, 9] and [10].

The anomaly detection is based on defining behavior of the network. The behavior of the network is in accordance with previously defined behavior, then it is accepted or else it triggers event in anomaly detection. Accepted network behavior is learned or prepared by specification of network administrator. Significant stage in defining network behavior is intrusion detection system engine ability to cut throughout different protocols at every level. Engine should be capable to know its aim and procedure protocols. Although this investigation of the protocol is computationally pricey, the advantages is it produces rising rule set like assist in lesser false positive alarm. Defining its rule set is an important disadvantage of the anomaly detection. The effectiveness of method depends on how nicely it is tested and implemented on every protocol. Rule defining procedure is as well as pretentious by dissimilar protocols employed by different vendors. Excluding these, custom protocols as well create rule defining a complicated job. For recognition to occur properly, the complete knowledge regarding accepted network behavior require to be implemented by administrators. But one time the rules are explained and the protocol is constructed then anomaly detection techniques will work properly.

Main benefit of anomaly detection over the signature detection is that a new attack for which a signature will not exist is identified suppose it falls out of standard traffic patterns. This is monitored when system detects novel automated worms. Suppose novel technique is spoiled with a worm, it generally begins scanning for other susceptible techniques at an accelerated rate filling network with malicious traffic, therefore causing event of a TCP bandwidth or connection abnormality rule.

There are many attacks in anomaly IDS. The anomaly intrusion detection is helpful for identifying attacks like:

- Buffer overflow
- Misuse of protocol and service ports
- DoS based on crafted payload
- DoS based on volume
- Other natural network failure

The above mentioned attacks are the different types of attacks found in the anomaly IDS. In our proposed system the buffer overflow attack is considering as the anomaly. Buffer overflow is the more general vulnerability exploited by attackers. The detail description of the buffer overflow attack is described below.

In programming and computer security, the buffer overflow is an anomaly, where a program at the time of writing data to a buffer, overruns boundary of buffer and overwrites adjacent memory location. Buffer is defined as; it is a given size of memory taken to load with data. Say a program is reading strings from file like dictionary; it might discover a name of big word in English and fix that to be the size of its buffer. The difficulty occurs when files contains string more than buffer. This might arise legally, where a novel, big word is accepted into dictionary, or when hacker adds string to damage memory. In the buffer over flow attack, the additional data sometime holds particular instructions for action intended by malicious user or hackers, for example the data could trigger a response that spoils files, changes data or reveal private information.

Algorithm 1: AODV routing protocol
1. **Input:** *Initialization of source node and destination node.*
2. *Source node will transmit RREQ (route request message) message to nearby node or destination node.*
3. *If the RREQ will not attain the destination node, it will confirm with the next neighbour node.*
4. *If the RREQ will attain the destination, the destination node will transmit RREP message to source node.*
5. *Source node transmit the data packet to nearby node or midway node.*
6. *Check for anomaly behavioural data packet.*
7. *If the anomaly behavioural nodes there in path, creates an alarm.*
8. *If anomaly behavioural nodes are not occurred in the path, it will verify that the anomaly nodes are present in network or not.*
9. *If there is no anomaly node in network, it will generate an alarm.*
10. *If anomaly nodes are present in network, it will forward data packet to next node or destination node.*
11. **Output:** *detect the anomaly IDS in the mobile Ad-hoc networks.*
12. *End algorithm*

Figure 5 depicts flow chart of anomaly detection method. The anomaly detection method, checks the anomaly behaviour data packets which is received from the

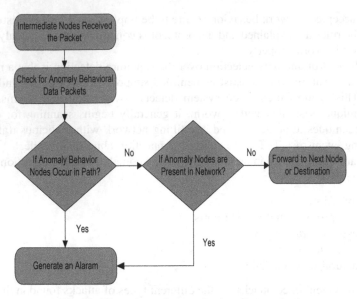

Fig. 5. Flow chart of anomaly detection method

intermediate nodes. If the anomaly behaviour nodes are not there in the path, then it checks for anomaly nodes in network. If it is present in anomaly behaviour, then it generates an alarm else it forwards to next node and calculates the false positives.

4   Experimental Result

Here first step is to initialize the network; there are 20 nodes in network for every node an identical ID is given (1 to 20) as is shown in Fig. 6(a). In initialized area selection of the source node and destination node are done as shown in Fig. 6(b). Once selection of source and destination is done, the source will send route request message to neighbour or destination node which is shown in Fig. 6(c). The Fig. 6(e) depicts command window display of route request message. Once route request message reaches to destination, the destination will send route replay to source which is shown in Fig. 6(d). Figure 6(f) shows the command window display of the route replay message. After route replay reaches to source a path will be generated from source to destination which is depicted in Fig. 6(g) and command window will display the updated path sequence which is depicted in Fig. 6(h). The source will transfer data packet to destination which is shown in Fig. 6(k) and the Fig. 6(i) shows the command window display of data transmission process. Every data packet is having their unique sequence. While transferring data, the data sequence will change and the buffer overflow is occurred which is shown in the Fig. 6(j). If the data sequence is changed and the buffer is overflowed the MATLAB code will display a notification that "data sequence is changed and buffer overflow occurred" which is shown in Fig. 6(m).

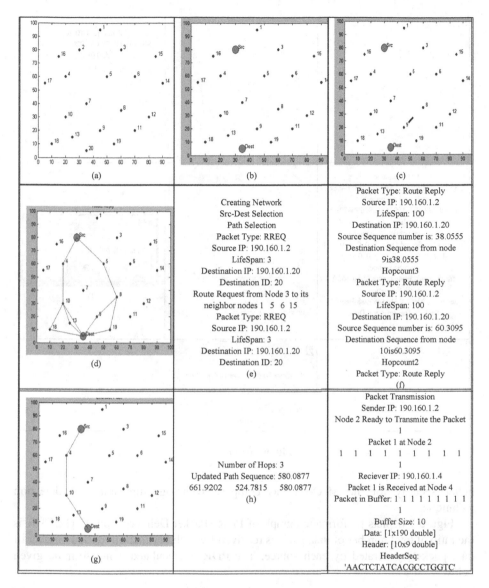

Fig. 6. (a) Network initialization; (b) Source and destination node selection; (c) Route request; (d) Route replay; (e) Command window display of route request; (f) Command window display of route replay; (g) Shortest path; (h) Command window display of updated path sequence; (i) Command window display of data transmission; (j) Command window display of data sequence change and buffer overflowed data; (k) Packet transmission; (l) Anomaly attack; (m) Buffer overflow

The buffer overflow is a kind of anomaly so then it will also display one more notification like "anomaly attack" which is shown in Fig. 6(l). Hence in this manner the recognition of the anomaly intrusion detection in the MANET is done resulting in

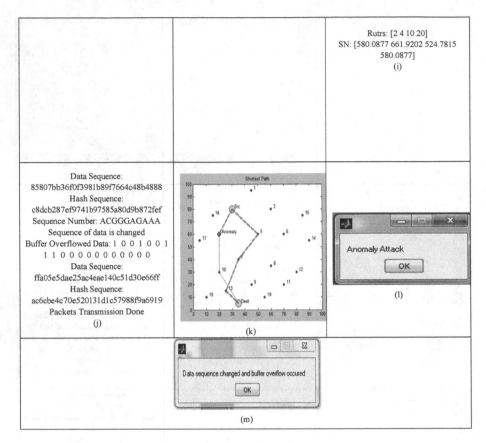

Fig. 6. (*continued*)

better security for the MANETs as compare with signature intrusion detection technique.

Figure 7 depicts performance graph of PDR (Packet Delivery Ratio). The PDR is the ratio of total number of data packets received by each destination to total number of data packets generated by each source. The PDR is calculated using formula given below:

$$PDR = \frac{N1}{N2} \tag{1}$$

Where, $N1$ is total number of data packets received by every destination, $N2$ is total number of data packets produced by every source. So by using the above formula the packet delivery ration is calculated. The proposed system achieves the PDR (Packet Delivery Ratio) of 97%. It gives the better PDR as compared with the existing system's PDR (95%) [11]. Throughput is the amount of data travelled successfully from one place to other in a given time period. The Fig. 8 shows the performance graph of the throughput rate.

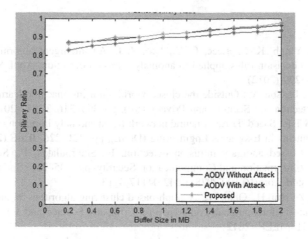

Fig. 7. Packet delivery ratio

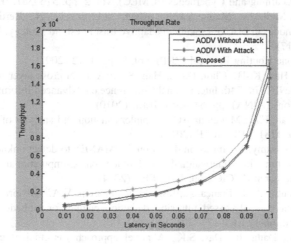

Fig. 8. Throughput rate

5 Conclusion

Usual intrusion detection contain a problem dealing with need of secure boundaries, threats from the cooperative nodes need of restricted power supply, centralized management scalability and capability. Because these problems, they are encouraged to introduce well organized Intrusion Detection System, which contain a novel method to recognize anomalous behaviors in the MANETs. The intrusion detection is a significant technique for security protection. It will give the better security for mobile Ad-hoc networks. In this paper better intrusion detection technique depending on the anomaly detection is introduced. The anomaly intrusion detection method is executed on the zone based AODV routing protocol. This detection system will provide the enhanced security for the mobile Ad-hoc network. The parameters like energy consumption and packet delivery ratio are calculated, which give the better result as compared with the existing systems.

References

1. Lin, S.-W., Yingb, K.-C., Leec, C.-Y., Lee, Z.-J.: An intelligent algorithm with feature selection and decision rules applied to anomaly intrusion detection. Appl. Soft Comput. **12** (10), 3285–3290 (2012)
2. Sommer, R., Paxson, V.: Outside the closed world: on using machine learning for network intrusion detection. In: Security and Privacy (SP), pp. 305–316. IEEE (2010)
3. Al-Janabi, S.T.F., Saeed, H.A.: A neural network based anomaly intrusion detection system. In: Developments in E-systems Engineering (DeSE), pp. 221–226. IEEE (2011)
4. Hu, J.: Host-based anomaly intrusion detection. In: Stavroulakis, P., Stamp, M. (eds.) Handbook of Information and Communication Security, pp. 235–255. Springer, Heidelberg (2010). https://doi.org/10.1007/978-3-642-04117-4_13
5. Mingqiang, Z., Hui, H., Qian, W.: A graph-based clustering algorithm for anomaly intrusion detection. In: 7th International Conference on Computer Science and Education (ICCSE), pp. 1311–1314. IEEE (2012)
6. Meng, Y.: The practice on using machine learning for network anomaly intrusion detection. In: Machine Learning and Cybernetics (ICMLC), vol. 2, pp. 576–581. IEEE (2011)
7. Khan, M.S., Midi, D., Malik, S.U.R., Khan, M.I., Javaid, N., Bertino, E.: Isolating misbehaving nodes in MANETs with an adaptive trust threshold strategy. Mob. Netw. Appl. **22**, 1–17 (2017)
8. Beijar, N.: Zone Routing Protocol (ZRP), vol. 9, pp. 1–12 (2002)
9. Shrestha, R., Han, K.-H., Choi, D.-Y., Han, S.-J.: A novel cross layer intrusion detection system in MANET. In: 24th International Conference on Advanced Information Networking and Applications (AINA), pp. 647–654. IEEE (2010)
10. Ehsan, H., Khan, F.A.: Malicious AODV implementation and analysis of routing attacks in MANETs, pp. 1181–1187. IEEE (2012)
11. Lalli, M., Palanisamy, V.: Intrusion detection for MANET to detect unknown attacks using genetic algorithm. In: International Conference on Computational Intelligence and Computing Research (ICCIC), pp. 1–5. IEEE (2014)
12. Viegas, E., Santin, A.O., França, A., Jasinski, R., Pedroni, V.A., Oliveira, L.S.: Towards an energy-efficient anomaly-based intrusion detection engine for embedded systems. IEEE Trans. Comput. **66**(1), 163–177 (2017)
13. Marchang, N., Datta, R., Das, S.K.: A novel approach for efficient usage of intrusion detection system in mobile ad hoc networks. IEEE Trans. Veh. Technol. **66**(2), 1684–1695 (2017)
14. Song, J., Zhu, Z., Scully, P., Price, C.: Selecting features for anomaly intrusion detection: a novel method using fuzzy C means and decision tree classification. In: Wang, G., Ray, I., Feng, D., Rajarajan, M. (eds.) CSS 2013. LNCS, vol. 8300, pp. 299–307. Springer, Cham (2013). https://doi.org/10.1007/978-3-319-03584-0_22
15. Zhou, C., et al.: Design and analysis of multimodal-based anomaly intrusion detection systems in industrial process automation. IEEE Trans. Syst. Man Cybern.: Syst. **45**(10), 1345–1360 (2015)
16. Bhuyan, M.H., Bhattacharyya, D.K., Kalita, J.K.: Network anomaly detection: methods, systems and tools. IEEE Commun. Surv. Tutor. **16**(1), 303–336 (2014)
17. Sen, N., Sen, R., Chattopadhyay, M.: An effective back propagation neural network architecture for the development of an efficient anomaly based intrusion detection system. In: International Conference on Computational Intelligence and Communication Network (CICN), pp. 1052–1056. IEEE (2014)

Abstract Model of Trusted and Secure Middleware Framework for Multi-cloud Environment

Deepika Saxena[1]([✉]), Kunwar Singh Vaisla[1],
and Manmohan Singh Rauthan[2]

[1] Uttarakhand Technical University, Dehradun, Uttarakhand, India
13deepikasaxena@gmail.com, vaislaks@gmail.com
[2] HNB Garhwal University, Srinagar, District – Pauri, Uttarakhand, India
mms_rauthan@rediffmail.com

Abstract. In the current world of digital advancement, almost every organization is leveraging the services (like storage, computation, networking etc.) from multiple traditional cloud service providers across the world. They are required to collaborate with numerous clouds providers, in order to achieve different variety of services as comply with their business. This imposes a great challenge as how to handle the complex business collaboration with multiple Clouds simultaneously, how to ensure trust and security concerning data storage, computation and networking in such an enormous inter-cloud environment. To efficiently tackle this problem, this paper introduces a trusted middleware framework. This middleware is conceptually designed to reduce the complexity of handling the range of services from many traditional cloud service providers. Here, middleware consists of distinct user-centric multi-cloud (UM-Cloud) for each individual user. UM-Clouds are accomplished to furnish or yield secure as well as transparent services to the user in the form of compliance and trust.

Keywords: Automated security · Middleware · Multi-cloud · Trust engine
UM-cloud

1 Introduction

Across the world, the complex computational sphere of cloud has captured almost entire business-market. Every organization ranging from big business tycoons to small scale business organization, public sector (Government) organization or private sector (e.g. multinational business) organizations are exclusively and painstakingly dependent on the services of cloud datacenters for their data or information storage, computational processing of their business data, all time availability of their data at all location and exchange of their business information beyond the world. There is no doubt in saying that the web (or network) of clouds has laid the backbone of the current urban civilization throughout the world. This scenario of the modern business world represents the big requirement of efficient, exhaustive, painstaking, secure, trustworthy and faithful working of clouds to support efficient and smooth functioning of every business and social organization. Looking towards traditional cloud service provider's

© Springer Nature Singapore Pte Ltd. 2019
A. K. Luhach et al. (Eds.): ICAICR 2018, CCIS 956, pp. 469–479, 2019.
https://doi.org/10.1007/978-981-13-3143-5_38

view, they generally distribute the user (e.g. organization)'s application over nearby companion clouds in order to offer faster result access or load-balancing or raising the scalability etc.

Also, cloud service providers inherently deploys several users application on same virtual machines (i.e. multi-tenancy) but each user feels that entire virtual machine is dedicated for his use only. These are some pragmatic situations that happens at cloud datacenters that raises security and trust compliance issues, which is unknown to common laymen user. User is completely unaware about the location of his data and security attributes (lock-ins) applied by the cloud service provider (CSPs). It becomes difficult to believe whether the CSP is trustworthy and strictly following the guidelines of signed SLA (Service Layer Agreement) or not. The parent CSP distributes and replicates the user (organization)'s confidential, secret and top-secret data on other closely located clouds (companion clouds) without giving any prior information regarding this to the user. This hampers extreme trust of the user.

User (organization) just knows the parent cloud service provider (CSP) with whom he has signed SLA-treaty is following all respective security measures as per jurisdictional constraints. After that, user faithfully consumes the services of parent cloud and deploys his organization's (public, private, secret and top-secret) data on the respective cloud. Then parent CSP deploys data of user as desirable or suitable to him in order to make his maximum profit and providing best possible service at cloud end. This kind of negligent or incautious attitude towards security of user's data and ignorance of trust obedience of various cloud service providers have risen up the very big issue of obligation of trust and security management, that even after signing the SLA agreement, they are negligent regarding user (organization)'s data security, computational security and networking security. Also, since the user's data is distributed across different clouds, where each different cloud service provider (CSP) has his own level of local cloud security. Moreover, the other clouds (which are involved by user's parent cloud as companion cloud) have not signed any official agreement or treaty with user (organization). That's why they are not abide by any rule and regulation regarding storage and security of user's confidential information.

To resolve this problem user (organization) switches from single cloud environment to multiple cloud environment. Making use of multiple clouds allows many benefits to the user, in terms of security and cost efficiency. Likewise, user can keep his public domain data on public cloud and for storing confidential, secret and top-secret data on private cloud. Also, he can place same data on more than one clouds (public or private clouds), to maintain reliability regarding his data. Now, each public cloud has their own rules for implementing security upon user's data and private cloud also follows their own security schemes. Moreover, since the organization has collaboration with both public and private clouds, it is desirable that there should be some facility or arrangement to communication and exchange of messages or information between them (as they belong to same user). Then, again there arises a demand of common trusted- negotiation platform between different clouds of same user.

The user (organization) here is not a single customer, in fact, user is a group of customers (e.g. employees, managers, DBA of organization, owner of organization, public domain users etc.) and each different customer has different level of access and authorization. The information meant for public domain is available to all and can be access easily by following some light security implications (like, password). The working details and other official data, confidential and secret information on private clouds with defined level of access policy for each customer and strictly applied security schemes. Organization can collaborate with multiple private clouds for storage of different categories of confidential information. But problem arises when the data exchange occurs within the organization and outside the organization between multiple clouds of the same user (organization). Briefly described above issues leads towards a very implicit need of middle-man to handle the deficiency and negligence of trusted or faithful collaboration and automated security while receiving services from multiple clouds.

To the best of our knowledge, there is no such appropriate solution available in the form of broker at middle or middleware to handle issues of trust and security management between user and respective multiple clouds. To efficiently tackle this problem, we are introducing a trusted middleware (broker layer at middle) that would bring each different CSPs and user (organization) at a common foundation of trust and security in between traditional CSPs and user.

This paper presents an abstract model of the ongoing research on trusted middleware framework in multi-cloud environment. This middleware will promise a healthy trustworthy relationship between several CSPs and user and will ensure automated security to the user. Initially, the user will contact middleware (broker or provider) layer and instantiate middleware with its (organization)'s requirement of type of data storage, type of security schemes on data computation, storage and transmission etc.

Middleware communicates different traditional cloud service providers (CSPs) in order to accomplish demands of user along with in-built trust and automated security at middleware. Middleware is composed of user-centric multi-clouds known as UM-Clouds. Middleware will incorporate separate UM- Cloud for each different user (organization). Now user is not required to take any strain of dealing with many clouds individually and if any cloud disobeys trust-compliance and SLA-treaty or officially signed documents by any means, the user is not need to indulge. Middleware is placed in between to take over all the issues of security and trust-compliance (if any protocol is broken) as per cyber-legacy and jurisdictional constraints.

The structure of the article is as follows: Sect. 2 is depicting literature survey, motivation for developing middleware for multi-cloud environment, challenges for multi-cloud and objective of middleware framework, Sect. 3 covers propose model of middleware framework. Finally, Sect. 4 presents conclusion of the article.

2   Literature Survey

Every business domains have started using cloud computing services for their data storage, data processing, information exchange and advertisement etc. or as a platform to deliver their services. As a result of this new business world, new services in cloud delivery model were introduced. The cloud services are also implemented in many exclusive ways on different deployment models. All these cloud services deploy data at different level in the field of business. As the number of cloud services are advancing, the number of users utilizing the cloud services and their expectation from the cloud are also increasing, thereby increasing the volume of data generated. Though, the data in the cloud may be under the control of the user logically, but actually, the data physically resides in the infrastructure of cloud service provider [1]. Trust is the strong belief in the compliance of any parameter to act as expected within a specified context [13].

Reputation management always plays an important role in developing cooperative and trustworthy relationships between users and service providers by minimizing chances of the risks [3]. Since, an entity can trust another entity based on a good reputation in the cloud network, we can utilize reputation to build trustworthy relations [7]. In the light of this it can be concluded that reputation can contribute, in the sense of reliability and performance, as a measure of trust-compliance. Our confidence in the system can be measured by trust, that a secure system performs as per our expectation. An efficient trust management system provides capability to change the unpredictable, highly dynamic cloud computation environment into a trusted and successful business platform. Therefore, as the scope of inter cloud computing enlarges to pervasive computing, there will be a need to assess and maintain the trustworthiness of the cloud computing parameters. The reputation scheme helps in building trust between user based on their past experiences and feedbacks from other users.

Singh, Sidhu have proposed compliance based multi-dimensional trust evaluation system (CMTES) is presented, which evaluates of trustworthiness of CSPs by monitoring the service compliance provided by the CSPs by using improved TOPSIS technique. The shortcoming is that here, cloud customer is appointed to evaluate the trust by collecting SLA compliance details of the cloud. In the light of this paper, if the cloud client needs to deploy services of multiple cloud, then he has to evaluate first each different cloud on trust compliance basis, this raises overhead at cloud customer end [2].

Ryutov, Zhou and Neuman have presented the ATNAC framework that combines adaptive trust negotiation and fine-grained access control for protecting sensitive resources in electronic commerce. This framework supports dynamic adaptation of security policies according to the suspicion level and system threat level. They have applied GAA-API and Trust Builder to prevent information leakage [22].

Demchenko, Turkmen, de Laat and Slawik defines inter-cloud security framework (ICSF) for multi-cloud data intensive application, where security infrastructure for multi-cloud application is defined. They have specified general security requirements like access control, security of credentials, single credentials for all distributed multi-cloud resources, data protection during whole data handling lifecycle, security session synchronization mechanisms, SLA and Compliance management, brokered and third party security services etc. They have also highlighted facts like cloud service broker, Trust Broker and Trust-introducer, Service Registry and Discovery, Federated identity provider and Inter-domain gateway etc. In the light of this paper, we can say that security issues are well defined, but not discussed in detail and Trust importance in multi-cloud application is discussed in short, hence, limitation is that trust is not absolutely integrated with security, which is must for inter-cloud or multi-cloud based application [5].

Balasaraswathi and Manikandan have proposed secured multi-cloud storage, which provides each customer with a better cloud data storage decisions, considering security and availability of data services. They have proposed security of user's data by splitting and distributing customer's data [9]. This paper has lot of limitations considering multi-cloud application security, as security during data transfer between multiple cloud is not mentioned, no trust significance discussed.

Cao, Yao, Chase, represents a trust management core for federation of clouds using logic {"CFlo"} based on SAFE logical trust framework. SAFE supports semantically rich certificates and logic based authorization engine implemented in a comprehensive framework which materializes logic sets as certificates and stores them as linked DAGs in a common key-value store [8]. This paper has brought logical approach in the form of SAFE which is independent of implementation. Fan and Perros has developed a novel trust management framework for evaluation of trustworthiness of CSPs utilizing subjective and objective trust in multi-cloud environment. Here, trust service-provider (TSP) collects local subjective and local objective trust for each single service provider, then evaluates global subjective and global objective trust taking feedbacks from whole cloud service-user in aggregation [20].

The major drawback here is that it is effective in case of single-cloud environment, it requires to be extended for multi-cloud. Also, this model is unable to completely prevent the untrustworthy malicious cloud service users. Chakraborty, Roy have proposed an SLA-based Framework for Estimating Trustworthiness of a Cloud. This framework extracts parameters from SLA and evaluates quantitative trustworthiness of each parameters separately as a fraction between 0 and 1. This is dynamic level of trust that can be tuned with session logs and can calculate trust based on individual consumer's policies [22]. The major drawback of this framework is that multiple cloud scenario is not considered here and also it has not been examined and implemented.

Wan, Zhang, Chen and Zhu have formulated security requirements for a vTPM migration process. They have proposed a novel protocol that is based on trusted channel to mutually authenticate between source and destination and takes property-based attestation of destination station for authenticated data exchange to a secure platform. Along with this, they have applied encryption, integrity checks and nonce to assure confidentiality, integrity and freshness of transmitted data [23].

In 2016, Zhang et al. have presented the very basic principle for multi-cloud data hosting is present by the "CHARM: A Cost-Efficient Multi-Cloud Data Hosting Scheme with High Availability [24]. Figure 1 shows the basic principle of multi-cloud data hosting. Here the basic principle of data hosting on multi-cloud is to distribute data across multiple clouds to gain redundancy and prevent vendor-lock-in. The key component in this model is "Proxy" which redirects the request from client application and coordinate data distribution among multiple clouds. Different clouds exhibit huge difference in terms of their services like pricing policies and work performance. For instance, Google cloud platform charges more for bandwidth consumption but Amazon S3 charges more for storage space and Rackspace provides all web operations free via series of REST ful APIs. The advantage of the CHARM multi-cloud model is that it provides guidance to the customers to distribute their data on multiple clouds in cost effective manner. CHARM makes fine-grained decisions about which storage mode to use and which clouds to place data in.

In 2012, Villegas et al. [25], have shown a layered multi-cloud architecture by creating federation at each service layer as shown in Fig. 2. At each layer, broker is present,

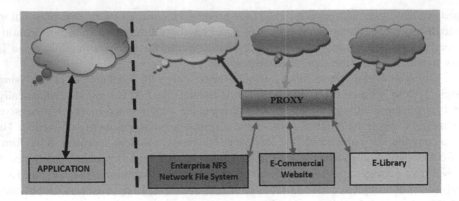

Fig. 1. Basic principle of multi-cloud data hosting.

who follows some pre-defined collaboration terms for successful inter-cloud federation. They have added federation of cloud model by showing how it works in delivering weather research forecasting (WRF). They have given conceptual view of decoupling SaaS, PaaS and IaaS clouds. For such federation, well defined policies and protocols must be defined. PaaS layer act as middleware and act as a bridge for vertical integration. It is a bridge between application and elastic infrastructure resource management.

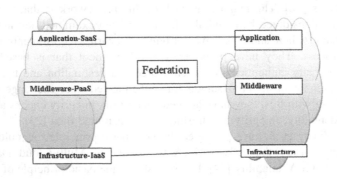

Fig. 2. Showing cloud federation layered model

For cloud security, other researchers have provided solution but they lack user-control security locks, so they are not capable of providing required level of security in multi-cloud environment. Fine-grained security settings are not defined to control protection of their cloud resources for e.g. security locks must prohibit transfer of confidential data types across jurisdictional boundaries. Most of the above research papers have described trust evaluation and security restricted to single cloud environment and not extended for multi-cloud environment.

In our middleware framework model for multi-cloud environment, we are applying automated security, preventing unauthorized access and trust mechanism to ensure jurisdictional or legal constraints SLA-based constraints etc. from all aspects while a user application is deployed in multi-cloud environment. This proposed middleware encapsulates all the complexities of handling or dealing with multi-cloud services.

Motivation for Proposing Middleware Framework

Benefits of adding middleware while attaining services from multiple cloud service provider are as follows: Firstly, UM- Cloud provides faster service deployment and increased homogeneity at service level from different CSPs. Secondly, customizability can also be increased as the user can select which virtualization security service or any other type of service to deploy, resulting in user-controlled security lock- ins. Thirdly, it avoids lower infrastructural operation overhead and provides independence from dealing with many traditional CSPs individually. Hence, we can conclude that this proposed middleware layer framework is a user (organization)-controlled infrastructure for running UM- Clouds leveraging services of computation, storage and networking etc. from both public and private CSPs with additional trust management and auto-mated security features.

Challenges of Multi-cloud

- API's differ: Different sets of resources are there, different formats and encodings, and several simultaneous version of single cloud exist.
- Abstractions differ: Network architecture differ- VLANs, topology differ, security grounds differ.
- Difference in storage architecture- local/attachable, disks and backups.
- Hypervisor and physical machines differ etc.
- Mismatch of cyber-laws of various interconnected clouds depending on their geographical location physically.
- *Interoperability*: The biggest challenge in cloud computing is the diversity of resources, management and rules and regulations of cloud providers, diverse SLAs, differences in security characteristics at various CSPs etc. Interoperability means the ability of diverse system to work in cooperation and serve the common output. Interoperability of multi-cloud has several heterogeneous dimensions:
- *Vertical interoperability* - Along the cloud stack, interoperability increases as we move from IaaS to SaaS. To deal with such heterogeneity, standardize platform and mapping interface layers are required.
- *Horizontal interoperability* - The inter-communication issues lying between various service providers, technically, physically, logically and legally etc. while con-tributing for multi-cloud.
- *Geographical location* - Across the world, thousands of data centers are geo-graphically distributed which vary in cost of electrical consumption.
- *Resource provider* - At various data centers, there exist heterogeneity in resource usage there logical and physical infrastructure.
- *Cloud Service provider* - Each different CSP follows his own SLA policies, man-agement rules, security features, cloud service cost etc.

Objective of Middleware

Trust management: UM-Clouds will offer trust management engine that would be responsible for imparting healthy trust relationship between user and different CSPs.

Automated security: Middleware should automatically manage heterogeneous cloud's security (from different CSPs) and deploy the same across provider domain (at traditional CSPs) end to ensure user decided security compliance.

User Privacy: It must also prevent traditional CSPs from accessing user's data without user's consent confirmation and their by guarding user privacy.

SLA documentation: Middleware should guarantee SLAs documentation in multiple cloud provider environment and promise secure network inter-connection.

3   Proposed Model of Middleware

This paper introduces a new middleware framework concept that follows the vision of user (organizational)-centric multi-cloud (UM-Cloud) ensuring trusted and automated security management. In our proposed middleware framework, a distributed layer of several UM-Clouds (user multi-cloud) is set-up between traditional cloud service provider (CSPs) and user.

Each UM-Cloud belongs to a distinct user (organization). In nutshell, middleware is a multi-cloud service provider i.e. UM service provider (or broker at middle) which deploys several UM-Clouds. A UM-Cloud is responsible for providing automated trusted security at hypervisor layer while running application on multiple clouds.

Here a suitable hypervisor is deployed to manage the inter-operability of services attained from various CSPs. UM-Cloud is configured with newly added trust and security engines. Since, this middleware is set-up as user-centric multi-cloud layer, the automated security and trust schemes are transparent and under control of the user. Hence, it offers unified control for automated security and trust-management engine across different clouds, which is independent of the underlying traditional CSPs. In the Fig. 3. This article depicts an abstract model of multi-cloud computing, where different public and private clouds like public cloud A, cloud B (private) and cloud C are representing traditional CSPs layer. Actually, in datacenters at each physical machine, cloud service provider deploy several virtual (VMs). And each single VM is shared by number of users. This is multi-tenancy, which is inherently present at each cloud (datacenters) as shown in the Fig. 3.

Though multi-tenancy provides economic benefits to the cloud service provider (CSP), it also brings up many security challenges. At bottom, User access layer is shown, where several users are present, who are accessing services from multiple clouds (public or private clouds). For accessing multi-cloud services, we have proposed multi-cloud layer, which deploys several user-centric multi-clouds or UM-Clouds consists of many virtual machines realized from different clouds to fulfill the demand of the user (organization). A UM-Cloud is a set of computation resources, storage resources and communication services that lets individual multi-cloud users run their applications and services over a distributed cloud.

At the middle, some service provider is available who takes all the responsibility of setting up UM- cloud for each user separately. Here, UM-service provider (UMSP) is

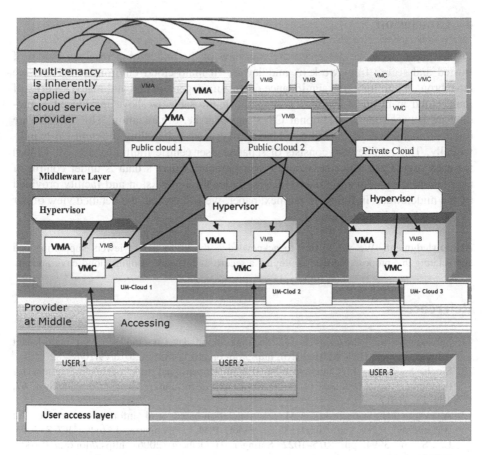

Fig. 3. Abstract view of Multi-Cloud architecture showing traditional cloud service provider at top layer, multi-cloud provider broker at middleware and access layer for user at the bottom.

acting as a broker at multi-cloud layer, who demands resources from actual CSPs and sets up the network for different user (like some organization) as desired by them. At top of each U-cloud there is a hypervisor resolving interoperability between different heterogeneous virtual resources taken from multiple clouds and is highly secure under the supervision of multi-cloud layer broker. In our middleware framework model, strictly separated UM- Clouds are deployed for each user. These UM-Clouds can communicate with each other over a secure channel. At each UM-Cloud, virtual machines (VMs) are realized with resources from underlying traditional CSPs. This middleware enables user to directly operate VMs (from different public or private clouds) regardless of their physical server hoisting at CSP.

4 Conclusion

In this paper, we have presented the overview of the undergoing research model of trusted and secure framework of middleware in multi-cloud environment. Here, we have brought into light, the significance of trust management and automated security of multi-cloud in business world. To accomplish the same we have introduced a middleware between many traditional CSPs and user i.e. organization. This middleware offers so many benefits including reducing overhead of handling different CSPs individually. This middleware consists of separate user centric multi-cloud (UM- Cloud) for each user. Here trust and security management of user's data is under control of user independent of many different CSPs, under the supervision and facility provided by the middleware. In future, in our next paper, we will present the detailed view of our UM-Cloud and its configuration.

Acknowledgment. We would like to acknowledge thanks to the reviewers supporting and appreciating this proposed idea of deploying a secure middleware in multi-cloud environment.

References

1. Selvakumar, S., Mohanapriya, M.: Securing cloud data in cloud enabled multi-tenant software service. IJST **9**(20) (2016). https://doi.org/10.17485/ijst/2016/v9i20/89782
2. Singh, S., Sidhu, J.: Compliance-based multi-dimensional trust evaluation system for determining trustworthiness of cloud service providers. Futur. Gener. Comput. Syst. **67**, 109–132 (2017)
3. Abawajy, J.H., Goscinski, A.M.: A reputation-based grid information service. In: Alexandrov, V.N., van Albada, G.D., Sloot, P.M.A., Dongarra, J. (eds.) ICCS 2006. LNCS, vol. 3994, pp. 1015–1022. Springer, Heidelberg (2006). https://doi.org/10.1007/11758549_135
4. Li, W., Ping, L.: Trust model to enhance security and interoperability of cloud environment. In: Jaatun, M.G., Zhao, G., Rong, C. (eds.) CloudCom 2009. LNCS, vol. 5931, pp. 69–79. Springer, Heidelberg (2009). https://doi.org/10.1007/978-3-642-10665-1_7
5. Demchenko, Y., Turkmen, F., de Laat, C., Slawik, M.: Defining inter-cloud security framework and architecture components for multi-cloud intensive applications. In: CCGrid 2017, Proceedings of 17th IEEE/ACM International Symposium on Cluster, Cloud and Grid Computing, pp. 945–952 (2017)
6. Jøsang, A., Ismail, R., Boyd, C.: A survey of trust and reputation systems for online service provision. Decis. Support Syst. **43**(2), 618–644 (2007)
7. Cao, Q., Yao, Y., Chase, J.: A Logical Approach to Cloud Federation. arXiv:1708.03389v1 [cs.DC] (2017)
8. Balasaraswathi, V.R., Manikandan, S.: Enhanced security for multi-cloud storage using cryptographic data splitting with dynamic approach. In: Proceedings of 2014 IEEE International Conference on Advanced Communication Control and Computing Technologies (ICACCCT) (2014)
9. Alaluna, M., Ramos, F., Neves, N.: (Literally) above the clouds: virtualizing the network over multiple clouds. In: IEEE NetSoft (2016)

10. Srirama, S.N., Batrashev, O., Vainikko, E.: SciCloud: scientific computing on the cloud. In: 10th IEEE/ACM International Symposium on Cluster, Cloud and Grid Computing (CCGrid 2010), p. 579 (2010)
11. Yuan, E., Tong, J.: Attributed based access control (ABAC) for web services. In: Proceedings of the 2005 IEEE International Conference on Web Services, ICWS 2005, pp. 561–569. IEEE Computer Society, Los Alamitos (2005)
12. Peterson, L., Wroclawski, J.: Overview of the GENI architecture. GENI Design Document GDD-06-11, GENI: Global Environment for Network Innovations, January 2007
13. Yang, Q., Cheng, C., Che, X.: A cost-aware method of privacy protection for multiple cloud service requests. In: 2014 IEEE 17th International Conference on Computational Science and Engineering (CSE), pp. 583–590 (2014)
14. Sousa, B., et al.: Toward a fully cloudified mobile network infrastructure. IEEE Trans. Netw. Serv. Manag. **13**, 547–563 (2016). ISSN 1932-4537
15. Iacono, L.L., Torkian, D.: A system-oriented approach to full-text search on encrypted cloud storage. In: 2013 International Conference on Cloud and Service Computing (CSC), pp. 24–29 (2013)
16. Baby, K., Vysala, A.: COBBS: a multicloud architecture for better business solutions. In: International Conference on Data Mining and Advanced Computing (SAPIENCE), pp. 347–352 (2016). C. J. Kaufman, Rocky Mountain Research Laboratories, Boulder, CO, private communication (2016)
17. Mostajeran, E., et al.: A survey on SLA-based brokering for intercloud computing. In: 2015 Second International Conference on Computing Technology and Information Management (ICCTTM). IEEE (2015)
18. Vijayakumar, V., WahidaBanu, R.S.D., Abawajy, J.: Novel mechanism for evaluating feedback in the grid environment on resource allocation. In: The 2010 International Conference on Grid Computing and Applications, 12–15 July 2010, (GCA 2010), pp. 11–17 (2010)
19. Grozev, N., Buyya, R.: Inter-cloud architectures and application brokering: taxonomy and survey. Softw. Pract. Exp. **44**(3), 369–390 (2014)
20. Fan, W., Perros, H.: A novel trust management framework for multi-cloud environments based on trust service providers. Knowl. Based Syst. **70**, 392–406 (2014)
21. Ryutov, T., Zhou, L., Neuman, C.: Adaptive trust negotiation and access control. In: SACMAT 2005, pp. 139–146. ACM 1-59593-045-0/05/0006 (2005)
22. Chakraborty, S., Roy, K.: An SLA-based framework for estimating trustworthiness of a cloud. In: IEEE 11th International Conference on Trust, Security and Privacy in computing and Communication, pp. 937–942 (2012)
23. Wan, X., Zhang, X., Chen, L., Zhu, J.: An improved vTPM migration protocol based trusted channel. In: The Proceedings of the 2012 International Conference on Systems and Informatics (ICSAI 2012), pp. 870–875 (2012)
24. Divya Shaly, C., Anbuselvi, R.: CHARM: a cost-efficient multi-cloud data hosting scheme with high availability. Int. J. Control Theory Appl. **9**(27), 461–468 (2016). https://doi.org/10.1109/TCC.2015.2417534
25. Villegas, D., et al.: Cloud federation in a layered service model. J. Comput. Syst. Sci. **78**(5), 1330–1344 (2012). https://doi.org/10.1016/j.jcss.2011.12.017

User Behavior-Based Intrusion Detection Using Statistical Techniques

Zakiyabanu S. Malek[1]([⊠]), Bhushan Trivedi[1], and Axita Shah[2]

[1] Pacific University, Udaipur, Rajasthan, India
zakiya.malek@gmail.com, bhtrivedi@gmail.com
[2] Department of Computer Science, Rollwala Computer Center,
Gujarat University, Ahmedabad, Gujarat, India
axitashah@gmail.com

Abstract. The objective of intrusion detection systems is to identify attacks on host or networks based computer systems. IDS also categorise based on attacks, if attacks pattern are known then signature-based intrusion detection method is used or if abnormal behavior then anomaly (behavior) based intrusion detection method is used. We have retrieved various user behavior parameters such as resource access and usage, count of input devices such as a keyboard and mouse access. The focus of this paper is to identify whether user behavior is normal or abnormal on host-based GUI systems using statistical techniques. We apply simple Aggregation measure and Logistic Regression methods on user behavior log. Based on our implementation, Evaluation show significance accuracy in the training set to result in confusion matrix using Logistic Regression method.

Keywords: Intrusion detection · Anomaly detection · Mean
Logistic Regression

1 Introduction

The signature-based intrusion detection identifies only known pattern while anomaly-based intrusion detection can identify or detect attacks by observing user, system or network activity and categorize it as either normal or abnormal [1]. In anomaly detection it compares users current behavior with stored profile [3]. For this an audit records are to be transferred in statistical form, dynamic user profile creation, and threshold assignment done now if any deviation occur from user's stored profile and current user behavior then an intrusion alert is generated [3]. It is more useful to discover unidentified attacks [4]. Statistical methods are not used for intrusion prevention [2]. It is used to find abnormal activity.

2 Related Work

Researchers work on Intrusion detection since 19's to improve its performance by increasing detection rate and reducing false alarm. To achieve these various statistical methods are used.

© Springer Nature Singapore Pte Ltd. 2019
A. K. Luhach et al. (Eds.): ICAICR 2018, CCIS 956, pp. 480–489, 2019.
https://doi.org/10.1007/978-981-13-3143-5_39

[6] analyzed user activity logs to identify the file and other resource access by the non-legitimate user by using averages, standard deviations, maxima, and minima. [1] followed the model [6] provide statistically and rule-based approach to detect intrusion where it includes more parameters like memory & CPU usage. [7, 8] work on [6] and identify abnormal user behavior activity. [9–11] create a user profile based on user's Unix command line. [12] uses OR Operation and AND operation to reduce false alarm. The above-discussed system does not support the GUI so there are many GUI based system which includes mouse dynamics and keyboard dynamics in user profiling [13–16]. [17] apply Chi-square distribution and Gaussian mixture distribution on performance log and counter log of the system to an intrusion detection system and achieve more 90% detection rate.

Statistical-based systems (SBIDs) identify user or system's authorized behavior and the behavior which are not in define range is consider as unauthorized. This is based on activity log analysis. In statistical-based anomaly detection user profile is created based on collected data and by observing data pattern system identify that given activity is normal or abnormal [4, 18–20]. Moments in statistics is Mean & standard deviation [21, 22]. Using a standard deviation with the hybrid intrusion detection technique it increases in detection rate as well as reduce 40% false alarm [23]. User profile created run time and updated regularly having threshold value [17]. If any deviation in user's stored profile and current behavior occur then an alert is issue.

The main advantage of the use of statistical profiles is that a prior knowledge of any vulnerability is not required. The system identifies about the normal behavior and then looks for deviation. The following Fig. 1 shows a general system flow in SBID.

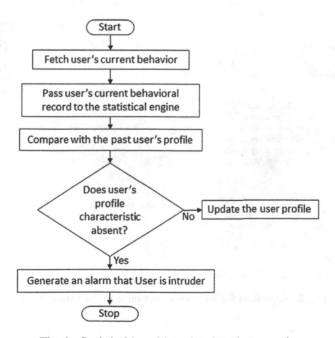

Fig. 1. Statistical-based intrusion detection scenario

As all the research on GUI bases user behavior intrusion detection provided constructive result but still it requires having a good data set that can be trained and more efficient methods to find intrusions. Hence we develop our own dataset. Our data set contain numeric values so we will use Aggregation measure and logistic regression methods for intrusion detection. The results of experiments illustrate that Logistic regression method obtains high detection rate with accuracy, by not compromising computational overhead time so more suitable for real-time IDS.

Section 3 proposes the model on Statistical-based Intrusion Detection. Section 4 specifies dataset, implementation, the experiment of a working system. Section 5 notify the result and discuss the experiment of the result. Section 6 concludes the research with future enhancement.

3   Proposed Model on Statistical-Based Intrusion Detection

In proposed model as shown in Fig. 2, we used store authorized user's log (Unix based command to retrieve parameter value) and generate numeric measures from the data log. Now system continuously monitored the current user behavior this current behavior is compared with the stored profile. If the difference between this two is significant then n alarm is generated and system considers that user as an intruder and stop allowing the access to the system but if there is no significant difference then the system will update user profile if required. To implement this there is two methods SIDE has considered: (1) Average, (2) Logistic Regression.

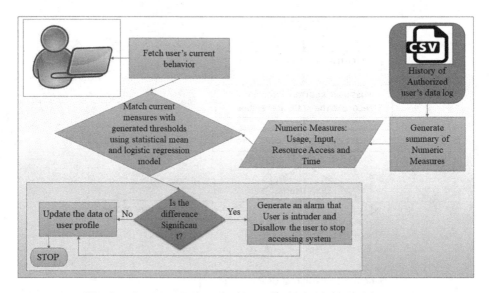

Fig. 2. Algorithm for intrusion detection using statistical methods

3.1 SIDE Mean

Mean or average value is used recognize middle position of data. It used to identify anomaly. The advantage of mean is, that the user's authorized behavior is not requires in advance.

3.2 SIDE Logistic Regression [SIDE LR]

Logistic regression estimates the probability that the user is authorized for set of values for the selected independent variables. It has single dependent variable and one or more independent variables. One of the popular statistical approaches is a fixed effect logistic regression model, which accommodates predictors for anomaly behavior [24].

4 Working of System

4.1 Dataset

Here, We have retrieved user profile numeric measures such as KeyCounter, typing speed, MouseClickCounter, MemoryUsage, IOUsage, CPUUsage, ProcessCounter, application counter, WebsiteCounter, FileCounter, DownloadInMB as an independent variable shown in Fig. 3. We have generated user log in comma separated file format. Every specified user activity is logged after every 10 s. User's log-in and log out time are also considered and stored in CSV file. Analysis of user profile dataset characteristic is specified in Figs. 4, 5 and 6.

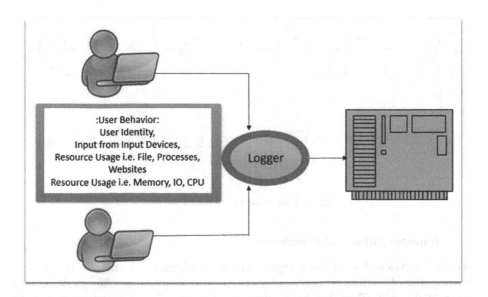

Fig. 3. User behavior numeric measures in SBID

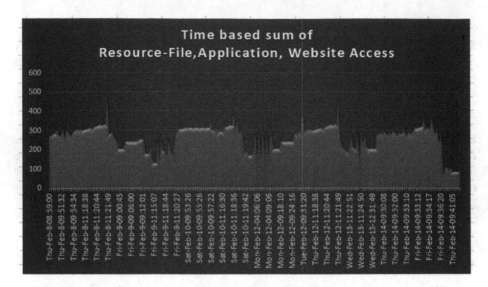

Fig. 4. Time based sum of Resource-file, process and website access

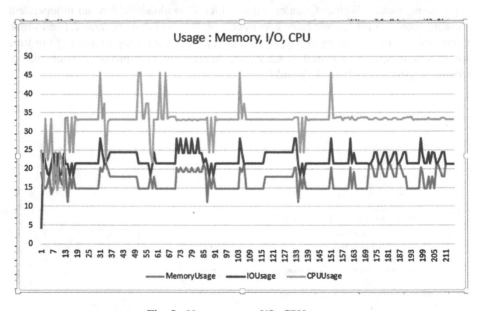

Fig. 5. User memory, I/O, CPU usage

4.2   Implementation and Experiment

We have developed a statistical engine which calculates the average of all the past training data of 10 different users and also generated logistic regression model in java using Weka API. Then We have taken 16 different attributed test cases for the

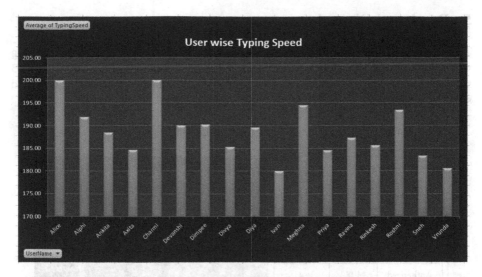

Fig. 6. User typing speed

experiment to the statistical engine to detect intrusion using the average method and Logistic Regression as shown in Table 1.

Table 1. Test Cases

Case#	Description of Test case
Case1	A Valid Record with all fields as valid
Case2	Changed UserName and Increased ProcessCounter
Case3	Changed UserName with Increased ProcessCounter
Case4	Increased KeyCounter, MouseClickCounter, IOUsage, CPU usage. Reduced ProcessConter, FileCounter.
Case5	An Invalid Record with all majority of fields as Invalid.
Case6	A Record with Invalid UserName and Invalid KeyCounter.
Case7	Changed Login time and Increased MouseClickCounter.
Case8	A record with Increased MemoryUsage
Case9	A record with Increased IOUsage
Case10	A record with Increased CPU usage
Case11	A record with Increased ProcessCounter
Case12	A record with Increased WebsiteCounter
Case13	A record with Increased FileCounter
Case14	A record with Increased DownloadSpeed
Case15	A record with Change in Username
Case16	A record with Change in LoginTime

5   Result and Discussion

To test the result of Logistic regression method, Along with our java program using weka API, we have generated a model using SPSS statistical tool even. Tables 2 and 3 specify confusion matrix and chart of logistic regression model result using weka and spss.

Table 2. Confusion Matrix and Chart of Logistic Regression in Weka

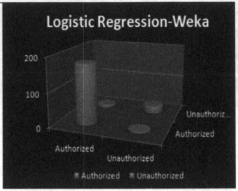

Logistic Regression-Weka	Authoriz ed	Unauthoriz ed
Authorized	178	4
Unauthorized	10	23

From the above discussion, we can say that result of intrusion detection can be derived from various methods. Now the question is the result of which method to be considered as a final result of intrusion detection. Here, we conclude the result of both the methods in Tables 4 and 5. Confusion Matrix given in Table 5 indicates that result generated using statistical mean is good when an unauthorized user is considered and logistic regression is considered good in the case of the Authorized user. Here, Result

Table 3. Confusion Matrix and Chart of Logistic Regression in SPSS

Logistic Regression -SPSS	Authorized	Unauthoriz ed
Authorized	179	3
Unauthoriz ed	7	26

of the statistical mean is dependent on the threshold value we consider to match, if the value difference is nearer then the correct result is achieved. Even Logistic Regression works better for the change in multiple attributes of the user profile.

Table 4. Result of the statistical engine from user's behavior data log with an actual result

Case#	Actual Result	Statistical Mean	Logistics Regression
case1	Authorized	Unauthorized	Authorized
case2	Unauthorized	Unauthorized	Authorized
case3	Authorized	Authorized	Authorized
case4	Unauthorized	Unauthorized	Authorized
case5	Unauthorized	Unauthorized	Authorized
case6	Authorized	Unauthorized	Authorized
case7	Unauthorized	Unauthorized	Authorized
case8	Authorized	Unauthorized	Authorized
case9	Authorized	Unauthorized	Authorized
case10	Unauthorized	Unauthorized	Authorized
case11	Unauthorized	Unauthorized	Authorized
case12	Authorized	Unauthorized	Authorized
case13	Authorized	Unauthorized	Authorized
case14	Authorized	Unauthorized	Authorized
case15	Authorized	Unauthorized	Authorized
case16	Unauthorized	Unauthorized	Authorized

Table 5. Confusion matrix

Confusion Matrix		Authorized	Unauthorized
	Authorized	9	0
Actual Result	Unauthorized	0	7
	Authorized	1	8
Using Mean	Unauthorized	0	7
	Authorized	9	0
Using Logistic Regression	Unauthorized	7	0

6 Conclusion

In the statistically based intrusion detection system, the stored patterns are not updated frequently hence it is easy to maintain. SBID will require more time to become accurate as user profile generation will require time. A threshold value also plays a major role of the success of SBID because to if a threshold is too high system will not generate an alert in necessary conditions and if too low the system will generate more false positives.

Using some predefined statistical methods like mean and standard deviation intrusion cannot be found accurately. For more reliable and accurate result, we have generated logistic regression model to detect intrusion. By applying Mean and Logistic regression method on user behavior we identify whether the user is authorized or unauthorized. These two methods give us acceptance region using which we can define the bounds in which user activity is normal and which user is performing abnormal activities In the future by applying machine learning techniques we will improve our result or provide comparison between machine learning and statistical methods.

References

1. Denning, D.: An intrusion detection model. IEEE Trans. Softw. Eng. **13**(2), 222–232 (1987)
2. Wafa, S.A., Naoum, R.: Development of genetic-based machine learning for network intrusion detection. World Acad. Sci. Eng. Technol. **55**, 20–24 (2009)
3. Gerken, M.: Statistical-Based Intrusion Detection. http://www.sei.cmu.edu/str/descriptions/sbid.html. August 2007
4. Axelsson, S.: Intrusion detection systems: a taxonomy and survey, Department of Computer Engineering, Chalmers University of Technology, Sweden, Technical report 99–15 March 2000
5. Umphress, D., Williams, G.: Identity verification through keyboard characteristics. Int. J. Man Mach. Stud. **23**(3), 263–273 (1985)
6. Anderson, J.: Computer Security Threat Monitoring and Surveillance. James P. Anderson Co., Fort Washington (1980)
7. Lunt, T.F.: Real-time intrusion detection. In: COMPCON Spring 1989 34th IEEE Computer Society International Conference: Intellectual Leverage, Digest of Papers, pp. 348–353. IEEE Press, Washington (1989)
8. Smaha, S.E.: Haystack: an intrusion detection system. In: 4th ACSAC, pp. 37–44. IEEE Press, Washington (1988)
9. Balajinath, B., Raghavan, S.V.: Intrusion detection through learning behavior model. Comput. Commun. **24**(12), 1202–1212 (2001)
10. Gunetti, D., Ruffo, G.: Intrusion detection through behavioral data. In: Hand, D.J., Kok, J.N., Berthold, M.R. (eds.) IDA 1999. LNCS, vol. 1642, pp. 383–394. Springer, Heidelberg (1999). https://doi.org/10.1007/3-540-48412-4_32
11. Tan, K.: The application of neural networks to UNIX computer security. In: Proceedings IEEE International Conference on Neural Networks, vol. 1, pp. 476–481. IEEE Press, Washington (1995)
12. Gu, G., Cardenas, A.A., Lee, K.: Principled reasoning and practical applications of alert fusion in intrusion detection systems. In: 2008 Proceedings ASIACCS, pp. 136–147. ACM, New York (2008)

13. Shavlik, J., Shavlik, M.: Selection, combination, and evaluation of effective software sensors for detecting abnormal computer usage. In: Proceedings 10th ACM SIGKDD, pp. 276–285. ACM, New York (2004)
14. Pusara, M., Brodley, C.E.: User re-authentication via mouse movements. In: ACM Workshop on Visualization and Data Mining for Computer Security, pp. 1–8. ACM, New York (2004)
15. Bergadano, F., Gunetti, D., Picardi, C.: Identity verification through dynamic keystroke analysis. Intell. Data Anal. 7(5), 469–496 (2003)
16. Vizer, L.M., Zhou, L., Sears, A.: Automated stress detection using keystroke and linguistic features: an exploratory study. IJHCS 67(10), 870–886 (2009)
17. Om, H., Hazra, T.: Statistical techniques in anomaly intrusion detection system. Int. J. Adv. Eng. Technol. 5(1), 387–398 (2012). ISSN: 2231-1963
18. Debar, H., Dacier, M., Wespi, A.: A revised taxonomy for intrusion-detection systems. Ann. Des Télécommun. 55(7–8), 361–378 (2000)
19. García-Teodoro, P., Díaz-Verdejo, J., Maciá-Fernández, G., Vázquez, E.: Anomaly-based network intrusion detection: techniques, systems and challenges. Comput. Secur. 28(1–2), 18–28 (2009)
20. Anderson, D., Frivold, T., Tamaru, A., Valdes, A., Release, B.: Next Generation Intrusion Detection Expert System (NIDES), software users manual., http://citeseerx.ist.psu.edu/viewdoc/summary?doi=10.1.1.26.5048. Accessed 19 February 2016
21. Qayyum, A., Islam, M.H., Jamil, M.: Taxonomy of statistical based anomaly detection techniques for intrusion detection. In: Proceedings of the IEEE Symposium on Emerging Technologies, pp. 270–276 (2005)
22. Jyothsna, V.V.R.P.V., Prasad, V.R., Prasad, K.M.: A review of anomaly based intrusion detection systems. Int. J. Comput. Appl., 28(7), 26–35 (2011)
23. Ashfaq, A.B., Javed, M., Khayam, S.A., Radha, H.: An Information-theoretic combining method for multi-classifier anomaly detection systems. In: IEEE International Conference on Communications, pp. 1–5 (2010)
24. Mok, M.S., Sohn, S.Y., Ju, Y.H.: Random effects logistic regression model for anomaly detection. Expert Syst. Appl. 37 7162–7166 (2010)

Three-Level Leach Protocol to Increase Lifetime of Wireless Sensor Network

Anamika Trehan[✉], Preeti Gupta, and Sunil Agrawal

Department of Electronics and Communication,
University Institute of Engineering and Technology, Panjab University,
Chandigarh, India
anamikatrehangndu@gmail.com, preeti.uiet@gmail.com,
s.agrawal@hotmail.com

Abstract. The wireless sensor network is the decentralized type of network which is deployed on the far places. Due to small size of the sensor nodes and far deployment energy consumption is the major issue of the network. The clustering is the most efficient technique which reduces energy consumption of the network. The cluster heads in the leach protocol is selected on the basis of distance and energy. The improved LEACH is the algorithm in which leader and cluster heads are selected which transmits the data to base station. In this work, the enhancements in the improved LEACH algorithm is proposed in which gateway nodes are deployed, the cluster heads will pass the information to gateway node and it will further pass information to base station. The simulation of proposed algorithm is done in MATLAB and it performs well in terms of energy dissipation.

Keywords: LEACH · Gateway · Energy efficient

1 Introduction

The network in which small-sized and less expensive sensor nodes are deployed is known as wireless sensor network. There are self-contained battery powers systems present within these sensor nodes. The sensor nodes process the input that is received from adjacent sensors. For transmitting the information gathered, this data is further transmitted to the base station of the network. Each node of these networks has several resource constraints such as there is limited bandwidth consumption, energy and processing capability of these sensor nodes [1]. There are some completely application based design constraints as well. The determination of deployment mechanism, network topology and size of the network are important factors on which the performances of these networks depend. Within internal scenarios, there are very less number of nodes. However, the external scenarios include large number of sensor nodes. [2] The communication of sensor nodes amongst each other and with the external base stations are both provided in these networks. The lifetime of network is affected directly depending on the battery of sensor node. To enhance the battery consumption of sensor nodes, there are several energy-based solutions protocols at different levels.

© Springer Nature Singapore Pte Ltd. 2019
A. K. Luhach et al. (Eds.): ICAICR 2018, CCIS 956, pp. 490–500, 2019.
https://doi.org/10.1007/978-981-13-3143-5_40

WSN is utilized by several other applications and in order to design the protocol that includes several constraints, several non-conventional paradigms are included. The classification of several routing protocols is done amongst various categories [3]. Amongst these, the basic type of classification is reactive and proactive types of protocols. The proactive routing protocols are utilized to provide routing paths and states previous to the demand of routing traffic. Reactive routing protocols are known as the protocols through which routing actions are triggered to transmit the data to other nodes The classification of routing protocols is done on the basis of source-initiation (Src-initiated) or destination initiation (Dst-initiated). The routing path that is initiated from source node is provided as per the demand of source node within the source-initiated protocol.In case of destination-initiated protocol; the routing path is initiated from the destination node. The routing protocols are classified into homogeneous and hetero-geneous as per the architecture of sensor network architecture [4].

Energy Efficient Techniques

a. **PEGASIS**

A greedy-chain based algorithm that is relevant to LEACH protocol is known as PEGASIS (Power-efficient Gathering in Sensor Information Systems). Following are some of the features of this algorithm:

- The base station is at far distance from the base station.
- There is similarity of all the sensor nodes available in the network and they include very limited amount of energy.
- There is no mobility amongst the sensor nodes available in this network [5].

Chaining and data fusion are the two various strategies included within PEGASIS, using any node, the leader of the chain within the algorithm can be chosen. The leader can be chosen amongst any of the nodes present. Due to the deployment of sensor nodes, the chains are constructed by greedy algorithms.

b. **LEACH**

Low Energy Adaptive Clustering Hierarchy (LEACH) is known as the hierarchal protocol through which the nodes are transmitted to the cluster head. Following are the two phases included in this protocol [6].

1. The Setup Phase: This phase organizes the clusters and selects the cluster heads. Each node checks whether it can be chosen as a cluster head or not using the stochastic algorithm in each round. There is no repetition of selection of a node as a cluster head once it has been chosen.
2. The Steady Phase: Within this phase, the data is transmitted to the base station. The time duration of this phase is longer than the existing phase such that the overhead across the network is minimized.

c. **Ant Colony algorithm**

The ant colony algorithm is utilizes the natural behavior of ants that communicate amongst each other using pheromone. Pheromone is the chemical substance that is released by ants which helps them in mobility. Initially when there is no release of pheromone, there is no knowledge about the length of branches. Once the shorter range is detected, the pheromone is released at higher rate [7]. Along similar paths, ants visit numerable times. The amount of pheromone released by large number of ants is the factor of which the behavior of ants depends. The positive feedback related to the path is provided through this method.

d. Particle Swarm Optimization (PSO)

On the basis of social behavior of group of birds, PSO algorithm is introduced. Various optimization issues are resolved using behavior of swarms in PSO. For providing a fitness function that provides best evaluation, the location of particle is located. The initial step of PSO is that initial parameters are provided in an irregular manner for each particle. For increasing the probability of providing an optimum solution space, the information relevant to the best old individual position and the global best optimum location is used. A better fitness space is used within the algorithm as a result of this approach [8].

2 Literature Review

Brar et al. [9] proposed in this paper, a directional transmission mechanism. The proposed approach is known as PDORP approach. The newly proposed protocol is generated by integrating the Power Efficient Gathering Sensor Information System (PEGASIS) and DSR routing protocols. The bit error rate, delay and energy consumption is minimized as per the results achieved through performance analysis proposed here. The throughput of the network is enhanced as a result of improvement in the QoS in these networks. Thus, the lifetime of network is also enhanced here as per the results.

Han et al. [10] reported that there are large numbers of applications in which the underwater WSNs (UWSNs) are utilized. This paper presents a study related to the already existing routing protocols. Further, comparisons are made amongst all the previously existing routing protocols and each protocol is studied as well. On the basis of route decision makers utilized, there are two broader categories in which the routing protocols are categorized. There are several improvements to be made in these networks as per the simulation results achieved. Novel approaches are to be proposed to achieve better results in the future work.

Harn et al. [11] proposed that to provide secure end-to-end data communication several techniques are thus proposed. However, due to several problems being faced yet in the applications, a novel approach is proposed here that includes group key pre-distribution approach. A path key which is known to be a unique group key is utilized here to protect the data available in complete routing path for transmission. To generate a path and path key, the sensors are authenticated using this protocol. There is minimization of time required to process the data through intermediate nodes using this protocol. This has proven to be a great advantage for these networks.

Yan et al. [12] presented in this paper that since there is very limited amount of battery provided within the sensors of wireless sensor networks, the increment of lifetime of network is very important. The author also presented the important properties, demerits and the applications of these networks. Further, the energy efficiency of routing protocols also faces several issues which are also presented. In comparison static WSNs, the mobile WSNs have provided improved results due to which the energy efficiency, balance and overall cost of these networks is also improved. Several enhancements have been made and results are evaluated through simulations.

Zhong et al. [13] presented the extensive application of wireless sensor networks issue to the vast development and emerging technology, it has been utilized it various different fields. The sensor nodes are deployed in this network which gathered all the data, further send to base station for the communication. Various methods have been proposed so far in order to mitigate the effects of major issues faced in the network. In detailed, they studied the energy efficient routing method in which multiple mobile sinks was used. In the several clusters the whole network was dividedin order to perform various experiments to show the effects of mobile sink on the network life time.

Arbi et al. [14] presented the technology using which data can be transferred from source node to the destination node using the sensor nodes which collect the data first from environment and further send it to base station, this network is termed as wireless sensor network. There is degradation in the quality of packets while transferring the data packets. Energy consumption is the major issue faced currently in this technology. For the communication purpose, this network is utilized in which the consumption of more energy is issue, due to which it is required to minimize the transfer rate of the packets from source to sink node. The development of more data reduction methods is required that helps in measuring the values of both source and sink node The difference between the sensed value and the predicted value has been measured using the threshold value. The techniques in this paper used in accordance with the type of sensed data such as for the data present in the non-linear system.

Jain et al. [15] studied an important concern of wireless sensor networks of the limited lifetime of the battery and maintaining the energy efficiency of the network. The several sensing nodes are deployed randomly in the hostile environment in order to sense the physical conditions such as temperature, pressure and so on. These sensor networks faced the issue of limited battery which is not possible for a human being to replace it as they are installed in the geographical region of hostile area. Therefore, once the battery exhausted, replacement process of battery cause major issues due to which this network is breakdown sometimes. Therefore, due to these reasons, they discussed the some energy efficient routing protocols for this network. There is reduction in the packet overhead, if there is updating in the routing tables frequently, which also minimizes the energy consumption rate of the network.

In the paper, introduction section describe about wireless sensor networks and their issues. In the second section, various techniques which are designed by the authors to increase lifetime of wireless sensor network are highlighted. In the next section, proposed methodology is described with the results of simulation. In the last section results are presented.

3 Proposed Methodology

The self-configuring types of networks that include small sized sensor nodes within them are known as wireless sensor networks. The major concern of these networks is the high energy consumption which is mainly because of the self-configuring nature of these networks. For minimizing the energy consumption of network, an energy efficient protocol used is LEACH. In order to minimize the energy consumption of network, several improvements have been made in LEACH protocol. Three-level architecture proposed in this enhancement in which the data communication process involves leader nodes, cluster heads and gateways nodes. Following are the various phases included in the proposed technique:

Phase 1: Cluster head selection

Within the network, the initial phase is the selection of a cluster head. Finite numbers of sensor nodes are deployed within the network. At the center of the network, base station is deployed. The messages are flood within the network by the base station. The signal strength of the network is calculated by the base station. The cluster head can be chosen from the nodes that have signal strength above to the threshold value. The below equation will define the threshold value [16]:

$$R_{CH} = R_{min} * \left[1 + \left(\frac{d_{BS} - d_{BSmin}}{d_{BSmax} - d_{BSmin}} \right) \right]$$ (1)

Here, the radius of cluster is denoted by R_{min}, the node's distance from base station is denoted by d_{BS} and the minimum distance from base station is denoted by d_{BSmin}. Further, the maximum distance from base station is denoted by d_{BSmax} [16].

$$F_{CH-value} = \alpha * N_{deg} + \frac{\beta}{MSD_{deg}} + \frac{\gamma}{d_{BS}}$$ (2)

Here, the number of neighbor nodes of specific node is denoted by N_{deg}. The mean distance of all nodes in network is denoted by MSD_{deg}. The three threshold values used here are α, β and γ which give 1 as total. Random values from 0 to 1 are generated by the sensor nodes of the network. When the condition given in Eq. 3 is satisfied, the sensor node will be satisfied as cluster [16].

$$K(i) > F_{CH-value}$$ (3)

The K(i) is the random value generated by the sensor node individually (Fig. 1).

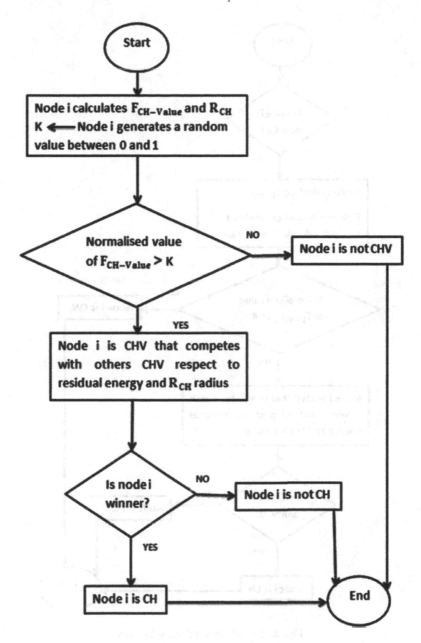

Fig. 1. Cluster head selection process

Phase 2: Leader node Selection

The selection of leader nodes in the network is the second phase of proposed technique. The nodes that are not chosen as cluster heads can be chosen as leader nodes. The data is collected from sensor nodes and passed to the cluster head with the help of these leader nodes. The Eq. 4 given below selects the volunteer leader node:

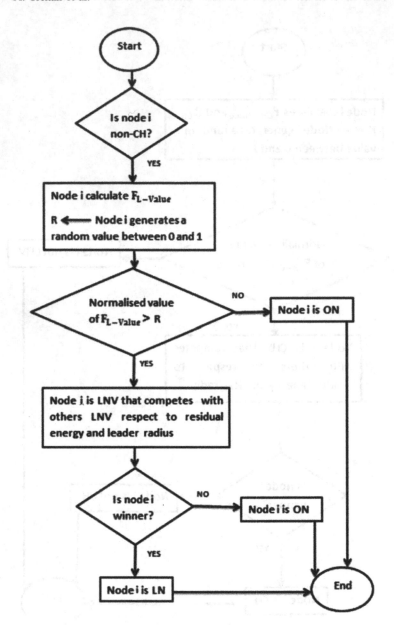

Fig. 2. Leader node selection process

$$F_{LN-value} = \eta * M_{deg} + \frac{\lambda}{K_{LN}} \qquad (4)$$

The numbers of nodes that can be volunteered as being chosen as leader nodes are represented by Mdeg. The numbers of nodes that fall under defined radius are denoted by K_{LN}. Two constants whose total will be 1 are denoted by η, λ. A random number will be generated from 0 to 1 by the nodes that are volunteered to be chosen as leader nodes. The leader node will be chosen amongst the nodes that satisfy the condition 5 (Fig. 2):

$$K(i) > F_{LN-value} \tag{5}$$

Phase 3: Gateway node selection

The gateway nodes are deployed in the network within the last phase of algorithm. On the basis of total number of nodes that are presented in Eq. 6, the gateway nodes are dependent.

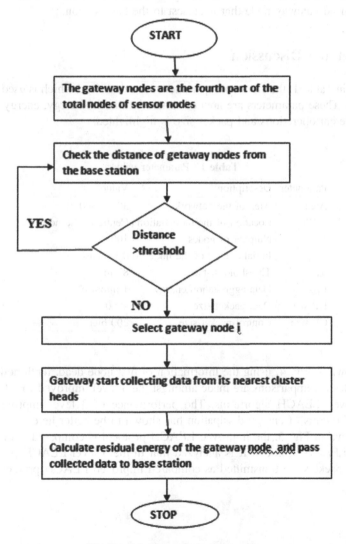

Fig. 3. Selection of gateway nodes

$$\text{Gateway}_{\text{nodes}} = \text{total number of nodes}/4 \tag{6}$$

The fourth part of total nodes is covered by gateway nodes. For transmitting data to the base station, the best node is chosen from all the gateway nodes. Equation 7 is used to calculate the distance between the base station and gateway node (Fig. 3).

$$\text{Distance} = \sqrt{(x(i) - x)^2 + (y(i) - y)^2} \tag{7}$$

The data will be aggregated from the normal sensor nodes with the help of leader nodes in the proposed approach. The sensed data will be forwarded to the cluster head nodes using leader nodes. The data will further by forwarded to the base station with the help of cluster head gateway node that is closest to the base station.

4   Result and Discussion

As shown in Table 1, the simulation parameters are described which is used to perform simulation. These parameters are area of simulation, initial energy, energy dissipation during different operations and packet size is highlighted.

Table 1. Parameter values

Parameter	Description	Value
Area	Area of the network	300 * 300 m
L-BS	Location of the base station	Centre of the network
N	Number of nodes	100
I_{nitial}	Initial energy of the node	0.1 joules
d_o	Threshold distance	87 m
E_{DA}	Data aggregation energy	1 nj/bit/m^4
DP size	Data packet size	4000
CP size	Control packet size	200 bits

As shown in Fig. 4, using the information of first node dead, tenth node dead and all nodes dead, comparisons are made amongst the 3 level improved LEACH protocol and improved LEACH algorithms. The performance of 3 level improved LEACH algorithm in terms of energy dissipation has shown to be better here.

As shown in Fig. 5, the improved LEACH protocol is compared with the 3 level improved LEACH protocol. It is analyzed that in the 3 level LEACH protocol more number of packets are transmitted as compared improved LEACH protocol.

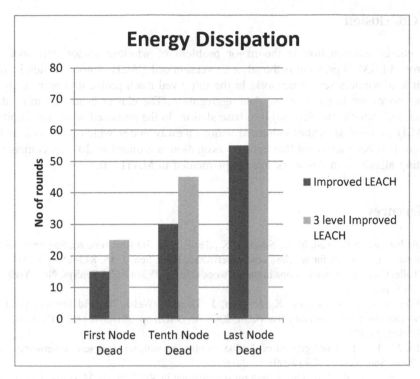

Fig. 4. Energy dissipation

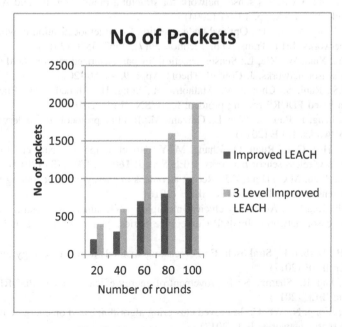

Fig. 5. Number of packets transmitted

5 Conclusion

The energy consumption is the major problem of wireless sensor networks. The improved LEACH protocol is the advance version of LEACH protocol which increase lifetime of wireless sensor network. In the improved leach protocol cluster heads and leader nodes are formed for the data aggregation. The cluster head transmit data to leader node which later forward it to base station. In the proposed work, the improved LEACH protocol is further enhanced using gateway nodes which pass data to base station. It is been analyzed that energy dissipation is reduced to 20% as compared to existing algorithm in this work after implemented in MATLAB.

References

1. Al Rubeaai, S.F., Abd, M.A., Singh, B.K., Tepe, K.E.: 3D Real-time routing protocol with tunable parameters for wireless sensor networks. IEEE Sen. J. **16**, 843–853 (2015)
2. Tolle, G., et al.: A macroscope in the redwoods. In: 2005 3rd ACM SenSys, New York, NY, USA, pp. 51–63 (2005)
3. Werner-Allen, G., Lorincz, K., Johnson, J., Lees, J., Welsh, M.: Fidelity and yield in a volcano monitoring sensor network. In: 2006 7th OSDI, pp. 381–396. USENIX Association, Berkeley (2006)
4. Li, M., Liu, Y.: Underground coal mine monitoring with wireless sensor networks. ACM Trans. Sen. Netw. **5**, 29 (2009)
5. Vicaire, P., et al.: Achieving long-term surveillance in VigilNet. ACM Trans. Sen. Netw. **5**, 9:1–9:39 (2009)
6. Xu, N., et al.: A wireless sensor network for structural monitoring. In: 2nd ACM SenSys, New York, NY, USA, pp. 13–24 (2004)
7. Liu, L., Zhang, X., Ma, H.: Optimal node selection for target localization in wireless camera sensor networks. IEEE Trans. Veh. Technol. **59**(7), 3562–3576 (2010)
8. Weng, Y., Xiao, W., Xie, L.: Sensor selection for parameterized random field estimation in wireless sensor networks. J. Control. Theory Appl. **9**, 44–50 (2011)
9. Brar, G.S., Rani, S., Chopra, V., Malhotra, R., Song, H., Ahmed, S.H.: Energy efficient direction based PDORP routing protocol for WSN. IEEE (2016)
10. Han, G., Jiang, J., Bao, N., Wan, L., Guizani, M.: Routing protocols for underwater wireless sensor networks. IEEE (2015)
11. Harn, L., Hsu, C.-F., Ruan, O., Zhang, M.-Y.: Novel design of secure end-to-end routing protocol in wireless sensor networks. IEEE Sen. J. **16**(6), 1779–1785 (2016)
12. Yan, J.J., Zhou, M.C., Ding, Z.J.: Recent advances in energy-efficient routing protocols for wireless sensor networks: a review. IEEE (2016)
13. Zhong, P., Ruan, F.: An energy efficient multiple mobile sinks based routing algorithm for wireless sensor networks. In: IOP Conference Series: Materials Science and Engineering (2018)
14. Arbi, I.B., Derbel, F., Strakosch, F.: Forecasting methods to reduce energy consumptionin WSN. In: IEEE (2017)
15. Jain, H., Jain, R., Sharma, S.: Improvement of energy efficiency using PDORP protocol in WSN. In: IEEE (2017)
16. Wu, W., Xiong, N., Wu, C.: Improved clustering algorithm based on energy consumption in wireless sensor networks. IET (2017)

Enhanced TESRP Protocol for Isolation of Selective Forwarding Attack in WSN

Harkiranvir Kaur[✉], Preeti Singh, Nidhi Garg, and Pardeep Kaur

Department of Electronics and Communication,
University Institute of Engineering and Technology,
Panjab University, Chandigarh, India
harkiransomal@gmail.com, {preeti_singh,
nidhi_garg}@pu.ac.in, pardeep.tur@gmail.com

Abstract. A wireless sensor network is the combination of large numbers of nodes connected to each other in order to communicate with other networks over a particular territory. Within the sensor networks there are two types of attacks which are active and passive attacks. The selective forwarding is the active type of attack in which malicious nodes drop some packets in the network which affect network performance which is considered in this paper. In this research work, technique of threshold is designed which detect and isolate malicious nodes from the network. The simulation results shows improvement in terms of dead nodes, throughput and packet loss.

Keywords: Security · Selective forwarding · Threshold

1 Introduction

Wireless sensor networks include several number of sensor nodes which are spread across the particular areas [1]. Several physical constraints like the temperature, moisture etc. from the surroundings are monitored with the deployment of wireless sensor networks.

In the WSN there is a base station which send and receive the data from the cluster head nodes in the network. As shown in Fig. 1 clusters are formed for a finite number of nodes and a cluster head is chosen. This head is responsible for aggregating the data sent by the nodes and transfering it to the base station. It is selected on the basis of energy of the node. It will keep on changing throughout the cycles of WSN. For several applications such as military services, self-monitoring home applications, medical services, and so on, the wireless sensor networks have been deployed in order to keep track of the regular changes occurring in these scenarios. The sensor nodes include batteries within them as a source of energy [3, 4]. Since, the size of battery is very small and there is limited amount of energy available, the deployment of sensor nodes in far places is not much beneficial. Thus, the efficient utilization of energy within these networks is a major concern [5]. Also the security of the wireless sensor networks is mandatory to be maintained for practical scenarios [6]. The security in WSNs is the major requirement such that secure communication can be ensured amongst the nodes. There are very less resources available within the sensor nodes and thus, the protection

© Springer Nature Singapore Pte Ltd. 2019
A. K. Luhach et al. (Eds.): ICAICR 2018, CCIS 956, pp. 501–511, 2019.
https://doi.org/10.1007/978-981-13-3143-5_41

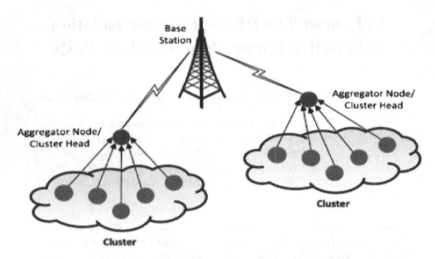

Fig. 1. Network model for WSN [2]

of important information that is gathered by them is a basic priority to be accomplished. There are certain functionalities that are to be provided by these networks. Because of certain vulnerabilities and opportunities available within the networks, it is possible for the attackers to attack these networks [7]. There are very less resources available within the sensor nodes and thus, the protection of important information that is gathered by them is a basic priority to be accomplished. There are certain functionalities that are to be provided by these networks. Because of certain vulnerabilities and opportunities available within the networks, it is possible for the attackers to attack these networks [8, 9]. The security of the system is needed for various reasons such as data confidentiality, data integrity and most important of all is that the network should be secure so the life of the network is increased as the secure environment would prevent the nodes from sending data again and again and thus utilizing less energy overall [10]. The network is prone to many types of attacks such as selective forwarding attack, sinkhole attack, blackhole attack, Sybil attacks and various other attacks. These attacks consume the energy of the nodes by making them transfer the packets again to the base station as the malicious nodes in the network drop the packets randomly [11]. Such attacks need to be combated to make the system reliable and more energy efficient. Various techniques have been proposed for different kinds of attacks in previous years [12]. This paper focuses on the selective forwarding attack and to detect more number of malicious nodes in limited time. In this, the network consumes less energy for packet transfer and the nodes have enough amount of energy for other computations and calculations and therefore the lifetime of the network is enhanced. The protocol is named as enhanced TESRP.

The paper is organized as follows. Section 2 will discuss the related work. Section 3 will present the proposed methodology and in Sect. 4 results and discussion is done. In the last Sect. 5 the work is concluded.

2 Literature Review

Kamble et al. [13] presented that there are several problems arising within the WSNs when they send data directly to the sink node. The major criterion of WSN is the collection of information. For reducing the amount of energy to be consumed and improving the lifetime of network, the energy effective information aggregation technique is utilized here. For avoiding any such issues relevant to energy, an energy effective technique is used here. With the help of forwarding data in aggregated format, the overall lifetime of wireless network is enhanced.

Rani et al. [14] presented that the energy efficiency as well as fault tolerance of protocols is modified due to the change in network topology. It is very important to maintain both the parameters and thus the attacks can be prevented from entering the network by proposing several approaches. Because of various attacks occurring in the networks, the energy is degraded. For avoiding any wastage of energy, several approaches such as cluster based approach is provided. The throughput is also maintained. In this paper, several approaches such as cluster based approach are provided. The throughput is also maintained through this approach and security is improved.

Joshi et al. [15] presented that there is less power being consumed due to the advancements in Micro-Electro-Mechanical Systems (MEMS), wireless communications, and digital hardware. By studying several investigation strategies, a definite study has been proposed. The various issues arising in the networks has been presented through this study. For gaining trust, reputation and provide security to the wireless sensor networks, huge study is presented in this paper. Within WSN, unified methodology has been utilized in any case. Further, to perform various calculations and eliminate the weight of power being consumed by reputation request, the base station is utilized. Also, the numbers of calculations being performed on sensor nodes are minimized through this approach.

Anand et al. [16] presented that are many resource constraints due to the deployment of nodes in remote areas and manner in which they are deployed. When one or more nodes misuse the transmission such that these nodes cannot be accessed by other resources, the Denial of Service (DoS) attack occurs in the network. This attack is identified in the proposed system by introducing a new methodology. In order to validate the nodes by retracing the routing path that was selected by the victim node as an internal attack, the Intruder Detection System was used. Thus, DoS attack was identified in this work and a secure and reliable data transmission method was provided from source to the destination.

Said et al. [17] proposed a new model for 3D wireless sensor networks through which heterogeneous sensors were deployed. Single sensing and multiple sensing were the two different methods controlled by this model. Further, this paper also presented the proficiency of WSN within several probabilistic distributions. OPNET and NS2 were used to generate a simulation domain for the proposed model. Both proficiency and execution were provided by Gaussian distribution as per the simulation results. Within both the evaluation approaches, Gaussian WSN has shown the best execution results in comparison to uniform WSN approach. There is least execution time found for beta and chi-square WSNs. The most important parameter is the end-to-end deferral in which the preferable execution is provided by uniform WSN in comparison to proposed approach. Thus, Gaussian sensors distribution can be used within 3D WSNs as per the simulation results achieved by the proposed model.

Biswas et al. [18] aimed to provide a study related to various types of security attacks occurring within WSNs and the effects caused by them. WSNs are highly prone to several types of attacks due to the manner in which they are generated and the nodes are deployed over the large area Different types of security attacks, their effects as well as the defense methods were presented in this paper. Further, the approaches used to avoid attacks in the networks are also reviewed in this paper.

Ahmed et al. proposed in this paper [19] a novel Trust and Energy aware Routing Protocol (TESRP) to detect as well as isolate the malicious nodes from the networks. To provide trust, residual energy and hop counts of neighboring nodes, a composite routing function is utilized in TESRP. The routing decisions are made with the help of this approach. The energy being consumed is minimized as per the simulation results. Further, there is improvement in throughput and lifetime of network as per the comparisons of several protocols with TESRP.

Li et al. [20] presented the wireless sensor network in this paper in which security is considered as the major issue in the physical layer as it is affected by the passive eavesdroppers. The presence of eavesdroppers' channels within the network is not known to transmitter. The physical layer security has been guaranteed in this paper due to the utilization of the multi-antenna relay. They assumed that relay works in full duplex mode and transmits artificial noise (AN) which is not followed in the existing work. They performed their work in both the stages of decode-and forward (DF) cooperative strategy. Therefore, for both the issues of power constrained and power unconstrained systems, they proposed the two optimal power allocation strategies in this paper.

Security is a major concern for the analysts in these papers. In order to construct a secure wireless sensor network framework, several ideas have been identified over the time. This paper focuses on selective forwarding attack and to detect more number of malicious nodes in lesser number of time.

3   Proposed Methodology

For increasing the lifetime of wireless sensor networks, it is very important to find out several energy-saving techniques. Through these approaches, either the throughput can be decreased or transmission delay can be increased through which the end-client can provide an inbuilt exchange. On the basis of number of queries being generated per mean time, the mobility of wireless sensor network can be done. By transmitting the query all across the sensor field, the detected data is transmitted by the sink node. The important information is sensed by sensor nodes and forwarded to base station within wireless sensor networks. Within the network, various active and passive attacks are possible due to the presence of malicious nodes. The active attack that results in dropping packets and forwards some packets to destination is known as selective forwarding attack. The throughput of network is minimized and energy consumption is maximized due to the occurrence of selective forward attack. Novel technique is proposed in this work for minimizing and eliminating the malicious nodes from network. A technique is proposed in the network depending upon the traffic analyzer and threshold values. On the basis of trust values of the nodes, the central controller is selected in this network. The trust value of the node is calculated on the basis of data packets being re-transmitted in the network. Each node is registered on the basis of IP, MAC address and current data due to the presence of central controller. With the help of central controller node, the bandwidth needed for communication is available. A secure and efficient path is created from the node towards the base station on the basis of two factors which are hop count and sequence number. The sensor nodes forward the data. Each node is checked randomly with the help of central controller. In a network, the malicious node is detected with the help of identifying the nodes that have threshold that is unequal to the decided threshold value. A multipath routing method is provided for eliminating such malicious nodes.

Proposed Algorithm

Input: Sensor nodes
Output: Detection of malicious nodes

1. Install finite number of sensor nodes in a network.
2. Select Central controller node ()
    i. For (i = 0;i = n;i ++)
    ii. No. of pkts = node(i)
    iii. If (node(no. of pkts(i) > no. of pkts(i + 1)))
    iv. Central controller node = node(i)
    v. End
3. Every node is registered with the central controller node with their MAC and IP address
4. Assign Bandwidth ()
5. For (i = 0;i = n;i ++)
6. Bandwidth of node(i + 1) = total bandwidth-bandwidth node(i + 1)
   End
7. Sensor nodes are checked by central controller randomly
8. if (node(bandwidth used = bandwidth alloted)
    1. if(Node(throughput < threshold throughput)
    2. malicious node = Node(i)
       else
    3. repeat step 8 to 9 until malicious node get detected
       else
9. End of for
10. End of if
11. End of if

Proposed Flowchart

A finite number of sensor nodes are installed in the network. Then the network is divided into fixed sized clusters and the cluster head is selected in every cluster. Select the central controller in the network that is the base station and record each node with the central controller. Now every sensor node is checked for vulnerability detection randomly. If it is detected then check the bandwidth consumed by the node. Again, if it is equal to the allocated bandwidth further check the throughput. If it is less than the

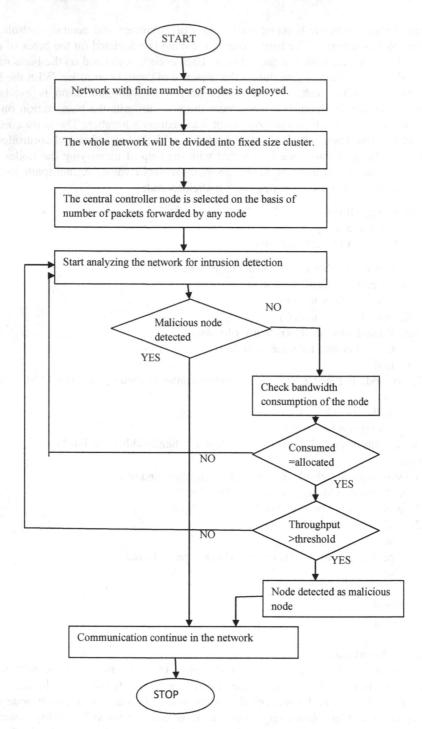

Fig. 2. Proposed flowchart

threshold value, the node is detected as a malicious node otherwise the steps are repeated. The formula for calculating the threshold is given as:

$$Pb = (avg - min)/(max - min);$$
$$P = Pb * max\_p \qquad (1)$$

The "avg" is the variable which defines the average data rate used in the simulation. The average data rate which is used in the simulation is 1 packet per 0.05 s. The "min" defines the lower bond value of the throughput. The "max" is the upper bound value. The "Pb" is the average throughput and when it is multiplied with the upper bound value then we get the threshold throughput. The "max_p" is the upper bound value of throughput (Fig. 2).

4 Results and Discussions

The ETESRP protocol is improved version of a well known protocol TESRP (A secure routing protocol with trust and energy awareness) protocol in which threshold based technique is implemented for detection of malicious nodes. These nodes are detected and isolated from network using the proposed algorithm. The active type of attack due to which the packets are dropped by the malicious nodes is known as selective forwarding attack. The performance is compared with TESRP [13].The simulation table presented below shows the various parameters being used in MATLAB for simulation (Table 1).

Table 1. Simulation parameters

Parameter	Value
Propagation model	Two ray ground model
Area	250 * 250 m
Number of nodes	100
Network type	Wireless networks
Range	250 m
Transmit energy	50 nJ/bit
Receive energy	50 nJ/bit
Initial energy	0.1 J
Amplification energy	10 pJ/bit/m^2
Data aggregation energy	5 pJ/bit/signal

As shown in Fig. 3, the simulation model is designed in which malicious node exists. The cluster head transmit data to base station. The malicious node drops certain packets in the network which reduce its efficiency. The green nodes define the cluster head and red nodes are dead nodes. The malicious node will keep on changing with every simulation.

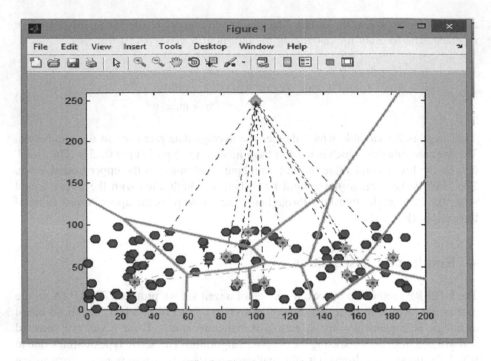

Fig. 3. Simulation model

Next the comparison results are discussed for number of dead nodes, throughput and packet loss.

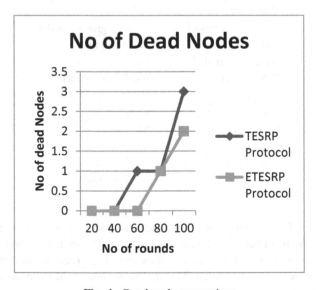

Fig. 4. Dead node comparison

Firstly, as shown in Fig. 4, the performance is analyzed on the basis of number of dead nodes in TESRP and ETESRP protocol. The number of dead nodes in TESRP is higher than that of ETESRP for the different rounds as less energy is consumed in the proposed protocol. In the 100th round dead nodes are 3 in existing protocol and in comparison to that only 2 are dead in proposed protocol.

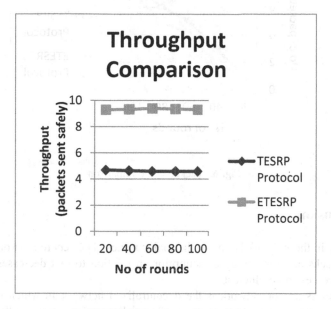

Fig. 5. Throughput comparison

Then in Fig. 5, the performance of TESRP protocol and ETESRP protocol is compared for throughput analysis. Due to isolation of malicious nodes from the network ETESRP protocol has higher throughput as compared to TESRP protocol. In existing protocol the throughput remains in the range 4–5 packets but in the proposed protocol it rises to the range 9–9.5 packets sent to the base station.

Next in Fig. 6, the packet loss of TESRP and ETESRP protocol is compared for performance analysis. The packet loss of ETESRP is less as compared to TESRP because the malicious nodes are detected in less time with respect to the existing protocol. Therefore, more number of packets is sent safely to the destination and hence packet loss is reduced.

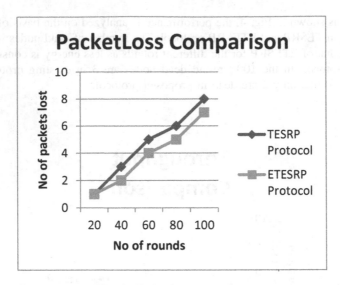

Fig. 6. Packet loss comparison

5   Conclusion

The security in the network is one of the major issues. The secure environment is less prone to attacks and the energy consumption in relation to that decreases. Hence the network becomes more efficient.

The wireless sensor network is the decentralized network in which sensor nodes sense information and pass to base station. The selective forwarding is the active type of which affect network performance. The novel technique is designed in this work based on the threshold values. The proposed technique is implemented in MATLAB. The simulation results shows improvement in terms of number of dead nodes, packet loss and throughput in comparison with the technique called TESRP.

References

1. Joseph, J., Vijayan, V.P.: Misdirection attack in WSN due to selfish nodes. detection and suppression using longer path protocol, vol. 4 (2014)
2. Rezvani, M., Ignjatovic, A., Bernito, E., Jha, S.: Secure data aggregation technique for wireless sensor networks in the presence of collusion attacks. IEEE Trans. Dependable Secure Comput., **12**(1) (2015)
3. Padmavathi, G., Shanmugapriya, D.: A survey of attacks, security mechanisms and challenges in wireless sensor networks. Int. J. Comput. Sci. Inf. Secur. **4**(1, 2), 1–9 (2009)
4. Abdullah, M.Y., Hua, G.W., Alsharabi, N.; Wireless sensor networks misdirection attacker challenges and solutions (2008). IEEE 978-1-4244-2184-8/08/
5. Sachan, R.S., Wazid, M., Singh, D.P., Katal, A., Goudar, R.H. Misdirection Attack in WSN: Topological Analysis and an Algorithm for Delay and Throughput Prediction (2012). IEEE 978-1-4673-4603-0/12/

6. Perrig, A., Stankovic, J., Wagner, D.: Security in wireless sensor networks. Commun. ACM **47**(6), 53–57 (2004)
7. Saleem, S., Ullah, S., Yoo, H.S.: On the security issues in wireless body area networks. Int. J. Digit. Content Technol. Appl. **3**(3), 178–184 (2009)
8. Martins, D., Guyennet, H.: Wireless sensor network attacks and security mechanisms: a short survey. IEEE (2010)
9. Kim, J., Caytiles, R.D., Kim, K.J.: A review of the vulnerabilities and attacks for wireless sensor networks. J. Secur. Eng. 241–250 (2014)
10. Sastry, A.S., Sulthana, S., Vagdevi, S.: Security threats in wireless sensor networks in each layer. Int. J. Adv. Netw. Appl. **04**(04), 1657–1661 (2013)
11. Karlof, C., Wagner, D.: Secure routing in wireless sensornetworks: attacks and counter-measures. Ad Hoc Networks Journal **1**(2–3), 293–315 (2003)
12. Sharma, K., Ghose, M.K.: Wireless sensor networks: an overview on its security threats. IJCA Special Issue on "Mob. Ad-hoc Netw." MANETs 42–45 (2010)
13. Kamble, S., Dhope, T.: Reliable routing data aggregation using efficient clustering in WSN. In: International Conference on Communication Control and Computing Technologies, pp. 246–250. IEEE (2017)
14. Rani, L., Rani, E.V.: A novel study on data flow routing with energy optimization under different attacks in WSN (2015)
15. Joshi, M., Patel, S.: Centralized signature based approach for wireless sensor network using rsa algorithm. Int. J. Technol. Res. Eng. **2**(8) (2015)
16. Anand, C., Gnanamurthy, R.K.: Localized DoS attack detection architecture for reliable data transmission over wireless sensor network. Wirel. Pers. Commun. **90**, 847–859 (2016)
17. Said, O., Elnashar, A.: Scaling of wireless sensor network intrusion detection probability: 3D sensors, 3D intruders, and 3D environments. EURASIP J. Wirel. Commun. Netw. **15**, 46 (2015)
18. Biswas, S., Adhikari, S.: A survey of security attacks, defenses and security mechanisms in wireless sensor network. Int. J. Comput. Appl. (0975–8887) **131**(17), 28–35 (2015)
19. Ahmed, A., Bakar, K.A., Channa, M.I., Khan, A.W.: A secure routing protocol with trust and energy awareness energy routing protocol. Mobile Networks and Applications **21**, 272–285 (2016)
20. Li, W., Liu, K., Wang, S., Lei, J., Li, E., Li, X.: Full-duplex relay for enhancing physical layer security in wireless sensor networks: optimal power allocation for minimizing secrecy outage probability. In: 2017 17th IEEE International Conference on Communication Technology (2017)

ITS-Application-Priority-MAC (ITS-APMAC) for Reliable Communication Over VANETs

Paramjit Waraich$^{(\boxtimes)}$ and Neera Batra

CSE Department, MMEC, M. M. University, Ambala, India
param.waraich@gmail.com, batraneeral@gmail.com

Abstract. V2V communication suffers due to various factors i.e. short range wireless links, Collision, dynamic topology and VANET's application compatibility with routing/MAC layer. Channel must be available for the safety applications and rest of slots may be allocated to other non-safety applications but MAC layer is not aware with the type of applications. So any application can access the medium at any time and MAC protocol manages the access to wireless medium. Unfair resource allocation to non-safety applications may interrupt the communication during critical circumstances like medical emergency/battlefield communication etc. Channel must be reserved for these types of application. In this paper, ITS-APMAC is introduced which can identify the application type and according to the rules, assigns the channel access to the applications.

Keywords: VANET · MAC · Safety application · IEEE-802.11p

1 Introduction

Intelligent Transport system (ITS) based applications can extend the capabilities of VANET but their performance suffers from the behavior of MAC layer. Researchers examined the traditional MAC protocol and later on it was modified to adopt the dynamic environment of VANET and new version is called IEEE 802.11p [23] but VANET still suffers from the following performance issues:

- Hidden terminal
- Expose Terminal
- Collision
- Highly Mobile Environment
- Transmission Range
- Unfair utilization of channel
- Road Topology

VANET based applications can be categorized in to following categories:
Standards for VANET based communication

1. **V2I Communication:** In this type of communication, vehicles interact with a fixed infrastructure nit, called Road Side Unit (RSU) (Figs. 1 and 2).

© Springer Nature Singapore Pte Ltd. 2019
A. K. Luhach et al. (Eds.): ICAICR 2018, CCIS 956, pp. 512–523, 2019.
https://doi.org/10.1007/978-981-13-3143-5_42

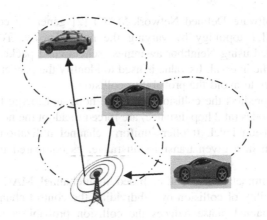

Fig. 1. V2I communication

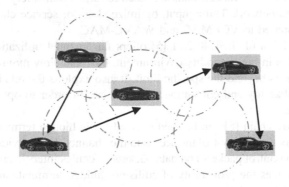

Fig. 2. V2V communication

2. **V2V Communication:** In this type of communication, vehicles interact with each other directly using short range wireless links. This type of communication suffers due to the behavior of routing and MAC protocols. Common MAC standards for VANET are as follow:

- IEEE 802.11p
- Multi-Rate MAC [14–22]

Now we will discuss the recent enhance related to the wireless communication over VANET.

2 Related Work

VMR-MAC [1] resolves the slot distribution issue using round robin method. Slots are allocated in a uniform manner and each node can utilize multiple slots with in a specific time frame. To avoid the collision, Slots are released at the end of time frame. It ensures the fair channel utilization thus results in minimum delay as compared to VeMAC.

Sdn-MAC (Software Defined Network-MAC) [2] generates collision alerts and updates the VANET topology by varying the node density. Topological data is dynamically updated using Neighbor awareness scheme and packet loss ratio is estimated over a specific interval. Its value is used to identify the packet drop location and topology is changes to avoid the probability collision.

CReMAC [3] predicts the collisions within 2 hops and merge the collision probability. After that nodes (at 2 hop distance) are forced to adopt the new slots, in order to minimize the collision level. It offers uniform channel utilization thus results less collision ratio with in a given transmission range, as compared to HER-MAC and VeMAC.

Multi-round elimination contention based multichannel MAC (VEC-MAC) [4] reduces the probability of collision by subdividing the control channel in to different phases: Service channel phase reduces the collision probability using multi round elimination contention, Safety message broadcast phase reserves the slots for emergency services and RSU broadcast phase is used to satisfy non-safety application users. It offers enhanced network Throughput, optimize slots for service channel, load optimization as compared to VCI-MAC and WAVE-MAC.

Enhanced version of IEEE-802.11 [5] offers fair channel utilization by enforcing the rules for nodes in high mobility environment. Fast and slow moving nodes cannot transmit the packets beyond the specific limit. It also exploits the relationship between transmission probability and contention window size, in order to optimize the packet transmission rate.

A 3-D Markov chain [6] can be used to resolve the hidden terminal problem. It is using a backoff method to control the access to the channel. It subdivides the upcoming transmission into control packets and data packets. It denies interspace time interval for each class. It reduces the probability of collision, hidden terminals and enhances the rate of successful transmission etc.

Efficient and fast broadcast (EFAB) [7] scheme reduces the collision ratio by merging the TDMA and CDMA schemes to improve the efficiency of MAC protocol. It can adapt the attributes of vehicles and regulate the broadcast services over control channel. It uses three hops neighbor information to allocate the slots for each upcoming node. Comparison of EFAB with HER-MAC shows that EFAB delivers higher PDR and it can also adjust the slot length automatically.

Self-sorting MAC protocol [8] can adopt the scalable VANET's feature and it regulates collision ratio just before data transmission. Node uses a queue processing method which can interact directly with channel to estimate the current processing length and after that a Threshold value is obtained for further queue processing using TDMA slots. Experiments show its efficiency in terms of less Delay and packet loss ratio.

Queue learning scheme (QL-MAC) [9] can provide the higher packet delivery ratio while minimizing the overall end-to-end delay. Contention window is dynamically adjusted to ensure the fair channel access. QL-MAC offers higher PDR with low Delay.

Heuristic and adaptive fuzzy logic scheme (HaFL) [10] method can dynamically adapts the network condition and adjusts the size of contention window. It uses MAC and PHY layers and collects the data about various parameters i.e. Collision ratio, SINR and current queue length etc. All these information is further use to control the level of congestion during transmission. Higher value of HaFL indicates the hidden terminal problem whereas its low value shows the transmission failure. HaFL offers higher rate of data transmission and Throughput with minimum delay.

Flooding over VANET may degrade the overall network performance and it also results in unreliable data transmission. Game theory [9] can be used to manage extra control overhead. According to this theory, each node observes the current network behavior and according to the collected statistics, network resources are utilized. Multiple nodes form a cluster and load is distributed to each cluster as per requirements. Experiments show that it can control the flooding overhead for VANETs.

Accuracy of channel sense may be affected due to the node's mobility [10]. MAC based cross layer solution integrates PHY and MAC layers to resolve this issue. This combination can handle the resource allocation issues efficiently as compared to KoN-MAC, CogMesh, and cluster-based MAC protocols.

Priority of channel access can be set using Adaptive Medium Access Control Scheduler (AMAC) [11]. It divides the upcoming streams into multiple sub classes to determine their data rate and transmission range. These parameters are further used to estimate the probability of collision ratio over a certain period. All this information is used to create the transmission schedule to minimize the collision level. Experiments shows that it is only suitable for short range communication and can maintain network performance as compared to Non Cooperative Cognitive Multiple Access (NCCMA).

TDMA-MAC [21] based Opportunistic transmission techniques can dynamically manage the available slots to the current node's density. In case of low node density, minimum slots are used but for large node density, additional slots are added for smooth communication thus results in low collision ration, higher successful transmission rate with minimum delay [12].

MAC layer plays an important role for VANET based delay tolerant sensor networks [13]. Sensors are deployed in each vehicle to cache the last behavior of transmission rate. This collected data is used to optimize the transmission power and buffer queue thus results in less power consumption and efficient data transmission.

2.1 Problem Formulation

Any node can access the wireless channel at any time and MAC protocol is responsible to manage the access to medium. End users may use any VANET application with any restriction. Table 1 shows some categories of these application. If entire channel is occupied by non-safety/other applications, than safety applications will suffer from starvation. If all resources are allocated to safety applications, than rest of all users may suffer from poor network performance. To cop up with this issue, there must be a provision which can identify the application type and manage its access over wireless channel in such a way that each user must have fair access to the medium.

Table 1. VANET application types

VANET application type	Purpose
Safety	Medical emergency Accident alerts
Non-Safety	Driver assistance, road map assistance, real time navigation,
Others	Advertisement broadcasting, Weather report application, news alerts, road condition alerts, traffic condition alerts

2.2 ITS-Application-Priority-MAC (ITS-APMAC)

ITS-Application-Priority-MAC (ITS-APMAC) scheme defines some rules which overwrite the behavior of existing MAC protocol. It uses following algorithms:

> **2.2.1 Priority Learning Algorithm (PLA)**
> **2.2.2 Decision Making Algorithm (DMA)**

2.2.1   Priority Learning Algorithm (PLA)

PLA is used for training purpose. It identifies all possible application types and set the priority for each one. Emergency applications have the highest priority, Assistance applications have the medium level priority and other (Alert) applications have the lowest priority. In case of collision state, according to the assigned priority, decision is made for channel access (Table 2).

For each possible application: vApp
If (vApp$_i$->Type:=SAFETY)
         Set vApp$_i$->Priority:=High
End If

If (vApp$_i$->Type:=NON-SAFETY)
         Set vApp$_i$->Priority:=MEDIUM
End If
If (vApp$_i$->Type:=OTHERS)
         Set vApp$_i$->Priority:=LOW
End If
End for

Table 2. VANET's application priority

VANET application type	Priority assumption
Safety	High
Non-safety	Medium
Others	Low

Case: Normal
Allocate Channel on the basis of FIFO method.

For each vAppi-> Type
Calculate Collision ratio: vCLR
Collision Threshold: vCTH
If (vCLR > vCTH) **then**
        Go to : Case: Collision
Else
        Go to : Case: Normal
End if
End For

2.2.2 Decision Making Algorithm (DMA)

In case of normal execution, FIFO method is used to allocate the channel w.r.t. priority. Collision ratio is monitored and if collision ratio increases then DMA is used to resolve

Table 3. Decision rules

State	Application type	Application priority	Decision
Collision	Safety	High	Allow
	Non-safety	Medium	Wait
	Others	Low	Denied

the conflicts over channel access (Table 3).
In case of collision,

Case: **Collision**

Safety application must have the highest priority among all other applications. So its collision ratio $vCLR_i$ is measured at different levels. If it is less than the Collision Threshold $vCTH_i$, channel access is granted but if it is equal to the $vCTH_i$, then WAIT status is set for that particular application, and if $vCLR_i > vCTH_i$, then channel access is denied.

If vAppi: SAFETY
        If (vApp$_i$->vCLR$_i$ < vCTH$_i$)
        vApp$_i$-> Decision: ALLOW
        else If (vApp$_i$->vCLR$_i$ = vCTH$_i$)
                vApp$_i$->nsWait++
            if (vAppi->nsWait> vTHw)
                vAppi-> Decision: DENIED
            else
                vAppi-> Decision: WAIT
            End If
        End if
End if

Non-SAFETY applications have medium level priority, to minimize the collision, their waiting period is increased. If waiting time exceeds from allowed Threshold, channel access is denied.

If vAppi: Non-SAFETY
      vAppi->nsWait++
      if (vAppi->nsWait> vTHw)
     vAppi-> Decision: DENIED
     else
      vAppi-> Decision: WAIT
    End If
End If

Other applications have the lowest priority as compared to others. To avoid the collision and starvation stage for these applications, channel access is denied.

If (vAppi: OTHERS)
      vApp$_i$-> Decision: DENIED
End If

If all applications have high priority then on the basis of collision ratio, channel access decision is made.

---

for each vApp$_i$ Calculate vCLR$_i$
    If (vApp$_i$->vCLR$_{i >}$ vCTH$_i$)
    vApp$_i$->nsWait++
    if (vApp$_i$->nsWait> vTHw)
        vApp$_i$-> Decision: DENIED
     else
          vApp$_i$-> Decision: WAIT
     End If
    Else If (vApp$_i$->vCLR$_{i <}$ vCTH$_i$)
       vApp$_i$-> Decision: ALLOW
    End If
End For

---

3   Simulation Configuration

See Table 4.

Table 4. Simulation parameters

Simulation parameters	Parameter values
Routing protocol(s)	AODV, GPSR, ZRP, OLSR
Terrain	4000x4000
Node density	30
MAC protocol	MAC-802.11p
Propagation model	TwoRayground
Traffic type	CBR, message agent
Packet size	1024
Queue type	DropTrail/Pri queue
Sampling interval	0.1 s
Simulation time	10 s
Network simulator	NS-2.35

4   Performance Analysis

Performance of ITS-APMAC was analyzed using different routing protocols i.e. AODV, GPSR, ZRP and OLSR under the various constraints.

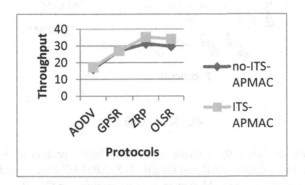

Fig. 3. Throughput

Figure 3 above shows the Throughput of different routing protocols with and without using ITS-APMAC. As per simulation results, Throughput of AODV and GPSR is marginally improved whereas it is increased for ZRP/OLSR. OLSR offers highest Throughput followed by ZRP and GPSR. AODV could not perform well.

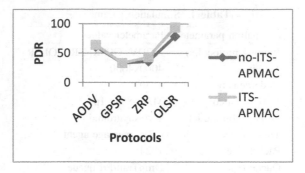

Fig. 4. Packet delivery ratio

Figure 4 above shows the variations in Packet delivery ratio of various protocols. OLSR and ZRP, both offered highest PDR as compared to AODV and GPSR. ITS-APMAC improves the PDR of individual protocol.

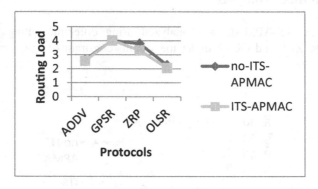

Fig. 5. Routing load

Figure 5 above shows the routing load of different protocols. It is highest for GPSR, followed by AODV, ZRP and OLSR. ITS-APMAC tried to reduce the overall routing load for each protocol. However, it is minimum for OLSR.

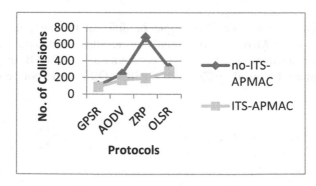

Fig. 6. No. of collisions

Figure 6 above shows the number of collisions occurred durign simulation w.r.t. each protocol.

It can be observed that with using ITS-APMAC, ZRP suffered from highest collision level, whereas GPSR has the lowest collision level. ITS-APMAC tried to reduce the collision level for each routing protocol and its level is smoothly increasing for individual protocol.

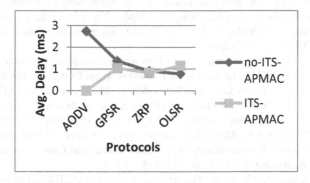

Fig. 7. Avg. delay

Figure 7 above shows the average delay for each protocol. Without using ITS-APMAC, it is highest for AODV, followed by GPSR, ZRP and it is minimum for OLSR. Using ITS-APMAC, AODV has the minimum average delay, followed by ZRP, GPSR and OLSR.

5 Conclusion

In this paper, ITS-Application-Priority-MAC (ITS-APMAC) was proposed for reliable communication over VANET. It uses PLA to identify the application type (Safety application/Non-Safety/Other) and sets their priority (HIGH/MEDIUM/LOW). DMA is used to enforce the rules (ALLOW/WAIT/DENIED) for each application and channel access is allocated according to the predefined priority. In case of highest collision level, channel access is denied for LOW priority applications followed by medium priority applications. Safety applications have the highest priority among others.

As per simulation results, ITS-APMAC enhanced the performance of each routing protocol. OLSR and ZRP performed well as compared to other protocols. Without using ITS-APMAC, ZRP and GPSR both have the highest routing load and using ITS-APMAC, it is declined.

In case of collision level, without using ITS-APMAC, ZRP has the highest collision level, followed by OLSR, GPSR and AODV has the lowest collision level. Using ITS-APMAC, collision level of each protocol was reduced to acceptable level, however, it is increasing gradually w.r.t. routing protocols.

Finally, it can be concluded that ITS-APMAC can ensure the reliable and collision aware transmission over VANET and it can be extended for V2I based communication.

References

1. Mao, Y., Shen, L.: VMR-MAC: a multi-round contention based MAC protocol for vehicular networks. In: IEEE Wireless Communications and Networking Conference, pp. 1–6 (2016)
2. Luo, G., Jia, S., Liu, Z., Zhu, K., Zhang, L.: sdnMAC: a software defined networking based MAC protocol in VANETs. In: IEEE/ACM 24th International Symposium on Quality of Service (IWQoS), pp. 1–2 (2016)
3. Avcil, M.N., Gurle, M.C., Soyturk, M.: Collision resolution MAC algorithm for vehicular ad hoc networks. In: IEEE 21st International Workshop on Computer Aided Modelling and Design of Communication Links and Networks (CAMAD), pp. 248–253 (2016)
4. Mao, Y., Yan, F., Shen, L.: Multi-round elimination contention-based multi-channel MAC scheme for vehicular ad hoc networks. IET Commun. 11(3), 421–427 (2017)
5. Siddik, M.A., Moni, S.S., Alam, M.S.: An efficient MAC protocol for provisioning fairness in vehicle to roadside communications. In: 9th International Conference on Electrical and Computer Engineering (ICECE), pp. 475–478 (2016)
6. Rathee, P., Singh, R., Kumar, S.: Performance analysis of IEEE 802.11p in the presence of hidden terminals. Wirel. Pers. Commun. 89(1), 61–78 (2016)
7. Nguyen, V., Oo, T.Z., Hong, C.S., Tran, N.H.: An efficient and fast broadcast frame adjustment algorithm in VANET. IEEE Commun. Lett. 6(1), 1–4 (2017)
8. Shen, Z., Zhang, X., Zhang, M., Li, W., Yang, D.: Self-sorting based MAC protocol for high-density vehicular ad hoc networks, vol. 1, no. 99, pp. 1–12. IEEE (2017)
9. Wu, C., Ohzahata, S., Ji, Y., Kato, T.: A MAC protocol for delay-sensitive VANET applications with self-learning contention scheme. In: IEEE 11th Consumer Communications and Networking Conference (CCNC), pp. 438–443 (2014)
10. Lim, J.M.Y., Chang, Y.C., Loo, J., Alias, M.Y.: Improving VANET performance with heuristic and adaptive fuzzy logic scheme. Wirel. Pers. Commun. 83(3), 1779–1800 (2015)
11. Dua, A., Kumar, N., Bawa, S.: ReIDD: reliability-aware intelligent data dissemination protocol for broadcast storm problem in vehicular ad hoc networks". Springer-Telecommun. Syst. 64(3), 439–458 (2017)
12. Zareei, M., et al.: CMCS: a cross-layer mobility-aware MAC protocol for cognitive radio sensor networks. EURASIP J. Wirel. Commun. Netw., 1–15 (2016)
13. Xiong, W., Hu, X., Jiang, T.: Measurement and characterization of link quality for IEEE 802.15.4-compliant wireless sensor networks in vehicular communications. IEEE Trans. Ind. Inform. 12(5), 1702–1713 (2016)
14. Zhou, C., Wang, Y., Cao, M., Shi, J., Liu, Y.: Formal analysis of MAC in IEEE 802.11p with probabilistic model checking. In: International Symposium on Theoretical Aspects of Software Engineering, pp. 55–62. IEEE (2015)
15. Geraets, M.: V2V and V2I communications—from vision to reality. In: Langheim, J. (ed.) Energy Consumption and Autonomous Driving. LNM, pp. 33–35. Springer, Cham (2016). https://doi.org/10.1007/978-3-319-19818-7_4
16. Rasheed, A., Gillani, S., Ajmal, S., Qayyum, A.: Vehicular ad hoc network (VANET): a survey, challenges, and applications. In: Laouiti, A., Qayyum, A., Mohamad Saad, M.N. (eds.) Vehicular Ad-Hoc Networks for Smart Cities. AISC, vol. 548, pp. 39–51. Springer, Singapore (2017). https://doi.org/10.1007/978-981-10-3503-6_4

17. Bäumler, I., Kotzab, H.: Intelligent transport systems for road freight transport—an overview. In: Freitag, M., Kotzab, H., Pannek, J. (eds.) Dynamics in Logistics. LNLO, pp. 279–290. Springer, Heidelberg (2017). https://doi.org/10.1007/978-3-319-45117-6_25
18. Jiang, H., Yang, Y., Xu, J., Wang, L.: Estimation of packet error rate at wireless link of VANET. In: Mukhopadhyay, S.C., Leung, H. (eds.) Advances in Networks and Communications. LNEE, vol. 64, pp. 329–359. Springer, Heidelberg (2011). https://doi.org/10.1007/978-3-642-12707-6_15
19. Singh, A., Kumar, M., Rishi, R., Madan, D.K.: A relative study of MANET and VANET: its applications, broadcasting approaches and challenging issues. In: Meghanathan, N., Kaushik, B.K., Nagamalai, D. (eds.) CCSIT 2011. CCIS, vol. 132, pp. 627–632. Springer, Heidelberg (2011). https://doi.org/10.1007/978-3-642-17878-8_63
20. Gozalvez, J., Sepulcre, M., Bauza, R.: Impact of the radio channel modelling on the performance of VANET communication protocols. Telecommun. Syst. **50**(3), 149–167 (2012)
21. Bhatia, A., Hansdah, R.C.: TRM-MAC: a TDMA-based reliable multicast MAC protocol for WSNs with flexibility to trade-off between latency and reliability. Comput. Netw. **104**(20), 79–93 (2016)
22. Purohit, K.C., Dimri, S.C., Jasola, S.: Performance evaluation of various MANET routing protocols for adaptability in VANET environment. Int. J. Syst. Assur. Eng. Manag. **8**(2), 690–702 (2017)
23. Cardoso, N., Alam, M., Almeida, J., Ferreira, J., Oliveira, A.S.R.: Performance evaluation of SIMO techniques in IEEE 802.11p. In: International Conference on Future Intelligent Vehicular Technologies, Future Intelligent Vehicular Technologies, pp. 91–100 (2016)

Trust Based Congestion Control Algorithm (TBCCA) in VANET

Ravi Pratap Singh$^{(\boxtimes)}$ and Dinesh Singh

Department of Computer Science and Engineering Motilal, Nehru National
Institute of Technology Allahabad, Allahabad 211004, India
ravimnnit2016@gmail.com, dinesh_singh@mnnit.ac.in

Abstract. Vehicular Ad Hoc network (VANET) is a promising technology mainly used to increase the safety of the vehicles, passengers, and etc. on the road. The safety and convenience services of VANET are supported through different type of messages. The high speed of vehicles results in the short time period available to exchange messages between the vehicles. All sorts of messages are broadcasted by the peer vehicles in the network, and those messages may causes channel overload, when vehicle density increases on the roads. In consequence of these, our channel gets highly congested which results in packet loss. The packet loss inside network is dangerous for many of VANET applications specially emergency noti cation services. It raises not only safety concerns but also results into degraded performance of VANETs. In our proposed algorithm Trust Based Congestion Control Algorithm (TBCCA), the priorities are computed independently in each vehicle for each message. Here a new trust parameter is considered in computation of message priority. The trust parameter is a ratio of sent and received messages, which determines how much a vehicle is contributing in congestion. The trust parameter not only aids in priority calculation but also helps in further broadcast of messages sent by trusted vehicles. Thus our algorithm controls congestion on the roads more efficiently. Our proposed algorithm has improved efficiency of VANET by controlling the congestion which reduced end to end delay by 7.778% and reduced packet loss by 8.333%. Our algorith also increased the throughput by 13.726%.

Keywords: Congestion control · VANET · Trust

1 Introduction

Today is an era of smart city. Smart city is an urban area which uses various methods to collect data from every aspect of city, and use this data to improve safety of public, better resource utilization, quality services, and etc. So ultimately smartness comes from collecting data, sharing this data and using this data for the betterment of city. One key dimension of smart city is smart roads and smart transportation. Data can be of many types that is generated by vehicles such as instant messaging, parking information, information about congestion on the roads, accidents on the roads, red light information, and so on [5, 15]. The communication between vehicles and other infrastructure components is needed for sharing the data generated by vehicles, and to implement smart road and smart transportation concept.

© Springer Nature Singapore Pte Ltd. 2019
A. K. Luhach et al. (Eds.): ICAICR 2018, CCIS 956, pp. 524–535, 2019.
https://doi.org/10.1007/978-981-13-3143-5_43

The need of communication between vehicles gave birth to Vehicular Ad Hoc Networks (VANETs). The VANET [7] is a technology which provides the means of communication between vehicles and other infrastructure components. The VANET is a sub-class of Mobile Ad Hoc Network (MANET). The MANET provides the means of communication between mobile nodes. The VANET only deals with the communication which involves vehicles. When vehicles communicate among themselves, it is called vehicle to vehicle (V2V) communication. When communication is between vehicle and infrastructure components like RSU (Roadside Unit), it is called vehicle to infrastructure (V2I) communication [5, 15].

The VANET uses Dedicated Short Range Communication (DSRC) [11] standard, which further employs IEEE 802.11p standard to facilitate the communication between vehicles. DSRC uses a 75 MHz bandwidth at 5.9 GHz to facilitate both type of communications (V2V and V2I) and transfer the messages over the control channel and service channel. DSRC bandwidth is divided into eight channels. The six service channels of 10 MHz are dedicated for transmitting non-safety messages, one control channel of 10 MHz is dedicated for transmitting safety messages, and one channel of 5 MHz is reserved for future uses. The DSRC channel allocation is shown in g 1. In VANET, two types of channels are used to transmit the messages: service channel and control channel. The control channel is used to transmit high priority messages whereas service channel is used to transmit other non-high priority messages. DSRC de nes transmission rate between 3 Mbps to 27 Mbps and transmission range between 10 m to 1000 m [11, 13, 23] (Fig. 1).

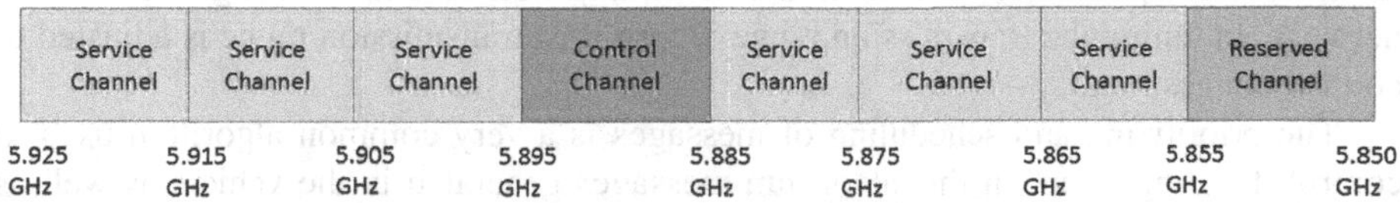

Service Channel	Service Channel	Service Channel	Control Channel	Service Channel	Service Channel	Service Channel	Reserved Channel
5.925 GHz	5.915 GHz	5.905 GHz	5.895 GHz	5.885 GHz	5.875 GHz	5.865 GHz	5.855 GHz	5.850 GHz

Fig. 1. DSRC channel allocation

The VANET have some special characteristics that are high mobility, high rate of topology change, frequent connection and disconnection, high rate of change in vehicle density. These characteristics give rise to challenges in, channel management, congestion control and data dissemination, which causes reduced performance in VANET [1, 4, 5, 12, 23].

Congestion [22] is the phenomena in which messages start to get drop instead of getting delivered to the receiver. The heavy increase in message transmission causes channel overload and Channels start to get saturated. In consequence of this congestion happens in VANET. Whenever emergency messages starts to drop then safety of drivers and other people on the roads gets compromised. This defeats the initial goal of the Vehicular Ad Hoc Network that is safety of driver and people on the roads. Thus congestion control algorithms are required to keep channel free from getting congested so that the reliable delivery of safety or emergency messages is ensured.

In this paper, congestion control algorithm is proposed to control congestion on the roads. In our algorithm we are controlling the number of messages broadcasted onto the

Vehicular Ad Hoc Network (VANET). Thus, congestion will be controlled altogether. We are also restricting the messages broadcasted by the untrusted vehicles from being further broadcasted.

Rest of the paper is organized as follows. In Sect. 2 we discuss related works done by other authors in this eld. Section 3 proposes a new algorithm to control congestion on the roads. Section 4 talks about simulation and results of the algorithm. Section 5 contains conclusion and Sect. 6 contains future scope.

2 Related Works

Prosperous amount of reasearch work has been carried out in the eld of congestion control in Vehicular Ad Hoc Network (VANET). The communication among peer vehicles and with infrastructure components is an important aspect for every research eld of the Vehicular Ad Hoc Network. Congestion control is an important area for VANET as it deals with communication in VANET.

The Congestion control algorithms are classified into two types of solutions (1) open-loop solution and (2) closed-loop solution. Open-loop solution avoids the congestion in network before congestion happens. Whereas closed-loop solution controls the congestion after congestion happens in the network [20].

Further, congestion control algorithms are classified into (1) tuning the transmission rate, (2) tuning the transmission range (3) prioritizing and scheduling messages onto the network, and (4) hybrid algorithms [16]. As name suggests in tuning the transmission rate algorithms, transmission rate is adjusted to control congestion in the network. In tuning the transmission range algorithms, transmission range is adjusted to control congestion.

The prioritizing and scheduling of messages is a very common algorithm used to control the congestion. In this algorithm messages generated in the vehicle as well as received from other vehicles, are assigned some priority. Once priority is assigned to each of the message, these messages are scheduled onto the network. It is an open-loop congestion control solution.

Hybrid algorithms [16] employ all or some of the previously described algorithms to make congestion control algorithm more efficient and effective. Hybrid algorithms are more effective compared to standalone algorithms as it combines the properties of all the used algorithm and provides a good congestion control which then leads to a better performance in VANET.

Torrent-Moreno et al. [21] proposed Distributed-Fair Power Adjustment for Vehicular environment (D-FPAV) congestion control algorithm. The algorithm is a closed-loop solution which employs dynamic adjustment of transmission range for beacon messages, to control congestion VANET. Thus, the algorithm compromises the performance of the applications which uses the information through beacon messages.

Sahu et al. [14] developed a algorithm called Network Coding Congestion Control (NC-CC) algorithm. Here, algorithm network coding is used to adjust the transmission range of beacon messages at the packet level. This algorithm controls the channel overhead by adjusting the beacon message transmission range.

Bouassida et al. [2] developed a algorithm in which messages are assigned priorities. The priority assignment was done on the bases of static and dynamic factors. Static and dynamic factors are calculated based on the content of messages and the network condition respectively.

Taherkhani and Pierrre [18] proposed a prioritizing and scheduling based algorithm in which messages are prioritized and then scheduled onto the service and control channels. The messages scheduling is done statically and dynamically. For dynamic message scheduling Tabu Search Scheduling (TaSch) algorithm is used in proposed algorithm.

Hsu et al. [8] suggested AOS (Adaptable Offset Slot) algorithm fro congestion control in Vehicular Ad Hoc Network. Jang et al. [9] proposed detection based Media Access Control (MAC) algorithm which employs CSMA/CA protocol.

Taherkhani and Pierrre [19] proposed another congestion control algorithm which employs machine learning [3, 10] algorithms. This algorithm runs on Road-side units (RSU) to control congestion on the intersections.

Some congestion control algorithms are based on Carrier Sense Multiple Access/Congestion Avoidance (CSMA/CA). CSMA/CA senses the channel for access ability for each message and controls the congestion by modifying the channel access ability. CSMA/CA protocol uses exponential back-off mechanism which is not efficient for beacon broadcasting [17]. This mechanism fails in the situations of high rate message transmission.

The prioritizing and scheduling algorithms show poor performance when number of vehicles increases. Since, the algorithm runs on each vehicle independently, when a vehicle sends its emergency message onto the channel, it can not stop other vehicles from sending their low priority messages. Therefore, when density of vehicles is very high, channel may be occupied by a large number of low priority messages leading to congestion [6].

3   Problem Statements and Solving Strategies

The road and highways have became congestion-prone areas as the number of vehicles on the roads are increasing every day. Congestion causes message drops in the VANET which increases the probability of emergency messages to drop or deliver with high delay. This may compromise safety of vehicles, safety of the people on the road and also compromises the performance of VANET. For controlling the congestion in Vehicular Ad Hoc Network we proposed a Trust Based Congestion Control Algorithm (TBCCA).

The TBCCA algorithm controls congestion by controlling the number of messages being broadcasted onto the network. The algorithm runs on each and every vehicle independently. IEEE 1609.4 Wireless Access in Vehicular Environment (WAVE) enables multi-channel communication in VANET. WAVE also prioritizes and schedules the various messages onto those channels. WAVE enabled multi-channels are service channel and control channel. So two queues are maintained service channel queue and control channel queue.

The Figure 2 shows the block diagram of Trust Based Congestion Control Algorithm (TBCCA).Trust Based Congestion Control Algorithm (TBCCA) module consists of two modules: (1) priority computation module and (2) scheduling module.

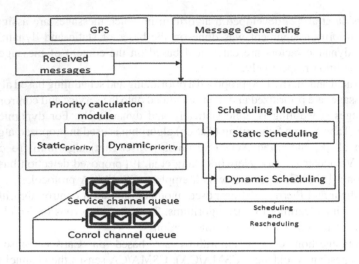

Fig. 2. Block diagram of TBCCA

3.1 Priority Computation Module

In Priority computation module, priority is calculated for each message whether it is generated by application in vehicle itself or received by the vehicle broadcasted by another vehicles. In our proposed algorithm calculation of effective priority (Priority$_{effective}$) is based on static priority, dynamic priority, trust value, and size of message.

$$Priority_{effective} = \frac{Static_{priority} \times Dynamic_{priority}}{Message_{size}} \tag{1}$$

Static$_{priority}$ is calculated according to the content of messages and type of the application which has generated the message. If the message belongs to category of Priority$_{low}$ then assigned Static$_{priority}$ value will be one (01). In case the message belongs to category of Priority$_{medium}$ then assigned Static$_{priority}$ value will be two (02). Further, if the message belongs to category of Priority$_{high}$ then assigned Static$_{priority}$ value will be three (03).

- **Priority$_{low}$**: Messages generated by low priority applications and messages generated by the high priority service application belong to this category. Low priority applications are instant messaging, parking spot locator, internet service provisioning, toll payment etc. High priority service messages/applications are map download, map upload, GPS correction, intelligent traffic control, and etc.
- **Priority$_{medium}$**: Low priority safety messages belong to this category. Low priority safety messages are lane change warning, stop sign assist, forward collision, left turn assist, right turn assist, and etc.
- **Priority$_{high}$**: Safety beacon messages and emergency messages belong to this category. The safety beacon messages are periodically broadcasted over the VANET to provide vehicular information such as speed, position, direction of vehicle, and etc.

Algorithm 1. Pseudo-code for calculating Static$_{priority}$

Input: Set of Messages M = $\{M_1, M_2, M_3, ..M_n\}$
Output: Set of Static Priority $S_P = \{S_{P1}, S_{P2}, S_{P3}, ..S_{Pn}\}$

1: **for** each message M_i in vehicle **do**
2:     **if** Message is generated by Low priority application **then**
3:         $S_{Pi} = 1$
4:     **end if**
5:     **if** Message is generated by Medium priority application **then**
6:         $S_{Pi} = 2$
7:     **end if**
8:     **if** Message is generated by High priority application **then**
9:         $S_{Pi} = 3$
10:     **end if**
11: **end for**

Dynamic$_{priority}$ is calculated based on the condition of VANET. The parameters which are considered to calculate Dynamic$_{priority}$ are vehicle velocity, direction of vehicle (sender and receiver), message validity and distance between the sender and receiver vehicles.

- **Velocity (V):** The velocity parameter, as name suggests, represents the velocity of the vehicle. If a vehicle is moving with higher velocity it will go out of the coverage area faster so, messages generated in such vehicle should be given high priority.

$$V = \frac{\pi \times R^2 + 2 \times R \times v \times dt}{\pi \times R^2} \tag{2}$$

Where R is Communication Range, and v is average speed of vehicle at time dt

- **Validity (A):** The validity parameter represents the validity of message. In other words remaining time for a message to be delivered before it becomes useless.

$$A = \frac{\text{Remaining time to the deadline}}{\text{Transferring time}} \tag{3}$$

- **Direction (D):** The direction parameter tells if the vehicles (Sender and receiver) are moving closer or moving away from each other. If they are moving away from each other than $D = 1$ and if they are moving closer to each other than $D = 0$.
- **Distance (S):** The distance parameter represents the distance between the vehicles (sender and receiver).
- **Connection Time (C):** The connection time parameter represents the time for which the sender and receiver vehicles will remain connected.

$$O = R_1 + R_2 - S \tag{4}$$

if $S > (R_1 + R_2)$

$$C = 0 \tag{5}$$

if $S <= (R_1 + R_2)$

$$C = (V_1 + V_2) \times (D_{i1} + D_{i2} - O) \tag{6}$$

Where $D_i = 2 \times R$ and O is overlapped range.

- **Trust Value (T):** Trust value is the ratio of received count of data packets and forward count of data packets.

$$T = \frac{\text{Received count of data packets}}{\text{Forward count of data packets}} \tag{7}$$

Now Dynamic$_{\text{priority}}$ will be calculated using following equation..

$$\text{Dynamic}_{\text{priority}} = \begin{cases} \frac{V \times T \times C}{(A+1) \times S}, & \text{if } D = 0 \\ \frac{V \times C \times T \times S}{(A+1)}, & \text{if } D = 1 \end{cases} \tag{8}$$

Algorithm 2. Pseudo-code for calculating Dynamic$_{\text{priority}}$

Input: Set of Messages M $= \{M_1, M_2, M_3, ..M_n\}$
Output: Set of Dynamic Priority $D_P = \{D_{P1}, D_{P2}, D_{P3}, ..D_{Pn}\}$

1: **for** each message M_i in Vehicle **do**
2:    Compute V // V: Velocity
3:    Compute A // A: Validity
4:    Compute T // T: Trust Value
5:    **if** Vehicles moving towards each other **then**
6:       $D = 0$
7:    **else**
8:       $D = 1$
9:    **end if**
10:   Compute C // C: connection time
11:   Calculate $Dynamic_{Priority}$
12: **end for**

3.2   Scheduling Module

For a reliable transmission of data, scheduling of messages is crucial. Due to the characteristics of VANET, it becomes a challenging task. Here, two queues are maintained (1) service channel queue and (2) control channel queue. The task of message scheduling is done in two steps (1) static scheduling and (2) dynamic scheduling. After applying both the steps on the queues, messages are ready to be transferred to the network. In step (1) static scheduling, messages are scheduled onto the queues according to the static priorities priorities. The messages with $Static_{priority}$ value one (01) are scheduled onto the service channel. Messages with $Static_{priority}$ value two (02) and three (03) are scheduled onto the control channel according to their priority as they are medium and high priority messages. The Figure 3 shows the static scheduling process in the scheduling module.

Step (2) dynamic scheduling is based on the computed priority, $Priority_{effective}$. The messages which are scheduled onto the queues in static scheduling are rearranged according to the calculated priority, $Priority_{effective}$ in descending order of the priority. After the rearrangement of the messages in the queues, messages are dequeued from the queues and transferred onto the respective channels.

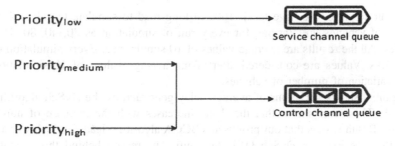

$Priority_{low}$ — Service channel queue

$Priority_{medium}$ — $Priority_{high}$ — Control channel queue

Fig. 3. Process of static scheduling

While rearranging messages in the queues using $Priority_{effective}$, we also check for the trust value for the vehicle. If messages are sent by the vehicle which is having trust value less then one (1) then the messages are discarded instead of sending further. This way we can block the messages sent by the vehicles which mostly contribute in congestion.

4 Experimental Results and Analysis

We have used ns-2.34 to implement those and simulate the algorithms. ns2.34 is a network simulator which provides enormous support for VANET. In our simulation environment at most 350 vehicles may exist. more than 350 vehicles will cause problems with simulation. Vehicles are equipped with Global Positioning System (GPS). Road has Roadside Units (RSUs) installed. Internet connectivity is available in all vehicles.

The results of our proposed algorithm Trust Based Congestion Control Algorithm (TBCCA) compared with the existing algorithm DySch, given by Taherkhani and Pierrre [18].

Simulation con guration parameters and their assigned values are listed in the Table 1 given below.

Table 1. Simulation configuration

Simulation parameters	Value
Simulation Area	1000 m × 1000 m
Total road length	1000 m
Number of vehicles	20, 40, 80, 160, 320
Vehicles speed	0–50 km/h
Transmission rate	3 Mbps
Bandwidth	10 MHz
Message size	511 Bytes
MAC type	IEEE 802.11p

In our scenario, we have taken 1000 m long road to simulate the algorithm. The number of vehicles are Varying for every run of simulation as 20, 40, 80, 160, 320 vehicles. All the results are average values of 10 simulations. Every simulation ran for about 40 s. Values are considered after taking average values of 10 simulations for every variation of number of vehicles.

Figure 4 shows variations of average delay generated by the DySch algorithm and TBCCA. The result shows that the delay increases with the increase of number of vehicles. Result shows that our proposed TBCCA algorithm leads to the lower average delay than the existing DySch [18] algorithm. The reason behind this is that Trust parameter causes the reduced number of packets in the network as it does not let a vehicle transfer the packets to the network when trust value is less then one.

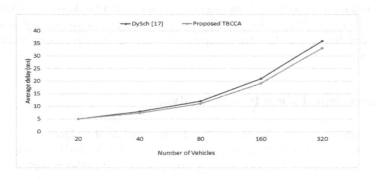

Fig. 4. Average end-to-end delay

Figure 5 shows the plot of the packet loss in DySch and TBCCA. By observing the figure we can say that by introducing the trust parameter we have decreased the number of messages in the channel which reduced the effect of congestion that resulted into less packet loss. For low density packet loss is equal for both strategies but as the density increases we can see the difference in packet loss by both the strategies.

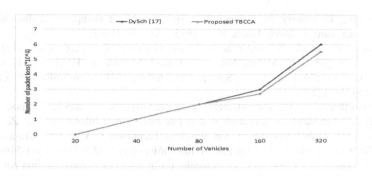

Fig. 5. Packet loss

5 Conclusion

We have proposed a modified DySch algorithm. In our proposed Trust Based Congestion Control Algorithm (TBCCA) we have introduced two new parameters, Trust parameter and connection time. Our proposed Trust Based Congestion Control Algorithm (TBCCA) controls the numbers of packets before sending them onto the channel which is not done in existing DySch [18] algorithm. Our proposed algorithm reduced end-to end delay by 7.778%, packet loss by 8.333% and increased throughput by 13.726%. The reason behind this improvement is controlling the number of packets being sent onto the channel. Our proposed algorithm check packets for trust value, if trust value is less then one then packets are dropped instead of scheduling them onto the service channel and control channel respectively. Thus our algorithm reduces the number of packets effectively, hence improving the congestion control ability of algorithm.

6 Future Directions

As it is a prioritizing and scheduling-based strategy it has a limitation that it does not prevent other vehicles from sending their low priority messages. This may lead to congestion in the channel while vehicles are on intersections. On the intersections number of vehicles is far more than the number of vehicles on the highway. So in future we can work to overcome this limitation.

References

1. Aragiannis, G., et al.: Vehicular networking: a survey and tutorial on requirements, architectures, challenges, standards and solutions. IEEE Commun. Surv. Tutor. **13**, 584–616 (2011)
2. Bouassida, M.S., Shawky, M.: On the congestion control within VANET. In: Wireless Days 1st IFIP, pp. 1–5 (2008)

3. Dougherty, J., Kohavi, R., Sahami, M.: Supervised and unsupervised discretization of continuous features. Mach. Learn. Proc. **1995**, 194–202 (1995)
4. Golestan, K., et al.: Vehicular ad-hoc networks(VANETs): capabilities, challenges in information gathering and data fusion. In: Kamel, M., Karray, F., Hagras, H. (eds.) AIS 2012. LNCS (LNAI), pp. 34–41. Springer, Heidelberg (2012). https://doi.org/10.1007/978-3-642-31368-4_5
5. Guerrero-Ibáñez, J.A., Flores-Cortés, C., Zeadally, S.: Vehicular ad-hoc networks (VANETs): architecture, protocols and applications. In: Chilamkurti, N., Zeadally, S., Chaouchi, H. (eds.) Next-Generation Wireless Technologies. Computer Communications and Networks. Springer, London (2013). https://doi.org/10.1007/978-1-4471-5164-7_5
6. Guo, J., Zhang, J.: Safety message transmission in vehicular communication networks. In: 17th ITS World Congress (2010)
7. Hossain, E., et al.: Vehicular telematics over heterogeneous wireless networks: a survey. Comput. Commun. **33**, 775–793 (2010)
8. Hsu, C.-W., Hsu, C.-H., Tseng, H.-R.: MAC channel congestion control mechanism in IEEE 802.11 p/WAVE vehicle networks. In: Vehicular Technology Conference (VTC Fall), pp. 1–5 (2011)
9. Jang, H.-C., Feng, W.C.: Network status detection-based dynamic adaptation of contention window in IEEE 802.11 p. In: Vehicular Technology Conference (VTC 2010-Spring), pp. 1–5 (2010)
10. Kodrato, Y.: Introduction to Machine Learning. Elsevier, Amsterdam (2014)
11. Liu, Y., Dion, F., Biswas, S.: Dedicated short-range wireless communications for intelligent transportation system applications: State of the art. Transp. Res. Rec.: J. Transp. Res. Board, 29–37 (2005)
12. Nassar, L., et al.: Vehicular ad-hoc networks(VANETs): capabilities, challenges in context-aware processing and communication gateway. In: Kamel, M., Karray, F., Hagras, H. (eds.) AIS 2012. LNCS (LNAI), pp. 42–49. Springer, Heidelberg (2012). https://doi.org/10.1007/978-3-642-31368-4_6
13. Qian, Y., Moayeri, N.: Design of secure and application-oriented VANETs, pp. 2794–2799 (2008)
14. Sahu, P.K., Hafid, A., Cherkaoui, S.: Congestion control in vehicular networks using network coding. In: IEEE International Conference on Communications (ICC), pp. 2736–2741 (2014)
15. Sattari, M.R.J., Noor, R.M., Ghahremani, S.: Dynamic congestion control algorithm for vehicular ad hoc networks. Int. J. Softw. Eng. Its Appl. **3**, 95–108 (2013)
16. Shen, X., Cheng, X., Zhang, R., Jiao, B., Yang, Y.: Distributed congestion control approaches for the IEEE 802.11 p vehicular networks. IEEE Intell. Transp. Syst. Mag. **5**, 50–61 (2013)
17. Stanica, R., Chaput, E., Beylot, A.L.: Congestion control in CSMA-based vehicular networks: do not forget the carrier sensing. In: 9th Annual IEEE Communications Society Conference on Sensor, Mesh and Ad Hoc Communications and Networks (SECON), pp. 650–658 (2012)
18. Taherkhani, N., Pierre, S.: Prioritizing and scheduling messages for congestion control in vehicular ad hoc networks. Comput. Netw. **108**, 15–28 (2016)
19. Taherkhani, N., Pierre, S.: Centralized and localized data congestion control strategy for vehicular ad hoc networks using a machine learning clustering algorithm. IEEE Trans. Intell. Transp. Syst. **17**, 3275–3285 (2016)
20. Tanenbaum, A.S., et al.: Computer Networks, 4th edn. Prentice Hall, Upper Saddle River (2003)

21. Torrent-Moreno, M., Santi, P., Hartenstein, H.: Distributed fair transmit power adjustment for vehicular ad hoc networks. In: 3rd Annual IEEE Communications Society on Sensor and Ad Hoc Communications and Networks, vol. 2, pp. 479–488 (2006)
22. Zang, Y., Stibor, L., Cheng, X., Reumerman, H.J., Paruzel, A., Barroso, A.: Congestion control in wireless networks for vehicular safety applications. In: Proceedings of the 8th European Wireless Conference, vol. 7 (2007)
23. Zeadally, S., Hunt, R., Chen, Y.-S., Irwin, A., Hassan, A.: Vehicular ad hoc networks (VANETS): status, results, and challenges. Telecommun. Syst. 50, 217–241 (2012)

Smart Cities in India: Revamping the Street Lighting System Using IOT

Akash Vashishtha, Saru Dhir[✉], and Madhurima Hooda

Amity University, Noida, Uttar Pradesh, India
vashishth.akash1997@gmail.com, sarudhir@gmail.com,
10madhurima@gmail.com

Abstract. Smart environment deals with the use of substantial technologies to take better care and being better informed of the surroundings. There has been significant work in this field having to be fully applied in today's world as widely as other technologies. The main issue is to shed light on is the bad weather conditions affecting the proper functioning of the system and how to make things better. This paper covers the specific spectrum of smart cities and environment - a very potential subset of IoT. Humidity sensors and LDR are used to improve the bad weather conditions. These sensors can sense the surroundings according to which the system will act. Microcontroller will be acting as the brain of the system.

Keywords: Internet of Things (IoT) · Smart environment · Smart lights

1 Introduction

With IoT, a brighter, better and technologically advanced future can be designed for the next generations. It can be known as a network of physical objects which can be operated through a network.

IoT allows all kinds of devices to act smartly and take combined decisions for a better user experience. This technology plays a big role in public sector services and can be used practically in almost every situation such as healthcare sectors, automobile sectors, industrial control, agriculture sectors etc. Now, IoT has a wide range of applications in a user's day to day lives such as smart parking in the automobile sector, industrial control (machine to machine communications), smart-phone tracing facilities, and smart traffic control and so on [9].

Environment is concerned with nature and a smart environment is technologically advancing the environment. Smart environment is basically using technology to preserve natural resources and put them to best use. The idea is to build a smarter surrounding with embedded sensors, displays, and computing devices so that a strong network foundation is set up for taking better care of the environment. It can be considered as a web interwoven with actuators, displays, computation elements which are generally embedded and interconnected over the internet and beyond for a better user experience and interaction, providing better access to control and manipulate the environment.

© Springer Nature Singapore Pte Ltd. 2019
A. K. Luhach et al. (Eds.): ICAICR 2018, CCIS 956, pp. 536–546, 2019.
https://doi.org/10.1007/978-981-13-3143-5_44

Smart Light is one of the biggest steps towards making our environment smart. To prevent the depletion of the resources in the environment, smart lights must be opted. These lights work on solar energy as they relate to solar cells and can sense objects which are incoming towards it as a result they can work only when they are needed to. This concept can provide a better future with almost all devices interconnected. Instead of fluorescent bulb, the smart lighting system uses LED which consumes less electricity than these bulbs. They drastically decrease the CO_2 emission which is beneficial in environmental, lighting performance and reduction in road accidents. These bulbs also emit CFCs which are very harmful for the planet. As these gases effects on a global level by causing global warming. Not only these system saves the environment, but also dramatically saves the economy of the country. They save electricity by using different techniques, which will eventually help not only the country but the whole planet. Since these systems collect real time data, we can easily get to know about the happenings in the surrounding. The sensors used in the smart lighting system will collect the heterogenous spatio temporal data which can help to take accurate actions required at the right time. The real time data can help us to prevent accidents as by using humidity sensors, lights will work under the bad weather conditions of Fog and rain. In this way, more accidents will be stopped before happening.

Forest fire detection, air pollution detection and control, snow level monitoring & avalanche precautions in cold areas, and earthquakes early detection are also some widely used applications of IoT in this field of making our environment smarter and better. Radio Frequency Identification plays a very crucial role in communication of the devices and objects that the IoT cover. These devices communicate using radio frequencies. An open signal is sent in the medium using a transcender and the other devices detect and receive it with the help of an antenna. With one open radio signal, one device can communicate with multiple devices at the same instant. When devices communicate with each other individually rather than a hub or a server to process and forward their requests, it provides a better and faster platform for intercommunication. As far as the wireless IoT is concerned, many different wireless communication protocols can be used by the devices to communicate with one another.

2 Existing Work

The existing profile of smart light consists of a lot of things which are discussed below in brief. Smart lights are getting more and more popular in the current era. The following is a brief explanation about the existing work on smart light.

1. LENSCAPE (also known as Lighting Enabled Smart City Applications and Ecosystem) framework is becoming quite popular now days [1]. This framework is widely used to connect streetlights wirelessly. LENSCAPE is basically made up of three parts i.e. OLNs (wireless outdoor Lighting Networks), sensors that collect HST data (Heterogeneous Spatio-Temporal data) and controllers which are used to actuate processes. The idea is to use different types of sensors which can be used to make lights more energy efficient. As these sensors can be used to detect lights and vehicles due to which they only work when they are needed. OLNs basically follow IEEE 802.15.4g standards. MATLAB is generally used for OLNs [1].

2. LoD (Light on Demand) is one of the most promising technologies which is getting used in making smart street lights [1]. According to this, Ultra Sonic sensors are used in order to detect cars on roads. When the sensor detects the vehicle, it automatically turns on the lights. They are cheap as compared to other smart light technologies and they sense the surroundings and provide the light intensity according to the requirement.

3. Light as a Service (LAAS) is widely used with smart light technology. The idea is to get data about the health condition of the hardware and lighting system by getting access to real time data [1]. LAAS can save people the inconvenience as when the device fails, it automatically sends the information and thus proper actions could be taken to rectify the faults.

4. Lights have become WiFi enabled. The market is already equipped with WiFi enabled LED bulbs. LED bulb once connected with holder, can automatically connect though a wireless network. Lights can be easily operated by the application provided by the company.

5. Dynamic street lights are becoming a trend now days. DSL enables getting an inter connected street lights which uses a fusion of sensors to indicate the Lighting or Luminosity, Human presence to control the street lights dynamically [4].

6. Solar Energy is widely used for the power source of the smart lights. The street lights are powered by solar batteries which are quite environment friendly. The idea to connect LED with solar batteries was the starting point of smart lights. Even now days, Lights are still powered with Solar batteries as it's a clear and econobabble source of Energy for street lights. The solar panels are generally made of a single crystal. There are two types of crystal which can be used to make solar panels i.e., Monocrystalline panel and Polycrystalline panel. Panels made up of Monocrystalline crystal are 18% more efficient as compared to panel made up of Polycrystalline crystal. The battery used in these systems are rechargeable batteries (Li Ion Phosphate Battery). These batteries have a longer lifespan and gets charged with the energy collected by the solar panels [5].

7. Communication protocols are used in smart lighting systems. These protocols help in gathering information and sharing of it from Local Control Unit to Control Center. Basically, there are two types of communications which are utilized in smart lighting system.

    7.1. **Long Range Communication:** It basically refers to the information sharing between the local control unit and control center. As Smart lighting system is big, it is generally divided into small parts termed as Local Control Unit. These units are under Control center. The local control unit gathers and transfers data with one another or it transfers it to control center [3]. Since when the transfer of data from local control unit to control center takes place, a long-range connection is established which is possible with the help of protocols such as WIFI, ethernet etc.

    7.2. **Short Range Communication:** It generally refers to the communication takes place between the devices that are close to each other. The local control unit and the Street Light (Lamp Unit) are in the line of sight so, the communication between these units can be termed as Short-Range Communication. It can be either wired or wireless. For e.g. (DALI) for wired and (LoWPAN, ZigBee) for wireless communication. These protocols are widey used in IoT enabled devices [3].

7.3. **Wireless Protocols:** The wireless protocols are based on IEEE standards 802.15.4 which defines Low Rate wireless personal area network. They come under the Physical layer and MAC Layer (Machine Access Control) of OSI model. ZigBee and 6LoWPAN are two IEEE 802.15.4 based protocols. Zigbee is more popular as compared to 6LoWPAN. It is a high-level communication protocol which was specified by ZigBee alliance. ZigBee uses 802.15.4 as Machine Access Control layer and provide services such as encryption, routing protocols etc. It can support up to 1024 nodes and has a bandwidth of 20–250 kbps. 6LoWPAN or (IP6 V) and Low-Power Wireless Personal Area Network allows the small IoT devices to communicate by using internet protocol. Data is transferred in the form of packets and after the transfer, an acknowledgement is sent for the confirmation of delivery. Not only 6LoWPAN allows small devices to communicate at a limited processing speed but it also reduces the implementation cost [11]. It is also based on IEEE 802.15.4 and can support up to 10000 ports. The bandwidth of 6LoWPAN is 250 Kbps and has a range of 200 m [3].

8. Systems with IR sensors are also introduced to detect human presence by detecting the heat signatures. As all the living emits some sort of thermal radiations. The radiations emit by the living beings are invisible to humans. These sensors can detect them, and the Lighting system will only work when they detect a heat signature of a living being. Not only for humans, this technology can be useful for animals. These sensors are normally connected with LDR so that lights will not work at the day time even after the detection of the heat signatures.

3   Issues in Existing Work

3.1   Bad Weather

Smart light is greatly affected by bad weather. It's one of the biggest problems faced by it. At the time of rain and excess fog at day time, lights are unable to work due to which many accidents take place.

Fog is one of the biggest concerns as if lights are unable to work in it which might lead to accidents. Road accidents and tragedies are on an increased rate during the past years. The average number of people killed in road tragedies were 16 in 2014, 21 in 2015 which too increased to 25 in 2016 in New Delhi. That's why it's important for street lights to work in day time also if fog occurs [7].

3.2   Security

Security is one of the major concerns in the field of IoT. Since the transmitted data do have a risk of malware threats. It's all depended on how encrypted the data is while transmission. Since smart lighting system is a part of smart city, so less security can cause data stolen. Black hats can get access to other systems through lights. So, it's important to encrypt the system effectively [10].

3.3 Efficiency of Solar Cells

Solar cells are great environment friendly technological equipment's which produce electric energy from sun rays. They are very efficient and on the other hand, expensive. Although they are a one-time investment, and their life span is for about 40 years, but the output might not always be sufficient as per the user's demand [6]. There are certain methods to increase the efficiency of the cells (discussed in the proposed work) but are not used often by the users.

4   Proposed Work

The main components which are getting used in the prototype:

4.1   Arduino

Arduino UNO R3 is an open source microcontroller board which can have up to 14 digital input/output pins. It is based on ATmega328 which a single chip microcontroller is. Arduino UNO R3 consists of a USB connection port, 16 MHz Crystal Oscillator,

Fig. 1. Arduino UNO R3

Power Jack and a reset button. It has a USB connection or external power supply. It works on the Arduino Integrated Development Environment (IDE). The IDE is written in Java Programming Language. The IDE supports the C and C++ language. It also consists of features such as text cutting, pasting, replacing etc. In IoT enabled devices, it can act as the brain of the system. Substitutes are available such as Raspberry Pi, but they are costly as compared to Arduino (Fig. 1).

Basically, Arduino is a physical programmable circuit board with software.

4.2 LDR

LDR (Light Dependent Resistor) is a kind of sensor which changes its resistance accordingly with the light falling on it. They are also known as Photoresistor (resistor which is used to indicate the presence and absence of light). It can be used in Smart lights due to which street lights automatically starts glowing at a certain level of the intensity of light. The collected data can be used to turn the light ON/OFF [2]. These are generally made up of semiconductors due to which they have light sensitive properties (Fig. 2).

Fig. 2. LDR

4.3 DHT11

It is a low-cost humidity and temperature sensor which has a thermistor which measures the air in the surrounding. After measuring the air, it gave the digital signal on the pin (data pin). It's easy to use and can be applied to the lights so that they can sense fog or rain. When the sensor will be displaying the reading of humidity more than 95% then it will be considered as either rain or fog. But it requires accurate timing to grab data [8] (Fig. 3).

Fig. 3. DHT11

4.4   HC-SR04

HC-SR04 is a low cost ultra-sonic sensor which can be used in smart lights to operate them only when they are needed. The sensor detects the objects coming forward and sends the signal to the light. When the objects come in contact within the range of 400 cm, system will detect it. The range is adjustable i.e. 4 to 400 cm. It consists of four pins i.e. TRIG pin, ECHO pin, UCC and GND pin. The purpose of Trip pin is to send a high frequency sound. When the sound gets to an object, it gets reflected and the echo pin receives it. That's how the whole thing works. There is an internal clock which starts ticking when trig pin goes high then low (for not less than 10 μs). 8 Cycles of 40 kHz sounds are send and it counts the duration for the echo to arrive. It can be used detect incoming cars and then the LEDs start glowing one by one according to the code [10] (Fig. 4).

Fig. 4. HC SR-04

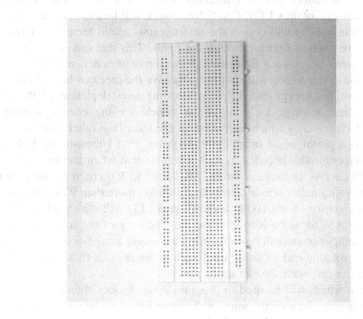

Fig. 5. Breadboard

4.5   Breadboard

Breadboard is the base for constructing electronic devices. It's solder less so; there is no need for soldering. Since there is no need of soldering so, it can be used again. It's easy to use and changes can be done easily in it. Size of the breadboard used is 175 x 67 x 8 mm and have 400 points for connection (Fig. 5).

4.6   Solar Energy Concentrator

It is a system which is used to increase the efficiency of the solar cells. As we know that solar panels are made up of one crystal and the panels which are made up of Monocrystalline crystal are 18% more efficient as compared to panel made up of Polycrystalline crystal. But to increase it more, we will use concentrators of sunlight with the panels. The System will use mirrors to increase the concentration of the sunlight. It can easily increase the efficiency up to 8–10%. Basically, mirrors/lenses are acting like the concentrator of sun light. The system uses concave mirror below the Cell and the reflected lights get absorbed by the cell as a result, improved Efficiency [6].

The vision for the betterment of smart lighting is to equip the smart lights with a humidity sensor (DHT11) [8]. The current scenario is that when the weather is bad, the sensors face a lot of difficulties communicating the right information to each other. Incorrect information provided by the sensors to the system as in case of roads and traffic might lead to serious accidents risking the lives of users (drivers & pedestrians both). The device will contain LED (Light Emitting Diode), sensors such as LDR (Light Dependent Resistor), DHT11 (Humidity Sensor), Ultrasonic sensors and hardware devices such as Arduino. LENSCAPE framework will be used to interconnect all the devices. These sensors will collect the heterogenous spatio temporal or real time data which will be used to switch ON/OFF the lights. This real time data can also be used in many other ways such as detecting the future weather and prevention of accidents to some extent which will automatically save the precious human life. These systems will save the energy and helps to stop the over depletion of the energy resources. As these systems are using Solar panels for the energy sources and rechargeable Li Ph batteries which have a better life span than other batteries.

Following is a prototype of smart lighting system with Ultrasonic and Humidity sensor. The microcontroller is coded in such a manner that when an object will be in the range of 400 cm (As the range of the HC SR-04 is 4 to 400 cm, it can only measure upto 4 m) or when humidity sensor detects the humidity more than 95% (Since in Fog or rain, humidity sensor shows 100% reading), then LED will start working (Fig. 6).

Another aspect to focus on is to increase the efficiency of the solar cells by concentrating the sunlight on the cell by either using a concave mirror or a lens. The mirror or lens has to be rotating and adjusting itself such as the angle is right to reflect/refract the sunlight on the cell since the sun keeps moving.

The software which will be used to program these devices should be end to end encrypted. In this way, the security issue for the smart lights can be overcome. Not only in street lights but also in-home lights which are connected to Wi-Fi must be encrypted in a well manner. In this way, the malware issues can be rectified. Compatibility issue can be resolved only if all the manufacturers agree on the same standards such as

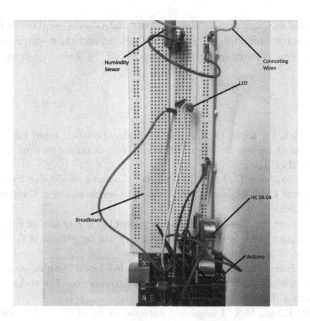

Fig. 6. Prototype

Bluetooth or USB. It's important to follow same standards for connectivity in making of devices. As if the devices follow different standards, then it will become quite difficult to connect the devices to each other.

5 Conclusion

The presented idea is to make smart light more efficient in the bad weather. By enabling these smart lights in the smart cities not only preserve our resources but also can help to gradually decrease the accidental rates in the area. The methods highlighted are Ultrasonic ranging in the field of IoT based Smart Lights and also used the technologies such as LoD (Light on Demand), LDR which changes the resistance accordingly with the light falling on it. Humidity Sensors used will help us to achieve relatively low accident rates, as they make our lights work in the conditions such as fog and rainfall. Concentrated Solar energy can be used to increase the efficiency of the solar cells. Relatively, using of LENSCAPE Framework in the street lights and implementing OLNs in it can help us to interconnect all the street lights which energy can be efficient. Although it could be a little expensive to implement OLNs, but it will be like a onetime investment. These systems collect the Hetrogenous Spatio Temporal or real time data which have many uses. Since the system works on real time data, working of Lights will be improved.

In future, the smart environment would be deeply investigated and studied. Improvements will be made in solar energy Concentrator. The communication protocols which will be required to make smart environment will be made better and further betterment in cost efficient networking between the objects. A thorough research will be done on the communication protocols for the long and short-range communications and how to implement them in the entire system of the Smart Lighting System.

References

1. Murthy, A., Han, D., Jiang, D., Oliveira, T.: Lighting-enabled smart city, applications and ecosystems based on the IoT. In: 2nd World Forum on Internet of Things (WF-IoT), pp. 757–763. IEEE (2015)
2. Abinaya, B., Gurupriya, S., Pooja, M.: IoT based smart and adaptive lighting in street. In: 2nd International Conference on Computing and Communications Technologies (ICCCT), pp. 195–198. IEEE (2017)
3. Sikder, A.K., Acar, A., Aksu, H.: IoT-enabled smart lighting systems for smart cities. In: 8th Annual Computing and Communication Workshop and Conference (CCWC), pp. 639–645. IEEE (2018)
4. Ouerhani, N., Pazos, N., Aeberli, M., Muller, M.: IoT-based dynamic street light control for smart cities use cases. In: International Symposium on Networks, Computers and Communications (ISNCC), pp. 1–5 (2016)
5. Bhaire, M.N., Edake, M.S.: Design and implementation of smart solar led street light. In: International Conference on Trends in Electronics and Informatics (ICEI), pp. 509–512 (2017)
6. Khatri, N., Brown, M., Gerner, F.: A solar energy collection system using optical fibers and a two-stage concentrator. In: Proceedings of the 25th Intersociety Energy Conversion Engineering Conference, pp. 173–178 (1990)
7. https://timesofindia.indiatimes.com/india/fog-related-crashes-getting-deadlier/articleshow/62407961.cms. Accessed 05 Apr 2018
8. Shradha, M., Dhir, S.: IoT for healthcare: challenges and future prospects. In: 5th International Conference on Computing for Sustainable Global Development (2018)
9. Tyagi, E., Madhurima, D.S.: Blue Eyes Technology: Impact and Applications. In: Presented in 5th International Conference on Computing for Sustainable Global Development (2018)
10. Krishna, S.B.V.: A systematic study of security issues in internet-of-things. In: International Conference on I-SMAC (IoT in Social, Mobile, Analytics and Cloud), pp. 107–111. IEEE (2017)
11. Lavric, A., Popa, V.: Performance evaluation of large-scale wireless sensor networks communication protocols that can be integrated in smart city. Int. J. Adv. Res. Electr. Electron. Instrum. Eng. 4(5) (2015)

A Power Efficient Solution to Counter Blackhole and Wormhole Attacks in MANET Multicast Routing

Rubal Sagwal[⊠] and A. K. Singh

National Institute of Technology, Kurukshetra, Kurukshetra, India
rubal.swt@gmail.com, aks@nitkkr.ac.in

Abstract. Routing is of prime importance in mobile ad-hoc networks as it is complex and the environment is extremely dynamic. On the other hand, multicast routing supports one to many communication and it is efficient with channel usage, bandwidth. Routing algorithms define how data travels in a multicast network. In this paper we take a close look at attacks in multicast networks and ponder up on techniques involved in making the operation secure. Power usage should be kept an eye on, as multicasting involves nodes operating at remote locations. The power consumption was made aimed to make as minimal as possible.

Mobile ad-hot networks are complex environments that are extremely dynamic. Routing is the first step in setting up a MANET and it is of paramount importance to do it securely and efficiently. Many algorithms have been proposed to secure the routing. However, the operation is still a grey block with multiple major security challenges. In this paper we take a deeper look at techniques in making more robust and secure.

Keywords: Mobile ad-hoc (MANET) · Heterogeneous nodes
Mobile nodes · Dynamic environment · Multicast routing protocol
Internal attacks · External attacks · Wormhole attack · Black-hole attack
MAODV

1 Introduction

In past few years computer networks security concern has been broadly discussed and made popular. The discussion has, though, usually involved only wired and static networks while concern related to MANETs have not been handled largely. Challenges such as routing, source to destination communication, message ex- change, group communication, key distribution require and grant privileges even make mobile ad-hoc networks more challenging. So, we can say that MANETs are considerably different from the wired networks.

MANETs are group or a collection of heterogeneous, independent, wireless mobile nodes that are self organizing and have different resource availability like battery power [1]. Nodes have different transmitting power, computational capabilities and communication range. The wireless and mobile nature provide freedom of moving anywhere to the nodes. The distributed and dynamic nature of mobile ad-hoc network enables it

© Springer Nature Singapore Pte Ltd. 2019
A. K. Luhach et al. (Eds.): ICAICR 2018, CCIS 956, pp. 547–556, 2019.
https://doi.org/10.1007/978-981-13-3143-5_45

to be deploy-able in various extreme and explosive environmental situations. Many applications have been found in many dominions such as environmental monitoring, workings of rescue system and military etc. [2]. Because the nodes involved here are mobile in nature and have a limited range of wireless communication, in MANETs, for communication they cooperate with each other.

In MANETs due to dynamic environment routing is deciding and vital task, where every node works as a host and as well as a router. We need a routing protocol always whenever a packet needs to transmitted to destination from source via number of nodes. Any two nodes that are in communication range of each other and can directly communicate are known as neighbor, otherwise multi-hop communication is used. To deal with such kind of network various protocols have been proposed which help not only for packet delivery but also packet delivery at correct destination. Routing is done by three ways in MANET, namely, unicast (one-to-one), broadcast (one-to-all) and multicast (one-to-many). Multicast routing is more efficient method to support group communication.

Multicast is a one-to-many communication technique, in which sender sends packet to more than one hosts, and thus planned for group oriented communication. Multicast routing in MANETs has several benefits. Unlike unicast, Multicast reduce the cost of communication by sending multiple copy of same data, saves bandwidth, helps to improve the effectiveness of the channel by minimizing consumption of channel capacity and less communication delay.

As we studied all essential tasks like routing, packet forwarding are done by nodes themselves. Compared to wired network, due to unavailability of centralized authority, no fixed boundaries and limited resources MANETs are more defenseless to security attack [3]. For all these reasons, security is essential requirement in MANETs. There are five most important security measures that require to be addressed in order to keep up a reliable and secure ad-hoc network environment, mainly are confidentiality, authentication, integrity, non-repudiation, availability and access control [4].

Security concerns of mobile ad-hoc networks are challenging in group communication where multiple senders and multiple receivers take place for communication. Attacks on multicast protocol can be classified as: 1. Unicast Attacks, where attackers major motive is not multicast operation of protocol but attack the unicast operation of the protocol; and 2. Multicast Attacks, where attackers main motive is multicast operation of the protocol. These attacks are dependent on specific protocol. These are not common to all multicast routing protocols; it can harm one or more multicast group internal operation. For example, in MAODV [5], it attacks the multicast group leader election, multicast group establishment and link breakage.

Security is crucial to facilitate efficient and effective multicast based application for multicast routing. Nevertheless, the exclusive features of such networks like shared wireless medium, peer-to-peer structural design and dynamic network topology introduces number of security challenges to construct secure multicast group. These non-trivial challenges force to focus on construct security solutions that help to achieve wide security without compromising the performance of the network. From last few years various security solutions have introduced for the security of the uncast protocols, these solutions cannot be directly fit into multicast protocols. So propose of this paper is to provide the security solution for multicast routing protocol attacks [6].

The rest of the paper is organized as follows. Section 2 presents a relevant related work. Section 3 presents brief overview on the main multicast operations of MAODV. Section 3 presents the objective and goals of the scheme, and the threat model. The proposed security countermeasures against the attacks are presented in Scct. 4. Section 5 contains the performance simulation study. Section 6 concludes the paper.

2 Related Work

In this section we briefly discuss about the various multicast protocols and then their security solutions. Finally, we listed out the addressed drawbacks which are allied with the related works that provide us the motivation for our work to address them.

Corson et al. [2], in this paper provides an overview of Mobile Ad-hoc Networks and emerging technologies. It introduces continuing motivations for mobile wireless system-based networking protocols. It also talks about several existing limitations of the MANETs and introduce several scopes of future work.

Taneja et al. [1], in this paper give an impression of various famous routing protocols, namely, DSR, TORA and AODV. It provides summery of these routing protocols by presenting their capabilities, functionalities, uniqueness and provide their performance analysis in terms of benefits and drawbacks.

Royer et al. [5] proposed an MAODV, which is a reactive multicast routing protocol for mobile networks that dynamically constructs a bi-directional shared multicast tree. It uses various control messages namely RREQs, RREPs, MACTs and GRPHs for multicast tree construction. It has several advantages like require low processing, less network utilization and less operating cost. Initially MAODV wasn't secure against various security threats but later on number of researchers proposed number of security solution for MAODV [7–10].

[3, 4, 11] in these papers define the possible Attacks on mobile ad hoc net- works and provide a brief comparison on these attacks. On the bases of the operations of network and activities of the attacks these are characterized as passive and active attack. It addressed five major security goals, they are mainly integrity, availability, confidentiality, access control and non-repudation that need to maintain for reliable operation of the network.

[11–15] proposed security solutions against unicast attack. They provide intrusion detection system for unicast attacks in MANETs.

[7, 16–19] provide various security solutions for multicast routing protocol of MANETs. They provide solutions for how to mitigate protocol dependent and independent attacks.

3 Objective

As discussed above many of the available techniques don't involve a runtime mechanism to guard against possible Rogue node attacks. In this scheme the proposal would be to make sure any Rogue node will be identified and identified with precision. Efficiency also plays a major part in reactive strategies.

– Goals

1. *An efficient system with no (or minimum) overhead:* Overhead alongside communication can degrade the system performance. When the aim is to counter DDoS/DoS a degraded performance might prove heavy on the End Users front. So the proposed scheme makes sure to identify malicious attempts with just an ack and a few fields alongside the ack packet. From this we achieve not just an efficient but a faster scheme at identifying malicious attempts.
2. *A system that identifies the Rogue node with precision:* it is important to identify the center of malicious activities. If we can identify the node with precision, reactive measures and forming the Multicast Group excluding Rogue node can be faster. This not only counters DoS but also makes sure the End User doesn't get a perception of an attack.
3. *Faster identification of attack:* Responding quickly to an attack can minimize the damage on system. So including this as one of the primary goals we aim at making a robust system that is impossible for damage, efficient at working. Being theoretically recoverable from an attack, the scheme works at giving perception of robustness.

To achieve the above goals, we propose a model that works in two phases. The paper hopes to address issues related to the secure operation of the scheme.

– Phases of Operation

1. Phase 1 (setup phase): This phase follows the standard process of setting up a multicast network. It involves nodes waiting for an election. Once the election is complete using one of the methods [5] we have a Group Leader and Group members. On a decision to multicast a message the leader node identifies the most optimal route. It then
2. Models routing packets and broadcasts them. On reception of these packets a bidirectional hierarchical tree is formed with all participant nodes that connect multicast group members possibly via non-group members. This makes each node aware of the ongoing communication. Once the agreement on this step is done and the trees are formed the system proceeds to the next phase where data is transferred in the form of Data packets (DP).
3. Phase 2 (Operation phase): The phase immediately follows setup phase where route and destination were identified. Each of the nodes involved in this phase has the primary responsibility of forwarding the packet and executing the code specific to packet forwarding. In the existing techniques [4] the forwarding operation has. MAODV is susceptible to attacks by outsiders as well as malicious insiders.

4   Countermeasures

In this section we present the proposed model to counter an ensuing attack. We also present the assumptions and modifications made to existing standard packets.

1. **Packet frequency estimation to counter worm hole attack:** In this method an ideal packet frequency is measured beforehand by the leader node. Along with the routing packets the value EF (Expected packet frequency) and a threshold t are sent. Once the operations phase begins, every node sees incoming packets, it then marks the frequency of incoming packets. RF (Received Frequency) is then calculated. Threshold value t makes sure we are not alerting the system on false positives. The threshold value must be chosen such that the value maintains a smooth operation of the system, while keeping the communication secure. If the

$$|RF - EF| < t$$

then the multicast system is operating as expected. If there is any deviation in the calculated error value an attack is suspected, because the packets might not have been following the optimal path discovered by leader node. The worker node (normal node/non-group member) then alerts or takes measures according to the contingency algorithm (Fig. 1).

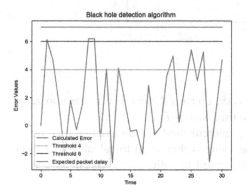
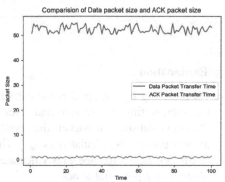

Fig. 1. Performance of wormhole attack detection

Fig. 2. Network usage by data packets and ACK packets comparison

Parameter	Description
f_E	Expected packet arrival frequency
f_R	Received packet frequency
T_n	Time stamp when nth packet is received
N	Total number of packets received
t_{avg}	Average time lapse among packets

Algorithm

| **Setup Phase:** |
| $CP\langle route, f_E, \tau \rangle$ |

Operation Phase:

On receiving first packet:

$n = 0$

$t_{avg} = 0$

$t'_{avg} = t_{avg}$

$T_{n-1} \longleftarrow$ *Time stamp when a packet comes in*

On every subsequent packet:

$++n;$

$t'_{avg} = \frac{t_{avg} \cdot (n-1) + (T_{n-1})}{n}$

Explanation

- On receiving the first packet the carrier node updates the count variable n to zero, the average time t_{avg} to zero and takes a time stamp T_{n1}.
- On every subsequent packet, the count is incremented and an average time delay among packets is calculated as t_{avg}. The value is then used to calculate reception frequency f_R. Difference thus calculated is used to estimate the threshold and to identify any potential attack.

2. **Two-hop Backward ACK to counter black hole attack:** The scheme follows a series of "two-hop" backward acknowledgements. For this scheme to work we propose to make changes with the Data packet. Data packet should now contain the hop count and ever node that forwards the packet decrements the hop count by 1 and forwarded. The hop count when a packet is received is saved and forwarded to the two-hop ancestor. Thus, when a node receives ACK back with remaining hop count the difference is counted. If the difference is not found to be 2, then an attack is ensued.

   We need to modify the data packet as: $DP = DP + Hopcount$. Where the hopcount is determined from the predetermined path to be followed to the destination.

5 Evaluation of the Scheme and Implementation

In this section we cover the performance evaluation of the specified schemes in terms of power usage, data usage and time taken to perform each of the operations. A home grown java based simulator running on Intel i5 machine with

4 GB memory was used for the evaluation. A Multicast network of 10 nodes was formed with an initial load of 120 MB data. The data is transmitted over the predefined paths to reach destination. Attack was induced on a random node chosen node by making the node route packets in the longer path. The results are documented and presented in the sections to follow.

Algorithm 1. Algorithm for detection of attack at Carrier node on arrival of each ACK packet

---

Input: DP - The data packet
Output: Build hop-count to detect an attack
 1: **fun**(DP)
 2: arrivalHopCount = DP.hopCount; // remaining hops are saved in memory
 3: DP.hopCount–; // hopCount on Data packet is decremented
 4: **forward**(DP, nextNode); // Data packet is forwarded
 5: **backAck**(arrivalHopCount, twoHopAncestor);

Algorithm 2. Algorithm for detection of attack at Carrier node on arrival of each ACK packet

---

Input: ACK - The acknowledge packet
Output: Alert if an attack is detected
 1: **fun**(hopCount)
 2: receivedHopCount = hopCount // an ack packet with hop count is received
 3: diff = receivedHopCount - arrivedHopCount // difference in ack and stored hop count is calculated
 4: **if** diff != 2 **then alert**();
 6: **end if** // if difference is not 2 alert the system

To understand the working of Wormhole attacks the simulation was divided into two sub-parts. Each scenario was simulated over 10 nodes and for 100 iterations. We have made note of time-stamp when each no of each of packets arrive at a node, and the delay was calculated. As a first part the threshold was considered to be at 4 ms delay, which was ambitious. The results showed a number of alert points. This can be seen clearly in the plot in Fig. 4. However, when we have brought up the threshold to 6 ms, the alerts were fewer and the nodes have alerted only when an induced attack was detected. Here, we have found an optimal threshold required for the smooth operation and detection of attacks.

The simulation showed clear indications of an efficient transmission in the form of ACK packets. Though this is an addition to the already existing techniques, our schemes make sure the lag will not be on network. Here we have a plot in Fig. 2 that shows the same. The ACK packets are as small as 0.1 to the originally sent data. This not only signifies as a light weight addition but considering the security improvements and robustness of the scheme ACK packets of this size can be an inclusion in already existing schemes.

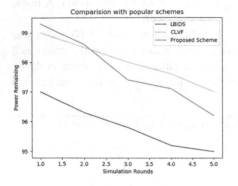
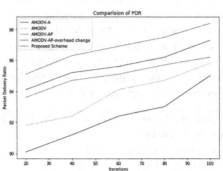

Fig. 3. Network usage by data packets and ACK packets comparison

Fig. 4. Comparison of PDR

5.1 Comparison of Proposed Scheme with Other Methods

In order to compare the power consumption and the repercussions of inclusion of an extra round of packet acknowledgement we chose two recent schemes in literature. Cross Layer Verification Framework (CLVF) [10] and LBIDS were chosen for the task. The results in Fig. 3 clearly show the scheme proposed by us performs better than LBIDS in every aspect. While the usage of power may surge occasionally we can see the same happening on rounds 3 and 6. There are clear indications of better performance than CLVF as well. Considering the extra load we are proposing with ACK packets this however is an acceptable performance.

In order to compare the packet delivery ratio Fig. 4 shows our proposed scheme has high PDR because of secure trust based finest route selection. For comparison we chose Basic Ad-hoc on-demand distance vector protocol [24], AOMDV-A (where A stands for Attack), AOMDV (Attack Prevention) and improved AOMDV-AP.

5.2 Power Efficiency

From the Fig. 4 we can clearly see that the proposed scheme fares well with the existing schemes. The scheme has consistently maintained a better power saving, where the slopes of curves do not drop as sharply compared to LBIDS. However, because of limitations and un-touched mechanism of nodes, we see a steep drop after the second iteration. This is an indication of one of the nodes being under attack. As an attack would cause the nodes to work more in providing with fake routes this change is seen.

6 Conclusion and Future Work

As a counter to popular attacks in MANETs we have proposed two algorithms which closely follow the well established schemes. The algorithms are expected to detect blackhole attacks and wormhole attacks in multicast networks. We have simulated these schemes and the results show how lightweight and robust the scheme is. These algorithms have met the defined objectives.

In the future we intend to extend the scheme for a wider lifetime of net- work and to include techniques that can support smooth functioning in network creation phase as well.

References

1. Taneja, S., Kush, A.: A survey of routing protocols in mobile ad hoc networks. Int. J. Innov., Manag. Technol. **1**(3), 279–285 (2010)
2. Corson, M.S., Macker, J.P., Cirincione, G.H.: Internet-based mobile ad hoc networking. IEEE Internet Comput. **3**(4), 63–70 (1999)
3. Jawandhiya, P.M., Ghonge, M.M., Ali, M.S., Deshpande, J.S.: A survey of mobile ad hoc network attacks. Int. J. Eng. Sci. Technol. **2**(9), 4063–4071 (2010)
4. Wu, B., Chen, J., Wu, J., Cardei, M.: A survey of attacks and countermeasures in mobile ad hoc networks. In: Xiao, Y., Shen, X.S., Du, D.Z. (eds.) Wireless Network Security. SCT, pp. 103–135. Springer, Boston (2007). https://doi.org/10.1007/978-0-387-33112-6_5
5. Royer, E.M., Perkins, C.E.: Multicast ad hoc on-demand distance vector (MAODV) routing. IETF Internet-Draft, draft-ietfmanet-maodv (2000)
6. Moamen, A.A., Hamza, H.S., Saroit, I.A.: Secure multicast routing protocols in mobile ad hoc networks. Int. J. Commun. Syst. **27**(11), 2808–2831 (2014)
7. Curtmola, R., Nita-Rotaru, C.: BSMR: Byzantine-resilient secure multicast routing in multihop wireless networks. IEEE Trans. Mob. Comput. **4**, 445–459 (2015)
8. Roy, S., Addada, V.G.K., Setia, S., Jajodia, S.: Securing MAODV: attacks and countermeasures. In: SECON, pp. 521–532 (2005)
9. Borkar, G.M., Mahajan, A.R.: A secure and trust based on-demand multipath routing scheme for self-organized mobile ad-hoc networks. Wirel. Netw. **23**(8), 2455–2472 (2017)
10. Jagadeesan, S., Parthasarathy, V.: Design and implement a cross layer verification framework (CLVF) for detecting and preventing blackhole and wormhole attack in wireless ad-hoc networks for cloud environment. Clust. Comput., 1–12 (2018)
11. Gheorghe, L., Rughinis, R., Tataroiu, R.: Adaptive trust management protocol based on intrusion detection for wireless sensor networks. In: 2013 RoEduNet International Conference 12th Edition: Networking in Education and Research, pp. 1–7. IEEE (2013)
12. Shakshuki, E.M., Kang, N., Sheltami, T.R.: EAACKa secure intrusion-detection system for MANETs. IEEE Trans. Ind. Electron. **3**, 1089–1098 (2013)
13. Marti, S., Giuli, T.J., Lai, K., Baker, M.: Mitigating routing misbehavior in mobile ad hoc networks. In: Proceedings of the 6th Annual International Conference on Mobile Computing and Networking, pp. 255–265. ACM (2000)
14. Al-Shurman, M., Yoo, S.-M., Park, S.: Black hole attack in mobile ad hoc networks. In: Proceedings of the 42nd Annual Southeast Regional Conference, pp. 96–97. ACM (2004)

15. Mo'men, A.M.A., Hamza, H.S., Saroit, I.A.: New attacks and efficient countermeasures for multicast AODV. In: High-Capacity Optical Networks and Enabling Technologies (HONET), pp. 51–57. IEEE (2010)
16. Sharma, P., Sharma, N., Singh, R.: A secure intrusion detection system against DDOS attack in wireless mobile ad-hoc network. Int. J. Comput. Appl. **41**(21), 16–21 (2012)
17. Shanthi, N., Ganesan, L.: Security in multicast mobile ad-hoc networks. Int. J. Comput. Sci. Netw. Secur. **8**, 326–330 (2008)
18. Vijayalakshmi, S., Albert Rabara, S.: Weeding wormhole attack in manet multicast routing using two novel techniques-LP3 and NAWA2. Int. J. Comput. Appl. **16**, 26–33 (2011)
19. Galera, F.J., Ruiz, P.M., Gmez-Skarmeta, A.F., Kassler, A.: Security extensions to MMARP through cryptographically generated addresses. In: GI Jahrestagung (2), pp. 339–342 (2005)
20. Marina, M.K., Das, S.R.: Ad hoc on-demand multipath distance vector routing. ACM SIGMOBILE Mob. Comput. Commun. Rev. **6**(3), 92–93 (2002)
21. Perkins, C.E., Royer, E.M., Barbara, S., Das, S.R.: Ad hoc on-demand distance vector routing. IETF draft RFC 3561, pp. 1–37 (2003)
22. Jetcheva, J.G., Johnson, D.B.: Adaptive demand-driven multicast routing in multi-hop wireless ad hoc networks. In: Proceedings of the 2nd ACM International Symposium on Mobile Ad Hoc Networking Computing, pp. 33–44. ACM (2001)
23. Sivakumar, K., Selvaraj, G.: Analysis of worm hole attack in MANET and avoidance using robust secure routing method. Int. J. Adv. Res. Comput. Sci. Softw. Eng. **3**(1), 235–242 (2013)
24. Sutariya, D.: Performance evaluation of multicast routing protocols in mobile ad hoc networks. Proc. Int. J. Comput. Netw., Wirel. Mob. Commun. (IJCNWMC) **6**(2), 45–54 (2016)
25. Patel, N.: Security technique for on demand multicast routing (SAODV). In: IJIRST (National Conference on Latest Trends in Networking and Cyber Security), NCLTNCS, pp. 101–104 (2017)

Security and Privacy

Change Point Modelling in the Vulnerability Discovery Process

Ruchi Sharma$^{(\boxtimes)}$, Ritu Sibal, and Sangeeta Sabharwal

Netaji Subhas Institute of Technology, Delhi, India
rs.sharma184@gmail.com, ritusib@hotmail.com,
ssab63@gmail.com

Abstract. The process of vulnerability discovery and its successful fixation is dependent on various factors like testing strategy, test case effectiveness, team constitution, efficiency, and environmental factors. These factors are prone to changes over the period of time. Change point analysis is the process of detecting this point at which the cumulative effect of factors affects the rate of change of vulnerability discovery. In this paper, we propose a mathematical model which captures point of switch or change in the regression. The practical utility of the model is confirmed by validating it on three real life software datasets. The results validate that the proposed model with change point consideration shows a better goodness of fit in comparison with mathematical models without change point.

1 Introduction

Quantitative assessment of the quality of a software plays a crucial role in providing a secure and reliable software [3, 4]. Vulnerability discovery models helps in this quality assessment of software by analyzing the trend of vulnerability occurrence. Vulnerabilities are the faults which have the potential of causing security breaches and hence obstructing the confidentiality, integrity or availability of crucial resources in a system which might further lead to monetary losses. Moreover, the information extracted as a result of these security breaches can be used by the attackers to cause damage. Therefore, testing of a software is continued even after it is released in the market so as to come up with patches which can fix the vulnerabilities that are residing in the software in its operational phase. This process of vulnerability fixation is preceded by vulnerability detection or discovery.

Various factors affect the process of vulnerability discovery. These factors may include strategy adopted, testing environment, effectiveness of test cases, skills of testing team, efficiency and many more [5–7]. VDMs are formulated to track their growth rate at any point of time during operational phase while taking in consideration some or all of these factors. The models are formulated while taking certain assumptions on the process [1, 2].

The parameters of these models represent various factors associated with the trend of vulnerability discovery [5, 7]. When VDM is applied in real software environment to predict the number of vulnerabilities it is usually carried out under the assumption that the parameters of the VDM will remain unchanged during the course of testing.

© Springer Nature Singapore Pte Ltd. 2019
A. K. Luhach et al. (Eds.): ICAICR 2018, CCIS 956, pp. 559–568, 2019.
https://doi.org/10.1007/978-981-13-3143-5_46

However this assumption may not hold true for all the cases. It may happen that once the process of testing is started, the team decided to include a more experienced and skilled member to be a part of the team. They may also introduce changes in the current testing strategies while adopting automated tools for better results. The basic motive is to come up with best possible results and this might lead to multiple changes during the testing process. Now, in such a situation, the model parameters estimated without considering these changes may not be able to give an accurate description of the testing progress. Owing to these changes some or all of the parameters used in the model may show significant variations that are usually observed in the operational environments [22].

The paper organization is as follows: Sect. 2 presents the existing related work, followed by notations, assumptions and framework of the proposed model in Sect. 3. In Sect. 4, the change point based vulnerability discovery model has been developed. Section 5 includes the numerical illustration of the proposed model and its analysis. Finally conclusion has been drawn in Sect. 6 based on the model development and analysis.

2   Related Work

Over the years, researchers have tried to come up with different mathematical models with varied assumptions for this process of vulnerability discovery. Anderson's thermodynamic model was the first model in the direction of modelling the process of vulnerability discovery [10, 21]. It was initially developed in the field of thermodynamics and later applied to model the vulnerability detection process. Though, it did not give appreciable results, it marked the beginning of research in this direction. Soon after the Anderson's thermodynamic model, Rescorla proposed two linear and exponential models which gave slightly better results. The most widely used model termed as Alhazmi Malaiya Logistic (AML) [1, 2]. Model came out in early 90's and gave commendable results. Their vulnerability [24] prediction results for windows operating system were very close to the actual number of vulnerabilities observed. They also proposed an effort based discovery model and called it Alhazmi-Malaiya Effort-based (AME) model but that does not show any improvement in results over AML. AML established that vulnerability discovery curve is sigmoid in shape due to 3 phases involving learning, linear and saturation. The results obtained using AML model were very close to the observed data.

Later, Joh et al. [13] used Weibull distribution function to model the process of vulnerability discovery but could not give appreciable predictions. Kapur et al. [14] gave two models and made a comparison with AML model. They developed these models using two different distribution functions. Shrivastava et al. [20] modelled a VDM using the famous AML model created around the stochastic differential equation. Kim [17] talked about the multiple versions of software during the modelling process. Sharma et al. developed a VDM using Gamma function and discussed differences in the process of vulnerability discovery for open and closed software systems [26]. Anand et al. [9] suggested a model for multiple versions of vulnerability discovery framework where they assumed that the total number of vulnerabilities of the nth version is sum of the vulnerabilities detected in the current version and remaining vulnerabilities that are detected in upcoming version.

In 2003, Shyur suggested that change point exists in the process of testing and hence should be considered during model development [7]. Change point models are extensively used in the hardware and software reliability study [22]. Here we are proposing this phenomenon of change point in specific area of Software Vulnerability discovery. In the existing work in this field, the models have been derived under the assumption of a constant detection rate [1, 2, 8–11, 13, 19, 24, 26]. Researchers proceeded with the assumption that the probability of vulnerability detection is equal for all the vulnerabilities while in the operational phase, and the rate at which they are detected does not change. However, in a real scenario, the Vulnerability detection rate relies on the skills of testing team, defect density, size of the program, factors of code expansion, team constitution, testing, testability of software etc. [7, 15, 18, 22, 25].

3   Methodology

In this study, we have used the methodology applied for reliability assessment in Software Reliability Growth Models [22] which is now being applied to Vulnerability Discovery Models as well [16, 20, 26].

Non Homogenous Poisson Process is a process in which the rate of arrival or detection of an entity is random with non-stationary increments. It shows all the properties of a Poisson process but the rate is a function of time. In this study, we have considered the process of vulnerability discovery as an NHPP. Since, the number of vulnerabilities detected by the testing team is random and in each time interval, the number of vulnerabilities found may not be stationary. The VDM is hence developed under the assumptions that hold true for NHPP processes. The various assumptions considered during model development are described in the next section.

3.1   Assumptions

The mathematical models are usually developed with certain predefined notions treated as model assumptions. These are the conditions that usually prevail and simplify the process of model development. The assumptions during model development are as follows:

  i Initially the number of vulnerabilities detected are zero i.e. at zeroth time instant, So, at $t = 0$, $V(0) = 0$.
 ii The total no. of vulnerabilities detected depends on the no. of unresolved ones.
iii The software has finite no. of vulnerabilities.
 iv The rate of vulnerability detection is not constant and it can change at any point.

3.2   Notations

$\bar{V}$:   Total number of Vulnerabilities present in the software.

$V(t)$:   expected no. of Vulnerabilities identified during the time interval $(0,t]$.

$r(t)$:   time dependent rate of Vulnerability removal per remaining no. of Vulnerabilities.

c: the point of change.

$D(t)$:   Cumulative distribution function of Vulnerability occurrence, with density function $d(t) = \frac{dD(t)}{dt}$.

4 Model Development

Recent study on change point model [22] suggested a methodology for developing the models with change point by giving an appropriate cumulative distribution function for the software vulnerability discovery times, $D(t)$. The exponential model with single change point is then developed from this framework.

As, per the Non Homogenous Poisson Process, the total count of vulnerabilities discovered with time is in proportion with the count of residual vulnerabilities in the software and the rate of detection. This is depicted by Eq. (1) below.

$$\frac{dV(t)}{dt} = r(t)(\bar{V} - V(t)) \tag{1}$$

Equation (1) above shows the general model without considering the phenomenon of change point.

While considering the notion of change point, the rate of vulnerability detection changes with time. Hence, in order to develop the single change point model, we take two different hazard functions for pre and post occurrence of change point. Using Eq. (1),

$$r(t) = \begin{cases} r_1(t) = \frac{d_1(t)}{1-D_1(t)} & 0 \leq t \leq c \\ r_2(t) = \frac{d_2(t)}{1-D_2(t)} & c < t \end{cases}, \tag{2}$$

Solving (1) using (2), with the initial condition $V(0) = 0$,

$$V(t) = \begin{cases} \bar{V}D_1(t) & 0 \leq t \leq c \\ \bar{V}[1 - ((1 - D_1(c))(1 - D_2(t))/(1 - D_2(c)))] & c < t \end{cases} \tag{3}$$

If $V(T)$ is defined by a logistic distribution function i.e.

$$D_1(t) = \frac{1 - e^{-r_1 t}}{1 - le^{-r_1 t}}, \quad 0 \leq t \leq c \tag{4}$$

and

$$D_2(t) = \frac{1 - e^{-r_2 t}}{1 - le^{-r_2 t}}, \quad c < t \tag{5}$$

For simplification, the shape parameter in the distribution taken can be presumed to be same for before and after the occurrence of change point. Now, the mean value function of the VDM with change point is

$$V(t) = \begin{cases} \bar{V}\left(1 - \frac{(1+l)e^{-r_1 t}}{1 + le^{-r_1 t}}\right), & 0 \le t \le c, \\ \bar{V}\left(1 - \frac{(1+l)(1+\beta e^{-r_2 c})}{(1 + le^{-r_1 c})(1 + le^{-r_2 t})} e^{-b_1 c - b_2(t-c)}\right) & c < t \end{cases} \quad (6)$$

This model represents a learning curve which is flexible and generally provides a decent estimation of software vulnerabilities and hence the reliability and security of the software. For mathematical simplification, it is assumed that the parameter l of the failure time distribution is not changed and hence taken as same for the distributions for before and after the change point. However it might be changed and the value of mean value function can be computed accordingly for any practical real scenario.

5 Parameter Estimation

Parameters are estimated for three different software data sets using Statistical Package for Social Sciences (SPSS).

5.1 Dataset Description

The data used for the estimation of parameters has been extracted from CVE Details and National Vulnerability Database (NVD) [12]. The data sets contain vulnerability data for three software namely, Adobe (D1), Windows XP (D2), and Mozilla Firefox (D3). For parameter estimation in existing and proposed model, we have used (MLE) maximum likelihood estimation which is based on Non-linear regression. The existing model without change point is depicted by Eq. (1) above and the proposed model with change point is given by Eq. (6) (Tables 1, 2 and 3).

Table 1. Parameter estimation results on D1

Parameter	Estimate without change point	Estimate with change point
$\bar{V}$	6168.235	3640.083
r_1	0.273	0.320
r_2	–	347.856
l	288.268	0.375

5.2 Prediction Capabilities

The capability of prediction of the proposed model with change point and currently existing model without change point are evaluated based on various comparison criteria for vulnerability prediction on the datasets used in this study.

Table 2. Parameter estimation results on D2

Parameter	Estimate without change point	Estimate with change point
$\bar{V}$	853.543	825.613
r_1	0.352	0.252
r_2	–	12.865
l	33.121	0.331

Table 3. Parameter estimation results on D3

Parameter	Estimate without change point	Estimate with change point
$\bar{V}$	2121.472	2314.820
r_1	.309	.124
r_2	–	22.360
l	52.139	.245

5.2.1   Criteria for Comparison

For gauging the capability of prediction for the exiting and proposed model, we have used following statistical comparison criteria.

Let n be the size of sample dataset, V_i is the no. of vulnerabilities by time t_i (as observed in original dataset) and $V(t)_i$ represents the estimated no. of vulnerabilities by time t_i.

(1) Bias

$$Bias = \sum_{i=1}^{m} \frac{V(t_i) - V_i}{m}$$

The difference between predicted & observed number of vulnerabilities detected at any instant of time i is Prediction error (PE). Bias is the average of PE's. A lesser value of Bias indicates better curve fitting and hence better prediction.

(2) Variance

$$Variance = \sqrt{1/m - 1(PE_i - Bias)}^2$$

The standard deviation of Prediction Bias is used as a measure of variance from the original dataset. Prediction Bias is the average value of all the prediction errors taken together. A lower value of variance means better prediction.

(3) Root Mean Square Prediction Error (RMSPE)

$$RMSPE = \sqrt{Variance^2 + Bias^2}$$

RMSPE is a measure of how closely the model predicts the observed values. A lower RMSPE value is desired as it suggests close predictions.

(4) Mean Square Error (MSE)

The difference between the observed data y_i, and the expected values $m(t_i)$ is measured by MSE as follows:

$$M.S.E. = \sum_{i=1}^{m} \frac{(V(t_i) - y_i)^2}{m}$$

Where k denoted the no. of data points. Lower the value of MSE, lower is the error in curve fitting and hence desirable.

(5) Coefficient of Multiple Determination (R^2)

The ratio of the sum of squares resulting from the trend model to that from constant model subtracted from 1 is defined as the Coefficient of multiple determination. Closer the value of R^2 to 1, better is the curve fitting and hence predictions.

$$\text{i.e. } R^2 = 1 - \frac{residualSS}{correctedSS}$$

Table 4. Comparison criteria results of model with and without change point (CP)

Datasets	D1 (Adobe)		D2 (Windows XP)		D3 (Mozilla Firefox)	
Comparison criteria	Without CP	With CP	Without CP	With CP	Without CP	With CP
Bias	0.287	4.74	41.56	11.71	−12.4	0.996
Variance	21.66	18.55	95.67	16.45	37.95	13.95
RMSPE	21.66	19.15	104.3046	20.19	39.95	13.98
MSE	439.8	344.9	8694.5	3398.4	1352.7	747.11
R^2	0.984	0.995	0.994	0.995	0.996	0.998

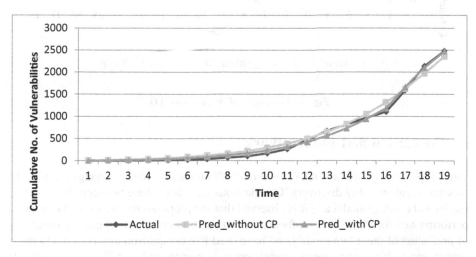

Fig. 1. Goodness of fit curve for D1

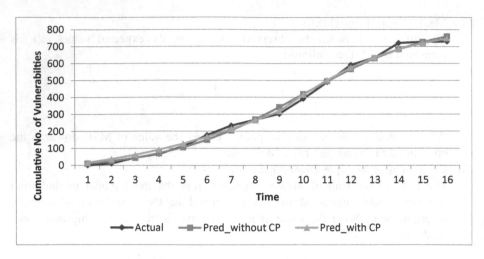

Fig. 2. Goodness of fit curve for D2

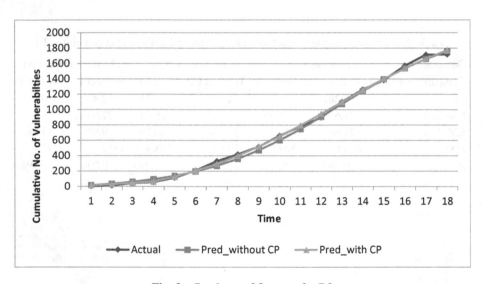

Fig. 3. Goodness of fit curve for D3

6 Conclusion and Future Work

This proposed work introduced a new model which uses the idea of change point in the process of vulnerability discovery. Comparisons have been done between the proposed model and existing model and it is observed that the proposed model with change point performs well for all the three software dataset used. In order to evaluate the capability of prediction of these two models, we have used five comparison criteria namely mean square error, bias, root mean square error, variance and coefficient of multiple determination, as shown in Table 4 above. For the first four criteria, a lower value suggests better curve fitting and hence indicates that the model is comparatively better. While for the last criterion, i.e., coefficient of multiple determination, a higher value indicates better curve fitting. As can be seen in Table 4 above, the proposed model shows better results for all the criteria over all the datasets. The goodness of fit curves are shown in Figs. 1, 2, and 3 for datasets D1, D2 and D3 respectively. It can be seen that the plot of predictions with change point almost overlaps the existing dataset while the predictions without change point do not overlap effectively with the data points. Hence, establishing that the phenomenon of change point exists during testing in the operational phase and vulnerability predictions can be effectively improved while modelling with change point considerations.

In future, this work can be enhanced by considering imperfect debugging and error generation during the process of vulnerability fixation. Patch analysis can also be considered in future while modelling the process of vulnerability discovery.

References

1. Alhazmi, O.H., Malaiya, Y.K.: Modeling the vulnerability discovery process. In: 16th IEEE International Symposium on Software Reliability Engineering (ISSRE 2005), pp. 10-pp. IEEE (2005)
2. Alhazmi, O.H., Malaiya, Y.K.: Application of vulnerability discovery models to major operating systems. IEEE Trans. Reliab. **57**(1), 14–22 (2008)
3. Musa, J.D.: A theory of software reliability and its application. IEEE Trans. Softw. Eng. **3**, 312–327 (1975)
4. Lyu, M.R.: Handbook of Software Reliability Engineering (1996)
5. Hsu, C.J., Huang, C.Y., Chang, J.R.: Enhancing software reliability modeling and prediction through the introduction of time-variable fault reduction factor. Appl. Math. Model. **35**(1), 506–521 (2011)
6. Musa, J.D.: Software Reliability Engineering: More Reliable Software, Faster and Cheaper. Tata McGraw-Hill Education, New York (2004)
7. Shyur, H.J.: A stochastic software reliability model with imperfect-debugging and change-point. J. Syst. Softw. **66**(2), 135–141 (2003)
8. Anand, A., Bhatt, N.: Vulnerability discovery modeling and weighted criteria based ranking. J. Indian Soc. Probab. Stat. **17**(1), 1–10 (2016)
9. Anand, A., Das, S., Aggrawal, D., Klochkov, Y.: Vulnerability Discovery modelling for software with multi-versions. In: Ram, M., Davim, J. (eds.) Advances in Reliability and System Engineering. Management and Industrial Engineering, pp. 255–265. Springer, Cham (2017). https://doi.org/10.1007/978-3-319-48875-2_11
10. Anderson, R.: Security in open versus closed systems—the dance of Boltzmann, Coase and Moore. Technical report, Cambridge University, England (2002)
11. Bhatt, N., Anand, A., Yadavalli, V.S.S., Kumar, V.: Modeling and characterizing software vulnerabilities. Int. J. Math., Eng. Manag. Sci. **2**(4), 288–299 (2017)
12. National Vulnerability Database. https://nvd.nist.gov/
13. Joh, H.C., Kim, J., Malaiya, Y.K.: Vulnerability discovery modeling using Weibull distribution. In: 19th International Symposium on Software Reliability Engineering, pp. 299–300. IEEE (2008)

14. Kapur, P.K., Yadavalli, V.S.S, Shrivastava, A.K.: A comparative study of vulnerability discovery modeling and software reliability growth modeling. In: International conference on Futuristic Trends in Computational Analysis and Knowledge Management, pp. 246–251. IEEE (2015)

15. Kapur, P.K., Sachdeva, N., Khatri, S.K.: Vulnerability discovery modeling. In: Quality, Reliability, Infocomm Technology and Industrial Technology Management, pp. 34–54. I.K. International Publishing House (2015)

16. Kapur, P.K., Garg, R.B.: A software reliability growth model for an error-removal phenomenon. Softw. Eng. J. 7(4), 291–294 (1992)

17. Kim, J., Malaiya, Y.K., Ray, I.: Vulnerability discovery in multi-version software systems. In: 10th IEEE High Assurance Systems Engineering Symposium. HASE 2007, pp. 141–148. IEEE (2007)

18. Kimura, M.: Software vulnerability: definition, modelling, and practical evaluation for e-mail transfer software. Int. J. Press. Vessel. Pip. 83(4), 256–261 (2006)

19. Rescorla, E.: Is finding security holes a good idea? IEEE Secur. Priv. 3(1), 14–19 (2005)

20. Shrivastava, A.K., Sharma, R., Kapur, P.K.: Vulnerability discovery model for a software system using stochastic differential equation. In: International Conference on Futuristic Trends in Computational Analysis and Knowledge Management, pp. 199–205. IEEE (2015)

21. Brady, R.M., Anderson, R.J., Ball, R.C.: Murphy's law, the fitness of evolving species, and the limits of software reliability. Technical report no. 471, Cambridge University Computer Laboratory (1999)

22. Kapur, P.K., Pham, H., Gupta, A., Jha, P.C.: Software Reliability Assessment with OR Applications. Springer, London (2011). https://doi.org/10.1007/978-0-85729-204-9

23. Krusl, I., Spafford, E., Tripunitara, M.: Computer vulnerability analysis. Department of Computer Sciences, Purdue University, COAST TR 98-07 (1998)

24. Alhazmi, O.H., Malaiya, Y.K., Ray, I.: Measuring, analyzing and predicting security vulnerabilities in software systems. Comput. Secur. 26(3), 219–228 (2011)

25. Huang, C.Y.: Performance analysis of software reliability growth models with testing-effort and change-point. J. Syst. Softw. 76(2), 181–194 (2005)

26. Sharma, R., Sibal, R., Shrivastava, A.K.: Vulnerability discovery modeling for open and closed source software. Int. J. Secur. Softw. Eng. (IJSSE) 7(4), 19–38 (2005)

Modeling Vulnerability Discovery and Patching with Fixing Lag

A. K. Shrivastava[1(✉)] and Ruchi Sharma[2]

[1] Fortune Institute of International Business, Delhi, India
kavinash1987@gmail.com
[2] Netaji Subhas Institute of Technology, Delhi, India
rs.sharma184@gmail.com

Abstract. Development of Secure Software was always a tedious task for IT industry. The insecurity issue of the software systems can be looked as two primary problems: vulnerability discovery and patching. Vulnerability discovery modeling tends to develop mathematical models that predict the behavior of vulnerabilities in a software system and patches are used to fix the vulnerabilities. In this work we are proposing a new approach to model vulnerability by categorizing them into two types (direct and indirect) based on how they are fixed by utilizing the vulnerability patching phenomenon with delay called lag time while fixing them after discovery. Numerical Illustration on a real life vulnerability data is provided to validate the proposed model.

Keywords: Vulnerability · Modeling · Discovery · Patching · Fix Lag

1 Introduction

During operational phase, the key attribute that can be used to measure the security of the system is the number of vulnerabilities present in the software [20]. If the number of vulnerabilities found is low, then the system is said to be more secure. Thus the extent to which the software is at risk is measured by the security level of the software which is in turn assessed by means of counting vulnerabilities [16]. Pfleeger et al. defined software vulnerability as a security defect that enables hackers to bypass the system without authenticity [24]. Bishop and Bailey [29] stated that a computer system contains various events that explains the current configuration of the attributes and changes their behavior according to the performed transaction. The authors have classified these events into authorized and unauthorized events wherein vulnerability is a characterization of authorized event that disrupt the confidentiality and integrity of the system.

Ozment stated that vulnerability modeling is analogous to software reliability growth model (SRGM) with an aim to increase the reliability of the system regardless of their operating environments [20]. We have observed that the concept of fault detection and correction process which is similar to vulnerability discovery and patching process in software security [21]. When vulnerabilities are reported, the first thing that comes into the mind of patch developer is "which vulnerability should be tackled first". For reducing the time and effort, MITRE Corporation has categorized all

© Springer Nature Singapore Pte Ltd. 2019
A. K. Luhach et al. (Eds.): ICAICR 2018, CCIS 956, pp. 569–578, 2019.
https://doi.org/10.1007/978-981-13-3143-5_47

the vulnerabilities so that a single comprehensive patch may fix the root cause of all the vulnerabilities within the group. In this work, we aspire to develop a standard approach for assessing the security of the system on the similar lines of reliability engineering. The investigation initially classifies the vulnerability modeling into two parts: vulnerability discovery and vulnerability patching. Vulnerability discovery modeling (VDM) predicts the cumulative number of vulnerabilities against calendar time. In contrast, vulnerability patch modeling (VPM) observes the cumulative number of patches with calendar time only. In this research we have used this idea to propose a new approach to predict vulnerabilities by categorizing them into two types i.e. direct and indirect with fixing lag. In the proposed model numbers of vulnerabilities are estimated using the fact that during patching process of direct vulnerabilities some more vulnerability gets fixed termed as indirect vulnerabilities. To assist with the aspect of patches, this work provides some vulnerability discovery and patching models that mathematically determine the intensity with which the vulnerabilities are patched. Here, we have provided some evidence to show the time lag between the vulnerability discovery and patching process. Rest of the paper is organized as follow: Sect. 2 discusses the related work done in this area of research. In Sect. 3 we have defined the notation, assumption and the modeling framework of the proposed model. Section 4 provides the combined model for direct and indirect vulnerabilities discovery and patching. In Sect. 5 numerical illustration of the proposed model is discussed. Finally conclusion of the work is drawn in Sect. 6.

2 Related Work

In past few decades, various researchers considered software security to be analogous with software reliability and developed the vulnerability discovery models on similar lines [8, 12, 15]. Anderson et al. examined and measured the security in open and closed systems by proposing a thermo-dynamic vulnerability discovery model [4]. The author have modeled the discovery rate on the basis of mean time between failure (MTBF) and defined the model analogous to SRGM. However, the author concluded that the there is no difference between open and closed system, both are similar in long run. Rescorla determined that the vulnerability finding is a better approach if it is followed by the white hat users [11]. He evaluated the economic effectiveness of finding and fixing rediscovered vulnerabilities on the developing organizations especially when they are identified by black hat users. The author has fitted a non-homogeneous poisson process (NHPP) reliability growth model to the observed vulnerability data to evaluate the vulnerability discovery rate over time. However, he proposed two statistical models i.e. Rescorla exponential (RE) and Rescorla Linear or Quadratic (RL or RQ) model that is later proved to be insignificant as they are not able to predict the behavior of all empirical data sets [11]. Ozment identified the OpenBSD operating system data set and stated that some vulnerability within the data set is dependent. However, he does not apply any VDM on the data set and considered the engineering tools to measure the software security [20]. Alhazmi et al. [1, 2, 14] attempted to develop a logistic VDM (known as AML model) that quantitatively evaluates the vulnerabilities trend over time. He also proposed a new metric i.e.

vulnerability density which is analogous to defect density. If the software has high vulnerability density then it is at major risk. The author divided the discovery process into three phases i.e. linear phase, learning phase and saturation phase. Later, he proposed an effort based vulnerability discovery model (known as AME model) that exhibits the environment changes with respect to the effort instead [1, 2]. However, these models are solely dependent on discovery time which seems inappropriate since there are various operational factors that may influence the vulnerability discovery process. Kim et al. [9] extended the work done by Alhazmi et al. [1] for single version by developing a new VDM for multi versions (known as MVDM). They proved that the behavior of vulnerability discovery rate for multiple versions is different from single-version modeling for open source and commercial software systems. Anand et al. [3] developed the idea of modeling multi version of vulnerability discovery in generalized way by using distribution function. Sutton et al. [26] proposed a methodology to discover vulnerabilities for any software applications with the help of fuzzy theory. Though authors have not developed any mathematical models for vulnerability prediction. Joh et al. developed a VDM that follows Weibull distribution and is known as JW model [7]. The model represents the asymmetric nature of vulnerability discovery rate because of the skewness present in probabilistic density function. Though, this model is also exclusively dependent on discovery time. Algarni et al. [10] scrutinized the factors that motivate the vulnerability discoverers to spend the effort in findings. As per the study, the discoverers are more attracted towards bug bounty programs that have become the main reason of their encouragement. However, they have not modeled the vulnerability discovery process. Massacci and Nguyen proposed a methodology to validate the performance of empirical VDMs [28]. The methodology focuses on two quantitative metrics that are quality and predictability analysis. The quality is measured on the basis of good fit and inconclusive fit while the predictive accuracy is measured on current and future horizon. However he does not proposed any mathematical model. Zhu et al. [23] proposed a mathematical model that predicts the software vulnerabilities and used the estimated parameters to develop a new risk model. Authors also determined the severity of vulnerability using logistic function and binomial distribution, respectively.

Other than vulnerability discovery there is another factor that affects the software security known as patching. Patching ensures that all the vulnerabilities affecting the system information are addressed and effectively removed [25]. It is the most effective countermeasure that improves the system security and avoids erosion of user's confidence. When highly exploited vulnerabilities are reported, then patches are supposed to be release frequently that do not provide any time for vendors to test them properly [13]. This introduces the risks to the patch installation process. Thus to understand the behavior of patches (developed for fixing highly exploitable vulnerabilities) there is a need to develop a mathematical vulnerability patching model that operates on successfully patched vulnerabilities with operational time. Kansal et al. [18] developed a vulnerability patch model by categorizing vulnerability into direct, indirect and unpatched vulnerabilities. Their model forms the relationship between the patch success rate and the number of patched vulnerabilities. The patch modeling helps vendors in proper patch management and scheduling. Earlier researchers have only focused on the factors that affects the patch release time theoretically. In this work, we will present a mathematical model that represents those underlying factors into account. These models also emphasize on the key aspects of the patching process, (1) Patching is conducted for discovered vulnerabilities thus vulnerability patching process should be considered in estimating the number of vulnerabilities, (2)There is always a time lag between the discovery and patching process. However, it is not important in case of zero-day vulnerabilities. Bhatt et al. [5] categorized vulnerabilities into leading and dependent type using the famous bass model time for modeling vulnerability discovery.

A parallel research to model the patch release time is also attracting researchers working on vulnerability discovery modeling. Various researchers have worked to represent the patch management economically. Beattie et al. proposed a mathematical cost model that extrapolates the best time to release the patches. The authors modeled the cost of vulnerability discovery due to attack and the cost of deprave due to flawed patches over time [22]. Telang et al. [27] quantified the losses faced by software vendors due to vulnerabilities disclosure. The authors also examined the patch value and determine the relationship between the vendor and user characteristics on market. Arora et al. [13] attempted to determine the time taken by vendor to release a patch theoretically with the help of some hypothesis such as the competitive and non-competitive vendors sharing common vulnerabilities, a threat of disclosure and large market size. The authors have concluded that the vulnerability disclosure is the major factor that effectively influences them to release patch early. Cavusoglu et al. [25] developed a game theoretic model that maintains a tradeoff between the cost and benefit of patch management to solve these issues. The authors have considered that the patch release and update policy is either time-driven or event-driven. In time driven approach, the vendors should distribute the patches periodically while in event driven, the vendors should distribute the patch when a fixed amount of vulnerabilities are discovered. Later, Okamura et al. [30] proposed a patch management model and extended the work done by Cavusoglu et al. [25]. Authors have modeled the vulnerability discovery process to evaluate the optimal patch release time in terms of cost. The work concludes the non-periodic patch release policy as a uniform approach. Dey et al. [19] developed optimal release policies for patches. They provided analytical model to determine the optimal patch release time. Okhravi and Nicol developed a patch management strategies based on number of vulnerabilities discovered [16]. They proposed an analytical model to determine the patch timing. Though they didn't use any specific model patch model but initiated the discussion for need of patch modeling. Wang et al. [17] presented a patching process in Industrial control systems. They deployed Famous Bass model to see the trend of patching behavior. In all the above described literature it was assumed that vulnerability discovery and patching are separate process and prediction of vulnerability has no effect due to patching. But in reality it has some impact which has been raised in few of the research work [5, 18]. In the next section, we present a framework for vulnerability discovery and patching with categorization of the vulnerabilities into direct and indirect vulnerabilities. Here we have proposed a new approach for modeling direct and indirect vulnerabilities discovery with a fixing lag in patching the discovered vulnerabilities. By direct vulnerability we mean to say the vulnerabilities which are directly reported to the vendor after their discovery. Indirect vulnerabilities are those which are discovered during the fixing of discovered vulnerabilities.

3 Modeling Framework

In this study, we have used the methodology applied in Non Homogenous Poisson Process (NHPP) based Software Reliability Growth Models which is now being applied to Vulnerability Discovery Models as well [21].

3.1 Assumptions

The assumptions during model development are as follows:

  i Initially the number of vulnerabilities detected are zero i.e. at, t = 0, V(0) = 0.
  ii The total no. of vulnerabilities detected depends on the number of remaining or unresolved vulnerabilities.
  iii The no. of vulnerabilities in the software is finite.
  iv Vulnerability detection rate is not constant and it can change at any point.
  v Vulnerabilities are of two types i.e. direct and indirect.

3.2 Notations

$\overline{V}$:   Total number of Vulnerabilities present in the software.
$V(t)$:   Expected number of Vulnerabilities detected in the time interval$(0,t]$.
$r(t)$:   Time dependent rate of Vulnerability removal per remaining Vulnerabilities.
$V_{d1}(t)$: Cumulative number of direct vulnerabilities discovered by time t.
$V_{d2}(t)$: Cumulative number of indirect vulnerabilities discovered by time t.
$V_{p1}(t)$: Cumulative number of direct vulnerabilities patched by time t.
$V_{p2}(t)$: Cumulative number of indirect vulnerabilities patched by time t.

3.3 Modeling Vulnerability Discovery and Patching of Direct Vulnerabilities

Based on the assumptions above we have the differential equation corresponding to direct vulnerabilities is given by

$$\frac{dV_{d1}}{dt} = r(t)(V_1 - V_{d1}) \tag{1}$$

Solving (1) using the initial condition we get

$$V_{d1}(t) = V_1 \left(1 - \exp\left(-\int_0^t r(s)ds \right) \right) \tag{2}$$

Where r(t) is the vulnerability detection rate for direct vulnerability and V_1 is the total number of direct vulnerabilities. We can obtain different $V_{d1}(t)$ by changing r(s) in Eq. (2).

Now vulnerability patching of direct vulnerability can be regarded as a delayed process of direct vulnerability discovery process (DVDP). The process of fixing the vulnerability by patch can be constant, time dependent or random. If the fixing lag is not random the vulnerability patching of direct vulnerability can be derived from DVDP as $V_{p1}(t) = V_{d1}(t - \delta(t))$. Otherwise we have $V_{p1}(t) = E_{\delta(t)}[V_{d1}(t - \delta(t))]$ if $\delta(t)$ is a random variable. In particular if we assume the fixing lag to be a exponential random variable i.e. $\delta(t) = \exp(ct)$ we will have

$$V_{p1} = c \int\limits_0^t V_{d1}(t - s) \exp(-cs) ds \tag{3}$$

Taking the derivatives of both sides with respect to t, we can obtain that:

$$\lambda_{p1}(t) = \frac{dV_{p1}}{dt} = c(V_{d1}(t) - V_{p1}(t)) \tag{4}$$

Which shows that expected number of vulnerabilities patched is proportional to the number of direct vulnerabilities discovered but not patched. Here c is the vulnerability patching rate.

3.4 Modeling Vulnerability Discovery and Patching of Indirect Vulnerabilities

Indirect vulnerabilities are those which are discovered after patching of corresponding direct vulnerabilities. Hence, the proportion of the indirect vulnerabilities which can be discovered in the Indirect vulnerabilities is equal to the proportion of the patched direct vulnerabilities in the direct vulnerability. Suppose the number of Indirect vulnerabilities is V_2. Then, the expected number of Indirect vulnerabilities to be discovered is $V_2 V_{p1}(t)/V_1$ up to time t. Furthermore, because direct and Indirect vulnerabilities are discovered by the same environment it is reasonable to assume that the vulnerability discovery rate for Indirect vulnerability is the same as that of direct vulnerability. Hence:

$$\frac{dV_{d2}}{dt} = b(t)\left(\frac{V_2 V_{p1}(t)}{V_1} - V_{d2}(t)\right) \tag{5}$$

On solving using initial condition of $V_{d2}(0) = 0$ we have

$$V_{d2}(t) = \frac{V_2 V_{p1}(t)}{V_1} - \frac{V_2}{V_1}\exp\left(-\int\limits_0^t b(s)ds\right)\int\limits_0^t \lambda_{p1}(s)\exp\left(\int\limits_0^s b(u)du\right)ds \tag{6}$$

Taking $b(t) = b$ we get

$$V_{d2}(t) = \frac{V_2 V_{p1}(t)}{V_1} - \frac{V_2}{V_1}\exp(-bt)\int_0^t \lambda_{p1}(s)\exp(bs)ds \qquad (7)$$

Based on the detection process of Indirect vulnerabilities, the corresponding patching process can be obtained as a delayed process as for direct vulnerabilities. Thus, with different assumptions for the debugging delay, $V_{p2}(t)$ of vulnerability patching process of Indirect vulnerability can be derived accordingly.

4 Combined Model

With the vulnerability discovery and patching model of direct and indirect vulnerabilities we can get the combined model. Here $\bar{V} = V_1 + V_2$, $V(t) = V_{d1}(t) + V_{d2}(t)$ and $V_p(t) = V_{p1}(t) + V_{p2}(t)$.

4.1 Time Dependent Fixing Lag (Model 1)

Now we will develop the combined model for the time dependent and random lag between vulnerability discovery and patching. As considering constant lag looks impractical. In practice, the vulnerabilities discovered in the after a long time gap is difficult to fix. To model such a phenomenon, we assume the fixing lag is dependent on the discovery time $\delta(t) = \frac{\ln(1+\gamma t)}{b}$ where $0 < \gamma < b$. Accordingly the vulnerability patching model for the two types of vulnerabilities are

$$V_{pi}(t) = V_{di}\left(t - \frac{\ln(1+\gamma t)}{b}\right) \quad i = 1,2. \qquad (8)$$

Under this assumption we have

$$V_{p1}(t) = V_{d1}\left(t - \frac{\ln(1+\gamma t)}{b}\right) = \bar{V}p\left(1 - (1+\gamma t)e^{-bt}\right) \qquad (9)$$

Based on Eqs. (6) and (9) $V_{d2}(t)$ can be derived. Then $V_d(t)$ for the combined vulnerability discovery process can be given as

$$V_d(t) = \bar{V}\left(1 - e^{-bt}\right) + \left(\bar{V}(1-p)\right)\left(bt + \frac{b\gamma t^2}{2}\right)e^{-bt} \qquad (10)$$

Now because $V_p(t) = V_d\left(t - \left(\frac{\ln(1+\gamma t)}{b}\right)\right)$ the combined model for vulnerability patching can be derived as follow

$$V_p(t) = \overline{V}p\left(1 - (1+\gamma t)e^{-bt}\right) -$$
$$\overline{V}(1-p)(1+\gamma t)\left(bt - (1+\gamma t)\ln(1+\gamma t) + \frac{b\gamma t^2}{2} + \frac{\gamma \ln^2(1+\gamma t)}{2b}\right)e^{-bt} \quad (11)$$

4.2 Exponentially Distributed Random Time Lag (Model 2)

As explained above the number of vulnerabilities patched during $(t, t + \Delta t)$ in this case is proportional to the number of vulnerabilities discovered but not patched at time t. Based on Eq. (3) $V_{p1}(t)$ is given by

$$V_{p1}(t) = \begin{cases} \overline{V}p\left(1 - (1+bt)e^{-bt}\right); b = c \\ \overline{V}p\left(1 + \frac{be^{-ct} - ce^{-bt}}{c-b}\right); b \neq c \end{cases} \quad (12)$$

$V_{d2}(t)$ can be derived on the basis of $V_{p1}(t)$ according to Eq. (7) and $V_d(t)$ is given by

$$V_d(t) = \begin{cases} \overline{V}p\left(1 - e^{-bt}\right) - \overline{V}(1-p)\left(bt + \frac{b^2 t^2}{2}\right)e^{-bt}; b = c \\ \overline{V}p\left(1 - e^{-bt}\right) - \overline{V}(1-p)\left(\frac{bcte^{-bt}}{c-b} + \frac{b^2\left(e^{-ct} - e^{-bt}\right)}{(c-b)^2}\right)e^{-bt}; c \neq b \end{cases} \quad (13)$$

From $V_{p1} = c\int_0^t V_{d1}(t-s)\exp(-cs)ds$ we note that $V_p = c\int_0^t V_d(t-s)\exp(-cs)ds$ also holds therefore $V_p(t)$ can be obtained as

$$V_p(t) = \begin{cases} \overline{V}p\left(1 - (1+bt)e^{-bt}\right) - \overline{V}(1-p)\left(\frac{b^2 t^2}{2} + \frac{b^3 t^3}{6}\right)e^{-bt}; c = b \\ \overline{V}p\left(1 + \frac{(be^{-ct} - ce^{-bt})}{(c-b)}\right) - \frac{\overline{V}bc(1-p)}{(c-b)^2}\left(\frac{(b+c)\left(e^{-ct} - e^{-bt}\right)}{(c-b)} + bte^{-ct} + cte^{-bt}\right); c \neq b \end{cases}$$
$$(14)$$

5 Parameter Estimation

Parameters of the model are estimated by using Statistical Package for Social Sciences (SPSS). The data set used for numerical illustration in this study is extracted from National vulnerability database (NVD) for most severe vulnerabilities (Common vulnerability scoring system (CVSS) score more than 8) of Google chrome from year 2009–2018 [6]. The parameter estimation results for model 1 & 2 are given in Table 1. For comparison purpose, we also fit the data by the two proposed models with simplified models of Model 1 & 2 with p = 1, which are abbreviated as Model 1' and Model 2' respectively. As we can clearly see from Table 1, the estimated parameter $\overline{V}$ (the total number of vulnerabilities) in the two proposed models 1 & 2 are close to each other. On the contrary, the models Model 1'& Model 2', which assume no dependent faults exist, produce quite large $\overline{V}$. Therefore, ignoring the indirect vulnerabilities patched in the model would result in incorrect total number of vulnerabilities. Also the result shows that the exponentially distributed fixing lag model fits the data set best.

Table 1. Parameter estimation results

Parameters	$\overline{V}$	b	c/γ	p	MSE
Model 1	63.21	0.013	0.0031	0.854	15.56
Model 2	64.44	0.024	0.032	0.793	7.88
Model 1'	78.36	0.1193	0.2330	–	47.1220
Model 2'	76.35	0.1404	0.1581	–	56.9210

6   Conclusion and Future Work

In this work a new approach for vulnerability prediction with respect to patching is developed. The proposed model considers the time lag between vulnerability discovery and patching and categorizes vulnerabilities into two types. The proposed model has been compared with existing models with no indirect vulnerabilities considered. The proposed model with indirect vulnerability considered performs well in comparison to existing models for the data set. This work can be further enhanced to determine the optimal patch release time considering the proposed model.

References

1. Alhazmi, O.H., Malaiya, Y.K.: Modeling the vulnerability discovery process. In: 16th IEEE International Symposium on Software Reliability Engineering. ISSRE 2005, pp. 10-pp. IEEE (2005)
2. Alhazmi, O.H., Malaiya, Y.K.: Application of vulnerability discovery models to major operating systems. IEEE Trans. Reliab. 57(1), 14–22 (2008)
3. Anand, A., Das, S., Aggrawal, D., Klochkov, Y.: Vulnerability discovery modelling for software with multi-versions. In: Ram, M., Davim, J. (eds.) Advances in Reliability and System Engineering. Management and Industrial Engineering, pp. 255–265. Springer, Cham (2017). https://doi.org/10.1007/978-3-319-48875-2_11
4. Anderson, R.: Security in open versus closed systems—the dance of Boltzmann, Coase and Moore. Technical report, Cambridge University, England, pp. 1–15 (2002)
5. Bhatt, N., Anand, A., Yadavalli, V.S.S., Kumar, V.: Modeling and characterizing software vulnerabilities. Int. J. Math. Eng. Manag. Sci. 2(4), 288–299 (2017)
6. National Vulnerability Database. https://nvd.nist.gov/
7. Joh, H.C., Kim, J., Malaiya, Y.K.: Vulnerability discovery modeling using Weibull distribution. In: 19th International Symposium on Software Reliability Engineering. ISSRE 2008, pp. 299–300. IEEE (2008)
8. Kapur, P.K., Yadavali, V.S.S., Shrivastava, A.K.: A comparative study of vulnerability discovery modeling and software reliability growth modeling. In: 2015 International Conference on Futuristic Trends on Computational Analysis and Knowledge Management (ABLAZE), pp. 246–251. IEEE (2015)

9. Kim, J., Malaiya, Y.K., Ray, I.: Vulnerability discovery in multi-version software systems. In: 10th IEEE High Assurance Systems Engineering Symposium. HASE 2007, pp. 141–148. IEEE (2007)

10. Algarni, A., Malaiya, Y.: Software vulnerability markets: discoverers and buyers. Int. J. Comput., Inf. Sci. Eng. 8(3), 71–81 (2014)

11. Rescorla, E.: Is finding security holes a good idea? IEEE Secur. Priv. 3(1), 14–19 (2005)

12. Shrivastava, A.K., Sharma, R., Kapur, P.K.: Vulnerability discovery model for a software system using stochastic differential equation. In: 2015 International Conference on Futuristic Trends on Computational Analysis and Knowledge Management (ABLAZE), pp. 199–205. IEEE (2015)

13. Arora, A., Telang, R., Xu, H.: Optimal policy for software vulnerability disclosure. Manag. Sci. 54(4), 642–656 (2008)

14. Alhazmi, O.H., Malaiya, Y.K., Ray, I.: Measuring, analyzing and predicting security vulnerabilities in software systems. Comput. Secur. 26(3), 219–228 (2007)

15. Sharma, R., Sibal, R., Shrivastava, A.K.: Vulnerability discovery modeling for open and closed source software. Int. J. Secur. Softw. Eng. (IJSSE) 7(4), 19–38 (2016)

16. Okhravi, H., Nicol, D.: Evaluation of patch management strategies. Int. J. Comput. Intell.: Theory Pract. 3(2), 109–117 (2008)

17. Wang, B., Li, X., de Aguiar, L.P., Menasche, D.S., Shafiq, Z.: Characterizing and modeling patching practices of industrial control systems. Proc. ACM Meas. Anal. Comput. Syst. 1(1), 18 (2017)

18. Kansal, Y., Kumar, D., Kapur, P.K.: Vulnerability patch modeling. Int. J. Reliab. Qual. Saf. Eng. 23(06), 1640013 (2016)

19. Dey, D., Lahiri, A., Zhang, G.: Optimal policies for security patch management. INFORMS J. Comput. 27(3), 462–477 (2015)

20. Ozment, A.: Improving vulnerability discovery models. In: Proceedings of the 2007 ACM Workshop on Quality of Protection, pp. 6–11. ACM (2007)

21. Kapur, P.K., Pham, H., Gupta, A., Jha, P.C.: Software Reliability Assessment with OR Applications. Springer, London (2011). https://doi.org/10.1007/978-0-85729-204-9

22. Beattie, S., Arnold, S., Cowan, C., Wagle, P., Wright, C., Shostack, A.: Timing the application of security patches for optimal uptime. LISA 2, 233–242 (2002)

23. Zhu, X., Cao, C., Zhang, J.: Vulnerability severity prediction and risk metric modeling for software. J. Appl. Intell. 47(1), 828–836 (2017)

24. Pfleeger, C.P., Pfleeger, S.L.: Security in Computing. Prentice Hall Professional Technical Reference, Upper Saddle River (2002)

25. Cavusoglu, H., Cavusoglu, H., Zhang, J.: Security patch management: share the burden or share the damage? Manag. Sci. 54(4), 657–670 (2008)

26. Sutton, M., Greene, A., Amini, P.: Fuzzing: Brute Force Vulnerability Discovery. Pearson Education, London (2007)

27. Telang, R., Wattal, S.: An empirical analysis of the impact of software vulnerability announcements on firm stock price. IEEE Trans. Softw. Eng. 33(8), 544–557 (2007)

28. Massacci, F., Nguyen, V.H.: An empirical methodology to evaluate vulnerability discovery models. IEEE Trans. Softw. Eng. 40(12), 1147–1162 (2014)

29. Bishop, M., Bailey, D.: A critical analysis of vulnerability taxonomies (No. CSE-96–11). California Univ Davis Dept of Computer Science (1996)

30. Okamura, H., Tokuzane, M., Dohi, T.: Optimal security patch release timing under non-homogeneous vulnerability-discovery processes. In: 20th International Symposium on Software Reliability Engineering, pp. 120–128. IEEE (2009)

An Implementation of Malware Detection System Using Hybrid C4.5 Decision Tree Algorithm

Ajay Kumar[✉], Shashank Sheshar Singh, Kuldeep Singh,
Harish Kumar Shakya, and Bhaskar Biswas

Department of Computer Science and Engineering,
Indian Institute of Technology (BHU), Varanasi 221005, India
{ajayk.rs.cse16,shashankss.rs.cse16,kuldeep.rs.cse13,hkshakya.rs.cse,
bhaskar.cse}@iitbhu.ac.in

Abstract. Malware (**Ma**licious Soft**ware**) is a program that can harm the computers/mobiles/networks and affects their normal functioning. As the computational needs are diversified, security threats are also getting complex to be detected. The traditional approaches require updation and are not able to cover the entire definitions of each kind of malicious code patterns. Therefore, an improvement in traditional approach is required to be incorporated. In this work, it is intended to search an adaptive approach by which the machine can learn and update itself from the last learning. Two different appropriate data models namely C4.5 decision tree and Bayes classifier have been used in this paper. Both the data models are promising and provide accurate classification with some limitations. To make improvement on it, a hybrid classification approach is designed using C4.5 decision tree and Bayes classifier. This work is implemented in JAVA and performance is evaluated on several parameters such as classification accuracy, space and time complexity. As per the obtained results, it is evident that the proposed technique is more accurate and efficient as compared to the respective implemented algorithms.

Keywords: Malware detection · Decision tree
Bayes theorem · Machine learning · Classification

1 Introduction

Malwares, also termed as malicious softwares, are basically computer programs that are designed to destroy the security of a computer or computers in a network [2]. Malware is a generic term represents several types of undesirable programs like viruses, trojans, worms, bots, and so on. The main motive of these programs can be economic targets or for promotional activities. There are a number of approaches recently developed for malware detection, some of them are signature-based techniques [11] and behavior-based techniques [4]. Most of the

© Springer Nature Singapore Pte Ltd. 2019
A. K. Luhach et al. (Eds.): ICAICR 2018, CCIS 956, pp. 579–589, 2019.
https://doi.org/10.1007/978-981-13-3143-5_48

commercial malware detection techniques are based on signatures. Signatures are sequence of unique bytes present within a malicious program in files which are already infected by malwares [18]. To find out the infected files, it is required to have a large database of malware signatures to determine whether a signature of malware is present or not. Signature-based malware detection methods are not effective for newly introduced malicious programs; additionally, these techniques are unable to find infection over the network. Furthermore, the computational complexity increases when we compare new input sample to the large malware database. Thus, a new technique is required to identify the behavior of the infected files in a computer or network. For this purpose, behavior analysis based techniques are developed to identify the malwares.

Basically, analyzing the behavior of malicious programs, machine learning-based approaches are utilized. The main advantages of these approaches are efficient classification between malicious and non malicious files and low computational complexity as compared to the signature based techniques. The machine learning has three key phases of the data analysis named as preprocessing, learning and classification. During preprocessing phase, data is processed in order to prepare the format of data which is acceptable with the algorithm. The next phase uses transformed data with the mathematical models or data models to identify the meaningful patterns from the available data. In classification phase, the meaningful data patterns, which we obtained after learning phase, are used to classify the malware files and benign (supportive) files. In this paper, behavior-based techniques are investigated for finding efficient and accurate classification of malwares. For this, different machine learning algorithms are evaluated and two most promising approaches namely C4.5 decision tree and Bayesian classifier are selected for further solution development. Both the techniques work differently but provide promising results when applied both in a particular order.

2 Literature Review

A malware detector normally tries to find malicious softwares or files based on APIs (Application Programming Interfaces) of the system or by other techniques. A major issue of this approach is to collect relevant information about malware. Additionally, call graph matching is an NP-complete problem and computationally complex. Using the call graphs of APIs of a system, Elhadi et al. [5] proposed a system to detect malicious files. In this approach, each malware sample is expressed as a call graph in which a node represents integrated api calls with the operating system resource and dependencies between such nodes are represented by the edges. After the call graph construction, similarity of the input sample is computed based on graph matching algorithm. To cope with the NP-completeness of the graph matching problem, graph edit distance algorithm is used. Simplification of reducing the computational complexity is based on integrated API call graph. Experimental results show classification accuracy as 98%.

The volume of malware is growing exponentially and creating serious security problems. Therefore, effective malware detection becomes an essential domain of research in digital security. The signature-based method fails to detect newly introduced malware which are more complex from earlier one. Santos et al. proposed a data mining-based method for the detection of unknown malwares [14] in which frequency of the opcode sequences are used. Furthermore, they described a technique for mining the relevance of opcodes and assess the frequency of each opcode sequence. In addition, the validation of the approach shows that proposed method is capable to detect unknown malware. Machine learning methods improve the detection speed and adapts new malwares. The performance of such approaches are based on the induction algorithms applied. To get benefits from different multiple classifiers and to exploit their strengths, Menahem et al. suggested an ensemble approach [10] that combines multiple classifiers in the system and results of these classifiers are also combined to compute the desired output. Authors performed experiments with different combinations of classifiers to optimize the classification accuracy and execution time. Recently Saxe et al. [15] introduce the concept of deep neural network with the Bayesian calibration model in malware detection system, performance evaluation of which shows a high detection rate of 95% with 0.1% false positive rate.

The recently developed systems work on Detection, Alert and Response (eDare). The key aim is filtering Web traffic from malicious softwares or files. A powerful network scanner is used to filter such files originating from known sources and the remaining traffic originating from unknown is filtered based on Machine Learning (ML) algorithms. Elovici et al. utilize Decision trees, Neural Networks and Bayesian Networks to analyze the malicious code patterns [3,6]. The suggested algorithm provides better results.

Mobile malware is growing much rapidly. This becomes more troublesome on Android platform because the android source codes are available to all i.e. open platform. Recently, lots of new malwares having advanced evasion capabilities are introducing day-by-day which are more difficult to detect by the traditional approaches. Yerima et al. investigated and proposed a model based on machine learning to detect such malwares [19] which is parallel in nature. A composite data model is constructed using parallel combination of heterogeneous classifiers. The performance of the data model under different combinations shows improvement in detection accuracy. Recently, Hou et al. [8] work on mobile malware detection extracts API calls from smali files and categorized into code blocks. They applied deep belief network, a deep learning approach on these code blocks to unknown malware detection system.

A major issue with a malware detection system is scalability as new malwares are introducing every day. To tackle this issue, Tamersoy et al. presented a new scalable algorithm viz. Aesop [17]. It uses a large dataset consisting of list of files obtained from the Norton Community Watch members and finds relations of those files that frequently appear together. The performance results show a 0.9961 true positive rate and 0.0001 false positive rates. Bai et al. proposed a new malware detection system based on 'format information' of portable executable files [1]. They extracted 197 features after analyzing the portable executable files. Large number of features degrade system performance, only relevant features are selected based on feature selection algorithm and trained with the classification algorithms. Experiment results show the classification accuracy to a high of 99.1%. The performance of detection scheme and its ability to detect unknown malwares make it more promising. Experimental results of identifying new malware are not accurate but still able to identify 97.6% of new malwares with 1.3% false positive rates.

Accuracy is not a major issue in process of comparing signature of new input sample with large database of signatures because a classifiers can be tuned to the desired level of false negative positive rates. Detection speed is the main problem in comparing signatures of large databases. As the adversarial dissimulation techniques of malware continue to evolve, computational complexity issues will soon show its limitations involved in emulation and parsing schemes [16]. The proposed approach resolves this issue of detection speed. It is on the ground that the less number of tree branches remains after prunning of decision tree.

Traditional C4.5 algorithm proposed by Quinlan [13] outputs a decision tree, in which an internal node represents a test on an attribute followed by its result on the corresponding branch and a leave node represents the final decision in terms of class label. The Naive Bayes classification algorithm is a powerful algorithm of which representation is based on the class probability and conditional probability hence the name probabilistic classifier. The assumption of independency among attributes sets its name to be naive although rarely found in real data. Crux of the algorithm is Bayes theorem proposed by Thomas Bayes.

3   Proposed Work

The proposed work is intended to find a novel approach to optimize the performance of detection rate. Optimization is based on the classification approaches of machine learning algorithm. It is also required to enhance the adaptability of the algorithm in terms of the computational complexity. Initially, the machine learning algorithms learn on specified patterns of data and prepare data model. The prepared data model is used to distinguish different patterns available in infected and benign files. In order to provide demonstration of the proposed technique, two different modules are prepared namely data preprocessing and proposed classification.

3.1   Data Preprocessing

Data preprocessing is done to make data more effective to be used in classification algorithms. In this module, data is processed for cleaning, transforming and enhancing the quality. A malware dataset that contains the malicious and normal opcode patterns, is collected from the internet source. This is a kind of labeled data which can be used with the normal text classification approaches. A relational attribute-based dataset is prepared by using the given samples in the dataset. But, in order to make it more effective, the data is preprocessed by the term frequency. The term frequency can be computed as

$$term \quad frequency = \frac{n_1}{n_2}$$

where n_1 is the total times a code token appeared, and n_2 is total amount of tokens available. In order to understand the preprocessing step, we consider an example:

Mov ax, 000h

Add [0ba1fh], c1

Push cs

Add [si + 0CD09h], dh

After preprocessing, the above example can be converted to following set of attributes given in Table 1.

Table 1. Example of preprocessing

Mov	Push	Add
1	1	2

After computation of term frequency, the above listed attributes are converted as given in Table 2.

Table 2. Example of finalized dataset

Mov	Push	Add	Class
0.25	0.25	0.50	Normal

3.2 Proposed Model

Several reasons limit the accuracy and applicability of traditional C4.5 algorithm and ID3 algorithm [12] (an earlier version of C4.5 proposed by Quinlan). One of them is the attribute selection measure used in these algorithms. ID3 algorithm applies information gain as selection measure that biases towards several outcomes [7]. C4.5 uses gain ratio that removes the problem of information gain but it motivates unbalanced splitting of attributes which results in unbalanced tree. To improve the accuracy we applied a hybrid approach in which naive bayes classification algorithm is used in conjunction with the traditional C4.5. The whole process of our model is depicted in Fig. 1.

Input Data. The input data or training sample is a raw data and it may be either in structured or unstructured format. The proposed model accepts structured data in the form of ARFF (Attribute-Relation File Format) data or the data in CSV (Comma Separated Value) format.

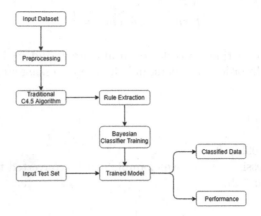

Fig. 1. Proposed data model

Preprocessing is used when the data available for modeling is not in appropriate format. Preprocessing step removes several types of the unwanted symbols inherently (or introduced by human error) present in the input data such as noisy data, missing values etc. Data available after the preprocessing is now appropriate for data modeling.

Traditional C4.5 Algorithm. The preprocessed input dataset is used as input to the C4.5 algorithm in the form of instance data. Instances are the objects of dataset row which are processed using C4.5 algorithm and converted to a decision tree. A sample decision tree is shown in Fig. 2.

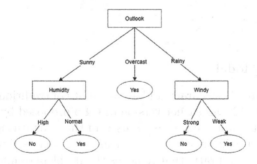

Fig. 2. Decision tree sample

Rule Extraction. The C4.5 algorithm generates output in the form of decision tree from which decision rules can be extracted. One unique decision rule is generated by traversing from the root to a leave node following each branch of the decision tree. This traversing process is used as a decision rule to classify the input samples. For example, the given sample decision tree in Fig. 2 can be converted to the following decision rules (if then else rules).

If Outlook = 'sunny' and humidity = 'high' then

Play tennis = 'No'

Else if Outlook = 'sunny' and humidity = 'normal' then

Play tennis = 'Yes'

End if

Bayesian Classifier Training. The extracted rules from C4.5 decision tree are evaluated again by Bayesian classifier. Bayesian classifier is probabilistic in nature and its represents each training sample in the form of class and conditional probability. For each training sample, it computes the probability of each class and the conditional probability (using Bayes theorem) given each class value. Finally, the training sample is assigned to the class having larger conditional probability value. This process is applied for all training samples in the datasets which results final trained hybrid model.

Test Set Input. Once the model is trained, it needs to be validated. For validation of the model, a completely new input sample (test set) is used. The test set is processed in the same manner as the training to compute the accuracy of the model. After the computation over test set input, if the predicted result is same as the observed output, classification accuracy is increased otherwise error is increased.

Performance. This is final stage of our model where k-fold cross-validation [9] is employed to compute the different performance metrics. This work evaluates the proposed model on accuracy, error, time, and space complexity.

3.3   Proposed Algorithm

Above steps in Algorithm 1 explain the overall process of the proposed model.

Algorithm 1. Hybrid C4.5 Algorithm

Input: Dataset D, Test Dataset T.

Output: Classified data.

1: A = [column, rows]
2: A = ReadDataset(D)
3: Pa = PreProcess(A)
4: [model, validation] = $Train\_C4.5(Pa, num\_folds)$
5: $B\_model = Train\_Bayes(Pa)$
6: $T\_rule = Extract\_Rules(model)$
7: $[R\_rule, Rindex] = ValidateRule(T\_rule, B\_model)$
8: $Ref\_rule = PrunRules(R\_rule, Rindex)$
9: $[Accuracy, ErrorRate, Decision] = R\_ruleClassify(T)$

Algorithm Description. The entire process of the proposed data model is summarized in the above steps. Inputs to the algorithm are input dataset and the test input. Line 1 declares matrix A with the similar size of rows and columns of the input dataset. Function ReadDataset(D) reads the data row and column-wise and the extracted contents of data is stored in matrix A. Data is preprocessed using function PreProcess(A) in line 3. This function accepts the matrix data A and returns the preprocessed data as defined in Sect. 3. Line 4 employs the C4.5 decision tree algorithm that accepts the preprocessed data and the number of folds as input arguments to validate the training process of the system. After successful training, this algorithm returns the decision tree data model that incorporates the learned patterns over the tree. Further line 5 employs $Train\_Bayes(Pa)$ function to train the Bayesian classifier using the preprocessed data. $Extract\_Rules(model)$ function in line 6 extract the rules form the decision tree. In line 7, $ValidateRule(T\_rule, B\_model)$ function is used to validate rules using the trained Bayes model, B_model and the rules extracted from the decision tree, T_rule. $PrunRules(R\_rule, Rindex)$ function in line 8 prunes the poor or ambiguous rules having arguments index, Rindex and the list of appropriate rules, R_rule. Finally R_rule Classify function is called to classify the new input testing set that returns Accuracy, Error rate and the Decisions of the input data.

4   Result Analysis

This section provides the comparative analysis between the proposed algorithm and the existing base algorithms (C4.5 and Naive bayes).

Accuracy. In the context of data mining, the classification accuracy of a model is defined as the number of data samples/instances correctly classified by the model.

Figure 3 shows the comparative performance of Bayesian classifier, Traditional C4.5 algorithm and proposed Hybrid C4.5 algorithm. The obtained result shows that Bayesian classifier and Traditional C4.5 algorithm provide less accurate results as compared to the proposed Hybrid C4.5 algorithm.

Error Rate. The error rate demonstrates the amount of data samples/instances misclassified by the trained data model. The comparative error rate is shown in Fig. 3b. Hybrid C4.5 algorithm shows less error rate as compared to traditional implemented classifiers algorithms. Thus the proposed method is much adoptable as compared to traditional classification techniques.

Memory Consumption. The amount of memory required by the algorithmic constructs for the selected algorithm (model) is known as the memory or space consumed by that model. The obtained result clearly shows that if the amount of data for training process increases, it leads to increment in memory consumption of the system. The Fig. 3c shows that the memory consumption of proposed Hybrid C4.5 algorithm is more than that of traditional C4.5 and Bayesian classification algorithm.

Learning/Training Time. The total amount of time required by the input data samples/instances to train the data model. This is also known as model

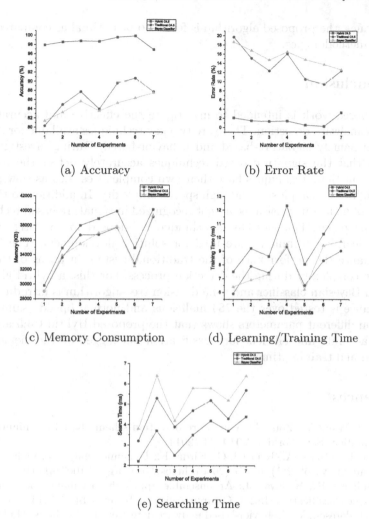

(a) Accuracy

(b) Error Rate

(c) Memory Consumption

(d) Learning/Training Time

(e) Searching Time

Fig. 3. Results on different parameters

learning time. Figure 3d shows the comparative training time of the proposed and the base algorithms. The learning (training) time of the proposed model is higher as compared to the traditional approaches.

Search Time. It is also known as the classification time which is the time required to classify a test set input based on the trained data model. The search time of the implemented algorithms are shown in Fig. 3e. Evaluated outcomes shows that the Hybrid C4.5 algorithm takes much less time to classify as compared to the traditional algorithm. This is because the less amount of tree branches are generated after the pruning process.

This section provided the results analysis of the proposed algorithm with respect to the other similar machine learning algorithms. According to obtained performance, the proposed algorithm is found to be optimal as compared to the existing methodologies.

5 Conclusion

The proposed work is intended to investigate the effective and accurate technique for malware detection. There are two key techniques available for malware detection namely signature-based and behavior-based. During investigation, it is found that the signature based techniques accurately detect the malicious patterns but these techniques have their own complexities such as slow processing or high time complexity and high space complexity. In addition to that new patterns of malicious programs are not recognized in signature based techniques.

In this paper, behavior-based technique is adopted for investigation and machine learning techniques are used for solution development. The key aim is to enhance the performance of the traditional system in terms of the space and time complexity during the detection process. For this, a hybrid algorithm based on Bayesian classifier and C4.5 decision tree algorithm is introduced. The performance is tested over the 783 malicious and normal opcode samples and results on different parameters shows that the proposed Hybrid C4.5 algorithm is more accurate and efficient for classification but lagged on the memory consumption and training time.

References

1. Bai, J., Wang, J., Zou, G.: A malware detection scheme based on mining format information. Sci. World J. **2014**, 11 (2014)
2. Bayer, U., Moser, A., Kruegel, C., Kirda, E.: Dynamic analysis of malicious code. J. Comput. Virol. **2**(1), 67–77 (2006). https://doi.org/10.1007/s11416-006-0012-2
3. Choudhary, R., Raikwal, J.: An ensemble approach to enhance performance of webpage classification. Int. J. Comput. Sci. Inf. Technol. **5**(4), 5614–5619 (2014)
4. Christodorescu, M.: Behavior-based malware detection. Ph.D. thesis, Madison, WI, USA (2007). aAI3278879
5. Elhadi, A.A.E., Maarof, M.A., Barry, B.I., Hamza, H.: Enhancing the detection of metamorphic malware using call graphs. Comput. Secur. **46**, 62–78 (2014). www.sciencedirect.com/science/article/pii/S0167404814001060
6. Elovici, Y., Shabtai, A., Moskovitch, R., Tahan, G., Glezer, C.: Applying machine learning techniques for detection of malicious code in network traffic. In: Hertzberg, J., Beetz, M., Englert, R. (eds.) KI 2007. LNCS (LNAI), vol. 4667, pp. 44–50. Springer, Heidelberg (2007). https://doi.org/10.1007/978-3-540-74565-5_5
7. Han, J., Pei, J., Kamber, M.: Data Mining: Concepts and Techniques. Morgan Kaufmann, Burlington (2011)
8. Hou, S., Saas, A., Ye, Y., Chen, L.: Droiddelver: an android malware detection system using deep belief network based on API call blocks. In: Song, S., Tong, Y. (eds.) Web-Age Information Management, pp. 54–66. Springer International Publishing, Cham (2016). https://doi.org/10.1007/978-3-319-47121-1_5
9. Kohavi, R.: A Study of Cross-Validation and Bootstrap for Accuracy Estimation and Model Selection, pp. 1137–1143. Morgan Kaufmann, Burlington (1995)

10. Menahem, E., Shabtai, A., Rokach, L., Elovici, Y.: Improving malware detection by applying multi-inducer ensemble. Comput. Stat. Data Anal. **53**(4), 1483–1494 (2009). https://doi.org/10.1016/j.csda.2008.10.015

11. Moskovitch, R., Feher, C., Elovici, Y.: A chronological evaluation of unknown malcode detection. In: Chen, H., Yang, C.C., Chau, M., Li, S.H. (eds.) Intelligence and Security Informatics, PAISI 2009. Lecture Notes in Computer Science, vol. 5477, pp. 112–117. Springer, Heidelberg (2009). https://doi.org/10.1007/978-3-642-01393-5_12

12. Quinlan, J.R.: Induction of decision trees. Mach. Learn. **1**(1), 81–106 (1986). https://doi.org/10.1023/A:1022643204877

13. Quinlan, J.R.: C4.5: Programs for Machine Learning. Morgan Kaufmann Publishers Inc., San Francisco (1993)

14. Santos, I., Brezo, F., Ugarte-Pedrero, X., Bringas, P.G.: Opcode sequences as representation of executables for data-mining-based unknown malware detection. Inf. Sci. **231**, 64–82 (2013). https://doi.org/10.1016/j.ins.2011.08.020

15. Saxe, J., Berlin, K.: Deep neural network based malware detection using two dimensional binary program features. In: Proceedings of the 2015 10th International Conference on Malicious and Unwanted Software (MALWARE), MALWARE 2015 pp. 11–20. IEEE Computer Society, Washington (2015). https://doi.org/10.1109/MALWARE.2015.7413680

16. Spinellis, D.: Reliable identification of bounded-length viruses is NP-complete. IEEE Trans. Inf. Theory **49**(1), 280–284 (2003)

17. Tamersoy, A., Roundy, K., Chau, D.H.: Guilt by association: large scale malware detection by mining file-relation graphs. In: Proceedings of the 20th ACM SIGKDD International Conference on Knowledge Discovery and Data Mining, KDD 2014, pp. 1524–1533. ACM, New York (2014). https://doi.org/10.1145/2623330.2623342

18. Ye, Y., et al.: Combining file content and file relations for cloud based malware detection. In: Proceedings of the 17th ACM SIGKDD International Conference on Knowledge Discovery and Data Mining, KDD 2011, pp. 222–230. ACM, New York (2011). https://doi.org/10.1145/2020408.2020448

19. Yerima, S.Y., Sezer, S., Muttik, I.: Android malware detection using parallel machine learning classifiers. In: 2014 Eighth International Conference on Next Generation Mobile Apps, Services and Technologies, pp. 37–42, September 2014

Secure Online Polling: Based on Homomorphic Encryption Using (n,n) Secret Sharing Scheme

Yogesh Kumar and Arun Mishra[✉]

Defence Institute of Advanced Technology (DU), Pune, India
yogeshkumar02691@hotmail.com, arunmishra@diat.ac.in

Abstract. Online polling or i-polling is the process of polling by using Internet. Many countries are trying to move from polling to i-polling, to make polling easy and fast. For key management system research community mostly uses (t, n) threshold secret sharing scheme, which enforces the presence of 't' number of authorities out of 'n' authorized members to construct secret key and use it to decrypt votes and completes the counting part of polling. However, it opens a new challenge, i.e. the probability of corrupting 't' people is more than 'n' because, in (t, n) secret sharing scheme, 't' is less than 'n'. A solution to such issue is proposed by making sure that other security objectives of polling have been addressed. For counting votes, Homomorphic encryption technique has been used in this work along with (n, n) secret sharing scheme and Paillier version of (n, n) secret sharing is proposed. This scheme enforces the requirement of presence of all 'n' number of authorized members in the making of the secret key. It is found that by using (n, n) secret sharing scheme the trust on polling system increases.

Keywords: Homomorphic Encryption
Multi-party secret sharing scheme · Online polling
Paillier cryptosystem

1 Introduction

There has been a lot of changes in the procedure of elections from ballot boxes—ballot machines—ballot servers. Use of ballot servers and internet for polling is known as online polling or i-polling (suggested as 'i' stands for internet). In online polling, which is considered in this work, authorized participants votes for 'In favor' or 'Not in favor' of an opinion. As online polling uses Internet and it can be accessed by cybercriminals or attackers or hackers too, we need strong cryptographic techniques (like Encryption for Security, Digital signature for Integrity etc.) to make sure following objectives are fulfilled [1]

1. Only authorized voters should be allowed to vote: before allowing a person to vote, it must be checked if the voter is an authorized person.

© Springer Nature Singapore Pte Ltd. 2019
A. K. Luhach et al. (Eds.): ICAICR 2018, CCIS 956, pp. 590–600, 2019.
https://doi.org/10.1007/978-981-13-3143-5_49

2. One Vote per Person: Only one vote must be recorded for one person.
3. Integrity of votes: Nobody should be able to change or falsify the vote, not even admin.
4. Privacy of voter: voter's identity should not be revealed.
5. Transparency of polling system: Polling process should be transparent and easy to understand.
6. Secrecy of the End Result: Result should not be revealed until voting is over.

Many countries like Estonia, New Zealand, UK, Japan, Australia etc. [2] are trying to make voting available on internet. This makes this topic important for present and future.

Most of the key management systems works on (t, n) threshold secret sharing scheme [3], where, it is assumed that 't' number of parties will not get corrupted. However the probability of corrupting 't' number of authorized members is more than 'n' members because 't' is less than 'n' and probabilty of corrupting less number of person is more. A key management scheme, which enforces the requirement of presence of all 'n' authorized members for constructing decryption-secret key, is proposed in this paper. This proposed solution reduces the requirement of 'n-t' number of honest member to '1' honest member and it also makes sure that it works by not leaving any required security objectives of polling.

2 Background

2.1 Assumptions

Some assumption are consider in this paper these are as follow

- Votes are considered in terms of "YES" ("1") for 'in favor' and "NO" ("0") for 'not in favor'. Where, '1' and '0' are decimal values.
- Voter already registered on Ballot server and possess user ID and Password.
- At least one authorized member out of 'n' is honest.

2.2 Paillier Cryptosystem

Paillier proposed a asymmetric key cryptosystem in [4]. It selects two large prime numbers 'p' and 'q' randomly, to generate public key 'n', where $n = p*q$. It selects 'g' randomly from multiplicative residue set of $Z_{n^2}^*$ This 'g' and 'n' is shared with public for encryption. For private key, it computes Carmichael totient [15] ($\lambda(n)$) of public key 'n' and then computes 'μ' as shown in Eqs. 1 and 2 respectively

$$\lambda(n) = LCM(p - 1, q - 1) \tag{1}$$

$$\mu = [L(g^{\lambda(n)} mod\, n^2), n]^{-1} mod\, n \tag{2}$$

where, $L(x, n) = \frac{(x-1)}{n}$ taken as L(x) throught the paper for simplicity and $x^{-1} mod\, n$ is multipliactive inverse of x modulo n

Encryption, Plaintext $m < n$, Random number r, $1 < r < n$

$$Ciphertext\, c = g^m r^n mod\, n^2 \qquad (3)$$

Decryption:

$$m = L(c^\lambda mod\, n^2)\, \mu\, mod\, n \qquad (4)$$

Relationship between encryption and decryption is described in [4].

2.3 Homomorphic Encryption

When some mathematical computation like addition or multiplication, is done over two or more ciphertexts, which are generated by encrypting plaintexts with same public key, we get a single ciphertext, which when decrypted give results in such a way as if we have performed computation on plaintext [5]. This scheme is used in online polling to count votes without decrypting individual votes and provide secrecy to votes.

In Paillier Cryptosystem [4], let 'c_1' and 'c_2' be two ciphertexts of mesaage'm_1' and 'm_2' as shown in Eqs. 8 and 9. If we multiply two ciphertexts we get.

Let, $c_1 =$ Encryption$(m_1, n) = g^{m_1} r_1^n mod\, n^2$
and $c_2 =$ Encryption$(m_2, n) = g^{m_2} r_2^n mod\, n^2$
$c = c_1 c_2 = (g^{m_1} r_1^n mod\, n^2)\, (g^{m_2} r_2^n mod\, n^2)$
$c = g^{m_1+m_2} (r_1 r_2)^n mod\, n^2$
When this ciphertext is decrypted with private key(see Eqs. 1 and 2), we get
$m = L(c^{\lambda(n)}\, mod\, n^2)\, \mu\, mod\, n$

$$\therefore m = \frac{L(g^{((m1+m2)\lambda(n))}(r_1 r_2)^{n\lambda(n)} mod\, n^2)}{(L(g^{lambda} mod\, n^2) mod\, n} \qquad (5)$$

From [4] we get Eqs. 6 and 7

$$\omega^{n\lambda(n)} mod\, n^2 = 1\, mod\, n^2 \qquad (6)$$

$$\frac{L(\omega^{\lambda(n)} mod\, n^2)}{L(g^{\lambda(n)} mod\, n^2)} = log_g \{ \frac{\lambda(\omega)}{\lambda(g)} \} \qquad (7)$$

Aplying Eq. 6 on Eq. 5, we get
$(r_1 r_2)^{n\lambda(n)} mod\, n^2 = mod\, n^2$
And by applying Eq. 7 on Eq. 5, we get
$\frac{L(g^{(m_1+m_2)\lambda(n)}}{L(g^{\lambda(n)} mod\, n^2)} mod\, n = log_g g^{(m1+m2)}\, mod\, n$
$\therefore m = (m_1 + m_2) mod\, n$
Hence, $m = m_1 + m_2$.

2.4 i-Voting [6]

i-Voting is online system of Estonia country. They started online voting in 2005. They have used envelop scheme for voting, where vote is first encrypted with public key of server and then digitally sign the encrypted vote before submission. Digital sign works as envelope for encrypted vote.

These digitally signed votes are collected by server. All digitally-signed-Encrypted votes are separated from envelope and encrypted votes are transmitted to other device for counting. This device is not connected with internet or any other device by any means. The only way to transmit encrypted votes from server to counting device is CD ROM or Pen Drive or other portable memory devices.

For counting, private key is constructed by using (t, n) secret sharing scheme [7]. It also facilitate auditing such that anybody can be able to audit the online voting without revealing the identity of the voter. However, it faces the challenge as mentioned erlier. Solution for this challenge is prpoposed in Sect. 3.

3 Proposed Method

In this paper, work is done on the key management system, where (n, n) secret sharing scheme is proposed for the solution of the challenge.

3.1 (t,n) Secret Sharing Scheme

In this system, there are 'n' participants. Out of all 'n', at least 't' number of participants should share their secret to construct complete secret.

In one scheme, trusted party 'T' generates private and public pair key. It divides private key into 'n' number of shares. And distributes these shares to all 'n' members [7]. Private key for decryption can be constructed only if at least 't' members out 'n' members share their secret share.

In other scheme all 'n' members generate key pairs. All of them participate in generation of public key. And then utilizes the property of (t, n) secret sharing scheme to construct private key. Here trusted party T is not required [8].

3.2 Proposed (n,n) Secret Sharing Scheme

In this proposed scheme all 'n' members will participate in constructing public key as well as private key as shown in Figs. 1(a) and (b) respectively.

3.3 Proposed Pilliers Version of (n,n) Secret Sharing Key

For such case we proposed a new key generation procedure in Paillier cryptosystem. Let us assume there are $A_1, A_2, ., A_n$ number of authorities.

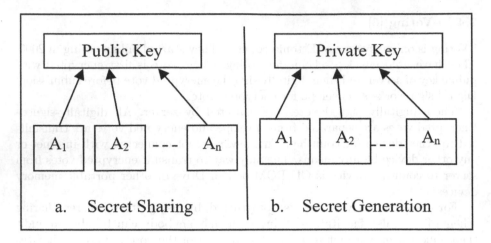

Fig. 1. a. Public key generation b. Private key generation

1. All Authorities constructs their key pairs (g_i, n_i) and private key (λ_i, μ_i), where i = {1, 2, 3, 4, n}
2. all authorities will share their public key 'n_i' and one combined public key is constructed. It is computed a $n = \Pi_{i=1}^{n} n_i$
3. 'g' is selected from $Z_{n^2}^*$ randomly

New Public key will be (g, n)

After encryption procedure is over, decryption key is needed. For that, all authorities have to share their private key $\lambda(n_i)$ [15] to construct private key.

$$\lambda(n) = LCM(\lambda(n_1), \lambda(n_2), .., \lambda(n_n)) \tag{8}$$

And then 'μ' is calculated in similar way as calculated in paillier cryptosystem (see Sect. 2.2). Here, we need to prove that $m' = m$

Proof. From decryption equation, we have,

$$m' = L(c^{\lambda(n)} \bmod n^2)\, \mu \bmod n = \frac{L(c^{\lambda(n)} \bmod n^2)}{L(g^{\lambda(n)} \bmod n^2) \bmod n}$$
$$= \frac{L(g^{m\lambda(n)} r^{n\lambda(n)} \bmod n^2)}{L(g^{\lambda(n)} \bmod n^2))\, \bmod n} \tag{9}$$

By applying Eq. 6, we get

$$m' = \frac{L(g^{m\lambda(n)} \bmod n^2)}{L(g^{\lambda(n)} \bmod n^2)\, \bmod n} \tag{10}$$

By applying Eq. 7, we get

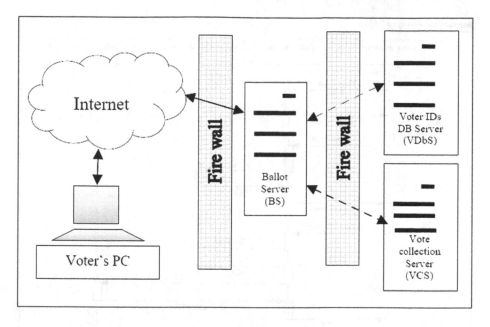

Fig. 2. System design

$$m' = \frac{\lambda(g^{m\lambda(n)}) \, mod \, n^2}{\lambda(g) \, mod \, n^2) \, mod \, n} = log_g g^m \, mod \, n$$

$$= m \, log_g g \, mod \, n \quad [\because log_a e^x = x \, log_a e] \tag{11}$$

$$= m \quad [\because log_a a = 1]$$

$$\therefore m' = m$$

By seeing above prove we conclude that (n, n) secret sharing scheme version of Paillier is possible.

3.4 Proposed Secure i-Polling System

It is inspired from Estonia online voting [6]. It also consist of three servers, one for handling requests named as Ballot server and another two for database and vote collection. As shown in Fig. 2 Voter's PC is connected with Internet so that voter can access the Ballot Server (BS). BS is connected with internet through firewall. Voting database server(VDbS) and Vote collecting server (VCS) connected with BS through another firewall. Here, second firewall will only allow packets coming from BS.

With such assumption, following steps are followed for polling Online which is shown in sequential diagram, Fig. 3.

1. Voter opens the polling link on browser and requests for polling page.
2. BS responds with polling page and asks voter to authenticate itself.

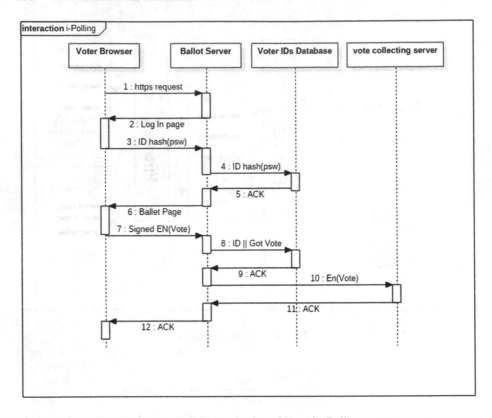

Fig. 3. Sequential diagram of working of i-Polling system

3. Voter submits her credentials for authentication.
4. BS authorizes the voter's identity by confirming from VDbS.
5. VDbS acknowledges the authenticity.
6. BS provides the ballot page for polling after confirming from VDbSr.
7. Voter choses yes or no as '1' or '0' respectively and encryption is done to the give choice with public key of BS. $C(v) = \text{Encryption(vote)} = (g^v r^n) \, mod \, n^2$ Where $v = \{0,1\}$, $0 < r < n$.
8. BS confirms digital sign of voter by decrypting signed vote with public key of voter.
9. ID of voter is sent to voting data base server to check if voter had already voted before or not.
10. VDbS acknowledges the voter's status.
11. If voter is voting first time, her encrypted vote is transferred to the VCS. At VCS all votes are collected and multiplied to get holomorphic encrypted result.

4   Previous Work

Banloh [9] explains how Banaloh cryptosystem have homomorphic properties. Johnson et al. [10], found that such technique does not satisfies all security expectations. They concluded in their research banaloh scheme is not secure against random forgery attack.

Adida [11], in 2008 proposed an online voting system, they call it Helios. It was the first open audit voting system based on web. It is publically available on web. Anyone can use it for their voting purpose. And any observer get ability to audit entire voting process. They also gave security and threat model of their system. The secrecy of votes is get compromised if some attacker hacks or compromises the server before election. They have used two techniques in their protocol Random Perturbation (Mix-Nets) and Homomorphic Encryption. However, for threshold decryption, trusted authorities are assumed in both cases. Also they are using centralized system which can be seen as bottle neck of the system.

Guerraoui et al. [12] in 2009, proposed a Decentralized Polling Protocol for polling problem in social network, where social network user participates in polling and don't want to reveals her identity. to do so they proposed Distributed scalable polling protocol(DPol), which is described in [12]. Their protocol can expose misbehaving nodes. DPol work accurately when number of dishonest nodes is less(i.e $B < \sqrt{N}$, where B represents number of dishonest nodes out of N nodes). We can clearly see their protocol also needs more honest members. However, it also spread light over the importance of Decentralized topology for polling.

Another Decentralized technology for voting is Blockchain-based Voting Systems. It's a theoretical approach, where votes are mapped as a cryptographic coin. Whoever collects more coins wins the election, described by Liu et al. in [13]. This Online voting is based on Bitcoin technology. Zhao and Chan (2015) [14] presented a protocol for a binary voting. Online voting, using Bitcoin technology is based on coloured coins that allow associativity of digital assets to Bitcoin addresses. Eligible voters will have colour coin to vote, they will start sending this coin when voting starts. Those coins are then transferred to a destination that corresponds to a candidate. They showed how identity of voter can be hide by using anonymous property of bitcoin technology. Limitation to this protocol is wastage of bandwidth and electric power by computing proof of work. And Security of Coloured coin/vote is not addressed. All of these researchers shows that there is requirement of system which is not centralized and not too big in decentralized topology.

5   Results and Conclucion

(n, n) secret sharing version of Paillier is implemented using python language and found following results.

5.1   Results

Let, there are '10' number of voters which will vote as given, Votes = {1, 0, 1, 1, 0, 1, 0, 1, 1, 0}, where '1' and '0' are decimal values, and '1' represents 'In Favor' '0' represents 'Not in Favor'

As we can see total number of voters in favor are '6', therefore sum of votes is $Sum(votes) = 1 + 0 + 1 + 1 + 0 + 1 + 0 + 1 + 1 + 0 = 6$

Let 'N' is the number of voting authorities and (g, n) is Public key. for simplicity 'g = n + 1' And $(\lambda(n),\mu)$ is New Private key.

Single cyphertext is computed from all encrypted votes as, $C = \Pi_{i=1}^{10} c_i$

where, $c_i = g^v r^n \, mod \, n^2$ and $v \in$ Votes R is the result, obtained after decrypting Single ciphertext, R = Decryption (C, private key)

KS is the Key Size in Bits obtained as,

KS = N* 32 Bits

As all 'n' members will participate in generation of key, the main key pair size will increase. For simplicity, we have kept key share size of each member to 32 bits. Experiment is done for N={1,2,3,............,25}, where we got desired results. We get our result equal to sum of In Favor votes from complete ciphertext as it can be found by adding plaintexts. We can also notice that size of key will increase with increase in number of authorities. According to the given shared Key Size, the assymetric key size for '4' number of authorized member was 128 Bits

Example, for N = 4, 128 bits key is generated Public key pair generated by A1 (n1 = 2570934623, g = 2570934624)

Public key pair generated by A2 (n2 = 1992404671, g = 1992404672)

Public key pair generated by A3 (n3 = 3478253803, g = 3478253804)

Public key pair generated by A4 (n4 = 2421452513, g = 2421452514)

Combined Public Key (n = 43142549830432150064072809199780914987, g = 43142549830432150064072809199780914988)

Encryption(1) = c1 = 18364362161967178878842130511962851832189223415728756988244739628174367933358

Encryption(0) = c2 = 71213752615340583962068406276746201067504147538897856751067112778090976541

Encryption(1) = c3 = 16035011676780462223283693770306479649695523707706813791824607503895473542226

Encryption(1) = c4 = 11719782754939966121045180295475324674771307363938849018669425681523965010836

Encryption(0) = c5 = 14854245615167939294937338353663339542860676917431612934618568429716431541046

Encryption(1) = c6 = 39875713422984487621540600854736611507173681071358681812029677927229108601866

Encryption(0) = c7 = 57716130236016707848218637023961371755167072350994620712137131513579933705356

Encryption(1) = c8 = 14314883128647919867557613533040345512014185967176109245570996991377020146776

Encryption(1) = c9 = 58892916222105242613299812959879118200206171198976

9622709337916901863578527l

Encryption(0) = c10 = 113860183797528390899427660818755915127099103516
223129530158434128539191061

Combined Cihertext C = 113860183797528390899427660818755915127099l0351
62231295301584341285391910061 mod n

Private key (= 431356026351846203689219580508364800000, = 45614196351491
774332619629573798248028022)

Decryption(C) = Result, R = 6

As we see in example it gives result as axpected. i.e Result = 6. It can also
be observed, everytime encrypted value is diffrent for same plaintext.

5.2 Conclusion

It is found that, by enforcing (n,n) secret sharing scheme, we increase the trust
on online polling system. Since we can't decrypt votes unless all authorities are
present.

In (t, n) scheme, if 't-1' number of authorities are dishonest, they could not
construct secret key [7]. It can be seen clearly from (t, n) scheme, remaining 'n-t'
number of members must be honest.

5.3 Future Work

This system relies on assumption that at least one authority need to be honest.
By implementing verification of authorities at every stage of key generation we
need not to rely on this assumption.

Also we can see, with increase in number of authorities. Size of key increases.
This can be improved in future.

References

1. Ansper, A., et al.: E-voting concept security: analysis and measures. Technical
   report EH-02-01, Estonian National Electoral Committee (2003)
2. Cheyne, C.: E-voting eventually? Online voting in (local) elections. Policy Q. **12**(4)
   (2018). https://ojs.victoria.ac.nz/pq/article/view/4633&gt. ISSN 2324–1101
3. Yang, C.-C., Chang, T.-Y., Hwang, M.-S.: A (t, n) multi-secret sharing scheme.
   Appl. Math. Comput. **151**(2), 483–490 (2004)
4. Paillier, P.: Public-key cryptosystems based on composite degree residuosity
   classes. In: Stern, J. (ed.) EUROCRYPT 1999. LNCS, vol. 1592, pp. 223–238.
   Springer, Heidelberg (1999). https://doi.org/10.1007/3-540-48910-X_16
5. Stuntz, C.: What is Homomorphic Encryption, and Why Should I Care? Embar-
   cadero, 18 March 2010. https://community.embarcadero.com/blogs/entry/what-
   is-homomorphic-encryption-and-why-should-i-care-38566&gt
6. General Framework of Electronic Voting and Implementation thereof at National
   Elections in Estonia, 20 February 2018. Accessed 11 Apr 2018
7. Shamir, A.: How to share a secret. Commun. ACM **22**(11), 612–613 (1979)

8. Pedersen, T.P.: A threshold cryptosystem without a trusted party. In: Davies, D.W. (ed.) EUROCRYPT 1991. LNCS, vol. 547, pp. 522–526. Springer, Heidelberg (1991). https://doi.org/10.1007/3-540-46416-6_47

9. Benaloh, J.: Dense probabilistic encryption. In: Proceedings of the Workshop on Selected Areas of Cryptography, pp. 120–128 (1994)

10. Johnson, R., Molnar, D., Song, D., Wagner, D.: Homomorphic signature schemes. In: Preneel, B. (ed.) CT-RSA 2002. LNCS, vol. 2271, pp. 244–262. Springer, Heidelberg (2002). https://doi.org/10.1007/3-540-45760-7_17

11. Adida, B.: Helios: web-based open-audit voting. In: USENIX Security Symposium, vol. 17, pp. 335–348 (2008)

12. Guerraoui, R., Huguenin, K., Kermarrec, A.M., Monod, M., Vigfússon, ý: Decentralized polling with respectable participants. J. Parallel Distrib. Comput. 72(1), 13–26 (2012)

13. Liu, Y., Wang, Q.: An E-voting Protocol Based on Blockchain. IACR Cryptol. ePrint Arch., Santa Barbara, CA, USA. Technical report 1043 (2017)

14. Zhao, Z., Chan, T.-H.H.: How to vote privately using bitcoin. In: Qing, S., Okamoto, E., Kim, K., Liu, D. (eds.) ICICS 2015. LNCS, vol. 9543, pp. 82–96. Springer, Cham (2016). https://doi.org/10.1007/978-3-319-29814-6_8

15. Friedlander, J., Pomerance, C., Shparlinski, I.: Period of the power generator and small values of Carmichael's function. Math. Comput. 70(236), 1591–1605 (2001)

Author Index

Printed in the United States
By Bookmasters